THE CIO, 1935–1955

THE CIO 1935–1955

Robert H. Zieger

The University of North Carolina Press

Chapel Hill & London

The paper in this book meets the guidelines for permanence and durability of the Committee on Production Guidelines for Book Longevity of the Council on Library Resources.

Library of Congress Cataloging-in-Publication Data

Zieger, Robert H.

The CIO, 1935–1955 / by Robert H. Zieger.

p. cm.

Includes bibliographical references and index.

ISBN 0-8078-2182-9 (cloth : alk. paper)

ISBN 0-8078-4630-9 (pbk. : alk. paper)

1. Congress of Industrial Organizations (U.S.)—History. 2. Trade unions—United States—Political activity—History—20th century. I. Title.

HD8055.C75Z54 1995

331.88'33'09730904—dc20   94-17949

                                    CIP

00 99 98 97 96   6 5 4 3 2

Contents

A section of illustrations begins on page 191.

Preface

The idea of writing a history of the CIO grew out of a summer seminar for college teachers that I conducted in 1981. As we discussed the role of organized labor in American history, 1930–80, we found ourselves remarking frequently on the lack of an archives-based history of the industrial union federation. Having just completed studies of AFL unions in this period, I decided that it was time for someone to take on the CIO. Since we held our sessions in the Walter P. Reuther Library conference room at Wayne State University in Detroit, the notion of writing a history of the CIO came naturally, even if in such a setting the project seemed daunting.

Now, a decade and a half later, the task is done. Its completion encourages reflection about the places to which research has taken me and the people who have helped me. I wish to thank the American Council of Learned Societies, the National Endowment for the Humanities, the Faculty Enrichment Programme of the Canadian government, Wayne State University, and the University of Florida for providing travel funds. In the summer of 1983 I held Summer Stipend from the NEH, which also sponsored the seminar out of which the project grew. The Office of Research and Graduate Education of the University of Florida helped defray the costs of photographic reproduction.

The list of curators, librarians, and archivists who helped me is long. In a previously published article on CIO research (see below), I provided a guide to sources and mentioned some individuals whose assistance was invaluable. I am particularly indebted to the staff of the Archives of Labor and Urban Affairs, Wayne State University, who for the first part of this project were also my academic colleagues. Betty Corwine, Renee Akins, Greg Kisling, and other members of the office staff of the Department of History at the University of Florida provided outstanding assistance.

Individuals who helped by sharing materials were John Barnard, Randy Boehm, and Gilbert Gall. Robert E. Zieger helped with some key research. Joan Man of the IUE helped me gain access to "missing" CIO Executive Board minutes, while Maier Fox, then research director of the United Mine Workers, helped make United Mine Workers and John L. Lewis records, in storage at the time, available for research. Lewis Bateman, executive editor of the University of North Carolina Press, took an early interest in this project and was a ready source of outstanding professional advice.

The following scholars have permitted me to cite unpublished work: Steve Babson, Thomas Dietz, Michael Goldfield, Rick Halpern, Roger Horowitz, Nelson Lichtenstein, Bruce Nelson, Judith Stein, Marshall Stevenson, Warren Van Tine, Jacob Vander Meulen, and Walter Yonn. Colleagues and friends who read and commented on parts of the manuscript also deserve thanks. LeRoy Ashby, David Colburn, Michael Goldfield, Pat Maney, Bob McMahon, and Marshall Stevenson helped in this way at crucial moments. The critiques of the University of North Carolina Press's readers, David Brody and Melvyn Dubofsky, were invaluable. For many years, the friendship of LeRoy and Mary Ashby, Pat and Elaine Maney, and Sam and Marion Merrill has been a constant source of encouragement and validation.

Happy is the person for whom love and work combine. My biggest debt is to my wife, Gay.

January 1, 1994
Gainesville, Florida

Abbreviations

AA	Amalgamated Association of Iron, Steel, and Tin Workers
ACTU	Association of Catholic Trade Unionists
ACWA	Amalgamated Clothing Workers of America
AFL	American Federation of Labor
AFL–CIO	American Federation of Labor–Congress of Industrial Organizations
CARD	Committee to Abolish Racial Discrimination
CIO	Committee for Industrial Organization (1935–38); Congress of Industrial Organizations (1938–55)
CPUSA	Communist Party of the United States of America
CWA	Communications Workers of America
ERP	employee representation plan
FBI	Federal Bureau of Investigation
FE	Farm Equipment Workers
FEPC	Fair Employment Practice Committee
FTA	Food, Tobacco, and Allied Workers
GM	General Motors
HUAC	House Committee on Un-American Activities
IAM	International Association of Machinists
ILA	International Longshoremen's Association
ILGWU	International Ladies' Garment Workers' Union
ILWU	International Longshoremen's and Warehousemen's Union
IUC	industrial union council
IUE	International Union of Electrical, Radio and Machine Workers
IWW	Industrial Workers of the World
LIU	local industrial union
LNPL	Labor's Non-Partisan League
Mine, Mill	International Union of Mine, Mill, and Smelter Workers
MRA	Moral Re-Armament

NAACP	National Association for the Advancement of Colored People
NDAC	National Defense Advisory Commission
NDMB	National Defense Mediation Board
NIRA	National Industrial Recovery Act
NLRB	National Labor Relations Board
NMU	National Maritime Union
NRA	National Recovery Administration
NWLB	National War Labor Board
OES	Office of Economic Stabilization
OPM	Office of Production Management
PAC	Political Action Committee
SOC	Southern Organizing Committee
SWOC	Steel Workers Organizing Committee
TWOC	Textile Workers Organizing Committee
TWU	Transport Workers Union
TWUA	Textile Workers Union of America
UAW	United Automobile Workers
UCAPAWA	United Cannery, Agricultural, Packing, and Allied Workers of America
UCWOC	United Construction Workers Organizing Committee
UE	United Electrical, Radio and Machine Workers
ULPC	United Labor Policy Committee
UMW	United Mine Workers
URW	United Rubber Workers
USWA	United Steelworkers of America
UTSE	United Transport Service Employees
WFTU	World Federation of Trade Unions
WSB	Wage Stabilization Board

THE CIO, 1935–1955

Introduction The Fragile Juggernaut

Organized labor.' Say those words, and your heart sinks," laments labor lawyer Thomas Geoghegan. "It was a cause, back in the thirties. Now it is a dumb, stupid mastodon of a thing, crawling off to Bal Harbour to die." Evidence of labor's decay is everywhere. Recruitment of new members is at a standstill. Once-powerful unions retrench and retreat. Laws passed ostensibly to encourage unionism now victimize activists. Cheering Tennessee autoworkers celebrate the defeat of a UAW organizing drive. A third of the delegates at the 1992 Democratic National Convention are unionists, but the AFL–CIO plays no visible role in the campaign and is absent from public discussion of the postelection economic summit and the new president's economic policy initiatives. "Even liberals, even progressives, do not seem to need us," mourns Geoghegan.[1]

It was not always thus. Beginning in November 1935 and for a decade thereafter, industrial workers organized powerful unions. Aided by a friendly federal government, workers staged innovative sit-down strikes and wrested contracts from some of the most bitter-end corporations. They created permanent industrial unions that boldly intruded into political and governmental arenas. They challenged managers and supervisors at work sites and on shop floors throughout the country. They staged mass demonstrations. Through their leaders, they pressed a social democratic public agenda. They often welcomed Communists and other radicals as their leaders and spokesmen. It was, recalled a veteran organizer a few years later, a golden age, an "era of invincibility," a time when "labor was on top and management underneath."[2] It was the classic era of the CIO.

The CIO stands at the center of the history of twentieth-century America. Its emergence was the key episode in the country's coming to terms with the "labor problem" that had commanded public attention since at least the 1870s. With a peak membership of nearly 5 million, the CIO represents the largest sustained surge of worker organization in American history. Its efforts led directly to the establishment of a system of collective bargaining within the context of regular economic growth that lasted for a generation. The explosion of unionism in the central industrial core of the economy transformed American politics, refigured the class-race nexus, and crucially influenced the U.S. role in the overlapping international crises of the 1940s and 1950s.

Within the labor movement itself, the impact of the CIO was equally great. The expansion of organized labor from its traditional narrow enclaves into the central industrial core transformed unionism in the United States. Associated with the coming of the CIO are the politicization of organized labor, the recasting of racial and ethnic dynamics of the labor movement, and the expansion of the collective bargaining agendas of U.S. unions. The CIO's contractual achievements set new standards for working people, whether unionized or not. The openness of the CIO initially to anticapitalist movements and the subsequent conflict within industrial unionism over the role of Communists and their allies decisively shaped the postwar agenda of organized labor and of the American polity more generally.

From its founding event – the famous punch that John L. Lewis delivered to the face of an AFL rival on October 19, 1935 – the CIO projected manly strength. Its picket line confrontations, its militarylike logistical innovations, its centralized organizing campaigns, and its enormous public demonstrations often made it seem like an irresistible juggernaut. Backed by the fiery rhetoric of John L. Lewis and the legendary militancy of 600,000 Mine Workers – "the shock troops of the labor movement" – the CIO in the 1930s appeared to contemporary observers as a powerful, protean force. "The working class of America came of age in 1937," wrote one enthusiastic observer. The uprisings of auto, steel, and rubber workers, added another, "brought the greatest upheaval in American industrial history." "The CIO," lamented a rival unionist in 1941, "is everywhere these days, spreading its poison and stirring up strife and confusion."[3]

This image of heroic – or disruptive – militancy is rightly associated with the CIO. Yet from the start, for all the power and strength that it projected, the new industrial union movement was in reality fragile and uncertain. Moreover, its agenda, even in its most heroic days, emphasized the achievement of detailed contractual arrangements with employers and the regularization of industrial relations. Its epic battles are more a testament to the hostility of corporate America to any form of union presence than to some primal bloodlust.

Often depicted by its friends and its enemies alike as a mighty force, in fact the CIO was rarely on firm institutional footing. Dependent on political and governmental forces over which it had little control, it lurched from crisis to crisis. It reached its greatest strength and institutional cohesion not in the conflictual days of the fabled 1930s but rather in the patriotic atmosphere of World War II. Its unions won their most expansive contractual gains after the CIO had expelled its Communist-leaning affiliates in 1949–50. It developed its most systematic and effective political impact in the allegedly placid 1950s as it was poised on the edge of merger with the AFL and as its legendary shop-floor militancy was being enmeshed in a web of formalized dispute resolution.

There exists a compendious literature on the history of labor during the CIO era, a body of work that over the past decade has expanded exponentially.[4] Led by Irving Bernstein, Walter Galenson, Joel Seidman, and Sidney Fine, an earlier generation of scholars ably chronicled and analyzed the origins of the industrial union project and charted its early years. More recently, Nelson Lichtenstein has subjected its World War II experience to searching analysis. Dissertations, monographs, and journal articles have examined the histories of key affiliates, notably the UAW, the TWU, the ILWU, the URW, the USWA, and the UE. Biographies of John L. Lewis, Sidney Hillman, Walter Reuther, Harry Bridges, and Lee Pressman analyze the roles of key CIO leaders. The activities of Communists and their allies have been the subject of an extraordinary outpouring of scholarly and politically engaged analysis, while historians have increasingly focused attention on racial, ethnic, and gender aspects of industrial unionism's course. Scholars likewise have been busily reexamining the political, governmental, and legal phases of CIO history, raising provocative new questions about the efficacy of governmental action in support of workers' activism and the trade-offs between union autonomy and state support for union building and collective bargaining. As the archival riches of the New Deal/World War II/CIO era grow, we can only expect further proliferation.

Yet there still exists only one history of the CIO, Art Preis's *Labor's Giant Step*, published in revised form in 1972. Preis was an acute journalistic observer. His book was written from a stance well to the left of virtually everyone associated with the CIO. Honoring activists who disdained bourgeois politics and mainstream unionism, it drips with contempt for the fallible men who led the CIO unions and with hostility toward the politicians and businessmen who cooperated with and confronted it. It celebrates a militant rank and file, forever contrasting what Preis saw as the inherent, if often disguised, radicalism of ordinary workers with the caution and duplicity of their leaders. Based on his own experiences and his coverage as a reporter of key events in CIO history, it made no pretense of archival grounding and was little concerned with analyzing the tough choices that always faced the men who led the CIO.

The CIO, 1935–1955, seeks to meet the need for an overall history of the CIO. It rests upon archival and oral history materials and exploits the outpouring of recent studies. At the same time, it taps into an older political science and industrial relations literature, which often serves as a corrective to a recent historiography that sometimes seems to disremember how hard it was to build unions in the mass production industries. It is my aim to recapture the experience of the past while at the same time responding to questions newly raised, notably about the role of race, the vagaries of governmental and legal developments, and the legitimacy of the anti-Communist postwar American consensus.

The book devotes roughly equal treatment to the three main subperiods of CIO history, namely the 1930s, the World War II era, and the final decade of separate CIO existence. A recurrent theme is the contrast between the CIO's more heroic and dramatic episodes, on one hand, and the industrial union project's always-uncertain institutional identity on the other. *The CIO, 1935–1955*, attempts to illuminate underlying forces in economic, demographic, and political life, while highlighting the human dimensions of the central episodes in the labor history of this period. It attempts to respond to the interpretive initiatives that have made labor history such an exciting field over the past generation while at the same time keeping faith with the people who lived in the 1930s, 1940s, and 1950s.

In the fall of 1955, on the brink of merger with the AFL, CIO partisans indulged frequently in retrospective assessments of their handiwork. A few held that the so-called merger was really, in the words of TWU president Michael Quill, "the tragic liquidation of CIO" and represented the abandonment of CIO ideals. But most expressed satisfaction with their past efforts and hope for the future. Nineteen fifty-five, proclaimed one widely circulated statement, "marks . . . two almost incredible decades, unmatched and unparalleled" in the gaining of "economic, social and political progress achieved on behalf of the nation's working men and women." President Walter Reuther was confident that CIO ideals would continue to animate organized labor, that the merger was a "new and glorious beginning." He could not, he told the delegates to the final CIO convention, prove that this would be so, for in the end, "This is a matter of believing."[5]

In this book I am not primarily concerned with explaining what has happened to the labor movement since the 1950s. I confine my analysis to the period that ended in 1955 when the CIO ceased to exist as a separate entity. This is the period I have studied extensively through examination of the archives and documents, the use of oral histories, and the reading of specialized studies. I feel confident about my judgments regarding the CIO's history in a way that I am not about the connection between this past and the open-ended future. To be sure, the history of the CIO offers ample opportunity for drawing lessons, and in the final section of *The CIO* I offer some opinions about the meaning of the CIO experience.

Questions abound. Did the CIO's ouster of its pro-Soviet affiliates in 1950 lead directly to its enfeeblement and, over the longer run, to the labor movement's descent into its current abyss? Did the CIO's reliance on a compromised Democratic Party squander the heritage that militant activism had bestowed upon it? Was the CIO enlistment in the Cold War and in the social economics of productivity embedded in it fatal to the long-term health of an autonomous and effective union presence in America? Is there any lasting useful heritage for progressives in the CIO project?

These are fascinating questions. In another forum, I do attempt some responses to these and related issues.[6] In this book, however, it is my aim to get the historical record of the CIO as right as I can. Its intended contribution to contemporary debate is to provide a reliable record of the past. Its challenge is to compel acknowledgment of the difficulty of the choices that historical actors faced.

1 Before the CIO

"It is clear . . . that we have to build another organization." The words were those of Hatters' president Max Zaritsky, but the sentiments were everyone's as industrial union supporters met in the wake of Franklin Roosevelt's overwhelming electoral victory in November 1936. The men who hoped to build a new labor federation had to respond to three broad concerns: the ambiguous legacy of industrial unionism, the character and proclivities of an industrial working class undergoing rapid and dramatic transformation, and the institutional and political developments that had occurred since the onset of the Great Depression in 1929–30. The remarkable labor activism and political upheaval of the early New Deal offered these men unique opportunities, but as they well realized, if they misstepped they might well find themselves doyens of a marginalized movement rather than pioneers of a new union frontier.[1]

THE AMERICAN WORKING CLASS IN THE 1920s

The industrial working class in the long decade after World War I underwent profound and rapid changes. During the period 1919 to 1933 working people experienced enormous changes in the pace and character of work, the patterns of industrial unrest, and the very composition of the labor force. The full implications of the second industrial revolution now became apparent. Thus, for example, employment in its characteristic industries, such as automobiles, rubber, petroleum, chemicals, electrical goods, and related sectors, expanded. Employment in the clerical, services, and governmental areas mushroomed. Meanwhile, employment in agriculture, extractive pursuits, and older industrial sectors such as cotton textiles and iron and steel making shrank.

In the 1920s the content of much industrial labor changed dramatically. Industry after industry registered almost incredible gains in productivity as more and more mechanical devices came on line. In manufacturing generally, production per man-hour grew by over 70 percent, and the real value added per worker grew by 75 percent; the average worker had 50 percent more horsepower at his or her disposal. Between 1914 and 1927 productivity in iron and steel grew by 55 percent, in automobiles by 178 percent, and in rubber tires by 292 percent. In the coalfields, mechanical cutters and loaders began to transform the miner's traditional tasks, while power-driven trams accompanied the industry's rapid expansion into the virgin fields of southern Appalachia. Textile manufacturers introduced electrically powered machinery at a rapid rate. The automobile assembly line swung into full operation, with vehicle production leaping from 573,000 in 1914 to over 5.3 million in 1929. In the latter year, the industry employed 447,500 workers, a number only three and a half times larger than the 1914 labor force. Major innovations in glass production, lumber handling, cigar manufacturing, and construction tools accounted for part of the great growth in productivity, but incremental changes involving cumulative small improvements contributed as well. In the 1920s integrated systems, linked by sophisticated electrical communications networks and powered by ever more efficient engines, became commonplace.[2]

Experts disagreed as to how to interpret these vast trends in human terms. Many people lamented the decline of the craftsman and the degradation of skill. Thus, sociologists Robert and Helen Lynd quoted the proprietor of a large midwestern machine shop discussing his workers' lack of pride in accomplishment. "They're just working. They don't know what for. They're just in a rut and keep on doing it."[3]

Not every observer of modern industry as it came of age in the 1920s agreed. The U.S. census showed a decline in the percentage of workers toiling in unskilled jobs and increases in both the semiskilled and skilled categories between its 1910 and 1930 enumerations. Children stayed in school longer, a circumstance that most manpower experts associated with rising skill levels. Industrial changes mechanized *jobs*, but they rarely deskilled *people*. The automobile industry, for example, changed dramatically from the early century days when metal, upholstery, and finish workers built each car by hand. Yet these workers, along with thousands of tool-and-die makers, continued in great demand in the expanding industry, partly because even the most mechanized industry required many traditionally skilled workers; partly because the expansion of mass production in most sectors was accompanied by a similar expansion in prototype, luxury, and specialty products; and partly because new processes inevitably demanded workers skilled in maintenance, repair, and adaptation.[4]

The very meaning of the term *skill* fell into contention. Critics of census and union definitions argued that what was defined as skill had less to do with the inherent character of work than with who was doing it: when women or immigrants took over tasks earlier performed by men, taxonomists began to classify the work as un- or semiskilled. Was secretarial work, involving meticulous labor with state-of-the-art typewriters, calculating machines, and accounting and filing systems, less skilled than typography? And what of the skills of interpersonal discourse, human management, and personal appearance, increasingly at a premium in a society moving rapidly toward white collar employment? Even in the industrial sphere, it was unclear that the stereotypical picture of the sturdily republican craftsman was any closer to reality than the national myth of the yeoman farmer.

In America, autonomy and opportunity had been associated with geographical mobility. Slaves were slaves, regardless of their particular tasks, most essentially because they had no option to exit. People were free when they could pick up and move on. Thus, autoworkers and textile workers, however mechanized their work, were freer than the tens of thousands of coal miners, trapped in rural environments and possessed only of skills that were ill-matched to the requirements of modern industry. Most economists argued that skill was less the ability to perform given tasks, no matter how much dexterity or experience went into the performance, than the ability to "learn how to learn." From this perspective, truly skilled workers actually welcomed technological innovation, sought the vocational training or education that allowed them to keep abreast, and exploited opportunities an expanding economy offered to upgrade their qualifications and capabilities.

The attitudes and policies of employers in many of the newer sectors of the economy changed as well. Several generations of industrial experience had revealed that even jobs that seemed to require little training or education were generally performed better by people with experience. Employers in fast-paced modern industry might discriminate against aging workers, but overall there was a tendency for large-scale employers to attempt to reduce labor turnover and to retain experienced workers. Some employers created internal labor markets, providing workers with mobility within the company into supervisory and even (though rarely) managerial positions. While abusive treatment of workers remained widespread, employers were increasingly aware that the training and experience, even among semiskilled workers, represented an important asset. In the 1920s, statistical indices showed characteristically sticky wage rates, as employers paid above strict market levels, partly no doubt to buy off potential militancy but partly also in recognition of the costs of labor turnover.[5]

The composition of the labor force running this complex and potent system changed dramatically after the war. After 1914 the great influx of southern and eastern Europeans slowed to a trickle. The exit of children from the industrial labor force continued. At the same time, however, large numbers of native rural dwellers, black and white, surged into the industrial sectors, and female employment expanded. In 1900, for example, about 17 percent of the labor force consisted of women, about half in domestic service. Three decades later, female participation had expanded to 22 percent of the labor force, or over 10.6 million workers, fewer than a fifth of whom were domestics. As women entered the labor force, children left it. Even in the southern cotton mills the labor force aged as men settled into permanent employment and the number of children in the mills dwindled.

Massive European immigration had given eastern and midwestern cities a distinctive cast. But wartime and postwar immigration restriction abruptly curtailed the influx from Europe. Demographic stabilization created an emerging second generation of ethnic workers, committed to life in America, increasingly distanced from old-world customs and familial traditions, and expecting the continuation of rising standards of security, prosperity, and mobility.[6]

The curtailment of European immigration opened opportunities for domestic and hemispheric migrants. Between 1917 and 1929 over a million and a half black Americans came north to work. Likewise, the mechanization of agriculture and the relative attractions of industrial wages and urban life drew thousands of white rural workers into the manufacturing centers. Mexicans filled some of the void left by the restriction of European immigration, migrating first to the growing fields of California and the Midwest but moving as quickly as they could from the sugar beet fields to the steel mills and auto factories.[7]

Industrial conflict abated. The period of World War I and its aftermath had been remarkable in its incidence of strikes and violence. Between 1916 and 1922 an average of 9 percent of American workers were involved in strikes annually, with the great 1919 strike wave involving over one-fifth of all workers in work stoppages.[8] After the massive coal and railroad strikes of the summer of 1922, however, industrial America quickly settled into apparent quiescence, as remarkable for its placidity as the earlier period had been for its turbulence. Between 1923 and 1930 the number of strikers engaged in stoppages dropped by over 80 percent. In 1919 there were 3,600 strikes involving over 4 million workers; in 1929 there were 921, involving fewer than 300,000. The index of strike activity declined steadily throughout the late 1920s, reaching in 1930 an incredible 637 strikes and 183,000 workers, who represented a minuscule .8 percent of the labor force.[9]

Equally notable was the rising prosperity of working-class America. In the 1920s real wages continued to rise. Between 1914 and 1929 the average number of hours toiled per week in manufacturing declined by about 10 percent. Skilled workers and increasing numbers of their semiskilled associates bought homes and automobiles. Those who worked in the newer sectors of the economy often had access to company-sponsored programs of medical care, housing, recreation, and stock purchase and increasingly enjoyed at least a modicum of job security. The labor force aged as child labor receded. The proportion of the foreign-born declined. With educational standards rising and with employers increasingly concerned about turnover, workers became less mobile geographically, gained more experience, and were more likely than they had been earlier to commit to an entire career in industrial employment.[10]

This America was no workers' paradise. Income distribution remained steeply skewed. Regional and sectoral exceptions to the general pattern in industrial prosperity, high (if officially unacknowledged) rates of unemployment, and boring, dispiriting, and often downright dangerous toil exacted a dreadful toll. Harsh discipline, chaotic job classification and assignment, arbitrary exertions of shop-floor power, and anxiety-producing rehiring and promotion practices kept millions of workers on the edge of insecurity and defeat. Even progressive employers imposed close supervision and accelerated the pace of work. Age, gender, and racial discrimination were rampant.

Everywhere except in a few unionized enclaves, workers lacked representation, legal job entitlements, and even the most rudimentary voice in the industrial decision-making process. The right to organize was nonexistent. Democratic representation, the rule of law, and the protection of individual rights were rarely to be found in mills, factories, and mines. Everywhere, it was open season on anyone who dared talk union.[11]

Moreover, in the 1920s once-strong unions suffered crushing defeats. The UMW lost 80 percent of its membership. Belligerent employers wiped out World War I-era union gains in textiles, meatpacking, metalworking, and pulp and paper making.

Despite declining strike incidence, however, laborite dissidence was hardly dead. The railroad brotherhoods and the politically cautious AFL participated in third party political action through the 1924 election. Throughout the new era of the 1920s, labor, radical, and ethnic subcultures flourished, rallying in defense of the Italian anarchist martyrs Sacco and Vanzetti, keeping alive the spark of unionism, and warning against the injustices and irrationalities of the now-triumphant business culture.[12]

Still, through the bulk of the decade in most of American industry there were no strikes and little apparent interest in the revival of laborite activism. After smashing the steelworkers' union in the great 1919–20 strike, the steel companies yielded the eight-hour day in 1923 and were untroubled by unions. In the automobile industry, a few radicals distributed shop papers, but by 1930 the vast auto labor force was 99 percent nonunion. Among the country's 100,000 rubber workers, similar conditions prevailed. The booming electrical appliance, farm equipment, and auto parts industries were no more hospitable.

Business leaders and their spokesmen in Washington such as Secretary of Commerce Herbert C. Hoover pronounced the end of the labor problem. In a 1928 campaign address, presidential candidate Hoover boasted that during the decade the nation had constructed 3.5 million new homes, electrified 9 million residences, installed 6 million telephones, and produced and sold to its citizens 7 million radio sets and 14 million automobiles. In the crisis-ridden postwar years "discontent and agitation against our democracy were rampant" and "fear for the future haunted every heart," but, he now proclaimed, an American working class more fully integrated into national life and culture than any comparable class in history bespoke the end of such strife and tribulation.[13]

Indeed, by the later 1920s, throughout the industrial heartland of the country would-be organizers and activists grew discouraged. Whole communities that only a decade before had nurtured rich and active socialist and working-class organizations were now quiescent. "There is no longer a Workingmen's Library or any other educational activity," reported the Lynds from Muncie, Indiana, quoting a despairing unionist who declared that "'the organized labor movement in [Muncie] does not compare with that of 1890 as one to one hundred.'" The situation was much the same in dozens of other cities and towns.[14]

Indeed, it was in new industrial cities such as Flint, Michigan, that the new era seemed most dramatically to have transformed the lives and mentalities of working-class people. Before the war the city had boasted a vigorous local craft union movement and had elected socialists to citywide office. In the 1920s, however, only construction and railroad workers were able to maintain their unions. The 40,000 men and women who poured into the city to toil in the new auto factories did not look to collective bargaining to advance their interests. Partly, of course, this was because Flint's major employer, GM, tolerated no union talk. But as important was the calculation that autoworkers made in their own minds: the industry's high wages bought the ability to participate in the emerging consumer culture. They did not regard the movies, the radio, the automobile, and the freedom from conventional moral and behavioral restraints that these marvels brought as tawdry or ignoble. Indeed, they embraced the culture and considered the hard work they performed to gain access an acceptable bargain. The demand for skilled workers in the tool-and-die shops and specialty labor markets continued, and opportunities for advancement into supervisory ranks existed. For younger men, running a lathe or even working on the assembly line represented an improvement over life on the farm.[15]

Akron's rubber workers viewed life in the modern industrial setting in similar terms. They took advantage of rubber companies' housing subsidies. They calculated piece-rate payment plans and collaborated with foremen to turn to their advantage upper management's sporadic efforts to bring scientific management to the shop floor. They viewed company unions as a means of gaining a voice in affecting the terms of their employment. Politically, rubber workers sought greater access to Akron's public services, educational facilities, and recreational opportunities, sometimes in alliance with corporate and local commercial interests, sometimes in opposition to one or the other.[16]

Workers in the electrical appliance industry also sought advantage within the emerging corporate dispensation. Innovative companies such as General Electric and Westinghouse developed elaborate corporate welfare programs, partly to discourage unionism, partly to reduce turnover and manpower costs.[17] Even southern textile workers showed signs of integration into the corporate system. The industry now employed fewer children and increased the proportion of adult males. Company-owned housing, once a scandal, became more substantial, exhibiting impressive rates of electrification and the installation of modern plumbing. The introduction of electrified machinery, "modern" methods of surveillance, and an intensified pace of work, it is true, triggered bitter strikes in the Piedmont, but during the decade southern textile workers made important strides in literacy, health, industrial experience, and even real wages. By the late 1920s the revolution in consumer culture had made deep inroads into the once-isolated mill communities.[18]

Still, many mass production industries slogged along with traditional methods of authoritarian supervision and bleak records of declining wages, heightened unemployment, and chaotic personnel policies. For the nation's 200,000 packinghouse workers, for example, the 1920s were a grim extension of previous experience. Pulp and paper workers lost their hard-won unions as industry giant International Paper Company destroyed them in a bitter five-year strike that lasted through much of the golden 1920s.[19]

Laborites puzzled as to how to come to terms with the new era. Increasingly it seemed impossible to convince workers that the labor movement had anything worthwhile to offer them. In contrast, corporate America proposed, and throughout much of the 1920s delivered, a lot. By the late 1920s the growth of welfare capitalism and company unionism, the apparent acquiescence – even satisfaction – of industrial workers with the new era regime, and the ability of commercial corporatism to provide not only basic necessities but an expanding array of entertaining, even liberating, artifacts and opportunities threatened to turn unions into musty anachronisms.[20]

THE DEPRESSION AND THE EARLY NEW DEAL

Economic catastrophe changed the equation. The collapse of advanced commercial and welfare capitalism transformed the nature of the bargain that the industrial workers had accepted. The devastating impact of the Great Depression soon overwhelmed even the most conscientious efforts of employers and government officials to maintain employment and wage levels.

By 1931 welfare capitalism was in full retreat. By 1933 fully one-quarter of the working population was unemployed. By the summer of 1931 Ford Motor Company had slashed its Detroit-area employment rolls from 128,000 to 37,000. Between 1928 and 1933 employment in the rubber tire and tube industry dropped by 48 percent. In this same period leading manufacturers of electrical equipment and appliances also slashed payrolls in half. Everywhere, part-time employment and reductions in the work-week artificially inflated the number of workers retaining jobs.[21]

The suddenness of depression and unemployment left workers perplexed and frightened. They responded diversely. Many took up alternative employment, driving cabs, digging ditches, and selling insurance until even these jobs disappeared. Those fortunate enough to work found that even enlightened companies pursued efficiency with a new ruthlessness, dismissing older workers, stepping up work norms, and ignoring workplace safety.

Workers looked in vain to business and governmental leaders for answers. City and state governments, private charities, and corporate stratagems for sharing work or providing garden plots pathetically failed to provide relief on a scale sufficient to alleviate suffering. For New Era workers, the consensus of the 1920s had promised a bargain: hard work and permanent commitment to industrial labor in exchange for high wages, family security, and participation in the consumer culture. But the failure of the system to deliver made it clear that the bargain would have to be renegotiated.[22]

But from whence would a new dispensation come? During the first three years of the depression there seemed no answer to that question. Certainly the Hoover administration provided little hope. Neither did the great corporations. Although leaders of some, such as Gerard Swope of General Electric, did advance complex proposals involving cartelization and government coordination of industry as necessary preconditions for recovery, corporate America's characteristic response was, ultimately, cutting wages, increasing the pace of work, and denying responsibility for the destitute and jobless.

What, then, of organized labor? Surely, working people might look to the labor movement for strategies to relieve distress and restore prosperity. But in fact labor's leadership showed few signs of responding to the crisis. By the 1930s, the AFL had been in continuous existence for a half-century. Despite sporadic outbreaks of mass organization, on the whole it had proven unresponsive to the concerns of the growing proportion of American workers who toiled in large-scale industrial settings, even though the AFL fiercely insisted that it and it alone could speak legitimately for all workers. Moreover, its ideology of "voluntarism," adopted in response to a repressive judicial system, rejected the kinds of public social programs that in other countries had provided working people with defenses against the vagaries of capitalist development.[23]

True, American labor history did include stirring episodes of mass organization. The term *industrial unionism*, in one sense merely descriptive of the effort to organize mass production workers, had been a rallying cry in behalf of a "new" unionism that would move beyond the craft workers who comprised the core of AFL strength to embrace the millions of semiskilled workers and operatives who made the modern industrial machine work. Indeed, dating back to the frenzied organizing days of the Knights of Labor in the 1880s, mass organization of workers regardless of skill, gender, or race had periodically swept the country. Early in the twentieth century the radical IWW had brought its message of all-embracing industrial unionism to the harvest fields, mines, mills, and factories.[24]

The AFL too exhibited industrial union tendencies. The UMW, among the AFL's largest affiliates, brought into its fold not only coal miners but the carpenters, electricians, transport workers, and general laborers who toiled in the often-remote mining sites. Craft unions such as the IAM and the United Brotherhood of Carpenters and Joiners at times opened their doors to operatives and semiskilled workers. After World War I, AFL leaders launched multiunion drives to recruit steel and packinghouse workers on a mass basis. Indeed, throughout its twentieth-century history, the federation experimented with institutional mechanisms that would reach out to the increasingly large proportion of nonskilled workers while at the same time protecting the traditional jurisdictions of its powerful craft unions.[25]

As of the 1930s, however, the dream of mass industrial unionism remained unfulfilled. The Knights of Labor was no more, and repression and defection had reduced the IWW to a corporal's guard. The CPUSA did launch industrial unions, but these were small, beleaguered organizations, under continual assault by the government, employers, and the AFL. Pro-union intellectuals and publicists continued to invoke the ideal of industrial unionism, holding that only with the mass organization of millions of industrial workers and their forceful entry into the nation's central economic and political arenas could the labor movement be revitalized. But with the UMW and other smaller industrially inclined unions reeling under the impact of the depression, there seemed few reasons for hope that organized labor could reinvent itself in response to this great social and economic collapse.[26]

Eventually, however, even conservative unionists began to appreciate the depth of the crisis. In 1932 the AFL's annual convention overrode the objections of traditionalists to endorse federal unemployment insurance legislation and federally mandated limitations on the hours of employment.[27] The federation's mild-mannered president, William Green, challenged those in power: "What do they expect us to do? To sit still? The fighting spirit of the labor movement is aroused," he proclaimed. "We are going to fight . . . with our entire economic strength."[28] But labor's most potent weapon, the strike, was of little use against unemployment. Nor did Green accompany his words with a program of worker mobilization.[29]

The only systematic response to come out of the organized labor movement was associated with the president of the ACWA, Sidney Hillman. An independent union unaffiliated with the AFL, the ACWA had been born in 1914. Under Hillman it organized workers of all skill levels and ethnic backgrounds in the urban men's clothing trades. Hillman early sought to translate union power on the shop floor into union-industry cooperation in establishing common standards of production, labor conditions, and marketing arrangements. He believed that only strong unions could regulate the industry and guarantee the high wages, stable employment conditions, and receptivity to technological innovation that the modern economy required. Declared Hillman in 1928, "A high standard of living is no more a question of mere justice. . . . It is essential to our system of mass production to create a consumers' demand for almost unlimited output." Throughout the 1920s Hillman and the ACWA worked closely with progressive intellectuals to promote this vision of labor-management relationships.[30]

The depression devastated the men's clothing trade as it devastated virtually every sector. Unemployment approached 50 percent, and the cutthroat competition, sweatshop labor, and exploitative homework that had characterized the pre-ACWA days returned. The union's pioneering unemployment insurance system quickly buckled. The ACWA's program of union-employer cooperation foundered. Declared Hillman early in 1933, "Our drifting toward chaos is being accelerated almost from day to day."[31]

Hillman had always understood, however, that no single industry could create an island of prosperity and rationality amid an economic system that always teetered on the edge of crisis. From his earliest days he had advocated a prominent role for the federal government in regulating and stabilizing industry. The wartime mobilization of 1917–18, in which he had been involved, proved to him the efficacy of a strong federal hand. During the 1920s, of course, Republican administrations had reduced the regulatory functions of government, but the depression revealed the folly of this return to laissez-faire. Thus, even as he sought with limited success to regroup his battered union and to bring order to the men's clothing industry, he argued that "no one industry can stabilize itself entirely by its own efforts." Hillman urged a coordinated program of shortening the workweek, establishing national standards for hours and wages, and instituting public works as a means of reducing unemployment and stimulating consumer demand. Basic to this program, of course, was workers' right to establish strong unions with which to promote their interests in this new industrial order. He urged workers to help themselves by joining unions and voting for candidates receptive to this progressive agenda. In 1932 the presidential candidacy of Franklin Roosevelt, long associated with liberal reform in New York state, offered a unique opportunity to advance Hillman's goals.[32]

Hillman was hardly a household name in the early 1930s. In any event, the substantial working-class support awarded Roosevelt in his defeat of Hoover reflected ongoing patterns of ethnic and class alignment rather than any clear programmatic preference.[33] But the AFL's shift toward enhanced governmental involvement in labor affairs, along with programs such as Hillman's and similar notions emanating from the UMW,[34] insured that when Roosevelt took office and actually faced the need to take dramatic steps, he would find important support among the ranks of labor.

Indeed, in its first three months in office the new administration launched critical relief and recovery legislation. Of greatest relevance to organized labor and to working people generally was the NIRA, signed into law on June 16, 1933. This sweeping enactment created the NRA, which was to oversee the restructuring of the entire nonagricultural economy through government-sponsored cartelization that would boost price levels and curb instability. A separate title of the law allocated $3.3 billion for public works construction. For workers specifically, the legislation offered the promulgation of codes in each industry regulating hours of labor and establishing minimum wage levels. Of particular significance for unionists,

Sections 7a and 7b proclaimed the right of workers to form unions of their choosing free of employer domination or manipulation.[35]

Working people responded fervently to this recovery program and to the apparent promises contained in its labor provisions. Through the second half of 1933 and into 1934 America experienced a remarkable surge in both union membership and industrial militancy. Within a matter of months the UMW rebuilt its shattered organization. Garment workers' unions, like the UMW outposts of industrial unionism within the AFL, expanded rapidly as well, with Hillman's ACWA doubling its depression-ravaged membership by the end of 1933. Even in mass production industries such as autos, rubber, steel, textiles, and electrical goods, workers quickly began to create unions and to seek affiliation with the AFL. Thus, between 1933 and 1935, AFL membership increased by 30 percent, reaching its highest total since 1922.[36]

In fact, neither the drafters of the NIRA nor President Roosevelt regarded its labor provisions as more than a restatement of progressive homilies. But workers acted differently. Not only did they create or rebuild unions; they displayed a militancy that had been little in evidence since the early 1920s. The strike totals of 1932 were doubled in 1933, and throughout the summer and fall of the early New Deal they continued to mount. In 1934 the upward trends continued, with massive and bloody confrontations in the longshoring, trucking, auto parts, and textile industries swelling the totals. Typically the contentious issues were not specific wages and hours provisions but, rather, the right to organize.

Employers fiercely resisted unionization. They fired activists, disrupted union meetings, and enlisted law enforcement authorities in antiunion campaigns, triggering bitter conflict. Designed and promoted as a vehicle to promote economic recovery through social harmony and government-sponsored collaboration, the NIRA seemed to have helped rekindle the savage class antagonisms of the past.[37]

Although government officials, employers, and even many labor leaders were surprised by these events, even before the arrival of the New Deal careful observers had charted a new restiveness among industrial workers. Deepening depression should have further shrunk the low 1930 level of strike activity, but instead both 1931 and 1932 revealed sharp increases. Because mounting unemployment had removed so many from the labor force, the increase in the number of walkouts in 1931 by a third resulted in a doubling in the percentage of the labor force involved. In 1932, in the telling category of "percent of working time" lost owing to strikes, the figure quintupled that of 1930. Southern textile workers, increasingly sub-

jected to intensified operations, launched a wave of strikes in 1929 that culminated in 1934 in the walkout of over 200,000. In 1931 and 1932 coal
miners left the West Virginia and Pennsylvania pits in increasing numbers,
sometimes led by Communists and other opponents of the official UMW
leadership of John L. Lewis. In the dreary winter of 1932–33 even open
shop Detroit erupted, with walkouts at key auto body and parts facilities
bringing out 12,000 workers and idling an additional 100,000 in the face of
savage police and employer reprisals.[38]

Contemporary observers found this militancy confusing. Was it merely
the most public manifestation of profound alienation with the basic features
of American life? The bitterness and intensity of these labor struggles made
such a view plausible. Certainly Communists and other radicals, some of
whom played prominent roles in the battles of the 1931–35 period, believed
so, or at least that the process of protest would soon educate workers as
to the systemic oppression inherent in the existing order. In their darker
moments, businessmen and their political allies were inclined to agree with
the assessment, if not with the idiom. Thus, to Hugh Johnson, director
of the NRA, the strike of San Francisco longshoremen that immobilized
the city in July 1934 was "a menace to the government" and "bloody
insurrection."[39]

Veteran laborites and close observers of industrial relations were more
skeptical. True, strike levels rose dramatically; but even in 1934 the vast
majority of workers were never on strike, and the time lost to work stoppages amounted to less than two-fifths of 1 percent of all work time. Union
membership was up, but even in 1935 it represented less than 10 percent of
the nonagricultural labor force. Social scientists produced seemingly contradictory evidence about the state of mind of American workers. Many
appeared to blame themselves for joblessness and economic failure. At the
same time, however, workers seemed determined to find ways to recapture
the relative prosperity and promised security of the 1920s, and polling and
interview data also revealed high levels of political and social protest.[40]

No observers were more interested in or more uncertain about the mood
of working-class America than the high-ranking functionaries of the labor
unions. The restiveness of the working class in the early depression years
challenged and engaged them on several levels. Most men and women with
responsible positions in the great majority of unions were deeply committed to mainstream American civic values. With few exceptions, they
accepted and even embraced capitalism as a legitimate and even privileged
economic system. They honored the American republic, endorsed the common understanding of the democratic process, and believed that America
offered to working people opportunities for achievement, prosperity, and

civic freedom unmatched anywhere. To leaders such as William Green, John L. Lewis, and Sidney Hillman the catastrophe of the depression posed a basic challenge to their most deeply held social values. Indeed, for them, while the new militancy swelled union ranks and breathed new life into the labor movement, it also posed dangers, both to the country as a whole and to organized labor.[41]

For many old-line leaders of the AFL, for example, the new wave of recruits was suspect. Many were of different ethnic origin than the Anglo, German, and Irish workers who dominated the craft unions that largely comprised the AFL and the railroad brotherhoods. Few newcomers had sustained experience with organized labor. Old-timers had seen great influxes of mass production workers in the past and had seen them drop away equally rapidly. "I find everywhere," observed the president of the pulp and paper workers' union, "among the workers that just as soon as they meet with some little obstacle they immediately become discouraged and quit." AFL officers imposed bureaucratic procedures on new members who were enrolled in its directly affiliated organizations, the federal labor unions, fearing that enthusiastic but inexperienced new members would too readily employ the strike weapon and thus court disaster.[42]

Indeed, it was true that the gains of 1933–35 often proved transitory. In the automobile and rubber industries, for example, by the end of 1934 thousands who had signed up in 1933 had defected. Established unions could not collect dues from new members, many of whom, a paper workers' organizer lamented "are almost as bad as bargain counter hunters. . . . They want value rec'd in advance." AFL traditionalists believed that these new recruits were simply too inexperienced, undisciplined, and vulnerable to establish stable unions without detailed guidance.[43]

Key AFL leaders, however, rejected such views. For Lewis, Hillman,[44] David Dubinsky of the ILGWU, and others active in organizations with industrial union traditions the counsel of caution was foolish. Younger men and women newly recruited into the federal labor unions that emerged in the wake of the NIRA in the mass production industries were impatient with cautionary admonitions. They believed that traditional craft demarcations were irrelevant. Moreover, the separation of skilled from semi-skilled workers deprived the latter of precisely those experienced, articulate, and often union-minded cohorts who might lead the way to effective organization. Moreover, critics charged, the leaders of the traditional craft unions, however diffident they might be in actually seeking to organize industrial workers, adamantly refused to cede jurisdiction to enable these workers to organize on their own.

Within the councils of the AFL, Lewis and other industrial union advocates now made repeated appeals for the organization of the unorganized, the waiving of jurisdictional boundaries, and the launching of mass campaigns. The AFL leadership did not reject these initiatives out of hand. Federation chieftains endorsed the idea of mass organization in principle, but whenever Lewis pressed President Green for concrete action, the AFL leadership held back. Any organization of the auto and rubber industry would have to separate the skilled workers and assign them to their appropriate craft organizations. Any organizing campaign would have to employ only the most senior and conservative representatives. Any effort to organize the crucial steel industry would have to pay scrupulous regard to the wishes and interests of the AA, a feeble but long-lived affiliate.[45]

The industrial turmoil of 1934 gave way to stasis in early 1935. In the spring of 1934 the AFL had persuaded impatient new unionists in the automobile industry to accept government mediation rather than risk a strike. When the federal Automobile Labor Board proved powerless to prevent the automakers from pressing their antiunion campaign, membership in the auto locals fell drastically. Reported one local leader in July, "Since March our membership has fallen away in appalling numbers. . . . Our treasuries have been drained. . . . The few remaining loyal members are discouraged." From the spring of 1934 through early 1935 the AFL disbanded some 600 of the local unions formed in the flush of NIRA optimism.[46]

To Lewis, Hillman, and their allies these losses were disastrous. In their view, the NIRA and the willingness of mass production workers to storm into the labor movement had provided the AFL with a unique chance to move to the center of American life. If organized labor did not respond now, it might never again have the chance. During the 1920s the labor movement had been shut out of mass production industry, where the bulk of the working class toiled. If the leaders of organized labor could not seize the opportunity that a favorable political environment now offered, these workers might well be lost forever to the labor movement. Whatever happened on the organizing front, these workers would always be voters and citizens. How could the labor movement hope to survive, let alone promote any ambitious agenda, without any access to its own natural constituency?

Lurking behind all this was a question: Where *would* the workers go if not into the labor movement? Would failure on the part of the mainstream labor movement open the doors to authoritarian radicalism? After all, the Communist Party enjoyed considerable cachet in some working-class areas, and the "workers' state," the Soviet Union, offered a seemingly glowing contrast to the despair of capitalist America. Perhaps, though, the German model would be more likely, with authoritarian political movements of the right claiming the loyalty of masses of disaffected and resentful workers who could turn to racialist or militaristic solutions to their problems.

Most likely, however, labor's failure to recruit mass production workers into strong industrial unions would give corporate America another chance. In the 1920s company unions had prospered, and in some industries they continued to flourish despite the agitation of the early New Deal.[47] How long until large corporations recovered and began systematic campaigns to co-opt their employees? Most industrial union advocates within the AFL had no serious plans to supplant the capitalist system; indeed, the vast majority wanted only to work out a modus vivendi with it that gave workers an independent voice and themselves the power and influence to which they felt entitled. But they did believe that this independent voice was necessary, and they did believe that if the AFL did not find the energy, will, and imagination to seize the moment and respond to the current opportunity, it would soon become marginal and irrelevant.[48]

During the first year of its existence, the CIO simultaneously exhibited both the pageantry and idealism of a great liberation movement and the determination to foster responsible, contractual unionism in the mass production sector. These two aspects of the early CIO were complementary, for the ability of American workers both to endure the hardship of raw confrontation and to create and sustain vehicles for the regular conduct of ordinary life in a complex corporate order were equally vital. The success of the CIO depended in large part on its ability to fire workers' imagination, dramatize its goals through public epics, and maneuver through the maze of changing legal and political boundaries to build an organization that would embrace a great diversity of workers while surviving in a hostile environment.

STARTING UP

This dual nature of the early CIO was evident in the events surrounding its birth. These involved simultaneously a spectacular fistfight and the rapid recruitment of high-ranking union officials and veteran activists who were as committed to orthodox conceptions of institutional behavior as they were to expanding labor's domain. Through the first four months of the CIO's life, its organizers and spokesmen made choices that both heralded the dawning of a new day and insured that the resulting institution would remain squarely within the ambit of the historic labor movement.

The fistfight occurred in Atlantic City, New Jersey, on October 19, 1935, toward the end of the AFL's annual convention. On that afternoon, John L. Lewis, the chief of the UMW, picked a fight with his counterpart in the Carpenters' Union, William L. Hutcheson. Actually the two men had much in common. Both were midwesterners and Republicans, and each presided as a hardheaded autocrat over his union. For the past year and more, however, Lewis had been the AFL's leading industrial union advocate, while Hutcheson epitomized the federation's orthodoxy.

In 1934 the AFL convention had seemed to respond to the pleas of Lewis and other industrial union advocates. It had endorsed the chartering of unions in auto, rubber, and other industries and had pledged to organize steel. But in the intervening year, little had happened. At the 1935 gathering Lewis had watched impatiently as the federation's old guard rejected appeals to launch aggressive campaigns among industrial workers. On October 16 he called on the AFL leadership to "heed this cry from Macedonia that comes from the hearts of men. Organize the unorganized," he challenged, "and in so doing you make the American Federation of Labor the greatest instrumentality that has ever been forged in the history of modern civilization to befriend the cause of humanity and champion human rights."[1]

By the nineteenth, as the convention wound down, however, it was clear that Lewis's rhetoric had been fruitless. The AFL leadership grew ever more contemptuous of the industrial union supporters, many of them young delegates representing federal labor unions in the mass production industries. Finally, Lewis had had enough. When his erstwhile crony Hutcheson sought to stifle an expression of dissent on the part of some young rubber workers, Lewis confronted him. The two large (but normally sedentary) men exchanged insults. Suddenly, the fifty-five-year-old Lewis vaulted a row of chairs, drew back his fist, and decked the sixty-one-year-old Hutcheson. Then, with delegates and reporters standing atop chairs to catch a glimpse of the action, Lewis turned, relit his cigar, and strode to the rostrum while Hutcheson's friends helped the bloodied Carpenter from the hall.[2]

Lewis's assault on Hutcheson, whatever its immediate motivation, underlined his policy differences with the federation leadership in the most spectacular way imaginable. Here was a violent disruption of the AFL's most solemn occasion, its annual convention. An intra-union debate on what sometimes seemed arcane questions of jurisdictional boundaries was now spectacularly dramatized. Remarked labor publicist Len De Caux, the fistfight immediately popularized the image of "the battling Lewis as a John L. Sullivan of industrial organization" among workers everywhere. They may not have followed the details of the AFL convention, De Caux observed, but "they did follow sporting events."[3]

The next morning, Lewis convened a breakfast meeting of forty or fifty supporters of industrial unionism. Three weeks later he invited a handful of AFL union leaders who had backed the industrial union minority position at the convention to gather at UMW headquarters in Washington. They formed a committee, headed by Lewis and with Charles Howard, president of the venerable International Typographical Union, as secretary. The three largest participating organizations, Lewis's UMW, the ILGWU, and Sidney Hillman's ACWA, each pledged $5,000 to back up the call for industrial unionism within the confines of the AFL. At Lewis's recommendation, they named John Brophy, a veteran union activist, as director of the new body, which they named the Committee for Industrial Organization.

The key figures in the CIO were all veteran unionists, steeped in the routines of the American labor movement. In addition to Lewis, attending the founding meetings of the new body were seven other union leaders, all heads of AFL affiliates. Three – Thomas McMahon of the United Textile Workers, John Sheridan of Mine, Mill, and Harvey Fremming of the Oil Workers – headed organizations that had few members and little influence. A fourth, fifty-six-year-old Howard, participated as an individual, neither seeking nor receiving his organization's official support for the CIO. Three leaders from the New York City-centered garment trades, Hillman of the ACWA, David Dubinsky of the ILGWU, and Max Zaritsky of the Hatters, Cap and Millinery Workers, rounded out the original group of CIO leaders. Dubinsky, Hillman, and Zaritsky were nominal socialists, but all of these men eagerly embraced the New Deal and the leadership of Franklin Roosevelt. While all were critical of AFL policies and leadership, none repudiated its traditional agenda of collective bargaining, centralized and authoritative union leadership, and fundamental support for basic American institutions (including private enterprise). None was associated with the syndicalist or localistic unionism that characterized the largely defunct IWW and that had cropped up in various parts of the country in response to depression conditions. The challenge for Dubinsky, Hillman, and Lewis was to tap into the current mass activism, provide it with disciplined leadership, and bring it into the ambit of a revitalized and assertive American labor movement.

To some, Lewis's forceful leadership of this endeavor seemed out of character. His criticisms of the AFL and his brawl with Hutcheson contrasted sharply with the orthodoxy of his career in the labor movement in the two previous decades. In the 1910s, for example, he had scrambled to the top of the UMW despite lack of broad rank-and-file support, largely through bureaucratic maneuvering. Through the 1920s, as the UMW declined, Lewis had clamped a rigidly repressive personal control over the union. Moreover, he had actively supported both Calvin Coolidge and Herbert Hoover.

Lewis's advocacy of vigorous organization of mass production industries, however, had both personal and institutional roots. On the most practical level, the revival of the UMW remained tenuous so long as the steel industry remained nonunion. U.S. Steel and other large corporations owned and operated so-called captive mines, which accounted for about 8 percent of total U.S. coal production. So long as these mines remained nonunion, they represented a threat to the UMW. By rationalizing production and perhaps by eventually bringing stability and security to coal mining, the big steel companies might well convince miners that union protection was not necessary for the achievement of improved working conditions and living standards.

By 1935 the UMW had gained important footholds in the captive mines, but so long as the steel industry remained antiunion, the union's success there, and by extension its overall collective bargaining posture, would be compromised. Coal operators in Alabama, for example, following the lead of the steel companies and their captive mines, were stonewalling the UMW – "trying to starve my people to death," Lewis told the AFL convention. By failing to make good on its promises to organize the steel industry, the AFL, in Lewis's view, was jeopardizing the UMW. "Our people are suffering," he declared, "and they are suffering . . . by the fact that the American Federation of Labor . . . has failed . . . to organize the iron and steel workers."[4]

More generally, Lewis believed that industrial and economic developments over the past generation posed a fundamental threat to the American polity and social order. Relying heavily on ideas generated by his close personal advisor, economist W. Jett Lauck, Lewis had come to believe that the republic itself was in danger. The staggering technological revolution of the 1920s, he held, had fundamentally distorted the nation's economic life. A cabal of bankers and financiers "working out its objectives silently, invisibly, and without official recognition" had come to dominate the American economy. In the effort to shield themselves from public scrutiny and regulation, the "Kings of Money and Lords of Finance" were perverting the Constitution and the Bill of Rights, corrupting the political processes, and regimenting the people. They would stop at nothing short of a "Tory Revolution."[5]

Invoking themes of conspiracy and defense of the virtuous republican order, Lauck and Lewis saw the labor movement as the only effective means of stopping this reactionary tide. "Our self-governing republic is at the cross-roads," they proclaimed. Only a strong labor movement could resist corporate domination. The New Deal offered hope, but "while organized labor is striving to endure its Valley Forge . . . these mercenaries of our dominant private banking groups, . . . the real rulers of America, are spending millions on false propaganda . . . for the purpose of betraying organized labor and democracy." In addition to this direct threat to republican values, the captains of finance and corporate pirates, by their exploitative policies, fostered the growth of Communism and other forms of "destructive radicalism."[6]

Hence Lewis's bitterness toward the AFL. While the very foundations of the republican order were in danger, the old federation clung to out-moded jurisdictional and procedural rules. The opportunity to empower the industrial working class was slipping away. Industrial unionism was more than a fight for higher wages and better working conditions; it was an "epoch-making crusade for humanity and democracy."[7]

How much of this did Lewis, not normally a man given to disquisitions on republican government, mean, or even understand? For all his oratory, declared one of his many critics, he remained "ruthless, unscrupulous, dictatorial" at heart.[8] Despite his eloquence, the best some of his critics would credit him with was a certain keen instinct for power. In this view, the opportunity that the activism of mass production workers offered was the opportunity Lewis saw for aggrandizing himself in the name of the toiling masses and at last realizing the ambitions for national leadership that, he believed, his talents entitled him to.

In Lewis's oratory, however, and in Lauck's various memorandums and drafts, lay a fundamental sense of crisis and of redemption through the means of organized labor that struck a powerful chord among other labor leaders impatient with the AFL's caution and delay. Whatever doubts they may have had about his motives, even men who had suffered grievously from Lewis's wrath now willingly came to his side. When Lewis stepped outside the confines of the AFL and conveyed his sense of peril and hope directly to mass production workers, as he did in a series of speeches and radio broadcasts early in 1936, he triggered a massive response.[9]

The other key figures in the early CIO, Dubinsky, Hillman, and Howard, spoke in diverse but overlapping idioms about their vision of industrial unionism. Howard and Dubinsky were both committed to using the CIO as a means of rescuing the AFL from itself. Dubinsky, whose union had wide jurisdiction in the women's garment industry, was critical of the AFL old guard's diffidence and hostility. Dubinsky believed that the penalty for the AFL's failure to organize mass production industry would be forfeiture, perhaps to the Communists, of this vast reservoir of membership. Closely linked to anti-Communist radicals in New York City's ideological and sectarian hothouse, Dubinsky sought always to combine the crusade for industrial unionism with anti-Communism and the retention of ties to the AFL.[10]

Howard shared Dubinsky's apprehensions about Communism. He believed that one way or another, "these workers will organize." Indeed, the organization of workers was simply part of a nationwide flood tide of organization, as people increasingly came to realize that in modern society only organized blocs could participate in decision-making processes. Howard also believed that many groups were actively seeking the franchise for representing working people. "The Townsendites are organizing," he warned; "the ex-service men are organizing . . . ; a number of agencies are organizing the wage workers."

The problem was that "organization of wage workers is the most difficult" kind of organization. Yet, since the passage of the NIRA, workers had in fact actively sought representation, only to find the AFL unresponsive. Thus, ironically, "the greatest obstacle at this time is the refusal of the American Federation of Labor" and its affiliates "to adopt more modern organization policies to meet modern conditions." Make no mistake, Howard warned: if the bona fide labor movement did not do the job, others would. Already, he asserted, company unions, independent unions, and other organizations "not in sympathy with the A. F. of L." had a combined membership of over 2 million workers. Even more alarming, failure of the AFL to act might well "force them to organize and accept a destructive philosophy under subversive leadership."[11]

Of all the influential early leaders, Hillman had the least substantial ties to the AFL. Along with fellow activists, he had created the ACWA in 1914 as an alternative to the AFL's corrupt and ineffectual affiliate in the men's clothing trade. For two decades Hillman had led an organization that was a pariah among AFL officials, a dual union. During that period, the ACWA had organized the men's clothing industry in New York and other eastern cities, bringing together workers of diverse skill levels and of a wide variety of ethnic identities. It had built a thick network of housing, credit, and insurance services, providing for its members a private version of the kinds of welfare state policies that Hillman advocated in public realms.[12]

It was natural, then, that after the ACWA was admitted to the AFL in 1933, Hillman quickly became a leading spokesman for industrial unionism. Replenished by the organizing gains achieved after passage of the NIRA, Hillman's forces provided able support for Lewis at the 1934 and 1935 AFL conventions. With the establishment of the CIO, Hillman became, after Lewis himself, the new body's most articulate, decisive, and generous supporter. Of all the original group of eight, perhaps even including Lewis himself, Hillman was initially the least concerned about placating AFL leaders and the least worried about facing sanctions at their hands.[13]

To do the daily work of this new CIO, Lewis reached out to former adversaries. In the 1920s Brophy, now fifty-two years old, had been a rank-and-file UMW leader with close ties to anticapitalist radicals. After Lewis defeated him for the UMW presidency in 1926, with the aid of questionable balloting procedures, and then drummed him out of the union, Brophy worked for a time as a salesman before Lewis brought him back into the UMW in 1933 as a troubleshooter and field representative. Experienced, able, and widely admired for his independence and integrity, Brophy was an obvious choice as director of the CIO's daily operations. For his part, the veteran activist jumped at the opportunity to help expand the labor movement. No longer threatened by rivals or nonunion operators in the UMW, Lewis, Brophy believed, could now afford to indulge his better side and give voice to an expansive vision of labor's role in society. "I am sold on him today," said Brophy, although he later recalled that "I had my fingers crossed all the time, of course." [14]

One of Brophy's first acts as CIO director was to name another veteran of the anti-Lewis wars in the UMW, Adolph Germer, as the new organization's first field representative. Fifty-four at the time of his new appointment, Germer had begun his career, which eventually included service as a labor editor and socialist and union organizer, by joining the fledgling UMW in 1894 at age thirteen. Only five years before the birth of the CIO Germer had been a key figure in a revolt of Illinois miners against Lewis's leadership and had suffered physical assault at the hands of Lewis's henchmen. But within days of the formal opening of the CIO office in Washington on November 18, Germer was on the job, circulating through the Midwest, reporting back to Brophy and Lewis on the state of union sentiment in the auto and rubber industries. [15]

After the turn of the year, another veteran UMW dissident, Powers Hapgood, became the second CIO field representative. Born in 1899, Hapgood came from a talented and socially committed family. After graduation in 1921 from Harvard, he worked in factories, on the docks, and in the mines of the United States and the United Kingdom. In the mid-1920s he joined dissidents in the UMW in an anti-Lewis program of democratic reform. Ebullient, idealistic, and irrepressible, Hapgood now joined his erstwhile companions in dissent, Brophy and Germer, willingly submitting himself now to the direction of Lewis. "Overnight," remarked veteran Lewis-watcher McAlister Coleman, "the magic formula of the words 'industrial unionism' was dissolving ancient grudges." [16]

Two other staff members played important roles in the early CIO. Katherine Pollak Ellickson, a thirty-year-old economist and labor education activist, was hired by Brophy immediately upon the formation of the committee to manage its office, conduct research, handle correspondence, and generally direct the organization's day-to-day business. Shortly after the turn of the year, Brophy appointed Len De Caux, a thirty-six-year-old radical journalist, to handle the committee's publicity and to produce copy for a CIO news service. [17]

These five early staff members each represented American labor's heritage of dissent. Through the 1920s Brophy, Germer, and Hapgood, of course, had agitated bravely in behalf of union democracy. Brophy and Hapgood had welcomed the support of Communists and other anticapitalist radicals and had castigated Lewis relentlessly for his cozy relationships with coal operators and with the Republican regime in Washington. Ellickson had been a participant in innovative programs of women workers' education. Her very presence at the inner circle of CIO activity flew in the face of laborite tradition. In the UMW, for example, no married women other than relatives of the leadership were employed. In fact, at the time he asked her to sign on with the CIO, Brophy did not know she was married, and Ellickson judiciously used her maiden name, Pollak. De Caux was a fiery, New Zealand-born and Oxford-educated Communist, a veteran of fifteen years of labor activism and journalism in the United States and abroad.

Despite the staff's collective record of dissidence, however, all operated well within the traditional boundaries of the labor movement. Brophy and Germer were social democrats who combined a commitment to social justice with a strong sense of order, propriety, and procedure. Hapgood subordinated his more expansive feelings to the job of building stable organizations. Ellickson quickly proved an able administrator and researcher; she had no particular feminist agenda and willingly accommodated herself to the priorities of the CIO leadership. De Caux had long before learned to perform as a professional publicist for labor organizations far more conservative than the new CIO.

NOVEMBER 1935–APRIL 1936

Between its founding on November 9, 1935, as a formal organization and the following spring, the CIO took on an increasingly autonomous institutional identity. Its transformation from a modest ginger group to a fledgling rival to the AFL came as a result of three central factors. The harsh reaction of the AFL to the CIO's early activities, the enthusiastic response of industrial workers to the CIO initiative, and the increasingly aggressive stance of Lewis and Hillman soon necessitated institutional development. The creation in June 1936 of SWOC marked the decisive step in the CIO's evolution into a rival labor federation.

At first the new committee was a modest affair. It would promote industrial unionism within the AFL. It would print material on the subject and support would-be industrial unionists facing craft union hostility. It would, for example, encourage federal labor unionists to participate in AFL meetings. It would promote industrial unionism in rubber, auto, steel, radio, and other mass production fields. It would do all this openly in an effort to bring the restless masses of industrial workers into a recast AFL.

From the start, however, AFL leaders denounced the CIO project. Federation officials had always insisted that they alone could legitimately speak for the American working class. Declared Green in 1933, "There is no other instrumentality set up or created through which Labor can speak its mind or express itself except through the American Federation of Labor."[18] From Green's first public response, which was carried in a letter to each committee member on November 23, 1935, through the AFL's Executive Council meeting in mid-January the next year, the AFL chiefs demanded that the CIO disband. While the council did appoint a committee to meet with CIO leaders individually, the AFL took no official recognition of the CIO. With Green's every statement came the message loud and clear: the primary problem facing the American labor movement was not that of organizing auto, rubber, and steel. It was the CIO.[19]

For the CIO this intransigence presented both a threat and an opportunity. The threat was obvious and, to men such as Howard and, especially, Dubinsky, serious. If the AFL did suspend or expel the CIO unions, the result would be a disastrous split in the House of Labor at a time of maximum peril. Elevated to an AFL vice-presidency in 1935, Dubinsky cherished his immigrant-based union's acceptance into the AFL's inner circle. Moreover, he distrusted some of the prevailing currents of worker activism and was concerned about possible Communist influence among workers with little union experience. In December he cautioned his colleagues that "we want the activities [of the CIO] carried on so the rank and file won't think they are in opposition to the A.F. of L."[20]

In the auto plants, rubber factories, and steel mills, however, nothing so validated the new CIO as the AFL's hostility. As Germer circulated through the industrial heartland, he heard the same story everywhere: the AFL was discredited. Workers demanded that their local unions remain intact and that skilled workers not be sorted out and handed over to the craft unions. The federation had had two years to build unions but had failed. "A gigantic mass organizational drive is essential to overcome the apathy and suspicion in the auto industry," declared autoworker activists. Unrestricted industrial organization was the only answer, declared a Flint unionist, for "workers believe that the present [AFL] setup is beyond repair & that an entirely new plan as advocated by Lewis must be used."[21]

Indeed, it seemed that the automobile industry of southeastern Michigan, where 300,000 autoworkers toiled for such corporations as GM, Ford, and Chrysler, would surely be a vital testing ground. In Flint, Pontiac, Detroit, and other auto cities autoworkers had turned toward organizations unconnected with the AFL. Thousands of skilled machinists and tool-and-die makers belonged to the Mechanics Educational Society of America, a militant union led by Anglo-Scots socialists. Thousands of Chrysler workers belonged to the Automotive Industrial Workers' Association, an organization that combined certain unionlike attributes with elements of social resentment associated with Detroit-area radio priest Father Charles Coughlin, who served as its chaplain and advisor. Germer's informants told him also that still another autoworkers' group flourished among Hudson Motor Company employees.[22]

In contrast, the newly chartered UAW, comprised largely of federal locals, had most of its membership in outlying areas, with little strength in critical southeastern Michigan. UAW local leaders resented the AFL's refusal to grant an unrestricted industrial charter and deplored the inept leadership of its Green-appointed head, Francis Dillon. Thus, the Detroit-area auto situation was volatile and dangerous. Unless some force – presumably the CIO – could bring about unification of its diverse elements and mobilize the great mass of autoworkers who belonged to no organization, this critical industry might fragment into warring factions and be lost to the labor movement. Although neither Brophy nor Germer said so openly, it was becoming increasingly clear that only by maximizing its distance from the AFL could the CIO hope to serve this purpose.

The combination of AFL attacks on the CIO and enthusiastic worker response to the committee's formation had a decisive impact within the CIO. From the start, Lewis responded belligerently to the AFL's thrusts. In late November he resigned from the AFL Executive Council. Early in December he made an offer to Green certain to infuriate his former UMW colleague. Lewis urged him to abandon his opposition to the CIO. "Why not return to your father's house?" Lewis asked. He, Lewis, would gladly relinquish the leadership of the CIO in favor of Green and guaranteed him an "honorarium [that will be] equal to that you now receive." Increasingly, Lewis framed CIO goals and activities in opposition to the AFL, carefully arranging the timing and staging of his communications and appearances so as to maximize their dramatic impact among industrial workers.[23]

Hillman drew essentially the same lessons as Lewis. As early as December he concluded that industrial unionism in auto and rubber depended on the CIO and that any backing down to placate the AFL would be fatal. When Germer and Brophy reported on the auto situation, Hillman urged that "this is the time to go in." "If we don't take some step now," he went on, "in two months people will say that the committee will do nothing."[24]

Germer heard the message: the closer the identification of the CIO with the AFL, the more skeptical and resistant were the workers. Conversely, every time John L. Lewis blasted the federation, enthusiasm for the CIO surged. With each fresh example of Green's intransigence and each new report of rank-and-file enthusiasm, the CIO took on the character of an autonomous center of labor activity.[25]

The first opportunity for the CIO to align itself with vigorous local militancy occurred, however, not in the auto industry but among rubber workers in Akron, Ohio. There in February and March 1936 thousands of Goodyear workers conducted an epic strike, which capped over two years of labor-management confrontation in the Rubber City. Throughout the fall of 1935 and into the winter, complex disputes erupted over the length of the workday, piece rates, and the disciplining of worker activists. At last, on February 14, the firing of 137 tire builders, who had refused to work in protest over Goodyear's disciplinary policies, triggered a revoltlike outpouring, with thousands of Akron workers taking to the streets, eventually establishing an eleven-mile picket line around the vast Goodyear complex. Between the formal beginning of the strike on February 18 and the settlement reached on March 21, Akron was the scene of both an epic working-class struggle and the CIO's first test under fire.[26]

The strike was not a simple tale of union versus management. The 3,000 Goodyear workers, along with their cohorts in the nearby Firestone, Goodrich, General, and other factories, were sharply divided amongst themselves. Hard-pressed local union leaders struggled to discredit a company union that over the years had attained some credibility. At the same time they attempted to channel the direct-action militancy of tire builders, many of them not union members, whose frequent job actions both sparked and complicated the strike.

As early as December, Germer's reports had highlighted the restlessness of rubber workers. The URW, a recent AFL affiliate comprised largely of federal labor unions born in the wake of the NIRA, had, like the UAW, been denied a full industrial charter. Its beleaguered leaders had watched the early enthusiasm ebb as the AFL's policy of cautious reliance on the federal government and cooperative relations with employers failed to bring meaningful collective bargaining or improvements in wages or working conditions. By 1936, like the autoworkers, rubber workers were fed up with the old federation and identified closely with the industrial union project.[27]

In view of the volatility of the situation in Akron, however, CIO support was of necessity double edged. On one hand, CIO leaders welcomed and stimulated the grassroots militancy that kept the rubber factories in turmoil. On the other, however, they worked hard to insure that the ultimate repository for the rubber workers' activism would be bona fide unions, led by responsible men and following accepted operating procedures and methods of accountability and governance.

There was much in the Akron situation that made these goals problematic. Deep into the strike, Goodyear management continued to support the Goodyear Assembly, an ERP that had been operating since 1919 and that had over the years claimed the loyalty of many veteran workers. On the other hand, many rubber workers trusted neither it nor the URW, depending, rather, on their own ad hoc workplace networks to force management to revise piece rates or resist disciplinary measures. Actual union membership at Goodyear was a small minority of the workforce, and the URW – which consisted mainly of the several large Akron locals – had few resources with which to support a sustained strike. Through the entire confrontation between rubber workers and employers lurked the ever-present threat of violence. Antiunion workers threatened to assault the picket lines. Firearms were omnipresent. Throughout the strike, declared organizer Rose Pesotta, dispatched to Akron by the ILGWU in behalf of the CIO, "we were standing on the brink of a smoking volcano."[28]

The direct CIO presence predated the strike itself. In December and January, Germer visited Akron several times, and as early as its December meeting, the committee targeted rubber as a key to its ambitions. On January 18 Lewis visited the city. His castigation of the rubber companies and the AFL fed the militancy of activists and drew cheers from the crowd of 2,000 workers. "Your destiny is in your hands," he told them; "I hope you'll do something for yourselves."[29]

Once the strike began, the CIO responded swiftly. The militancy of the Goodyear tire builders drew Brophy and Germer to Akron, with the latter settling in as a full-time advisor. Soon Hapgood joined him, his irreverent attitude a constant irritant to Goodyear officials. In addition CIO affiliates dispatched veteran organizers to assist in the struggle. Leo Krzycki, one of Hillman's top troubleshooters, and Rose Pesotta, a veteran ILGWU organizer, came for the duration. Germer enlisted the services of McAlister Coleman, a labor publicist and newspaperman. Before the end of February, Brophy sent a check for $3,000 – 20 percent of the CIO's entire operating budget – to the URW for strike support.[30]

The Goodyear strike, which lasted until March 21, was an epic struggle. Strikers established a cordon around the entire complex, setting up strong points to which they gave such names as "Camp Roosevelt," "John L. Lewis Post," and "Mae West Post." On February 24, when 150 law officers tried to breach the picket lines, over 5,000 strikers and supporters faced them down. Reported the local newspaper, union partisans were armed with "ten pins from bowling alleys, sawed off billiard cues, short but stout clubs," and other weapons. The vast picket line required complex logistical support and an elaborate warning system. Some strikers were designated as "call boys." These men sped from house to house, mobilizing reinforcements. Strike leaders used the radio to scotch rumors, convey news of meetings, and report on the strike's progress. Pesotta rented a downtown theater, and rubber workers put on nightly skits and musical programs, their Appalachian background evident in the banjo and accordion selections and the yodeling and clog dancing that prevailed. Dramatic mass meetings, in which thousands of rubber workers debated proposed terms of settlement, punctuated the last week of the strike.[31]

Victory came on March 21. The actual settlement, which provided for modest revisions in working hours and limitations of future company changes in the workweek, was something of an anticlimax. Goodyear refused to sign an actual contract or to dismantle the Goodyear Assembly. The union agreed to withdraw wage demands. For the URW and the rubber workers, however, the very fact of concluding a settlement through the consent of the workers while building a vigorous organization from among the disparate strains of worker unrest constituted a great victory.

Germer and other CIO representatives had little to do with the actual strike settlement. Indeed, Germer often misread the temper of the workers, supporting on several occasions company offers that the rubber workers shouted down in mass meetings. At the end of the strike he remained uneasy, feeling that the URW was too much dominated by a spirit of irresponsible militancy. "Our next job," he wrote Brophy, "is to bring more order and discipline into the organization." For Pesotta, the very vagueness of the agreement settling the strike would soon redound to the benefit of those seeking responsible unionism. Lack of definition, she predicted, would lead to more strikes and sit-downs. When employers complained, veteran unionists would be able to explain that without signed contracts, workers would be free to protest in the traditional way. Before long, she expected, "the company would see to it that the whole rubber industry had a closed shop," which would at once guarantee union security and workplace discipline.[32]

SWOC

The second major CIO initiative occurred in the steel industry. The formation of SWOC in June 1936 marked the irrevocable transformation of the CIO into a rival center of union power. Here too the industrial union body combined the high drama of public confrontation and innovative tactics with the promulgation of careful and authoritative rules and regulations designed to create a stable organization in the shortest time possible.

Steel was the litmus test for industrial unionism. Steel was the quintessential heavy industry, employing a half-million workers in its various subdivisions. It was central to manufacturing and increasingly important in coal mining, and the steel industry was run by some of the most fervently anti-union businessmen in the country. The very fact that organized labor had suffered crushing defeats in 1892 and 1919–20 both complicated the task of winning the allegiance of steelworkers and made victory imperative.[33]

In theory, the situation in steel was ideally suited for the original CIO program. The CIO had only to encourage the AA to organize its jurisdiction aggressively and to offer support. Since the AFL had gone on record repeatedly as favoring a steel drive, it seemed on the surface at least that the CIO might pursue its goals without having to challenge the federation outright.

Moreover, steelworkers clearly wanted representation. In the steel towns of the Midwest and Pennsylvania, thousands of steelworkers, many of them second- and even third-generation veterans of the industry, detested its instability of employment, its arbitrary disciplinary, promotion, and job assignment policies, its confusing pay schedules, and the general lack of security. Thousands had responded to the NIRA by joining AA lodges. By February 1934 the AA boasted a membership of over 50,000, a twelvefold increase in less than a year.[34]

Big Steel, however, refused to deal with unions. The AA's new membership totals were in many areas ephemeral, and soon conflict between new recruits and the lethargic veteran leadership dominated the association's affairs. Steel companies quickly created ERPs, or company unions, as a means of complying with NIRA's strictures about worker representation. By the end of 1934 these ERPs claimed over 90 percent of workers in basic steel as members, while AA membership fell drastically.

Like most company unions, those established in response to the NIRA were designed to contain and co-opt workers' demand for representation and to preclude independent organization. Steelworkers understood these motives, yet many found the ERPs plausible vehicles for their concerns. The very creation of representation plans validated the discussion of a wide range of issues in the plants, and whatever their limitations, the ERPs did constitute a form of industrial organization, with all workers in a given plan enrolled in one organization. Moreover, the passage in July 1935 of the Wagner or National Labor Relations Act held out the possibility for autonomy in the company unions because the new law prohibited overt company support for labor organizations and outlawed a number of management practices standard in the conduct of ERPs. By the beginning of 1936 neither the AA nor the AFL enjoyed much support among steelworkers and seemed powerless to prevent the workers in this crucial mass production industry from falling irrevocably outside the ambit of the labor movement. Steelworkers, Brophy declared, were eager for organization, "but many workers are becoming heart-sick from hope deferred."[35]

Plummeting AA membership and continued AFL inertia accelerated Lewis's frustration. In February 1935, for example, he warned the Executive Council that "if we do not take some action the . . . steel workers are going to take it that we have given up hope." To be sure, Green did advance a plan and urged AFL affiliates to contribute $750,000 toward organizing steelworkers. But AFL leaders ignored it, and the federation could raise only $8,625.[36]

CIO initiatives in steel ran on two tracks. Brophy monitored the situation, assessed rank-and-file sentiment, and kept tabs on the AA and the AFL. He warned in April 1936 that "a waning of enthusiasm and disillusionment with the Committee [i.e., the CIO] may result among the company union members, independent groups and Amalgamated lodges whose hopes have been aroused by our previous activities." The company unions might well evolve into permanent organizations, insuring that steelworkers would not take their rightful place in the House of Labor.[37]

In the meantime Lewis had begun to move forcefully. In February he issued a challenge first to the AFL, then to the AA. The CIO would contribute $500,000 (actually it would be UMW money) to a steel campaign. The campaign would bypass the craft unions' jurisdictional claims and organize steelworkers permanently into one industrial union, presumably a revamped AA. It would have as its director someone independent of the parochial AA leadership, presumably someone close to Lewis.[38]

When the AFL, predictably, proved unresponsive, Lewis made a direct offer to the AA: cast your lot with the CIO, he insisted, and cooperate with its efforts to organize steel. In return, he promised, the AA would have representation in the campaign and would reap the ultimate benefit of the masses of new members. Seventy-eight-year-old AA president Michael Tighe balked, fearing that his union would disappear in the proposed setup. Throughout April and May AA members agitated in behalf of CIO affiliation, while Brophy and other Lewis aides intensified the pressure on the old leadership. Thus, one CIO advocate warned the AA's second-in-command, "the present is one of these crucial moments in the history of the labor movement." If the AA did not embrace the CIO, it would "be swept aside." Early in June the AA leadership capitulated.[39]

On June 12 Lewis announced the formation of SWOC, a unique institutional creation. The committee would be a separate entity, covered broadly by the CIO umbrella but with its own governing board, consisting of members appointed, in effect, by Lewis and representing the unions contributing to it. In fact, four of the board's eight members, including director Philip Murray and secretary-treasurer David J. McDonald, came from the UMW. The AA had two members, with the other two representing the ACWA and the ILGWU. The committee's initial funding came almost entirely from the UMW, which contributed a half-million dollars and detailed three dozen organizers to work with SWOC.

SWOC differed from all previous organizations in mass production industries. Unlike earlier radical industrial unions, it endorsed standard collective bargaining goals. At the same time, unlike the AFL, it appealed directly to the steelworkers, recognizing that mass recruitment and shop-floor power alone could bring Big Steel to the bargaining table. It had the forceful backing of the UMW and its now-bulging treasury, insuring a ready supply of cash, experienced organizers, and, most importantly, the vigorous support of the nation's most powerful and energetic labor leader. Unlike the National Committee for Organizing Iron and Steel Workers of 1919–20, SWOC could ignore crippling AFL jurisdictional regulations. It would function as a centralized, authoritative body, dispatching organizers, dispensing money, generating publicity, and recruiting workers directly into its ranks.[40]

The creation of SWOC was a bold move. It marked the irrevocable break with the AFL. If nothing else, the new organization's unilateral declaration of its intention to ignore the jurisdictional claims of other unions and to recruit all steelworkers into one union made it impossible for Green to compromise with the CIO on the question of steel or anything else.

Lewis punctuated the CIO's bold initiative with scathing public ridicule of AFL president Green. Lewis responded savagely to an attack Green made on the CIO's plans to organize steel. In a public letter issued on June 6, Lewis expressed mock astonishment: "It is inconceivable that you intend doing what your statement implies, i.e. to sit with the women, under an awning on the hilltop, while the steel workers in the valley struggle in the dust and agony of industrial warfare." To threats that the UMW and the other CIO unions would face suspension from the AFL, Lewis responded with mock amazement that Green, a UMW member for over forty years, "would be a party to such a Brutus blow."[41]

When Green defended the AFL's unwillingness to follow Lewis's lead, the CIO leader resumed his insults. "Your lament," he intoned, "is that I will not join you in a policy of anxious inertia. . . . [But] candidly, I am temperamentally incapable of sitting with you in sackcloth and ashes, endlessly intoning, '*O tempora! O Mores.*'" The carefully chosen rhetoric, replete with obscure but impressive-sounding Latin locutions and images of a passive, feminized Green, posed starkly the contrast between the lusty young CIO and its bold leader and the effete, dithering AFL and its be-fuddled chief.[42]

Yet the CIO drive in steel actually displayed keen concern with the traditions of the mainstream labor movement. After all, SWOC was a device for bringing workers into unions and for engaging in collective bargaining. Its first policy statement emphasized that the organization sought only "to establish a permanent organization of the workers for the orderly and peaceful presentation and negotiation of their grievances and demands." SWOC was "composed of responsible representatives of many of the Country's greatest labor organizations," which had "a long record of success in carrying through collective bargaining with a minimum of industrial strife."[43]

SWOC promised a "centralized and responsible" organizing campaign. Some labor advocates believed that the time was ripe to create more participatory forms of worker organization. They hoped that the CIO would spearhead a sweeping social transformation. But no one associated with SWOC, the CIO's first great institutional embodiment, even contemplated such a prospect. Instead, SWOC's founding documents and early strategy sessions made it abundantly clear that not only did the new organization embrace the essential goals of the AFL, it would follow hierarchical patterns of union governance and organizing strategy. All decisions were to be made by Murray; all funds were to be dispersed by and sent to SWOC headquarters in Pittsburgh; all appointments for organizing posts came from the top. Indeed, in terms of union structure, the most innovative aspect of SWOC was not some turn toward democracy but, rather, the creation of a highly centralized organization, with little provision for local union initiative or rank-and-file participation.[44]

In mid-June SWOC moved into the field. The first of its projected 200 organizers, many of them UMW veterans and others recruited from the ranks of the Communist Party and its short-lived Steel and Metal Workers Industrial Union, filtered into the steel towns and mills. SWOC began publishing a newspaper, established a research department, and employed a full-time legal counsel, the able Lee Pressman, a former Communist recruited by Lewis. At a CIO board meeting early in July, Murray reported that "astonishing results have been attained in two weeks." A lavish corporate publicity campaign designed to discredit SWOC boomeranged, helping by its very extemism to validate the new union among steelworkers. Murray and his assistants reached out to public officials, leaders of ethnic and religious groups, and company union activists to spread the CIO's message of organization and responsible collective bargaining.[45]

Actual progress in the field was slow, however. Skeptical steelworkers exhibited little of the mass enthusiasm that Akron's rubber workers had shown earlier. "It was hard work," recalled one organizer, "continual plugging away. It was a crusade without the Crusaders." SWOC began to focus its attentions on gaining influence within the company unions. Although by the end of the year SWOC claimed 125,000 members in basic steel, its actual dues-paying constituency was a fraction of that figure. Thus, for months after SWOC's dramatic birth, the fate of the CIO's most ambitious undertaking remained uncertain, as SWOC leaders sought to find a way, Murray remarked, to "banish fear from the steel workers' minds" and to persuade Big Steel to accept the new steelworkers' union as its unavoidable bargaining partner.[46]

THE ELECTION OF 1936

Through most of 1936, politics permeated CIO activity. Lewis, Hillman, and the others believed that Franklin Roosevelt's reelection was absolutely critical to their success. Republican victories, which in the spring seemed eminently possible, might well abort the whole CIO enterprise. Every union affiliated with the industrial union body lined up behind Roosevelt.

Lewis in particular threw himself into the campaign. In May, along with Hillman and President George Berry of the AFL Printing Pressmen's union, he announced the creation of LNPL, ostensibly a multiunion organization established to support Roosevelt and other progressive candidates. In reality there was little AFL participation in LNPL, and most of its funding – at least $600,000, a staggering sum in the mid-1930s – came directly from the UMW. Lewis met frequently with Roosevelt and in September and October toured industrial areas and made nationwide radio speeches in FDR's cause. In the weeks before the November 3 election Murray devoted the manpower and resources of the steelworkers' union primarily to getting out the vote.

LNPL was both part of and distinct from the overall CIO initiative. In theory it was an independent organization open to all who shared its left-liberal agenda. It had no institutional connection with the CIO per se. At the same time, however, all CIO leaders enthusiastically endorsed it, and the organizers who campaigned so energetically in the steel towns of Ohio and Pennsylvania did so as CIO representatives.

Moreover, the vast financial scale and innovative character of LNPL closely paralleled the new style of union activism associated with the CIO. LNPL channeled its money directly to the Roosevelt campaign and to the campaigns of other progressive candidates rather than serving as a fundraising arm for the Democratic National Committee. Lewis took his message directly to the workers. "I salute the hosts of labor who listen," he told a vast radio audience in July. "My voice tonight will be the voice of millions . . . economically exploited and inarticulate." Would American workers gain democratic representation in the workplace, he asked, or "shall [they] serve as indentured servants for a financial and economic dictatorship?"[47]

In November Roosevelt won overwhelmingly, carrying most industrial centers, many with massive majorities. Workers contributed heavily to FDR's triumph and to the election of large Democratic majorities in Congress and of progressive governors such as Frank Murphy in Michigan and George H. Earle, Jr., in Pennsylvania. Experts were unclear as to precisely how large Roosevelt's debt to labor was. There was substantial evidence, for example, that working-class support for FDR existed in large measure apart from any endorsement of him by labor organizations. Indeed, in many organizing campaigns union representatives reversed the equation, telling workers that Roosevelt wanted them to join the union. In an election in which Roosevelt captured 60 percent of the two-party vote and 523 electoral votes, even labor's contribution could hardly have been decisive. Organized labor gained enormously through the president's reflected glow. In 1936 no labor partisan seeking to align his movement with the political preferences of his constituency could fail to embrace Roosevelt, regardless of the Democratic Party's less than progressive reputation.[48]

The election victory permitted the CIO to redirect attention to the steel campaign. "We know we must capitalize on the election," Lewis told his associates a few days after the balloting. "The C.I.O. was out fighting for Roosevelt and every steel town showed a smashing victory for him." With Roosevelt safely reelected and with prolabor legislation such as the Wagner Act seemingly secure from repeal or dismemberment, the way was clear for the CIO to move forward.[49]

At the same meeting Brophy summarized CIO progress since the organization's inception just a year earlier. In rubber, autos, steel, radios, and other industries, Brophy declared, the AFL policy had been one of drift, inertia, and "craft segregation." Gains of the 1933–34 period were being lost. In steel, company unions "were moving steadily in the direction of independent [i.e., non-AFL] organization."

The CIO had appeared on the scene just in time. In Akron, CIO involvement provided "the backing that made victory possible for the determined and heroic strikers." The fact that the CIO represented "powerful, nationwide organizations," such as the UMW and the ACWA, gave workers hope in their struggles against "the huge, anti-union corporations" and contrasted sharply with the parochialism and localism that continued to dominate the AFL old guard.

Yet Brophy reaffirmed that the CIO's aim remained "to organize workers into the A.F. of L." The CIO had confined its activities to the absolutely critical situations in auto, rubber, steel, and radios where the fate of organized labor's future seemed to be in the balance. In steel, Lewis and the CIO had sought with excruciating patience to work with and through the AFL. When it finally created a separate body to organize steelworkers, it had done so with the consent and involvement of the enfeebled AA. Murray followed with a measured assessment of SWOC accomplishments, pointing out the special difficulties involved in recruiting local organizers and in attracting black workers, long victimized by the AFL's discriminatory practices.[50]

Overall, the tone of the postelection meeting was sober. As Katherine Ellickson later remembered it, the CIO leaders believed that "they had won at the ballot box, but [they wondered if they] could . . . win at the plants." "The C.I.O.," Murray remarked, "was formed in desperation," as a last-ditch effort to bring mass production workers into the House of Labor. The CIO dare not fail, Hillman added, for this "may be the last opportunity to organize."[51]

The CIO leadership understood that they did not control events. Would the AFL officialdom proceed with its campaign to destroy the CIO? Would the Wagner Act stand the test of constitutionality at the hands of a conservative Supreme Court? Would the Roosevelt administration provide vigorous support? Or would Big Steel be successful, as it had been so regularly in the past, in its campaign to smash the new union? Above all, the question that loomed most pregnantly was this one: In the mills and factories, on the assembly lines, and in the neighborhoods of industrial America, would the workers continue to respond to the unique mixture of trade union traditionalism and bold initiative that the CIO offered? Could the House of Labor accommodate the industrial masses and would they choose to dwell within it?

3 Over the Top, 1936–1937

The events of the year after Roosevelt's reelection put the CIO over the top. Breakthroughs in the automobile industry and the steel industry early in 1937 brought industrial unionism at last to the heartland of the economy. In addition, unionists in other mass production industries and key service sectors, notably electrical appliances, longshoring, meatpacking, and transportation, made significant advances. These victories unleashed a wave of organizing that made the CIO a household word and seemed to vindicate the bold initiative that Lewis and his cohorts had launched in 1935.

OF GAINS AND LIMITS

Disturbingly, however, the great victories of 1936 and 1937 soon proved less than complete. Barely months after U.S. Steel signed an agreement with SWOC, the so-called Little Steel companies, which employed over 150,000 steelworkers, turned back SWOC in a bloody strike that culminated in the unpunished murder of ten Chicago strikers. Even as autoworkers rejoiced over the coming of collective bargaining to industry giants GM and Chrysler in the spring of 1937, Henry Ford's toughs were bludgeoning UAW organizers in Dearborn and escalating the reign of terror inside the plants of the second largest automaker. Tiremakers continued to resist the URW in Akron, and the important aircraft and farm equipment sectors remained largely nonunion. A CIO drive aimed at bringing industrial unionism to southern textile workers soon bogged down.

There were many reasons for CIO success in auto, steel, and other industries, and as many for frustration and failure in these and other sectors. The CIO surge drew its strength from the determination of industrial workers to achieve greater security and dignity in their workplaces. It was aided by a broadly pro-worker constellation of political forces as demonstrated in the labor-backed victories not only of FDR but of governors in the large industrial states. It drew upon the astute leadership of Lewis and his colleagues who ably combined behind-the-scenes negotiations with fiery appeals to an aroused working class. The CIO drive benefited also from fortuitous timing, coming as it did amid a period of rising economic indicators that weakened the appetite of key employers for industrial conflict.

These same factors, however, also blunted this initial CIO threat. Democratic politicians pulled back from outright alignment with the new labor movement, influenced partly by continuing alliances with the rival AFL and partly by class and party dynamics that worked against too close a relationship to militant unionism. The very success of the CIO against GM, U.S. Steel, and Goodyear encouraged mass production workers and industrial union leaders to move more boldly against unorganized firms than circumstances made prudent. An expanding economy encouraged some industrialists to bargain, however reluctantly, with the CIO, but the drastic recession that began in the fall of 1937 stiffened corporate resolve to resist unionization.

Of all the factors contributing to CIO success and frustration, however, the behavior of ordinary workers was the most perplexing and volatile. Workers were angry, restive, and determined to effect changes. Through the 1930s, surveys and polls found that working-class Americans were moving to the left. The enormous blue collar vote for Roosevelt and other industrial state Democrats in the 1936 elections provided ample evidence. The outpouring of letters to Franklin and Eleanor Roosevelt, unprecedented in American history, also revealed the growing class consciousness and populist radicalism of blue collar America.[1]

Workers' activism on the picket lines and in the streets reinforced these findings. Early chroniclers of the CIO hammered home the theme of an aroused and united working class. Journalist Mary Heaton Vorse stressed the spontaneity and solidarity of working-class behavior in Flint, Akron, and the steel towns of Ohio and Pennsylvania. "There is an awful power and might in this age-old drive for freedom," she declared of the industrial union crusade. "It is like a force of nature[,] irresistible as a tide." Veteran publicist Edward Levinson wrote of "the masses in rubber, auto, and steel centers" whose solidarity and militancy brought about "the greatest upheaval in American industrial history." Levinson told his readers of Flint's autoworkers girding for battle against the company-corrupted police in the great sit-down strike of early 1937. Carrying lead pipes, barrel staves, and clubs, they gathered near the Fisher Body plant to resist the enforcement of an antiunion injunction. "Like the Minute Men of '76 and as fully determined that their cause was righteous," Levinson wrote, "they had seized whatever weapon lay at hand and rushed off to battle." Declared publicist Len De Caux, "In major CIO struggles . . . the workers reacted as members of a working class in combat."[2]

Despite these vivid characterizations, however, militancy, solidarity, and class consciousness were not universal among industrial workers. Even in the relatively favorable climate of the mid- to late 1930s, joining a union was a risky business. Even the passage in July 1935 of the National Labor Relations Act, with its apparent protection for union advocates, failed to annul the fear that infected blue collar communities. The actual conduct of organizing campaigns and strikes usually rested on a handful of committed activists, with most workers, understandably, hanging back until favorable odds had developed.

Moreover, despite their leftward drift, workers retained strong attachments to the central features of American society. Veneration of FDR expressed faith in him as a benevolent father rather than as a class avenger. At the height of CIO dynamism, in July 1937 a public opinion poll found that 53 percent of lower income workers preferred the AFL's conservative William Green as a leader of labor to the CIO's wrathful John L. Lewis. A 1941 Gallup survey revealed that a majority of working-class respondents identified Henry Ford as a greater friend of the working man than John L. Lewis. Radical political candidates rarely achieved more than marginal support. Throughout the mid-1930s the mainsprings of worker activism centered in the modern industrial core of the economy, usually in locales and sectors on the road to recovery from the worst ravages of the depression. Workers in autos, steel, rubber, and electrical appliances saw in the new unions an effective means for achieving a more stable and secure version of the relative prosperity of the 1920s. Thousands of their coworkers, however, remained uncommitted, carefully weighing the shifting balance of power in the workplaces and industrial communities.[3]

Union campaigns often had as much difficulty in attracting workers as in battling employers. Western Pennsylvania steelworkers doubted SWOC's ability to change the balance of power inside the mills. Memories flashed back to the defeats of 1919 and even to the Homestead disaster of 1892. "What we hoped would be a torrent [of SWOC memberships] turned out . . . to be a trickle," reported one officer, adding that "the steelworkers did not fall all over themselves to sign a pledge card with SWOC." In dozens of mills the union threw up picket lines to collect dues from reluctant coworkers. "They would sign a card," said one union activist, "and when it come time to pay their dues they wouldn't. . . . We [the union officers] sat around a pot-belly stove getting splinters in our ass passin' the hat tryin' to get [money to buy] coal."[4]

Even workers in the fabled sites of CIO militancy, Flint and Akron, often proved less than enthusiastic. In the wake of the URW's remarkable victory over Goodyear in the spring of 1936, turmoil raged in the Ohio city's huge tire factories. True, job actions were frequent. But hundreds of rubber workers remained loyal to the companies and to the company unions, while many more remained on the sidelines, waiting to see how the struggles within the plants and community would turn out. Indeed, the very militancy that made Akron rubber workers legendary stemmed at least in part from the precariousness of union commitment, as union supporters and opponents battled.[5]

Similar patterns emerged in Flint and Detroit. The great majority of Flint autoworkers, for example, played no active role in the great sit-down of December 1936 to February 1937. Far larger numbers of GM workers opposed the strike than belonged to the UAW, while many more were (in the words of a union activist) "just sort of watching."[6]

The situation was similar in Detroit and other auto centers. In Anderson, Indiana, for example, home of two GM parts plants that employed over 11,000 workers, few workers joined the UAW locals in the months following that city's sit-down strike. In Norwood, Ohio, and Hamtramck, Michigan, the enthusiasm of the spring of 1937 petered out, and union building became a slow and uncertain process. Management blunders were often more important than unionist enthusiasm. Henry Kraus, a UAW publicist and chronicler of the Flint strike, depicted the confrontation against GM as a spontaneous rising of the auto center's working class but in the end stressed the courage and dedication of a handful of union militants and the reluctance of the broad majority of autoworkers. Clayton Fountain, an activist at Chevrolet Gear and Axle in Detroit, found that fear and caution dominated his coworkers. It was not until he was fired and then reinstated, appearing in the shop sporting a UAW button, "months later, when there was no danger of getting fired, [that] they all became good union members."[7]

Workers exhibited complex and shifting patterns of response to the new union initiative. The southern textile labor force, heir to a long tradition of local activism, seemed to combine impatient militancy and resigned acceptance of managerial dominance. In electrical appliances, early breakthroughs by the CIO's UE did not lead to wider organization. In short, a seeming paradox characterized the first great CIO surge, with an enormous welling up of activist sentiment coexisting with distressing apathy and unwillingness of workers to sign membership cards and pay dues.[8]

Workers were not cowardly or misguided. They had to be convinced that the union could be and, more importantly, could remain an assertive presence on the shop floor, assembly line, or loading dock. Employers exerted power seemingly effortlessly every day. Could the new unions translate their sudden success into permanent countervailing power? Workers sympathetic to the CIO watched hopefully, looking for signs of a dramatic shift in the balance of power. The reinstatement of fired activists, the humiliation of a hated foreman, or the open display of union buttons had a powerful appeal to these secret sympathizers.

Others, however, continued to view the employer as the fundamental source of sustenance. What right did a self-righteous minority have to change a workplace regime that benefited many workers? They sought to replace a familiar workplace hierarchy with a new one that was at best untried and at worst would put company loyalists under the thumbs of outsiders and hostile coworkers. To these oppositionists the union had to demonstrate simply that it could compel their acquiescence. In a thousand workplaces the CIO challenge evidenced itself in this department-by-department, work-group-by-work-group redefinition of power relationships. It well behooved ordinary workers to hedge their bets until the still-untested union could demonstrate that it would be as potent a force in the day-to-day lives of the workers as were their foremen and supervisors.[9]

SIT-DOWN

The sit-down strike of automobile workers in Flint, Michigan, in the winter of 1936–37 powerfully illustrated the crosscurrents of militancy and diffidence that characterized the industrial working class. At the same time, it exhibited the combination of picket line activism, skillful negotiating, and favorable political and economic forces that gave the CIO its distinctive character and made possible its early success. The juxtaposition of the great public drama played out on the frozen streets of the Michigan auto center, on one hand, and the results of this enormous working-class victory – a sketchy one-page contract – epitomized the two polar, yet complementary, tendencies within the CIO, namely the anger and resentment of large portions of the working class and the modesty of their goals. Likewise, the combination of sharp confrontation and practical acceptance of limited contractual gains revealed the high degree to which John L. Lewis and his CIO cohorts were in close tune with the notions of moral economy that animated blue collar activism in the New Deal period.

The automobile industry loomed large in the plans of Lewis and his colleagues. Employing more than a half-million workers, it was the quintessential mass production industry. The assembly line, though in fact employing but a fraction of the industry's labor force, epitomized the workplace characteristic of the second industrial revolution. The industry had pioneered in the application of new methods and technologies in machine tooling, metallurgy, corporate structure, and marketing. In labor relations the automakers combined innovative workplace restructuring and redefinition of skills with old-fashioned union bashing.[10]

The drastic mechanization of the auto industry in the period immediately before World War I had both expanded production exponentially and driven craft unions of metalworkers out of the plants. Through the 1920s organized labor played no role in its labor relations regime. The combination of management's determination to prevent union development, the relatively high wage structure and booming levels of production and employment of the 1920s, and the inability of the AFL to generate any organizing impetus insured a nonunion environment.[11]

During the high-wage 1920s the industry had attracted large numbers of young, energetic, and ambitious first-generation industrial workers. German and Anglo-Scots machinists, metalworkers, and tool-and-die makers took advantage of America's weak vocational education and apprenticing practices and filled the expanding need for their skills in the plants of Ford or GM. Immigrants and rural Americans alike found good wages and a taste of modern consumer capitalism in the midwestern auto plants. The work was hard and discipline harsh, but many felt they had made a reasonable bargain in exchanging the limited prospects of the farm or European homeland for work in Ford's or GM's plants.[12]

The depression changed this calculation. Auto and parts makers responded to the crisis by laying off workers, tightening discipline, and ratcheting up the pace of work. Even during prosperous times, autoworkers suffered from seasonal unemployment. Now competition for jobs grew fierce. Employers chose the younger job applicants; Detroit drugstores put in extra stocks of black shoe polish in time for the fall rehiring season, as older men attempted to cover graying hair. In the plants, those fortunate enough to gain work found production norms heightened, shop-floor discipline harsher, and conditions more dangerous. Skilled workers now performed repetitive tasks and earned a fraction of what they had made before. The opportunity to abandon a bad job and hire on with another automaker was gone.

For many workers, however, the system's irrationality and injustice were the hardest to bear. While autoworkers and their families suffered, GM stockholders continued to reap dividends. Arbitrary treatment, demands for personal and sexual favors, and religious, ethnic, or personal favoritism characterized the recruitment, discipline, discharge, and rehiring of workers. In many auto plants, security officers used harassment, surveillance, and sheer physical brutality to squelch dissent. Racketeers and shakedown artists preyed upon workers, often with the active connivance of supervisors.[13]

As the depression deepened, autoworkers protested deteriorating conditions with strikes and marches. Section 7a galvanized union sentiment. Although the AFL had no autoworkers' union as such, its representatives signed up new recruits in the federation's federal labor unions, unions directly affiliated with the AFL that had historically enrolled workers who did not fit into any existent jurisdictional category or for whom representatives of their appropriate organization were unavailable. Declared one frank Cleveland unionist, "I do not think there was any real urge for unionism until the [NIRA] law made it . . . look like it was going to be possible to have a union without a lot of discharges and so forth." By the end of the summer, William Collins, an AFL functionary appointed by Green to oversee the surge of unionism in autos, was reporting membership of over 100,000. Flint activists counted 20,000 new recruits in the five GM plants in that critical center of production.[14]

But the heady enthusiasm of this early burst of organization quickly ebbed. Company spies were everywhere. Workers soon realized that federal legislation had changed little and that unionists enjoyed no protection under the law. "A great many people at that time," recalled an auto union activist, "believed that a union was like a slot machine. . . . If you did not hit the jackpot, you walked away." Too many workers, declared one militant organizer, substituted a "child-like faith in the President" for sustained commitment to the union. New locals in Flint and elsewhere soon withered. By early 1934 it was business as usual in the city's Chevrolet, Buick, Fisher Body, and AC spark plug plants, with the union presence now confined to a few diehards.[15]

Autoworkers had anticipated corporate hostility. What they were unprepared for was the ineptitude of the AFL and the powerlessness of government. Green dispatched bland second-raters to oversee the recruitment of autoworkers. These men proved as fearful of the aroused rank and file as they were credulous about government's good intentions and optimistic about management's willingness to welcome the AFL. A government-sponsored and AFL-endorsed agreement in March 1934 that left power relationships in the plants unchanged further discredited the AFL and the NRA. In Flint, the unions formed in the immediate wake of Section 7a, the "NRA babies," lost over 90 percent of their members.[16]

Disillusionment with the AFL was deep. Declared one Flint activist at the end of 1935, "Workers believe that the present [AFL] setup is beyond repair."[17] Not only had federation leaders been ineffective; in addition, it became increasingly clear that the AFL hierarchy had no intention of permitting the establishment of a true industrial union of autoworkers. The machinists' union claimed the skilled men and undermined the federal auto unions. President Green *said* that he understood the demand for industrial unionism, but he invariably gave the fledgling mass production workers homilies rather than effective support. "He who keepeth his head," he counseled unionists in Massachusetts, "is stronger than he that taketh a City. Remember gentlemen keep your head and respect jurisdictional rights."[18]

At its October 1934 convention the AFL had declared its commitment to organizing auto and other mass production workers, and in August 1935 the federation had in fact acceded to the wishes of the scattered federal auto unions by granting a charter to them under the rubric of the International Union, United Automobile Workers. But restrictions hedged the charter, requiring the parceling out of metal finishing, upholstery, tool-and-die, and other skilled workers to their respective craft unions. By the time of the CIO's birth in November 1935 the UAW consisted of small local unions throughout the Midwest and had little strength in the auto capital, Detroit. The UAW had no membership in the savagely antiunion Ford Motor Company plants and but a handful of beleaguered members in Flint, the strategic hub of the GM empire.

In the absence of a vigorous AFL presence, organizations of skilled workers and of employees of particular companies sprouted, especially in Detroit. The Mechanics Educational Society of America, the Automotive Workers' Industrial Association (centered in Detroit Chrysler plants), and other local bodies kept alive the spark of collective action. In other places, company unions, initiated by auto companies as a means of formal compliance with Section 7a, held sway. The CIO's representatives and officers feared that disillusionment with the AFL could well result in a permanent loss of this core industry's huge workforce to the House of Labor.[19]

In 1936 several factors combined to stir union hopes. The activities of the CIO, the URW victory, and the launching of the steel campaign in the summer energized auto activists. An upturn in the economy and expanding auto sales tightened labor markets, making the companies more vulnerable to pressure. The Roosevelt campaign, with Lewis eloquently aligning the industrial union movement with the revered president while auto industry magnates ostentatiously financed the Republicans and openly reviled the New Deal, sharpened the "us versus them" feelings of autoworkers. "The thing that is outstanding and impresses me," declared Brophy early in the year, "is the widespread and sustained response of workers' interest on the subject of industrial unionism."[20]

The Roosevelt landslide was crucial. FDR's victory in the most class-divided presidential contest in memory demonstrated the vulnerability of big business. Moreover, in Michigan, liberal Frank Murphy, mayor of Detroit, had defeated a conservative Republican opponent for the state's governorship, thus depriving employers of the guarantee of support by public authorities to which they had become accustomed.

Soon after, militants in the sprawling Fisher Body plants began to harass supervisors. Work groups pulled quickie strikes. Whole departments walked out when management tried to discipline activists. Within a month of the election, membership had multiplied tenfold. In the Fisher Body plants, noted a UAW activist, "union buttons began to sprout like dandelions everywhere." In December 3,000 new members signed up.[21]

At the end of that month, the guerrilla warfare between aroused unionists and GM management came to a head. Through the late fall, autoworkers in Kansas City, Atlanta, Cleveland, and Detroit had been backing up their demands for union recognition with sit-down strikes. Sit-downs offered decided advantages over outside strikes. Seizure of a work site shut down production at once, and as long as strikers occupied the facility, they were free from the picket line violence. Moreover, sit-down strikes masked the union's numerical weakness, for they permitted a militant minority to demonstrate in the most dramatic way possible the power of the union. UAW leaders, at once encouraging and seeking to channel the suddenly explosive militancy, wanted a coordinated strategy of work stoppages to force GM to recognize the union. But in December, events happened too quickly for meticulous planning. As union strength grew in Flint's Fisher Body No. 1 and No. 2 plants, some workers now seemed eager for confrontation. Would workers obey a strike call? asked a UAW representative of a local activist. Were they ready? "Ready?" Bud Simons replied. "They're like a pregnant woman in her tenth month."[22]

On December 30, 1936, workers took control of Fisher Body plants No. 1 and No. 2. Rumors that GM was about to remove critical dies from Fisher No. 1 so as to guarantee continued production in case of a strike spurred the move. Timing their action for the afternoon shift change, unionists surged into the plants, calling on fellow workers to drop their tools. They shut off machinery, expelled company guards and foremen, and occupied the two buildings. Now in control of GM's means of producing bodies for popular Chevrolet, Pontiac, and Buick models, the occupiers vowed to remain in the plants until GM recognized the UAW.

The six-week strike that followed resulted in the first significant union contract wrested from a major automaker. Eventually the UAW added another plant to its list of occupied territory. As GM production plummeted, that of its chief rivals, Ford and Chrysler, spurted upward as they exploited the buoyant automobile market of early 1937. On two separate occasions the company secured court injunctions, ordering workers to vacate the plants, only to have the first discredited when CIO legal counsel Lee Pressman disclosed that the issuing judge was a GM stockholder. Autoworkers simply ignored the second injunction, expecting that Governor Murphy would not risk the bloodshed that vigorous enforcement of it would have brought.[23]

The sit-downers displayed remarkable élan, comradeship, and solidarity. They fought off police assaults by turning fire hoses on the attackers and by hurling heavy door hinges and tools from second-floor windows. They organized entertainment and exercise programs. They turned car bodies and seats into bedrooms. In their act of protest, they recovered some of the human connection that mass production industry had systematically leached out of the work experience. Declared one sit-downer, "It was like we were soldiers holding the fort. It was like war. The guys with me became my buddies." Meanwhile, outside the plants the sit-downers' coworkers and families mobilized in their support. With the help of sympathetic restaurant owners, UAW wives fed the strikers. More dramatically, a newly organized Women's Emergency Brigade at times confronted mayhem-bent police physically, turning back attacks on the sit-downers.[24]

The CIO itself played a limited role in the actual conduct of the strike. A remarkable group of UAW activists such as Wyndham Mortimer, Bob Travis, Victor Reuther, Genora Johnson, and Henry Kraus provided day-to-day leadership. It was an autoworkers' affair, reflective of the distinctive mixture of victimization and resolve that characterized worker activism in this boom-and-bust modern mass production industry and its recently created communities.

But the battle line of the sit-down strike stretched well beyond Flint. Federal officials, most notably Secretary of Labor Frances Perkins and President Roosevelt himself, sought settlement. Reporters flocked to southeastern Michigan as the nationwide implications of the stalemate in the plants became clear.

In this aspect of the strike, the CIO, and especially John L. Lewis, played a critical role. In January 1937 the CIO remained a skeletal organization. The steel drive, still very much in doubt, claimed its primary attention and most of its resources. The UMW and the other industrial unions had shoveled huge sums into Roosevelt's campaign, and the steel drive was costing over $100,000 per month. Insofar as the situation in the automobile industry was concerned, the CIO *was* John L. Lewis, who personally conducted the complex negotiations involving GM executives and state and federal officials that eventually ended the strike.

In his capacity as the CIO's chief spokesman, Lewis performed brilliantly. He quickly grasped three fundamental points: the sit-down strike provided the UAW and the CIO with a degree of power that could not be surrendered without tangible concessions from GM; striking workers rallied under the CIO banner because they believed that it would stand behind them and not cut the ground from under them, as many believed the AFL had done in 1934; and as important as the struggle on the picket lines and in the plants was, the ultimate fate of the strike lay with public authorities in the Michigan capital, Lansing, and Washington, D.C.[25]

Lewis confined his involvement to working with and through government officials to bring GM to the bargaining table. He insisted that the plants would not be vacated until GM had agreed to recognize the union as exclusive bargaining agent. GM officials tried to persuade Murphy, and union leaders indirectly, to have the sit-downers abandon the plants as a condition of subsequent negotiations. The governor and federal officials pressed Lewis to order the workers to leave.

Lewis would have none of it. The essential point, he insisted, was this: GM had proved repeatedly that it respected only power, and right now, in January and early February 1937, it was the autoworkers who exercised it. Since 1933, he pointed out, GM had spent over $1 million in espionage services. It had colluded with the Flint police first to freeze the strikers out, then to assault them physically. In other Michigan cities its security agents were daily brutalizing union supporters. If the strikers left the plant, GM would "negotiate" only in some pro forma meeting that would result in no permanent recognition. "To recognize the union for an hour is no lasting gain," the CIO president told Murphy. "They will not make a concession" on any substantive point, Lewis believed, unless the union continued to wield the tangible power that alone could compel recognition. In the protracted negotiations that Lewis conducted with Murphy, Secretary of Labor Perkins (and through press conferences and releases, President Roosevelt), and, eventually, GM officials, he held as firmly to these bedrock positions as the autoworkers did to the Fisher Body plants.[26]

The agreement that ended the strike on February 11 was a one-page document. It stipulated no drastic change in wages or conditions of employment. But it did obligate GM to recognize the UAW as the only legitimate labor organization in the plants affected by the strike for a period of six months. The UAW could use the very fact of having wrested such an agreement to extend its membership both throughout GM facilities and among other automakers. While the agreement specified no precise system of handling workers' grievances, by extending recognition to the UAW it did grant de facto legitimacy to the union activists who took on the role of shop stewards. The February 11 agreement was a giant step toward the goal of bringing industrial unionism to the auto industry.[27]

The auto agreement was powerful vindication of the CIO course. Few believed that William Green could have stood up to GM as Lewis had.

Indeed, the AFL's claim, on the eve of the settlement, that skilled auto-workers should be separated from the UAW and turned over to AFL craft unions further discredited the old federation. Victory weakened company unionism in auto production and cut the ground from rival labor organizations. The UAW, proudly flying the CIO flag, had earned the right to undertake the still-daunting task of organizing the entire auto industry.

In the months immediately after the Flint settlement the UAW made major strides to do exactly that. One by one major plants operated by Packard, Hudson, Murray Body, and a dozen other auto and auto parts makers fell into line. The plum, however, was Chrysler, with its workforce of over 100,000. In March, emboldened by earlier successes, UAW members occupied the corporation's Detroit plants. With Lewis again doing the high-level negotiating under Governor Murphy's aegis, Chrysler eventually agreed on April 6 to a GM-like settlement.[28]

By late spring 1937 the UAW seemed headed for overwhelming victory. Dues-paying membership leaped from just over 60,000 at the end of 1936 to over 150,000 in May. Confident stewards and activists faced down supervisors, threatening them with work stoppages, slowdowns, and other reprisals. As more and more workers now brandished UAW dues buttons, other workers, perhaps lukewarm about the union, acknowledged the UAW's new power and signed on.[29]

In fact, however, the enthusiasm of the immediate post-Flint months proved evanescent. GM instructed its managers to contest the union at every turn within the broad terms of the contract. Ford stepped up its intimidation of union activists. In May, at an overpass leading to the Rouge complex just outside Detroit, company thugs savagely beat UAW organizers attempting to distribute leaflets. The militancy of autoworkers sometimes played into management's hands, and the internal life of the UAW seethed with dissidence, as would-be leaders and long-frustrated workers struggled for position in the new order. Ever concerned with the establishment of stable union bodies, Adolph Germer reported sourly throughout the fall on the escalating factional fighting within the UAW. "Flint is in turmoil," he told Brophy. "The people who really built the organization are pushed out," only to be replaced by "dummies." A fascistlike organization, the Black Legion, continued to have influence in some Flint locals. GM chairman Alfred Sloan, Germer noted darkly, had boasted that before the February 11 contract had run its six-month duration, company pressure and internal factionalism would have destroyed the UAW, and the veteran Germer did not consider Sloan's to be an idle boast.[30]

Still, autoworkers had gained a vital foothold and boosted the CIO's stock. The initiative for the sit-down strike and the subsequent advances had come from local activists and UAW leaders, but the successes of the winter and spring would have been inconceivable without Lewis and the CIO. As dramatic and important as the automobile sector was, however, steel was still the CIO's primary focus, and here the victory or defeat of industrial unionism lay directly in CIO hands. For, unlike the grassroots UAW, SWOC was from top to bottom a direct creature of John L. Lewis and the CIO.

STEEL

CIO victory in steel followed immediately upon the heels of the Flint settlement. The agreement between SWOC and U.S. Steel signed on March 2, 1937, was no less stunning and vindicating than the GM contract three weeks earlier. "If we can break the Hindenburg line of [American] industry – steel – everyone knows how far we can go in organizing millions," Lewis had declared in November. Indeed, like the auto settlement, that in steel unleashed a wave of organization that swelled union ranks and gave powerful legitimacy to the CIO project.[31]

Again, however, as in auto, the agreement raised as many questions as it answered. SWOC's route to victory was quite different from that followed by the UAW. Steelworkers exhibited much less activism at the local level than did autoworkers. Early in their campaign SWOC leaders concentrated on working through the various ERPs. In steel as in auto Lewis played a key role in arranging the final settlement, but the bargain between the CIO chief and U.S. Steel's chief executive officer, Myron Taylor, appeared more a deal negotiated between fellow executives than the direct fruits of worker activism.

In steel as in auto, organizing fervor followed pathbreaking settlement. Also as in auto, the limits of the early CIO's power and appeal soon became evident. Like the UAW, SWOC was unable to extend its sway through key sectors of the industry. In particular, Little Steel fought SWOC without quarter. The strike that resulted from SWOC's efforts to bring Little Steel to terms began in May, but by July it had ended in bloody defeat. Even here, however, the increasingly effective workings of the National Labor Relations Act helped SWOC to keep alive a union presence and to lay the groundwork for eventual recovery.

In launching the drive to organize steel in the summer of 1936, Murray and his associates had dispatched squadrons of organizers, held mass meetings, and sought out local activists in the mills. Increasingly, however, SWOC leaders realized that U.S. Steel's company unions held the key to success. Thus, in November SWOC organizers began to cooperate with and, they hoped, to co-opt these bodies. Meanwhile, the CIO exploited the victories of Roosevelt and New Deal Democrats in the gubernatorial races in Pennsylvania[32] and the Midwest to convince cautious steelworkers that a new era in political and industrial life had arrived. In addition, CIO people worked closely with the staff members of the U.S. Senate's special committee examining employer abuses of workers' rights, the La Follette Committee, in highly publicized investigations of the steel communities. It cultivated leaders of ethnic and fraternal organizations in the steelmaking areas, using their endorsements as badges of legitimacy. Finally, Lewis used his growing reputation as the authoritative voice of industrial workers to convince U.S. Steel executives that only by dealing with the CIO could they restore order in their plants.[33]

In the end it took all these maneuvers to achieve the rudiments of collective bargaining in steel. SWOC depicted armies of steelworkers surging into the new union, but in reality the going was slow. On July 2 Murray boasted that "astonishing results have been attained in two weeks." Six weeks later he had to admit that "there is no remarkable showing in dues-paying members." In its first three months SWOC distributed 700,000 pieces of literature and passed out over 100,000 membership cards but could count only 15,300 members, about 3 percent of the total in basic steel. During this period SWOC expended over $200,000 and took in a total of $9,200 and indeed soon curtailed the collection of dues and initiation fees in an effort to swell its paper membership.[34]

By November Murray acknowledged that SWOC's campaign had gone awry. Normally organizers tried to work through influential local activists with previous union experience. The core of union supporters then tested the limits of company authority. They wore union buttons to work. They defended fellow workers in disputes with foremen. They recruited new members continuously. Such activists faced reprisals, but when a popular union supporter was fired, the dismissal would itself often galvanize union sentiment. The identification and recruitment of these activists, then, was the critical first step in building SWOC presence in the mills and, declared Murray, in creating a stable union that would be able to "discipline . . . an army of 500,000 steel workers to secure collective bargaining."[35]

Here, SWOC faltered. In part the difficulty had to do with the nature of work processes in steel. The mills typically housed a wide variety of operations, few of which involved masses of workers doing the same thing. Big mills might employ thousands of workers, but the typical employee spent his time in a small work group, usually a tight-knit body. Here the foreman, often exploiting ethnic or neighborhood ties, combined favoritism and arbitrary discipline to keep control. It was not easy for outsiders to locate and recruit work group leaders, nor could a handful of union militants in a steel mill achieve the kind of shop-floor power that was sometimes possible in the more centralized and homogeneous work environment of an auto plant or a tire factory.[36]

Moreover, steelworkers had been beaten repeatedly in their efforts to build unions. To the heirs of the defeats of 1892, 1902, 1909, 1919, and 1934, the new CIO merited a healthy skepticism. In the towns of western Pennsylvania, reported two veteran unionists, steelworkers valued stability and regularity of employment above all else. Living in "soot-covered houses in the shadow of the mills and hanging from the hillsides," long-term steelworkers had learned "not to join unions rashly." CIO representatives sought to reassure cautious workers and skeptical corporate executives alike that the new union wanted to avoid strikes. Still, steelworkers held back. Thus, Murray reported, "it was well neigh impossible to recruit a competent organizing staff from the ranks of the steel workers."[37]

The organizers that the UMW and other unions supplied could not fill the vacuum. Although at its peak the steel drive employed as many as 400, many of these men found recruitment in the steel centers frustrating and unproductive. They did have success in rousing steelworker political activity in behalf of Roosevelt and gubernatorial candidate George Earle, but recruitment into the union was less successful. Even when steelworkers did sign union cards, they were reluctant to pay SWOC's $3 initiation fee and dollar-a-month dues. "These organizers," Murray admitted, "have had to go through a period of readjustment and re-education which in some cases, has proven difficult [and] . . . painful."[38]

A good part of the problem was that in steel, far more so than in auto, the company unions represented a plausible alternative. By mid-1935 over 90 percent of the workers in basic steel were enrolled in ERPs. To be sure, steel companies had originally sponsored these organizations so as to resist outside unionism. But in U.S. Steel's plants in particular, by 1936 the ERPs had begun to take on a life of their own. Company officials had come to see the company unions as useful means of learning about daily life in the mills. So long as they did not challenge management's basic shop-floor prerogatives or make general wage demands, the ERPs helped to blunt the SWOC challenge.

For many ordinary steelworkers, these company unions had an appeal. Since the company paid the bills, no dues were required. Company unions were risk free; indeed, employers actively encouraged and in some cases virtually coerced participation. In the eyes of thousands of steelworkers, the ERPs were not necessarily less legitimate or effective than so-called bona fide unions, especially since, unlike the AFL, they did not fragment workers into arcane craft compartments.

Of course Murray and SWOC claimed that *they* were different. But the CIO was, after all, a self-proclaimed appendage to the AFL, and the AA was an integral part of SWOC. Moreover, many activists believed, company-sponsored organizations could become autonomous bodies and could force employers to make significant concessions.[39]

Through 1936 and into 1937 these company unions provided the main arena in SWOC's struggle for legitimacy. U.S. Steel officials began to realize that in creating company unions that were sufficiently credible to offer genuine appeal to their workers, they were leaving themselves vulnerable. With SWOC forever looming in the background, company officials had little choice but to treat workers' representatives, chosen in ERP elections, as legitimate spokesmen. Increasingly, ambitious, articulate, and often union-minded men dominated company union affairs. They pressed ever broader demands, constantly exposing the vulnerability of the ERP program to charges of company domination and insincerity. They insisted upon companywide and areawide organizations and convened multiplant conferences despite company discouragement. They made wage demands. They pressed grievances. They compelled company officials to vacate company union meetings and insisted that accurate minutes of meetings be published, including speeches by union-minded ERP representatives.

The company unions posed a powerful, double-edged challenge to SWOC. On one hand, union activists could win leadership positions. There they could claim credit for concessions while agitating for a real union when the company turned them down. But elsewhere in American industry, notably in the telephone and petroleum industries, company unions had proven long lived and even popular. If the steel ERPs attained credibility among the workers, bona fide unionism might forever be foreclosed in America's most basic industry.[40]

Thus, through the fall and winter of 1936–37 SWOC concentrated on gaining control of the ERPs. Murray directed SWOC field representatives to cultivate ERP activists. "I am convinced," he told his organizers, "that hundreds of them are willing and anxious to cooperate." In the Chicago area, many ERPs came over to SWOC en masse. In Pittsburgh, SWOC members and sympathizers encouraged company unionists to make far-reaching demands. ERPs boiled with conflict as pro- and anti-SWOC company union factions whipsawed company officials. In some of U.S. Steel's midwestern mills, aggressive company union activists achieved a degree of shop-floor power unrivaled by SWOC locals. SWOC co-opted company union leaders with staff jobs, relying on them to bring their followers into the union.[41]

As in the automobile industry, the resolution of the industrial relations crisis in steel relied heavily on Lewis. In leading the CIO, Lewis had broken with tradition. Yet in reality he was no scourge of the establishment. He sought entry into the decision-making centers, not their destruction. In his personal life he embraced capitalism's benefits, cultivating the well-to-do and influential and referring to himself as an "executive," not as a labor leader. Thus, on January 9, when Lewis unexpectedly encountered U.S. Steel president Myron Taylor in the dining room at Washington's posh Mayflower Hotel, reporters were on hand, for this was exactly the sort of place that Lewis frequented.[42]

The two men had much to discuss. SWOC's campaign was making inroads into Taylor's company unions, but the process was frustrating, protracted, and costly. Perhaps when Taylor understood that the centrally controlled SWOC would replace the current discord with stability, he would break with the industry's fifty-year opposition to organized labor. As the leader of the UMW, Lewis was proud of his ability to control the union's historically turbulent membership. Perhaps Taylor would now understand that the CIO and SWOC were his best options.

For his part, Taylor had no personal stake in the company's union-busting past. He was a financier, not a steelmaker. In 1933 he had followed the advice of the corporation's personnel relations director to promote company unionism. But by 1937 company unionism was boomeranging. Production suffered as activists stepped up their demands. With economic indicators rising, U.S. Steel, which had seen its market share erode even before the onset of the depression, simply had to operate at full throttle. With a prolabor administration in Washington and prolabor governors in the large steel states, and with the La Follette Committee exposing U.S. Steel's reliance on espionage and its stockpiling of tear gas and small arms, the repression option was singularly unappealing. But here was Lewis, like Taylor an authoritative executive dressed in a three-piece suit, offering a way out of the corporation's dilemma. Union recognition would be, to say the least, an unorthodox solution, but then new conditions required new approaches.[43]

Events in Flint and Detroit soon claimed Lewis's attention. For the next five weeks Taylor followed the auto negotiations closely. The militancy of the autoworkers, the vigor of the CIO, and, perhaps most tellingly, the attitude of President Roosevelt and Governor Murphy impressed him. Thus, when the two men next conferred, on February 17, less than a week after the GM-UAW settlement, Taylor was ready to come to terms with Lewis, and over the weekend of February 27–28 they clinched a deal. U.S. Steel would grant a 5 percent wage increase, the forty-hour week, and time and a half for overtime. The corporation recognized SWOC as bargaining agent for its members and agreed to the establishment of a grievance procedure. The corporation remained free to deal with nonunion employees through other organizations or individually. The agreement would apply immediately to U.S. Steel itself and would be extended, following detailed negotiations, to major subsidiaries. On March 2 it was made public at a signing ceremony in Pittsburgh involving SWOC president Murray and U.S. Steel president Benjamin Fairless.

This remarkable agreement had profound repercussions. Insofar as the steel industry was concerned, the agreement compromised the giant corporation's historic leadership. In accordance with long-established practice, Taylor had informed executives of several Little Steel companies of the progress of discussions, but they had dissented from his policy of negotiation with Lewis. SWOC, they pointed out, was having trouble recruiting members; a simple wage increase would deflate the drive once and for all. With the signing of the agreement on March 2, executives of Republic, Inland, Bethlehem, and other steel firms, which traditionally had followed the giant corporation's lead in all major industrywide matters, broke ranks with U.S. Steel and resolved to fight SWOC to the finish.

Within the CIO also, the agreement, welcome as it was, created uncertainty. Some observers who followed the talks between the two executives wondered what the method of negotiation and the fact that steelworkers had no opportunity to ratify, reject, or amend the agreement implied for the future of SWOC. Was SWOC a genuine steelworkers' union or simply an appendage to Lewis's UMW? The Lewis-Taylor settlement was arranged with no involvement on the part of rank-and-file leaders or even, it seemed, the head of SWOC itself, Philip Murray. Marginalized in these negotiations, Murray might never gain the stature and respect that real leadership of a mass steelworkers' union would require.[44]

In itself, the contract that Murray and Fairless signed was actually weaker than the one the UAW had wrested from GM. But the establishment of formal relations between SWOC and the company and especially the establishment of a grievance procedure tipped the balance in behalf of the CIO organization. Throughout U.S. Steel's empire workers now recognized that SWOC would be a daily force in shop-floor life. Covert union sympathizers joined up; antiunion workers retreated to the sidelines. Moreover, U.S. Steel executives soon came to regard SWOC as a stabilizing force in the mills, and while they did not quickly grant additional concessions, they exhibited little of the postcontract antagonism that characterized GM's relationship to the UAW.[45]

Though the Lewis-Taylor agreement and the resulting contracts affected only U.S. Steel employees directly, their impact on other steelworkers was powerful. Throughout the industry, and especially in the smaller fabricating, processing, and manufacturing sectors, workers flocked into SWOC. Soon the new union was granting charters in every kind of metalworking subindustry. By June 1937, SWOC regional director Clinton Golden observed, there were unions among metal toy workers, locomotive builders, and iron foundry workers as well as among those who made diesel engines, turbines, tin cans, bedsprings, hardware, cutlery, air conditioners, air compressors, metal signs, railroad cars, metal pipes, steel chain, oil well machinery, steel castings, and a bewildering variety of other products. SWOC now had over 150 contracts in at least twenty-nine distinct categories of metalworkers. Golden warned that this rapid, unplanned growth could quickly boomerang. By organizing a few producers in a given sector now, SWOC had implicitly accepted the obligation to organize the entire trade. Failure to do so would expose organized locals to nonunion competition, which would either drive the organized employers out of business or force the union to negotiate weak contracts with them. Weak contracts, in turn, would disillusion new union members and perhaps deal a fatal blow to SWOC's long-run success. "I personally feel," he told Katherine Ellickson, "that right now the future permanency of the Union is in grave danger." SWOC, he believed, had "grown and expanded and assumed responsibilities clear out of proportion" to its ability to "properly direct and guide this huge army of the rawest kind of Union recruits."[46]

The U.S. Steel agreement also encouraged activism in the mills of the Little Steel companies. In the large Jones & Laughlin works at Aliquippa, Pennsylvania, for example, notice of the agreement had an immediate and profound effect. Known as "Little Siberia" because of its reputation for antiunion savagery, the Aliquippa plant employed 10,000 steelworkers. Since 1933 union activists and company police had fought running battles, and in 1936 the SWOC local had filed extensive briefs with the new NLRB, charging Jones & Laughlin with systematic violations of the provisions of the Wagner Act. The Lewis-Taylor agreement spurred immediate membership growth. After eight weeks of negotiations in which SWOC sought the basic terms contained in the Lewis-Taylor agreement, steelworkers struck on May 12 in a massive display of solidarity. Unionists and family members gained control of the city streets and plant entrances, assaulting those who attempted to remain at work. After only a two-day shutdown, Jones &

Laughlin signed a contract along the lines of the U.S. Steel settlement. Little Steel, it seemed, as Murray had predicted in March, was on the verge of "complete unionization." The Little Steel companies, he had said, might "balk a little and cry a little, but they will come around."[47]

Jones & Laughlin proved the exception, however, not the rule. The Little Steel companies, led by Republic Steel, unleashed a bitter and violent campaign of opposition. In all, about 186,000 workers toiled in the works of Bethlehem, Republic, Youngstown Sheet and Tube, National Steel, Inland Steel, and American Rolling Mills. Aroused activists urged SWOC leaders to compel Little Steel to recognize the union through a militant strike. Lewis, however, along with national SWOC leaders, was hesitant. Union sentiment remained spotty and the Little Steel firms were powerful. In the employer-dominated steel towns they would no doubt control the newspapers, local government, and law enforcement. Company agents had infiltrated many SWOC locals, and Little Steel officials were rapidly stockpiling small arms and tear gas.

The Little Steel companies also moved to preempt the union. In mid-May they announced that they would freely grant the raises and the changes in working hours contained in the U.S. Steel settlement. To thousands of ordinary steelworkers, these economic gains were seductive. A strike over an abstraction such as union recognition seemed confusing, even wrong-headed.[48]

The showdown with Little Steel found SWOC financially exhausted. It had borrowed at least $1.5 million to bankroll the steel drive. But at a conference on May 26 in Youngstown, SWOC plant representatives confronted Murray with overwhelming strike sentiment. Some plants were already out, protesting Republic Steel lockouts in Canton and Massillon, Ohio. "We've had a hell of a time holding the men in," reported one delegate. "If I go back without word to go out . . . tonight, I will get my throat cut."[49]

The resulting strike was the CIO's first direct test. The Akron strike of 1936 and the Flint sit-down had been grassroots affairs, with the CIO playing a secondary role in both cases. Little Steel, however, was a different matter entirely. SWOC was a direct arm of the CIO, and steelworkers referred to themselves as members of the CIO, not of SWOC. A lengthy strike would require a lot of money, coordination among widely separated centers, and a precise mixture of raw militancy and careful strategy.

In the end, SWOC and the CIO were not equal to the task. Support for the strike was inconsistent, and funds for strikers' relief soon dried up. The companies effectively recruited strikebreakers. In Ohio, Democratic governor Martin Davey and local officials in Massillon, Canton, Youngstown, Cleveland, and elsewhere bowed to company demands that they protect workers seeking to enter the mills. The companies and the public officials, who increasingly served as strikebreaking agents, resorted to brutal and even deadly means to beat back the SWOC drive.[50]

In the period between the onset of the strike for recognition that began on May 26 and the middle of July, lethal violence, most of it perpetrated by company guards and city police, swept the midwestern steel centers. On Memorial Day 1937, Chicago police killed or wounded dozens of steelworkers and sympathizers. In Cleveland, Youngstown, and Massillon, lawmen also killed steelworkers. All told, the summer of 1937 added 18 dead to the long list of labor's martyrs that totaled at least 550 men, women, and children killed in the struggle for union or in protest over their treatment by employers since the mid-1870s.[51]

The violence in Chicago was the worst. There, city police, housed, fed, and even armed by Republic Steel, confronted an essentially peaceful and certainly unarmed march of strikers and supporters protesting restrictions on picketing. A newsreel, never released to the theaters but seen by journalists and members of the La Follette Committee, documented the gruesome violence. After a brief exchange of words with one striker, a policeman is seen turning his back on the march and saying something. "Then suddenly," wrote a journalist who saw the film, "without apparent warning, there is a terrific roar of pistol shots, and men in the front ranks of the marchers go down like grass before a scythe. The camera catches approximately a dozen falling simultaneously in a heap." After gunning down forty of the marchers, the police charged into the frightened, fleeing mass of men, women, and children, beating people with billy clubs. Policemen slugged stricken marchers, first battering the wounded with truncheons, then hurling them into patrol wagons. In all, they killed ten, wounded another thirty, and clubbed dozens more. "Can it be true," Lewis asked the next day, "that striking workmen may be shot down at will by the very agents of the law? . . . Is labor to be protected or is it to be butchered?"[52]

Several weeks later in Massillon, the forces of law and order struck again. There, on the night of July 11, following a misunderstanding that involved the failure of a union supporter to dim his car headlights, police opened fire without warning into the peaceful, even festive, crowd that gathered nightly near union headquarters. "Let them have it, boys. Break them down," yelled a trigger-happy auxiliary police leader, and his men poured rifle and shotgun fire, as well as tear gas canisters, into the crowd. One officer raked the street and houses with submachine gun fire. Sporadic shooting kept up the rest of the evening. Those leaving union headquarters for medical help were fired on. "The kitchen of the union hall was spattered and smeared with blood," reported an observer. Three men were killed, an unknown number wounded. "How did it happen?" asked scholar Robert Brooks, a careful chronicler of the steel industry. How could one "group of American citizens in police uniform coldbloodedly sho[o]t down another group dancing in the street to the music of a fiddle, a mandolin, and a big bass viol?"[53]

By mid-July the strike against Little Steel was a lost cause. In Canton, Youngstown, Massillon, Cleveland, and Warren, Ohio; in Monroe, Michigan; in Johnstown, Pennsylvania; in Buffalo and Lackawanna, New York; and in other steel centers throughout Illinois, Indiana, and the other industrial states, employers refused to sign agreements and workers straggled back into the mills. SWOC did achieve a de facto contract at Inland Steel's Indiana Harbor, Indiana, plant, but otherwise the results of the violence of the summer of 1937 seemed a sad reprise of the catastrophes of 1892 and 1919.[54]

SWOC's defeat in Little Steel did not end the CIO drive, however. In contrast to the aftermath of these other defeats, the period after the Little Steel strike was characterized by ongoing union activities both in the mills and in legal forums. In U.S. Steel and its major subsidiaries, SWOC used the grievance procedures to expand membership. Despite the harrowing setback in Little Steel, SWOC was strong enough to begin collecting per capita tax (dues) and to begin to pay back the loans that had sustained it in its first year. In October Murray reported that the steel union had chartered over 1,000 local unions and was administering 439 collective bargaining agreements. Membership figures remained shadowy, but SWOC claimed that its contracts covered over 300,000 workers, although in general the ratio of actual dues-payers to paper members was roughly one to two.[55]

Local SWOC activists functioned aggressively, even in Little Steel plants. In some places SWOC locals received de facto recognition as foremen and supervisors had no choice but to deal with popular union stewards on a day-by-day basis. In U.S. Steel plants, which dealt formally with the union, SWOC leaders used their official status to show recalcitrants the value of membership. SWOC demonstrated daily its ability to make a difference on the shop floor and thus proved practically that the balance of power within the steelworks had shifted.

Moreover, the new federal labor law reinforced this activism. In April 1937 the Supreme Court had validated the National Labor Relations Act in a case involving SWOC and Jones & Laughlin. Thereafter, members and staff of the NLRB aggressively pursued unfair labor practices cases. Here SWOC's centralized and rather bureaucratic style paid off. In the critical months following the Little Steel defeat, SWOC set Meyer Bernstein, an energetic young college graduate, to work on the myriad of NLRB cases involving discrimination and harassment of unionists. SWOC attorney Lee Pressman and a small staff of aggressive young lawyers worked closely with Pressman's former colleagues in the Agricultural Adjustment Administration who now held key positions on the NLRB staff. Favorable decisions by the board and in the appellate courts on these cases regularly buoyed SWOC's standing in even nonunion mills, providing proof that the old regime in the steelworks was gone forever. Discharged union activists often won substantial back pay awards and returned triumphantly to their jobs. Resort to the legal arena reinforced SWOC's and the CIO's status as the protector of workers' rights and as a substantial and vigorous actor in the industrial relations regime.[56]

Local unionists and SWOC leaders gave no stock to the argument that governmental intervention might undermine worker militancy or somehow compromise the union.[57] Such arguments might be heard among civil libertarians, radical laborites, and even among old-time AFL functionaries, but workers and SWOC officials alike believed that they needed every advantage they could get to complete organization of steel. They understood all too well that raw courage was no match for corporate power. The partial removal of labor-management conflict from the point of production to the hearing room stopped the killing. Although the mills of justice ground slowly, they produced back pay awards totaling millions of dollars and, more importantly, the growing recognition among steelworkers that SWOC and its allies in the federal government were a permanent force in their industrial lives.[58]

As the second anniversary of the founding of the CIO approached, the industrial union body's promoters could look back with pride of accomplishment and ahead with hopes for the future. Under the leadership of Lewis and Hillman, it had changed the rules governing labor's political activities, and its identification with Roosevelt's overwhelming victory was already paying dividends. In the industrial arena the CIO's combination of dramatic confrontationalism and low-keyed persuasion had brought unionism for the first time in the century into the heart of mass production industry. True, the CIO still had to wrest collective bargaining from Ford, Little Steel, and major rubber companies. While some calculations credited the CIO with over 3 million members, Lewis, Murray, Hillman, and their cohorts knew all too well that much of that membership was composed of workers who had been in unions before the launching of the industrial union body. If the breakthroughs in auto, rubber, and steel were critical, the fate of the CIO also rested with tens of thousands of other industrial workers in the nation's packinghouses, textile mills, car barns, wharves, appliance factories, and other work sites. Even as the CIO fought its great battles in Chicago, Akron, Flint, and Pittsburgh, it was active as well in these other sectors, and the fate of industrial unionism there did as much to shape the character of the new unionism as the spectacular achievements in the big three basic industries.

4 The Diverse Arenas of the CIO, 1936–1938

The dramatic origins and spectacular successes of the early CIO resonated throughout working-class America. During the period 1936–38 the CIO supported or launched organizing initiatives among longshoremen, electrical appliance workers, metal miners, textile workers, packinghouse workers, food and cannery workers, and others. While the Pennsylvania-to-Michigan industrial corridor remained central to the CIO's emerging identity, these initiatives brought the industrial union body forcefully into the urban centers of the East Coast, the manufacturing and shipping centers of the West Coast, and the mines and factories of the South as well. These diverse locales and circumstances brought the CIO into contact with a range of ideological, racial, gender, and sectional concerns that often posed new and difficult problems for the men who had originated the CIO and who conducted its affairs. The necessity to respond to unexpected and diverse organizing opportunities impelled the CIO's founders, in effect if not in name, to formalize their break with the AFL and to adopt increasingly elaborate institutional structures.

In expanding its scope the CIO both responded to and sought to initiate grassroots activism. Just as the contrasting characters of the auto and steel drives reflected different patterns of CIO support and rank-and-file initiative, so the expansion of industrial unionism partook of sharply diverse regional, racial, and sectoral realities. In some places, the new banner of the industrial union body was eagerly seized by energetic activists and carried with little material support from Lewis and his associates. Elsewhere, however, the CIO sought to breathe life into latent organizing possibilities, pouring money and resources into centrally directed campaigns modeled after that of SWOC.

CREATING A CIO STRUCTURE

The victories over GM and U.S. Steel soon forced the CIO to adopt a more coherent and explicit structure. In the spring and summer of 1937 the enthusiasm for industrial unions outside the rubber-steel-auto triangle impelled CIO leaders to make basic decisions concerning its scope, procedures, and institutional character. By fall 1937 the CIO had created a system of regional directors, had formed state and local coordinating bodies, and had expanded drastically both its Washington office staff and its contingent of field organizers, which now numbered over 200 in addition to those employed in SWOC. It was separate from the AFL in everything but name. The CIO, boasted Philip Murray in October, had 4 million members, 6,000 local unions, 64,000 democratically elected local officers and stewards, and 3,000 agreements with employers. "We are the dominant labor force in this nation," the SWOC chief asserted.[1]

Throughout the hectic days of 1936 and 1937 the CIO's small central staff attempted to formulate coherent policies to govern the explosion of worker interest. In the wake of the steel and auto settlements, Brophy reported, "Groups of workers all over the country are besieging organizers of the C.I.O." Requests for CIO support and affiliation from workers of every description poured into the Washington office. "As the years go by," Katherine Ellickson reported John L. Lewis as saying, "this period will be marked as epoch[al] in [the] life of labor organizations."[2]

Yet explosive growth created problems. CIO leaders did not want to be confused with the radical IWW, with its reputation for promiscuous organizing and undisciplined behavior. Nor did they want to antagonize friendly or powerful AFL unions. Charles Howard, whose Typographical Union remained in the AFL, worried about "unauthorized activities" among new recruits. In mid-1937 Adolph Germer warned that "every CIO representative is looked upon as a walking strike," a circumstance that would quickly frighten off potential recruits and make the achievement of stable bargaining relationships difficult. The CIO, said Hillman, had "to do something if we are to keep control of the situation." Too often the decisions about whether the CIO would enter a given field were being made, observed Katherine Ellickson, by "organizers . . . in the field . . . under the pressure of demand."[3]

In response to these dilemmas the CIO began in the spring of 1937 to elaborate its bureaucratic structure. At a meeting on March 9 the CIO committee addressed itself to both the expansion of opportunities that its recent successes had stimulated and the increasingly hostile posture of the AFL. The federation was demanding that its state and local bodies expel all local unions having ties with the CIO, and AFL affiliates were imposing boycotts on products coming from CIO-organized shops. Brophy urged that his office be authorized to establish local and state CIO coordinating bodies analogous to the AFL's central labor councils and state federations. "Hundreds of local groups of all types are clamoring for charters," he noted, and organizers had responded as best they could: SWOC had enrolled drugstore clerks, and the UAW signed up corset makers. Brophy believed the time had come to establish a formal structure. "The C.I.O.," he insisted, "must have its own representatives . . . and follow orderly procedures."[4]

His superiors agreed with him. While Young Turks in the new industrial unions urged an aggressive challenge to the AFL, Lewis, Hillman, and the others opted for a more cautious approach. The CIO would not respond to workers in the construction trades or in other industries where an active AFL affiliate was present. It would set up state and local bodies only when the AFL expelled CIO locals. But Brophy was now authorized to issue charters to individual groups of workers falling outside the jurisdiction of the established unions. Moreover, the CIO would now name regional representatives to guide and service these LIUs and to coordinate CIO activities.[5]

Over the next seven months, this new structure took shape. In the Washington office Katherine Ellickson reported that requests were pouring in from "marginal groups outside of the basic industries." Brophy began issuing LIU charters in wholesale lots. From early May through mid-July the CIO received 564 charter applications, the vast majority directly from grassroots workers' bodies, with CIO field representatives often doing little more than providing application forms. By October Brophy reported that he had issued over 600 LIU charters covering 225,000 members. These included 139 unions in the food processing field, 92 in lumber and wood products, 37 in paper products, 36 in laundries and dry cleaning establishments, 29 in stone, clay, and glass works, and others scattered among hotel and restaurant workers, optical and novelties fabricators, cemetery laborers, and a wide variety of miscellaneous trades.[6] This remarkable surge of activism echoed the expansion of the AFL's federal labor unions after the passage of the NIRA in 1933 and reminded labor veterans of the helter-skelter growth of the Knights of Labor in the mid-1880s.

These new LIUs played an important role in shaping the CIO's institutional identity. Had CIO leaders encouraged SWOC, the UAW, the URW, and other affiliates to take in disparate groups of workers, the industrial union body might have turned into more of a geography-based, as opposed to industry-centered, organization, along the lines of the old mixed assemblies of the Knights of Labor. In some parts of the country in fact a sort of regional unionism did take hold. Thus, in southeastern Minnesota and in Rhode Island, meatpacking and textile workers, respectively, spearheaded successful communitywide mobilizations of their areas' working class.[7] The decision instead to create separate unions for these diverse groups of industrial workers followed traditional trade union practices followed by the AFL.

Accepting hundreds of thousands of diverse industrial workers into the

CIO required the erection of an administrative and institutional structure for their servicing, again along AFL lines. Normally a local union affiliated with a national or international union such as the UMW or the ACWA received the advice and services it needed from the international union. The costs of these services were paid for by the per capita tax levied on the members of and collected by local unions.

But the AFL's federal labor unions and the CIO's new LIUs were not part of any national or international union. They received their services directly from the national federation. CIO field representatives and regional directors would have to be responsible for these matters. In June the CIO set the monthly dues for direct affiliates at fifty cents per member per month, ten times the amount charged to its national and international unions, a disparity that reflected the costs of the special services the CIO would have to provide directly affiliated unions. In turn, this meant that in a normal month the 225,000 LIU members were contributing over $110,000 to the CIO, while the industrial union federation's remaining membership of 2 million supplied only about $100,000.[8] In theory this could be a fair arrangement. But as the AFL had found in its relationships with its federal labor unions, this disparity in financing caused endless resentment and conflict, as did the anomalous nature of the LIUs as appendages to a labor organization established by and ostensibly in the interests of workers enrolled in national and international unions.[9]

The importance of the decision to create LIUs went further. The men and women who established the CIO's initial bureaucratic procedures believed the AFL's mistreatment of federal labor union members had been among the federation's most grievous sins. It was in support of the protests of these fledgling industrial unionists that Lewis had challenged William Hutcheson at the 1935 AFL convention. The federation charged high dues, provided little service, and imposed rigid bureaucratic rules. Craft unions chronically picked off groups of skilled workers and undercut federal labor union locals in joint bargaining situations.[10] If the CIO were to do right by its directly affiliated members, it would need a vastly expanded corps of organizers as well as regional directors and an augmented Washington staff. "If we are charging .50 cts. per month per capita," observed Katherine Ellickson, "we must extend [a wide range of organizational, legal, and administrative] aid to all locals we accept into affiliation," an arrangement that would entail drastic expansion of the CIO staff both in Washington and in the field.[11]

Thus, declared the first issue of the CIO organizers *Bulletin*, "The C.I.O. has recently entered a second phase of its activities by issuing charters to workers in miscellaneous industries." Brophy began appointing regional directors and field representatives to oversee and service these new recruits. By October 1937, he reported, there were 200 field representatives directly on the CIO central payroll "for work in the miscellaneous industries where no C.I.O. national or international union exists as yet." In the past seven months it had appointed a regional director for each state as well as ten subregional directors. In March it had had a staff of seven who occupied about 2,600 square feet of office space in two Washington buildings; now it employed fifty people in the capital, and its new headquarters on Connecticut Avenue covered 7,300 square feet. In addition to the expansion in its field and Washington staff and facilities, the CIO had issued charters to over eighty-two IUCs, city/county bodies analogous to the AFL's city central labor unions. These coordinated CIO bodies now operated in Birmingham, Los Angeles, San Francisco, Milwaukee, Toledo, St. Louis, Buffalo, Baltimore, Philadelphia, and elsewhere, and Brophy urged the prompt creation of IUCs in all major industrial centers.[12]

This expansion in the CIO's activities and elaboration of its institutional identity both signaled and sealed its break with the AFL. For Lewis, Murray, and certainly the younger leaders of the newer unions, association with the AFL was a dead letter. Everywhere, declared one of the new regional directors, the "CIO answers . . . a demand from the American workers for stream-lined unionism" and had "taken deep root" in its brief history.[13]

At the same time, however, the decisions taken during the summer and fall of 1937 insured that the new CIO would remain well within the labor movement's historic patterns. The CIO's affiliates would be confined to particular jurisdictions. Its geographical representation would be expressed through city central and state bodies that paralleled those of the AFL and not through some sort of mass regional mobilization. Initiation fees and per capita dues might be suspended during the organizing period, but the men in charge of the CIO insisted that soon the new organization must become self-financing. The shop-floor organizations of CIO unions would follow clear lines of authority. While sit-downs, strikes, and demonstrations might be temporarily necessary, the CIO stood for stable contractual relations and was committed to taking labor disputes off the streets and into the courtrooms and negotiating chambers. In a proposed master plan for the institutional structure of the CIO, never adopted but characteristic of the priorities prevalent in the turmoil-filled year of 1937, SWOC secretary-treasurer David McDonald advanced as central matters of CIO policy the "continuation of the classical American economic system, . . . preservation of American business institutions[,] . . . [and] continuing opposition to economic philosophies which seek to destroy the present economic system in America." In their public speeches and appeals to workers, Brophy advised,

CIO representatives were to downplay references to picket line heroism and to emphasize that CIO unions "*observe their contracts*" and sought only to bring prosperity, order, and a "peaceful atmosphere" to industrial communities.[14]

The CIO leaders were products of the very labor movement that they sought to revitalize and expand. They were little attracted to either anticapitalist politics or fundamental institutional experiments. They thought they knew their constituency, which, they judged, was angry, not alienated. Its militancy was directed above all else at the attainment of security, stability, and dignity on the job. The structure that took form in the summer of 1937 fit comfortably into both the broad traditions of the nonradical labor movement and the bureaucratic imperatives of a complex industrial and governmental order.[15]

THE WEST AND THE SOUTH

By March 1937 it was clear that CIO success had stiffened the old federation's hostility. As the AFL acted against CIO locals in labor councils and as AFL unions launched sometimes violent boycotts against CIO-produced or -handled goods, Lewis and Brophy broadened their organizing agenda to include disaffected unions nominally affiliated with the AFL. Thus the new industrial union organization became what its founders had disavowed, a rival labor federation. Moreover, in seeking entry into new geographical sectors, CIO leaders had to confront complex interunion and ideological questions. As a result the CIO's institutional identity became increasingly shaped by the need to accommodate ambitious and contentious leaders of established labor organizations and to seek recruitment of workers outside the central industrial core.

Events on the West Coast posed an immediate challenge to the industrial union project. Unless the CIO was to be confined to the industrial heartland, it had to establish a presence on the Pacific. The UAW, the URW, and SWOC all had large potential memberships there, and as CIO clothing and garment workers' locals were driven out of central labor bodies along the coast, the need for industrial union development grew. Moreover, tens of thousands of lumber and sawmill workers, airframe and aircraft workers, packing and cannery workers, shipyard workers, and miscellaneous industrial and service workers seemed to be ripe for industrial unionism. Even the motion picture industry of southern California seemed susceptible to the CIO appeal.[16]

But California and Washington were far from the center of CIO operations and had no established UMW infrastructure. For a presence on the

West Coast, the CIO would have to rely on established organizations that were either outside the AFL ambit or willing to break with the old federation. Indeed, in California and the Pacific Northwest there already existed a militant and left-leaning union movement that seemed to fill the bill splendidly. In the summer of 1934 a massive dockers' strike, eventually involving sailors, teamsters, and other workers, had shaken the San Francisco waterfront. After three weeks of savage conflict, bay area longshoremen won union recognition and, most critically, control over their own hiring halls.[17]

The leader of the San Francisco local of the ILA was Harry Bridges, a tough, radical, Australian-born sailor and docker. Bridges believed it essential that the seagoing and shoreside trades unite to fight shipping and goods-handling companies. Following the Great Strike of 1934, Bridges secured from the New York-based ILA the directorship of all West Coast longshoremen's locals. In September 1935, along with other maritime unionists, Bridges engineered the creation of the Maritime Federation of the Pacific, a multiunion body designed to coordinate organizing and collective bargaining strategy and, perhaps, to serve as an industrial union spearhead.[18]

Bridges had bold ambitions. Using the longshoring locals as a beachhead, the Longshoremen would "march inland" to organize warehousing, packing shed, and other goods-handling workers. Eventually agricultural and food processing workers would be brought in. The ILA's 1934 victory had triggered union enthusiasm in the logging camps, sawmills, and shipyards all along the West Coast. "We are beginning to organize for something bigger than the ILA itself," declared one of Bridges's lieutenants. "Once such a union is formed . . . we will become really invincible." A prominent shipping magnate agreed: "Bridges and his group will control the distribution of the country and whoever controls distribution rules the country."[19]

Thus Bridges and his Longshoremen seemed ideal vehicles for CIO activity on the coast, but in reality several factors clouded the situation. Most importantly, as late as the summer of 1937 Bridges remained unwilling to break with the AFL. True, the New York-based ILA was among the most corrupt and collaborative of all American unions. However, Bridges believed that he could work within the AFL to expand the West Coast influence and eventually to control the entire ILA, whose membership on the Atlantic and Gulf Coasts far surpassed that of Bridges's West Coast branch.

Moreover, the West Coast ILA locals enjoyed friendly relations with AFL shipyard and seagoing unions. Bridges continued to believe that the Maritime Federation of the Pacific might serve as an industrial union nucleus within the AFL. Thus, throughout the latter part of 1936 and into

1937 Bridges played a complex game, maneuvering against West Coast rivals, negotiating with CIO officials, yet carefully maintaining his AFL connections.

Political and ideological matters colored the CIO's relationship with Bridges. The Longshoremen's leader and many of his close associates were ardently pro-Soviet. Some, including Bridges himself,[20] many thought, were members of the CPUSA. Meanwhile, in March 1937 another water-front organization, the International Union of Marine and Shipbuilding Workers, had been granted a CIO charter. Not only did its socialist leader-ship consider their organization the proper vehicle for industrial unionism on the West Coast, they detested Bridges and his cohorts for both their Communist sympathies and their lingering AFL commitments. Still an-other radical maritime organization, the Sailors' Union of the Pacific, was headed by Harry Lundeberg, a fiery syndicalist who likewise had no use for the ILA's Stalinoid West Coast leadership.[21]

The policy of working through someone so closely identified with the Communist Party triggered dissent in some CIO circles. If the CIO named Bridges as its West Coast director, he would no doubt select Communists and their allies for positions as organizers and staff members. He would link up with an emerging CPUSA-oriented agricultural and cannery workers' union beginning to stir in the central valleys and with Communist-influenced lumber and sawmill workers' organizations in the Pacific Northwest. But would a Bridges-led West Coast CIO adequately support mainstream CIO unions such as SWOC, the UAW, the URW, and the ACWA as they sought to organize in the West? Bridges's attitude toward the Shipbuilding Work-ers, which he sought to marginalize even as his longshoremen's union en-croached on its jurisdiction, was not encouraging on this score. Politically, the Bridges-led West Coast CIO would inevitably follow the Communist line, making alliances with mainstream politicians problematic.[22]

In the end, however, there was no real alternative to Bridges. Lunde-berg's Sailors were too weak and Lundeberg himself too self-willed, while the Shipbuilding Workers would have to start from scratch on the West Coast. For all his fiery radicalism, Bridges was a shrewd bread-and-butter unionist. Brophy and Lewis concluded that only by working with Bridges and paying the price that he cleverly negotiated – the CIO's official desig-nation of him as West Coast director – could the industrial union body gain a foothold in this critical area.[23]

As for Lewis, he acknowledged no Communist problem. If Communists got out of line, he believed, he could deal with them, as he had done in the UMW. Bridges, who enjoyed a good reputation among West Coast employ-ers for honoring contractual obligations and for keeping rein on his militant membership, was someone he could work with. In the hectic days of 1937 Lewis was glad to have a Bridges in California and, for the time being at least, was little inclined to inquire too closely into the specifics of his politics or operating policies.[24]

CIO expansion into the Far West came as the result of an arrangement with a leader with a strong power base. Expansion into the South, however, presented quite a different challenge. Movement south was equally essential. Tens of thousands of metal miners, steelworkers, textile workers, food and tobacco workers, pulp and paper workers, furniture workers, and other industrial workers toiled in low-wage jobs. As UMW members had learned bitterly in the 1920s, cheaper southern labor undermined collective bargaining gains elsewhere. Historically low-wage industries, such as cotton textiles, not only jeopardized the higher standards of northern workers in the same industry but established regionwide patterns that weakened wages and labor standards in other industries, directly in the South and indirectly elsewhere.

There was also a political dimension. With its one-party system and its widespread disfranchisement of lower-income voters, the South was a conservative bulwark. Powerful southern committee chairmen and city and regional bosses, little troubled by prospects of rank-and-file voter rebellion, brokered effectively with the Roosevelt administration, making sure that federal money flowing into the South remained under their control and disturbed as little as possible existing relations of racial and class power.[25]

Southern elites and political chieftains detested unions. Discriminatory AFL craft unions and the rigidly segregated railroad brotherhoods reinforced racial norms. Established economic and political elites regarded any gesture toward expansion of union influence in mass production industries as a fundamental challenge to their power. Dixie did have vigorous traditions of labor protest. Most recently and relevantly, between 1929 and 1934 the southern Piedmont, in whose mills toiled over 200,000 cotton textile workers, had rocked with strikes and demonstrations. In September 1934, cotton mill workers had conducted a brave, militant strike. Its defeat, in which the AFL's weak United Textile Workers played an equivocal and vacillating role, was a spectacular example of organized labor's disappointment over the results of the New Deal's early experiment in worker empowerment.[26]

The attention of CIO leaders focused on these textile workers. The Piedmont mills, scattered over a 300-mile stretch that extended from southern Virginia to northern Alabama, represented the South's largest contingent of industrial workers. Without textiles, any industrial union initiatives in the South would be marginal; but a vigorous textile workers' union could spur the subsequent organization of metal miners and food, chemical, furniture, paper, and other industrial workers.[27]

Another factor added to the attractiveness of a textile campaign. Since its modern growth in the Piedmont, dating to the 1880s, the industry had employed few black workers. Thus one of the most difficult obstacles to organizing southern workers – the seemingly irreducible barrier of racial antagonism – was not a factor in textiles.[28] CIO activists, from Lewis down, supported biracial unionism and actively sought to recruit black workers into the auto, steel, and other emerging CIO organizations. But bringing industrial unionism to the South would be a far less daunting prospect with the region's leading industry largely unburdened by the racial issue.

Even so, organizing southern textiles would be hard. By 1930 over 75 percent of the nation's cotton textiles were produced in Dixie, but the leading manufacturer accounted for only 3 percent of total production. Southern entrepreneurs relied on the region's low wages and lack of unionization for competitive advantage. Workers typically lived in isolated communities and were dependent on their employers for housing, medical care, and public services. In such environments, of course, employers' control of public officials, newspapers, and police forces discouraged labor organizers.[29]

Over the years the AFL's United Textile Workers had enjoyed little success in the South. Its leaders hardly understood the distinctive circumstances of their southern textile workers; indeed, charged some southern activists, the organization sought only to do enough in the South to protect northern wage rates and to discourage employers from moving operations to Dixie. In any event, the union was weak, underfunded, and, a 1937 CIO analysis found, "saddled with factional fights . . . [and] incompetent organizers."[30]

In March 1937 the CIO began to focus on the textile industry. The United Textile Workers had been among the unions forming the original CIO, but it was ill led and bankrupt. Thus, at Hillman's behest, the CIO governing board created TWOC, which was modeled on SWOC. Hillman would serve as its chairman, and funding would come primarily from the ACWA and the ILGWU.[31]

Organizing textiles, however, even with a centralized and well-financed CIO in charge, presented unique difficulties. "Textiles" was a congeries of discrete subsectors with distinct geographical, industrial, and labor force characteristics. Indeed, there were over 6,000 "textile" plants in twenty-nine states, presenting a bewildering variety of economic circumstances and organizing problems. Altogether they employed over 1 million workers. On one hand, Hillman and other CIO officials appreciated that the ultimate test of a successful drive was victory in the South. On the other hand, however, was the reality that nonsouthern and noncotton sectors of the industry – woolens, silk, hosiery, synthetic fabrics, and dyeing – presented far more plausible initial targets for successful organizing and collective bargaining than did cotton textiles.[32]

In theory, Hillman and his ACWA cadres were well equipped to deal with such diversity. They had pioneered in the organization of a multi-employer, mass production industry. Along with the ILGWU, which also supplied significant financial and organizational support for TWOC, the ACWA had been able to remove wages from the competitive calculus and to convince many employers that the union was a source of stability and discipline in an unruly industry.[33]

From the start, however, the campaign faltered. Although the South represented the greatest challenge, Hillman and his colleagues devoted almost 70 percent of their organizers to the northern sector, where unionism had a long history. The implicit theory of the campaign was that initial success there would provide the financial and experiential momentum for a subsequent campaign in the South.[34]

Even so, TWOC did not ignore Dixie. Of the 500 organizers employed as the campaign gathered steam, about 150 were in fact assigned to the South, 112 in the heart of the Piedmont. The TWOC chairman appointed A. Steve Nance, a Georgia Typographer of impeccable Dixie lineage, to direct the Atlanta-based drive in the Piedmont. Unlike in the steel drive, Communists were screened out. Lewis and Hillman recruited prominent southern liberals, such as Rev. Witherspoon Dodge and social activist Lucy Randolph Mason, to speak for the CIO and thus reinforce the southern character of the TWOC drive.[35]

Through 1937 and into 1938 the going was slow. "This is like a different world from New York" – the seat of TWOC headquarters – reported Lucy Mason from the Piedmont. Even the validation of the Wagner Act in April failed to force southern employers to stop their blatant antiunion actions. They drove union supporters from company houses, colluded with police to harass and assault organizers, encouraged the clergy to denounce the CIO, and fired union activists. Manufacturers, reported a textile trade paper correspondent, would fight to the "last ditch to save themselves and their organization from unionism."[36] Southern organizers had started optimistically. Over its first six months, however, the campaign established only a handful of Piedmont locals. By October TWOC had fewer than 2 percent of southern cotton textile workers under contract. In the fall, business turned down suddenly and steeply, hitting textiles with devastating force. At the end of the year TWOC research director Solomon Barkin reported that the industry was operating at only 53 percent capacity. In the South employers stepped up workloads, a practice that normally ignited militancy but one they could now implement with impunity in view of the distress of the mill towns.[37]

Misfortune did not mean defeat. Unionists awaited a business upturn and relied on the NLRB to reinstate victimized activists. But unlike the case in steel, TWOC could point to no stunning breakthrough. It had made no dramatic gains, especially in the South, and its performance, for all the vigor and purpose exuded by the CIO, seemed no better than that of the United Textile Workers, the AFL, and the NRA.

Defenders of Hillman and TWOC believed that the textile initiative had simply run into bad luck and bad timing. "The CIO may yet discover," wrote one sympathizer early in the campaign, "that compared with southern textiles, steel was a playful kitten." The severe depression, the bitterness and sheer illegality of employers' actions, and the fear and diffidence of mill workers, they believed, were clearly responsible for the no doubt temporary frustration of CIO hopes.[38]

TWOC representatives vowed to stay the course. They believed that southern workers were cautious about the CIO because of its reputation for militancy. "It is difficult for anyone who does not know the South intimately," warned Lucy Mason, "to realize that moderate statements of the CIO cause gain . . . more friends and influence than the more militant pronouncements." Hillman constantly preached the virtues of moderation, professing to believe that "management will cooperate with the workers" when the real TWOC-CIO program got a fair hearing.[39]

Critics on the left were not convinced. In other southern industries, industrial unionism was making greater headway. Left-wing unions, with little direct encouragement from the CIO itself, were enjoying some success in organizing on a biracial basis. In the tobacco factories of North Carolina and the iron mines and smelters of Alabama these organizations began laying the foundations for vigorous local unions. Rather than shying away from the racial factor, as the official CIO focus on textiles did, these unions recognized that it was precisely among African Americans that the greatest hope for aggressive industrial unionism rested. They believed also that it was wrong to see the southern working class as diffident and conservative. When guided by committed radicals unafraid to confront tyrannical bosses, southern workers could be as militant and steadfast as any others. The official CIO line of moderation and appeasement of southern elites, they argued, sent southern workers the message that the vaunted CIO was simply another chapter in the long-discredited AFL tactic of attempting to recruit workers by cultivating employers.[40]

By early 1938 the CIO could claim a beachhead of sorts in the South. The UMW boasted 100,000 southern members, and the U.S. Steel agreement had brought tentative recognition to iron and steelworkers in the corporation's Alabama subsidiaries. Left-wing unions of food and tobacco and metal mining workers had made inroads in North Carolina and Alabama. Locals of the ILGWU and the ACWA were scattered throughout Dixie, each with a handful of members, and the new industrial unions such as the UAW and the URW were attempting to spread into the handful of auto and rubber factories of Alabama, Georgia, and Texas. The crucial textile industry, however, remained nonunion. By the end of 1937 the CIO was solidly placed in the eastern and midwestern industrial heartlands and had achieved a lively presence on the West Coast, but its southern flank remained insecure.[41]

OPPORTUNITIES AND CHALLENGES

"The C.I.O.," John L. Lewis told the General Executive Board of the ILGWU early in 1937, "has let loose great forces." Even before the victory over GM and the settlement with U.S. Steel, the men and women associated with the CIO believed that at last organized labor and the vast millions of workers for whom it claimed to speak were on the verge of achieving their rightful place in American life. Reported the editor of *Justice*, the ILGWU newspaper, in Lewis's presence "one felt labor's destiny nearing a realization."[42]

Throughout 1937 and 1938 Lewis and his associates sought to actualize these broad possibilities. Virtually every industrial sector and geographic area generated pressure for expanded CIO activity. By mid-1938 the CIO was active in radios and electrical appliances, oil, forest and wood products, pulp and paper, urban transport, utilities, chemicals, metal mining, shoes, meatpacking, agriculture, shipbuilding and repairing, diverse metal trades, farm equipment, warehousing and goods distribution, newspapers, office and professional work, and public employment. In some of these areas it absorbed independent or disaffected AFL unions or dissident splinters of AFL unions. In other sectors, notably meatpacking, it established organizing committees patterned after SWOC and TWOC or chartered new, self-governing unions. In still another format, the UMW created a special unit, District 50, to recruit men and women whose work involved coal-derived chemicals.

There were notable success stories among this helter-skelter growth. In the radio manufacturing and electrical appliance industry, centered in Pennsylvania, New Jersey, New York, and Massachusetts, for example, a rich mixture of federal labor unions, former company unions, and Communist-influenced "independent" unions fused in mid-1936 to form the UE. The UE enjoyed uncommonly good leadership from among seasoned Communist Party union organizers and young, ambitious non-Communist activists. In addition, important sectors of the electrical appliance industry, notably General Electric, soon proved willing to cooperate with the new union, seeing it as a means of improving communication between management and workers and of stabilizing conditions in an industry that prided itself on its modern and humane record of labor relations.

The UE, to be sure, had its share of hostile employers. Like Ford, Republic Steel, Goodyear, and International Harvester, Westinghouse, the second leading electrical equipment manufacturer, refused to sign a labor contract. By the late 1930s, however, the UE had in fact organized its key plants and was bargaining on a de facto basis with the company. In the summer of 1936 the UE gained a foothold in the Radio Corporation of America only after a difficult three-week strike. Among several substantial, although smaller, employers, such as Emerson Electric and Maytag appliance, the fight for union was protracted and, in some cases, unsuccessful. But in comparison with the SWOC campaign, which left eighteen unionists dead, or southern textiles, with its lengthy roll of union martyrs, the radio and electric industries were easy going. In other industries, observed a UE activist from Erie, Pennsylvania, "when people joined a union, they were taking a chance of getting fired. Things like *that* never happened out here."[43]

Another significant industrial sector, meatpacking, followed a more complex and turbulent route into the CIO. Meatpacking had a troubled history of industrial relations, especially in the center of its operations, Chicago. The AFL union for packinghouse workers was the Amalgamated Meat Cutters and Butcher Workmen of North America. This union had originally represented butchers and meat dressers who worked in the neighborhood abattoirs and retail shops that dominated pre-1890 meatcutting. As mass production methods took over, however, huge meatpacking corporations employed vast numbers of unskilled and semiskilled workers. These men and women came from all quarters of Chicago's diverse ethnic communities. Strikes in the 1890s and early 1900s left a legacy of interethnic rivalry and widespread suspicion of the union, which at times tried to unite skilled butcher workmen with mass production workers but which also sacrificed the interests of mass production workers at critical junctures.

During World War I another wave of mass organization and labor conflict had swept the stockyards and packinghouses of Chicago. By now about a third of the packinghouse workers were black men, many of them employed in the dangerous and dirty, but strategic, jobs on the kill floors. Union militants built a new, biracial industrial union, stressing solidarity and shop-floor activism. Unionists kept this agenda alive through the difficult postwar period but suffered crushing defeat at the hands of the packers in a decisive 1921–22 strike.[44]

The New Deal revived union hopes. The Communist Party's Packinghouse Workers Industrial Union became active, and in the wake of the NIRA the Amalgamated Meat Cutters moved tentatively back into the plants of big packers such as Swift, Armour, and Wilson. By the mid-1930s many of the ethnic tensions that earlier had characterized packinghouse unionism had abated in the common misery of the depression. Black workers soon emerged as a particularly militant force. Able Communist leaders greeted the launching of the CIO enthusiastically. As one activist remarked, after the UAW's victory in Michigan "everyone wanted to know when the CIO was coming out to the Yards." SWOC's contract with U.S. Steel and its vigorous presence in the Chicago-Indiana steel mills further fueled industrial union sentiment in the packinghouses.[45]

At first, however, the CIO leadership was ambivalent. The Amalgamated Meat Cutters was a "friendly" AFL affiliate that had supported Lewis's position in AFL councils. Activists in Chicago and the Midwest pressed CIO functionaries to embrace meatpacking workers, who, they argued, were prime candidates for industrial unionism, and in the summer of 1937 SWOC in Chicago had begun to recruit packinghouse workers. By the fall SWOC Midwest director Van Bittner, a legendary old UMW warhorse, had become enthusiastic. "May I take up the packinghouse industry[?]" he asked Lewis, promising a membership of 200,000 in the Chicago area alone if the CIO launched a full-scale, SWOC-like drive. Lewis approved and soon after the CIO established the Packinghouse Workers Organizing Committee, modeled on SWOC.[46]

Other notable initiatives during the hectic 1936–37 period included a vigorous union of rapid transit workers in New York City, the enrollment of thousands of chemical and coal tar workers into District 50, and a small but hopeful foothold of biracial metalworkers' unionism in Alabama. Groups of disaffected government employees and white collar workers, impatient with the hat-in-hand approach of their AFL unions, gained CIO charters in 1937. Food, tobacco, and agricultural workers in California and North Carolina, often guided by zealous and courageous Communists, enjoyed at least sporadic success in establishing unions in sectors whose racial and gender divisions made organizing difficult in the face of intense grower and packer hostility. Lumber and sawmill workers in the Pacific Northwest and farm equipment workers in Illinois, Iowa, and Wisconsin mobilized under the banner of fledgling CIO affiliates that also relied heavily on Communist-oriented activists.[47]

The CIO per se was involved in these diverse activities in diverse ways. For example, in the radio and electrical industry the CIO presence was confined largely to moral support and free advice. The New York City TWU, which affiliated in May 1937, required no financial or organizing support from the CIO but did use its mystique in organizing the city transit system. "The CIO charter was a magic wand," declared TWU president Michael Quill, "that worked miracles."[48]

In some sectors, notably oil and meatpacking, the CIO did contribute organizers and financial support. Even so, the recession beginning in the fall of 1937 and the heavy continuing expenses associated with the steel and textile drives limited tangible support. In white collar and government employment as well as in agriculture, Lewis and his associates advanced money for organizing activities but had little direct influence in these campaigns. Moreover, the priorities of the official CIO did not always jibe with the goals and aspirations of local unionists and indigenous leaders. In the meatpacking industry particularly, Bittner's cautious leadership clashed with the militancy of left-leaning activists. Since in the case of the Packinghouse Workers Organizing Committee the CIO's top-down governance was combined with minimal financial and organizational support, the relationship between restless packinghouse locals in Chicago and the national organization remained troubled.[49]

In truth, the CIO's great surge following its auto and steel breakthroughs was wider than it was deep. The wrenching recession of 1937–38, vigorous AFL response to CIO gains, the protracted nature of most NLRB proceedings, and the sheer fact that joining a union remained, for millions of workers, a chancy and problematic act combined to blunt the industrial union spearhead. Even before the new year, Lewis's UMW functionaries, who exercised increasing control over CIO finances and procedures, began cutting back the staff, laying off organizers, and stanching the flow of funds into SWOC, TWOC, and other dependent bodies. Observed Lewis's executive assistant in November, "The CIO is carrying a right smart load with . . . the United Mine Workers carrying all deficits." Brophy spent much of early 1938 cutting back office expenditures, laying off organizers, and reducing support for affiliates' organizing campaigns.[50]

In the original mass production industries that the CIO targeted, organization remained incomplete. Firms that had been forced to recognize the union argued that concessions to the UAW or the URW would render them uncompetitive so long as major rivals remained union free. Ford continued to thwart the UAW, which had to rely on unfair labor practices cases before an inundated NLRB to keep its presence alive. In rubber, Goodyear played a similar role, as the giant meatpacker Armour did in that sector. Several large steel companies held out, notably Bethlehem and the infamous Republic. Employers such as GM and Firestone that had had to recognize the union were hardly reconciled to its permanent presence. During the recession they worked hard to limit the scope of collective bargaining and to reclaim worker loyalty.

The going was even slower in meatpacking, textiles, oil, wood products, agriculture, and other even less organized sectors. A resurgent AFL began to challenge the CIO. In the shipyards, sawmills, pulp and paper plants, and elsewhere, AFL representatives used the CIO threat to persuade employers to sign backdoor contracts with them. Elsewhere, control of the building trades and local transport enabled AFL organizers to enforce boycotts against CIO-produced or -handled goods.[51]

The wide extent and diversity of the CIO's early activities also posed significant internal dilemmas for the new labor federation. The role of Communists, for example, continued to trouble traditional unionists. In the UE the number two and three slots were occupied by Communists Julius Emspak (secretary-treasurer) and James Matles (director of organizing). Michael Quill, who headed the TWU, leaned heavily on party labor functionary John Santo, a gifted tactician. New unions in woodworking, farm equipment, maritime trades, agriculture, government, and office work all had Communists among their top leadership, while in packinghouse, metal mining, and the UAW, party members were prominent among the second rank. Veteran unionists such as Dubinsky, Adolph Germer, and, increasingly, John Brophy grew uneasy. As early as July 1937 one of Dubinsky's West Coast officers charged that the CIO "is fast becoming a [Communist outpost] . . . in Los Angeles." Lewis's own aides noted that the party regarded the CIO as "their most fertile field" and that "there is no question but that they are boring from within."[52]

Warnings poured in from veteran labor activists, journalists, former Communists, and other CIO sympathizers. In January 1938 Benjamin Stolberg, a veteran labor journalist and socialist, published a series of articles in Scripps-Howard newspapers assessing the progress of the CIO and warning of the dangerous influence of the Communists. Brophy, he charged, was a "tool" of the party. The appointment of Bridges as West Coast director had opened the way for the CPUSA to play its usual "divisive and desperate game." The key arena, he believed, was the UAW, where Stalinist cadres struggled to contest the anti-Communist leadership of President Homer Martin.[53]

Lewis paid little attention. Indeed, he increased his already heavy reliance on Pressman, brushing aside information about the lawyer's Communist associations. He seemed to accept with equanimity the participation of Communists in the steel drive and in the new affiliates. In the late 1930s the CPUSA put aside its revolutionary rhetoric as it sought to build the broadest possible antifascist coalition. Why not, then, use Communists' impressive talents as organizers and activists in the cause of industrial unionism? After all, asked Lewis rhetorically when questioned about the wisdom of permitting the Communists a role, "Who gets the bird, the hunter or the dog?"[54]

The Communist issue generated much public controversy. Other troublesome issues, however, remained in the background Thus, for example, the new movement's relationship with female workers and African Americans, while gaining little open public recognition, posed problems that were at the heart of the definition of "industrial unionism" that CIO advocates promoted.

On the surface the "race issue" was an easy one for the CIO. CIO leaders were not caught in the racist hiring and recruitment practices that characterized the AFL's building and metal trades unions or the railroad brotherhoods. Industrial unionism, whether in its Knights of Labor or IWW incarnations, had featured cooperation across racial lines. The circumstances of mass production industry, in which increasing numbers of blacks were integral to production processes, made obvious the need for color-blind unionism. The institutional father of the CIO, the UMW, had a long, if spotty, record of biracial organizing and, along with the other founding CIO unions such as the ACWA and the ILGWU, rejected the racial exclusivism that characterized most of the railroad, craft, and construction unions.[55]

Black workers toiled in most of the industries that constituted the CIO's main targets. They comprised about 15 percent of steelworkers, 25 percent of Chicago packinghouse workers, 4 percent of automobile workers, and significant proportions of employees in garment manufacturing, food processing, tobacco working, and general industrial labor, especially in the South. Often more important than sheer numbers was the strategic location of black workers, either with particular employers or in certain sectors of the production process. In the automobile industry, for example, Henry Ford employed large numbers of blacks, especially at his River Rouge facility, where they accounted for about a tenth of the 60,000-man workforce. In Chicago meatpacking plants, black workers were concentrated on the kill floors, toiling in dirty, dangerous, and disagreeable conditions. These positions, to which discriminatory hiring and promotion policies relegated them, were critical to the production processes of the entire meatpacking industry, for they controlled the flow of carcasses through an entire facility. In steel, although the proportion of black workers was slowly declining from the peaks reached in the mid-1920s, they still accounted for a high proportion of the workers in the critical blast furnaces and rolling mills.[56]

Thus, to the men who launched the CIO, the *importance* of black workers in industrial America was clear. To them the CIO's basic message applied with particular force to black workers, in view of their particular victimization at the hands of corporate America. However, although Communist and other radicals sometimes attempted to address the particular concerns of blacks, most CIO officials and organizers tried to minimize the racial character of the CIO enterprise. They believed that the rising tide of unionism would benefit all workers. Industrial unionism held out equal rights for all, special treatment for none. To be sure, intelligent organizing *tactics* might well require the use of African American (or native southern or Italian-speaking) organizers to meet particular circumstances, but African American workers were, finally, workers first and Negroes second.[57]

CIO organizers and officers were often unsure about the response of black workers to their appeal. There were no more militant CIO supporters than the African Americans in Chicago's packinghouses. The UMW could count about 35,000 African Americans among its half-million members, and in Alabama several thousand black iron mine and smelter workers provided the mass base for the CIO's Mine, Mill there.[58]

In the critical mass production arenas, however, the racial situation was less promising. For example, black steelworkers often expressed loyalty toward employers and skepticism toward unions. "'Negroes here,'" concluded one veteran organizer in Pennsylvania, "'are the hardest race on earth to organize.'" Murray fretted that "we have not made satisfactory progress" among blacks. Still, blacks recognized that the steel companies pitted workers against one another along racial lines, and the more resourceful and sensitive organizers found younger black workers more responsive than their cautious elders.[59]

SWOC's leaders and organizers recognized the need for new approaches to blacks. They had some success in enlisting churches and fraternal organizations in behalf of the union. In the Pittsburgh district, organizers reported, SWOC efforts were paying off as black steelworkers were joining the union at higher rates than were whites, although in neighboring Ohio, with fewer African Americans, the reverse was true. During the Little Steel strike, blacks in the Chicago area were notable for their tenacious support for the walkout. Elsewhere, however, racial antagonism exploded. In Johnstown, Pennsylvania, an African American journalist reported frequent "clashes between white and Negro workers," only a handful of whom joined the strike. Particularly tense were relations between blacks and Eastern European ethnic workers, so frequently competitors for jobs.[60]

In the automobile industry also, black workers were hesitant or hostile. The relatively few African Americans who worked there were not significant factors in the early struggle for union. At Ford, black workers initially proved loyal to Henry Ford. Alone among the automakers he had provided opportunities for stable employment and even advancement into skilled and supervisory work. He contributed to black philanthropies. Critics charged that these gestures were cynical and insincere, but the fact remained that as of the mid-1930s Ford provided more jobs, more opportunities, and more support for the black community than all of the other Detroit-area employers combined.[61]

UAW leaders often voiced egalitarian views. Declared president Homer Martin, "Negro workers have all the benefits and rights of our union. . . . We feel very, very strongly on this matter." But blacks remained suspicious. Despite the positive reputation of John L. Lewis and the UMW, observed a black journalist in 1937, African American workers were "still reluctant to cast their lot with the union."[62] As the UAW faced the daunting task of attempting to organize Ford's River Rouge complex, the black workers who toiled there posed a critical problem despite the union's recruitment of a gifted cadre of African American organizers and its increasingly close collaboration with the NAACP.[63]

The birth of the CIO and the creation of SWOC, both so obviously imbued with the UMW heritage, did help to change black workers' attitudes. Black workers and reformers alike increasingly felt that only in New Deal programs and in the mobilization of lower-income people of all ethnic backgrounds could they participate in programs that offered a way out of the depression. As organizations that might well upgrade the status and compensation of employed blacks, the new industrial unions merited support. Moreover, as African American votes increasingly swung into the Democratic column, the CIO was a natural ally. Some left-wing organizers believed that the CIO might have made more rapid progress with a more direct, race-centered appeal. But the leaders of the CIO believed that it was their historic task to bring color-blind equality and empowerment to the industrial scene even as the American political system proclaimed it in public arenas.[64]

If the men leading the CIO charge were cautious on the issue of race, they were virtually silent regarding gender. Despite the lack of public discussion, however, embedded within the CIO enterprise were very real notions about the industrial and domestic roles of women in the labor movement and in American society generally. The CIO leadership made early choices concerning the role of women in the labor movement that helped to establish the boundaries of the industrial union enterprise.

Much as the males who led the CIO might wish it otherwise, women were significant factors in the workforce. The remunerated labor force was over one-quarter female, with the vast majority of women workers concentrated in low-wage occupations, notably in some of the CIO's primary fields of operation. True, there were virtually no female coal miners, steelworkers, or rubber workers. No women worked as stevedores or merchant seamen. But even in the automobile industry, largely a male preserve, almost 30,000 women, comprising 6.5 percent of the labor force, were employed. Electrical appliances employed over 100,000 women, fully one-third of its labor force, while 40 percent of textile workers were women. In the needle trades, home of Hillman's Clothing Workers and Dubinsky's Garment Workers, women comprised well over half of the labor force. Meatpacking increasingly employed women as wrappers, dressers, slicers, and packagers. Thousands of agricultural workers were females, and the white collar, governmental, and retail sectors, into which some CIO activists hoped to expand, were major employers of women.[65]

The significance of gender went beyond the matter of working women in their roles as potential union recruits, however. The wives and other female relatives of male union members played critical roles in the classic strikes of the early CIO. In Flint, for example, UAW organizers had early recognized that enlisting the support of strikers' wives was crucial. SWOC organizers too recognized the key importance of steelworkers' wives. Union appeals stressed the CIO's pacific intent and its commitment to domestic virtues. A steelworkers' union, pledged Bittner, "means the ownership of homes, with the comforts every wife and mother desires." Steelworkers' wives, he instructed, should "realize that it is their duty to lend every aid and assistance" to SWOC. Organizers established women's auxiliaries and community groups to mobilize support for the campaign. Since in the typical working-class household women kept track of family finances, this focus on women's domestic role was not misplaced.[66]

For the most part the men who launched the CIO had traditionalist views of the economic, social, and political roles of women. They embraced the family wage concept that had been at the heart of the AFL's perspective on gender. The employment of married women represented a defeat for the working-class household. The UAW, acknowledged a local officer, was bound by its contract to represent women. Still, he continued, "some day . . . I hope we will reach that economic ideal where the married woman will find her place in the home caring for children, which is God's greatest gift to women and her natural birthright."[67]

Not every CIO functionary held to so categorical a view of women's roles. Younger activists especially, more likely to have had experience with women as coworkers, tended to be less bound by stereotypes. Communists, while by no means free of the generation's gender biases, proved more willing than most to contemplate women in positions of leadership and responsibility. New York City UE activist Ruth Young, for example, was an influential early leader, while the ILWU employed writer Tillie Olsen as its education director. In the United Office and Professional Workers, a while collar affiliate with strong Communist ties, Eleanor Nelson served as secretary-treasurer. The social democratic needle trades unions, with their large female memberships, also made room for female representation. In the ACWA Dorothy Bellanca rose to the executive board, and the union employed a small group of women organizers. In the ILGWU Rose Pesotta served as an organizer through the heyday of the early CIO and won a reputation for vigor and effectiveness.

Even in these unions, however, women's roles were severely circumscribed. In the UE, which pioneered in many aspects of women's union activity, male suspicion of women activists remained strong. Recalled one UE activist, those women who showed ambition and ability had a difficult time. "I was not accepted by the other representatives of the UE," observed Mary Voltz. "They were men. And they tried very hard to make me into an office clerk." Pesotta grew increasingly disillusioned with the male-dominated leadership of the ILGWU. She reminded her boss, David Dubinsky, of his complaints that the old AFL Executive Council had treated him as the token Jew, adding that in the ILGWU, "I am considered the [token] *Woman* and at times I feel just as comfortable as you did."[68]

What was true in relatively cosmopolitan organizations such as the UE and the ILGWU was even more prevalent in the UMW and the inner councils of the national CIO. Coal mining and steelmaking were men's work, and so was labor organizing. Married women had no place in a UMW office, except when the union's bitter internal conflicts made it prudent to put a trusted relative on the payroll. For all important or confidential work, male clerks were recruited.[69]

Despite ample evidence of women's activism, most CIO functionaries insisted on relegating them to the periphery. In the wake of the Flint victory, for example, thousands of Detroit-area clerks, tobacco workers, waitresses, and hotel employees waged spirited sit-downs of their own. In the large eastern cities, office and professional workers' unions, with high percentages of female members, conducted aggressive campaigns for recognition and improved standards. From the early experience of the UE, Agricultural and Cannery Workers, and the UAW came abundant examples of female activism. Yet the view persisted that women were peripheral to the CIO's central goals. Official CIO pronouncements demanded "equal pay for equal work," but more eloquent and revealing was the sign carried by a male CIO picket and published in the *CIO News*: "Restore Our Manhood," it implored. "We Receive Girls' Wages."[70]

In the mid- to late 1930s few feminist voices criticized the CIO. Indeed, most laborite women approved of the focus on male-dominated core industry and the marginalization of the concerns of female workers. It was not part of the CIO enterprise to challenge prevailing notions of unionism as an essentially male enterprise and, implicitly, as a working-class prop to generally prevailing structures of patriarchy. To be sure, the CIO did organize women workers, and some active in the CIO afforded women activists a greater degree of recognition and opportunity than any labor organization since the Knights of Labor. But an organization so powerfully influenced by the manly world of the coal miner and the steelworker simply was not open to the kinds of possibilities that a more capacious redefinition of gender roles might have permitted.[71]

The CIO's early experience with race and gender provided vivid evidence of what it was and was not. The leading figures in the CIO would inaugurate no revolution in labor's scope of action, institutional character, or relationship to distinctly disadvantaged or vulnerable groups. At the same time, however, the CIO was clearly the most vigorous, expansive, and inclusive force that the mainstream labor movement had produced in over fifty years.

By the spring of 1938 CIO leaders were ready to dispense with the fiction of continued association with the AFL. In the fall of 1936 the federation had suspended and then expelled the CIO unions. It was driving CIO unions out of city central and state federation bodies, and its affiliates were waging war against CIO organizations. Since March 1937 the CIO had been operating politically, legislatively, and organizationally apart from the AFL. Lewis, Hillman, and Murray had held back from formalizing the break in part because the rush of events was too swift for the leisurely holding of a convention. Moreover, Charles Howard and David Dubinsky, two important members of the original CIO committee, had never abandoned hope of reconciliation with the AFL.

By the spring of 1938, however, no such possibility remained. At a meeting convened in Washington, D.C., in April, representatives of the CIO unions adopted a resolution calling for a formal constitutional convention to be held in the fall. The AFL, Lewis noted, was asserting that the CIO was merely "a papered organization" that had no legitimacy or standing in the House of Labor. "It was time," Lewis declared, "for the C.I.O. to decide its own destiny." With the country still struggling in recession and with events in Europe casting an increasingly ominous cloud over America, the country needed direction and boldness. America, the resolution asserted, needed "an aggressive, efficiently administered, progressive labor movement." In the fall, when the CIO adopted its constitution and formally institutionalized its spectacular achievements, it would have one.[72]

5 Stasis and Schism, 1938–1940

In the period after the CIO's early victories and bitter defeats, ideological forces and differences among leading figures in the CIO about both domestic and international politics fractured the industrial union organization. The formal establishment of the CIO as the Congress of Industrial Organizations in November 1938 provided only a thin facade of unity. As the Roosevelt recession lingered into 1939, membership totals remained stagnant. John L. Lewis grew distracted from CIO affairs, leaving much of the day-to-day work in the hands of family members and UMW retainers. The departure of the ILGWU in 1938 and near-fatal internal conflict within the UAW slowed industrial union development. As the nation drifted toward war, disagreement between Lewis and Hillman over the CIO's relationship to the emerging national security state erupted into open conflict.

In the fall of 1940 the UMW chief repudiated Roosevelt and subsequently surrendered the reins of the industrial union federation to his long-term assistant, Philip Murray. The outbreak of war in Europe also posed new challenges. Accelerated military production stimulated workers' demands and held out the prospect of rapid completion of the organization of the central industrial core. Meanwhile the CIO's influential Communist contingent geared their shifting policies to the rapidly changing situation abroad and asserted them forcefully within the industrial union federation.

THE CONVENTION

The band of the Brickville, Pennsylvania, UMW local struck up "Happy Days Are Here Again" as Lewis strode to the podium to address the opening session of the CIO's long-awaited constitutional convention on November 14, 1938. As the Committee for Industrial Organization, the CIO had had no formal institutional identity. Now, legitimized by a new constitution, its adherents believed, the CIO would redefine the role of the central labor federation. It would amass a great warchest, launch potent organizing drives, and claim, in Lewis's words, "increasing participation in the functions of government." "Today," he told the cheering delegates in Pittsburgh's Islam Grotto auditorium, "we fit the roof tree in a mighty new house of labor."[1]

In establishing itself now as a discrete labor federation, the Congress of Industrial Organizations shattered the fiction of a single House of Labor. The constitution, produced under the direction of general counsel Lee Pressman at the behest of Lewis, did depart from the AFL model. For example, whereas unions affiliated with the AFL paid a monthly per capita tax of one cent to the federation, those in the CIO were assessed five cents, thus permitting a far more active central federation. The CIO, observed twenty-seven-year-old James B. Carey, president of the UE, would "have more central authority, and [would] engage in organizational activity" of unprecedented dimensions.[2]

In fact, the CIO of the late 1930s was mired in recession, incomplete organization, and internal controversy. Moreover, close students of the new constitution pointed out that, rhetoric aside, it actually followed the AFL model in important respects. A board comprised of the presidents of affiliates would govern the CIO between its yearly conventions. True, there were different arrangements for the CIO's executive officers than those prevailing in the older federation, but it was uncertain that the CIO's provisions for leadership were clearly more progressive and dynamic than those that had served the AFL. In any event, the new federation, like its older counterpart, was just that – a federation. Clearly, power in the CIO resided where it lodged in the AFL, namely in the potent national and international unions that embraced the bulk of the membership and paid the necessary dues to finance its operations. Perhaps the industrial union project would permit the CIO eventually to transcend the decentralized structural arrangements that had dominated the labor movement since the nineteenth century, but nothing in the CIO's constitution, or in its heavy dependence on Lewis and other autonomous leaders, guaranteed, or even prefigured, such a course.[3]

In the new CIO the chief executive was, in theory, less dependent on the national and international unions, since there was no provision in the new document for paying him a CIO salary. Thus, presumably, he would continue, as was the case with Lewis, to lead one of the affiliated unions, thus, presumably, freeing him from close scrutiny and dictation by the affiliates. At the same time, however, simultaneous leadership of both a large international union and the CIO would tax even the most dynamic leader. Moreover, of course, the dual status would clearly compromise his ability to serve as honest broker or conciliator in intraunion conflicts.

Still, so long as Lewis headed the CIO, such an arrangement was compatible with a strong and decisive executive. Lewis headed the CIO's largest, most solvent, and most stable union, the UMW. Although at the time of its formal creation the industrial union federation claimed 4 million members, in fact it collected per capita tax on little more than one-third of that number. The UMW members contributed $30,000 a month to the CIO, an amount that often accounted for over half of its revenue. Moreover, the UMW had lent or given vast sums to SWOC and other struggling affiliates and provided the salaries for scores of CIO organizers and members of the Washington staff.

Thus, whatever the claims of the new constitution, clearly the CIO remained heavily dependent on Lewis and his Mine Workers. Indeed, developments within the CIO before the adoption of the new constitution tightened the UMW's (and hence Lewis's) control. Beginning late in 1937 UMW functionaries such as Lewis's brother-in-law J. R. Bell, his brother Dennie Lewis, and his 26-year-old daughter Kathryn Lewis began to assume key responsibilities. At the end of the year, Katherine Ellickson, whose work in the Washington office had provided the early CIO with much of the continuity and institutional identity it possessed, was released. Brophy found increasingly that Bell, who served as CIO comptroller, Dennie Lewis, and John L. Lewis's executive assistant Walter Smethurst were making critical decisions about CIO affairs without consulting him. Also noteworthy was the growing role of thirty-one-year-old Lee Pressman, who retained close ties with the pro-Soviet left and enjoyed direct access to Lewis.[4]

Lewis's conduct of CIO affairs grew secretive and arbitrary. He did not involve his CIO colleagues in formulating a public response to the Roosevelt recession of 1937–38. His political moves became increasingly erratic as his growing disappointment over the administration's economic and defense policies brought him into conflict with Hillman, Murray, and most other CIO influentials.[5]

Critics in the AFL claimed that by the middle of 1938 there was little to the CIO as an organization. Asserted one of Lewis's bitterest foes in the old federation, "The impression . . . [is] that the CIO remains in the main a sort of large holding company, in which the miners held the controlling shares." Journalist Benjamin Stolberg put it more succinctly: "John L. Lewis is the CIO."[6] Indeed, it was in part to answer these critics that Lewis arranged to hold the Pittsburgh convention.[7]

In an important sense, then, the new constitution ratified the existing arrangements. Lewis would continue to function as CIO president while heading the UMW. But his position as UMW leader occupied most of his time. He almost never appeared at CIO headquarters, and some labor reporters and insiders detected a note of weariness and impatience in Lewis with regard to the CIO. The constitution called for two vice-presidents, also nonsalaried, with loosely defined duties, and a secretary. The vice-presidencies were filled by Sidney Hillman and Philip Murray. Hillman's ACWA provided, after the UMW, the CIO's most generous financial support and consistent payment of per capita tax. Murray's SWOC remained deeply in debt to the CIO and to the UMW, but he was using SWOC's highly centralized command structure to tighten his grip on its growing membership. The convention rubber-stamped Lewis's selection of the youthful James B. Carey as secretary.

In fact, the secretaryship had generated some mild controversy in the otherwise harmonious convention. Alone among the top offices, it could carry with it a CIO-paid salary, although in fact Carey retained his position and the compensation that went with it from his home union.[8] In view of Lewis's apparent lack of attention to CIO affairs, the secretaryship might well become the office of the de facto head of the CIO. If so, John Brophy seemed to many the natural choice for this job.[9]

Lewis had no desire to create an independent center of power in the CIO, however. Brophy, like Lewis and Murray, was a Mine Worker, and the CIO head believed that the new mass production unions needed representation in the CIO's inner councils. Carey was a Catholic liberal whose youth and identification with such causes as civil rights made him an ideal national spokesman. That Carey seemed devoted to Lewis and was a particular favorite of Kathryn Lewis added to his appeal, as did his growing association with members of the Roosevelt administration, most notably Eleanor Roosevelt.

The formal establishment of the Congress of Industrial Organizations raised more questions than it answered. A viable industrial union federation without Lewis seemed unthinkable, yet the UMW chief appeared to be losing interest in the CIO. International developments and the growing debate over foreign and defense policy tightened tensions among industrial unionists. Membership growth stopped, and the industrial core remained only partially organized. The biggest question of all faced CIO partisans: Could it weather these storms and achieve a stable institutional identity apart from the powerful figure of John L. Lewis?

TROUBLES

The CIO was not a healthy organization at the time of its constitutional convention. The continuing recession stalled membership growth, dried up dues payments, and encouraged employers to roll back the union tide. Internal conflict ravaged several unions, notably the UAW. The textile campaign bogged down, while SWOC made little progress. Dues payments were a chronic problem. Observed Lewis in June 1939, "The financial nightmares around this . . . organization have been serious enough month after month and pay day after pay day, simply because somebody has been getting a free ride." [10]

Meanwhile the AFL mounted a potent counterattack. Unions such as the Carpenters, the Electrical Workers, the Machinists, and the Teamsters often outorganized CIO rivals. Moreover, by the summer of 1938 the ILGWU was drifting back into the AFL fold. John P. Frey, head of the AFL Metal Trades Department, noted with satisfaction that "there has been a widespread unwillingness on the part of members of many C.I.O. unions to pay dues." [11]

The CIO's membership and financial situation during the two years after the convention remained precarious. Leaders boasted of over 4 million members, but in truth during this period the CIO did not even reach the 2 million mark. The UMW and the ACWA regularly accounted for around 40 percent of the dues-paying membership. Before 1941 the accumulation of workers actually brought into unions under the aegis of the CIO rarely reached a million. Until that year the UAW, SWOC, and the URW typically had a combined dues-paying membership of under 200,000, fewer than Hillman's ACWA alone. TWOC and its successor CIO union, the TWUA, publicly boasted of having over 300,000 workers under contract, but in reality its sporadic dues payments to the CIO reflected membership of under 40,000. Bridges's ILWU was a stable and strategically important union, but its membership was tiny, numbering about 20,000. The UE paid on under 80,000 members. Indeed, when the ILGWU left the unofficial CIO fold in late 1938, it took with it 12.5 percent of the industrial union body's membership. [12]

CIO officials never released realistic membership figures. They used a variety of devices to inflate apparent totals. A favored ploy was to speak of workers under contract, a category that inevitably included large numbers of workers who were not in fact union members. Another method was to use the rubric of "exonerated" members, that is, members who were temporarily excused from paying dues, usually because of unemployment. So, for example, in 1938 SWOC paid per capita tax on 82,000 members but carried an additional 400,000 steelworkers as exonerated, even though it had never collected a dollar from the vast majority of these men. Lewis and his aides kept these bookkeeping arrangements from public scrutiny (and, indeed, from other members of the CIO's hierarchy), but journalists and AFL rivals made pretty accurate estimates of the actual state of affairs. [13]

There was some justification for keeping membership figures obscure. Building a steelworkers' union, for example, was a monumental undertaking. SWOC collected no dues from among thousands of supporters in Republic and Bethlehem plants. Shop stewards and union officials had to attempt to collect the per capita tax each month, dollar by dollar. Failure to pay dues, however, did not necessarily indicate antiunion feeling. Thus observed one SWOC official, "Steel workers will go out and die for the union in the excitement of the picket line, but they'll be damned if they'll pay another dollar to 'that lousy shop steward.' "[14]

Spotty membership totals, of course, translated into financial precariousness. The CIO never in this period collected a fraction of the per capita tax needed to finance its operations. It was dependent always on UMW subsidies, doled out in the form of outright loans or grants to affiliates or to the CIO, assignment of UMW-paid organizers, and generous subscriptions to CIO publications.[15]

Simply on the basis of the formal collection of per capita tax, dependence on the UMW was clear enough. Thus, from the time the CIO began to collect monthly dues in the spring of 1937 until its formal constitutional beginnings nineteen months later, it received about $1.355 million in per capita tax from affiliates. The UMW was responsible for $570,000, or 43 percent. In addition, in 1937 the UMW pumped over $1.2 million of loans into the CIO, as well as advancing substantial sums to SWOC. Through 1940, per capita tax from the UMW accounted for at least one-third of the CIO's monthly income.[16]

Just as the CIO depended on the UMW, so many of its affiliates depended on the CIO. By late 1939 SWOC had run up at least $2.5 million in indebtedness, an amount equal to about three times the CIO's annual dues collections from its affiliates. In contrast, affiliates such as the UAW, the URW, the UE, the ILWU, and the TWU were largely self-financing. On the other hand, many of the newer affiliates were costly indeed. Between mid-1937 and September 1941 the CIO paid out almost $900,000 more in subsidies to some nineteen new affiliates than it received from them in per capita tax. Minuscule public sector unions, for example, absorbed over $190,000 in this period, and other small organizations of communications, technical, utilities, and office workers absorbed another $215,000. The CIO contributed $138,000 to the textile drive during this period, on top of the half-million dollars paid directly by the ACWA.[17]

The problem with this state of affairs was not so much the indebtedness per se. After all, organizing workers cost money. But there appeared to be no coherent plans for these expenditures. Since Lewis and the UMW controlled CIO finances, they also controlled the organization's agenda. Was the public sector a sensible choice for the investment of nearly $200,000? Did it make sense to siphon off $120,000 to assist tiny groups of communications and technical workers? Most spectacularly, how could the expenditure of over $313,000 to subsidize a hopeless CIO campaign to challenge the AFL's entrenched construction workers be justified? Since Lewis was providing the money, however, no one could question the disbursements or the conduct of these marginal organizations.[18]

Stolberg and others noted that large sums flowed to affiliates whose leadership was associated with the Communist Party. Thus the CIO ran up large deficits in assisting the American Communications Association ($80,000), a union of architects and technical workers ($40,000), the Farm Equipment Workers Organizing Committee ($41,000), a white collar workers' union ($39,000), and the two public employee unions ($190,000). On the other hand, Bridges and the ILWU complained that Lewis-supplied CIO subsidies were encouraging rival organizations to encroach on their jurisdiction, thus, in their view, needlessly fragmenting potential CIO memberships.[19] Meanwhile, UAW leaders questioned why the CIO was subsidizing a separate union for farm equipment workers, whose workplaces and employers were located in the UAW's midwestern heartland.

There seemed no pattern to the CIO's support of new unions other than Lewis's whims. His efforts to launch a CIO construction workers' union in the summer of 1939 seemed particularly quixotic. On the surface it seemed a bold step forward, but this was in reality an empty gesture. He created UCWOC without consulting his CIO colleagues. Its founding manifesto was a progressive document, promising to challenge the notoriously corrupt, racist, and anachronistic AFL building trades organizations. UCWOC would eliminate restrictive work practices, jurisdictional wrangling, racial exclusion, and collusive bargaining. The time was ripe, for no doubt the impending expansion of American military capability would require a vast expansion in the heavy construction industry.[20]

From the beginning, however, Lewis sent mixed signals about UCWOC. Some observers speculated that its creation was in retaliation against the AFL for its recent chartering of a dissident union of Illinois coal miners. If so, however, why did Lewis pour almost $170,000 in CIO resources into it during its first year? Moreover, Lewis increasingly made support for UCWOC a test of loyalty among his CIO colleagues, most of whom wanted no part of a battle against the AFL's building trades unions. But if Lewis were in earnest about UCWOC, why did he put his brother Dennie Lewis, his notoriously inept and unimaginative bodyguard, in charge?[21]

Normally Brophy might have moderated these moves. But in October 1939 Brophy was replaced as the CIO's director by Allan S. Haywood, a veteran UMW organizer and Lewis loyalist. Increasingly now Lewis's circle called the shots. Bell initiated cutbacks in the CIO staff in response to the lingering recession. Dennie Lewis assigned office space and dispatched organizers. Kathryn Lewis regulated access to Lewis himself. Haywood, in contrast to Brophy, had no standing outside the world of the UMW. He was Lewis's creature in a way that Brophy had never been.[22]

By mid-1940 the CIO was floundering at the top. Indeed, in 1939 and 1940 disquieting rumors circulated that perhaps Lewis might be ready to write off the CIO. His increasing reliance on a small inner circle of relatives and confidants, his ouster of Brophy, and his arbitrary patterns of decision making moved the CIO ever further from autonomy and internal cohesion.

Even so, few in the CIO could contemplate an industrial union movement without Lewis. Thus, when in October 1939 Lewis announced to a shocked Executive Board that he had decided to resign as CIO president, his colleagues begged him to remain in charge. For whatever the limitations of his day-to-day stewardship, CIO leaders believed that he remained their only hope for eventual success.[23]

DEFECTIONS

Throughout the pre–World War II period, internal conflict characterized the CIO. Clashes of personality, ideology, interest, and opinion regarding America's response to the outbreak of war in Europe created multiple and intersecting lines of fracture. Early evidence of CIO factiousness appeared in the course of the UAW following its great victories in the winter and spring of 1937. Soon after, the CIO lost one of its most important affiliates, the ILGWU. Its president, David Dubinsky, refused to bring the ILGWU into the new CIO and began to drift back into the AFL.

Conflict in the UAW extended from just after its breakthrough victories in 1937 until the early months of 1940. Rival blocs were divided along personal, ideological, and ethnocultural lines. In addition the recession of 1937–39 fed both protracted shop-floor conflict and the ambitions of automotive executives to undo the results of the 1937 strikes. With a potential membership of over a million, the UAW was crucial to the entire CIO project, and its internal tribulations eventually forced Lewis and other top CIO leaders to intervene directly in its affairs.[24]

The struggle involved primarily rivalries among the young and ambitious founders of the UAW. President Homer Martin, thirty-four years old at the time of the Flint strike, was a popular, erstwhile Baptist preacher and GM worker from Kansas City. Martin played a limited role in the epic encounter with GM, but after the strike he consolidated his power. Martin led the ostensibly apolitical Progressive Caucus, which from 1937 through early 1939 held a majority of the positions on the union's executive board. Martin's popularity was particularly strong among older workers, Anglo-

American autoworkers, and unionists of traditional religious and social orientation, although his increasingly bizarre and secretive behavior eventually alienated even many erstwhile supporters.[25]

The Progressive Caucus soon became a vehicle for one of the more esoteric and ambitious left-wing sects to populate the 1930s. Headed by former CPUSA general secretary Jay Lovestone, the Communist Party (Opposition) had since its inception in 1929 been a vociferous foe of the Stalinist CPUSA. Lovestone peppered Lewis, Brophy, and other CIO influentials with news of Communist ambitions, focusing in particular on the conflict within the UAW, where it was indeed true that CPUSA members played a significant role in the union's factional conflicts.[26]

Lovestone got nowhere with Lewis, but he struck paydirt with Dubinsky and with Homer Martin. As early as March 1937 Martin began placing Lovestone's adherents in key UAW slots. Since Martin's opponents in the UAW did indeed include influental leaders who were either Communists or closely identified with the party, the former preacher needed little prodding from Lovestone.[27] Thus, through the late 1930s the UAW found itself squarely in the middle of complex maneuverings among rival left-wing groups.

Indeed, the UAW was a hotbed of ideological conflict. Some prominent UAW leaders, notably Richard Frankensteen and Richard Leonard, were genuinely nonideological. Others, however, notably the young Reuther brothers, Walter, Roy, and Victor, were initially members of the Socialist Party of America. These gifted young men eventually broke with the socialists, but they and their followers retained an essentially social democratic outlook. Convinced that Martin's continued leadership of the union spelled disaster, they caucused with the Communists, but this arrangement was always fragile. For their part, the Communists and their allies regarded the Reuthers as untrustworthy and in 1938 turned away from the Reutherites to conclude an alliance with the opportunistic Frankensteen. The Nazi-Soviet pact of August 1939 both symbolized and gave impetus to the widening rift between the erstwhile allies.

The conflict in the UAW was not primarily about ideology, however. At root it involved the running of the union itself. Insecure and inexperienced, Martin sought validation of his position through increasingly authoritarian moves against his opponents and through collective bargaining approaches to employers that bypassed the shop-floor democracy that was the UAW's proud hallmark. Victor Reuther and Wyndham Mortimer, two bona fide heroes of the Flint strike, were demoted and sent to outlying assignments. In the fall of 1937 Martin formed an alliance with Frankensteen, who had a large following among Chrysler workers, naming the burly martyr of the

Battle of the Overpass assistant president and giving him the prestigious job of organizing Ford. Martin stacked the executive board with his adherents, spied on his enemies, and red-baited his opponents relentlessly.

Meanwhile the effects of the Roosevelt recession triggered sharp conflict within the auto factories. Layoffs were rampant. Dues paying fell, and local unions began to disintegrate. Employers, with GM leading the way, used the recession to test the new union. Never reconciled to the UAW, GM executives and foremen often skirted the frail boundaries of the 1937 contract in assigning work, disciplining workers, and scheduling layoffs. UAW workers retaliated. Between March and June 1937 they conducted over 170 sit-down strikes, presumably in violation of the contract, in GM plants alone. For the next two years auto plants seethed with protest against GM's heightened work norms and antiunion actions. Rather than building solidarity among autoworkers, however, often these informal and unsanctioned job actions ended up pitting one section of a plant against others, as foremen and company officials charged the careening UAW with inability to control its disputatious adherents. Membership totals plummeted and dues payments fell.[28]

Martin was no match for GM bargainers. In August 1937 he negotiated an agreement (the original February agreement ran for only six months) that contained harsh disciplinary measures against accused wildcat strikers. GM workers angrily rejected it, whereupon in March 1938 Martin imposed upon them another agreement that included much-diluted worker protections. He refused to submit it to the divided executive board or the GM locals.

Through 1938, continued recession and internal conflict ravaged the UAW. In June Martin suspended five opponents from the executive board, whereupon Reuther and four others announced that they too would boycott it. In July and August Martin held a "trial" of his opponents. Throughout Detroit and Flint, pro- and anti-Martin forces slugged it out, quite literally at times, for control of local unions. Meanwhile an increasing number of locals, loyal to one or another of the suspended board members or disgusted with Martin's actions, continued to send their monthly per capita dues payments to ousted secretary George Addes. "Hell has broken loose in the U.A.W.," declared one close observer.[29]

Until now, apart from sending Brophy and Germer at separate times to attempt to conciliate the factions, Lewis had kept out of the UAW's difficulties. In September, however, the CIO chief dispatched Murray and Hillman to Detroit to work out a settlement. With this action, Lewis was in effect exercising a receivership over the UAW and clearly was determined to get rid of Martin.[30]

By 1939 two separate UAW executive boards were meeting, and the CIO-sanctioned, anti-Martin board named Chrysler local leader Roland J. (R. J.) Thomas acting president. In March the rival forces held separate conventions. The desperate Martin was openly dickering with the AFL, which tendered him a loan of $25,000, amid reports that he was negotiating a backdoor contract with Henry Ford.

Even the departure of Martin, however, did not end the divisiveness within the UAW. The remaining leaders contested for control of the union. A year earlier, the Communist faction had cut its ties with the Reutherites and had embraced their (and Reuther's) former rival, Richard Frankensteen, now a fugitive from the Martin camp. Now the Communist-Frankensteen alliance was arrayed against the Reutherites, and for a time it appeared that either George Addes, a popular Toledo-based leader who cooperated closely with the Communists, or Wyndham Mortimer, a veteran Communist, had the inside track for the presidency.[31] However, Hillman and Murray, acting for Lewis, engineered a compromise that permitted Thomas to remain president and gave the secretaryship to Addes and a majority on the executive board to the Communist-Frankensteen forces. Soon after, Thomas appointed anti-Communist Walter Reuther director of the UAW's GM Department, the most prestigious and important of its company units, and the various factions within the UAW-CIO settled down to an uneasy cohabitation.[32]

In the aftermath of these developments Martin's now AFL-affiliated UAW challenged the UAW-CIO in NLRB elections. From August 1939 through April 1940 the UAW-CIO overwhelmed its rival, piling up victories by as much as twenty to one. This balloting eliminated the UAW-AFL as a significant force in the auto industry. Meanwhile, brightening economic prospects and a brilliantly devised and led strike of skilled tool-and-die makers against GM in the summer of 1939, engineered by Walter Reuther, solidified the UAW-CIO and eliminated the prospect of the CIO's flagship union succumbing to internal rivalry and renewed corporate attack.[33]

Only about 17,000 UAW members went with Martin out of the CIO and into the AFL. The unwillingness of the ILGWU to participate in the founding of a separate CIO, however, deprived the industrial union federation of a quarter-million dues-paying members[34] and increased its financial dependency on the UMW. The departure of the ILGWU was virtually a foregone conclusion, given the decision to constitute the CIO as a separate labor center.

Dubinsky believed this was a time of "grave crisis" for the labor movement. The onset of the recession, the slowing of the New Deal's domestic momentum, and the increasingly evident horrors of Nazism made healing the split in the House of Labor imperative. Dubinsky and the ILGWU had supported the CIO project from its inception and had contributed significant resources to it. But Dubinsky's agenda had always been more modest than that of Lewis or the new unionists surging into the CIO. He deplored Lewis's more provocative pronouncements and grew increasingly uneasy over the role that Communists were playing in CIO affairs. Close to Lovestone, Dubinsky loaned ILGWU funds to the Martin-led UAW in the factional struggle. He believed that so long as the industrial union project did not take the form of a separate labor center, the chances for peace with the AFL were great.

Dubinsky complained that Lewis had become increasingly arbitrary in his conduct of CIO affairs. In a January 1938 speech he charged that he and the ILGWU "have never been consulted as to policy, procedure, issuance of charters and strategy." Dubinsky resolved to resist Lewis's ambitions even if opposition made him "a minority of one."[35]

In the fall of 1937 AFL and CIO representatives had conducted unity negotiations. Dubinsky had placed great hope in these discussions, but in reality they had little chance of success. AFL spokesmen insisted on the dismantling of newer CIO affiliates and would never agree to granting industrial jurisdiction to the established CIO unions. For their part, CIO negotiators, led by Murray, pressed for drastic constitutional revision in the AFL as their price for unity. Dubinsky blamed Lewis for the talks' breakdown, but in fact the two sides were never close to agreement.[36]

As CIO functionaries planned the founding November convention, Dubinsky continued to criticize Lewis. Throughout the country, ILGWU locals held back from participating in the IUCs. "Our Union," he told a local union leader in March, "does not intend to leave the CIO," but it was hard to see what choice Dubinsky would have when a permanent CIO was established. In August Lewis attended a secret ILGWU board meeting, but the only result was to feed rumors that Dubinsky was no longer paying per capita tax to the CIO and was on the verge of reaffiliating with the AFL. Although in fact the garment workers' union temporarily continued its financial contributions, its nonparticipation in the November convention signaled the end of its three-year sojourn with the CIO. At a board meeting on the eve of the CIO gathering, the ILGWU reaffirmed its opposition to a permanent CIO and announced that it would remain unaffiliated with any national union center. The original CIO, Dubinsky told a radio audience on November 13, "had a definite mission to accomplish. . . . It will [now] assume a new status and we refuse to join such a move." For the time being, the ILGWU would remain friendly toward both federations.[37]

The experiences of the UAW and the ILGWU revealed the tentative and incomplete nature of the CIO accomplishment of 1935–37. Involving as they did ideological, tactical, and political issues, these two episodes underscored the great extent to which the CIO enterprise remained vulnerable to the powerful social, political, and ideological currents that raged through this pregnant period. The CIO's public pronouncements continued to exude confidence, but its internal fissures bespoke disarray and uncertainty.

SHAKE-UP

The UAW and ILGWU episodes were soon dwarfed by the escalating conflict between the two leading figures in the original CIO, Lewis and ACWA head Sidney Hillman. The war in Europe, which began on September 1, 1939, formed the backdrop to a series of confrontations between the two men that raised basic questions about the essential character of the CIO and the relationship of the labor movement to the emerging national security state. Involving as it did the CIO's posture with regard to the U.S. military buildup, appropriate forms of worker activism, relations with Franklin Roosevelt and the Democratic Party, and the nature of the institutional character of the CIO, the Hillman-Lewis feud far transcended the personalistic terms in which most contemporary journalists, politicians, and unionists spoke of it. Still, the personalization of the conflict was not entirely misplaced because Lewis and Hillman embodied two profoundly different conceptions of the modern labor movement and articulated these conceptions in highly individual and dramatic terms.

This was an extraordinary period for laborites generally. Eager to take advantage of the tightening labor markets that the military buildup brought, industrial unionists were determined to make wage gains and to complete the organization of the central industrial core. Problems of manpower development, defense plant site selection, the awarding of military contracts, and industrial conflict insured that labor would take center stage. President Roosevelt's selection of CIO vice-president Sidney Hillman as the chief representative of organized labor in the mobilization apparatus he created in mid-1940 insured that federal policies and the course of the CIO would be inextricably interwound.

Profound and ever-shifting international crises permeated the increasingly conflictual world of the CIO. The emergence of the horrific Nazi state in Germany sent shock waves through an American labor movement, many of whose members and leaders were of Eastern European and/or Jewish heritage. In addition, the impact of relations between the Soviet Union and the German reich reverberated powerfully in America. The stunning announcement on August 23, 1939, of the German-Soviet Non-Aggression Pact quickly reversed the stand of the CPUSA and placed the party, its labor union adherents, and their allies in opposition to U.S. aid to the Western allies. American Communists and their associates now backed intensified worker militancy, even (or, their enemies said, especially) in the defense industry and even as other laborites were committing themselves ever more openly to the government's military buildup and President Roosevelt's policy of support for the Western allies.

Among CIO leaders Hillman identified most closely with the administration's foreign policy positions. He believed fervently that only rapid American military buildup could thwart Nazi ambitions and that only Franklin Roosevelt could lead the American people in this time of maximum peril. He sought, both as a CIO official and, after May 1940, as part of the Roosevelt administration's defense mobilization machinery, to enlist organized labor in behalf of a vigorous program of increased production. Moreover, he believed, loyalty to FDR would eventually pay off in expanded union membership and influence. In 1940 these views pitted Hillman against John L. Lewis, whose anti-Roosevelt and antiwar utterances grew increasingly strident and uncompromising.

Lewis was an isolationist. He believed that British imperialists were plotting with Wall Street Anglophiles to bring America into the European bloodbath, as they had done in 1917. He regarded FDR's foreign and defense policies, which edged ever closer to U.S. intervention, as tragically mistaken if not consciously dishonest.

During the early building of the CIO, such provincial and conspiratorial views mattered little. Increasingly, however, the world intruded on America and on the CIO project. Only months after the milestone events of the early CIO, the achievement of contracts with GM and U.S. Steel, the Japanese attacked China. In March 1938, as Lewis and Dubinsky debated the merits of establishing a permanent CIO, Germany annexed Austria. Throughout the remainder of that year and through most of 1939, as the CIO weathered the factional conflicts in the UAW and attempted to stabilize itself financially and institutionally, Hitler's demands on Czechoslovakia and Poland escalated and the Soviet Union concluded its historic pact with the reich. President Roosevelt identified the United States increasingly with the anti-Axis cause. With the outbreak of war in September 1939, and especially after the shocking German defeat of France in June 1940, the administration embarked on a feverish program of military expansion.

For Lewis, these developments offered opportunity and peril. Throughout the defense buildup Lewis encouraged worker activism. He spurred the completion of organization in autos, steel, farm equipment, and other industrial sectors and moved to bring the so-called captive coal mines (those owned and operated by steel manufacturers) into union shop agreements with the UMW.

In Lewis's view, however, the defense boom imperiled the labor movement even as these opportunities emerged. Throughout the latter 1930s to the eve of Pearl Harbor, Lewis warned of the dangers. Repeatedly he drove home the same message: "If it is our mission to save Western Civilization, then let us begin by saving it right here in our own country" through improving living standards, abolishing racial discrimination, and democratizing the political process. At the UMW convention in January 1940 he lashed out bitterly at the president, who, he charged, was on the verge of "taking our young men and making cannon fodder out of them." The government, he declared, sought "to kill off the virile, energetic youth of the nation in a war . . . so that the rest of the population older in years will be more docile and more easily exploited."[38]

Both Lewis's general antiwar views and his increasingly strident condemnation of the president brought his conflict with Hillman to a head. Hillman simply had a different understanding of the nature of the German threat than did the Iowa-born, isolationist, provincial Lewis. Moreover, the once-socialist Hillman viewed government-labor collaboration as a positive good. Presiding over a union whose decentralized industry stood on the fringes of the central economic core, Hillman looked to government for enforcement of workers' rights and labor standards. In contrast, Lewis's use of government to rebuild the UMW and launch the CIO had been largely situational. Coal, he believed, was so crucial to the industrial economy that once reestablished the UMW could stand on its own. As foreign affairs loomed ever larger on the political scene, Hillman tightened his embrace of the Democratic Party even as Lewis pulled back.[39]

After the defeat of France in the spring of 1940, labor's role in national defense and its political and institutional relationship with the administration took on new urgency. Late in May 1940 Roosevelt appointed Hillman to serve as labor representative on the NDAC, created to coordinate escalating military production. Both the manner of Hillman's appointment and his role in the government raised basic questions about the CIO's relationship to Roosevelt and the national security state.

Hillman accepted the appointment while retaining the presidency of the ACWA. He believed that labor support was critical in both the political and the international agendas of the Roosevelt administration. To Hillman, it was a testament to the CIO's great achievements that one of its own had been chosen to assume such heavy responsibilities.

And the responsibilities were heavy. FDR wanted the ACWA president to mediate between AFL and CIO unions, to devise and implement plans for manpower use, to develop programs for the augmentation of the skilled labor force, and to arrange settlements for industrial disputes in defense plants. As a labor activist, of course, Hillman would press labor's case in administration circles. He would use his access to the president to oppose corporate leaders and military procurement officers who would abandon labor standards and award fat contracts to corporations that violated labor laws. At the same time, however, he was now a government official and did have to work through the often-frustrating labyrinths of bureaucratic decision making and backstairs dealings to gain his point. In the final analysis, he was charged with facilitating military production. There was, in his view, no fundamental conflict in his roles as labor leader and defense mobilizer. He believed fervently that collective bargaining, decent standards, and strong unions enhanced industrial efficiency. Hillman believed that both labor's and the nation's interests dovetailed, as did his dual roles as union leader and public official.[40]

Lewis, however, did not share Hillman's sense of national peril or his commitment to the administration. Convinced that Roosevelt was leading the country to disaster, the CIO chief focused much of his hostility toward the government on Hillman. He believed that Roosevelt was using Hillman to co-opt workers and reshape the labor movement. Throughout the summer and fall of 1940 Lewis and Hillman confronted each other at labor gatherings and in the public press, each seeking to advance his definition of the CIO's relationship to the national security state.[41]

Lewis found ample evidence to support his belief that the president was attempting to reshape the labor movement to suit his own political objectives. Picking Hillman without even a show of consultation with Lewis was an egregious case in point. The question of labor unity constituted another. Hillman believed that international crisis and the need to reelect Roosevelt now necessitated reconciliation, a view that Roosevelt shared. Convinced that AFL negotiators were determined to liquidate the CIO, Lewis believed that in his advocacy of labor unity Hillman was acting as a messenger for the administration and was willing to compromise the basic integrity of the whole CIO undertaking.[42]

Hillman's actions on the NDAC drew immediate fire from Lewis and his allies. Much of the conflict between the two labor chieftains focused on the seemingly straightforward issue of the government's awarding of military contracts to firms that chronically violated federal labor laws. In each major industry, key employers had remained unorganized following the CIO's spectacular breakthroughs of 1937. Little Steel companies continued to promote company unionism. The Ford Motor Company, International

Harvester, Goodyear Tire and Rubber, Allis-Chalmers (a large producer of naval engines), and others resisted unionization, often employing blatant discrimination and even physical assault against union activists. Since 1937 unions such as the UAW, SWOC, the FE, and the URW had repeatedly won NLRB rulings for unfair labor practices against such employers, but the companies in turn used legal appeals to delay judgments and keep the unions at bay.

In addition, Lewis and other CIO leaders charged, defense contractors regularly violated the provisions of the 1936 Walsh-Healey Act, a measure that required government contractors to adhere to specific standards of wages, hours, and working conditions. Notorious labor law violators such as Ford and Bethlehem Steel seemed favorites of the military procurement authorities, together receiving over 10 percent of the business generated by new military orders in 1940. Bethlehem, declared SWOC president Murray, was "laughing at the law" and "its plants are running amuck with a thousand and one systems of espionage" designed to thwart the steelworkers' union. For laborites, observance of these federal laws was critical. In 1917 government officials had persuaded the AFL to agree not to exploit wartime conditions to disturb existing patterns of labor-management relations. Corporations that had successfully resisted the earlier union onslaught now claimed that the military emergency required a freeze in existing patterns of worker-management relations. Unless the CIO made its move now, it might never fulfill its ambitions.[43]

Beginning in 1939 Lewis pressed Roosevelt to deny military contracts to labor law violators, but the president responded cautiously. Since in most cases court actions involving alleged labor law violations were still pending, the offending corporations were not technically guilty of crimes. Standard government procedure required that contracts be granted to lowest bidders. New legislation, declared FDR, was the only means by which any injustice could be remedied. Lewis and CIO counsel Lee Pressman had indeed sought amendments in 1938 to the Walsh-Healey Act requiring the government to consider adherence to the law in granting contracts, but their failure then had convinced them that the legislative route was a dead end.[44]

When Hillman assumed his responsibilities in June 1940, Lewis renewed his demand. Through the summer, with Roosevelt locked in a close presidential race and heavily reliant on labor support, Hillman tried to hammer out a solution. With rank-and-file pressure building for strikes against Bethlehem Steel and other notorious union-resistant firms, Hillman at last gained Roosevelt's endorsement of a statement to be issued in the name of the NDAC on labor policies in defense mobilization. Released to the press on August 31, 1940, the document declared that "all work carried on as part of the defense program should comply with Federal statutory provisions affecting labor." Supplementary statements and advisory rulings by the Department of Justice stipulated that, all things being equal, NLRB findings of noncompliance with the provisions of the National Labor Relations Act would disqualify labor law violators in the competition for defense contracts.[45]

On October 1 Hillman triumphantly told the press that "Army and Navy contracts will no longer be given to companies violating the Federal labor laws." But Lewis quickly pointed out that the statements announcing the government's position fell far short of a commitment to penalizing labor law violators. Existing contracts, which totaled in the hundreds of millions of dollars, would not be affected. Moreover, all of the government's statements were so studded with qualifications that they amounted to little more than pious hopes that the military procurement agencies would suddenly turn into aggressive watchdogs. Most importantly, Lewis noted, the various declarations of the NDAC said nothing about enforcement.[46]

Congressional and military response to the NDAC's policy statements soon forced Hillman to back off from even this mild endorsement of labor's rights. On October 8, just a month before the presidential election, Congressman Howard Smith of Virginia, head of a special House committee investigating the alleged excesses of the NLRB, summoned Hillman, the service secretaries (Frank Knox of the Navy and Henry L. Stimson of the War Department), and Attorney General Robert Jackson to explain the meaning of the NDAC's rulings. Jackson, Knox, and Stimson quickly backed off from any but the most innocuous interpretations of the Hillman-developed program. Hillman confined himself to generalizations about the need for labor-management unity, invoking the theme of cooperation in a forum notorious for its hostility to the CIO and all it stood for. Thus, complained Murray, Hillman's initiative had accomplished nothing because "under the driving attack from this Committee and the press, the government policy was completely nullified."[47]

Lewis and Hillman clashed most dramatically on the political front. Throughout 1940 Hillman worked tirelessly, first for Roosevelt's unprecedented third term nomination, then for his election. Lewis's vocal and pointed hostility created an enormous factor of uncertainty at the heart of the campaign. His outspoken advocacy of labor militancy and, especially, his bitter-end isolationism stuck responsive chords among workers. Throughout 1940 Hillman appeared at major CIO gatherings, always with the same message: as much as he admired and respected John L. Lewis, he remained loyal to FDR; fascism had to be stopped; under Roosevelt, organized labor had made unprecedented gains; having gained access and recognition, the CIO would be foolish to permit disagreements over particular points of public policy to cause it to abandon its association with FDR.[48]

Through the spring and into the summer, Lewis searched for an alternative to Roosevelt. He first attempted to launch a boom for Montana senator Burton K. Wheeler and later declared "that the working people of the United States need and want the leadership of Herbert Hoover."[49] But well into the fall campaign Lewis confined himself to his multipronged attacks on Roosevelt and Hillman, keeping his own counsel about where he might throw his weight in November.

Within the CIO the contrast between the organization's political operations in 1940 and those of 1936 could not have been greater. Now the CIO offered no endorsement, contributed no money, and confined its organizers to union building and strike support. The CIO's Communists now depicted the president as a stooge for British imperialism. Murray, Brophy, CIO secretary James B. Carey, the rising star of the UAW, Walter Reuther, and most others personally supported Roosevelt, but the CIO per se played no coherent role in the campaign.

On October 25 Lewis finally revealed his hand. On a nationwide, multinetwork radio broadcast eleven days before the balloting, he declared his support for the Republican nominee, utilities executive Wendell Willkie. He spent most of the broadcast blasting FDR. The president, he asserted, welcomed war as a means of diverting attention from his own failure. His reelection "would be a national evil of the first magnitude."[50]

Lewis's speech hit the nation like a thunderbolt. Communists applauded. Lewis's loyal followers in the UMW and the CIO, including Lee Pressman and Allan Haywood, backed his stand. But elsewhere, disbelief and antagonism reigned. One New Jersey CIO leader charged that Lewis had "betrayed organized labor . . . for Wall Street," and New York City CIO activists branded him a "Benedict Arnold." Murray and UMW secretary-treasurer Thomas Kennedy quietly reaffirmed their support for FDR, while William Green reveled in the CIO's division and discomfiture. Indeed, the only major labor leader to declare himself for Willkie was the Carpenters' William L. Hutcheson, Lewis's victim in the fistfight that had launched the CIO five years earlier. The Lewis announcement was a defining moment for the CIO. He explicitly made his endorsement of Willkie a test of his political leadership in the labor movement. "Sustain me now," he implored the CIO members in his audience, "or repudiate me," and he pledged (or threatened) to step down from the CIO presidency (but, tellingly, not from that of the UMW) if its membership did not follow his lead.[51]

Was the CIO to remain an adjunct to Lewis's grand, but increasingly erratic, vision? Or was it to become ever more enmeshed in the complex politics of the Democratic Party and the national security state? Never did the membership of the industrial union federation have an opportunity to pass direct judgment on the CIO's leadership or the policies the organization pursued. But the election of 1940 did constitute a kind of plebiscite, invoked by Lewis himself. Would the CIO rank and file support Roosevelt and labor leaders who were willing to work for the achievement of union goals within the prevailing political context? Or would they repudiate the president in favor of Lewis and the combination of opportunism, isolationism, and adventurism that he embodied? When the votes were tallied and the blue collar districts showed unmistakable, if somewhat reduced, commitment to the president, Lewis had his answer.[52]

Whether Lewis would in fact step down from the presidency of the CIO, however, remained uncertain. At the annual convention, two weeks after the election, the lengthy conflict between Lewis and Hillman came to one of its periodic heads, with the future leadership of industrial unionism in the balance. Many of the 2,600 delegates were convinced that an irresistible movement to draft Lewis was afoot. Outsized "We Want Lewis" buttons appeared on countless lapels. On November 18 a forty-three-minute ovation greeted Lewis when he entered the hall. Delegates waved placards, staged parades, and chanted "Lewis is our leader! Lewis is our leader."[53]

In his remarks to the convention Lewis was unabashed by his electoral repudiation. He lashed out at the then-absent Hillman and the ACWA delegates in remarks that seemed to some implicitly anti-Semitic. He suggested that they were about to follow Dubinsky out of the CIO. The rhetoric was vintage Lewis: "And now above all the clamor comes the piercing wail and the laments of the Amalgamated Clothing Workers," he sneered. "Dubinsky," Lewis declared, "took the easy way. . . . If there is anybody else in the CIO who wants to take the easy way, let them go," a pointed reference to widespread speculation that Hillman's ACWA would follow his needle trades cohorts back into the old AFL.[54]

Alarmed at the show of strength for Lewis, Hillman rushed to Atlantic City. Continued Lewis leadership, he believed, meant disaster for the CIO and for the labor movement. Saddled with a large Communist contingent determined to prevent aid to Hitler's enemies and with impeding the defense buildup, a Lewis-led CIO would run headlong into a powerful national security state and alienate the president. The next day he addressed the convention. "The Amalgamated will stay in the CIO!" he pledged. Defending his record on the NDAC, Hillman sought to deflate the draft-Lewis boom with words of conciliation and flattery. "I have considered my association with John L. Lewis the greatest privilege," he declared. More than anyone else, he intimated, he regretted Lewis's decision, made before

50 million radio listeners, to step down as CIO president, but he knew that once Lewis had made his pledge, he would stick by it. Thus, Hillman concluded, since Lewis's departure was inevitable, "it is my considered judgment that when John L. Lewis steps down there must be a demand for Phil Murray" to take his place.[55]

It was a shrewd and effective speech. It bought time for anti-Lewis delegates to lobby against any draft. It reminded the uncommitted of the seemingly headstrong and arbitrary nature of Lewis's October 25 pronouncement. It reassured Lewis loyalists that the CIO would experience a smooth transition and that Lewis would remain a powerful force. Three days later, nominated by Lewis himself, a tearful and uncertain Murray was chosen president of the CIO by acclamation.[56]

What would a post-Lewis CIO look like? Could Philip Murray, the soft-spoken, fifty-four-year-old Irish-Scots Catholic immigrant, reach a modus operandi with the government, straighten out the CIO's chaotic financial and membership affairs, mediate the escalating dispute between the CIO's Communists and their increasingly vocal critics, and push forward with the complex organizing, bargaining, and political work that confronted the CIO? Murray, for all his loyalty to Lewis, had quietly supported the president in 1940 and had shown himself responsive to the claims of the military buildup in the escalating showdown between SWOC and the Little Steel companies. At the same time, however, it seemed clear that Lewis's presence would remain powerful, and UMW functionaries remained in place throughout the CIO. In his acceptance speech on November 22 Murray seemed to justify the fears of Lewis's critics. In a long, rambling address, he declared himself unfit for the great responsibilities that the CIO presidency entailed. "I think I am a man," he said, suggesting to some of his listeners that he remained in thrall to the powerful father figure whose career he had served for over twenty years.[57]

By the time of the CIO's November 1941 convention a new regime was in place, one that valued stability, administrative coherence, and friendly and cooperative relations with the emerging national security state and the Democratic Party. The Murrayite CIO was deeply committed to improving the standards of industrial workers. At the same time the new leadership regarded defeating the Axis as integral to that project and to their equally important goal of injecting laborite power and influence into the heart of the American political and economic system.

Pursuit of these aims raised questions about the CIO's ability to fulfill the agenda of 1935. The CIO alliance with the Roosevelt administration paid off but also bound the union body in an increasingly intricate governmental and political apparatus. In 1941 under Murray's leadership the CIO became a coherent, fully functioning, and self-financing union entity as it never had been and likely could never have been under Lewis. But the bitter departure of the UMW in 1941–42 deprived it of a powerful counterforce to its necessary, but problematic, enmeshment in the wartime ideological and governmental consensus.

THE INDUSTRIAL WORKING CLASS IN 1941

The ability of the CIO to complete its project of organizing the mass production core of the American economy depended on the responses of American workers to its appeal. As U.S. entry into the war impended, these men and women evidenced a great variety of condition, character, circumstance, and *mentalité*. They combined solid support for FDR with strong isolationist currents. They resented much about their current status and treatment yet consistently endorsed the broad contours of the American economic and social system. Very much divided by skill, gender, race, ethnicity, and sectoral occupation, they had many common interests nonetheless, even if they did not exhibit unified responses as frequently as labor activists preferred.

On the eve of war, over 20 million Americans toiled in industrial and related occupations. About 3 million made basic steel and other metals and metal products, vehicles, electrical appliances, rubber tires, textile products, and garments. Another three-quarters of a million processed the nation's food products. Over 4 million transport and goods-handling workers were closely integrated into the industrial core. Over 3 million construction workers built the country's roads, airports, industrial plants, offices, and residences.[1]

Seventy-five percent of these workers were men. About 7 percent were African American. In the East and Midwest well over half were immigrants or first-generation offspring of immigrants. In cities such as Buffalo, Chicago, Detroit, New York, Philadelphia, and Pittsburgh most lived in distinct ethnic neighborhoods. Ethnic identity was also evident in the world of work as labor market segmentation and hiring practices followed residential and kin patterns of the community. African American workers commonly toiled in the least secure, most hazardous, and least remunerative jobs. Italian, Polish, Jewish, and other "new immigrant" peoples suffered also from discrimination and prejudice in the allocation of work and opportunity.[2]

The restrictive immigration laws of the 1920s and the onset of prolonged hard times produced significant changes in the composition of the working class. During the 1930s the average age of industrial workers rose. At the same time, the second-generation offspring of the "new" immigration of 1890–1914 began to emerge as distinct actors in work sites and neighborhoods. These young men and women exhibited attitudes and patterns of behavior that sharply distinguished them from their parents' generation. They were, for example, more likely to vote and helped to form the core of the Roosevelt vote of the 1930s. They spoke English as a first language and had more, and more American, education than their elders. They were more likely to mingle with outsiders and to accept and even value interethnic collaboration in social, workplace, and, eventually, labor activities. They were less prone to accept the authority of the boss and more responsive to union appeals.[3]

Some ethnic workers toiled in highly distinctive circumstances. Mexican immigration had increased in the 1920s in response to the exemption of Western Hemisphere workers from the general immigration acts. Throughout the southwest and even into the steel, auto, and meatpacking plants of Detroit and Chicago thousands of Hispanics added to the already-rich ethnic mix. In the Southwest both Mexican citizens and Americans of Mexican descent formed the backbone of the labor force in copper mining and smelting. Mexican and Mexican American workers harvested, processed, and canned the produce of California and the Southwest. Hispanics fought discrimination, establishing a rich tradition of communal and labor activism.

Their distinctive circumstances posed both opportunities and challenges to CIO unions, such as Mine, Mill and the UCAPAWA.[4]

African American workers also comprised a distinctive and highly significant group. In the South they were key elements in the growing pulp and paper, tobacco, canning and food processing, metal mining and smelting, and lumber products industries.[5] Although the depression had slowed black migration to the North and West and had had the effect of reducing the presence of African American workers in industrial employment,[6] they remained significant. In some industries, notably foundry work and meatpacking, their labor was critical to the entire production process. Elsewhere they remained an abundant "reserve army" of labor. By the eve of the war, at Ford, International Harvester, and in the burgeoning shipyards African American workers were critical to the success of industrial unionism.[7]

The nation's 14 million female workers were overwhelmingly concentrated in low-wage and insecure industrial and service trades. As garment, textile, food processing, and light industrial workers many were members of CIO unions or targets of CIO organizing. Since the late nineteenth century increasing proportions of the female labor force consisted of married women, who in 1940 constituted over one-third of the total. More and more women found themselves the sole or main support of families. However, even the rising volume of military production of 1941 seemed at the time to have little to offer women workers. Women seeking industrial employment, observed one official, were more likely to be a nuisance than a help for the defense effort; the main problem would be how to "give the women something to do to keep their hands busy . . . – then maybe they won't bother us."[8]

In 1941 industrial workers enjoyed a relatively good economic year. A combination of war-induced expansion, wage advances in response to union militancy and tight labor markets, and a delay in the inflationary effects of expanded production boosted take-home pay to all-time record levels. As late as January, unemployment had stood at almost 8 percent, but by the time the Japanese bombs fell, that figure had been halved. In basic industry in 1941 the average wage earner made about 74 cents an hour and, for the first time since the onset of the depression, averaged over forty hours of work a week, thus bringing home about $30.00. Automobile workers were among the income elite, averaging $1.04 an hour, while those in basic steel earned about 95 cents. Rubber tire workers made almost as much as autoworkers, while packinghouse workers stood well down the list, earning just about the national average. Coal miners did better than the average manufacturing worker, earning an hourly wage of 99 cents, although miners toiled ten fewer hours of work per week than did their factory counterparts and thus brought home only a dollar or so more weekly.

The men and women who toiled in more fragmented industries producing nondurable goods lagged well behind. Paper box makers earned 61 cents an hour, tobacco workers just over 50 cents, garment workers about 60 cents, and cotton textile workers a mere 46 cents. Retail and service workers brought up the nonagricultural rear, as laundries, hotels, retail stores, and dyeing and cleaning establishments paid wages ranging from 35 to 50 cents an hour. Of course these trades were significant employers of female workers, whose earnings averaged under 60 percent of those of male workers.[9]

Industrial workers' experiences in the 1930s had been mixed. Even the upturns in 1933–34 and 1936–37, which had brought employment and income levels close to those of 1928–29, had proved ephemeral. In the sharp recession of 1937–39 workers had lost ground rapidly, with unemployment soaring in 1938 to 19 percent.

Still, the depression had a differential impact on various sectors of the working class. Thus, for example, after the depths of the depression in 1931–33, long-term unemployment was concentrated among workers without skills or education who were either just entering the labor market or were above age forty-five. For employed workers, always the majority, the buying power of their wages had been improving since 1933 and by 1935 had permanently surpassed 1929 ratios.[10]

The steel industry was a particularly good example of uneven effects. The shift toward lighter and more flexible steel products required by the canning, automotive, and consumer goods industries opened new lines of development even as heavy steel production flattened. Throughout the late 1930s, the peak years of these technological wrenchings and their attendant high levels of unemployment in many communities, hourly wage rates for employed steelworkers continued to rise.[11]

War-related production brought generally brightening prospects. Between 1938 and 1941 weekly hours rose 14 percent, with time-and-a-half pay now mandated by federal law fattening pay packets. In 1941 the average yearly income for manufacturing workers was $1,479, up almost $220 from the year before. As early as the end of 1939, reported two veteran observers of the depression-ravaged steel industry, "'Glory hallelujah!' . . . is how World War II was greeted" by steelworkers in one hard-hit Pennsylvania town.[12]

Even with the defense boom, however, workers lived close to the bone. Full employment for the average industrial worker brought in under $1,500 annually at a time when standardized budgets projected that the average family needed over $2,000 annually for a no-frills level of living. For cotton textile, food processing, service, and garment workers, simple survival remained the only realistic goal. In 1939, when the average yearly income for manufacturing workers was $1,250, 58.5 percent of the working men and almost 80 percent of the women received less than $1,000. Another 2.5 million people made do on sub-subsistence public relief project wages.[13]

Consumption patterns revealed a working-class America that was fabulously privileged by world standards yet far removed from the plenty and security that corporate America had promised. The 1940 census revealed, for example, that almost a third of the nation's dwelling units had no running water or indoor toilet facilities. Two-fifths had no shower or bathtub, almost 60 percent lacked central heating, and over one-fourth lacked either mechanical or ice refrigeration. Government family budget watchers reported that impoverished black women in the South spent about $2 per year on clothing.[14]

Even "high wage" core industrial workers scrimped to make ends meet. A steelworker family with the statistical average of 2.5 children could afford a new coat for mother and father every six years and a new pair of shoes for each child every two years. The mother could buy two housedresses a year and the father a workshirt annually and two dress shirts every three years. An old used car provided transportation to and from their five-room rented apartment. If only the father were employed, the family income would cover just 80 percent of the modest family budget requirements.[15]

This steelworker family, struggling to avoid debt, however, did enjoy some apparent amenities that would have made it the envy of millions of workers elsewhere in the world. The possession of an automobile, for example, was beyond the dreams of the vast majority of British workers, and yet in the United States 65 percent of median earners had cars. Workers' dwellings were plain, yet with indoor plumbing and with more rooms than family members,[16] they afforded a degree of privacy and convenience rare elsewhere.

There were trade-offs. By 1940 an automobile, for example, was hardly a luxury. Deteriorating public transportation and expanding urban sprawl made an automobile a virtual necessity. For many the car was less a symbol of freedom than a drain on resources. Relatively low levels of public services and facilities in the United States were particularly disadvantageous to working people.[17]

Ambivalence of condition was matched by ambivalence of *mentalité*. American workers were eager to resume the advance that the depression had interrupted. Sensitive to unfairness and exploitation, they were nonetheless committed to the American business system. In public opinion polls throughout the late 1930s and early 1940s, lower-income Americans regularly expressed a distinctive perspective on public issues, generally but irregularly to the left of the general public. At the same time they evidenced no deep-seated sense of outrage or injustice.[18]

Even the theme of class itself revealed workers' ambiguous – or perhaps nuanced – consciousness. Thus, when in March 1939 pollsters asked a sampling of the public to what *social* class they belonged, 88 percent chose "middle" and only 6 percent "lower." Yet in the same question sequence, 31 percent of the respondents identified themselves as members of the lower *income* class and another 21 percent in the lower-middle category. Workers thus evinced a realistic understanding of the hierarchies of wealth and income while at the same time insisting on their inclusion in the central arena of social citizenship.[19]

In particular questions of politics and economics, working people regularly staked out positions to the left of their fellow Americans in the upper- and middle-income ranges. In virtually every poll, for example, lower-income and union voters provided Franklin Roosevelt with his margins of victory over Republican contenders, actual or suggested. They evidenced far stronger support for the Wagner Act, the expansion of presidential power, and an enhanced role for the federal government in economic matters than did the general public. On questions dealing with a range of issues from corporate wealth to access to medical care, working people registered distinctive, liberal perspectives.[20]

Yet this was hardly a lower class alienated from existing arrangements. Workers overwhelmingly reported that their employers were paying them fair wages. On many public issues they expressed views remarkably similar to those of middle- and upper-income interviewees. Thus, for example, in the winter of 1939–40 lower-income Americans led all income groups in supporting enhanced defense expenditures, favoring an increased military budget by almost five to one. On the tough question, asked in the fall of 1941, of what was more important, staying out of war or preventing a German victory, unionists, like the population generally, gave the latter option a two-thirds advantage.[21]

Throughout the immediate prewar period working-class Americans viewed skeptically the institution putatively representing their interests, the labor movement. Lower-income workers and union members alike opposed granting Works Progress Administration workers the right to strike and were with the majority that opposed the right to strike on defense work. In the spring of 1941 84 percent of lower-income respondents believed that union leaders possessed too much power. Blue collar and lower-income respondents strongly supported the work of HUAC and overwhelmingly favored the restriction of political and constitutional rights of Communists. A September 1938 poll revealed that almost two-thirds of lower-income respondents favored William Green over the CIO's John L. Lewis. By the eve of the war the UMW chief had become no more popular among workers, as evidenced by a November 1941 survey of workers' opinions in the captive mines strike. "Do you think John L. Lewis was justified in calling this strike?" pollsters asked skilled and unskilled workers. Eighty-four percent of those with an opinion said No.[22]

Public opinion polls and election results did provide important clues as to the *mentalité* of prewar American workers. But polls of the late 1930s and early 1940s ignored some of the most basic concerns of working people. Thus while workers were asked if they considered their wages and hours of employment fair, they were never questioned about their attitudes toward work itself. Did workers consider the patterns of command, discipline, and redress fair and reasonable? Did they find fulfillment or at least comradeship and purpose in their work? Were workers grudging, alienated participants in the industrial system, constantly inventing new methods to restrict output and otherwise undermine the corporate-conceived system of mass production? Or were they ambitious and energetic men and women, eager for material gain, without fundamental objection to shop-floor arrangements, seeking at most reform in the direction of greater stability and rationality in matters of compensation, job tenure, discipline, and promotion?[23]

Since the late nineteenth century, reformers had been tinkering with methods of improving recruitment and retention of workers, job satisfaction, workplace discipline, and worker loyalty. The depression exacerbated concerns about the nature of work and workplace authority, for now it was hard for workers to protest poor conditions by switching jobs. Hence, of course, matters such as the order of layoffs, favoritism by foremen, and workplace discipline took on elemental importance.[24]

America's sprawling economy insured that workers and unions would face diverse circumstances. Corporate reformers and human relations experts, however, believed that American industry had been moving toward ever fairer and more rational personnel policies. But the nation's factories, mills, mines, and workshops in the 1930s too frequently remained afflicted with favoritism, arbitrary discipline, and insecurity to convince working people that their interests were best entrusted to their employers.[25]

In the metalworking heart of the 1940s economy, for example, highly variable patterns of employee relations were evident. As early as the 1920s, electrical appliance companies had worked hard to convince employees that their interests were coterminous with those of the firm. The automobile industry, in contrast, had generally relied on the industry's high-wage and low-skill profile to keep the supply of workers coming. Within the automobile industry, however, differences among firms were increasingly apparent. Ford, a pioneer in a kind of coercive paternalism, had degenerated into an authoritarian empire in which economic necessity and physical intimidation kept the assembly lines moving. Chrysler, in contrast, set up "works councils" after the passage of the NIRA in hopes that they would promote harmonious communication between managers and workers. GM followed still another pattern, especially after the UAW's early victories. There, astute managers recognized the value of orderly workplace procedures, although they resisted both the fledgling UAW and any form of formal worker representation.[26]

Still different conditions prevailed in steel. The industry's lack of true mass production work routines made supervision by top management difficult. Rapid technological change introduced in the 1930s exacerbated the industry's always-erratic patterns of job structure, wage schedules, and work-site discipline. Thus, at Bethlehem Steel's Sparrows Point (Baltimore) facility in 1937–38, the 2,200 men in the "hot" mill watched as a new strip mill came on line, enabling the company to produce more tin sheet with 84 percent fewer workers. The superintendent told the hot mill workers that "you . . . ain't gonna get the good jobs on the strip mill because the big bosses think you might slow down production." The fortunate caught on as laborers, earning a fraction of their previous pay. Callous in its treatment of these skilled workers, Bethlehem inadvertently helped SWOC in its efforts to convince steelworkers that a union would protect them from such arbitrary treatment.[27]

Authoritarianism ruled the American workplace. It was true that aggressive unions could assert substantial control. Increasingly, the West Coast longshoremen, relying on union hiring halls, employers' vulnerability to delays in unloading, and the close-knit work groups and communities that characterized the docksides, carved out considerable autonomy in their arduous work. UAW stewards gained a reputation for shop-floor activism, while the Chicago stockyards' African American kill floor workers, members of the Packinghouse Workers Organizing Committee, made inroads into the arbitrary work regime of the city's big meatpackers. The quickie strikes, wildcat walkouts, and spontaneous sit-downs of the Akron rubber workers became legendary.[28]

In the end, however, management held the cards. The very language of the emerging contract unionism exhibited the power imbalance between even a strong union and management. No early CIO contracts even hinted at a union role in production decisions, the layout of work, the timing of operations, or other central elements of management prerogative. Initiative for discipline remained in managerial hands. The terminology in contract language was revealing: the most common general category of offense was invariably "insubordination," a term that validated the hierarchical power relations even as the contract sought to moderate and rationalize their operations.[29]

Without unions, workers had little redress. Democracy was little evident in the day-to-day organization, conduct, and governance of work. "My boss," recalled one UAW activist, "was an S.O.B." Hat squarely fixed on his head, he spoke to workers only in criticism. "No one had the right to talk back, the right to question decisions, the right to dissent." In a widely circulated story in the late 1930s one blue collar worker is asked why he plans to vote for FDR. Simple, the worker responds: "He understands that my boss is an SOB."[30]

There was ample evidence to support this generic worker's opinion. The experiences of the depression had put a premium on security of employment, which in turn made seniority a central concern of industrial workers. With job mobility diminished, workers focused on job rights though length of service as their most significant protection. Just as vehemently, many employers resisted any interference in the right to hire and fire. Union appeals stressed this phase of workers' moral economy. Thus, addressing Ford workers in its 1941 organizing campaign, the UAW called forceful attention to the company's notorious system of favoritism. It had maintained "pct" lists of workers who survived layoffs or received early callbacks. Under a UAW contract, the union asserted, "the foreman can't set up a patronage system so that the boys who buy him drinks get to work and the boys that won't lick his boots get laid off."[31]

What made the translation of dissatisfaction with shop-floor conditions into support for union activism difficult, however, was the differential degree of frustration and the diverse backgrounds and interests of workers in any large, multisection plant. In the Detroit-area automotive industry, for example, there were sharp ethnic cleavages among the skilled tool-and-die makers to whom others often looked in struggles with management. After World War I the auto companies had recruited heavily from the European metalworking industry. In general, skilled workers of German background tended to identify strongly with their employer and to see their future in terms of movement into supervision and management, while Anglo-Scots workers, recruited often from the radical but declining shipbuilding and engineering industries in England's north and in Scotland, kept alive patterns of laborite militancy and radical politics.[32] In general, first-generation immigrant workers tended to be less willing to challenge managerial authority than workers of second-generation standing.[33] While activists and radicals worked to encourage worker solidarity, much evidence accumulated indicating that workers primarily identified with their firm in its competition with other firms, or even with their department or section of the plant. Gender, racial, and ethnic divisions were rife, especially where these coincided with functional divisions in the workplace.[34]

Union activists invoked the term *industrial democracy* to characterize their project. By it they meant creating fair and orderly procedures to govern the daily lives of workers in such matters as wage determination, access to training and promotion, layoffs, job assignments, and discipline. They had no intention of introducing syndicalist notions of workers' control of the production process any more than they might champion plebiscitary democracy in the civic arena. Repeatedly, CIO organizers reported, it was obtuseness, intransigence, and insensitivity on the part of management that rallied workers to the union cause.[35] But managerial ineptitude was not guaranteed. To the extent that the drive for industrial unionism rested on misguided managerial policies and actions, it was vulnerable. As early as the 1920s, large-scale employers had begun to acknowledge that even in mass semiskilled production work, experience paid a premium in productivity and that with reductions in labor turnover came important benefits. Standard Oil, AT&T, Eastman Kodak, du Pont, and other industrial giants had introduced and were elaborating personnel regimes that aimed to reduce the arbitrariness and insecurity of blue collar employment. These efforts sought to build worker loyalty through stock distribution, company-sponsored recreational and medical services, and in-plant rites of recognition and reward. Throughout industrial America, the proportion of supervisory and administrative personnel in the workforce increased. Leading companies published detailed employee handbooks, specifying rights and obligations. Indeed, the first contract between the UE and General Electric consisted of the existing company employment rules. In the 1930s and 1940s most corporate managers clung to arbitrary practices, but the CIO did not fare well where employers introduced genuine reforms in personnel policies.[36]

In the pressurized atmosphere of 1941 the loyalty of the industrial working class was of central importance. Workers who had joined the new unions in the mid-1930s now expected them to pay off in the form of higher wages and better conditions. Thousands of others remained to be recruited. Could the CIO, under a new leadership and beset by internal conflict, AFL counterattack, and hostile employers, capture their loyalty and complete the agenda sketched out in 1935? With military production pumping $2 billion monthly into the economy and labor shortages beginning to appear, the new CIO leadership prepared for the next round.

ORGANIZING AGAIN

Completing the organization of the industrial core was basic to the entire CIO undertaking. As things stood at the beginning of 1941 the breakthroughs of 1936–37 remained uncertain in their long-range meaning. Unionism in GM, Chrysler, U.S. Steel, Firestone Rubber and Tire, and other firms in which the early CIO had enjoyed success would remain tenuous without successful organization of Ford, Goodyear, Little Steel, and other corporate giants that had successfully resisted the earlier onslaught.

In the spring of 1941 the Autoworkers and the Steelworkers made decisive breakthroughs, at last forcing Ford, Bethlehem Steel, and other Little Steel companies to recognize their unions. Ford and Bethlehem succumbed to industrial unionism because of a combination of circumstances, many unique to the period of rapid military buildup. Rank-and-file activism in Ford's River Rouge complex and in mills of Bethlehem and other steelmakers confounded the corporations' faltering antiunion programs. At the same time the NLRB proved its value to industrial unionism as, led by Steelworkers' and CIO counsel Lee Pressman, labor lawyers won a string of victories in cases that systematically rejected a wide range of antiunion practices and resulted frequently in the reinstatement, with pay, of fired union activists.

The initial CIO drive had stalled in the summer of 1937. On May 26 Henry Ford's thugs had brutalized UAW organizers attempting to pass out leaflets at the Rouge, located just west of Detroit. Thereafter, UAW factionalism, the crippling 1937–38 recession, and Ford's heavy-handed authoritarianism had kept the Autoworkers at bay. In steel, although U.S. Steel dealt cautiously with SWOC, Republic, Inland, Bethlehem, and other companies continued to resist SWOC inroads. In electrical appliances, although the UE did gain contracts with General Electric, the recalcitrance of the other major producer, Westinghouse, frustrated the union's efforts to move beyond its vague initial contracts. International Harvester, the farm equipment leader, remained obdurate, as did meatpacking giant Swift and major tire producer Goodyear. The southern textile drive remained stalled, while in Iowa the Maytag appliance company turned back the UE. Indeed, it was by no means clear that the CIO upheaval of 1935–37 had changed anything permanently.

The military buildup and rising levels of employment through 1941, however, permitted swift advance. Through the first eight months of the year, strike totals leaped upward. Organized workers, whose basic wage levels had remained at best static through the late 1930s, now at last saw the possibility of gaining tangible advantages from their union membership. Moreover, the burgeoning shipyards, the booming aircraft factories, and scores of other facilities employed tens of thousands of potential new recruits for an expanding labor movement.

Union membership surged. Between June 1940 and December 1941 organized labor gained about a million and a half new recruits, increasing the membership of unions by over a quarter. The CIO's share of this rising tide was substantial, perhaps as many as a million new members. Equally important was the stability of membership, and hence of dues paying, that the new growth brought. As the UAW at last brought Ford under contract in the spring of 1941 and as SWOC won victory after victory in Little Steel, these bellwether CIO organizations were now able for the first time to concentrate on collective bargaining rather than on sheer survival as their primary activity. The bringing of Westinghouse, International Harvester, Goodyear, and several important shipyards, aircraft factories, and southern textile firms into the CIO orbit added to membership totals and solidified the CIO's position.

Few of these corporations succumbed without a struggle. The Ford campaign was illustrative. For almost four years after the UAW's victory over GM in Flint, septuagenarian Henry Ford had relied upon his "Service" Department of 3,000 men, a paramilitary force that featured thugs and ex-convicts, to suppress unionism in his plants. Nowhere was Ford Service more blatant and workers more bitter than at the fabled Rouge. Erected in the 1920s this vast facility had miles of railroad tracks, ore-boat docking stations, and giant smelters, blast furnaces, and rolling mills. It boasted the world's largest concentration of machine tools, made its own steel and glass, and rolled thousands of Fords off its assembly lines annually. Employment fluctuated between 60,000 and 90,000 workers.

After the UAW's abortive effort in 1937 to organize the Rouge – universally recognized as the key to victory throughout the Ford empire – the two sides waged guerrilla warfare in its shops and in the courts. Factionalism, along with the dampening effects of the 1937–38 recession, kept the union on the defensive. Espionage and sheer physical brutality discouraged unionists. For their part UAW leaders sought to keep the union presence alive while repeatedly filing charges with the NLRB against Ford for labor law violations. Communists and other radicals, many of them Anglo-Scots immigrants imbued with the brass-knuckles militancy of the British left, were particularly effective in creating incidents that the skillful UAW legal staff could use in NLRB and court proceedings.[37]

The CIO's direct role in bringing the union to the Rouge was limited. In September 1940, however, Lewis dispatched UMW representative Michael Widman, a gifted organizer, to assist the UAW, along with a pledge of $50,000 in CIO (which is to say, UMW) financial support. Throughout the fall and winter of 1940–41 Widman collaborated with the new UAW leaders to rouse union sentiment in the Rouge and in the larger Detroit community. Meanwhile, in the legal arena the UAW won a series of cases against Ford, many requiring the reinstatement of victimized unionists who invariably returned to their jobs triumphantly, sporting outsized UAW buttons and suggesting in the most tangible way possible that the federal government stood with the UAW and against Henry Ford.[38]

The struggle to win Ford workers for the UAW was complicated by the racial composition of the labor force in the Rouge. About 6,000 African American workers toiled there, many in the crucial foundries and rolling mills. Many blacks considered Ford a benefactor of the African American community and were skeptical of the union. UAW efforts to enlist local and national leaders of the NAACP in behalf of the union cause were effective, especially since among the small cadre of pro-union blacks in the Rouge was a group of vigorous and militant young men who had cut their activist eye teeth in the Detroit NAACP's youth branch. UAW-NAACP appeals did not convince most of the Rouge's black workers to join the union. Nonetheless, the innovative UAW-community alliance and the recruitment of black organizers broke Ford's monopoly on the loyalty of his African American labor force.[39]

By the spring of 1941 Ford was on the defensive. NLRB and court rulings emboldened the UAW. By March unionists in some departments had forced supervisors to deal with stewards in the settlement of grievances or face constant disruptions in work routines. Autoworkers' threats of retribution against company police were increasingly credible. When on April 1 some recently reinstated activists were fired again, rolling-mill workers walked out en masse. Widman and the UAW leaders at first urged caution, but shop-floor protest grew and they quickly endorsed the walkout. Thenceforth Widman and the UAW conducted a bold campaign that combined traditional picketing, auto caravans that ringed the huge facility, and flyovers by airplanes. Skillful publicity linked the union cause to national defense and cast Ford himself as a de facto ally of the fascist dictators. "The UAW is dealing with Hitler's Henry," proclaimed one CIO leader, pledging the destruction of the company's "industrial dictatorship." On April 10 the company agreed to NLRB elections, with Ford apparently hoping that yearlong cultivation of Homer Martin, now head of an AFL autoworkers' union, might pay off. But new CIO membership applications flooded into headquarters of UAW Rouge Local 600. In the labor board election on May 21 the UAW-CIO captured over 70 percent of the 74,000 votes cast. Over the next three weeks the CIO swept the follow-up elections at Ford facilities in the Detroit area and around the country.[40]

SWOC too completed its organization of the basic steel industry. A rising tide of unionist sentiment besieged Bethlehem Steel, the industry's second largest employer. In the spring of 1941 a renewed SWOC drive, tapping into the pent-up militancy of thousands of steelworkers and using SWOC's critical role in defense production as a lever, brought Bethlehem into the union fold. Rank-and-file walkouts, involving 13,000 workers in the Lackawanna, New York, plant in February and 19,000 at Bethlehem, Pennsylvania, on March 25, demonstrated that despite years of harassment and frustration, steelworkers had kept a unionist commitment alive. The Bethlehem walkout and another soon after at the Johnstown, Pennsylvania, works were protests over the company's efforts to promote its company unions. Authoritative federal court decisions required Bethlehem Steel to dissolve these bodies, leaving the corporation with no alternative but to agree to NLRB elections. Throughout the summer and fall steelworkers voted for SWOC by margins of up to 80 percent.[41]

The SWOC offensive carried over into the other Little Steel employers, with Youngstown Sheet and Tube and Inland Steel agreeing to accord recognition when an NLRB check of SWOC's membership cards revealed that huge majorities in both companies had signed up. Republic Steel quietly followed suit, with 70 percent of its 46,600 workers now belonging to the steel union. Just as important, SWOC built upon worker militancy to expand and solidify its position in U.S. Steel. Since 1937 it had held bargaining rights for its members only and just in certain plants. In some places, such as U.S. Steel's important Homestead, Pennsylvania, mill, only a handful of SWOC members kept the flag flying. But here, too, latent union sentiment burst forth. At Homestead, protests against layoffs brought dues payments pouring into union coffers and overnight revitalized the SWOC local. In April, eager for military contracts and faced with an aroused workforce, U.S. Steel signed an improved contract with SWOC.[42]

The spring-summer victories in Ford and Bethlehem were reminiscent of the CIO's 1937 triumphs. Now, however, significant collective bargaining advances accompanied these organizational gains. In this respect the victory over Ford was the most impressive and the most inexplicable. The company agreed to a sweeping redefinition of workers' rights. Wage provisions guaranteed Ford workers the highest wages in the automobile industry. Ford agreed to union-written provisions governing seniority, grievance handling, and compensation for downtime. Moreover, Ford granted the UAW both a union shop agreement and a dues checkoff, stunning concessions especially in view of the still-rudimentary character of the UAW's contracts with GM and Chrysler. The Ford agreement embodied virtually everything unionists could plausibly have hoped for.[43]

Indeed, so amazing was this agreement that veteran labor observers smelled a rat. Perhaps Ford's chief negotiator, Service Department head Harry Bennett, believed that after the enthusiasm had passed, his men would be able to control the UAW locals. Perhaps Henry Ford's son Edsel Ford, nominally president of the company, had intervened in an effort to use the union as a stabilizing force in the faltering company, whose workplaces had become increasingly irrational and chaotic. In any event, the new contract, with its no strike provisions, would presumably put an end to the constant shop-floor warfare and would permit the company to bid successfully for lucrative military contracts.[44]

Other collective bargaining advances were less spectacular but nonetheless significant. A four-week strike by the UMW in April won a 15 percent basic wage increase. By the end of April U.S. Steel, GM, General Electric, and other companies had boosted wages by at least 10 percent. In July the Packinghouse Workers gained a 7 percent pay boost on top of an 8 percent raise granted by the packers only three months before. Maritime, wood, oil, and other CIO workers also made substantial wage gains, thus contributing to the 17 percent gain in annual earnings experienced by production workers in 1941 over the previous year. The renewed CIO offensive, reminiscent of the heady days of 1937, surged into diverse industrial sectors. Thus, readers of the *CIO News*'s May 19, 1941, edition learned, perhaps doing a double take as they read, that "Marx Bows to CIO Toy Workers."[45]

Through this turbulent spring, laborites rejected the notion that workers should moderate their demands to accommodate the needs of military production. Lewis championed militant action. Communists and their allies proclaimed the need for intensifying militancy. "Take it easy, boys, but take it," was the advice of the troubadours of the pro–Soviet left, the Almanac Singers, in their paean of defense-plant militancy, "Talking Union." Even Philip Murray declared upon assuming the CIO presidency, "I am not going to permit any restraint to stand in my way," while warhorse CIO organizer Van Bittner urged aggressiveness, "defense program or no defense program."[46]

Corporate leaders hoped that the growing strike wave might trigger governmental intervention against organized labor. Backed by military leaders, they urged the administration to clamp down on the mounting unrest. Congressional committees weighed antistrike proposals, and public opinion polls revealed that a substantial majority of Americans, including blue collar workers, held strikers responsible for lagging defense production.[47]

There was no general crackdown, however. Rejecting the advice of his secretary of war, Roosevelt frustrated congressional antistrike legislation. Instead he relied primarily on exhortation and mediation to keep workers on the job. As a result the CIO grew increasingly enmeshed with the federal machinery created to oversee defense production. In the complex and often bitter conflicts involving adamant corporations, militant workers, ambitious unions, and determined war mobilization functionaries, critical aspects of the CIO's relation to the state and its maturing character as a labor organization emerged.

By the spring of 1941 Hillman was serving, with GM's William Knudson, as codirector of the chief war mobilization agency, the OPM, the successor agency to the NDAC. Hillman worked hard to frustrate the efforts of Pentagon and corporate hardliners to commit the government to a harsh antiunion line. Despite his militant rhetoric, Murray also projected himself as a labor statesman, seeking only justice for workers and uninterrupted production for the arsenal of democracy. In the fall of 1940 he had delayed initially planned strike action at Bethlehem Steel in deference to the military's needs, and when rank-and-file workers hit the bricks the next spring, he was well situated to portray himself as an honest broker. Moreover, his succession to the presidency freed the CIO from the incubus of Lewis's anti-FDR stance.

Several episodes involving the UAW in the winter and spring of 1941 laid bare the complexities of defense-production industrial relations. In the late winter of 1940–41 a major confrontation in Milwaukee involving UAW Local 248 and the Allis-Chalmers company came to a head. Some 7,000 workers toiled in the Milwaukee plant of Allis-Chalmers, which had just been awarded a $40 million contract to build turbines for U.S. Navy destroyers. Insofar as both the company's managers and the relatively highly skilled workers were concerned, military necessity was irrelevant to their dispute. Company president Max Babb was determined to operate his business on a nonunion basis despite a recent NLRB victory for Local 248. For their part, Allis-Chalmers workers regarded changes in the company's production processes, which were sure to be accelerated in the fulfillment of its Navy contracts, as threatening to their hard-won skills and substantial shop-floor power. Thus, on January 21, 1941, the dismissal of union activists triggered a sustained work stoppage.

In view of Babb's repeated efforts to undermine Local 248, the union leadership, in which a pro-Soviet group figured prominently, demanded some sort of union security provision as its price for ending the strike. Babb regarded such an arrangement as blackmail. Caught between a determined union leadership, an angry rank and file, and a corporate leadership resolved to resist the UAW, Hillman sought to end the strike. He attempted to convince frustrated naval and military officers and cabinet representatives that union security would restrain, rather than encourage, worker militancy. Ignoring him, on March 27 Knudson and Secretary of the Navy Frank Knox peremptorily ordered the plant reopened. In response only 15 percent of the workers reported, and for the next three days fighting raged along the picket lines. The governor of Wisconsin called in national guard units and ordered the plant closed once again. At last, early in April, the NDMB, a tripartite body created to carry forth the mediation work with which the OPM had been increasingly saddled, arranged a settlement involving a modified form of union security but not before the strike had triggered harsh anti-CIO outpourings in Congress and in the defense mobilization establishment.[48]

The North American Aviation controversy was even more contentious. The UAW had ambitious plans to expand into the mushrooming aircraft and airframe industry. However, the CIO union faced a powerful rival, the AFL's IAM. In the 1930s this influential craft union was a major obstacle to expansion of the AFL into mass production industry.[49] Indeed, it was in good part out of frustration with the Machinists that autoworkers had demanded a separate union and, eventually, enlisted with the CIO.

By the time of the defense buildup, however, the IAM had begun to respond to the challenge of organizing industrial workers. The aircraft and airframe industry offered it a particularly tempting field. Between 1937, when the Machinists began actively to recruit aircraft workers, and the beginning of 1941 employment grew from about 30,000 to over 200,000, with more workers entering the burgeoning California plants each day. Moreover, the work process in the aircraft industry called for higher proportions of skilled workers than was the case on the automobile assembly lines. Each airframe was constructed individually. Aircraft engines, usually produced in facilities entirely separate from the airframes and shipped, often thousands of miles, for final assembly, were more complex than automobile engines and called for much finer tolerances and more hands-on work by skilled machinists. Thus the airframe and aircraft industry was a natural field for the IAM, whose membership expanded from under 90,000 in 1935 to over 150,000 by 1940.

In the fall of 1940 the UAW launched a concerted campaign in the industry, focusing its organizing energy on Douglas Aircraft and North American Aviation in southern California. By then, however, the IAM was already a force on the West Coast. In 1934 the AFL had transferred to it several federal locals, notably a 1,500-worker unit at the Boeing Aircraft works in Seattle. In 1937 it gained another local at Lockheed Aircraft in Los Angeles, in good part because the company feared inroads by the UAW and granted the IAM preferential access to its employees.[50]

Within the UAW, organizing aircraft workers had an important internal aspect. The West Coast was promising territory for the Communist-influenced components of the UAW and the CIO. The pro-Soviet ILWU was firmly in control of the docks and had ambitious plans to extend inland to the packing sheds and processing points. Their leader, Harry Bridges, served as West Coast director for the CIO. A Communist-led CIO union of agricultural and cannery workers was active in the fertile valleys. Other small West Coast waterfront and communications unions, all with a strong pro-Soviet orientation, were closely enmeshed with Bridges's powerful union. In the Pacific Northwest, Communists and their allies played significant roles in the CIO's International Woodworkers of America, then engaged in a bitter rivalry with the AFL's Carpenters' union for the allegiance of thousands of lumber, wood processing, and sawmill workers. A strong Los Angeles local of the CIO's United Furniture Workers was led by pro-Communists, as were the CIO's fledgling entertainers' and technicians' unions in Hollywood. Both the Los Angeles and the San Francisco IUCs were heavily pro-Soviet.[51]

The major anti-Communist CIO unions, notably the SWOC, the ACWA, and the TWUA, had little membership on the West Coast.[52] The establishment of a strong UAW presence there would help tip the scales within the UAW in the emerging struggle between pro- and anti-Communist factions. New UAW president R. J. Thomas put Wyndham Mortimer, a leading figure in the UAW since its inception, in charge. The fifty-four-year-old organizer was a Communist, as were the UAW's West Coast director, Lew Michener, and the president of the North American Aviation local. The prominence of Communists in defense organizing was controversial, especially in view of the CPUSA's hair-trigger responsiveness to the foreign policies of the Stalinist USSR. But Mortimer argued that his political preferences had nothing to do with union activity. "Some persons," he remarked sarcastically, "think anyone who wants more than $20 a week is a Communist."[53]

California aircraft wage rates varied wildly from employer to employer and even within the same facility. Union competition combined with an expanding workforce to breed fierce militancy, to the great distress of war production authorities. Rival UAW and IAM organizers faced great pressure to promise dramatic increases in pay.[54]

The strike at the North American Aviation complex in Inglewood was the most controversial of the job actions of the defense buildup period. Early in the year the UAW had narrowly defeated the IAM for representation rights. North American, which was turning out one-quarter of all U.S. fighter planes, stonewalled the negotiations. Its starting wage of fifty cents an hour was far below prevailing rates. Late in May, with negotiations at a standstill, workers overwhelmingly authorized a strike. UAW national officials, now led by Vice-President Richard Frankensteen, wanted no part of a walkout in a major defense plant, especially since only a few days earlier on a national radio broadcast President Roosevelt had announced a state of national emergency and had denounced those impeding defense production. Apprehensive too that the West Coast aircraft industry was becoming a center of Communist strength in the union, they readily collaborated with federal officials to delay the strike until after the NDMB could make recommendations.

By now, national UAW officials had sent Mortimer out of the area and were handling negotiations directly. Even so, local unionists soon took matters into their own hands. Since the election six months before, over 4,000 new workers had joined the North American labor force, a number easily shifting the balance of power if the UAW did not deliver a strong contract. Convinced that the NDMB and the company were stalling and goaded by the IAM, on June 5, UAW members ringed the plant with picket lines. Military and defense mobilization officials immediately urged the president to send in troops.

Roosevelt, however, was not eager to follow this advice. Conferring closely with Sidney Hillman, the president preferred to give the UAW and the CIO time to end the walkout. Prodded by Hillman's warnings about the pressure for military intervention, Frankensteen and other UAW and CIO officials spent four days trying to get the aircraft workers back on the job. They suspended the local leadership and ordered UAW members to pick up their tools. Frankensteen charged that "infamous agitation and vicious underhanded maneuvering of the Communist Party" was responsible for the strike. But at a mass meeting on June 8, workers greeted Frankensteen with resounding boos and catcalls, and the next day, despite tear gas and police escorts, only a third of the plant's workers obeyed the union's back-to-work order. Roosevelt mobilized the California national guard. Twenty-five hundred soldiers seized the plant and with fixed bayonets cleared a path through the picket lines, breaking the strike in a massive display of force.[55]

In Hillman's view the situation in Inglewood was one in which a responsible union needed help in disciplining unruly members who might have been influenced by radicals. The government dispatched troops so as to permit the NDMB to arrange a settlement. In this case the troops were actually upholding the authority of bona fide unionism. The *Daily Worker* accused the government of "bringing a military dictatorship to our very doorsteps," while Lewis denounced "the use of the United States Army to break strikes with their bayonets in the backs of American workingmen." But to Hillman, the sorry North American situation, which resulted after all in a reconstituted UAW local and in a contract that brought substantial wage increases through NDMB recommendations, merely marked the outer limits of the difficult and complex process of give-and-take that inevitably characterized industrial relations in this uniquely dangerous and critical time.[56]

The Allis-Chalmers and North American Aviation situations encapsulated all of the major themes coming to a head in the middle of 1941. With scores of other episodes in that strike-torn year, they exhibited the tensions arising when worker militancy, union discipline, and powerful claims of national security collided. They involved AFL–CIO rivalry, increasingly assertive federal mobilization organs, and sharp controversies surrounding the role of Communists and their allies at a time of dramatically shifting international developments, and all of this played out during a time of seemingly unstoppable Nazi and Japanese military advance. The Japanese war machine, linked to those of Germany and Italy through the Tripartite Pact of September 1940, continued its brutal campaigns against the Chinese and stood poised to plunge into Southeast Asia. The *Wehrmacht* dominated Europe, supplied by a Soviet Union that faithfully met the economic provisions of the 1939 German-Soviet Non-Aggression Pact. The *Luftwaffe* pounded British cities, and after the German attack on the Soviet Union, the international situation seemed even more desperate. "We must realize," declared a CIO convention resolution in November, "that Hitler today is as close to Moscow as the town of Flint is to the City of Detroit."[57]

The CIO, far more than its AFL rival, stood in the middle. It was the CIO that was primarily engaged in organizing the heavy industrial sector at the heart of defense production. CIO leaders were torn between the desire to maintain industrial union solidarity and the suspicion that Communists such as Mortimer, Michener, and the leaders of the woodworkers' union might be sabotaging the defense effort. At the very least, these radicals lent legitimacy to the de facto Nazi-Soviet alliance and to the bizarre notion that fascism was, in Soviet foreign minister Molotov's words, "a matter of taste."

Like the CIO's first breakthroughs of 1936–37, its resurgence on the eve of World War II was the product of complex and diverse factors. Now, like then, a bedrock rank-and-file activism was crucial. Determination to create or rebuild strong unions was unmistakable. The mass strikes, the rejection of company unionism, and the massive NLRB votes clearly indicated the commitment of auto, steel, packinghouse, maritime, electrical, lumber, and other mass production workers to the furtherance of the CIO project.[58] Indeed, to radical journalist Art Preis, who covered many of the organizing campaigns of 1941, this raw militancy alone explained the successes of 1941. "These gains," he declared, "were won despite the union leaders," whose primary aim, he believed, was to appease government officials.[59]

In fact both government and the union leadership played positive roles in the CIO's revival. The legal arena was crucial. True, NLRB proceedings were often slow. At the same time, however, the existence of the NLRB, whose three members and whose legal staff were deeply sympathetic to the cause of industrial unionism, gave organized labor for the first time an arena other than the picket line in which to meet its adversaries. Victories in the legal arena were precious, subjecting the once-impregnable antiunion corporations to humiliating defeats. "When I hear Wagner bill went constitutional," a journalist quoted an Aliquippa, Pennsylvania, steelworker in 1937, "I happy. . . . I say good, now Aliquippa become part of the United States." Murray believed that the fact that "unionism in the steel industry was able to survive the tribulations which beset it in 1937 and 1938 . . . is due in no small part to the existence of the National Labor Relations Act."[60]

In the American industrial relations environment of the late 1930s and 1940s, exclusive reliance on shop-floor militancy would have been risky indeed. Too many workers held back and the corporations were too strong.[61] The only unionists who raised questions about the possibly corrupting and co-opting effects of federal labor law were AFL conservatives, fearful of disruption of traditional, sometimes collusive, arrangements. For the overwhelming majority of labor activists, federal labor law was a spectacular boon, the handmaiden to and encourager of worker militancy and not some sinister co-optive force.[62]

The critical role played by the NLRB highlighted the importance of a positive association with the federal government. NLRB members were presidential appointees and, of course, its appropriations entailed congressional scrutiny and debate. Beginning in 1939 the House Rules Committee held an exceedingly hostile investigation of the NLRB. Business spokesmen charged that the new agency fomented rather than ameliorated labor unrest. Joining the critique of the NLRB, AFL representatives called for changes in the law to limit the board's power to establish bargaining units, thereby hoping to preserve traditional craft demarcations in the face of the industrial union onslaught. Hostile witnesses attacked the CIO as a subversive, violent, and sinister organization.[63]

Indeed, the defense buildup and the labor unrest that attended it triggered all sorts of attacks on the labor movement. The cabinet service secretaries and army and navy representatives on presidentially appointed defense mobilization bodies insisted on curtailment of the right to strike. Declared the chairman of the House Judiciary Committee in March, when faced with "enemies of the nation in the factory or elsewhere," he and his colleagues "would not hesitate one split second to enact legislation to send them to the electric chair." Public opinion polls overwhelmingly backed restrictions on job actions, with respondents blaming unions primarily for military production delays. Congressional conservatives, encouraged by their strong showing in the 1938 elections, declared CIO counsel Lee Pressman, "started a race as to which one could report out the most drastic [antilabor] measure in the quickest time." With CIO secretary James Carey hopping from hearing to hearing, both congressional chambers considered bills that would destroy organized labor's legislative gains of the 1930s. In early December 1941 the Smith Bill – according to Pressman "probably the worst of all" – passed the House by a two-to-one margin.[64]

In confronting these attacks the CIO needed friends in the government, and it needed leaders who could combine real power in the factories and on the picket lines with a reputation for moderation and sober judgment. In the real world of industrial America on the brink of global conflict, labor relations, like every other aspect of defense production and military mobilization, was part of an intricate political process. CIO leaders could not afford the alienation that John L. Lewis had chosen; they could not afford to regard the complex patterns of militancy, threats of repression, and opportunities for laborite advance as a zero sum-game in which every union concession fundamentally compromised some mystical laborite essence.

In this respect the CIO was fortunate in the two men who served as its primary spokesmen during 1941. Both CIO president Philip Murray and former vice-president Sidney Hillman, now serving as codirector of the OPM, combined political influence and leadership of large unions. Staunch Roosevelt Democrats, both men were respected in the shops and mills and welcomed in the counsels of government. While the UMW tested the outer limits of governmental forbearance, Hillman and Murray sought with considerable success to fend off punitive measures while consolidating the recent round of CIO advances.[65]

For Hillman the whole point of building the CIO was to attain the strength and credibility that permitted access to the decision-making arenas. That compromise and give-and-take were required was obvious. Attacked by Lewis as a back-stabbing lackey of the administration, the ACWA chief was convinced that cooperation with the administration and support for military production combined patriotism and common sense.[66]

Murray too sought to negotiate the powerful currents in which the CIO operated. He presented himself as a patriotic industrial statesman, seeking justice for his members while they produced the tanks and ships the country needed. He used the angry activism that rippled through the steel and auto shops to impress corporate leaders and government officials with labor's resolve and potency. At the same time, however, Murray believed that the attitude of the federal government would be decisive if the CIO were to avoid the defeats that had also made 1937 so memorable. Armed with favorable court and NLRB rulings but always cognizant of the potential of government for repression, Murray sought to use this latest outburst of worker discontent to establish industrial unionism irrevocably in steel and other mass production industries. The best way to accomplish this end and to make sure that *this* time union achievements would not be swept away in the next recession or the next spasm of repression was to encase it in union shop agreements and to give the 1941 breakthrough a solid political underpinning.

To be sure, the course taken by Hillman and Murray was dangerous. Involvement with the government and with a multitendency Democratic Party would involve compromise and disappointment. But from mass organization, now largely accomplished, came political power, and from political power came the ability to defend, protect, and advance labor's cause. They believed that the future, despite the menace of Hitler and the yappings of corporate reactionaries and congressional bumpkins, was a progressive future. American workers had much to defend in a treacherous world, and the CIO was was their most potent weapon in that effort. Besides, there was a war on.

CHANGING THE GUARD

In 1941 the CIO began to function for the first time as an autonomous institution. Upon taking over the reigns at the end of 1940, Murray had found that CIO finances were desperate and its governance chaotic. Determined to end reliance on the UMW, he promised to put the CIO on a sound, independent footing and to build a "real, true organization." But doing this brought the leaders of the CIO into even sharper conflict with John L. Lewis.[67]

The Lewis–Hillman conflict rolled on through 1941, as always a personal encounter that embodied fundamental disagreements about the character of the labor movement and its relationship to the state. As in the past, controversy centered on Hillman's role as a federal official. Closely related were conflicts over the CIO's institutional arrangements, especially involving the organization's financial circumstances.

Throughout 1940 and 1941 Lewis and his allies lost few opportunities to attack Hillman. The ACWA leader and his allies, they charged, were attempting to lead the CIO on its knees back into the AFL, and their worshipful attitude toward FDR threatened labor's autonomy. Within the CIO, Hillmanites tried to dominate political activities and to control key IUCs in New York, New Jersey, and Pennsylvania. According to Lewis, Hillman was attempting to turn Murray against his former chief. Indeed, he charged, Hillman and his associates were "sticking the knife into the CIO."[68]

In his capacity as associate director of the OPM, Hillman was vulnerable to attack. His inability to extract an effective ban on the awarding of defense contracts to labor law violators weakened his credibility, as did his efforts to restrain worker militancy and his association with union-busting corporate executives and defense officials. Indeed, as the head of only a medium-sized union whose industry was on the periphery of the mobilization effort and who owed his government position solely to President Roosevelt, Hillman had drifted far from the brass knuckles world of the labor movement. "Hillman is a pretty good little fellow and pretty fair," condescended Secretary of War Stimson.[69]

Another source of bitterness was Hillman's treatment of the claims of UCWOC in the defense construction field. Since its inception in 1939, UCWOC had received generous UMW and CIO subsidies but had gained little membership. Yet the Lewis-controlled *CIO News* lost few opportunities to praise UCWOC.[70]

In reality, however, UCWOC, as Hillman readily understood, had no real presence in the labor movement, despite Lewis's efforts to promote it. Thus, in the fall of 1941, Hillman dealt exclusively with the powerful AFL building trades unions in hammering out defense construction labor agreements. In response, UCWOC head Dennie Lewis, John L. Lewis's brother, sneeringly referred to him as "one of the so-called great leaders of the CIO," who was "using his office . . . to disrupt, stop[,] and destroy the UCWOC."[71]

For their part, though, Hillman and his allies found much to criticize in the behavior of Lewis and the UMW. In 1940 the *CIO News*, ostensibly the organ of the entire organization, slavishly trumpeted Lewis's bizarre political moves. Moreover, charged Hillman's second-in-command at the ACWA, under Lewis, CIO finances were a mystery, with Lewis's brother-in-law handling funds with no accountability. The entire organization was run as a ramshackle UMW subsidiary.[72]

At first most CIO leaders backed Lewis in this running conflict. After all, virtually all of the top CIO officers owed their jobs to Lewis, and most were still members of the UMW, whose blood loyalties were powerful indeed.[73] At a Lewis-called conference in July 1941 Hillman was almost universally condemned for his role in the North American strike. Lewis loyalists ridiculed Hillman for his allegedly inept running of the textile campaign and for its financial embarrassments. With Lewis in charge, asserted Director of Organization Haywood, the CIO needed no bureaucratic financial structure, for "we can go get $30,000 from him when we are hard up and need it."[74]

For the time being Murray remained the UMW loyalist. He dutifully supported the UMW in the spring 1941 soft-coal strike and the bitter captive mines strike of the fall. In November, when Hillman's NDMB rejected Lewis's demand for a union shop in the captive mines, Murray angrily resigned from it. He routinely lent his name to organizing appeals and press releases trumpeting the accomplishments of UCWOC and District 50, even after other CIO unions complained that these UMW initiatives poached on their jurisdictions. Declared Lewis, "Phil's all right."[75]

Murray was determined not to be a rubber stamp for Lewis, however. In 1940 he had not followed Lewis's political lead but instead had stumped for FDR. By the end of 1941 it was hard to resist the conclusion that Lewis's political and organizing moves were designed to embarrass and perhaps even to sidetrack the CIO. As SWOC gained firmer footing, Murray emerged as a labor leader fully comparable to Lewis and the AFL's William Green. Long in Lewis's shadow, he increasingly came to see the presidency of the CIO as the highlight of his career and the CIO itself as the legitimate repository of labor's highest aspirations.

Underlying Murray's growing estrangement from Lewis was his belief that administration defense and military policies were fundamentally correct and were fully compatible with – indeed, essential for – the achievement of labor's goals. Lewis's pronouncements on foreign affairs often seemed bizarre, even sinister. "It would be a fearful thing," he told a reporter as the *Wehrmacht* surged into the USSR and the *Luftwaffe* blasted England, "if the British won this war." Hitler, he believed, was a passing phenomenon who "would not attempt world domination." In contrast Murray profoundly feared German victory and believed that American might was essential in the defeat of fascism.[76]

Indeed, as the country moved toward war, Lewis's outspoken antiadministration views increasingly embarrassed other CIO leaders. The June 22,

1941, Nazi attack on the USSR dissolved the Lewis-Communist alliance, and CPUSA forces in the CIO lined up behind the once-despised Hillman's defense mobilization efforts. Lewis's public opposition in August to the extension of Lend-Lease aid to the USSR deepened the hostility of his pro-Soviet former allies.[77]

The captive mines strike, which flickered off and on between September and December, further tested CIO solidarity. Murray and other CIO leaders sympathized with Lewis's efforts to gain union shop status for the 53,000 miners employed directly by U.S. Steel and other large corporations that mined much of their own coal. Certainly they believed that union security was the key to a fair and efficient industrial relations regime.[78]

Nonetheless, Lewis's conduct of the strike raised troubling questions. Throughout the protracted controversy Lewis combined demands for categorical CIO support with attacks on CIO leaders who backed the foreign and defense policies of the administration. The strike, conducted amid daily heightening international tensions, provoked violent antiunion expressions in the press and in Congress, and it did threaten to impede military production at a time of deepening crisis. Eventually Roosevelt found a formula for resolution. On the morning of December 7, even as Japanese planes were bombing Pearl Harbor, the president's handpicked arbitrator, John R. Steelman of the U.S. Conciliation and Mediation Service, issued a decision that brought victory to Lewis. But UMW triumph left bitterness within the CIO over Lewis's imperiousness and his seeming lack of concern over the national emergency.[79]

Indeed, throughout late 1941 and into the early months of 1942, conflict flared between Lewis and the CIO leadership. As the main body of the CIO identified itself ever more closely with the government and the military effort, it drifted ever further from Lewis and the UMW. Even before Pearl Harbor, ILWU president Harry Bridges proclaimed that disagreements with government actions "will not affect our policies" of all-out production to defeat fascism. After Pearl Harbor the rhetoric escalated: boasted *News* editor Len De Caux, the "CIO is proud to take the lead for all out production for victory." While the Mine Workers never openly opposed military preparations, Lewis continually stressed labor's autonomous rights and his determination to resist subordination to governmental priorities. Increasingly Lewis acted as if cooperation with the government was tantamount to capitulation, and his wrath shifted from the beleaguered Hillman to his erstwhile comrade, Philip Murray.[80]

There were many reasons for a break between Lewis and the CIO. Differences over foreign and defense policy, labor's relationship to Roosevelt, and the running of the CIO itself grew ever greater. From the start of his tenure as CIO president, Murray had been at least implicitly critical of Lewis's stewardship of the CIO. Immediately on assuming the presidency Murray began to end CIO dependency on the UMW and to withdraw support from marginal Lewis-sponsored affiliates. Poignant personal factors complicated their growing antagonism as well. Lewis, for example, came to believe that there was a "poison squad in the headquarters of the C.I.O.," headed by John Brophy. This cabal, he charged, sought "to besmirch the character and impair the standing" of himself and those who supported him. A personal meeting between Lewis and Murray in October 1941 in a nearly deserted Atlantic City hotel failed to satisfy either man, and both came away convinced that the other was on the verge of a decisive break.[81]

Lewis expressed his growing estrangement from the CIO in tangible ways. UMW-controlled IUCs lashed out at the CIO leadership. Lewis pressed forward with organizing plans that bypassed or undermined CIO bodies. Thus in August 1941 he reorganized the UMW's District 50, which had been created in 1936 ostensibly for recruitment of workers in industries that used coal by-products and chemicals, appointing his daughter Kathryn Lewis as its secretary-treasurer. A marginal organization during its first five years, District 50 now began receiving generous funding from the UMW, carried on the books as advances to the CIO. He pulled UMW organizers away from CIO projects and put them to work for District 50, still charging their salaries to the CIO. It began to appear that Lewis was creating a sort of second CIO that was beginning to challenge the official CIO for the allegiance of workers in chemicals, paper, utilities, and other areas.[82]

After the United States entered World War II, Lewis stepped up this anti-CIO campaign. In January, for example, without any consultation with Murray, he announced an implausible but highly publicized plan for "accouplement" of the AFL and CIO that called for the retirement of both Murray and AFL president William Green. Soon after, he directed subordinates to submit a bill to the CIO for over $1.6 million, the amount he claimed the UMW had lent the CIO in its early days. The Mine Workers, he assured Murray and Secretary-Treasurer James Carey, did not expect immediate payment; they would simply withhold their monthly per capita tax payment of $30,000 for the time being, perhaps until the debt had been paid.[83]

These initiatives stunned the CIO establishment. The accouplement scheme was preposterous, patently designed to capture headlines and humiliate Murray. The sudden raising of the question of the CIO's financial relationship to the UMW was even more disturbing. After a search of the books, Murray acknowledged the great financial contributions of the UMW to the CIO but rejected Lewis's peremptory demand for repayment.

"I am told that most of [it] . . . was used to feed the hungry, clothe the naked and shelter the homeless during bitter struggles on the part of the workers to establish their unions," he intoned. Arrangements made before Murray took over were so poorly documented that it was impossible to make a correct accounting. The CIO Executive Board rejected Lewis's repayment ultimatum, declaring that clearly "the coal miners did not and do not consider the advances which they made to enable other and less fortunate workers to achieve economic freedom through union organization to be a debt to be repaid in dollars and cents."[84]

Even more outrageous than Lewis's sudden financial demands was his method of dealing with Murray. The CIO president received no direct communication from his long-term cohort; he learned of Lewis's scheme only when intermediaries presented brusque remittance notices. The whole affair, Murray conceded, "hit me pretty hard. . . . I felt like a lost soul, that's how I felt." Recalling the day in November 1940 when he took over the CIO's reins from Lewis, Murray reported that "he held my hand; he clasped it very firmly and tears were coursing down his cheeks when he said, 'I am handing over to you . . . a perfectly solvent organization.' " That statement, of course, was as bogus as Lewis's current financial claims. "I think," Murray concluded, "it is perfectly wicked."[85]

By this time Murray had concluded that Lewis was maneuvering to force a break. Lewis's UMW henchmen, he asserted in May, were "spreading poison and seeking to disorganize instead of organize." Soon after, SWOC, technically still a direct arm of the CIO, transformed itself into the USWA, an autonomous CIO affiliate, with Murray, of course, named president.[86]

Murray's action provided Lewis with an opportunity to formalize openly his break with his former cohort and with the CIO. He charged Murray with slandering him and the UMW, sabotaging District 50 and UCWOC organizing drives, and generally betraying his trust as a UMW vice-president. During the week of May 25, in a strange ritual held in the basement conference room of the UMW Washington, D.C., headquarters, Murray was removed as a UMW vice-president and stripped of his membership in an organization to which he had belonged for thirty-five years. Once Lewis's most trusted and devoted associate, Murray was now only the "former friend" of the UMW potentate.[87]

The rhetorical wars continued. In June Murray compared Lewis to Hitler. For his part Lewis professed to be weary of the tiresome wailings of those who now led the once-mighty industrial union movement he had created. "Life is too short for me to answer the yappings of every cur that follows at my heels," he told his UMW members. Let the "lap dogs and the kept dogs and the yellow dogs" who now ran the CIO bed down with their governmental masters. As for him, he had only contempt for the "miserable mediocrities of the CIO."[88]

The estrangement of John L. Lewis and the UMW from the CIO was a dramatic event. "Lewis," wrote an early biographer, "was [the CIO's] . . . founding father, its emotional symbol, its commander-in-chief." The UMW's role in the CIO went beyond its tangible support for industrial unionism. The struggles of the coal miners, in both England and America, provided the rich lode of myth and history that working-class leaders, orators, and balladeers drew upon. The UMW's 600,000 members included blacks, immigrants, and long-term Anglo-Americans. Its migrating sons and daughters had carried the union message with them to Akron, Pittsburgh, Flint, and Detroit. From Murray, Haywood, Brophy, and Bittner down to IUC officers, the CIO's leadership was dominated by Mineworkers.[89]

Indeed, until 1941, in most things except name the CIO *was* the UMW and John L. Lewis. Now, however, the UAW and the Steelworkers had more members than the UMW, and the UE was almost as large. Murray's administrative and financial reforms eliminated dependency on the UMW. By the first anniversary of Murray's ascendancy, the CIO boasted a $300,000 surplus and could conduct its affairs on a regular and businesslike basis.[90]

In some respects the UMW departure seemed a blessing. Gone was a major impediment to good relations with the Roosevelt administration. The departure of UMW representatives from CIO committees and IUCs removed a constant source of disputation and even obstructionism. No doubt the UMW's District 50 would now challenge the CIO openly in the organizing field, and few of his former colleagues underestimated the powerful appeal that Lewis had for industrial workers. Still, open competition was better than internecine warfare. Moreover, most indications showed that the best and the brightest organizers and activists who had come from the UMW into the CIO were not eager to return to the byzantine and parochial world of the miners' union.[91]

In the mid-1930s the interests of the UMW and the new CIO had seemed identical. By 1941, however, the interests of the new industrial unions had come to depart sharply from those of the UMW. Steel, auto, rubber, textile, electrical, and other mass production workers needed close association with the Roosevelt regime. In order to achieve what the UMW already had – stable memberships, union security, a seat at the table – they needed to accommodate themselves to the Roosevelt administration and to the defense buildup. They could no longer afford the incubus Lewis now represented. "Mr. John L. Lewis today," declared one CIO board member in June 1942, "is the No. 1 enemy against all labor."[92]

Nineteen forty-one had indeed been an eventful year for the CIO. It was a firmly established institutional entity with a solid financial footing. With the organizing surge of 1941 its claims to speak for the industrial working class rang true as never before. Its spokesmen and representatives were recognized figures in the country's political and economic power centers. Its commitment to the administration's military and diplomatic agenda was unequivocal, and its enmeshment in the state apparatus grew apace. What was in store for a CIO without Lewis? Would the powerful wartime political and economic pressures just beginning to be felt further suck the industrial union federation into a government-defined and -sanctioned role in American life? Or could the CIO, still proud of its rebel heritage and its independence, strike a balance between its enlistment in the antifascist crusade and its claims as an autonomous voice of the industrial working class?

World War II had a powerful impact on industrial workers and the CIO. For workers it brought four years of relatively full employment and heftier pay packets. It eroded traditional ethnic identities and encouraged the development of broad notions of racial and religious toleration. It brought workers forcefully into a mobile, consumerist, syncretic culture and into far more regular and intimate contact with the national government than ever before. Conflict and disruption accompanied these changes, but the industrial working class that emerged from the global conflict was less provincial, more tolerant, and more expectant of material gain than it had been in 1940. It was at once more regimented, better organized, and less willing to put up with scarcity, unemployment, and hard times.[1]

THE CIO AGENDA, 1941–1942

During World War II the fulcrum of the CIO changed. For the first time, even before the departure of the UMW, the membership from "new" unions surpassed that of the original CIO 1935 sponsors. In this shift Murray was a fortuitous leader, for he partook of both the old world of the labor movement and the emerging world of industrial unionism. The CIO was now clearly aligned with the government and the Democratic Party. With the creation of its PAC in 1943, it moved into an American version of participation in a governing coalition. In its role as a central federation of industrial unions, the CIO both furthered and was affected by these transformations. The war resolved its chronic membership and financial problems. It solidified and confirmed the industrial union federation's status as a critical factor in the central manufacturing core of the economy and as a key contestant in the competition for power, privilege, and influence in the post–New Deal political economy.

At the same time, inherent in wartime developments were important limits to both the immediate scope and the long-term possibilities for the role in American public life envisaged by the CIO's leaders. The war brought thousands of new workers into the factories and mills, many of them little interested in unionism and unaffected by the stirring events of the 1930s. Government policies and the unions' own hunger for stability fed the bureaucratization of labor relations, increasing the distance between leadership and membership characteristic of corporate institutions whatever the sincerity of their formally democratic values. The war delegitimated the shop floor as the primal arena of workers' struggle and elevated the voting booth and the hearing room. It brought tens of thousands of African American workers into the industrial heartland and unleashed bitter racial conflict among CIO members. The war, in short, simultaneously gave a foundering CIO a new lease on life and created drastically new and challenging environments in which it functioned.

Few elements in American public life were more eager to prosecute the war than the leadership of the industrial union body. As Philip Murray told the 1942 convention, "This Nation had at least one powerful organization already on the march against the evil forces of the Axis powers. . . . The CIO had acted while others hesitated."[2] Here was no reluctant workers' movement, requiring cajolery or repression to get it to march in the front ranks.[3]

The war also offered opportunities for union advance. Expanding military production filled the ranks of the industrial unions. Labor's friend, Franklin Roosevelt, was commander-in-chief. The war against fascism was a people's war, and no organ of American life, industrial unionists believed, had a better claim to speaking for ordinary people than the CIO.

Wartime was a time of peril as well, however. National crisis strengthened the hand of antiunion corporations and catapulted military priorities to the top of the public agenda. Superpatriotic reactionaries infested Congress. Public opinion seemed fixated on the unions' occasional missteps and tolerant of corporate excesses. Even working people expressed far more criticism of "union bosses" than they did of business leaders.[4]

Moreover, those who guided the CIO were aware that the war exposed the industrial union project to intense internal stresses. It transformed many workplaces and created hundreds of new ones. It disrupted communities and established new neighborhoods as additional factories, mills, and shipyards came on line. The CIO was committed to orderly processes. Could a labor force fractured by racial, ethnic, gender, and sectoral divisions and subjected to enormous wartime pressures remain sufficiently cohesive? At a CIO conference held less than a week after Pearl Harbor, Murray expressed some of these apprehensions. If complex workplace, compensation, and scheduling problems were not fairly addressed, "we would have a rebellion here . . . comparable perhaps to the Japanese war." Murray pledged to do everything he could to expand production while "trying to keep war down in the CIO."[5]

The CIO response to the onset of war was to exploit its relationship with

Roosevelt and secure and expand its membership while enlisting whole-heartedly in the war effort. This program consisted of four key elements: increasing production, collaborating with the government in developing and implementing labor relations machinery, expanding CIO membership, and building a permanent structure of labor involvement in national politi-cal and economic decision making. Achievement of these goals required a delicate balancing of interests. Thus, for example, CIO organizers and spokesmen would have to temper the militancy of organizing campaigns with the awareness that strikes might impede military production and in-vite reprisals. Conversely, cooperation with delay-prone governmental dispute-resolution machinery could alienate impatient union members.

No leading figure in the CIO of late 1941, except perhaps Lewis, doubted the need for U.S. entry into the war. "Labor," declared Murray shortly after Pearl Harbor, "is determined to place itself in the forefront in the battle of achieving maximum production." Fascism and militarism directly imperiled American workers. The war, observed UAW activist Victor Reuther, "was just another phase of the long historical struggle of people to free themselves from authoritarian rule and win a measure of individual freedom."[6]

CIO statements accused corporate managers of holding back on military production to accommodate expanding domestic consumer markets. All the more reason, then, for the CIO to take the initiative. If increased wartime workloads violated traditional labor standards, declared ILWU president Harry Bridges, that was part of the price to be paid for victory. Some would call the new norms a speedup, he admitted, but "we are not ashamed of it." Chimed in Julius Emspak, secretary-treasurer of the UE, the primary task of the CIO was "to build a disciplined army for production."[7]

Productionist ideas were not new to the wartime CIO. Hillman's career in the ACWA had been devoted to expanding the union's role in the decision-making processes of the clothing industry. Under the guidance of SWOC regional director Clinton Golden, Murray had in 1940 coauthored a book with liberal engineering expert Morris L. Cooke entitled *Organized Labor and Production: Next Steps in Industrial Democracy*, while two years later Golden and SWOC research director Harold J. Ruttenberg published *The Dynamics of Industrial Democracy*. Both books argued the case for dis-ciplined unionism as a central component of rational industrial develop-ment in a modern economy. Murray spoke and published extensively in behalf of industry councils, joint labor-management bodies that would co-ordinate allocation of resources, plan production techniques, and eliminate wasteful duplication of facilities and unprofitable marketing practices. Al-though geared to the immediate needs of defense production, Murray's industrial councils were rooted in liberal corporate Catholic thought, particularly as adumbrated in Pope Pius XI's *Quadragesimo Anno*, a 1931 encyclical stressing the rights of labor within the context of cooperative institutional arrangements.[8]

Walter Reuther soon emerged as a leading critic of corporate and governmental production policies and as a forceful spokesman for labor participation. Director of the UAW's important GM Department and head of a 30,000-member Detroit UAW local, Reuther believed that complex modern production problems required the detailed involvement of technical experts and experienced workers if industry was to free itself of underemployment, waste, and profiteering. In the fall of 1940 he advanced an ambitious plan designed to show how the automobile industry, with the cooperation of the UAW, could drastically increase production of military aircraft while continuing to meet the expanding domestic market for automobiles. Reuther's scheme featured involvement of workers' representatives in the design, retooling, and layout of production.[9]

Murray and Reuther lost few opportunities to promote these proposals. "The industry council set-up," said the CIO president in July 1941, "is more adaptable to the needs of American enterprise and American labor than anything ever yet conceived in the mind of man." Industry councils were the first step and "will prove to be a boom [*sic*] to the cause of labor . . . because it gives to labor for the first time . . . representation in the field of industry and in the field of government." Reuther asserted that the war crisis demonstrated the necessity for involvement of workers in managerial decision making. "We have to insist we be given a voice in these councils," he asserted. "We can do this job."[10]

Achieving this new status, however, would not be easy. The powerful corporations with which CIO unions bargained were not even reconciled to collective bargaining, much less to union participation in decisions affecting production. To realize the goal of participation, the CIO needed three things: expanding membership, union security, and governmental backing. Fortunately for Murray, Reuther, and the others, wartime circumstances maximized the prospect of attaining each. Thus, the CIO's ready adoption of the No Strike Pledge, offered gratuitously in the wake of Pearl Harbor, and its active participation on the NWLB, established by presidential order on January 12, 1942, laid the basis both for its wartime program and its ongoing claims for representation in decision-making arenas.

Expanding membership seemed the easiest requirement to satisfy. Production of aircraft, tanks and other military vehicles, naval vessels, munitions, electronic gear, and armaments brought tens of thousands of war workers into factories earlier organized by the UAW, the UE, and the Steelworkers. In addition, smaller affiliates, notably the Marine and Shipbuilding Workers, the FE, and Mine, Mill, were well placed to gather new recruits. The beleaguered TWUA found wartime conditions favorable to recruitment even in the South.

Through most of the war, CIO membership increased. It grew from 1.8 million in 1939 to 3.9 million in 1944, despite the loss of Lewis's 600,000 coal miners. UAW figures in the same period went from 165,000 to over 1 million, while the USWA tripled its membership, reaching over 700,000 in 1944. UE membership leapt from under 50,000 in 1939 to 432,000 at the peak of the conflict. The Textile Workers (83,000 to 216,000), Mine, Mill (under 30,000 to 98,000), Packinghouse Workers (39,000 to 100,000), and Shipbuilding Workers (35,000 to 209,000) likewise made dramatic gains. Reporting at the end of 1943 that the CIO books showed a membership expansion of 44 percent over the past year, Murray boasted "that this is the most glowing picture ever to be recorded in the annals of labor." Solvency followed recruitment, for by the end of 1943 the treasury showed a surplus of over $600,000.[11]

The second desideratum, union security, was complex and contentious. In CIO unions, this goal was usually expressed as a bargaining demand for the "union shop." Golden and Ruttenberg spelled out its essence in *Dynamics of Industrial Democracy*: "Membership in the union shall be a condition of employment in any given bargaining unit where a majority of eligible workers voluntarily belongs to the union." Management remained free to hire anyone it pleased, provided that "after an agreed upon period . . . all new workers shall join the union." Members were then obligated to pay their dues and remain in good standing, subject to discharge if they failed to fulfill these obligations.[12]

The union shop was a means of stabilizing membership and removing from the employer the temptation to play nonmembers against members. Since the Wagner Act obligated a union to represent all workers in a given bargaining unit, the union shop reassured the pro-union majority of workers in an organized shop that there would be no "free riders" among their coworkers. Unionists drew an analogy between political citizenship and industrial citizenship. The majority in the shop, like the majority in a political unit, made choices in free elections that bound all. Thus, the union shop was necessary to extend real democracy from the civics books into the nation's mills and shops.

More to the immediate point, union advocates argued that the union shop was necessary for the effective working of the government's wartime labor relations machinery. Without union security and its companion, the dues checkoff, even leaders who deeply wanted to cooperate with productionist priorities had to accommodate dissident groups of workers whose withholding of dues acted as a kind of blackmail. "The union," instructed Golden and Ruttenberg, "assumes the responsibility to see that no stoppages of work occur, that all workers adhere to the contract machinery to settle grievances peacefully, and that wages and other vital cost factors are pegged generally for the life of the contract." The presence of nonmembers in a union plant invited conflict and weakened the union's ability to meet these responsibilities.[13]

"The union shop is the big issue confronting management and unions today," declared Golden and Ruttenberg, and the tangled labor-management-government negotiations that characterized the immediate prewar and early war months drove home the truth of their observation. The UMW's quest for the union shop triggered the captive mines strike of the fall of 1941, and similar demands in defense industries occupied much of the attention of the NDMB. Organized labor's adoption of the No Strike Pledge immediately after Pearl Harbor gave the matter even greater urgency, for without some form of union security to replace the relinquished strike weapon, unions – particularly the new CIO unions – were uniquely vulnerable to fluctuating memberships and employer manipulation. The new NWLB thus found itself confronting the problem of union security in a series of important cases through the first half of 1942.[14]

Indeed, even having the NWLB consider union security was a triumph for laborites. In acrimonious discussions held under government auspices on December 17 and 18, unionists and employers were deadlocked on this issue, with employers arguing that no wartime labor board should consider union security. Murray retorted, "We have given all we can give here. We have given up the right to strike." The conference broke up without agreement, but when the new NWLB began meeting in January its four public members held, along with the four labor members, that the new agency would have to consider union security, since it was the most contentious and disputatious matter dividing labor and management.[15]

In a series of decisions, virtually all aligning the eight public and labor representatives against the four management appointees, the NWLB put in place a system of union security that substantially met the goals of the labor movement. Called "maintenance of membership," it provided that in union-represented workplaces all members of the union would have to sustain their membership during the life of the collective bargaining contract. These decisions accepted the essence of organized labor's view that the exigencies of wartime labor relations, if not necessarily the character of modern economic life per se, required the stability and predictability that union security promised.[16]

Maintenance of membership protected new unions from rapid fluctuations in worker support and gave evidence of the federal government's positive position. "If it was not for the union security given to our unions by the National War Labor Board we wouldn't have 5,000,000 dues-paying members [sic] in the C.I.O.," asserted Van Bittner, a CIO representative on the NWLB later in the war.[17] Thus, with rapidly expanding membership, solid union security provisions, and impressive evidence that the federal government recognized the key importance of the labor movement in the conduct of the war, the likelihood of the CIO joining the constellation of power brokers dominating the American political economy seemed strong.

In the summer of 1942, Steelworkers' monthly dues buttons carried the slogan "Remember Bataan," a grim reminder that allied forces were still reeling under the Axis onslaught. But Philip Murray could nonetheless contemplate a better day. "When the war ends," he told his colleagues, "we will be able to . . . participate in the eventual settlement" and in shaping postwar society. The military situation might be bleak, but the prospects for the CIO seemed bright.[18]

AMONG THE RANKS, IN THE PLANTS

Throughout the war, Murray and his associates sought to mediate between the shop-floor and plant-gate concerns of their members and the broader interests of the CIO and of a nation at war. Negotiating their way through often-explosive episodes of grassroots turbulence while successfully practicing patriotic labor statesmanship tested their personal abilities and the CIO's fragile institutional arrangements. In particular the wartime strikes of CIO workers and the often-related issue of the status of black workers in war industry and in the expanding industrial unions posed challenges that helped to define the ongoing character of industrial unionism.

The CIO was something of an abstraction to many workers, a proud rubric rather than a concrete entity. It played virtually no role in collective bargaining and was only sometimes involved in organizing. The vast majority of CIO members belonged to locals affiliated with the national and international unions primarily responsible for these critical activities. Still, by the middle of the war the CIO embraced nearly 4 million members, and to the government, the press, and the public its leaders spoke for them.

The CIO surge reached into many areas of local and community life. In cities such as Akron, Flint, Detroit, San Francisco, Chicago, and the steel towns of Pennsylvania, Ohio, and Indiana the arrival of the CIO sometimes resurrected patterns of union organizing that had linked community with workplace. In smaller cities such as Covington, Virginia, Winston-Salem,

North Carolina, and the meatpacking centers of Iowa, Kansas, and Nebraska the appearance of CIO unions such as the Paperworkers, the Cannery and Agricultural Workers, and the Packinghouse Workers brought the promise (or threat) of changes far beyond the packing shed or production line.[19]

The CIO, as provided in the 1938 constitution, did have an arm that reached into local communities, the IUCs. In a given geographical area these bodies brought together representatives of the local unions of CIO affiliates, which paid a small per capita tax that funded the council's activities. IUCs were charged with coordinating support for local strikes and organizing campaigns, keeping track of legislative and political developments, maintaining a CIO presence in civic and community affairs, and transmitting information between the national CIO and local unionists. State IUCs exercised the same functions on the state level, and in states with large CIO memberships, such as Michigan and California, they played major roles in lobbying, public relations, and political life. In January 1941 Murray appointed John Brophy, replaced in 1939 by Lewis as CIO director, as national director of the IUCs. As of the fall of 1944 the CIO boasted 36 state IUCs and 232 local and area councils.[20]

On an organization chart the role of the councils might have seemed clear and direct. In practice, however, these bodies were hotbeds of disputation and conflict. Usually the local and state councils functioned largely as arms of the most powerful unions in the area. The UAW soon dominated the Wayne County (Detroit) and Michigan IUCs, while the ILWU controlled the San Francisco Bay area councils and, though less unilaterally, the California state IUC. The Bay Area Council reflected the pro-Communist orientation of the longshoremen's union and its energetic leader, Harry Bridges. The Detroit and Michigan councils mirrored the ideological and political rivalries that characterized the UAW. Chicago's IUC too roiled with controversy along left-right axes, as pro-Soviet delegates representing such strong local organizations as the FE, the UE, and the Packinghouse Workers often found themselves in conflict with representatives of the Steelworkers, the ACWA, and other anti-Communist unions. The New York State IUC was largely controlled by the Clothing Workers, sometimes in uneasy alliance with Communist-influenced unions such as the TWU, the NMU, and the Fur and Leather Workers, sometimes (as in the 1939–41 period) in sharp conflict with them. For years Hillman opposed the establishment of a separate New York City IUC, fearing that locally powerful CPUSA-oriented unions would dominate it.[21]

Local unionists often regarded the councils as irrelevant to their members. Council meetings were often poorly attended and informally run, permitting highly motivated activists to dominate the agenda. Anti-Communists charged that the party directed its cadres in local unions to seek control of councils and through them press the current Soviet line. Certainly, in areas of Steelworker or ACWA strength, the councils directly reflected the policies and preferences of these unions.[22]

Even strong and united councils, however, often played a minor role in the lives of CIO workers. War workers faced enormous problems in housing, child care, transportation, and medical services. In the San Francisco area shipyards, for example, tens of thousands of new workers and their families poured into such cities as Richmond, California, straining housing and community services. The shipyards of Mobile, Tampa, and Jacksonville, modest prewar facilities, drew thousands of new workers who quickly overburdened housing and social services. Rapid expansion of southern California's aircraft industry created similar conditions. In the Detroit area the labor force exploded between 1940 and 1943 from under 400,000 wage earners to 867,000. Over 90,000 toiled at the Rouge and another 44,000 at the nearby Willow Run bomber factory, a mile-long complex hastily constructed in rural Washtenaw County. Housing shortages, rising crime rates, racial tensions, and other evidences of social pathology abounded.

Surveys of workers' attitudes in industrial centers in 1942 revealed a discouraging pattern of cynicism, powerlessness, and resignation. The majority of workers were deeply suspicious of management and the government. Over a third of these workers, many enrolled in labor organizations, had similarly negative views of unions. "Participation in the common cause," the government's Office of Facts and Figures reported, "was subordinated to self-interest," a fact that its analysts considered "deeply corrosive." "All anybody ever did," wrote two close students of the impact of wartime conditions on people's behavior, "was to fight . . . to keep their own humble ways of life unchanged." Throughout the war the CIO and many of its affiliates sought to combat apathy and resignation through morale-building meetings, literature, and union-run blood, war bond, and armed forces support drives.[23]

For most members of the CIO, however, the critical test of union membership was not in the neighborhood or the community but in the workplace. The vast manpower needs of the military frequently had the result of recomposing the workforce and restructuring work processes, often in bewildering new ways. Under pressure to produce munitions and military equipment rapidly, employers were less concerned than usual with labor costs. Experienced foremen went off to military service or advanced into newly opening middle management slots. Inexperienced supervisors now confronted confused war workers, many of them fresh rural migrants, African Americans, and, increasingly, women. Detroit area UAW locals were suddenly overwhelmed with new members, few of whom were aware of or interested in the union's heroic past. "At the bomber local [Local 50, at the Willow Run aircraft factory]," observed a UAW official, "the majority are paying $1 a month for the privilege of working. They have no understanding at all of the union and are probably a little mystified as to how they ever got into it." [24]

Despite workers' overall support for the war and despite the No Strike Pledge, literally thousands of job actions erupted in defense industries. From the beginning of 1942 until September 1945 nearly 7 million workers took part in over 14,000 strikes. Even in the desperate days of 1942 American workers conducted nearly 3,000 work stoppages. In 1943 the number leaped by 25 percent, while the next year a record 4,956 strikes were recorded. The sheer number of strikes was impressive testimony to the unwillingness of working people to permit government officials, patriotic slogans, or even their own union leaders to define the terms under which they would toil.

At the same time, other measures of strike activity indicated that strikes were compatible with broad commitment to the war effort and its productionist goals. Thus, for example, 1944's strike wave involved 7 percent of the entire workforce, almost as high a proportion as the classic strike years of 1937 and 1941. Yet these strikers stayed out for an average of only four days, less than half the 1941 average and barely more than a quarter of the 1937 figure. Thus, while engaging in a record *number* of strikes, workers in 1944 lost only a minuscule .09 percent of *working time*, the lowest proportion since the late 1920s. The only strike that even gave the appearance of jeopardizing essential war production was the 1943 soft-coal walkout; even so, UMW members were out on strike for only twelve days, and they dug a record amount of coal that year. [25]

The day-to-day indignities in the hectic wartime workplaces triggered most job actions. Disputes over production standards, treatment by foremen, wage classifications, job assignments, disciplinary actions, and standards of health, safety, and comfort multiplied. Workers discovered that without the strike weapon their unions had lost much of their leverage with employers. Indeed, workers soon realized, maintenance of membership could insulate the union leaders from rank-and-file concerns. With the No Strike Pledge in force, employers stalled on grievances and encroached on workers' shop-floor rights. As a result of these conditions, said Murray, "our people continue to engage themselves in all sorts of strikes and stoppages and interruptions of production." [26]

Most wartime strikes were short, averaging three to four days and in many cases lasting only over one shift. Many involved workers in only one department or on one shift; the handful of large-scale, concerted walkouts, such as those of Akron rubber workers in May 1943 and of 10,000 Detroit Chrysler workers a year later, were exceptions. Although a handful of non-Communist leftists sometimes attempted to provide political direction to these walkouts, these strikes seldom had any broader agenda. They did not indicate opposition to the war effort or even approval of strikes per se: while workers justified their own job actions, they evinced impressive support for the No Strike Pledge overall and frequently voiced criticism of other workers employing the strike weapon.[27]

Throughout the war CIO members accounted for over 50 percent of all strikers, although at any given time the industrial union federation contained at most a third of all organized workers. Moreover, since the CIO was active in precisely those industries involved in military production, these strikes were among the most widely publicized (and condemned) of the conflict. Among CIO unions, dissension flared most frequently in the UAW, especially in its southeastern Michigan heartland, a crucial military production center. In 1944, for example, 10 percent of all strikes, involving 25 percent of all workers on strike and accounting for 20 percent of lost time, were Michigan affairs. One estimate found that almost two-thirds of all Michigan UAW members spent some time on strike that year. "The mere mention of Detroit," wrote one furious overseas soldier to the Motor City's mayor, "brings nothing to mind but strikes."[28]

Strikes were more common where the requirements of military production necessitated large-scale refitting and reorganization of workplaces. Insecure or faction-ridden union leadership was positively associated with strike proneness, as the wartime experience of the URW and the UAW indicated. On the other hand, the textile and garment industries, both with centralized union leadership and relatively unchanged workplace regimes, had few strikes.[29]

Communists and their allies were particularly fervent in upholding the No Strike Pledge. The relative absence of job actions in the electrical appliances industry reflected the UE's strong pro-Soviet leadership and the industry's long-term patterns of incentive wage payments, which mitiated some of the effects of inflation. Leaders in other CPUSA-oriented unions, notably the Fur and Leather Workers, the FE, Mine, Mill, and the TWU suppressed strike talk rigorously. Thus, in mid-1943 TWU president Michael Quill, normally a feisty tribune of rank-and-file activism, declared, "I think we should shout our no-strike pledge louder than ever before in order to help win this war." The West Coast longshoremen followed a different pattern. A CPUSA-oriented leadership agreed to substantial increases in workloads. At the same time, however, rank-and-file control of job sites insured the retention of traditional practices with little need to resort to job actions.[30]

The case of the steel industry was particularly intriguing. No CIO union had a stronger centralized leadership than the United Steelworkers of America, as SWOC was renamed after its May 1942 constitutional convention. But legitimate grievances over wages, working conditions, and shop-floor treatment festered. The quality of life in the mill towns eroded, and wartime conditions highlighted the industry's complex and often arbitrary wage classification systems. At the end of 1943 Murray began tolerating and even tacitly encouraging strike preparations so as to put pressure on the government to permit wage increases. By the end of December as many as 150,000 USWA members had left their jobs in short-term strikes that eventually led to favorable action on demands for retroactive wage increases. In general, however, Murray and the Steelworkers' leadership suppressed strike activity effectively. In other key sectors of CIO strength and critical military production, notably airframe and shipbuilding, strikes of any kind were few.[31]

CIO spokesmen never tired of stressing the statistically minute percentage of time lost to strikes and the impressive production records compiled by industrial workers. Still, wartime strikes were deeply problematic. Eighty percent of the public and almost two-thirds of union members favored antistrike legislation. CIO leaders regularly denounced strikes. "Sometimes," said Murray, "it is even necessary for an International Union to employ disciplinary measures to restrain Local Unions from engaging themselves in strikes." Workers, conceded Mine, Mill president Reid Robinson, had legitimate grievances, but "nothing could be more dangerous to our trade-union movement . . . than a breakdown of the no-strike policy," no matter how great the provocation.[32]

One variety of rank-and-file wartime strike action was particularly disturbing to CIO leaders, the so-called hate strikes directed by white unionists against African Americans. During the war, employment of blacks expanded enormously. Participation in manufacturing, which in 1940 stood below predepression figures, had by 1944 expanded 150 percent. In that year over 1.25 million black workers, 300,000 of them women, worked in industry. As late as the summer of 1942 blacks held under 3 percent of the nation's war-related jobs, but by 1944 that figure had tripled. In the key wartime industries such as aircraft, military vehicles, shipbuilding, steel, and munitions, blacks comprised from 5 to 13 percent of the labor force.[33]

Black membership in CIO unions rose. At the peak of wartime industry, the CIO's membership of just under 4 million included 300,000 blacks, about 7.7 percent of the total. The million-member UAW led all unions in black members with 100,000, while the USWA counted perhaps 70,000. Other significant enrollers of African Americans included the Marine and Shipbuilding Workers and the United Packinghouse Workers, each with about 20,000. The virtually all-black UTSE counted about 12,000 wartime members, while smaller CIO affiliates such as Mine, Mill and the TWU had from 3,000 to 5,000 African Americans.[34]

African Americans were particularly important in such places as Detroit, Chicago, Memphis, Mobile, and Winston-Salem. Many CIO activists, especially those associated with the CPUSA, identified strongly with the concerns of black Americans. Others simply realized that African American workers were often critical to union success and that organizations such as the NAACP merited cultivation. In either case, civil rights and industrial unionism quickly developed reciprocal relations, with the presence of the CIO often energizing somnolent civil rights groups and with African Americans educating CIO representatives as to the close relationship between civic and social discrimination and workplace injustice.[35]

Winston-Salem, North Carolina, provided a particularly apt example of the fusion of industrial unionism and the struggle for racial justice. In 1943 black workers led a potent strike that forced the pivotal R. J. Reynolds Tobacco Company to the bargaining table. The UCAPAWA, mobilizing the African American majority, won a bitterly contested representation election. Its organizers linked the struggle for workplace democracy with opposition to segregation and discrimination. The very act of voting in an NLRB election highlighted black exclusion from North Carolina ballot boxes. Aggressive shop stewards were backed by a racially egalitarian union and color-blind NLRB regulations. In the community, newly empowered black workers challenged the behind-the-scenes style of the older generation of black leaders. "We feel we are the leaders instead of you," union members told the pastors and businessmen who had hitherto spoken for the black community.[36]

In Detroit the UAW-NAACP alliance that helped to defuse racial tensions during the 1941 Rouge organizing drive continued through the war years. Throughout southeastern Michigan, black workers linked job site grievances, a growing quest for power and influence within CIO unions, and mounting participation in race protest and civil rights activities. An influx of working-class members transformed the once-elite-dominated local NAACP. At Rouge Local 600 and in other UAW plants Communists led in recruiting black leaders into its local organizations, which in turn functioned as civil rights ginger groups.[37]

In Chicago, too, the CIO presence, largely in the form of militant packinghouse workers' unions with large black memberships and CPUSA-oriented and race-conscious activists, challenged segregation. In Memphis vigorous biracial unionism spearheaded by the UCAPAWA and the racially progressive NMU asserted a CIO presence that began to test the city's political and social racial order. In the iron ore mines outside Birmingham as well, the Mine, Mill locals, resting on a black majority, asserted both workplace and civil rights. In the San Francisco Bay area the CPUSA-oriented ILWU sought to build an all-embracing Popular Front civic culture that advanced progressive racial policies while expanding the role of the ILWU in the life of the community.[38]

The black-white alliance combining industrial unionism and civil rights, however, was often deeply problematic, especially in the South. Caution prevailed wherever white workers were in the majority. In the steel mills and pipe and fabricating shops of Birmingham, the USWA confined its wartime activities to improving contracts, a focus that particularly benefited black workers, most of whom toiled in low-wage jobs. Likewise, in Fort Worth's stockyards and meat packing plants, the Packinghouse Workers largely shelved the international union's ambitious civil rights agenda, restricting its wartime efforts to bread-and-butter matters. In Mobile the Marine and Shipbuilding Workers backed down, in the face of violent opposition from among the local's white majority, from its initially aggressive civil rights advocacy.[39]

Throughout the war racial tensions loomed large. "Where minority group workers are employed," observed a CIO statement on race relations, "the union's job is often more difficult."[40] Black workers and job seekers aggressively sought fair treatment in hiring and promotion. In the spring of 1941 A. Philip Randolph, head of the AFL's Brotherhood of Sleeping Car Porters, threatened a massive march on Washington to protest discrimination in the defense industry. The ensuing creation of the FEPC by executive order both encouraged black workers and stimulated further protests. Supported by civil rights groups, African American workers launched dozens of protests and strikes. As early as the summer of 1941 walkouts in Detroit's Chrysler and Dodge plants eventually impelled the UAW to support the claims of African American workers for fair treatment in transfers and upgrading. The Rouge, where in April 1943 3,000 black workers struck for expanded job opportunities, remained a center of racial activism. In rubber factories and steel mills throughout the Midwest, blacks also staged walkouts and protests that forcefully brought their grievances to the attention of government officials and union leaders.[41]

Most race-related walkouts, however, were conducted by white workers attempting to prevent the hiring or upgrading of blacks. With its huge influxes of southern whites and its expanding black population, wartime Detroit twice exploded into bloody rioting in disputes over housing and recreational facilities. In 1942 and 1943, employers, in response to manpower demands and pressure on the part of federal officials, CIO leaders, and black unionists and community groups, began cautious expansion of opportunities for African Americans in war work. The appearance of former janitors or cafeteria workers running a drill press or lathe often triggered white workers' hostility. In the spring and summer of 1942, hate strikes, usually • surrounded with rumors of Ku Klux Klan activity, erupted throughout Detroit. At the Hudson Motor Company, the Dodge Main plant, and Timken Roller Bearing white UAW members hit the bricks, the autoworkers' vaunted militancy now exercised in the cause of bigotry. In other plants also, harassment, sometimes supported or at least tolerated by local UAW leaders, accompanied the entry of black workers into new departments. In June 1943 25,000 Packard employees, who produced aircraft engines, poured out of the plants to protest upgrading of black workers.[42]

Detroit was not alone. In May 1943 white workers at the Mobile yards of the Alabama Dry Dock and Shipbuilding Company rioted when twelve blacks were promoted to welding positions. In July 1943 white workers at the Sparrows Point (Baltimore) shipyards of Bethlehem Steel struck over the hiring and upgrading of blacks, while in December at the nearby Point Breeze Western Electric plant whites staged a walkout to demand segregation of toilets. Other outbursts occurred in Gary, Aliquippa, and the old Wobbly stronghold of Butte, Montana. In the summer of 1944 the longest and most bitter racially motivated strike erupted in Philadelphia when hundreds of white streetcar employees revolted against their TWU leaders and staged a raucous strike after eight African Americans had been promoted to motormen.[43]

In response to these racial tensions CIO leaders addressed the concerns of African American workers in ways unprecedented in the American labor movement. The CIO's 1941 convention expanded the industrial union federation's commitment to racial equity by forcefully condemning discrimination in hiring as a "direct attack against our nation's policy to build democracy in our fight against Hitlerism." It lost few opportunities to contrast the CIO's racial enlightenment with the rival AFL's treatment of black workers. The CIO, proclaimed its recruiting literature, offered "new hope" for black workers. "The CIO," it insisted, "is a people's movement. . . . It does not ask questions of race or color or creed or origin. . . . The CIO welcomes you."[44]

At its November 1942 convention the CIO institutionalized its concern with African American workers by creating CARD. The impetus for the establishment of this body came from the increasing number of black workers in the industrial unions and growing evidence that black workers would assert their demands for equality of treatment in hiring and work assignments on the picket line. The affiliation in 1942 of the UTSE, a union of predominantly African American baggage handlers and railway terminal employees, gave the CIO its first black officer, Willard Townsend, who joined the Executive Board that year.

Moreover, at the May founding convention of the USWA, black members had convinced Murray that the union had to address black workers' concerns. In response he appointed Boyd L. Wilson, a veteran organizer, as his personal advisor in the field of race relations. Meanwhile Townsend pressed upon Murray the need for the industrial union federation to back its public statements with concrete action. In the summer Murray asked Townsend and CIO secretary-treasurer James B. Carey to investigate racial problems as they affected the CIO and to make recommendations for action. Their report to the Executive Board in September called for the creation of a permanent CIO committee and highlighted the importance of the political and governmental role in addressing racial problems. Thus Carey and Townsend recommended that the new committee marshal CIO support for expanding and strengthening the FEPC.[45]

Murray accepted the recommendation. He named Wilson; Ferdinand Smith, the West Indian-born secretary of the NMU; and James Leary of Mine, Mill to join Carey and Townsend in constituting the new permanent committee, CARD. Declared the UAW's Walter Reuther, racial discrimination "must be put on top of the list with union security and other major union demands" in contract negotiations. With the auto industry's racial tensions beginning to peak, Reuther stressed the importance of "get[ting] this message down to the people in the factories." Murray pledged that the CIO would intensify its expanding commitment to industrial and political civil rights.[46]

Throughout the remainder of the war CARD's activities exhibited both the innovative character and the limited scope of CIO racial initiatives. As CARD's director the committee chose George L.-P. Weaver, a thirty-year-old African American who had been serving as Townsend's assistant in the UTSE. Under Weaver's direction CARD sponsored conferences to promote racial understanding; marshaled support for the federal government's antidiscrimination activities, notably the FEPC; and produced and distributed literature. Its statements stressed good citizenship, reasoned appeals, and moderation. It issued no fiery denunciations, nor did it seek to mobilize blacks for militant confrontation. Thus in its 1943 pamphlet, *Working and Fighting Together Regardless of Race, Creed, or National Origin*, CARD addressed the problem of segregated dining facilities. Acknowledging that "there may be strong [rank-and-file] sentiment in favor of providing separate eating facilities," the pamphlet rejected segregation. Workers' acceptance of arbitrary division in any area implicitly legitimated management's divide-and-rule tactics generally. It acknowledged that whites feared that "Negro men will molest white women workers." But, declared CARD, these irrational prejudices were not "consistent with the general [CIO] policy."[47]

The members of CARD believed that workers would respond to appeals to patriotism and common sense. Union activists had an obligation "to encourage the friendly association of workers during lunch periods through frank discussion of these and other related problems." Dignified treatment of all workers, prompt response to minor racial episodes, and frequent reminders of the need for union solidarity would surely blunt the force of prejudice. "Union observance of these simple fundamentals," CARD assured local leaders, "will destroy all fears of race friction," whether owing to "the presence of women workers" or other factors. CARD's pamphlets and other publications said little about the most significant and contentious subjects of wartime racial friction, discrimination in hiring, disputes over job assignments, and the upgrading of African Americans.[48]

CARD largely avoided intervention in racial controversies on the local level. Instead CARD encouraged affiliated unions, their locals, and the IUCs to form their own antidiscrimination committees. By 1945 CIO affiliates and councils had created at least 100 of these bodies.[49]

CARD's most pointed activity was to promote the inclusion of contract language prohibiting discrimination in hiring. This was a difficult issue because most employers opposed any union involvement in hiring. Most CIO unions had never considered the hiring process as falling within the scope of collective bargaining. However, civil rights organizations correctly regarded access to jobs as the most critical industrial question facing African Americans. Thus CARD drafted model contract clauses with antidiscrimination language. The Packinghouse Workers, the URW, and the Marine and Shipbuilding Workers soon established hiring discrimination clauses as basic contractual demands. Others, however, held back, not wanting to risk offending the white majority. Murray's USWA never pressed this issue, and even the progressive UAW rarely achieved more than vague and unenforceable antidiscrimination clauses. Weaver and the committee believed that quiet suasion was the key to progress in this area, and as the war progressed, they grew less publicly vocal.[50]

Far more vigorous were CARD efforts to rally support for the FEPC. Initially lodged within the War Manpower Commission, the FEPC had only limited authority. It had no separate budget and little autonomy, but congressional, employer, and war mobilization critics assailed it as a bureaucratic monstrosity impeding the war effort. Its first chair, Louisville publisher Mark Ethridge, saw his job as that of shielding FDR from civil rights zealots. The FEPC did have two vigorous black members, Milton Webster of the Sleeping Car Porters and Chicago alderman Earl Dickerson, and along with the CIO's John Brophy and members of its small field staff they refused to permit Ethridge entirely to sidetrack the body. In February 1943 Roosevelt responded to mounting criticisms by appointing a new chair and placing the FEPC directly within the presidential office. Even so, the committee lacked power. Influential southern congressmen attacked it relentlessly, and the administration regarded it as a do-gooding sideshow.[51]

The FEPC, with all its faults, however, proved invaluable to CIO unions. Its hearings on discriminatory treatment of minority railroad, smelter, shipyard, and other workers, many of whom were held captive in collusive and openly discriminatory AFL closed shop agreements, helped sharpen the CIO's image as the friend of the black worker. Brophy's work on the FEPC and the appearance of CIO officials rendering testimony in behalf of black, Chicano, and other minority workers contrasted with the AFL's evasions and denials. Especially after the FEPC's reorganization, CIO leaders faced with the resistance of white workers found the committee an important ally in their efforts to upgrade and promote black workers. A strengthened FEPC would ease racial tensions within the unions by shifting primary responsibility for enforcing shop-floor equality from the union to a federal agency, thus clothing the drive for equity with emblems of patriotism and an aura of bureaucratic inevitability. Of course CARD lost few opportunities to highlight the CIO's ardent support for the FEPC.[52]

At the heart of CARD's approach was an essentially economic response to workplace racial problems. Townsend, Weaver, Carey, and most of the others serving on CARD held that African American workers were workers first and members of a victimized minority group second. CARD's literature invariably asserted the demand for fair treatment of black workers within the context of standard collective bargaining and economic policy goals. For example, it insisted that efforts to secure justice for blacks in no way compromised seniority rights, even though past patterns of racial discrimination would clearly disadvantage black war workers in the no-doubt bumpy transition to a peacetime economy. CARD's program meshed closely with the civic-minded, gradualist, and class-essentialist views of the CIO's central leadership.[53]

CARD did take strong stands in broader social arenas, devoting considerable attention, for example, to promoting nondiscriminatory public housing. But when it came to the workplace and the union hall, CARD, in common with Murray, Reuther, and most other non-Communist CIO leaders, discouraged racial militancy. The notion that race played some special, festering role in American industrial life and that black workers and unionists had special claims to representation and opportunity was foreign to them. The "colored man" who passes your house on his way to work each morning, a widely distributed wartime CARD pamphlet assured its readers, was just like everyone else. He needed to provide food, clothing, and shelter for his family. "If there is any [money] left, he will make a contribution to the Church . . . [and perhaps] go to a movie, or to a baseball game." He wanted only to be given a fair shake.[54]

Not everyone in the CIO orbit agreed with this perspective. Certainly, black activists regarded CARD's approach as naive. Walter Hardin and George Crockett, Jr., who represented the UAW on the committee at different times, urged more forthright advocacy of black workers' rights. In general, unions whose leadership was in or close to the Communist Party evidenced particular concern for the rights of black workers. Although Communist-oriented unions rarely risked shop-floor confrontations over race or anything else that might jeopardize output, they did more than other affiliates to address the distinct interests of black workers. Moreover, pro-Soviet unions made special efforts to recruit blacks into leadership roles and to insure African American representation on negotiating teams, grievance committees, and other union bodies. Thus, for example, at the 1943 convention of the UAW, Communists joined black activists in pressing for the election of an African American to the union's executive board. Proponents of such a move believed that the distinctive problems of African American workers required that they have a permanent, constitutionally legitimated presence in the union's ruling circles. Certainly the way in which the USWA, and the CIO itself for that matter, treated its antidiscrimination troubleshooters underlined the legitimacy of this view. In the USWA, for example, over two years passed before Boyd Wilson was granted office space and secretarial help. Although Murray acknowledged that the task of looking after the interests of black workers and investigating racial conflict was "Herculean," he admitted that Wilson was "required . . . to carry his office around in his pocket." Within the CIO itself, Weaver had to conduct CARD's business in the headquarters hallways, a visible symbol of both the CIO's public declarations for racial justice and its less impressive tangible support for the project.[55]

Despite their critics' frequent charges to the contrary, Communists were hardly guilty of expediency in their advocacy of African Americans' interests. CPUSA-oriented unions in the South faced overwhelming condemnation for their principled stands against segregation. Affiliates such as the UCAPAWA, Mine, Mill, and the NMU worked hard to organize black workers, recruit African Americans into leadership roles, and convince their white members of the ethical and practical virtues of interracial cooperation. Indeed, John Cort, a young Catholic activist otherwise deeply critical of the CIO's Communists, came to their defense. "Most Communists," he told his readers, "believe very strongly and sincerely in racial equality." The defenders of the rights of black workers, he added, will "lose more political support than they gain, since they obviously offend more whites than they please Negroes." [56]

In all, the CIO's World War II record in the arena of race was positive but problematic. In the South, apart from Communist-led or -influenced Mine, Mill and UCAPAWA locals, the CIO trod lightly. Elsewhere, some unions such as the NMU, the UAW, the URW, the Packinghouse Workers, the Marine and Shipbuilding Workers, and the TWU compiled strong records of supporting the workplace demands of their growing African American constituencies. These organizations on the whole combated the racism that instigated hate strikes and other kinds of racial harassment that often accompanied the recruitment and upgrading of black workers. CIO unions in Baltimore gained great credibility among the city's African Americans through their support of black members' rights in the shipyards, steel mills, and electrical factories. In Detroit, not only did UAW president R. J. Thomas and most of his otherwise divided executive board act vigorously against hate strikers, but the UAW reaffirmed its egalitarian commitments in the community by outspoken support of integrated housing and opposition to racial violence. On the national level, consistent CIO support for the FEPC and other federal antidiscrimination initiatives, along with CARD's activities, strengthened industrial unionism's affiliations with civil rights organizations such as the NAACP. Indeed, the CIO approach to racial tensions, emphasizing as it did moral suasion and the acceptance of African Americans as coworkers, contributed to the emergence and expansion of a broad wartime legitimation of cultural pluralism. [57]

Wartime CIO leaders believed that racial intolerance was an atavistic throwback. They believed that CIO-facilitated economic progress would erode prejudice. They rejected special measures to provide specific redress or opportunities for blacks. A united industrial working class working hand-in-hand with a liberal government would overcome bigotry. No leading figure in the wartime CIO sensed that the vast demographic changes and economic restructurings seemingly chronic in twentieth-century America might require redefinition of traditional notions of republican fairness and union aspiration. Deeply imbued with a sense of the tragic insofar as it related to class, they rarely sensed its presence in the area of race.[58]

In different ways both the strikes over wages and working conditions and the hate strikes troubled CIO leaders. In both cases, workers were not acting according to the script that the CIO's convention resolutions and the public statements by its top leaders had written. The CIO stood for responsible unionism, worker participation in industrial and public decision making, racial tolerance, and national harmony on the basis of orderly and democratic procedures. There was no room for angry wildcatters, disputatious local unionists, and Klan-inspired bigots.

Perplexity of the leadership over violations of the official version of good sense and good unionism reflected its increasing distance from the rank-and-file unionist. In part this separation was a natural result of the bureaucratization and enlargement of the scope of labor relations that came with the expansion of the labor movement. But during the war collective bargaining increasingly became a shadow ritual, with disputes sent to the NWLB. CIO leaders had to fight the tendency to see the government officials with whom they dealt as their primary constituency.[59]

The expansion of the industrial labor force and union security provisions brought into the unions thousands of new workers with little interest in or commitment to the labor movement. Turnover rates, especially in the early months of the war, were dizzying. How could a union leadership, whose vision of its role in American life was often forged in the embattled days of the 1910s, 1920s, and 1930s, relate to the problems of the young people, women, rural migrants, and other inexperienced workers whom they now represented?

Throughout the war the CIO leadership struggled to find ways to convey the federation's overall program to rank-and-file workers. The *CIO News* reached largely those in leadership positions. The IUCs proved poor vehicles for transmitting and rallying support for CIO positions. Local unions often failed to establish labor-management and antidiscrimination committees. CIO leaders frequently spoke of mobilizing masses of ordinary workers to pressure federal agencies such as the NWLB. "Their interest has to be stirred," Murray asserted. "The fact of the matter is," he said in the summer of 1944, "that the members of the National War Labor Board have not been hearing from the membership of the United Steelworkers of America."[60]

Rank-and-file opinion *was* hard to ascertain and interpret. On one hand, there were the strikes, over 500 in 1943 and 1944 in the Murray-led USWA and hundreds more in the UAW. But militancy and activism on both the shop floor and racial questions was episodic and unfocused, lacking coherent political content. The same workers who staged angry walkouts disapproved of wartime strikes. Workers continued to support FDR and the war effort; indeed, CIO members bought war bonds at a rate over 20 percent higher than the general public and showed little sympathy for any alternative politics.[61] In general, workers held to positions on a wide range of issues considerably to the right of their leaderships, that of race being the most dramatic example.[62]

There was, however, no large-scale rejection of wartime union leadership. In February 1945 the UAW, whose members were the most strike prone of any CIO affiliate, held a mail referendum on the No Strike Pledge. About 25 percent of the membership returned the postpaid ballots, with the pledge gaining a vote of support by a 65 percent margin. Even recision advocates admitted that the balloting was reasonably fair and that the vote was a legitimate reflection of rank-and-file opinion, although neither side had much to say about the revealing fact that almost 75 percent of the dynamic union's membership, legendary for its outspokenness, had not voted at all.[63]

More general public opinion polls also sent mixed messages. Overall they revealed significant divisions between union leaders and union members, although the patterns were often murky. Both leadership and rank and file clearly favored a broadly productionist view of labor's role in the war. Thus, for example, a February 1942 report revealed that both groups considered the prompt settlement of disputes and the boosting of production in order to win the war the most important question faced by organized labor. Leaders were two and a half times more likely to regard the battle against antilabor legislation as a top priority than were union members, while the latter were three times more concerned about the need to eliminate radicals and gangsters from union ranks.[64]

In questions relating to the activities and character of unions, rank-and-file members, to say nothing of working-class citizens more generally, revealed much skepticism. Two-thirds of union members polled opposed dues checkoffs. By a 65 percent margin, union members agreed that there should be federal laws against so-called featherbedding, a position anathema to their leaders who generally regarded the term as a loaded one that did not fairly describe labor's views on issues of staffing and job norms. Union members opposed the closed shop in a July 1945 poll by a three-to-two margin. Throughout the war, union members overwhelmingly supported the proposition that union affairs and finances should be subject to close regulation by government.[65]

Such findings, of course, were consistent with the theme of rank-and-file [?] [too early] rebellion against bureaucratic unionism. But even on questions that seemed to be of direct concern to themselves, workers gave responses that suggested that the questions relating to union governance and control were interpreted to refer to unions' general economic *power* and not to their treatment of ordinary members. When queried about the "Little Steel Formula," for example, only 38 percent of union members who said they had heard of it could give any sort of roughly correct definition, and among them a bare 50 percent believed that the government wage policies (against which Murray and other CIO officials raged so bitterly) should be changed to permit wage increases. Moreover, workers generally and union members more specifically came down heavily in favor of repression of strike activity. Throughout the war, union members voiced support for strike regulation by margins of two to one. In May 1943 an even greater proportion agreed that *advocacy* of a strike in a war plant should be made a crime.[66] At the end of May 1943 unionists in war plants responded positively to the question as to whether they would like to see their labor organizations change their way of handling things. The Gallup organization's question was ambiguous but no more so than the meaning of the ranks' response.[67]

WARTIME TRIBULATIONS

Throughout the war the CIO leadership was faced with the difficult task of balancing its members' interests with wartime production requirements. It had to steer through the complex and frustrating circuits of federal labor relations programs while attempting to meet the demands of an aggrieved membership. The wartime dispensation compromised the unions' traditional roles and penalized militant activism. Overall, however, industrial workers prospered. Union membership expanded dramatically, and industrial workers exhibited impressive loyalty to the CIO even in the face of wartime pressures and end-of-the-war dislocations.

At least temporarily the war delegitimated labor's militant idiom. On the eve of the labor upsurge of the 1930s John L. Lewis vowed to act as "captain of a mighty host" and frequently referred to the UMW as "the shock troops of the labor movement." The term *rank and file* derived directly from military usage. The aggressive term *strike* was apparently derived from rebellious seventeenth-century maritime workers' confrontations with overbearing officers. Labor songs and myths celebrated manly courage, physical bravery, and raw confrontation. As recently as mid-1941, auto, steel, wood, and other CIO workers had written epic new chapters in the saga of laborite struggle. To be for labor meant marching on picket lines, facing police truncheons, and fighting for workers' rights.[68]

The No Strike Pledge changed all that. There was an irony here: labor's participation in an actual war required that its leaders abandon the military paradigm. Young Americans were dying and Hitler was evil incarnate. The No Strike Pledge, said Philip Murray in 1944, was "sacred," and so it seemed to the vast majority of working people and union leaders.[69]

If the ethical imperative to foreswear the strike weapon were not enough, there loomed the practical consequences of strikes. From the earliest days of the war, opinion polls, congressional debates, and the press crackled with antilabor feeling. Congress buzzed with proposals to freeze wages, increase hours, and hamstring unions. Reviewing a spate of proposed restrictive laws in March 1942, Murray told his colleagues that "all of them [are] maliciously and premeditatively . . . designed to destroy you." Without self-limitation on job actions, organized labor, which escaped the war without most of these dire threats being implemented, could hardly have fared so well.[70]

The federal machinery created to deal with the overlapping problems of manpower, production, labor relations, and economic stabilization was complex and cumbersome. Organized labor's direct interests centered in the NWLB, created by presidential order on January 12, 1942, and throughout the war the board remained the CIO's primary forum in dealing with problems of union status, wages, shop conditions, and related matters.[71] At the same time, however, other wartime agencies significantly affected its interests. The War Manpower Commission, created in the spring of 1942, for example, wrestled endlessly with the problem of labor scarcity and issued rulings establishing the standard workday, limiting labor mobility, and otherwise affecting workers. The War Production Board, established in January 1942, sought to oversee conversion of production facilities from civilian to military use. It pressured unions to forgo established premium pay practices and to adopt production-based ("incentive") wage payment plans. The Office of War Mobilization, which FDR created in May 1943, was a kind of superagency, serving as an arbiter of last resort in disputes among government officials, military procurement chiefs, and civilian producers.

Workers most directly felt the hand of government in the area of "economic stabilization." This term referred to the effort to control inflation, a chronic wartime problem, through some combination of price fixing, wage controls, subsidies, and punishment of black marketeering and price gouging. The Office of Price Administration[72] initiated price, rent, and wage controls and implemented a system of rationing. Never granted definitive authority, however, it often ran afoul of congressional critics, who carved out specific areas, notably agricultural products, that were subject to only weak price regulation.

President Roosevelt himself sought with mixed success to exert leadership in the area of stabilization. Throughout 1942 he pressed Congress for legislation to implement a seven-point program, which featured increased taxes, price and wage controls, rationing, compulsory war bond purchases, and the discouragement of consumer credit. He urged and eventually sought to implement through executive order a salary cap of $25,000, largely a symbolic gesture. In October 1942, after Congress passed price stabilization legislation, Roosevelt created a separate body, the OES, and charged its director, former Supreme Court justice James F. Byrnes, with formulating policies that would stabilize prices and wages at levels prevailing during the first nine months of 1942. Byrnes soon announced that the NWLB would bear primary responsibility for wage stabilization.[73]

This mixture of congressional and administrative action against inflation generated as many problems as it solved. Congress had always shown special sensitivity to the demands of farmers for high price supports and for low-wage agricultural labor. Even the most sweeping administrative proclamations recognized the need to adjust prices and wages in special circumstances. Regional variations, unwillingness to freeze substandard wages, competitive pressures, problems of enforcement, and other factors made the stabilization ship chronically leaky. Even FDR's sweeping "Hold the Line" executive order of April 8, 1943, which enhanced the OES's authority, failed to end conflict over stabilization or to halt the upward creep of wages and prices, although in the final twenty-eight months of the war consumer prices rose at a rate less than one-fifth of that of the war's first two years.[74]

Within the crucial NWLB the CIO played the key role. Its affiliates were overwhelmingly engaged in war production, while a huge slice of the AFL's membership was in the construction trades, which fell outside the NWLB purview. Thus the key issues that the board debated and tried to resolve, notably wage stabilization and maintenance of membership, were of the most vital interest to the CIO. Its representatives were ardent participants in board deliberations and equally ardent defenders of the board as an instrument for the achievement of CIO goals. They were also active on the regional boards that the NWLB created early in 1943.[75]

The operations of the stabilization program at once enhanced the status and importance of the CIO and subjected it to divisive pressures. Matters of wage determination and forms of compensation were to be decided not at the collective bargaining table but in NWLB offices. In these sessions it was the CIO, not the affiliated unions, that served as the voice of industrial union members. Even, as was usually the case, when the CIO's regional board members were in fact on the payroll of one of its affiliates, they derived their status from their character as CIO, not UE or UAW, representatives. Board policies insisted on this arrangement. The very structure of its operations raised the status of the CIO as a corporate entity to an importance that the industrial union federation did not actually have according to its own constitution, operating traditions, or, at times, resources.[76]

Philip Murray himself embodied this enhanced status. In this respect, his dual role as leader of the USWA and of the CIO reinforced the sense that the CIO was the sole legitimate voice of industrial unionism. Basic steel, of course, was the most crucial of all wartime industries. In addition, Steelworkers produced ships, guns, munitions, and dozens of other military weapons and components. Moreover, the centrality of steel made it natural that when the NWLB addressed itself to the problems of wages in basic steel, as it did in the summer of 1942 and again throughout 1944, its actions set general wage patterns. Thus Murray enjoyed recognition as the voice of industrial unionism as well as direct access, along with his AFL counterpart, William Green, to stabilization authorities and to the president himself.

Status and access, however, came at a price. If Murray and his associates spoke for industrial labor, they were also held responsible for the behavior of industrial workers. At the same time, their members considered them accountable for the decisions that the NWLB handed down. Since those decisions increasingly derived from the board's character as an inflation-fighting agency, CIO leaders found themselves caught between the rock of NWLB priorities and the hard place of rank-and-file discontent. Noted UAW chief R. J. Thomas, "Collective bargaining did break down, and a feeling of blind exasperation developed" among workers.[77]

In itself, this situation was not unusual or even particularly regrettable. Even in peacetime, at any level of the labor movement above that of the intimate work group, leaders had to steer between rank-and-file sentiment – often itself complex and internally conflictual – and the realities of a given collective bargaining environment. Top leaders of unions were both elected officials and administrators of complex and multitendencied organizations. Even imperious leaders such as Lewis had to acknowledge these dilemmas.

Of course the war made these problems infinitely more acute. Labor representatives had to weigh the government's claims very heavily in their calculations. To be sure, an occasional militant voiced disdain for the claims of military necessity. "If I had brothers at the front who needed the 10 or 12 planes that were sacrificed [during a recent strike], I'd let them die," declared a UAW local leader in New York. But far more representative was

Murray's view, expressed in October 1942, that "everyone who works for a living has burned into his very soul the full appreciation of what this war is about," for civilization itself "is now being threatened by Hitler and his hordes." This basic understanding of the war as a working people's war ensured that governmental priorities carried enormous weight.[78]

The CIO's privileging of the government's agenda, however, exacted a steep price. If workers could not take advantage of conditions of full employment, when could they hope to make progress? In March of 1942, for example, the CIO succumbed to governmental pressure and urged its affiliates to voluntarily give up contractual provisions for "premium pay," which typically provided for time and a half for all Saturday work and double time for all Sunday work. Later in the war CIO unions agreed to explore favorably with their employers the negotiation or expansion of wage incentive plans as a means of encouraging greater productivity. Yet to their chagrin CIO leaders found that many AFL unions resisted government demands. In July 1942 the UAW's arch rival, the IAM, used this issue to defeat the Autoworkers in a key representation election among 17,000 Buffalo aircraft workers. Sneered an IAM leaflet, "The CIO sacrifices worker's [*sic*] pay, worker's overtime as the CIO's contribution to the war effort. Big of them, huh?"[79]

Stung, the UAW voted at its August convention to rescind its abandonment of premium pay unless all other unions complied, a pointed reference to the IAM. One government observer reported that high-ranking UAW officials had told him that "we should not be surprised if strikes started breaking out . . . to gain reinstatement of premium payment for Sundays and holidays." CIO leaders pressured FDR to order an end to all premium pay, which the president did in an executive order of September 9, 1942. By doing so, of course, they put themselves in the uncomfortable position of collaborating in lowering wages.[80]

Equally disputatious was the incentive wage situation. In industries such as electrical appliances workers willingly accepted the expansion of existing incentive pay programs. Such systems provided a means of increasing wages while boosting production and staying within the government's wage regulations. Autoworkers, however, believed that incentive pay plans were merely schemes to speed up work and fragment the workforce. The efforts of top UAW leaders to promote incentive plans triggered sharp conflicts among the rank and file, who eventually forced recision of UAW endorsement.[81]

Basic wage rates were, however, the central arena of contention. NWLB treatment of USWA claims in 1942 and again in extensive 1944 hearings set the basic patterns of wartime wage policy. Here, as in all its relationships with federal bodies during the war, CIO leaders sought to defend their members' interests while upholding the No Strike Pledge, a task that often proved impossible and sometimes led to union reprisals against rebellious members. "Where . . . efforts to end wartime strikes failed," boasted R. J. Thomas, "the unions refused to defend those who were guilty."[82]

The NWLB handed down its first major wage decision in steel on July 16, 1942. It grew out of wage disputes between the USWA and several Little Steel companies. The USWA had been successful in bringing such corporations as Republic, Bethlehem, and Youngstown Sheet and Tube to the collective bargaining table only during the period of defense production. In the process of organizing in the spring of 1941, steelworkers had struck several of these key steel, ship, and munitions producers, but once the issue of representation was settled in the USWA's favor, negotiations had become stalemated. After U.S. entry into the war, of course, the threat of an authorized strike disappeared, with the Steelworkers now turning to the NWLB for equitable resolution of their wage demands.

The board's tripartite structure insured that the Steelworkers would get ample hearing for their claims. At the same time, however, it meant that political and bureaucratic imperatives would shape the board's decision. Thus the passage of the Price Control Act on January 30, 1942, and the president's April 26 announcement of his anti-inflation program powerfully influenced NWLB deliberations. The board's public members, led by its chair, New York lawyer William Davis, regarded inflation fighting as a critical function. Thus while the board dutifully reviewed elaborate USWA materials that made the case for a 12.5 percent wage increase, the four public members, to say nothing of their employer counterparts, regarded any such figure as wildly inflationary.

The ultimate award pleased no one but established a formula for wage determination that served throughout the war as the basis for the NWLB's policies. Board experts calculated that from January 1, 1941, to May 1, 1942, the cost of living had increased by 15 percent. Since, however, workers in basic steel had received wage increases averaging 11.8 percent during that period, new wage increases would make up the difference between those wage gains and the rise in prices. In addition, though, the board observed that inflation tended to hit steelmaking communities disproportionately, thus justifying an additional wage increase of 2.3 percent to go with the 3.2 percent that represented the difference between 1941 wage increases and the cost of living. Thus the final award was for wage gains of 5.5 percent, far below the 12.5 percent that the USWA had urged.

This decision quickly gained the rubric Little Steel Formula and established the boundaries in which struggles over wages were conducted throughout the war. CIO representatives argued that the board used grossly inaccurate figures in calculating increases in the cost of living. Moreover, they pointed out, the board's choice of a base period beginning on January 1, 1941, stacked the deck against workers, for at that time depression-era levels of unemployment and living standards still prevailed. In response, NWLB statisticians pointed to inaccuracies in the USWA's figures. The four employer board members warned of catastrophic inflationary implications of even the Little Steel award. In truth, all parties shoehorned detailed data into arbitrary definitions of living standards, wage schedules, cost of living estimates, and the like. Indeed, the only thing formulaic about the Little Steel Formula was its role as a political formula that would provide each of the three parties with enough to convince their respective constituencies that they were fighting the good fight.[83]

President Roosevelt initially established the NWLB as a quid pro quo for the No Strike Pledge. Deprived of the strike weapon, organized labor needed a prestigious forum for the presentation of its interests and an authoritative mechanism for the resolution of disputes. In fact, the early operations of the NWLB up to and even including the promulgation of the Little Steel Formula had realized the expectations of most labor leaders. The four public members of the board enjoyed liberal and even prolabor reputations.[84] Maintenance-of-membership rulings were decidedly pro-union, and despite the results of the steel cases, Murray and his colleagues regarded the NWLB itself as a legitimate and generally responsive body.

As the war progressed, however, the role of the NWLB changed. The new controls legislation of October 1942 and the creation of the OES weakened the board's ability to respond to labor's claims. Increasingly, the NWLB seemed simply an instrument for limiting wages. When subsequent presidential and OES actions in the first half of 1943 reinforced this restrictive mission, the dilemma of its CIO supporters became more acute.

Indeed, it was this changing character of the NWLB that John L. Lewis and the UMW seized upon in justifying the coal strikes that erupted in April 1943. Failure to establish fair labor relations machinery, Lewis proclaimed, had produced "a policy . . . that fattens industry and starves labor, and then call[s] upon labor patriotically to starve." Three times in the spring and summer of 1943 Lewis led his soft-coal miners out amid almost hysterical public and governmental denunciation. The strike's settlement in November included wage provisions that breached the Little Steel Formula.[85]

The coal strikes highlighted the growing CIO dilemma. CIO leaders joined in the criticism of Lewis and remained committed to working within the government-established apparatus. Yet the evidence continued to mount that the NWLB had become primarily an anti-inflation agent. Meanwhile, workers expected the unions to which they paid dues to produce tangible benefits for them. Declared Murray in November 1944, his office was being "literally deluged" with resolutions from CIO unionists all over the country, "begging and pleading and praying for relief from these yokes of bondage" forged by restrictive wage policies and NWLB delays.[86]

In January 1944 the USWA formally petitioned the NWLB for approval of a 17 percent increase in basic wage rates, presenting voluminous studies to document deterioration of living conditions in the steel communities. Amid heavy administration and congressional pressure to curb inflation, the board began a protracted internal debate in an effort to balance the claims of frustrated workers, adamant employers, and disapproving stabilization officials. After a year of deliberations, the board reaffirmed the Little Steel Formula, denied the Steelworkers' request for general wage increases, and granted only improvements in shift differentials. With heavy sarcasm, one CIO representative conveyed "the appreciation of the CIO for the extreme patience of the public members in the long deliberation of this case."[87]

Throughout the last two years of the war, debate raged within the CIO over its relation to the government's stabilization policies. Responding to rank-and-file pressures, UAW and TWUA leaders argued for reconsideration of the No Strike Pledge. In June 1943, when Congress expressed its disapproval of the coal strikes by enacting antiunion legislation, the UAW-dominated Michigan State CIO Council passed a resolution favoring recision of the pledge. TWUA leaders advocated taking perverse advantage of the new Smith-Connally Act's restrictions on union autonomy as a means of protesting stabilization policies and NWLB complicity in them. The law imposed a thirty-day waiting period between the holding of a strike vote and an actual walkout. Why not, urged TWUA president Emil Rieve, flood the NLRB with strike ballots? Of course, workers would not actually hit the bricks, but their overwhelming endorsement of strike action would send a message. Added his colleague George Baldanzi, "We are not talking about strikes, we are talking about tactics."[88]

In the winter of 1944–45, with the NWLB logjammed, workers' disillusionment peaked again. Both the UAW and the TWUA executive boards passed resolutions calling for an end to the No Strike Pledge and for repudiation of the NWLB. Rieve argued that unless the NWLB and the OES broke free of the Little Steel Formula, workers would face the inevitable postwar recession economically disadvantaged and contemptuous of their unions' inability to protect their interests. The September 1944 UAW convention adopted a resolution providing for a referendum among UAW members on continuation of the pledge.[89]

As leader of the USWA and of the CIO, Murray shared in the frustration and anger of his fellow unionists. To be sure, he told his colleagues in 1944, he had access to all the top administration officials, including the president. Invariably, Roosevelt expressed concern for the plight of steelworkers reeling under the impact of wartime inflation. But "somehow or other after I leave there is always somebody around . . . who gets to talk to him later, and nothing happens." OES director James Byrnes and other top advisors believed that union leaders overstated the degree of rank-and-file dissidence while at the same time badgering them to suppress strikes and punish strike leaders. Complained Murray, the NWLB could not enforce its rulings "and so they call upon all of the resources of these international unions [and the CIO] to police these damnable and most obnoxious directives." The so-called wage stabilization program was acting only to impoverish workers. "The end," he vowed, "must come and it should come immediately."[90]

Murray's frustration with the government program extended beyond its wage policies. Certain aspects of wartime labor relations seemed to him to threaten the very existence of a free labor movement. Thus, for example, in January 1944 FDR endorsed national service legislation that would have overridden union security and seniority provisions and imposed sweeping criminal penalties on workers who did not obey government directives. Despite his ardent support for Roosevelt, Murray lashed out at the president, declaring that fascism is "actually jumping out at us."[91]

Also objectionable was a pattern of congressional favoritism toward the rival AFL. In 1943, for example, Congress adopted a measure that overrode NLRB rulings invalidating backdoor AFL contracts. These collusive arrangements trapped tens of thousands of workers in the federation's racially discriminatory and notoriously undemocratic metalworkers' unions and threatened to drive the USWA, Mine, Mill, and the Shipbuilding Workers out of booming war production facilities. The No Strike Pledge, Murray affirmed, was sacred, but "I am not going to supinely lay down on the flat of my back and let these people step on my face." If CIO unions were "going to be placed in jeopardy by acts of governmental agencies, I am going to fight, and I am going to ask my people to fight, for the right to live," he pledged.[92]

In the end, however, the CIO stuck closely to the No Strike Pledge and continued its commitment to the NWLB. The men leading the CIO believed that the war effort demanded uninterrupted production and that strikes broke faith with America's fighting men. They believed that their alliance with FDR was crucial if they were to resist the ferociously antilabor currents sweeping the country. They believed that alternative strategies, such as unleashing shop-floor militancy to compel more favorable governmental action, were unrealistic. Hillman, no longer an administration official, argued that workers would defend *their* strikes while condemning those of co-unionists. "Make up your mind," he advised, "that is the situation." Even Walter Reuther, a sharp critic of the pledge, acknowledged that "no labor movement can strike against the government . . . without literally crucifying itself."[93]

In March 1945, with the UAW and TWUA resolutions calling for CIO repudiation of the NWLB before him, Murray declared that "the most unprecedented actions have been taken by the President . . . to force recognition of labor . . . , all of which directly related themselves to the operations of the National War Labor Board." Added Bittner, "The no-strike pledge is the only weapon that organized labor has in this country during the war, and [if] you destroy your no-strike pledge . . . you have no weapon left." Speaking directly to UAW and TWUA representatives, Murray drove home the point: CIO departure from the NWLB would play into the hands of employers and greedy AFL rivals. "The wolves," Murray warned, "are just around the corner, and they have got a ravenous appetite and they are ready to eat you up."[94]

Throughout this extended debate within CIO circles, the most vehement supporters of the pledge were the Communists and their allies. These men and women often appeared to regard surrender to governmental directives as a positive good. The pro-Soviet leadership of some affiliates went well beyond the formal requirements of the No Strike Pledge to endorse national service legislation, speedups, incentive pay plans, and an extension of the pledge into the postwar period. In 1943 the Communist Party sent organizers into the soft-coal fields to encourage back-to-work sentiment among UMW members, and in 1944 Bridges ordered ILWU members to help break the CIO's lone sanctioned wartime strike, a walkout against NWLB-defying Montgomery Ward by the Wholesale and Retail Employees affiliate. Bridges proclaimed that the country needed more, not less, regimentation of labor. "Militancy," agreed Reid Robinson of Mine, Mill, meant only one thing: maximum production in the crusade against fascism.[95]

The most vocal critics of the No Strike Pledge and the CIO's overall policy of collaboration with the administration were the Trotskyists among its ranks and on its fringes. Numbering at most a few hundred, they included a high percentage of articulate veterans of the labor and ideological conflicts of the 1930s and 1940s. Seeing in the wartime strikes a potentially radical militancy, Trotskyists directed their most impassioned attacks on Communists and their allies but held the non-Communist CIO leaders to be little better. Declared journalist Art Preis, "They were quite prepared to sacrifice labor's basic rights." These men sought only "to fool the workers into believing than an appeal to the tiger's sense of 'justice' and 'righteousness' might get it to curb its appetite for fresh, raw meat."[96]

Although they exerted little influence in the CIO, Trotskyist observers did give voice to key issues that the CIO's course raised. Early in the war they applauded Lewis's defiance of the No Strike Pledge and the NWLB. *Labor Action*, a lively and well-informed leftist paper, hailed the Mineworkers' 1943 strikes and greeted the wide-front organizing efforts of the UMW's District 50 as an alternative to which workers betrayed by the AFL and CIO could turn. "The rapid growth of District 50 and its 'all inclusive' character," the paper declared, "has frightened the CIO leadership out of its wits."[97]

Lewis's break with the CIO and his defiance of the administration had a powerful appeal for industrial workers. CIO officials, contrasting their treatment in NWLB cases with Lewis's victory in the 1943 strikes, assailed the board for treating (in Van Bittner's words) "a God damn traitor better than they were going to treat" those who loyally upheld the pledge. Both AFL and CIO functionaries reported nervously on the appearance of Lewis's organizers throughout the East and Midwest. Warned UAW president R. J. Thomas, "Too many of our people are afraid of that guy." In May 1943 Philip Murray observed that only recently Lewis had boasted "that it was only a question of time until he succeeded in taking away from the . . . CIO some of its most important affiliates."[98]

The CIO fear of opportunistic rivals was not confined to concern about Lewis. AFL affiliates were often less willing than their rivals to sacrifice in the name of the war's larger purposes. The IAM continued to battle the UAW for aircraft workers, contrasting its hard-line position on wage incentives and premium pay with the CIO affiliate's more "statesmanlike" accommodation to the government's anti-inflation program. Moreover, "independent" unions such as the National Federation of Telephone Workers, not parties to the pledge and unrepresented on the NWLB, did resort to strikes and thus gained ground at the expense of CIO rivals.[99]

In the end, however, none of these challenges proved fatal. District 50 failed to fulfill either Lewis's ambitions for it or the fears of its rivals. By the end of the war it could claim a membership of only about 50,000. With regard to other rivals, far more disadvantageous to the CIO than any backlash against its pro-administration policies were the special rules favoring the AFL Metal Trades Department and the Boilermakers, adopted by Congress in 1943 (the Frey Amendment), that impeded CIO affiliates from challenging their rivals in the western metals and shipbuilding industries. Even so, despite the AFL's successes in the aircraft factories and shipyards, the UAW, the Marine and Shipbuilding Workers, and the CIO generally expanded enormously during the war. "Maintenance of membership provisions of the thousands of collective bargaining contracts approved by the War Labor Board," Murray reminded his colleagues in 1945, have "helped build this organization . . . from a paltry million and a half [in 1940] to its present proud . . . five million." [100]

As the war entered its final months, however, adherence to the No Strike Pledge became more problematic. With the surrender of Germany on May 7, 1945, and with Japan helpless before U.S. air assaults, the number and size of job actions mounted. For CIO leaders, however, the answer was not recision of the No Strike Pledge or defiance of the administration. It lay, rather, in remaining true to their wartime course while promoting a distinctive CIO program for the postwar world. Their successful creation of an effective political action committee [101] established the mechanism for the continuing exercise of influence. Declared Hillman, "It is the last mile of the race that will co[unt] . . . in the public mind." [102]

Even as the war ended, no one in the CIO paused to make up a balance sheet as to the conflict's impact on industrial workers and industrial unions. By most measures the CIO and most of its affiliates waxed fat during the war, and industrial workers enjoyed unprecedented regularity of employment and increased income. In 1942 the CIO laid out $300,000 for a Washington headquarters building, and by 1944 its annual budget had soared past the $1 million mark. By mid-1945 it could boast of cash reserves of over $1.5 million and contained just under 4 million members. Wartime peaks of the CIO's big three – the UAW, the USWA, and the UE – accounted for a combined total of almost 2.4 million members. Even more encouraging, however, was the performance of the TWUA, which counted over 200,000 members in the last year of the war, over 80,000 in southern locals.

The achievement of maintenance of membership and the expansion of rudimentary prewar systems of grievance arbitration gave the wartime CIO gains an institutional permanence and industrial unionism a degree of stability and legitimacy unparalleled in American history. These gains did much to allay apprehensions that organizing and bargaining success would evaporate as they had after World War I. In the words of Van Bittner, whose reputation as veteran of a thousand organizing campaigns gave his opinion special weight, "What a difference . . . from just a few years ago, so far as organizing workers and maintaining unions in America is concerned." [103]

Lewis and the radical critics of CIO policies depicted an industrial working class abandoned by a leadership intent on currying favor with corporate America and its political lackeys. In fact, however, within the confines of the No Strike Pledge and the labor relations system prevailing during the war, Murray and his colleagues fought hard for their members. They treated the NWLB and other federal agencies as battlegrounds, arguing the case for fairer wage treatment and highlighting the culpability of employers for the chronic unrest. At times, to be sure, they grew discouraged. Thus, in June 1944 Murray lamented that CIO efforts to change administration policies had "been confined . . . to . . . indulging ourselves in these platitudes . . . , talking to each other about the justice of our claims, going over to the White House" to little apparent effect.[104]

In fact, CIO representations did have an effect. CIO unions made important gains for their members during the war. In 1942 the War Manpower Commission accepted labor's view that the forty-eight hour week, with time-and-a-half pay over forty hours, constituted the wartime norm for defense workers. Overtime provisions boosted take-home pay by as much as 30 percent. NWLB members responded to Steelworkers' claims in behalf of low-wage workers, boosting substandard pay, and to reducing differentials between high- and low-wage workers, also part of the CIO agenda. Incentive pay plans, though anathema to many workers, were often laxly administered by employers more concerned with getting out the product than with enforcing strict performance norms. After all, recalled one electrical worker, the "companies didn't give a shit. They'd make a lot of money" through cost-plus government contracts anyway. The expansion of vacation benefits, which during the war were usually taken in the form of double-time pay, also contributed to the fact that industrial workers' take-home pay, despite heavier wartime taxes and mandatory war bond deductions, exceeded the rise in the cost of living. Between 1940 and 1944 the amount paid by employers to workers increased by over 100 percent, while monetary earnings in the manufacturing sector increased by two-thirds. Auto, steel, electrical, and other manufacturing workers boosted their real income by 20 to 27 percent, with workers in lower-wage sectors outstripping their higher-wage cohorts.[105]

Wartime conditions also enabled CIO unions to make progress on broad wage and bargaining issues as well. Thus, for example, the Steelworkers sought (and the NWLB approved) wage adjustments always on a cents-per-hour basis rather than on a percentage basis, compressing the notoriously wide differentials between common and skilled labor. Regional disparities through which steelworkers in Alabama were paid wages 20 percent below those of their counterparts in Pittsburgh and Chicago narrowed. Moreover, the NWLB's desire to deal with labor and management at the broadest level possible dovetailed with the CIO's commitment to industrywide bargaining and to its efforts to bring coherence to crazy-quilt patterns of wage determinations and job descriptions prevailing in much of the industrial core.[106]

Of course, as critics pointed out, gains in this direction came at the price of plant- and department-level shop-floor autonomy. Local activists often complained about the shifting upward of decision making. Thousands of wartime strikes involved the specific grievances of particular sections, departments, and work groups and had little connection to overall union strategies. Even before the war this tension between general-level CIO or international union ambitions for coherence, regularity, and rule making had run afoul of the CIO's other tradition of shop-floor activism. Thus, for example, the UAW's Walter Reuther remarked of the achievement of a provision providing for binding arbitration contained in the 1940 contract with GM, "We put up quite a battle to get it from the Company, and we put up quite a battle inside our organization to get the workers to accept it." Autoworkers, Reuther added proudly, were militant. "They believe in direct action," but UAW leaders, beset by work stoppages in violation of contractual provisions, believed that it was time "to grow up." Labor, the UAW vice-president pledged in 1942, had no designs on managerial prerogatives. Indeed, a strong and centralized union movement "can be a very important policing agency" in the effort to maintain regular production and shop-floor discipline.[107]

In truth, a good deal of the history of the CIO, war or no war, was bound up with the tension between local concerns and grievances, on one hand, and industrywide or national programs on the other. Was it possible for industrial unionism to combine the energy and enthusiasm associated with grassroots protest with the bureaucratic elaboration seemingly needed in dealings with the federal government and big corporations? Wartime conditions certainly raised these questions forcefully and established important precedents. At the same time, however, the war did not invent these issues. As elected leaders in a rapidly expanding labor federation, Murray and his cohorts believed that they had the workers' mandate to continue along the path that combined collaboration with the Roosevelt administration with sharp dissent from many of its particular decisions and practices. They were proud of their leadership both in the specific realm of the labor movement and in the mobilization of the American people in the fight against fascism. They believed that the wartime CIO was laying the basis for an industrial relations regime that, free of wartime distortions, would bring rising standards for their members and ever greater influence for the labor movement.[108]

Whether they were right, of course, depended on many things. Through 1945, work stoppages mounted in number and intensity. Congressional attacks on unions grew ever more strident. Newspapers and public opinion polls seemed unaware of workers' sacrifices and singled out unions for blame. Said director of organization Allan S. Haywood in July, "We are sitting on top of a powder keg." Workers, noted Murray, were becoming rebellious, but war's end was no time to give way to a spate of uncoordinated strikes. The CIO had to meet the postwar world with a broad program advocating full employment, income security, fiscal and social welfare reform, and the expansion of the scope of collective bargaining to include increased worker representation in corporate decision making. "To my mind," he declared, "it is the biggest single undertaking that we have ever attempted in the history of the C.I.O." [109]

WARTIME POLITICS

With Sidney Hillman in the vanguard, CIO leaders increasingly focused on the political arena for the resolution of wartime dilemmas. Sporadic efforts to mobilize workers to apply direct pressure on wartime stabilization agencies went nowhere. But the establishment in 1943 of a political action committee was designed to insure Roosevelt's reelection, roll back a mounting conservative electoral tide, and mobilize war-frustrated members into a militant crusade that would carry the progressive agenda into the postwar period.

Frustration with government policies often led to angry rhetoric on the part of CIO leaders. "I say fight, and I mean fight," Murray exploded when confronted with egregious governmental favoritism shown to AFL rivals. But the angry words led to CIO endorsement of strike action on only one occasion. [110] Some affiliates did test the No Strike Pledge. In February 1945, for example, President Emil Rieve withdrew TWUA representatives from regional labor boards, as southern locals protested the NWLB's inability to force employers to adhere to its decisions and its wage directives. Piedmontwide strike votes in March demonstrated massive support for a textile walkout, but before one could actually begin, the OES permitted the NWLB to grant both basic wage increases and fringe benefit improvements. [111]

However, it was not strikes that CIO leaders had in mind when they spoke of militancy. Rather, laborite aggressiveness now took on an intensely political meaning. New Deal reforms, success in bringing central core employers under contract, and the growth of grievance arbitration meant that, war or no war, strikes and picket lines were becoming less important than lawyers' briefs and economists' projections. Outside the Communist Party few in the CIO favored extending the No Strike Pledge into the postwar period, but clearly influence over legislation, public policy, and the judicial environment would count for more than traditional kinds of activism. During the war, CIO leaders embraced the political turn, directly by seeking to activate their members to effect changes in stabilization policies and more generally by creating innovative political action vehicles.

In the former task they enjoyed little success. No one in the CIO ever devised any coherent plan for bringing rank-and-file opinion to bear against obnoxious NWLB or OPM policies. Murray, presumably the one man who could make things happen in the CIO, was forced to admit as late as mid-1944 that "the members of the National War Labor Board have not been hearing from the membership of the United Steel Workers of America." The CIO leadership found no way of disabusing mobilization officials of their notion that labor chiefs were exaggerating shop-floor rebelliousness so as to loosen up wage restraint policies. The USWA, the UE, the UAW, and the national CIO allocated $100,000 to publicize their case against prevailing wage stabilization policies through billboards, newspaper advertisements, and radio spots, but CIO leaders were never able to send the message to Washington that the physical mobilization of thousands of workers might have conveyed.[112]

Actually, despite Murray's frequent complaints about workers' unwillingness to march against Washington, even his interest in mass mobilization was sporadic. None of the CIO wartime conventions directly addressed the problem, nor did Murray ever name an action committee to promote and coordinate grassroots activities. In reality, other kinds of rank-and-file mobilization took priority. The strike waves of 1943 and 1944 sent union representatives scurrying about, coaxing or forcing local unionists back to work and placating federal authorities who threatened to revoke maintenance-of-membership clauses if they failed. The typical CIO union, said Murray in January 1944, had become "a fire department." Indeed, "a very substantial portion . . . of the monies collected by each of the international organizations [in dues payments] is now being used to enforce the directives of the National War Labor Board . . . which we do not believe in."[113]

Routine activities also claimed the time and energy of union activists and representatives. The creation in 1943 by the NWLB of twelve regional labor boards, the appointment of labor assistants to the War Production Board's Industry Divisions, and the activities of other federal agencies drew heavily on the CIO's thin reserves of experienced functionaries. As of late 1944 almost 500 CIO members sat on Office of Price Administration advisory bodies, 2,000 were active in local rationing boards, and a full tally of CIO members serving on plant-level transportation committees "would," observed Murray, "round up a total of many thousands." War Production Board-sponsored labor-management production committees, CIO War Relief committees, and Red Cross, war bond, and other plant and community programs involved thousands of man-hours. True, noted Murray in his 1944 report to the CIO convention, "a great many CIO members have developed their abilities and grown in stature," but the combined demands of governmental agencies and the unions' own bureaucratic needs spread the talent pool thin.[114]

Moreover, this public-spirited and patriotic activity drew especially on the industrial union body's most energetic and idealistic people. Pro-Soviet unions such as the UE and the ILWU, whose local activists had often led in progressive organizing campaigns, were now deeply involved in community and war-support activities. Working in cooperation with employers to expand production, encourage war bond sales, and conduct blood drives helped to expand production and speed U.S. aid to the beleaguered Soviets, goals superior, in their view, to mobilizing dissidents to confront the NWLB. Harry Bridges articulated these themes in his inimitable idiom: "We can't dilly-dally around, and we can't make it fuzzy," he instructed. As for the ILWU, its representatives "have quit being business agents first, they are business agents second, they are speedup men first."[115]

The CIO, however, was more successful in creating a strong political arm during the war. Indeed, wartime conditions made politics the most logical and attractive arena for the furtherance of the CIO project. Mobilization of protest against the NWLB might backfire, weakening a friendly, if flawed, agency. But a campaign to reelect Franklin Roosevelt and to put liberals in Congress was one that union officials, staff representatives, and rank-and-file workers could embrace with enthusiasm.

Establishing a successful political action arm was no easy matter, however. Politically active in the 1930s, the CIO had not permanently institutionalized its political operations. Its vehicle in the first half-decade was LNPL, which was not formally part of the CIO apparatus. By the time of Lewis's endorsement of Wendell Willkie in October 1940, however, it had become a casualty of the Hillman-Lewis conflict.[116]

Since the inception of the CIO, debate over industrial unionism's relationship to the two-party system had been incessant. Leftists in Michigan, New Jersey, New York, and elsewhere called for a repudiation of the corrupt and southern-dominated Democrats. In New York, CIO unionists in 1936 had created the American Labor Party, formed by leaders such as Hillman and Dubinsky as a means of marshaling progressive forces and demonstrating their weight and influence. New York's laws permitted a candidate's name to appear under more than one party designation. Thus, American Labor Party voters could still support progressive Democrats but have their totals separately registered. In the long run, some observers speculated, the American Labor Party might provide the nucleus for a true third party having as its constituency base the mass unions that had emerged or been revivified in the 1930s. In Michigan, UAW activists looked with envy across the border to Ontario where in 1943 the socialist Co-operative Commonwealth Federation nearly captured the industrial province's premiership.[117]

In reality, however, there was little possibility of nationwide labor party development. During the war all but a small leftist fringe supported Roosevelt. Advocates of third party activity could draw no comfort from public opinion polls, which revealed virtually no support. The most cohesive and articulate block of nominal radicals in the CIO, the Communists, opposed any initiatives that might weaken the administration. They worked actively against even proposals that sought to couple support for the president with efforts to elect independent laborite progressives. Indeed, in 1943 the CPUSA disbanded, becoming a "political association" that was to work only within the established political spectrum.[118]

Thus, with some of the more divisive aspects of political action in abeyance during the war, the path was clear to create a permanent political apparatus. In the 1942 elections the Republicans had gained forty-four House and nine Senate seats, mostly at the expense of northern liberals. "When you come to examine the result of the recent election," lamented one CIO union leader, "you will find the entire element we cleaned out . . . in 1932 and 1936 are back stronger than ever."[119]

Liberal losses had immediate legislative repercussions. The soft-coal strikes, which began on April 1, 1943, fueled antilabor sentiment and swiftly resulted in antiunion legislation. In mid-June Congress passed the War Labor Disputes Act (Smith-Connally Act), which mandated a thirty-day waiting period between the holding of a strike vote and a walkout, provided for government takeover of military production plants threatened by labor disputes, barred strikes and strike advocacy in federally run facilities, and limited political activities of labor unions. Actually the law would have little immediate effect, since, after all, the CIO remained committed to the No Strike Pledge. But unionists were bitter at having their loyal productionism rewarded with such a stinging public rebuke. Murray squelched talk of repudiating the pledge, at one point threatening to resign if the Executive Board took this step. He pointed out that President Roosevelt's veto had kept faith with labor, and he urged political mobilization as the CIO's primary means of punishing its congressional tormentors.[120]

Indeed, CIO men increasingly pinned their hopes on the president as the defender of liberal values. His reelection in 1944 was imperative but, thought Hillman and other laborites, distressingly problematic. One of the prime reasons for progressive defeat in 1942, they believed, was the low voter turnout. Low registration and poor voter turnout were prevalent in industrial districts. Hillman, though eased out of the administration in 1942, remained a passionate Roosevelt supporter and even before the passage of the Smith-Connally Act began attempting to move the industrial union federation into a more active political posture so as to counter these trends.[121]

In July 1943 these multiple lines of interest in more assertive political action came together at a special CIO Executive Board meeting, called in the wake of the passage of the Smith-Connally Act. In the previous November Murray had appointed Brophy, CIO legislative director Nathan Cowan, and Research Director J. Raymond Walsh as a committee to make recommendations concerning the CIO's political operations. Their December 30 report had called for the creation in all international and local CIO unions of legislative committees and for the eventual establishment of a permanent CIO national political arm. The Brophy-Cowan-Walsh report, whose major recommendations the CIO Executive Board approved in January and February 1943, did not rule out the possibility of the eventual formation of a labor party but stressed instead the need to gear up for the crucial 1944 presidential election.[122]

At the post-Smith-Connally meeting, Murray had secured unanimous support for the creation of the PAC, a body to be headed by Hillman as chair and UAW president R. J. Thomas as treasurer. The other committee members were Van Bittner, Sherman Dalrymple, president of the URW, Albert Fitzgerald, president of the UE, and David McDonald, secretary-treasurer of the USWA.[123]

The PAC both departed from and reinforced traditional laborite patterns of political action. Unlike the AFL's political operations, which were largely confined to publicizing to members the labor records of candidates and to insider lobbying on issues of direct institutional interest, the CIO body would be an open, public operation, soliciting support from non-CIO unionists and from the progressive public. Moreover, while it would be nominally nonpartisan, everyone associated with it knew that it would function in close cooperation with the Roosevelt and liberal elements in the Democratic Party. Indeed, through early 1943 Hillman had coordinated his work in establishing a CIO political arm with the president and his advisors. Moreover, CIO political operatives would actively participate in intraparty platform, policy, and candidate selection processes, pressing the broad agenda of the industrial union movement. This was to be a concerted effort to inject the CIO's ideological and programmatic agenda directly into the Democratic Party's bloodstream.

Still, PAC stopped short of formally aligning itself with the Democratic Party. In some states this diffidence was more theoretical than actual. In Michigan, CIO and UAW operatives began steeling the weak Democratic Party with a powerful and decisive laborite presence. In Minnesota, CIO people, led by UE Communists and their allies, were decisive in engineering a merger of the weak Democratic Party and the robust but erratic Farmer-Labor Party. Everywhere PAC operatives collaborated with Democratic Party leaders.

Nonetheless PAC remained broadly within traditional American boundaries for laborite politics. It did not run candidates and remained formally nonpartisan, even supporting a handful of Republicans and a few nonpartisan hopefuls. It rejected third party possibilities, whatever the lingering hopes of some CIO radicals. "Ours is an educational movement. . . . We have no desire to organize another political party," Hillman reassured the 1943 convention delegates.[124]

Throughout the latter half of 1943 and through 1944, under Hillman's energetic leadership CIO-PAC mobilized industrial unionists. Smith-Connally made direct union financial contributions in general elections illegal, but the law apparently did not apply to primaries. Moreover, "non-partisan" registration and education campaigns, aimed at working-class voters, PAC operatives were convinced, would inevitably increase the liberal electorate.[125]

With strike levels rising and with growing frustration over stabilization policies, the CIO leadership saw PAC as the primary means of mobilizing the membership. Thus Hillman and his aides sought to make PAC a means through which patriotic support of the war effort, the reelection of Roosevelt, and the reaffirmation of the CIO's progressive goals would be fused. The same activities that produced Democratic turnouts would rekindle rank-and-file activism, refocusing it from strike-producing shop-floor confrontation to edifying civic action. "The greatest crusade ever seen in America should take place," said PAC member Van Bittner, "a crusade comparable to our organizing crusades." Political action, he pledged, was "a rededication of our lives to the fundamental objectives of the New Deal."[126]

To this end, national PAC urged affiliated unions to create local PAC bodies. Early in 1944, for example, the USWA assigned fourteen of its international representatives to PAC work. These men visited local unions, persuaded public officials to conduct in-plant registration drives, and worked through local union leaders and shop stewards to establish local PACs. These local bodies then began to distribute literature, arrange for candidate forums, seek media coverage, and generally alert the membership to the importance of the forthcoming election. Locals in a given city or county would coordinate activities through IUCs, which also were to establish PAC arms. Declared the Steelworkers' political action manifesto, "The gigantic sleeping political strength of our membership must be awakened."[127]

In the spring primaries PAC boasted of impressive victories in congressional contests. It claimed credit for the defeat or withdrawal of several notoriously antiunion politicians, notably Texas representative Martin Dies. In general, however, PAC concentrated on registration and voter turnout. Local PACs contacted nonvoting members. They worked with candidate and Democratic Party organizations to distribute literature, facilitate registration, and bring voters to the polls. In 1943 and 1944 national PAC churned out some 85 million pieces of literature for distribution to union members and their families.[128]

These activities were costly, of course. Within four months of PAC's founding, the CIO and the affiliated unions had pledged nearly $700,000. In addition, each union carried on its own PAC activities. But Hillman and his associates hoped that as the PAC campaign worked its way into the locals, hundreds of thousands of ordinary union members would welcome the opportunity to participate by contributing a dollar for PAC. Thus, fund raising would serve to bring the PAC message into the union members' homes, solidifying grassroots support for Roosevelt and reforging workers' bonds with the CIO project.[129]

PAC literature urged a recommitment of workers' energy and enthusiasm in behalf of liberal goals. Patriotic themes suffused its increasingly sophisticated pamphlets and posters. The message, wrote publicity director Joseph Gaer, consisted of "One Dozen Simple Propositions," which included the affirmations "Democracy is good," "Earning and spending are political matters," "A big vote is a good vote," and "Education for Political Action requires organization." Declared research director J. Raymond Walsh, the labor movement had a special obligation "to help protect the nation against the forces of evil and reaction."[130]

The graphics that accompanied the PAC campaign vividly depicted these themes. Keynoting the CIO effort was a pamphlet entitled *This Is Your America*, which presented the people and places of the republic in a benign soft focus. Scenes of tranquil countrysides opened and closed the publication. Glimpses of mighty industrial complexes alternated with views of rippling fields of grain and mammoth dams. But, the publication declared, true Americans loved America not for her scenery or wealth or power but, rather, for her people. Apart from a small inset of Sidney Hillman, the pamphlet contained only photographs of American workers and their families. A textile worker tended her spindles. A resolute millwright fastened bolts to a giant machine. A miner, his begrimed faced split into a broad smile, headed home after work. A young African American woman, her welder's mask flipped up, beamed optimistically. Workers relaxed around the potbellied stove; a family, its prewar coupe in prominent focus, picnicked in the park. Workers voted in a union meeting.[131]

The text was brief. It enlisted those depicted, as well as the reader, in the crusade for social justice and common decency. It rejected racial and ethnic prejudice. It aligned the CIO with the struggle to "build a better America and a better world." It closed with a civics lesson: "Find out all you can about the people who run for President and the Congress. Find out which ones are for the workers and for the common people. Then vote for the right people."[132]

The illustrations for such publications as *Every Worker a Voter, The People's Program for 1944*, and *A Woman's Guide to Political Action* mixed traditional and innovative genres. The front cover of *Political Action Primer for All Americans* featured a bold drawing of a muscular worker's arm stretching toward the Capitol, grasping a pencil and marking a ballot, thus linking a traditional figure of the worker's physical power with the newer emphasis on civic action. In the interior graphics, sturdy but hardly superhuman workers and their genial families rang doorbells, stuffed envelopes, and cast ballots.[133]

Every Worker a Voter employed a lighter, even comic approach. Engagingly drawn figures illustrated the link between political action and the preservation of hard-won shop-floor rights and benefits. Artist "Ajay" depicted the ordinary man, clad not in overalls and hardhat but in a modest business suit and sporting a friendly smile, seeking a decent life. Comic renderings of a satanic figure impeding voter registration and of Hitler, Tojo, and a black-coated figure labeled "Reaction" aimed at ridicule rather than revulsion. The pamphlet did contain several renderings of distinctively working-class figures, one a woebegone debtor victimized by wartime inflation, the other an overall-clad worker sporting a jaunty CIO cap and brandishing newly grown political action biceps. Even this depiction of potency, however, was more comic than awe inspiring. At the end of the pamphlet, a smoking cannon labeled "political action," manned by the determined, suit-coated citizen, forces the surrender of the ludicrous, goosestepping Axis triumvirate. Clearly, labor's cause now required far less brawn and truncheon-defying courage, calling instead for the ordinary skills and resolve of the alert citizen.[134]

Sophisticated PAC materials relating to gender and race appealed to women and blacks to join in a civic crusade. In *A Woman's Guide to Political Action* both text and drawings championed the rights of women. PAC rejected the notion that after the war, women should be relegated to purely domestic pursuits. Both as homemakers and as wage earners, the pamphlet held, women had particular reasons for supporting the CIO-FDR effort. Only a government-promoted full-employment economy could provide the good jobs that working women needed. Only New Deal-like programs for child and health care could ease women's family burdens. Only well-enforced price controls and government subsidy programs could fight the wartime inflation that ravaged family budgets. "Since the inception of our Republic," declared Murray, "women have been on the forefront of every progressive movement. . . . Without their participation and help our great international unions of today would not have been realized." [135]

The pamphlet's illustrations drove home the theme. Its one drawing of the domestic scene showed an enslaved housewife literally chained via a nose ring to a kitchen sink piled high with dirty dishes. In contrast, dignified drawings depicted women wielding rivet guns and enjoying workplace comradeship. With women expected to comprise over 50 percent of the 1944 electorate, the artist rendered sober sketches of women citizens toting up politicians' voting records and spreading the PAC message. A line drawing showed a woman's feet casually crushing a swastika-patterned serpent. The back panel featured a studious young woman examining PAC's publications, obviously preparing to play her role in the liberal crusade.[136]

PAC's main publication relating to African Americans was the only one that featured photographs rather than drawings. *The Negro in 1944* was a remarkable thirty-page publication printed on scarce glossy paper. It depicted African Americans in all walks of life, invariably in attractive and edifying settings, many of them integrated. Black medical students gathered on the steps of Howard University. Black servicemen and -women, unionists, and schoolchildren fought, marched, and played. Photographs highlighted integrated social settings. Pictures of Marian Anderson, General Benjamin Davis, and other African American celebrities were included, and several shots showed black executives and officials in conference with FDR and other leaders. But the emphasis was on the ordinary soldier, sailor, worker, and housewife. In a day when the major media included blacks only in exotic and/or pathological contexts, *The Negro in 1944* was a remarkable and even pathbreaking effort.[137]

PAC's sophisticated appeals to women and blacks, along with its more generic materials, conveyed both overt and implicit messages. Most obviously, of course, they sought to mobilize workers, their families, and allies into a broad political coalition to reelect FDR and lay the groundwork for a revitalized postwar New Deal. Their very presence highlighted the CIO's new emphasis on political action, and their high quality of writing and production drove home the seriousness of this industrial union effort.

More implicitly, they reflected the CIO's general movement away from raw, class-conscious politics toward a more pluralistic conception of labor's goals. Wartime conditions encouraged, even demanded, stress on the theme of national unity. True, PAC literature often attacked corporate looters and political reactionaries, but even these materials shifted away from explicitly class appeals toward a view of workers as participants in a broad civic coalition. In a war for the world, prejudices against women and blacks were intolerable. The cure for the problems of a democracy was more democracy – elimination of poll taxes, more expeditious voter registration, more effort to get out the vote, an expanding economy, and a potent union movement that would supply employment at good wages for every American. Thus, the image of the worker as a brawny superman rarely appeared in the PAC literature, while that of the ordinary citizen took center stage.[138]

Despite the energy, innovation, and enthusiasm of the PAC crusade, however, its immediate results were ambiguous at best and even downright disappointing. Few workers shared PAC's sense of civic crusade, and many believed that a union had no more right to attempt to influence political behavior than did an employer or a church. Despite the efforts of Hillman and his brigades of PAC staff operatives, the dollar drive that was to fill PAC war chests and renew the CIO mission yielded only 5 percent of the CIO's political action budget, with the rest supplied by the unions' central offices and a national citizens PAC that Hillman created to mobilize support among nonlabor sympathizers.[139]

Among the broad public, PAC's civic-minded appeal attracted little positive support. Conservatives attacked PAC as a Communist-dominated attempt to cram a collectivist agenda down the throat of the body politic. Republican strategists charged that powerful union chieftains had dictated FDR's choice of a running mate, requiring him to "clear it with Sidney [Hillman]." If the CIO supported a candidate, pollsters for the Gallup organization asked a representative sample of Americans in May 1944, would you be more inclined to vote for him? Ten percent responded positively, 53 percent negatively; among Democrats, 14 percent regarded a CIO endorsement as a positive recommendation, while three times as many held the opposite view.[140]

It was, of course, the results on November 7 that CIO and PAC leaders cared most about. Here the news was mixed. With the reelection of Roosevelt they could legitimately claim vindication and victory. True, Roosevelt's popular vote shrank from 1940's total of 27.244 million to 25.602 million and his margin of victory from 5 million to 3.5 million. But the Democratic Party held its own in the Senate and gained twenty House seats along with governorships of several large states. Murray was quick to claim a major share of the credit for PAC: "It did the greatest job of registering and voting that has ever been done in the history of the United States of America." "November 7," declared Hillman, "was our Battle of Britain, our Stalingrad."[141]

Indeed, some important voting indicators seemed to support these claims. Thus, for example, the counties in which PAC was most active bucked the national trend by increasing Roosevelt's 1944 margins over those of 1940. Moreover, as Murray observed, the total voter participation of 47.7 million confounded experts who forecast more modest totals. Gains in Congress and the state houses seemingly checked the reactionary tide that had been rolling in since the 1938 congressional elections.[142]

Yet other evidence suggested that the PAC effort had fallen far short of the ambitions of CIO leaders. There was little difference in turnout or voting patterns between a group of districts with heavy CIO memberships and PAC activity and districts in which PAC had not been active. In seventeen of the twenty-eight states in which PAC activity had been greatest, there was little evidence that the CIO's efforts had had any effect. Indeed, some analysts observed that Democratic candidates in districts where PAC had not been active actually registered slightly higher margins of support than did those where PAC concentrated its efforts. Throughout the latter stages of the campaign and in its aftermath, journalists, politicians, and CIO officials pointed to myriad problems in implementing the PAC strategy. After the tally, PAC advisor former congressman Thomas Amlie concluded that "on the Congressional level the various campaigns . . . have been conducted in a wholly ineffectual manner."[143]

In the end the PAC effort was hardly the kind of crusade that CIO leaders envisaged. Certainly it seemed to do little to hinder strike action, which continued at a disturbingly high rate throughout the electoral season. While workers awarded Roosevelt their votes, there was little evidence in the election returns that the CIO-PAC vision of worker-citizens united across racial and gender lines in support of an unambiguously liberal program was shared by the masses of CIO members. Hillman told the victory-savoring 1944 CIO convention delegates that their commitment to PAC must be continued and intensified. "Our generation," he intoned, "is confronted with a challenge and opportunity unparalleled in all history," that of making the liberal and humane features of the People's Program the nation's central agenda in the postwar years. But in view of the mixed signals that working-class America had sent in response to the PAC effort in 1944 and in its continued testing of the No Strike Pledge, the realization of this vision would remain as problematic in the future as it had been in the past.[144]

In November 1944 David McDonald, Murray's personal aide and general CIO and USWA factotum, told the delegates to the Chicago convention of the CIO about his recent War Department-sponsored tour of the European battlefields. A handsome, gregarious man of forty-two, McDonald had been hired in 1923 as Murray's secretary. The son of a steelworker, he had toiled only briefly in the mills. After completing high school, he studied bookkeeping, stenography, and office procedures. He enrolled in the Carnegie Institute drama program, hoping to translate his fleshy good looks into a career in films, but instead he became Murray's assistant in the UMW. In 1936 Lewis appointed him secretary-treasurer of SWOC, and he retained this post when the USWA succeeded SWOC in 1942.[145]

Other Steelworker officials distrusted the handsome McDonald. He often appeared vainglorious and deceitful, masking his lack of contact with rank-and-file workers and his shaky grasp of conditions in the mills with boastful orations and alcohol-enhanced bonhomie. But he was loyal to Murray, and in the rough-and-tumble of the UMW and the USWA, loyalty was a prime virtue. During the war, McDonald served as Murray's trouble-shooter, errand boy, and mouthpiece. He bullied or cajoled wildcat strikers, sweet-talked government officials and corporate executives, and appeared endlessly at rallies, bond drives, broadcasts, and press conferences to proclaim the Steelworkers' determination to set record production totals despite the unfair treatment meted out by the NWLB and the OES.

In this capacity as Murray's fill-in, McDonald found himself first in London, then with Allied forces in Normandy in July and August. Normally a bombastic and self-aggrandizing speaker, McDonald spoke simply and movingly about his experiences. In London a German rocket had killed 157 people in the apartment house adjacent to his hotel. During the tour through France McDonald and the others came frequently under German artillery fire.

The enormity and poignancy of what he witnessed stirred McDonald. The strength of the German defenses on the Normandy beaches astonished him. Here were acres of land mines, reinforced cannon and machine gun emplacements, miles of barbed wire, and thousands of tank traps. "It is absolutely unbelievable that men could fight through these things," he told his audience.

The magnitude of the Allied operations was awesome. Thousands of ships filled the English Channel. Huge drydocks and port facilities worked around the clock. Vehicle assembly pools, storage depots, and repair and refitting works had turned northern France into a vast industrial complex. Disabled trucks, tanks, and gun caissons littered the roads. Columns of prisoners, many of them teenagers, shuffled back from the battlefront.

The human dimension affected him powerfully. "We saw perfectly heartbreaking sights," he related: a French woman, soaked to the skin, with frightened children clinging to her skirts, wheeling her few earthly possessions, seeking shelter; a horribly wounded American soldier waiting at a field hospital to have his arm amputated; two army captains, minutes after coming off the line, eyes blazing, "filthy dirty with dirt in their fingernails where they had been clawing into the ground." McDonald and his colleagues attempted to talk to these men, but the soldiers only said, "'We killed them bastards – we killed them bastards,' with all the hatred they could muster."[146]

Reflecting on the experience McDonald remarked, "If the purpose of that trip was to stoke up the home-front war effort, it certainly worked with me." He redoubled his efforts to keep workers on the job. Vignettes of the suffering and heroism he had witnessed, he believed, lent him eloquence as he "raced all over the country to make sure there were no wildcat strikes or anything else that might slow down the flow of war goods."[147]

In effect, since Pearl Harbor the CIO had been operating on the fundamental premise evident in McDonald's report. The war was a stupendous undertaking, in both its physical magnitude and its political and moral consequences. It overshadowed everything. During the war, union leaders did many things they did not like doing. They foreswore the strike weapon. They suppressed worker activism and disciplined strikers. They cooled their heels as bureaucrats decided the wages and working conditions of union members. The war dictated their course, and their consciousness of its terrible suffering and its insatiable appetites caused them to yield to its imperatives, patiently, if not gladly.

War brought not only sacrifice and restraint, however. It brought expanding memberships and bulging treasuries, thicker pay envelopes and regular employment, and prestige and influence to the CIO leadership. It created the conditions that both required and permitted the establishment of a permanent political action arm. True, the war resurrected the prestige of American's corporate establishment. At the same time, however, it stabilized a troubled industrial union project and gave its new leadership reason to believe that organized labor's wartime record, along with its war-created numerical, financial, and institutional power, had for the first time in American history brought bona fide representatives of ordinary working people permanent entrée into the nation's decision-making councils.

Akron rubber workers celebrate the victorious end of their strike against Goodyear, March 1936, in the fledgling CIO's first major test. (ALUAWSU)

Sit-down strikers, Flint, Michigan, winter 1937. (ALUAWSU)

Basking in FDR's election victory, CIO leaders chart their next step in a November 1936 meeting. Shown here are (clockwise, at the table) Charles Howard, Sidney Hillman, John L. Lewis, Philip Murray, and David Dubinsky. (LMDC)

Chicago police count the casualties after their assault on unarmed steelworkers and their families, Memorial Day 1937. Paramount News suppressed newsreel film of the incident on the grounds that its public exhibition "might very well incite local riots." (ALUAWSU)

By 1938, the breach between the AFL and the CIO was wider than the aisle that here separates Lewis from the bespectacled William Green. (ALUAWSU)

In the 1930s, John L. Lewis stood alone among labor leaders and attained a public presence surpassed only by that of FDR himself. These Labor Day 1938 paraders in Toledo, Ohio, a CIO stronghold, spoke for thousands of industrial workers. (ALUAWSU)

Transition: Philip Murray succeeds John L. Lewis at the November 1940 CIO convention in Atlantic City, in the wake of FDR's third term victory. (PSULA)

Despite the efforts of pickets like those shown here, Ford resisted the UAW until the spring of 1941. Only during the military buildup of 1940–41 did the CIO complete its organization of workers in auto, steel, rubber, and other central core industries. (ALUAWSU)

California national guardsmen break the UAW picket line in the North American Aviation strike, Inglewood, California, June 1941. (*Los Angeles Times*; ALUAWSU)

On the second anniversary of the attack on Pearl Harbor, these ILWU members take a few minutes off to give blood and buy war bonds. (ILWU)

This World War II steelworkers' convention exhibit graphically depicts the CIO's commitment to victory in the people's war against fascism. (PSULA)

CIO PAC campaign billboard, Atlanta, fall 1944. For CIO members, FDR embodied both antifascism and hope for a better world. (SLA-GSU)

Eleanor Roosevelt and Philip Murray at the 1944 CIO convention in Chicago. Throughout its history, the CIO relied heavily on its association with liberal Democrats, to the dismay of third party advocates. (GMMA)

The CIO's wartime focus on political action downplayed the traditional image of the brawny worker and portrayed workers as civic activists. The 1944 pamphlet "Every Worker a Voter" made this shift clear. (Joseph Gaer, *The First Round* [New York: Duell, Sloan and Pearce, 1944])

In "A Woman's Guide to Political Action," the PAC shelved the CIO's usual domestic ideology, contrasting the drudgery of housework with the comradeship and purpose of wartime factory employment. (Joseph Gaer, *The First Round* [New York: Duell, Sloan and Pearce, 1944])

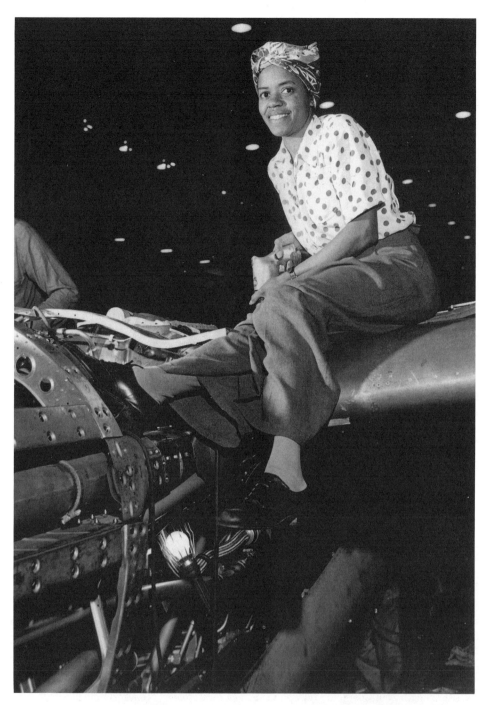

World War II gave women and African Americans an unprecedented opportunity to work, although temporarily in the case of many women, in high-wage industrial employment. This California aircraft worker was among over 300,000 black women toiling in war production. (ALUAWSU)

These packinghouse workers were among the 2 million CIO members on strike in 1945–46. (SLA-GSU)

Walter Reuther celebrates his narrow victory in the race for UAW president, March 27, 1946. Reuther's election encouraged anti-Communists within the CIO. (GMMA)

SHALL THESE MEN TELL YOU WHAT TO DO?

GEORGE BALDANZI of New York, on the right, is vice-president of the TWUA (CIO), and is vice-chairman of the drive in Southern Textile mills. On the left is a man called SMITH (probably Smithkowlski), of San Francisco, California, who is the big shot chairman of the drive in the State of North Carolina. Look at them . . . take a good look, emplyees of the Eastman mill . . . do you think they want to help you, and YOU?

Can't You Just See Yourself Crushed Under the Thumbs of These Fellows if You Vote C. I. O.?

Let's Vote 'Em Out of Eastman, Ga.

No tactic was too despicable, as this handbill attests, in the effort to thwart CIO attempts to organize southern workers after World War II. (SLA-GSU)

Recruitment of African American workers, most of whom toiled in dirty and unhealthy conditions, was critical for the CIO. These men are pouring castings for engine blocks at a Buick foundry in the 1930s. (ALUAWSU)

George L.-P. Weaver (right), secretary of the CIO's Committee to Abolish Racial Discrimination, and Assistant Director of Research and Education Kermit Eby testify in favor of fair employment practice legislation, 1947. (GMMA)

This giant telegram was the contribution of the American Communications Association, a small CIO affiliate, to the futile effort to defeat antiunion legislation in the spring of 1947. (GMMA)

Gadsden, Alabama, rubber workers line up to reaffirm their CIO affiliation in one of the elections required by the Taft-Hartley Act in 1947. Even after the heyday of rank-and-file unionism, CIO unions retained the loyalty of their members. (SLA-GSU)

Secretary of State George C. Marshall, surrounded by (left to right) James Carey, UAW chief Walter Reuther, ACWA president Jacob Potofsky, and Philip Murray, after addressing a responsive CIO convention in Boston, October 1947. Conflict over the emerging Marshall Plan played a crucial role in the showdown between the CIO's pro-Soviet and anti-Communist elements in 1948–49. (GMMA)

A PAC activist campaigns for Truman in Wheeling, West Virginia, 1948. The CIO often had trouble generating rank-and-file enthusiasm for its political agenda. (GMMA)

Efforts on the part of CIO unions such as the UAW to raid ousted pro–Soviet affiliates were often bitterly resisted by members of the pariah unions, as these East Moline, Illinois, farm equipment workers attest in a 1952 confrontation. (ALUAWSU)

Shop stewards, URW Local 12, Gadsden, Alabama, 1950. As CIO contracts became more formalized, union power receded from the shop floor and shop stewards increasingly played secondary roles in contract administration. (SLA-GSU)

In the 1950s, the CIO sought to become an integral part of community life. This Detroit baseball team was sponsored by URW Local 154. (ALUAWSU)

CIO president Walter Reuther, with general counsel Arthur Goldberg seated to his left, demanding repeal of the Taft-Hartley Act, January 1954. (ALUAWSU)

Leaders of the late CIO. Seated, left to right: Executive Vice-President John V. Riffe, President Walter Reuther, and Secretary-Treasurer James B. Carey. Standing, left to right: ACWA vice-president Frank Rosenblum, Oil Workers' president O. A. Knight, Rubber Workers' president L. S. Buckmaster, TWUA chief Emil Reeve, ACWA president Jacob Potofsky, CWA president Joseph Beirne, TWU leader Michael Quill, and the Steelworkers' David J. McDonald. The shade of Philip Murray oversees. (ALUAWSU)

These UAW women gather in November 1955 to assert their rights in an industrial union movement that was often obtuse in matters of gender. (ALUAWSU)

Walter Reuther looks happier than George Meany as the two leaders celebrate the merger of the AFL and the CIO in December 1955, but Reuther's hopes for a renewed surge of organizing were unrealistic. (ALUAWSU)

8 After the War

At the CIO's first postwar convention, held in Atlantic City in November 1946, Philip Murray glowed with pride at industrial unionism's achievements. The assembled delegates, he declared, constituted "the greatest parliamentary body of workers anywhere in the universe." The CIO's success during World War II and its turbulent aftermath, he affirmed, "demonstrates the fitness of our organization to arise to the needs of any occasion."[1]

Murray had reason for pride. The CIO survived and even flourished in the face of difficulties reminiscent of those that had destroyed wartime gains a generation earlier. In 1945–46 the industrial unions born in the 1930s waged effective strikes against powerful corporations. If they could not truthfully claim unambiguous victory, they could, and did, contrast their success in this round of industrial conflict with the devastation and disaster of an earlier time. The CIO was here to stay.

In other arenas, however, optimism was less justified. In 1946 and 1947 the CIO's political and legislative arms proved inadequate to the tasks of expanding the welfare state and preventing antilabor legislation. The limits to the industrial union project were also evident in 1946 when the CIO's efforts to move massively into the South quickly bogged down. These setbacks revealed starkly the continuing potency of the opposition to industrial unionism among employers and their allies and the drastically changed political and social climate prevailing in postwar America. Perhaps most ominous, however, was the extent to which these postwar battles – the relatively successful strikes no less than the legislative and organizational failures – revealed the CIO's internal divisions and exposed the institutional uncertainty that lay at the heart of the industrial union body itself.

POSTWAR STRIKES

The great strike wave of 1945–46 had four critical results for the CIO. The very fact of the survival of the new unions was the most important. Other results were less positive, however. Inability to achieve the industry-wide and even economywide bargaining structures that CIO leaders favored was a major disappointment. Likewise, the inability of labor and liberal forces to commit the federal government to playing a broad, coordinative role in the shift from wartime to peacetime economic life frustrated industrial unionists. Finally, the timing, conduct, and resolution of the postwar strikes revealed the extent to which the CIO remained less a unified center of industrial union than a congeries of disputatious labor unions.

Throughout the summer and fall a wave of strikes marked the transition from war to peace. Cancellation of military orders and cutbacks in the workweek quickly brought unemployment and sharp reductions in take-home pay. Joblessness and fears of postwar recession did not lead to defensiveness, however, but rather to renewed militancy. After V-J Day in August, strike totals that were already high veered sharply upward. In September, for example, the number of idle man-days stood at 4.3 million, more than double the rising August figure.[2]

In the final four and a half months of 1945 the nation lost over 28 million man-days to strikes, over double the number for 1943 and 22 percent higher than all of 1941, the previous recorded peak. In November the 180,000 UAW members struck GM. In January a half-million steelworkers joined the procession, as did over 200,000 electrical workers and 150,000 CIO packinghouse workers. During the period from July 1945 to March 1946 over two-thirds of all strikers were members of CIO unions.[3]

Amid the industrial conflict, CIO leaders sought to build new structures of industrial accord. Thus Philip Murray and rising UAW leader Walter Reuther advanced redefinitions of industrial unionism's role in the modern economy. Murray's vision rested upon hopes for a smooth transition from war to peace and on business-labor collaboration, with the federal government providing general oversight even as its fiscal and social policies promoted a full-employment economy. Reuther's outlook involved a willingness to exploit worker discontent and to use public opinion to force corporate America to submit to greater accountability to labor and to the public. In either case, reconversion, it seemed, provided industrial unionists with the opportunity to push the CIO project beyond its existing boundaries.[4]

Despite these hopes, however, the war's end brought familiar scenes of mass strike action, frantic and slap-dash efforts at governmental intervention, and jerry-built compromise solutions. Warring elements in the federal government struggled to control the administration's industrial relations policies. Core corporations fought to limit organized labor's power. Angry workers rejected elaborate proposals to confine the fight for upward wage adjustments to bureaucratic procedures. Thus, the strikes of 1945–46 were a running confrontation that revealed as much discord within the CIO as it did antagonism toward employers.[5]

Critical aspects of this round of conflict *were* different, however. These walkouts were on the whole peaceful. The steel strike, which ultimately affected 750,000 steel and fabricating workers, featured few mass demonstrations or violent confrontations. Steelmakers made little effort to recruit strikebreakers or to smash picket lines. The same was true in the auto industry, as disciplined ranks of autoworkers shut down the world's largest corporation, which for its part made no effort to oust the UAW or recruit strikebreakers.

There were exceptions. The UE and the Packinghouse Workers faced more intense opposition and more readily invoked 1930s-style militancy. Newspapers regularly featured dramatic scenes of picket line clashes in industries as diverse as longshoring and motion pictures. Workers in Rochester, New York, Oakland, California, Stamford, Connecticut, and Lancaster, Pennsylvania, mobilized communitywide support for strikes against union-bashing employers. Indeed, some business leaders and radical publicists did perceive a renewal of the root-and-branch struggles of the past.[6] But on the whole the 1945–46 strikes contrasted sharply with previous defining moments such as 1877, 1886, 1919, 1934, and 1937 in the history of America's industrial relations.

In part the relatively strife-free character of the postwar strikes reflected the revolution in labor law of the 1930s and World War II. Public policy now endorsed collective bargaining, and the federal government was in the hands of allies of organized labor. The general public had no stomach for a return to naked repression.[7]

More important, however, was the support that rank-and-file workers awarded to their unions. In previous episodes of industrial conflict in basic industry, repression and union-busting exploited the uncertain response of workers. Ethnic divisions, differing assessments of the chances of eventual union victory, and competing loyalties rooted in differing work experience often made the efforts of management to discredit or undermine a fledgling union effective. In hundreds of battles over industrial unionism stretching back to the nineteenth century the key issue had been union recognition. Now, by virtue of the successful struggles of the 1930s and 1940s, as reinforced with effective legal machinery, *that* issue was not in doubt, at least in the core regions of CIO strength.

Even though recognition was not a fundamental issue, much was at stake. The nature of permanent structures of collective bargaining in basic industry remained to be established. At what level would the critical bargaining take place – the plant, the firm, the industry, or perhaps some superindustry stratum? What was negotiable under the rubric *collective*

bargaining? Work processes? Investment decisions? Profit-and-loss calculations? How far did federal protections for unions and federal requirements
that the parties bargain in good faith extend? What was the nature of workers' rights to their jobs? How would peacetime collective bargaining work
on the shop floor, where in mass production industry it had little history?
What, exactly, did contractual unionism entail? For the CIO, the distinctive
importance of the strikes of 1945–46 lay in the partial answers they provided to these questions.

Wages stood at the heart of the postwar CIO bargaining agenda. During
the war, basic wage rates had eroded. Only the opportunities for overtime,
upgrading, and regular employment had enabled workers to maintain income. Victory meant abrupt cancellations of factory orders. In the year after
the end of the war fully one-quarter of all civilian workers experienced unemployment. The CIO publication *Economic Outlook* observed that the
sudden spring 1945 shutdown of the huge Willow Run bomber plant, operated by Ford in exurban Detroit, meant that "nobody wants the more
than 20,000 human beings who go with the plant" or the 80,000 others in
plants that supplied the bomber factory. Between V-E Day and October
1945 take-home pay plummeted by 23 percent.

To the Keynesians who increasingly articulated economic policy for the
CIO, these conditions were dangerous, unnecessary, and easily remediable.
They were dangerous because the lesson learned during the depression,
namely that mass purchasing power was the critical factor in sustaining
economic growth, was being ignored. They were unnecessary because the
nation had enormous unmet needs that these experienced and dedicated
workers could provide. They were avoidable because corporate America
could afford substantial basic wage increases – up to 38 percent by one CIO
calculation – without any need for inflation-promoting price increases.[8]

Restoring purchasing power and keeping faith with workers who had had
to bear the brunt of wartime stabilization policies, Murray declared, was
"perhaps the most important question confronting the nation today." In
the fall the industrial union federation spent over $100,000 on a publicity
campaign designed to convince the country of the justice of its position.
Nationwide radio programs broadcast the CIO message.[9]

CIO collective bargaining goals were part of a broader agenda. Fearing a
return to the conditions of the 1930s, industrial unionists urged the government to stimulate economic growth and to expand security, housing, and
welfare programs. Thus in July the Executive Board enthusiastically endorsed legislation that would require the government to maintain full employment.[10] In addition the CIO leadership promoted the concept of the

guaranteed annual wage as a collective bargaining counterpart to such legislation. As conceived of in CIO circles, the guaranteed annual wage constituted a kind of social contract with leading corporations in cooperation with the federal government. A broad commitment to employment security at high wage levels would require negotiation at the highest corporate and union levels and would constitute an overarching charter of labor based on industrywide and perhaps even economywide arrangements. According to TWUA vice-president George Baldanzi, "We all agree . . . that this whole problem of annual and full employment should be pretty much the whole drive of the C.I.O. going into this next year." [11]

Murray and most other top CIO leaders believed that this ambitious program could be accomplished without strikes. Said Bittner, mass strikes were "the last thing that anybody that has the welfare of the labor movement and the welfare of the country at heart would want." Declared the *CIO News* in April, "It's Industrial Peace for the Postwar Period." The wartime CIO had demonstrated both its toughness and its patriotism. Could there be any doubt as to its vital role in the achievement of a democratic and progressive workplace rule of law? [12]

In mid-1945 there was some reason for optimism over the attainment of these goals. Influential business spokesmen seemed eager to enter high-level accords with labor leaders. Thus, for example, in March 1945 Murray, along with his AFL counterpart William Green, signed a "Charter" with Eric Johnston, president of the United States Chamber of Commerce. By the terms of this document, "business" endorsed collective bargaining and foreswore intentions to overturn the Wagner Act. "Labor" affirmed managerial prerogatives in the workplace and continued the No Strike Pledge. In the end, however, most employers repudiated this charter, and the gathering strike wave quickly revealed workers' opposition to extension of the pledge; but as late as August Murray continued to work with Green, Johnston, and federal officials to salvage some sort of top-level accord. [13]

For much of the summer and early fall of 1945 Murray and his colleagues fluctuated between hopes of a relatively strike-free transition and a growing realization that events were spinning out of control. The industrial union body never promulgated a manifesto outlining its course in the reconversion period, nor were there authoritative planning and coordinating sessions among the influential affiliates. Murray himself functioned both as head of the CIO and chief of the USWA, at once the advocate of labor-management collaboration and the elected leader of a union seething with discontent. Even as he attempted to enlist the government in support of the CIO wage agenda, strikes erupted with increasing frequency. In August and

September alone, for example, autoworkers launched at least ninety unauthorized walkouts in Detroit area plants, including one at Kelsey-Hayes, a parts manufacturer, which soon idled over 50,000 Ford workers as well as the 4,500 Kelsey-Hayes strikers.[14]

The last legitimate hope of avoiding a strike-torn reconversion was a labor-management conference, arranged by the administration to convene on November 5. Truman hoped that a high-level gathering of labor leaders and employers could create mechanisms to process industrial disputes and facilitate a smooth transition into peacetime production. In a radio message on October 29 he expressed confidence that "if labor and management will approach each other, with the realization that they have a common goal, and with the determination to compose their differences in their own long range interest, it will not be long before we have put industrial strife behind us."[15]

Murray welcomed such a top-level conference. He wanted nothing more than to have the CIO accepted as the authoritative spokesman for industrial workers and to deal on an equal basis with equally authoritative employers. Murray believed that such an arrangement would provide workers with democratic representation and industry with disciplined and responsible workers. It was time for the American economy to acquire a governing structure consonant with its great size, scope, and accomplishments. With an active and friendly government managing demand through progressive tax and fiscal policies and pursuing an energetic program of public housing, social welfare, and labor market support, a broad corporate-labor relationship was the logical next step. Thus when Truman asserted that labor and management "have a common goal" and urged them to "compose their differences in their own long range interest," he had no more avid backer than Philip Murray.[16]

In convening the conference Truman stressed its voluntaristic character. He urged the corporate and labor elite to establish "some impartial machinery for reaching decisions on the basis of proven facts and realities." The American people, he warned, "never expected anything like the amount of strife which has been threatened." Resorting to the passive voice, he insisted that "a way must be found of resolving . . . [labor-management] differences without stopping production."[17]

From the start, however, the conference served more as a forum for contending parties than a catalyst for consensus. Management delegates sought revision of the Wagner Act and protection of employers from unfair union practices. They vowed to defend managerial prerogatives and to resist union efforts to address questions of labor process. Moreover, these corporate leaders flatly rejected companywide, much less industrywide, patterns of bargaining, dimming Truman's and Murray's hopes for labor-management harmony.[18]

Murray faced a difficult and, as it turned out, impossible task. He had somehow to win the conference to the CIO's high-wage position, retain the federal government's role as a price control agent, and appease militant unionists, many of whom were on strike or preparing to hit the bricks. At an early meeting of the conference's executive committee, the CIO head introduced a resolution to commit the body to the CIO's wage increase agenda, arguing that this was the only way to prevent a full-fledged strike wave. Only this course, Murray argued, would permit the conference to function as the president apparently envisioned, that is, as a means of achieving industrial peace during the difficult postwar transition.[19]

Murray's only hope of success, and it was a slim one, was that Truman would back his approach. During the war Senator Truman had been a leading critic of corporate abuses, and important members of the administration shared the CIO view that wage increases were both needed and grantable without price rises. Indeed, Murray based his resolution directly on remarks by the president on October 30 that appeared to endorse this view. But Truman's aides quickly distanced the administration from any explicit endorsement of the CIO position. Employers, of course, opposed it root and branch. Particularly devastating, however, was the hostile response of William Green and John L. Lewis, who rejected his call for ongoing federal regulation of collective bargaining. Indeed, Lewis charged that "what Mr. Murray and the C.I.O. are asking for is a corporate state." "This Conference," reported an administration observer early on, "can be wrecked by the bitterness attendant to a floor debate of wage policy." Insofar as the administration hoped to use the gathering as a means of short-circuiting the growing strike wave, he was right.[20]

The *New York Times* had sent its top labor reporter, the legendary Louis Stark, to cover the conference proceedings in Washington, D.C. But the epicenter of postwar industrial relations quickly shifted from the Department of Labor building in Washington to Detroit, where the UAW girded for battle against GM. Relegating the increasingly arcane conference discussions to the inside pages, the *Times* followed the intricate auto negotiations on page one. "The 'Big Three' of the automotive industry," declared reporter Walter Ruch, are "locked in a battle of such economic importance as to permit hardly any overstatement." George Romney, president of the Automobile Manufacturers of America, intoned that never since the Civil War had the country "faced a more anxious winter than in the critical days ahead."[21]

Throughout the latter stages of the war, UAW members had grown increasingly hostile to the NWLB and to the No Strike Pledge. Thousands greeted V-E and V-J Days with spontaneous walkouts, in effect canceling the pledge. The UAW executive board soon endorsed this grassroots rebellion, and dozens of strikes, many officially sanctioned by the union, erupted.[22]

Conflict in the auto industry, however, was not merely a case of workers and union against management. The UAW itself roiled with controversy involving personal ambitions, bargaining strategies, ideological disputes, and the union's long-range political agenda. President R. J. Thomas, a delegate to the Washington conference, supported Murray's efforts to find a strike-free means of achieving wage increases and a permanent basis for labor-management cooperation. Unauthorized strikes, he believed, undermined the CIO's position at the conference and invited repression and counterattack. "Discipline and order within the ranks of labor must be regained," he told local unionists early in September, because "if the present unruly condition is permitted to increase, the Union will be destroyed." UAW members, however, defied Thomas and continued to challenge both the UAW leadership and their employers.[23]

These outbursts quickly became tangled in UAW politics. The director of the union's GM Department, thirty-eight-year-old Walter Reuther, saw in autoworker activism an opportunity to advance a broad personal and social agenda. A talented and often inspiring activist, Reuther had been a shrewd critic of the No Strike Pledge and now welcomed the ending of wartime restrictions. Said his brother Victor, his closest ally and advisor, "It is time to debunk the notion that labor can meet in parlays with government and management [and,] by some miracle, fashion a compromise that will keep all parties happy and contented." The time had come for a showdown with corporate America, as well as for Reuther's own bid for leadership in the UAW and, more generally, in the emerging postwar political economic order.[24]

To the Reuthers, the flux of the reconversion period offered a unique opportunity to rewrite the rules governing the management of the American economy and the political and social order that it undergirded. War had in an important sense "socialized" the economy, for it had revealed the extent to which the public interest permeated the modern economic system. The events of the 1930s and 1940s precluded any return to some golden age of laissez-faire capitalism. But what would the new rules be? Who would devise them? If American history was any guide, business interests would quickly seize the initiative.

Now, for the first time, the country had a powerful industrial union movement. It was uniquely positioned to speak for working people and to link up with other progressive groups. How, however, could labor's shop-floor strength be translated into social and political power? To Murray and Thomas the angry militancy of rank-and-file workers was a liability, since it complicated their efforts to make broad-based arrangements with the government and corporate leaders. To the Reuthers, however, that very militancy held the key to labor's advance to the next level of influence in American life. Workers' just wage demands could force a rewriting of the social contract. When a corporation such as GM claimed that it could not afford to pay its workers more money, Walter Reuther declared, it should be required to open its books, to prove its case.[25]

Reuther's call for scrutiny of the corporation's records implied a consultative right for unions. He also held that if the company's profit statements were of legitimate concern to the union, other aspects of its operations, such as production and investment decisions, should also be subject to union scrutiny. Thus Reuther's call for public examination of the corporation's books also linked the union to its broader public. *Workers'* wages and living standards were part of the public record, and UAW members, Reuther claimed, recognized their responsibility to keep wages in line with productivity and legitimate profits. His demand that GM open its books was a claim on behalf of the American people that this giant corporation be held similarly accountable.[26]

Reuther's endorsement of militant activism and his urging of a broad-front attack on GM reverberated loudly within the contentious corridors of the UAW. Reuther believed that under Thomas the UAW had lacked vision and that Communists exerted too much influence. An articulate anti-Communist, Reuther saw the UAW and the CIO as the critical components in a labor-led liberal transcendence of the New Deal dispensation. He did not reject the notion of eventual labor-management-government coordination of economic structures and decision making. He was, however, firmly convinced that the continued irresponsibility of big business, the vacillation of the Truman administration, and, above all, the legitimate restiveness of workers mandated a season of conflict before the industrial unions could achieve their legitimate place in an enlightened new order. As head of the UAW's critical GM Department, he was uniquely positioned to implement his agenda.[27]

The GM strike, while officially endorsed by the UAW executive board and ritually supported by Murray and other CIO leaders, divided both the autoworkers' union and the CIO. Inside the UAW, Reuther's opponents believed that his belligerent posture and his demands that GM open its books needlessly provoked the corporation and protracted the strike. Indeed, UAW leaders charged with conducting negotiations with the other two leading auto companies, Ford and Chrysler, claimed that the demands of the GM strike had weakened their own bargaining positions. Since the beleaguered UAW depended heavily on dues payments and strike assessments from its employed members, Reuther insisted that strike action against Chrysler and Ford be rejected at virtually all cost. Seizing on the union's vulnerability, the two auto companies bargained aggressively, with Ford eventually gaining important management rights provisions that weakened the union's presence on the shop floor.[28]

The GM strike underlined the lack of unity within the CIO also. Despite Executive Board resolutions and frequent public statements, the CIO never established any general bargaining strategy. Early in December, at the instigation of UE leaders, Murray invited them and Reuther to Pittsburgh to discuss common approaches. The Communist-oriented UE leadership, who also bargained with GM, was deeply suspicious of Reuther and eager to forestall a confrontation with GM pending developments involving its main bargaining partners, Westinghouse and General Electric. They embraced Murray's more cautious approach and from the start were critical of Reuther and the UAW for "jumping the gun" against GM. "It [was and] is [still] true," reflected Murray after the strikes, "that there is no coordinated policy developed in the CIO, as to what the over-all program should be with respect to wages."[29]

After the start of the GM strike Murray still tried to assert at least a semblance of central CIO direction. He also sought to mediate between the UAW and GM, hoping that a quick settlement would leave intact his program for a relatively smooth transitional period and would refurbish the image of the CIO as the authoritative voice of industrial unionism. He urged Reuther and GM representatives "to get down into collective bargaining meetings and slug it out there without bringing news men in and sticking there until they reached an agreement." He advised them to "confine themselves solely to the more practical aspects of collective bargaining" and to stop playing to the press and the public.[30]

This advice went unheeded, and Murray soon had to face his own strike in steel. Indeed, by December Murray and most other CIO leaders had become reconciled to the likelihood of major walkouts in steel, electrical appliances, farm equipment, meatpacking, and other heavy industries. Most CIO unions had armed their leaders with strike votes, the Steelworkers' coming at the end of November. With 60,000 Oil Workers already out and with the GM strike running at full tilt, mid-January loomed as the strike deadline for steel and the other major sectors. As these strikes broke out or loomed on the horizon, CIO leaders had to tread a narrow line in their relations with the government. With the failure of general exhortation and of the Labor-Management Conference, the president now turned to industry-specific strike-delaying proposals aimed at keeping workers off the picket lines. CIO leaders, including Murray and Reuther, while denouncing Truman's more far-reaching proposals, continued to attempt to use the administration's initiatives to advance their claims.

On December 3 the president sent a special message to Congress calling for antistrike legislation. In industries affecting the public interest, his proposal went, the secretary of labor would certify to the president those disputes in which a strike or lockout threatened. The parties were thereby prohibited from any work stoppage for a period of thirty days. During this time a presidential fact-finding board would gather evidence and issue nonbinding recommendations. Truman believed "that in most cases, both sides would accept the recommendations," as had usually been the case with similar boards serving the railroad industry under the terms of the Railway Labor Act of 1926.[31]

Murray and other CIO leaders quickly rejected this initiative. It was one thing to agree voluntarily to a No Strike Pledge during wartime and quite another for Congress to force men to stay at work. Not even the odious Smith-Connally Act had taken this step. Shortly after the president's message, Murray took to the airwaves to express fundamental CIO opposition to "this type of compulsory legislation." Although public opinion polls showed overwhelming support for antistrike legislation – one poll showed that 70 percent of union members favored the president's proposal – Congress failed to respond.[32]

CIO unionists, however, were far more amenable when Truman appointed fact-finding boards without the antistrike and cooling-off provisions. Even before his December 3 message the president named a board to investigate the oil strike. When Congress rejected his request for coercive legislation, he appointed similar bodies, first in the GM strike, then in the steel and meatpacking walkouts. Noncoercive investigation, CIO leaders reasoned, could only bolster their cause. They were confident that objective analysis would support the case for hefty wage increases without corresponding price boosts. Moreover, since 1933, federal involvement had been beneficial to unions, and there was no reason to doubt that it would be so now. Thus, from the start the CIO unions cooperated with panels investigating the auto strike and the impending walkouts in steel, meatpacking, and farm equipment.[33]

Truman's efforts, however, failed to bring about a quick auto settlement or to prevent the other strikes. A December 8 conference of UAW GM locals defiantly rejected Truman's back-to-work appeal, while later in the month GM officials walked out on the auto fact-finding board when it sought access to corporation books. In mid-January 400,000 CIO electrical and meatpacking workers walked off their jobs. On the twenty-first, after having earlier acceded to the president's request for a delay, Murray led a half-million steelworkers out. During that month the nation lost 19.75 million man-days to strikes, while in February the figure jumped to 23 million. This represented a staggering 3 percent of available working time, and these walkouts constituted the most massive sustained strike episode in American history. By February 1 over a quarter of the CIO's entire membership was on strike.[34]

After such a lengthy buildup, the actual walkouts were something of an anticlimax. It soon became clear that these would not be classic picket line conflicts reminiscent of Homestead, Ludlow, Flint, and South Chicago. No major corporation hired replacement workers or attempted to breach picket lines. For their part, Reuther, Murray, and the UE leadership rejected the demands of militants for mass mobilization and provocative confrontation. The USWA headquarters in Pittsburgh, for example, issued a twenty-six-point set of instructions to district directors and local unions. It demanded scrupulous observance of all local picketing ordinances and advised local unions to make arrangements with management to admit service and maintenance workers into the plant. It warned against picket line drinking, provocation of the police, and inflammatory statements to the press. "Any necessary demonstrations or mass meetings," it advised, "shall be [held] under the supervision of the [international] Union Representative or District Director exclusively."[35]

Even so, the scope and strength of even orderly strike conduct was impressive. Radical journalist Art Preis recorded the scene along the Monongahela River near Pittsburgh. "For the past three days," he reported on January 23, "these plants have sprawled lifeless." The giant open hearths emitted no flames or smoke, but Preis vividly recorded the "friendly fires, meant to warm and comfort pickets in the long, freezing vigil of the near-zero night" that dotted the industrial landscape. The employers kept a constant queue of putative maintenance men and watchmen filtering through the union checkpoints, presumably to suggest business as usual. But union pickets stopped them one by one, carefully inspecting passes, constantly reinforcing the point that they controlled entrance to the mills.[36]

As tightly as the international unions controlled the individual strikes, there was no overall CIO coordination of this massive movement. Indeed, as the strikes ground on, the leader of the three main CIO unions in the metal and durable goods core of the economy, the UAW, the USWA, and the UE, saw his counterparts as competitors rather than allies. Each man sought to outdo the others and made decisions in response to federal fact-finding initiatives and corporate counterproposals solely on the basis of their direct impact on his own union.

The UE and the UAW both bargained with GM, since the electrical union represented some 30,000 workers at GM's Frigidaire Appliance Division. Clearly the behavior of one union held critical implications for the bargaining posture of the other. UE leaders were convinced that Reuther's anti–Communist enthusiasms were driving his strategy, and they resented his failure to consult them in precipitating the GM strike. They tied themselves to Murray and what they termed the "official" CIO policy of holding off strike action. For his part Reuther charged that *they* were undercutting the legitimate demands of the autoworkers by failing to join the original strike. When on February 9 the UE settled with GM for a wage increase of 18.5 cents – a penny lower than the increase recommended on January 10 by the president's auto panel in the GM strike – Reutherites were furious. Declared brother Victor, UE leaders had "met secretly with General Motors executives" and executed "a double-cross . . . , a sellout of the 150,000 GM auto workers." UE officers angrily denied these charges, asserting that "the record is clear: UE-CIO stood ready at all times to negotiate jointly, strike jointly and settle jointly," but these overtures were "repeatedly declined by the head of the UAW-GM Department," Walter Reuther.[37]

Murray carefully separated the Steelworkers' interests from those of the UAW. As early as September USWA secretary-treasurer David McDonald warned the union's district directors: "*Do not talk steel prices.*" "The Steelworkers can get out of this situation . . . as much as the Automobile workers will get out of theirs," Murray declared, without spending months on the picket line. "Our fight in the steel industry is an altogether different fight than the kind of a fight the Automobile Workers have to make," he insisted.[38]

Murray complained that the UAW leader had repeatedly undercut efforts to coordinate CIO strategy, "all of which," he declared, "was calculated to create more difficulty." In late January the story circulated that Murray had worked behind the scenes to cut back a recommendation made by a presidentially appointed fact-finding panel for the auto strike, presumably because it might award the UAW more than he was seeking for the USWA. Tracing this tale to GM president Charles E. Wilson, Murray was less upset with Wilson, "a man of evil mind," than with UAW leaders because they had believed the rumor and "circulate[d] this statement, a diabolicil [*sic*], vicious lie."[39]

Settlement of these strikes relied heavily on government intervention. Fact-finding boards advanced the basic conditions of settlement, and the administration's eventual approval of price increases persuaded the big corporations to agree to terms. At first Truman's panels for the auto and steel industries seemed to make little progress. Both made recommendations that went well beyond management's original offers and were silent on the ability-to-pay and price-relief issues. Both U.S. Steel and GM rejected these government proposals, charging that without assurances of price relief the 17.5 percent wage increases proposed by the boards would be suicidal. Murray became increasingly bitter toward his bargaining opponents. After U.S. Steel had rejected the president's recommendations, he exploded. "American industry," he charged, has "deliberately set out to destroy labor unions, to provoke strikes and economic chaos, and [to] hijack the American people." A Big Business cabal, he told USWA leaders, "wants to take the seat of Government out of the city of Washington back to Wall Street. . . . There is a firm determination on the part of Big Business to take this Government over."[40]

Less apocalyptical, Reuther was equally bitter. Indeed, well after guarantees of price relief had permitted a settlement in mid-February between the USWA and the steel companies, GM and the UAW continued to battle it out in Detroit's conference rooms, as autoworkers entered their third month on the streets. GM refused to grant the embattled Reuther even the semblance of victory. Corporate bargainers stuck fast to the 18.5 cents per hour to which the UE and USWA had agreed, while Reuther continued the fight for an additional cent, the amount recommended in January by the president's automobile panel. One cent per hour hardly seemed worth protracting the strike, but Reuther was determined that long-striking autoworkers' sacrifices would be rewarded. "Maybe you will be able to make Frigidaires," a reference to GM's home appliance products whose workers the UE represented, "but you will not be able to make Chevrolets with an offer like that," he snarled in mid-February. But in the end the UAW too settled for the standard wage increase of 18.5 cents per hour. Of course GM, like steel and the other major employers, had the assurance of administration officials that further weakening of federal price controls would compensate them for these wage concessions.[41]

These strikes were at once the death knell of the old industrial relations regime and the herald of a new order. The sheer magnitude and solidarity of the strikes evidenced workers' power. Less than a decade before, embattled CIO activists had pulled off miracles of resourcefulness and tactical maneuvering to win partial, tenuous victories (in Flint) or had suffered devastating and lethal defeats (in Little Steel). But now, CIO workers had shut down two of the world's most powerful corporations. Whatever the rivalry at the top, the rank and file held firm. Preis's revolutionary hopes were misplaced when he rhapsodized that "the industrial workers demonstrated that their organized power could command the nation," but he was not wrong to see in these impressive strikes "a new power in the land."[42]

Moreover, CIO workers won substantial wage increases. The CIO research department counted over 1.7 million members covered by new contracts that boosted wages between 15 percent and 20 percent. Despite the defeat of Reuther's open-the-books initiative, the CIO continued to promote more effective regulation of economic activity and to assert a right of consultation and involvement in basic decision making. Its more advanced proposals might not be realized, but the irreducible premise of its existence was that industrial workers should have a powerful voice in determining the conditions under which they toiled. These strikes forcefully and effectively asserted this point.[43]

In important respects, however, these accomplishments were part of an older agenda. Though they bargained hard, corporate leaders did not contest the CIO unions primarily on these grounds. It was, rather, in the area of control, both of corporate policies and shop-floor conditions, that they saw the new frontiers of labor-management rivalry. Here industrial unionism's record was less impressive. Exactly how far the Open the Books campaign might have extended was never clear because GM never regarded this demand as negotiable.[44]

Another control matter, however, was more contentious, and here too the major corporations emerged victorious. The rise of the CIO and turbulent wartime conditions had convinced managers that aggressive unionists were wresting important prerogatives from supervisors and other company officials. A widespread movement among foremen toward unionization alarmed business executives. At Ford an aggressive new management team characterized its relationship with the union an "unhappy experiment" and succeeded in writing provisions into the new contract that curtailed the union's ability to defend workers in disciplinary proceedings. Chrysler likewise gained "company security" provisions, and while the GM contract contained none of these stipulations, the biggest of the automakers had been working since the late 1930s to confine the union to the narrowest possible definition of its role. Clearly, corporations would not compromise "managerial prerogatives," and they held a very expansive sense of what that term meant.[45]

At the time that the management rights provisions were written into the Ford and Chrysler contracts, their long-range meaning was uncertain. No contract could unambiguously define shop-floor relations, and a strong union such as the UAW retained powerful weapons with which to counter overzealous foremen and managers. Moreover, upper-level union leaders themselves were at best ambivalent about shop-floor activism. During the war, for example, it was the union that had disciplined violators of the No Strike Pledge and hate strikers. The whole effort of the industrial union project was to bring clear, rational, and coherent practices to American workplaces otherwise notable for favoritism, confusion, and arbitrary treatment. Any modern labor organization had to balance between workers' rights and the general efficiency of the plant. Conversely, many industrial managers themselves repudiated the old drive system that relied on force and fear to get out the product. Still, workplace issues would clearly be important in the emerging industrial relations regime, and in this regard the settlements of the strikes of 1945–46 contained an ominous subtext.[46]

The 1945–46 strikes also revealed much about the CIO itself. In the broadest national forums the CIO spoke with one voice. It promoted a coherent list of legislative and collective bargaining goals, and CIO leaders all argued for greater participation in basic decision making. The achievement of these ambitions, of course, implied the existence of an internally unified industrial union movement.

The strikes of 1945–46, however, exhibited no such unity. Murray wore his CIO hat largely for public relations purposes but put on his USWA hard hat when it came to actually dealing with U.S. Steel. Reuther could not possibly have pursued his goals under the direct aegis of Murray and the national CIO. The lurking issue of Communism divided the UAW internally and poisoned relations between it and the UE. During the war, with public relations and dealings with governmental bodies taking precedence over collective bargaining as industrial unionism's central concern, the CIO had seemed a cohesive entity, but the return to peace meant business as usual for the embattled labor federation. The discipline and loyalty of thousands of striking workers projected power and unity, but in the end the CIO was less a mighty host than a fragile juggernaut.

FACING SOUTH

The failure in 1946 of the CIO's ambitious drive to expand substantially its membership in the South also revealed the limits of industrial union power. A southern organizing campaign aimed to unionize low-wage southern workers, to protect the contract gains made by CIO affiliates in other sections of the country, and to transform the region's political climate. The CIO sought to advance the cause of industrial unionism through steady recruitment and carefully planned NLRB elections. It abjured the fiery rhetoric and provocative tactics of the 1930s and attempted to divert attention from racial matters. From the start, however, the bitter opposition of southern elites, the uncertain response of white workers, and the CIO's lack of resources and internal unity frustrated initially high hopes.

Although the campaign's director, Van Bittner, claimed significant membership gains in the South, CIO efforts left the key textile sector virtually unaffected. The southern campaign lingered until 1953, but by the end of 1946 it had become a sideshow. Just as the strikes of 1945–46 revealed the limits to buoyant ambitions with regard to the nation's general structures of decision making, so the outcome of the southern campaign suggested the passing of the era of mass organization.[47]

Since the inception of the CIO in 1935 the South had seemed a natural field for industrial unionism. The South's labor force of 14 million persons included 375,000 mine and quarry workers, over 1.25 million manufacturing workers, and 700,000 transport workers. Textiles alone employed over a half-million, three-quarters in the cotton mills. Loggers; sawmill, furniture, and other woodworkers; and pulp and paper workers numbered nearly a half-million. A quarter-million tobacco and food processing workers; smaller but significant pockets of steel, nonferrous metal, electrical, and vehicle and heavy equipment assemblers; and thousands of shipyard, dockside, and warehouse workers also attracted CIO interest. Petrochemical and aluminum production soared, and northern-based manufacturers of consumer durables increasingly opened southern plants to serve local consumer markets. In the 1930s the South advanced relative to the rest of the country in its proportion of industrial workers, its share of wage payments, and other indices of increasing wealth and economic vigor.[48]

At the same time, the South posed unique problems. Race divided the southern labor force and tested the CIO's egalitarian commitments. Apparent weakness of traditions of union activism, antagonistic state and local political structures, and highly competitive conditions in the key industries instilled caution. Initial CIO activities in the South were confined to workers whose recruitment could be undertaken as a direct extension of organization elsewhere.

The UMW blazed the southern trail. By 1935 the union had established biracial locals even in Alabama and had brought the southern operators into broad regional wage and bargaining arrangements. By the eve of World War II about 18 percent of the UMW's total membership was in southern locals, and the union was playing a significant role in the politics of Kentucky, Tennessee, and Alabama.[49]

The Steelworkers also enjoyed some success in Dixie but largely because of events outside the region. In March 1937 SWOC gained recognition at Tennessee Coal & Iron, a U.S. Steel subsidiary, as a direct result of the Lewis-Taylor agreement. SWOC developed biracial locals among Tennessee Coal & Iron workers and in Birmingham-area pipe, plate, and specialty mills. However, until World War II SWOC was able to do little to expand this beachhead.[50]

There were other CIO initiatives in the South. From its inception in 1937 until 1939, TWOC devoted about 15 percent of its $2 million war fund to southern operations. Said TWUA president Emil Rieve, "There can be no labor movement in the South unless textiles is the foundation." Yet by May 1941 only about 5 percent of the South's 350,000 cotton textile workers were under contract, and even fewer were dues-paying members of TWOC's successor, the TWUA. The South, lamented Rieve, "seems like a bottomless pit."[51]

More optimistically, the UCAPAWA recruited scattered groups of tobacco and food processing workers. A handful of ACWA and ILGWU locals struggled along. In the late 1930s the International Union of Mine, Mill, and Smelter Workers built a biracial organization among 4,000 Alabama iron ore miners and smelter workers. Small groups of furniture, oil, and tobacco workers, along with outposts of river boatmen, newspaper reporters, and maritime workers, also flew the CIO banner.[52]

The CIO suffered sharp setbacks as well. Efforts to organize autoworkers, rubber workers, longshoremen, and pulp and paper workers largely failed. In these southern forays CIO unionists found that the NLRB, so useful elsewhere, was of limited value. A 1938 *CIO News* editorial proclaimed that the industrial union body was "the predominant labor movement of the South," but the reality was quite different. In all, by the eve of World War II the CIO had about 150,000 southern members, about 5 percent of its total, 10 percent of all southern union members, and about 1.5 percent of the region's nonagricultural labor force. Well over half of this total belonged to the UMW, whose ties to the CIO were snapping.[53]

World War II, however, brought dramatic gains for the CIO in the South. By the end of the conflict, CIO membership in Dixie stood at around 225,000, a remarkable figure in view of the 1942 departure of the UMW from the CIO, which took at least 100,000 members off its rolls. In cotton textiles, the number of workers covered by TWUA contracts expanded by over 42,000, and the union won several impressive NLRB election victories. The UCAPAWA built an energetic biracial local of several thousand R. J. Reynolds workers in Winston-Salem, North Carolina, and a vigorous multiplant union in Memphis. The Oil Workers' union made rapid headway in the expanding refineries of Louisiana and Texas, boasting by 1944 that it had more than doubled its prewar membership of 18,000. The USWA solidified its Alabama locals and formed new ones among the iron, foundry, and aluminum workers of neighboring Tennessee. The Shipbuilding Workers exploited opportunities among the South's war-expanded labor force. A new organization in the pulp and paper industry captured several large mills, including the largest such facility in Virginia. The Rubber Workers established strong locals in Memphis and Gadsden, Alabama, and the UAW made inroads in the South's expanding aircraft plants in Texas and Georgia.[54]

Central headquarters CIO interest in the South was both recurrent and vague. Beginning in 1939, annual conventions asserted the importance of Dixie, and CIO leaders periodically advanced hopeful plans of action. "The organization of the workers in the South," read a unanimously passed 1941 convention resolution, "is the no. 1 task before the CIO." Two years later Murray boasted that "splendid progress is being made," but as in the past, no program of action followed these words.[55]

Relative neglect of the South, however, was a luxury the CIO could not afford in the postwar era. For example, how long could the war-engorged TWUA sustain a membership of 400,000 with only token representation in the South, where wage rates trailed far behind those paid to northern workers? As a 1939 CIO prospectus declared, "As long as the south remains unorganized, it constitutes the nation's Number One economic problem and is also a menace to our organized movement in the north and likewise to northern industries."[56]

Political considerations were powerful as well. Conservatives dominated southern congressional delegations, and their seniority born of the South's one-party politics gave them a stranglehold on the key committees. It was true that the large New Deal majorities elected in 1934 and 1936 permitted passage of Social Security, National Labor Relations, and Fair Labor Standards legislation often over southern opposition. Even so, however, the extensive exemptions from coverage contained in these measures owed in large part to southern insistence that agricultural workers and domestic employees be exempted. Southern states and localities thus could, and did, establish low benefit levels so as to insure a steady supply of captive low-wage labor for their farms and factories. Local Works Progress Administration administrators purged relief rolls when planters needed harvest labor. Indeed, despite the obvious benefits of New Deal programs, in the South they often served to perpetuate poverty, dependency, and racial exploitation.[57]

The Democratic Party itself was also a battleground. Throughout the World War II era, southern congressmen, newspapers, and business leaders warned of PAC efforts to mobilize black voters and poor whites. CIO-PAC, fumed North Carolina senator Josiah Bailey in 1944, "will seek to purge us and every other self respecting and honest man who runs for office." It was true that in the 1944 primary elections PAC did help to oust fiercely anti-union Democratic congressmen in Texas and Alabama.[58]

Industrial unionists could hardly afford complacency, however. The results of both the 1938 and 1942 congressional elections had strengthened Dixie's conservative congressional delegations. In 1945 determined southerners foiled efforts to strengthen the federal government's role in workmen's compensation and employment service matters. In February 1946 a southern filibuster defeated the CIO-supported effort to create a permanent FEPC. President Truman, while verbally endorsing the progressive alternatives, refused to confront the southern legions. With these setbacks in mind Allan Haywood stressed "the absolutely essential need of increasing the activity of southern workers in line with the program of the CIO Political Action Committee."[59]

The actual shape of a southern campaign emerged in the fall of 1945 and the spring of 1946. In September Murray appointed a committee consisting of McDonald, Carey, Emspak, George Addes, Haywood, and two TWUA officers to assess postwar organizing opportunities. Reported McDonald, the unionists quickly decided that "the best place for the CIO to undertake organizing . . . would be in the South." The region's low wages, its potential for industrial growth, and its negative role in politics and legislation made it the obvious choice. "Practically all of you," McDonald observed to the CIO's Executive Board, "have had considerable experience in the South, and you know what happens in Congress." Detailed studies by Haywood indicated that "the South seemed to be the place which must be tackled."[60]

Through the winter and spring of 1946 these ambitions took tangible shape. In March the Executive Board endorsed the committee's concrete recommendations. Among these were the establishment of a permanent SOC, whose key members included Haywood, Carey, McDondald, presidents R. J. Thomas (UAW) and Albert J. Fitzgerald (UE), TWUA secretary-treasurer William Pollock, and ACWA vice-president Jacob Potofsky. Van Bittner was named director, to be assisted by George Baldanzi, a thirty-nine-year-old TWUA vice-president, fresh from leading a successful campaign to organize 13,000 cotton mill workers in southside Virginia. The CIO and the affiliated unions would contribute $1 million, assessed according to the affiliates' size, to be used primarily for the dispatch of 200 organizers. It would be, McDonald advised, "a straight organizing campaign" that would recapture the glory days of 1936–37. Bittner and Baldanzi would deploy teams of organizers to preselected target areas. These teams would then "proceed to organize everything in sight." Once the team had established functioning unions, the various affiliates would send in their field representatives to integrate them into ongoing operations.[61]

Organizers would collect an initiation fee of $1.00 from each recruit, except military veterans, who were exempt. Dues of $1.50 per month would also be assessed. This money would be funneled back into the organizing campaign. SOC would work closely with international unions with membership potential in the South, with the drive's Atlanta headquarters resolving jurisdictional questions and coordinating the work of SOC and international union representatives. Of course, in view of the importance of textiles, TWUA would play a critical role.[62]

Through the spring, Bittner set out to implement these plans. The USWA ($200,000), the ACWA ($200,000), and the TWUA ($125,000) were the largest contributors, with the CIO itself along with the UAW and the UE paying $100,000 each. Baldanzi established the Atlanta office, applications for organizer posts poured in, and pledges of support and requests from internationals that their jurisdiction receive priority came thick and fast. SOC leaders sought to recruit military veterans and men of southern nativity as field representatives in hope of deflecting the inevitable charges of radicalism and carpetbagging. But sifting through the applications was no easy task. Warned the SOC office in April, it was "not to be expected that 200 organizers can be immediately recruited and assigned to the South," and the committee cautioned sternly that "any organizer who gets drunk and/or makes a fool of himself, automatically is fired."[63]

The results of the 1945–46 strikes encouraged optimism. "We have every reason to believe these CIO wage victories will result in more demand for CIO organization among unorganized workers than followed the sit-downs in 1937," southern regional director Paul Christopher declared. An April *Wall Street Journal* report that the NLRB "had entered into an alliance [with the CIO] to spur the multi-million dollar union organizing drive in the South," though not in fact true, reflected the buoyant atmosphere. "This is the most important thing that has happened in this Country," declared a Virginia unionist. On June 3 Bittner issued the proclamation that set things in motion. "You are," he told his organizers in tones reminiscent of General Eisenhower's message to the troops before the Normandy landings, "now part of this great crusading movement in behalf of humanity. No people in the history of our country has ever had a greater responsibility for the betterment of all America than you have. . . . Let the campaign of organization roll on."[64]

Beneath the confident facade, however, lay conflicting assumptions about the nature of the undertaking. Was the southern drive a militant crusade or a sober business proposition? Would it work exclusively through legal and sanctioned channels, or would it defy the established southern order and pin its hopes, as the sit-down strikers had in the 1930s, on creative chaos? What role would there be for the CIO's Communists and their allies who had built small but impressive enclaves of aggressive biracial unionism in Dixie? Relatedly, would SOC use the well-established militancy of black workers as the spearhead of the drive? Or would it marginalize blacks in hopes of attracting the white majority?[65]

At first the southern drive did seem an attempt to rekindle the spirit of the 1930s. The unofficial term "Operation Dixie" conjured up images of an army with banners marching against the bastions of exploitation and privilege. Normally cautious David McDonald demonstrated a talent for pugnacious prose. "Like a champion fighter, we can't rest but must continue to bore ahead [and] ORGANIZE THE SOUTH!" he proclaimed. The South would be "attacked." CIO cadres would "just sweep through the area, go on and organize everything in sight." The *CIO News* called it a "Holy Crusade."[66]

"We can bring . . . [the spirit of the CIO] back to the period of 1937," proclaimed Haywood.[67] Yet in important respects CIO and SOC leaders systematically misread the experience of the glory days. They conveniently forgot the widespread apathy, fear, and indifference that workers had often shown. For understandable reasons they passed over John L. Lewis's contributions as well as the important roles that friendly federal officials, unique economic circumstances, and skillful (and sometimes fortuitous) legal maneuvering had played in the breakthrough victories of 1937.[68]

Postwar CIO leaders also slighted the work leftists had done for industrial unionism. For example, radicals had comprised at least one-third of SWOC's original cadre of organizers. In the South, they had helped to build some of the most active and vigorous local unions, but SOC's leaders kept Communists and those close to them at arm's length.[69]

SOC and CIO functionaries in fact never directly addressed the related questions of race, radicalism, and confrontationalism. But in effect they did answer them by virtue of the assumptions with which they set about their task and the basic framework they established. Thus, for example, the repeated stress that the southern drive was, in the words of an early manifesto, "to be purely an organizational campaign" carried key implications. The insistence that there were to be "no extra curricular activities – no politics – no PAC – no FEPC, etc." associated with the drive sent a clear message that black workers were to be peripheral and that SOC would attempt to build unions strictly around bread-and-butter issues.[70]

The injunction against political agitation was a coded way of marginalizing the left. CPUSA-oriented affiliates such as Mine, Mill and FTA had pioneered in linking industrial unionism and civil rights. They often spearheaded southern PAC drives and were thus particularly associated with the FEPC and other civil rights initiatives, presumably anathema to white workers. "I think the PAC in South Carolina is about as useful as Bill Green as a CIO organizer," Bittner declared, and he ordered SOC functionaries to sever their PAC ties. Thus the "no politics – no PAC – no FEPC" rule, with its eloquent "etc.," sent clear, if indirect, signals.[71]

SOC did welcome black recruits. CIO functionaries recognized the important role that blacks played in southern industry. In the South, however, CIO leaders avoided any implication of linkage between union membership and broader social purposes. "We are not mentioning the color of people," declared Bittner. Insofar as the CIO was concerned, he asserted, "there was no Negro problem in the south." SOC would recruit everyone "because they are God's human beings and are workers." Bittner and other mainstream CIO functionaries criticized the leaders of the FTA, the NMU, and Mine, Mill for pushing their advanced civil rights agenda. Continued agitation of racial questions, Bittner told FTA president Donald Henderson, "is hurting our drive and I am not going to allow anything to interfere with the organization of the workers into CIO unions."[72]

The campaign largely bypassed those industries in which large numbers of blacks toiled. The textile industry was the primary target, and its labor force was overwhelmingly white. Yet other southern industries, notably lumbering, pulp and paper, food and tobacco processing, and chemicals, employed thousands of African Americans, men and women who had repeatedly proved themselves eager and steadfast recruits to industrial unionism. Baldanzi discouraged blacks from applying for organizers' slots, and other SOC officials were only marginally more encouraging.[73]

The privileging of textiles, the marginalization of the left, and the relegation of blacks to a subsidiary role shaped every aspect of the campaign. These factors insured that the CIO southern foray would play by the established rules. Bittner, Baldanzi, McDonald, and others on the original committee did little to prepare their troops for a protracted struggle. "An organizing campaign in the South will require planning, organization, and concentration of effort beyond anything CIO had done up to this time," observed Haywood, but in fact SOC made little provision for actually training its representatives or anticipating some of the distinctive features of southern antiunion resistance.[74]

SOC officials assumed that, like in the northern plants of the 1930s, organizers would readily find dedicated union sympathizers upon whom they could build in-plant committees that would in turn recruit coworkers and neighbors. "The South is ripe and ready," declared Haywood. Thus in his instructions to organizers North Carolina director William Smith stressed the need for "a well disciplined, constructive organizing campaign," orderly dues collection, and regular filing of weekly reports.[75]

Experienced southern hands backed away from heroic rhetoric. "This is not an invasion of workers from the North to the South," Baldanzi insisted. "We must clear up . . . the erroneous impression that this is an 'Operation Dixie.' " Southerners had to be reassured that the CIO did not mean strikes, violence, radicalism, and turmoil. CIO publicity featured the activities of Lucy Randolph Mason, a Virginia-born CIO emissary who combined stalwart support for the union with quiet efforts to educate employers and community leaders about organized labor. SOC employed John Ramsay, a lay Protestant activist, "to meet with the ministerial association[s] and other representatives of the church and explain . . . what the CIO really is." Declared Baldanzi, "I would rather have a less spectacular campaign, but one which . . . is well planned and proceeding methodically."[76]

On the whole, SOC did pursue exactly this strategy. Still, the great fanfare with which Operation Dixie was launched and the militant rhetoric that seeped out of the board meetings helped to alert the South's antiunion legions. Employers, public officials, and journalists treated SOC as if it were Sherman's second march to the sea. The initials *CIO*, asserted some southern religionists, stood for "Christ Is Out." Warned the Southern States Industrial Council, the CIO invasion promised blacks "social and economic equality" while threatening to destroy "our democratic institutions." The victory of industrial unionism, this influential business group predicted, would be the "kiss of death" to hopes for regional economic progress.[77]

After its long gestation and the elaborate process of recruitment of organizers, the actual operation of the southern campaign was something of an anticlimax. The teams of organizers dispatched into Alabama, Georgia, and the Carolinas in the summer of 1946 more resembled loosely coordinated commando raids than an irresistible juggernaut. In a note of sober realism McDonald acknowledged that "a force of two hundred men scattered over the South would not even begin to touch the problem" and that in view of "how quickly you can spend one million dollars, it does not seem to be so much money."[78]

Organizers soon faced the harsh realities of attempting to spread the gospel of industrial unionism in the South of the mid-1940s. Textile workers proved unresponsive and even hostile. In-plant committees were often impossible to establish. Organizers bravely stationed themselves at the plant gates, handing out leaflets and soliciting signatures on membership cards. They visited textile workers' homes after hours. But the inability to locate cadre groups within the mills underlined the position of CIO men as outsiders and quickly left them exposed and isolated.[79]

Organizers attempted to put the best face on things. They were heartened when only a few workers discarded their leaflets or when workers agreed to accept copies of union newspapers. But whereas CIO leaders had spoken of enthusiastic waves of union recruitment, organizers quickly learned to have more modest expectations. Reports from North Carolina in July were typical: "Moving a little slow, but we are still signing up a few each week." "Gained some good leads and made some progress on build-up." In more candid moments, however, organizers grew pessimistic. "'I wish you wouldn't come to my house no more,' " one man reported being told by a potential recruit. In Greensboro, North Carolina, another organizer was assaulted by antiunion workers, who told him, "'We don't need you. You're going to cost us our jobs.' " "I'm beginning to think our problem is to get out of here alive," he reported.[80]

Meanwhile, back at headquarters, SOC officials remained optimistic. Late in June Secretary-Treasurer Sherman Dalrymple reported that "our Drive . . . is progressing rapidly and favorably." Two weeks later, North Carolina director William Smith was "very enthusiastic about the situation." At the end of July Bittner claimed victories in 49 NLRB elections, with 107 additional pending. Employers no doubt would try their old antiunion tricks, but, claimed Regional Director Smith, "the CIO is too strong in the south to allow that sort of conduct to take place in these towns."[81]

This optimism was misplaced, however. SOC achieved its early NLRB successes in places where organizing had preceded the southern drive. CIO operatives quickly learned the limitations of federal laws in the South. Even where workers signed union cards, organizers found little relationship between the card count and the resulting ballot. In too many cases, Bittner reported, "men [have] signed cards . . . just to get rid of our field men and then these people either do not vote at all or vote against our union." There was no substitute for the establishment of a strong local union that could keep a union presence alive in the event of a temporary setback, but, of course, strong local unions were precisely what the CIO could *not* build in the Piedmont.[82]

In theory, the unfair labor practices provisions of the National Labor Relations Act could provide a remedy. In the 1930s a steady stream of victimized CIO members triumphantly returning to work after vindication in labor board proceedings had revealed the vulnerability of employers and the strength of government-backed unions.[83] But 1946 was not 1938 and North Carolina was not Michigan. Even in the 1930s, textile employers had proved unusually skillful in stringing out NLRB proceedings and deflecting the union's legal challenges even as they blunted its on-site thrust. Bittner instructed directors to avoid unfair labor practices cases. "We cannot," he told them, "expect the NLRB to organize and win elections for us," although in fact the NLRB had played a crucial role in the late 1930s. In effect SOC was gambling that swift victories would quickly build pro-union momentum. But too often employers' final appeals and mysterious rumors were more important than careful cultivation of workers in deciding the outcome of elections.[84]

In the crucial textile sector, SOC met with virtually universal defeat. Early in August workers at three medium-sized North Carolina mills voted against CIO representation. On August 6 at the Sidney Blumenthal Company plant in Caramount the tally was close, with TWUA losing to "no union," 260 to 219. Immediately after, however, the CIO lost two additional elections in nearby Rockingham by votes of 315 to 95 and 496 to 105. Increasingly, through the late summer and into the fall police harassment, community hostility, and growing evidence of workers' indifference and even antagonism deflated the early optimism.[85]

Despite these setbacks North Carolina director William Smith and other SOC leaders hoped that a dramatic victory at the big Cannon Mills in Kannapolis, North Carolina, would turn the tide. In June Smith and Baldanzi dispatched ten organizers there, two-thirds of their North Carolina textile contingent. Reinforced in August, these men worked diligently for four months. But none of the CIO representatives could find lodging in Kannapolis, a company-dominated town. It was impossible to position organizers with any regularity at all the relevant gates in the sprawling enterprise. Team members projected an image of sober respectability. They attended local churches. They were always well dressed and modest in demeanor. Yet nothing worked.

Part of the problem was that workers were genuinely fearful of owner Charles Cannon's pervasive spy network. In addition many – perhaps most – Cannon employees seemed to accept the paternalism and antiunionism of their employer. Wages and regularity of employment in Kannapolis compared favorably with those at other textile centers, including those under TWUA contract. "The desire to improve present material conditions is almost non-existent," lamented the local campaign's director. Cannon workers "seem to be insulated . . . from liberal ideas." In August Smith declared that "there is a spirit of victory" in Kannapolis, but organizers' reports were in fact discouraging to the point of despair. When the CIO went down to a crushing defeat on October 9, the effect was devastating. "I, frankly, am worried and heartsick," Smith admitted. "I never wanted to do anything more in my life than to do a real job in the textile industry." Without in-plant organization and with Cannon's aura of invincibility enhanced by the feeble CIO showing, there seemed little hope of renewing the fight.[86]

Indeed, by the fall the whole campaign was sputtering. True, there had been scattered victories in tobacco processing, fertilizers, and wood products. In September in Oak Ridge, Tennessee, the CIO defeated an AFL rival to win bargaining rights in the Atomic City's largest chemical plant. From the Southwest, Bittner reported that "I attended very fine meetings in Texas and Arkansas and the organization is rolling there." But given the assumptions under which SOC had been conducting the campaign, victories in other industries were of marginal importance when coupled with defeat in textiles. From May 15 until the end of 1946 the TWUA won but twenty-one of its forty-seven southern elections, and the twenty-six it lost were in the larger plants. Overall the TWUA was outvoted by about 9,500 to 6,500, and these 16,000 textile workers represented only about 4 percent of the industry's total. "We seem," lamented Smith, "to be able to win elections in every other industry . . . [, but] unless we crack some of the major textile mills in the State, the rest will not mean too much."[87]

The textile failures underlined the campaign's financial burden. By the fall the TWUA alone was paying out at least $95,000 a month. SOC field operations alone were taking at least $100,000 a month. By November, less than six months after the actual campaign had started, the CIO had laid out over $800,000.[88]

Moreover, the campaign did not generate the revenues that its originators had anticipated. As late as November only two-thirds of the original assessment had been paid in. In the field, organizers normally forwent collecting the $1 initiation fees that were supposed to accumulate as a revolving fund. Despite Bittner's chronic hectoring, SOC representatives usually waived the fee, with the result that by November only a little over $21,000 had come in.[89]

The postwar conservative political tide peaked on November 6 with the election of the first Republican Congress since 1930. "We can overcome the election results by putting every ounce of energy and all the intelligence that God has given us in our organizational work," Bittner insisted, but in fact SOC's dwindling revenues soon forced a drastic cutback. At the November 1946 convention the rafters of Atlantic City's convention hall rang with pledges to press ahead. "We have a calm determination," Murray declared. "There just isn't anything that is going to stop the workers of the South in their desire to belong to CIO organizations." In fact, however, Murray and the board forced Bittner to slash the monthly budget by 50 percent, and in December state directors began laying off organizers. By Christmas the SOC staff had been cut by 126, and the monthly outlay had dipped below $100,000.[90]

The defeats and the financial crisis did not end the campaign. SOC's organizers plugged away, and Bittner continued to plead the South's cause in national CIO circles. Late in 1947 he told the Executive Board that "it is a war in the South," and he continued to claim successes. Membership gains during the first seven months, he asserted, were in triple figures, and by its first anniversary, CIO ranks had been augmented by the addition of 280,000 new southern members.[91]

Whatever the merits of these claims, by the end of 1946 it was clear that the southern drive had fallen far short of the expectations of its originators. The average plant in which the CIO sought NLRB certification employed fewer than 140 workers. In these elections almost as many southern workers voted "no union" as for the CIO. Despite massive expenditures, the CIO made only the most marginal gains in textiles. "The advent of the Southern Organizing Drive I thought . . . was the answer to our prayer," observed the Packinghouse Workers' southern regional director. But by year's end he had concluded that "the Drive is bogging down completely, having concentrated their work on Textile, their gains have been almost negligible."[92]

Brave words and pledges of continued effort were never in short supply. "We are going to do it, we must do it, and nothing under God's sun is going to stop this mighty movement from doing it," Murray reaffirmed. But if "doing it" meant laying a solid foundation for powerful industrial unions in the South and helping substantially to overcome the region's backward industrial relations, conservative political orientation, and repressive racial order, the CIO's southern campaign had failed.[93]

There were enough minor successes and certainly more than enough evidences of violations of workers' rights to permit Bittner and his colleagues to hide, even from themselves, the dimensions of CIO defeat in Dixie. But rather than invoking Sherman's march through Georgia, CIO operatives recalled the dark days of the American Revolution. "When you are discouraged," Bittner told a disheartened subaltern, "just think of George Washington . . . and what he had to go through." "Keep your chin up . . . [and] just keep slugging," he advised, reminding the organizer that "there finally was a Yorktown."[94]

The CIO never conducted a full-scale review of its southern effort. But unionists associated with the dozen or so affiliates in which pro-Soviet leaders were prominent pointed to the drive's lack of red-blooded militancy, its isolation of the left, its overwhelming concentration on textiles, its lack of political content, and its failure to exploit black workers' enthusiasm. They suggested a different approach. Instead of futile assaults on the textile citadels, why not throw resources into areas of previous success? Why not, for example, make use of black workers' proven support for the CIO to extend organization into food processing, wood and lumber working, transport and goods handling, and tobacco working?

An aggressive campaign, linking civil rights to industrial unionism, would enable the CIO to exploit rather than disguise its political progressivism. It could directly challenge Jim Crow. The beachheads of biracial unionism, these leftists contended, would eventually force changes in the political climate. With flourishing unions in food processing, tobacco, wood products, metalworking, and perhaps even agribusiness sectors, southern organizing would no longer be starved for funds. But alas, the fixation on anti-Communism and the determination to appear respectable deprived the CIO of precisely its most effective weapons.[95]

In fact, though, there was no chance that the Murray-led CIO would seriously contemplate such a program. The huge financial contributions of the TWUA and the ACWA, as well as the extensive experience that those two affiliates had logged in the South, insured the primacy of textiles. Moreover, the TWUA *had* made gains during World War II. Scattered CIO success in the small nonferrous metals sector and low-wage food and tobacco processing, where the CIO faced fierce competition from a revivified AFL Tobacco Workers Union, offered little realistic hope of providing a spearhead for industrial unionism. By 1946 suspicion of motives and judgment of the pro-Soviet leadership of several CIO unions was rife, and there was no possibility that Murray, Hillman, Haywood, Bittner, and the rest of the core leadership would turn over hundreds of thousands of dollars to organizations led by men such as FTA's bombastic Donald Henderson and Mine, Mill's mercurial Reid Robinson. UE, the only effectively led large pro-Soviet affiliate, had little involvement in the South, and the ILWU, repulsed from earlier forays into the Gulf Coast ports, exhibited little interest in the southern drive.

True, there were isolated occasions in which forthright commitment of industrial unionists to the cause of the South's African Americans paid dividends. But racial feeling among southern white workers was potent. Unless a workplace held a large black majority, SOC's course of stressing pure-and-simple gains and soft-pedaling the CIO's progressive political agenda made obvious sense.

To be sure, a confrontational campaign might have challenged the southern racial and economic order. But in a political arena that was, in contrast to that of the mid-1930s, veering sharply to the right, and with a much-chastened NLRB nervously defending itself from charges of pro-CIO bias, the option of aggressive militancy was risky. Moreover, the postwar CIO was not the organization to follow such a path. CIO leaders viewed their organizing efforts as part of a partnership led by the federal government to bring the South into the nation's mainstream. The Tennessee Valley Authority, the Fair Labor Standards Act, the government's National Emergency Council's 1938 *Report on Economic Conditions of the South*, the massive wartime spending in Dixie, and the activities of the NLRB and the NWLB were all of a piece. The southern organizing campaign fit into the pattern that would transform Dixie not by frontal assault but by building progressive, responsible, modern institutions.[96]

Enthusiasts spoke of the campaign in the South as a "Holy Crusade," but in reality CIO leaders believed that the time for laborite revivalism had passed. With a solid footing in the Democratic Party, with labor law at last seemingly endorsing collective bargaining, and with a proud record of wartime patriotism, the CIO was not going to revert to the street tactics of the 1930s. A more confrontational campaign would have been more heroic, but such a campaign was not one that the God-fearing organizers of SOC, or the union leaders who paid their salaries, could contemplate in 1946.

POLITICAL DEFEAT

By the end of World War II, politics had emerged as the CIO's crucial arena. "Our main mission in life," declared the Executive Board in July 1945, "our No. One mission, at least, is to organize the vote, to interest the voters, to get the voters registered, and to get the voters to the polls." Yet the immediate postwar years brought frustration and defeat on the political-legislative front. Initially the apparent success of the new political action committee in the 1944 elections had buoyed the hopes of industrial unionists. However, electoral defeats on the local level and in the 1946 congressional and state races, along with a steady stream of legislative setbacks, culminating in the Taft-Hartley Act of 1947, soon dashed them.[97]

The establishment of PAC in 1943 and its success in the 1944 elections had left many questions about the nature of the CIO's political operations. PAC chair Hillman, along with most of the pro-Soviet CIO leaders, envisaged PAC as the spearhead of a broad progressive coalition, with its own apparatus and institutional identity. Hillman believed that it should tighten its ties to progressive citizens' groups and function relatively autonomously as the spearhead of a broad liberal bloc. The CIO's Communists, their allies, and others on the anticapitalist left often hinted that PAC could be the core of a third, progressive political party.[98]

Increasingly, however, Murray, Secretary-Treasurer James Carey, and other CIO leaders moved to subordinate PAC to the CIO itself. A 1945 report by John Brophy, which Murray endorsed, flatly rejected third party ambitions and insisted that the national CIO exercise tight control over PAC activities. Murray's acceptance of Brophy's recommendations committed the CIO to a policy of close central direction of PAC activities and, implicitly, to the marginalization of the pro–Soviet left.[99]

So long as Hillman, who regarded PAC as his personal operation, lived, CIO political operations remained unsettled. But when the ACWA president died at age fifty-nine on July 10, 1946, Murray quickly reshuffled PAC. Henceforth a five-man executive board comprised of USWA secretary-treasurer David McDonald, his counterparts in the UAW, UE, and TWUA, and Jack Kroll, Hillman's chief PAC aide, would oversee its operations. Kroll, an ACWA functionary from Cincinnati, became PAC's director. An able tactician, Kroll served as an employee of the CIO, reporting to the Murray-appointed committee of CIO leaders.[100]

Throughout the immediate postwar period, things did not go well for the CIO in the political and legislative arenas. Thus in the summer and fall of 1945 national PAC and local CIO bodies put at least $200,000 into Detroit in an effort to elect UAW vice-president Richard Frankensteen mayor. This campaign was the most concerted effort on the part of any CIO body to elect a CIO leader to a major public office since at least 1937. Detroit was the quintessential CIO city, and it seemed only reasonable that the industrial union surge of the 1930s and 1940s should bring political power. "If you will work and vote for the election of Richard T. Frankensteen," wrote a UAW editorialist, "perhaps we can have a labor victory as well as our British fellow workers." But after an impressive primary showing, Frankensteen fell victim to his opponent's race-baiting, the unwillingness of AFL unions to support a CIO man, and poor voter turnout, losing narrowly in the November general election.[101]

The CIO fared no better in achieving broad legislative goals, and the CIO postwar vision was broad. "Are we going to master our economic system?" Murray challenged the Senate Banking and Currency Committee at the end of the war. In addition to equitable taxation policies, the nation needed massive programs of public housing, national medical provision, and school, highway, and hospital construction. Minimum wage, unemployment, and social security coverage needed to be expanded, streamlined, and improved. The federal government had to acknowledge responsibility for maintaining high levels of employment. The nation's impressive technological and military achievements, Murray declared, would be meaningless if the nation were "unable to prevent little children in the workers' homes from being undernourished."[102]

Repeatedly, CIO leaders asserted their views not only on matters of fiscal and economic policy but on civil rights, regional development, atomic energy, military manpower, and other critical concerns. Working through the Legislative Department, created at the 1942 convention, through the IUCs, and through PAC, CIO leaders sought to mobilize local union leaders, and through them the rank and file, to influence lawmakers. Every issue seemed imperative. As Congress debated future control of atomic energy in November, for example, IUC director Brophy called the councils into action: "Democratic control of the most important source of power ever discovered . . . may well depend upon what organized labor . . . does about this matter in the next few weeks," he instructed.[103]

Rarely, however, did the CIO find a responsive audience. Beginning with the enactment in July 1945 of bills that granted generous relief from high wartime corporate taxes, through the virtual abandonment of price controls a year later, the Democratic 79th Congress frustrated virtually every item on the CIO's agenda. In February 1946 hopes for a permanent FEPC fell victim to a southern filibuster. Congress also rejected efforts to expand and further federalize unemployment compensation and employment service programs. Despite the CIO's accurate forecasting of unemployment trends and the solid factual basis for its proposals, Secretary-Treasurer James Carey charged, "We were kicked in the teeth" by Congress.[104]

CIO leaders and other labor-liberals pinned particular hopes on passage of a full employment bill introduced in the summer of 1945 by Senators Robert F. Wagner and James Murray. This measure embodied the emerging Keynesian consensus among laborites and liberals, which saw as imperative an expanded federal role in maintaining purchasing power as the key to postwar prosperity. It stressed the boosting of lower-income purchasing power and, at least implicitly, sought to compensate for the system's seemingly chronic tendency toward unemployment by charging government with responsibility to provide jobs. On August 22, in lengthy testimony before the Senate Banking and Currency Committee, Murray spelled out the CIO's postwar vision. He told the senators that "high income of the mass of people [is] an economic necessity." The Full Employment Bill would keep faith with FDR's Four Freedoms by "adding an Economic Bill of Rights to our Political Bill of Rights." Along with the other planks in the CIO reconstruction platform the bill was a first step in the effort "to modernize America." People had a right to decent employment, he asserted, and "I insist that all the resources of the government should be applied to make it effective."[105]

By the time President Truman signed the Employment Act on February 13, 1946, however, the measure bore little resemblance to the original. Full employment now became simply a desideratum, along with avoiding inflation and upholding free enterprise. The creation of the Council of Economic Advisors did acknowledge a federal role in economic performance, but gone was the crusading sense of militant Keynesianism contained in the Senate bill and that Murray's testimony expressed. Equally disappointing was Congress's systematic dismantling of wartime price control machinery, with the passage in July 1946 of an enactment that all but ended the Office of Price Administration's power to affect prices of a broad range of agricultural and consumer goods. An August 1946 analysis prepared by the CIO Research Department detected a "widespread and sinister conspiracy on the part of organized employers . . . to depress real wages . . . and to torpedo the living standards of all the people." [106]

The remedy for legislative setbacks, of course, was political action. CIO and PAC functionaries believed that the broad public naturally supported the foreign and domestic policies associated with Franklin Roosevelt and the New Deal. "It is a matter of historical record that the people of the United States are naturally progressive," Kroll asserted early in 1946. [107]

In the wake of Hillman's death, however, the CIO's political operations sputtered. In August PAC-supported candidates did well in the West Virginia Democratic primary but suffered devastating defeat in adjoining Virginia. The *CIO News* predicted a massive labor victory in the fall elections, but the leaders of the heavily political UE made a more somber assessment. "The Union . . . has made a miserable showing," they reported, both in collecting voluntary contributions and in explaining the CIO agenda to their members. [108]

Without Franklin Roosevelt at the head of the ticket, the liberal cause seemed to drift. Heightened international tensions competed with postwar economic dislocations for public attention. Most CIO activists clung to hopes for continued cooperation among the wartime allies, but fear and suspicion of the USSR was rampant among the public. The CIO contained important pro-Soviet elements, along with many others who believed that the Truman administration's policies vis-à-vis the Soviet Union represented a sharp break with those of FDR. On the other hand, the CIO membership included hundreds of thousands of men and women of Polish, Czech, Slovak, and Ukrainian extraction, many of whom were fiercely anti-Russian and anti-Soviet. Most of these workers and their families were at least nominally Roman Catholic, and the church was becoming increasingly vocal in its anti-Communism. [109]

The events of the fall 1946 election campaigns vividly revealed the tensions at work within the CIO's political operations. Kroll stepped up efforts to build a streamlined and efficient PAC machine. He sought to keep attention focused on the misdeeds of congressional conservatives. In August CIO-sponsored rallies highlighted workers' victimization at the hands of conservative forces in Congress. In October Kroll pledged that CIO-PAC "will build ward and precinct apparatus and basic organization in every town and community . . . to carry the Roosevelt program forward."

Matters of foreign policy inevitably intruded, however, and initially at least it seemed that the standard wartime CIO line was still serviceable. "There are no 'off-years' in the battle against fascism, against reaction at home and war-mongering abroad," Kroll insisted. At the end of September PAC participated in a national progressive conference that highlighted left-wing criticisms of the Truman administration's foreign policies. PAC statements regularly condemned "the maintenance [by the United States] of a far-flung and world-wide system of military bases." Such statements, however, seemed now uncomfortably similar to strident Soviet denunciations of the United States, a similarity brought home when a front-page article in the October 18 *New York Times* reported the Soviet government's praise for PAC-endorsed candidates.[110]

The results on November 5 were disastrous. For the first time since 1930 Republicans controlled both houses. The CIO's machinery functioned only sporadically. Financial contributions were disappointing, and workers remained apathetic. PAC-backed candidates won only eight of the twenty House races in districts containing high proportions of CIO members. In the House, organized labor lost six friendly Democrats from the Committee on Labor, sure to be a key arena in the ongoing effort on the part of conservatives to scuttle or gut the Wagner Act. Licking his wounds, Kroll reassured his troops that CIO-PAC "is not a temporary organization. We are here to stay." But clearly ebullient CIO hopes for a renewal of the New Deal had given way to a grim determination to ride out the impending right-wing counterattack.[111]

The cost of such a devastating defeat for labor-liberalism was the renewal of efforts to amend or even scrap the Wagner Act. Since the late 1930s, Congress had repeatedly considered proposals to redress the allegedly pro-labor 1935 National Labor Relations Act. The Ball-Burton-Hatch Bill, for example, introduced in June 1945, would have imposed drastic limitations on the right to strike, revived the labor injunction, and bolstered employers' ability to fight unionization.

The strikes that greeted the end of hostilities further fueled antiunion sentiment. In the final session of the 79th Congress and in the first four months of the 80th Congress, seventy-three labor policy bills were introduced, most designed to chasten the unions and amend the Wagner Act. In the spring of 1946 Congress passed the Case Bill, which provided for unprecedented intrusion of federal authorities into labor disputes and curtailment of the right to strike. The House narrowly upheld President Truman's

June 11 veto, but hostility toward organized labor and determination to change drastically the New Deal dispensation in labor affairs was obvious. Thus the wholesale defeat of PAC-supported candidates sent a chilling message to an industrial union body that owed its success in good part to favorable governmental policies. "With the election of the 80th Congress," declared a resolution at the CIO's mid-November convention, "the anti-labor conspiracy of American employers . . . has gained new impetus." Delegates vowed a fight to the finish against "the sinister reactionary forces which seek to destroy labor through repressive legislation."[112]

It did not take long, however, for the new Congress to adopt antiunion legislation. The Taft-Hartley Act, passed over President Truman's veto on June 23, 1947, represented a grab-bag of provisions, many of them derived from earlier proposals. A complex law, it aimed to curb the political and economic activities of unions, to strengthen employers' ability to resist unionization, and to place the internal workings of labor organizations under greater direct federal scrutiny. It prohibited union contributions to candidates in primary and general elections, thus strengthening and making permanent the restrictions on political activities contained in the lapsed Smith-Connally Act.

Its main thrust, however, was in the realm of collective bargaining and industrial relations. Unlike the House version, the final bill affirmed the Wagner Act's endorsement of collective bargaining and retained the NLRB as the agency charged with implementing federal labor law. Taft-Hartley expanded the NLRB from three to five members and required that NLRB rulings follow legal rules of evidence. It also took the NLRB's legal arm, its general counsel, out of the board's jurisdiction and established it as a separate entity. The new law included a list of unfair union practices. It enabled employers to initiate decertification proceedings through the NLRB, hitherto a right available only to workers. It greatly expanded the ability of both employers and the NLRB to seek injunctions against unions, thus undermining some of the protections gained by labor in the 1932 Norris-LaGuardia Act. It explicitly gave employers the right to attempt to dissuade workers from supporting a union. Taft-Hartley recreated the former U.S. Conciliation Service, previously within the Department of Labor, as the Federal Mediation and Conciliation Service, now an independent agency, and it greatly expanded the president's power to force unions to delay strike action for up to 140 days in disputes that he regarded as "national emergencies."

The new law also banned strikes stemming from jurisdictional disputes among unions and banned secondary boycotts. These provisions, along with prohibitions against so-called featherbedding (i.e., union-required overmanning), related primarily to the parochial world of the AFL craft, transport, and construction unions and had little meaning in the CIO's mass production industries. But two other provisions, a section permitting states to outlaw union security provisions in collective bargaining contracts and the requirement that all union officers seeking access to NLRB facilities and services sign an affidavit stipulating that they were not Communists, held important implications for industrial unionists. Already, several states, led by Florida and Arkansas, had adopted so-called right-to-work measures, outlawing any form of union security. Federal law required unions to bargain and process grievances for all members of the bargaining unit; thus this provision of Taft-Hartley threatened to impede organizing campaigns, since a right-to-work state prevented the majority of workers in a bargaining unit from protecting themselves against so-called free riders, fellow workers who benefited from union contracts and services but who refused to join and hence to contribute financially. In addition to adding to the difficulty of organizing previously nonunion workers, right-to-work legislation (or state referenda) sent a clear antiunion signal.[113]

The anti-Communist affidavit was particularly offensive because it implied that unionists were uniquely suspect. The law did not require employers or their agents or lawyers to swear to their loyalty to the United States, but it did require that representatives of American workers go through a demeaning ritual that seemed designed to impugn their patriotism. Of all the provisions of Taft-Hartley, this one rankled most bitterly among laborites. Yet if union leaders did not sign the affidavit, they opened their organization to threats of raiding by other unions whose leaders had signed and to decertification proceedings on the part of employers. Without the affidavit, the union could not bring unfair labor practices cases before the NLRB, could not petition for a representation election, and could not use any of the other services that their tax dollars and those of their members made possible. Thus the affidavit provision denied workers rights guaranteed to them in other provisions of the same legislation.[114]

In testimony before a Senate committee in February Murray and his fellow CIO officers set forth the CIO case against this legislation. They criticized those who focused on such minor issues as secondary boycotts, featherbedding, and jurisdictional strikes, pointing out how little affect any of these matters had in the real world. Concentration on these peripheral issues, Murray believed, was part of a process by which "this Nation has been blanketed with a steady barrage of propaganda" aimed at discrediting the entire labor movement. The attack on union security, Murray argued, was counterproductive, since only with their institutional stability assured could unions afford to enforce shop-floor discipline and take the long-range view in relations with employers.

The fact was, Murray argued, that the strikes and inflation of the post-war period stemmed from irresponsible corporate behavior, inept and uncertain government policies, and the failure to extend the beneficial social and economic policies of the New Deal. Nothing in the proposed legislation even pretended to deal with these pressing matters. Employers had compiled a long record of flouting the provisions of the National Labor Relations Act. It was they, and not the unions, who had brazenly ignored or repudiated the recommendations of presidential commissions in 1945 and 1946, thus triggering the postwar strike wave. Even now, employers throughout the South were engaged in systematic victimization of union-minded workers and chronic violations of federal labor law in their effort to stop the CIO's southern campaign. Yet organized labor was singled out as the "culprit."[115]

As Taft-Hartley ground inexorably toward final passage in May and June, CIO general counsel Lee Pressman extended Murray's critique in a series of penetrating briefs and presentations. Pressman warned CIO leaders that much of what was dangerous about Taft-Hartley lay hidden in its seemingly esoteric language regarding administration and procedure. By widening employers' rights of access to workers in the representation election process, by establishing a list of unfair union practices, and by imposing on the NLRB lawyerlike standards of evidence in its findings of facts, the new law would inevitably plunge labor relations into a morass of legalistic proceedings. Even under the Wagner Act, employers had been resourceful in finding ways to avoid the clear intent of the law. They had learned that unfair labor practices cases stemming from discrimination against union activists, firings of union-minded workers, and similar acts could be strung out for years before court appeals were exhausted.

Since the late 1930s the NLRB itself had been retreating from its initially enthusiastic promotion of industrial unionism. Now an expanded board, saddled with an independent legal counsel who might work at cross-purposes from the board majority, would have even more reason to maintain a position of "neutrality" rather than implementing Wagner's clear mandate in behalf of unionism and collective bargaining. Henceforth it would be harder to organize workers, harder to protect union activists, and harder to represent union members. The great irony was that so-called conservatives, who had made careers out of criticizing the intrusion of the federal government into private matters, had created a grotesque new machine that would soon "convert . . . [federal] courts into forums cluttered with matters only slightly above the level of the police court."[116]

The Wagner Act, Pressman told the CIO leadership, "has not been weakened or emasculated." Instead "the Wagner Act as such has been repealed" in everything but name. In its place there was now "a government instrument conceived, designed, and intended to be an instrument of oppression against the trade unionists and the workers." Said Murray, it was only a matter of time before employers moved to cripple the industrial unions and roll the clock back to 1933. In Oklahoma a CIO regional director grimly predicted that the legislation "will completely wipe out Unionization [and that] all Industries will be about the same thing as concentration camps." Bittner was even more apocalyptical: with the enactment of this legislation, the old warhorse declared, "you have Fascism in its ultimate form right here in the United States."[117]

Throughout the debate over Taft-Hartley, CIO leaders had sought to mobilize the membership to pressure Congress and the president. In March the Executive Board declared April "Defend Labor Month," calling upon affiliates, local unions, and IUCs to stage rallies, distribute literature, put on radio programs, and conduct letter-writing campaigns. "Only the fullest political mobilization and firmest resistance of the people . . . can prevent this catastrophe," the board declared, calling on CIO activists to serve "as shock troops in battalions of citizens." "The drive against labor is on," Kroll told his PAC cadres, calling upon them to mobilize "thousands of Paul Reveres and Minute Men of 1947!" In May Murray appealed to a nationwide radio audience for the "immediate rallying of support from millions of Americans" to urge a presidential veto.[118]

In Detroit and other CIO centers, angry activists planned protest strikes and mass demonstrations. The UAW staged monster rallies, with over 200,000 CIO members and sympathizers jamming the Motor City's Cadillac Square on April 24. Indeed, the UAW executive board, despite the caution of newly elected president Walter Reuther, sanctioned a work stoppage as part of this rally; between two and seven o'clock, auto plants employing a half-million workers fell silent. Caravans of workers departed from the West Coast, gathering recruits along the way, for a show of force in Washington, D.C. Union members from around the country wrote, wired, or called CIO headquarters urging a national protest strike. With major coal and telephone strikes running full tilt in the spring of 1947 and with thousands of workers in Michigan, Iowa, California, and Illinois walking off the job to protest Taft-Hartley, many echoed the sentiments of Detroit UAW local activist Tony Czerwinski in believing that aggressive mobilization against antiunion legislation could lead to a "resurgence of militancy and fighting spirit."[119]

The CIO leadership, however, discouraged resorting to the strike weapon, relying instead on normal channels of political protest. Murray, Kroll, Reuther, and most others in the CIO's top leadership believed that politically inspired work stoppages in violation of collective bargaining contracts were irresponsible and dangerous. "I have never felt that lending comfort to wildcat strikes promoted the welfare of a union," Murray said in June. The CIO used the PAC apparatus to bring unionists to Washington to lobby their representatives and senators. Regional CIO functionaries coordinated letter-writing and petition campaigns. But, as Murray reported to the 1947 CIO convention, the CIO "has disapproved in most cases of mass demonstrations, caravans and the like."[120]

Militants and leftists scored the CIO leadership for its unwillingness to engage in confrontational tactics. "Murray," sneered journalist Art Preis, "could summon only petitions, postcards, and prayers." He charged that the leaders of the AFL and CIO "feared to summon 15,000,000 workers, with their hands on the basic means of production and distribution, to assert their potential power" in the effort to defeat Taft-Hartley. Vocal radicals believed that the time had come to cut loose from the institutional tethers imposed by collective bargaining contracts and the rituals of bourgeois politics and to confront the system root and branch.[121]

Despite the dire predictions of impending fascism and the denunciation of Taft-Hartley as a "slave labor" law, the official CIO did not take these steps. To some extent this was because its angry rhetoric was conscious hyperbole. At the same Executive Board meeting in which he depicted Taft-Hartley as a step toward fascism, Murray said, "I don't think the world is going to end. . . . What the hell – pendulums swing and we have our cycles in life, and we [have] got to make the best of it, using the tools at hand."[122]

Moreover, mass mobilization was risky. UAW activists could jam Cadillac Square, but what would they do for an encore? In the end, how many CIO members and their families would sanction a direct challenge to the political system? True, polls did indicate a clear class division regarding Taft-Hartley, with manual workers alone among the occupational groups surveyed favoring presidential veto of the bill. Even so, however, almost 40 percent of the workers polled supported the measure. Moreover, the 80th Congress, for all its faults, had been elected by the American people in a free election. There would be an 81st Congress. There was redress within the system. The CIO's leaders simply were not men who would jeopardize what they and their members had gained since the 1930s for the sake of defiant gestures.[123]

Taft-Hartley was a warning and a stimulus. With at least thirty state legislatures considering legislation to restrict union activities, the CIO had to redouble its political efforts. PAC had to work more closely with the IUCs, which in turn had to follow central CIO policy more faithfully. Voter registration had to be stepped up. The voluntary $1 PAC contribution campaign had to shift to high gear. Every local union had to establish a political action committee, and CIO members had to become more active in ward, precinct, and block organizations and in efforts to generate a voter turnout of 60 million in 1948. "All of the energies, all of the fighting instincts . . . [of the CIO] must be thrust into this operation," namely the defeat of Taft-Hartley legislators. "In 1944 our members were active; but in 1946 apathy reigned supreme," said Murray. The lesson for 1948 was clear.[124]

Several provisions of Taft-Hartley provoked confusion among unionists. The requirement of an anti-Communist affidavit on the part of officers of unions wanting to do business with the NLRB struck a heavy blow. Unionists who were Communist Party members, of course, ran the risk of perjury if they signed, but many others, including Murray himself, bitterly resented being compelled to abjure disloyalty. He refused to sign the affidavit, thus depriving the USWA of NLRB services and laying the union open to AFL raiding. David McDonald, Murray's aide, believed that without the benefit of NLRB elections, organizers would have to put away their "white collars and good suits" and don "those leather jackets that we used back in 1936, '37, '38, '39, '40, and '41, when we built the union."[125]

UE leaders likewise refused to sign and urged all CIO organizations to shun the NLRB. Director of organization James Matles, a member of the Communist Party, argued that solid union organizations and close contact between leaders and rank-and-file members would protect nonsigning unions from raids and would quickly dissuade employers from initiating decertification procedures. But if CIO leaders caved in, signed the affidavit, and made use of the corrupted NLRB, he predicted, workers would rightly question their courage and would be hesitant to enlist in the campaign to repeal Taft-Hartley.[126]

Uncertainty over the impact of Taft-Hartley highlighted the emergence of political activities as a central arena of CIO concern. The great strikes of 1945–46 had simultaneously proven the vigor and staying power of the unions created in the 1930s and revealed the limits to what they could accomplish through collective bargaining. The sputtering postwar southern drive revealed the difficulties of extending organization in the postwar environment. Political and legislative setbacks were also discouraging, but CIO leaders remained convinced that aggressive political action programs would eventually pay rich dividends. Repeal of Taft-Hartley, revitalization of the NLRB, and expansion of New Deal social programs depended on political mobilization of the working people of the country. CIO members, said Jack Kroll, "must talk politics with our neighbors just as we discuss the latest news or baseball scores." PAC pledged to provide a million block workers for the 1948 presidential election campaign.[127]

Politics could be divisive, though. As foreign policy issues and related matters of domestic loyalty came to dominate public discussion, the long-standing tensions between pro-Soviet and anti-Communist elements in the CIO loomed ever larger. If political action was to be the CIO's chief response to Taft-Hartley, could the industrial union federation find ways in which the radically divergent worldviews of its Catholics and secularists, its anti-Stalinist liberals and social democrats, on one hand, and its Communists and their allies and collaborators on the other might be accommodated? Everyone, at least rhetorically, favored organizing the unorganized. All CIO adherents were determined to push back the existing frontiers of collective bargaining and to achieve greater security, higher wages, and better conditions for the membership. In purely domestic political affairs, the CIO was united in its quest for stronger civil rights legislation, the expansion of the welfare state, and the repeal of Taft-Hartley. But when it came to attitudes toward the USSR and CIO response to the Truman administration's foreign policies, CIO unity proved ephemeral. By mid-1947 severe strains were evident. With the rise of third party politics and the intensification of the Cold War over the next eighteen months, they proved overwhelming.

9 The CIO and Its Communists

Between the end of World War II and the fall of 1950 the role of Communists and their allies in the industrial union federation occupied center stage. Until 1948, the CIO's pro-Soviet and anti-Communist wings continued to observe an uneasy truce. But in 1949 and 1950 the CIO expelled eleven affiliates, which enrolled nearly a million members, on the grounds of Communist domination. Critics of the CIO leadership charged that the purge of the "left" unions deprived the industrial union federation of some of its most effective activists and that the preoccupation with Communism fatally compromised the CIO's claim to leadership in struggles for social justice, civil rights, and class equity. According to anti-Communists, however, the CIO had no choice but to distance itself from the brutal and authoritarian Stalin regime in the Soviet Union and its apologists within the industrial union movement.

The process by which the issue of Communism came to dominate and eventually to split the CIO was protracted and complex. It involved personal and institutional conflicts, fierce ideological disagreements, and fundamental differences over the nature and purposes of unionism. In its most general formulation, it was part of a broader conflict within the international left that had been raging since the Russian Revolution. Its particular character in the postwar U.S. environment, however, was determined in large part by the mounting politicization of industrial unionism and by international developments that compelled unionists to make basic choices about highly disputatious matters of foreign policy and thus about the character and direction of the CIO itself.[1]

THE COMMUNIST PRESENCE IN THE CIO

Although many of them initially opposed the formation of the CIO, Communists and their allies quickly found a home in the rebel union grouping. The CIO program of energetic industrial unionism, antifascism, and coalition with progressive political and social forces coincided with the tactical agenda of the CPUSA. Communists played major roles in building key CIO affiliates, such as the UAW, the UE, the ILWU, and the Packinghouse Workers, while general counsel Lee Pressman retained close ties with

CPUSA officials. By the end of the war, Communists and their allies[2] controlled or heavily influenced most of the big-city IUCs and were influential in political action operations. Critics charged that in shielding Communists from public criticism and permitting them to affect the CIO agenda, Murray and his aides lent them legitimacy and served their ends.[3]

During the period of U.S. participation in the war the Communist issue receded. The party itself enlisted wholeheartedly in the war effort. Under the leadership of General Secretary Earl Browder, the party reformulated itself as a "political association" in hopes that U.S. Communists could now be part of legitimate politics. Thousands of new members joined party organizations, and Communists operated more openly and more freely than ever before.[4]

Industrial unionism remained a focal point of postwar Communist activity. Party members, though comprising less than 1 percent of the CIO, served in significant leadership positions. Thus, for example, the staffs of such unions as the UE, the FTA, the ILWU, the Office and Professional Workers, and several other affiliates were heavily populated with Communists. In the UE, both the secretary-treasurer and the director of organization were Communists, as were several regional directors. Communists led the FTA, Mine, Mill, and the Fur and Leather Workers. Just before the 1946 convention the organ of the anti-Communist ACTU, which was well-informed on these matters, counted thirteen unions in the strongly anti-Communist camp, with a total membership of 2.625 million, and fourteen in that of the pro-Soviet camp, whose members totaled 1.4 million. The 1.2-million-member UAW led a list of eleven divided or undecided unions, with a total of 1.58 million members. Joseph Loftus, a *New York Times* correspondent specializing in CIO affairs, estimated that "the left controlled between ninety-two and 100" of the 305 delegates at the convention.[5]

Many progressive-minded leftists, not members of the party, closely allied themselves with their Communist colleagues. Indeed, the line between party members and allied activists was unclear. In part this was because many party members kept their membership secret. Others dropped in and out of the party in response to the degree of persecution that Communists suffered or tactical circumstances that sometimes made open party membership a liability. Many active leftists who never belonged to the party so admired the Soviet Union and so valued their association with Communists that they hewed as close to the party's position as any member.

Critics charged that Communists were incapable of being good trade unionists, since they invariably put defense of the USSR at the top of their priorities. But in fact the actual record of Communist union leaders and

Communist-oriented unions within the CIO compared favorably with that of their non-Communist counterparts. It was true that Communists and their allies often formed a cohesive bloc within a union or a local and that they caucused before meetings, exploited parliamentary procedures to gain organizational advantage, and used every opportunity to promote their programs. Certainly, Communist union officials were in regular contact with party leaders. In local and industrial union council meetings Communists were notorious for bringing issues of marginal immediate union concern, issues that affected, for example, the foreign policy interests of the Soviet Union, into protracted and sometimes exhausting debate. It was also true that during the war Communists had been particularly ardent in their denunciation of strikes, their promotion of incentive wage plans, and their advocacy of cooperative labor relations.[6]

Still, the overall record of Communist-influenced unions with respect to collective bargaining, contract content and administration, internal democracy, and honest and effective governance was good. Rank-and-file Communists exhibited a passionate commitment to their conception of social justice. As a group Communists and their close allies were better educated, more articulate, and more class conscious than their counterparts in the CIO. Communist-influenced unions such as the ILWU, the FTA, and the UE were notable for fair and efficient administration, innovative cultural and educational programs, and positive responses to the distinctive problems of minority and female workers. Often it was only the insistence of Communists and their allies that forced CIO bodies to address such "extraneous" matters as civil rights and civil liberties. The Communists, remarked one of their fiercest opponents, "were good organizers technically and in terms of spirit, aggressiveness, and courage. They were, for the most part, on the right side of battles legislative and social" and were "good trade unionists . . . financially honest and dedicated." Added a southern party leader after his break with Communism, "It is paradoxical that the organization of such a union [i.e., the FTA's Local 22, a vigorous and democratic biracial tobacco workers' unit] was made possible by a political party whose ideal, the Soviet Union, had converted unions into managerial tools to facilitate the control and exploitation of workers."[7]

In regard to race and gender the Communist-influenced CIO affiliates stood in the vanguard. Mine, Mill leaders insisted on full equality in Red Mountain, Alabama, locals, in defiance of local custom and the preferences of many white members. FTA's locals in Memphis and Winston-Salem pioneered in linking workplace struggles to campaigns for racial justice in the community. FTA's work with its large proportion of female members exhibited a commitment to gender equality rare in the labor movement of the

1940s. On a larger scale the UE, with its 150,000 or so female members, brought women into at least secondary leadership roles and led the way in seeking job protection and pay equity. The NMU, consistently within the pro-Soviet orbit into the late 1940s, battled aggressively for its African American and other minority members. Locals with vigorous Communist presence in the UAW and the Packinghouse Workers fought hardest for the rights of African Americans within both the union and the community. Communists in the UAW also pressed for black representation on the union's executive board.[8]

The CPUSA-influenced CIO affiliates were also more advanced than their counterparts in their grasp of the changing character of the labor force. Affiliates with substantial numbers of white collar and professional workers – the UE, the Office and Professional Workers, the United Public Workers, and the American Communications Association – were Communist influenced and/or led. Men and women from these unions urged CIO leaders to pay sustained attention to the banking, insurance, clerical, professional, and public workers flooding into the labor market.[9]

There was, it is true, an institutional and disciplinary link between the apparatus of the CPUSA and those members of CIO unions who were Communists. Communists held that their relationship to the CPUSA was no different from the relationship of Democratic unionists to the Democratic Party or Catholic or Jewish laborites to their respective religious organizations. But this analogy was disingenuous. Communism was, after all, a disciplined international movement, not merely a collection of progressive-minded individuals. There were sharp limits to the willingness of any individual Communist to question party positions. American Communists sought unceasingly to understand and apply international Communism's requirements. Thus, for example, postwar signals from the prestigious European and Soviet Communist Parties triggered an abrupt shift in the orientation and leadership of the CPUSA. In 1945–46 Browder was dumped, with his longtime rival William Z. Foster assuming de facto control. Only months before the object of adulation among party members, Browder was ousted from the party in February 1946 as a "social imperialist."[10]

Indeed, from the party's inception in 1919, American Communists had dutifully responded to international Communist prescriptions. The outbreak of World War II in 1939 and the attack twenty-two months later on the USSR by Germany had underscored the subservience of the CPUSA to Stalin's foreign policy. Believing as they did that the Soviet Union was the legitimate repository of the hopes and aspirations of working people everywhere, American Communists made no apologies for their prompt accommodation to Soviet developments, although their critics and even erstwhile sympathizers often found the public rationales behind such shifts devious and unconvincing.

These sudden shifts in the party line had particularly significant implications for party members and their allies in the CIO. As the putative spearhead of proletarian revolution, the Communist Party naturally emphasized its role in the labor movement. Thus those Communists who in the 1930s and 1940s had achieved influence in the CIO merited particular distinction. Men such as "Red Mike" Quill of the TWU; Donald Henderson of the FTA; Emspak, Matles, and regional director William Sentner of the UE; Maurice Travis of Mine, Mill; and others in the ILWU, NMU, and white collar unions led organizations with tens of thousands of members and exerted real power and influence. On one hand top leaders of the CPUSA regarded them as unusually useful in the effort to change American society and educate American workers. On the other hand, of course, these unionists were successful in good part precisely because they were effective in achieving the contractual advances that their members expected. World War II posed a tough test for Communist laborites, for their party-urged embrace of incentive pay plans, increased work norms, and total avoidance of strikes often pitted them against rank-and-file workers as well as political rivals.

In the postwar period the labor connection remained critical. Influential Communist publications and Soviet officials spoke somberly of the inevitable showdown with imperialist capitalism, now headquartered in the United States. Yet other authoritative signals from abroad indicated that Communists should continue to collaborate with non-Communists in social and political organizations and in the labor movement, particularly the CIO.

Influential elements in the CIO had never reconciled themselves to a permanent Communist presence. Secretary-Treasurer James B. Carey, deposed as president of the UE in 1941 largely through the influence of his erstwhile Communist allies, bombarded Murray with warnings about the Communists. Walter Reuther used anti-Communism as the basis for his narrow election to the presidency of the UAW in March 1946. Emil Rieve of the TWUA, along with many of the secondary leaders in Murray's own USWA, hammered away at Communist influence. In October 1946 anti-Communists formed the CIO Committee for Renovative Trade Unionism, designed to expose and combat the Communists. Influential too were members of ACTU, a union-support organization prominent in New York, Detroit, Pittsburgh, and other CIO centers. Its members, clergy and laity alike, had actively supported fledgling CIO unions. After the war, however, the expansion of Soviet power, with its repression of the church, helped to galvanize ACTU into becoming a leading anti-Communist force in CIO circles.[11]

Indeed, the post–World War II showdown between Communists and their allies on one hand and anti-Communist elements was no sudden bloodletting. In the 1920s, fierce battles had raged in New York's garment workers' unions between anti-Bolshevik socialists and Communists and their allies. During the same period Lewis had waged war on Communists and those who cooperated with them in his rise to unchallenged power atop the UMW. For their part, American Communists in the late 1920s and early 1930s had savagely attacked non-Communist unionists as "social fascists" and had created dual unions in coal mining, the needle trades, meatpacking, and other industries in efforts to supplant AFL organizations.[12]

Still, in the aftermath of World War II, Communists believed that Murray's dedication to CIO unity and his relatively ecumenical attitude toward politics protected them from frontal attack. This "center-left" alliance continued a troubled life throughout 1946 and into the next year. American Communists hammered away at the Truman administration's policies with regard to the Soviet Union, and they joined liberals and laborites in criticizing Truman for his ineffectual domestic programs. For the most part, they kept their attacks on Truman within the boundaries of two-party debate. They sometimes spoke of the desirability of forming a third party, but none closed the door on the possibility of finding a progressive Democrat to replace Truman.[13]

In September 1946 Truman dismissed Secretary of Commerce Henry A. Wallace from the cabinet, citing a speech that the former vice-president had just given in New York that implicitly criticized the administration's "get tough" approach to U.S.-Soviet relations. For Communists and their allies, the martyred Wallace proved a splendid repository for their political hopes. An FDR Democrat, he embodied the liberalism of the 1930s in a distinctive postwar progressive idiom. At the same time he was a credible prospect for the 1948 Democratic presidential nomination; thus Communists and other left-oriented laborites could indulge their antagonism toward the administration while remaining within the ambit of the Democratic Party.[14]

If Communists and their allies were to continue to function within the CIO, Murray's role was critical. Of even greater importance than the institutional and administrative power he wielded was his reputation as the fair-minded guardian of the industrial union project. To be sure, the CIO president regarded the intensity with which many Communists pressed the cause of black workers and the affection they exhibited toward the USSR as bizarre at best and sometimes downright sinister. In the UMW, he had willingly implemented John L. Lewis's draconian anti-Communist policies.

In the late 1930s he had eliminated Communists from SWOC. During the war his fury over Bridges's endorsement of national service proposals and his rage over the ardor with which men such as the Fur and Leather Workers' president Ben Gold embraced the No Strike Pledge led journalists and anti-Communist CIO leaders to expect him to break openly with CPUSA-oriented unionists.[15]

Murray did not consider the Communist issue central, however. Rail as he might at Bridges, he supported the ILWU leader in his decade-long battle against deportation. Like most progressive-minded Americans, he hoped for continuation of the wartime collaboration between the United States and the USSR and even declared that "I shall never attempt to criticize Russia or her form of government." He believed that strident anti-Communism played into the hands of labor's enemies. If the CIO's Communists and their allies were not entirely trustworthy, they were important parts of the progressive community as it faced the reactionary challenge.[16]

Still, Communists and their allies could never be complacent about their status with Murray. Murray's close association with increasingly vocal Catholic anti-Communist unionists and their clerical allies suggested trouble for pro-Soviet unionists, as did the vociferous anti-Communism that permeated the staff of the USWA. At a late September 1946 conference called to celebrate progressive unity in the election campaigns, Murray disconcerted Communists and their allies with sharp criticisms of Soviet foreign policy and its U.S. defenders. At the November 1946 CIO convention he engineered the adoption of a resolution proclaiming that the delegates "resent and reject efforts of the Communist Party or other political parties . . . to interfere in the affairs of the CIO."[17]

Also worrisome to those seeking to further the cause of progressive unity within the CIO was the constant presence of a vociferously anti-Communist AFL. Federation leaders charged that Communists dominated the CIO's inner councils, pointing accusingly to the influence of Lee Pressman and Len De Caux in CIO headquarters and to important roles played by party members and sympathizers such as Julius Emspak and James Matles in the UE, Harry Bridges in the ILWU, and second-line leaders in the UAW. President William Green, Secretary-Treasurer George Meany, and ILGWU president David Dubinsky constantly embarrassed CIO partisans by foregrounding the evils of Stalin's USSR and by insisting on the complicity of American Communists in the vast crimes perpetrated there. Unambiguously supportive of the anti-Soviet orientation of U.S. foreign policy, AFL officials exerted constant pressure on the CIO to move in the same direction. Moreover, Dubinsky and his ideological advisor, former Communist general secretary Jay Lovestone, lent Walter Reuther and other

CIO anti-Communists verbal and financial support in their battles with pro-Soviet elements.[18]

Indeed, Reuther's emergence among the top circle of CIO leaders signaled an escalation of Communist/anti-Communist tensions. Born in 1907, the UAW leader had migrated as a young man from the family home in Wheeling, West Virginia, to Detroit. With his younger brothers Roy and Victor, Walter had worked in the Motor City's auto shops, attended classes at Wayne University, and participated in the city's rich socialist and labor life. In the mid-1930s Walter and Victor had worked for fifteen months at the USSR's Gorki automobile complex. An active participant in the formation of the UAW, Walter Reuther emerged by the late 1930s as a major figure in the union. His leadership in 1939 of a crucial strike of Detroit-area skilled tradesmen catapulted him to directorship of the union's prestigious GM Department and to a UAW vice-presidency. Throughout World War II he was an outspoken and well-informed critic of American industry's lethargy in producing needed military equipment and an ardent advocate of worker codetermination. His leadership of the 1945–46 GM strike furthered his reputation as a militant and resourceful activist, and his bold, although unsuccessful, campaign to force GM to open its books to public scrutiny marked him as an unusually innovative union leader. His narrow victory at the March 1946 UAW convention over incumbent R. J. Thomas, who had accepted support from the UAW's dynamic Communist element, positioned Reuther to go after the Communists and their allies in the broader arena of the CIO.[19]

While in the USSR the Reuthers had expressed some sympathy with the Soviet Union, and in the UAW's savage factional conflicts of the late 1930s they often cooperated with Communists. By the end of the decade, however, the Reuther brothers had become staunch and vocal anti-Communists. In part their anti-Communism derived from UAW factional politics. In the struggles that kept the UAW in chaos until the eve of World War II, the union's Communists had emerged in a stable alliance with President R. J. Thomas and Secretary-Treasurer George Addes. The Reuthers believed that the union could only reach its potential if freed from Thomas's unimaginative leadership and from the influence of Communists and their allies, who were always ready, the Reutherites charged, to subordinate the interests of its members to the vagaries of the party line. During the war Walter Reuther attacked Communists and their friends for supporting incentive pay plans and acquiescing in abuse of the No Strike Pledge by employers.[20]

Reuther's anti-Communism, however, was not limited to these kinds of issues. Virtually alone among the CIO's prominent anti-Communists, Reuther could boast broad experience in international labor and socialist affairs. His sojourn in the Soviet Union gave him and his able and articulate brother Victor particular authority in matters relating to Communism. The cataclysmic events of the late 1930s and the early 1940s encouraged them to see the factional struggles in the CIO in the context of international developments. At a time when many on the left ignored, denied, or soft-pedaled the wholesale imprisonments, bloody purges, and mass murders conducted by the Stalin regime, Reuther continually reminded his fellow unionists of the underlying character of the Soviet system. He used CIO forums to press the connection between Stalin's regime and the machinations of Communists within the labor movement and American society generally. Thus, for example, at the 1940 CIO convention the thirty-three-year-old Reuther had attacked the Soviet Union's de facto alliance with Nazi Germany and the CIO's Communists for their apologies for the Russians. In 1943 he joined Carey, Dubinsky, and other anti-Communist labor leaders in taking up the cause of Victor Alter and Henryk Erlich, Polish-Jewish socialist leaders murdered by Stalin.[21]

To Reuther, and to CIO activists who agreed with him, the battle with the CIO's Communists was a struggle for the heart and soul of the left. Reuther identified closely with leaders of the British Labour Party and with continental social democrats and socialists, root-and-branch enemies of the Communists in the brutal ideological conflict that had raged on the European left since 1917. The worst crime of Communism, he believed, was its corruption of the very language of socialism in service of a cynical and murderous regime. Its greatest victims were workers, trade unionists, and socialists, betrayed in the name of proletarian revolution. American Communists accepted the norms and practices of democratic politics only because their relative weakness in the United States gave them no option. A confrontation with them could not long be delayed. Certainly no rhetorical slap on the wrist, as contained in the 1946 convention resolution, could serve as an adequate response to what were to Reuther fundamental differences over the nature of unionism and the definition of free society.[22]

FOREIGN POLICY, POLITICS, AND THE CIO, 1946-1948

The showdown between pro-Soviet and anti-Communist elements, however, came not as a result of high-minded debate over the future of the left but, rather, because of the intrusion of questions of foreign policy and related domestic political affairs into the CIO. In one sense, matters of foreign policy were peripheral to labor unions in the United States. Even the CIO, which had always claimed a broader and more inclusive sense of public citizenship than the AFL, was overwhelmingly concerned with collective bargaining and directly related legislative matters.

The events of the 1930s and 1940s, however, inevitably sucked even the most practical trade unionist into the vortex of foreign policy. In 1940, disagreements over foreign and defense policy and presidential politics had triggered Lewis's departure from the CIO and Murray's elevation to its presidency. During the war, of course, the CIO had embraced the Grand Alliance and FDR's vision of a peaceful postwar world based on continuing U.S.-Soviet cooperation. Now, however, mounting U.S.-Soviet antagonism dragged a reluctant CIO into the international arena and forced its leaders to make hard and divisive political choices.

The maintenance of CIO unity depended heavily on the absence of serious controversy, both in Democratic Party and CIO circles, in questions relating to foreign policy. "Following the end of the war," recalled Murray at the end of 1947, the CIO "decided to abstain temporarily from making decisions and giving vent to opinions in international affairs." So long as FDR lived and the wartime alliance remained firm, the potentially warring wings of the CIO could remain together. But now international tensions claimed the center of the political stage.[23]

CIO leaders initially favored U.S.-Soviet cooperation. In September 1945 a CIO delegation visited the USSR, touring Soviet factories, talking with unionists, and enjoying a "confab with Molotov" in an effort "to strengthen our movement's ties with the Soviet trade unions." World peace, CIO literature proclaimed, was "Everybody's Business," and the United States, the United Kingdom, and the USSR were the "main cornerstones of world organization." PAC's "People's Program" for the 1946 election campaign highlighted the need for mutual accord and proclaimed, "Our goal is peace." Criticisms of the Truman administration for provocative actions toward the USSR were frequent, and warnings about the dangers of militarism and international capitalist exploitation permeated CIO gatherings. "The common people . . . demand that there be a fulfillment of the basic policy of our late President Roosevelt for friendship and unity among the three great wartime allies. . . . We reject all proposals for American participation in any bloc or alliance which would destroy the unity of the Big Three," read the foreign policy resolution adopted at the 1946 convention by "a very large majority."[24]

Complementing these statements was the CIO's enthusiastic participation in the WFTU, established in October 1945. Gathering in Paris, representatives of the labor movements of the victorious Allies created this body to replace the International Federation of Trade Unions, which had died in the 1930s. Boycotted by the AFL on the grounds that "unions" from the USSR were nothing more than fronts for the government, the founding conference gained prestige by the active participation of the British Trades Union Congress, the eldest of the Western labor federations and the union arm of the Labour Party that now governed the United Kingdom. The CIO's energetic participation in the WFTU gave tangible form to the determination of its leaders to cultivate peace and harmony through interunion association. The CIO delegation included several consistent pro-Soviet unionists, among them Joseph Curran of the NMU, Reid Robinson of Mine, Mill, Albert Fitzgerald of the UE, and legal counsel Lee Pressman. Heading the delegation, however, was Hillman, and serving enthusiastically on it were such staunch anti-Communists as Emil Rieve, John Green of the Marine and Shipbuilding Workers, and Thomas Burns of the URW, along with Murray's central office representatives John Brophy and Allan S. Haywood. James Carey served as the CIO delegation's secretary and authored the glowing report that the group submitted to the CIO Executive Board in November.[25]

For men such as Carey the struggle with Communists within the CIO did not necessarily require a showdown with the USSR. The domestic Communists of the United States, Carey believed, were devious and unprincipled. He used the resources of his office to fight them, collaborating with the FBI. But on the international scene, Carey believed, the CIO had no choice but to encourage practical cooperation with the Soviets and to hope that one day the WFTU "might even get the Soviet trade unions to . . . eventually serve . . . the interests of the people of the Soviet Union."[26]

From the start, however, conflict accompanied CIO participation in the WFTU. AFL critics, after all, were right in charging that the Soviet unions were direct representatives of a Soviet state that permitted no autonomous civic institutions. Their enormous membership figures, inflated precisely because of their official functions in the Soviet system, and the prestige that the USSR had won by virtue of its role in the defeat of Germany, gave the Soviet All-Union Council of Trade Unions great prestige among European workers. WFTU statements and publications routinely condemned Western missteps in foreign policy while ignoring the USSR's behavior in Eastern Europe, to say nothing of the Soviet regime's treatment of its own workers. U.S. Department of State officials prodded anti-Communists, such as Carey and CIO international affairs director Michael Ross, to confront the Soviets and their allies, as did the British Foreign Office with regard to the Trades Union Congress. For their part, the Soviets and their allies backed off from their more extreme anti-Western expressions and in fact offered little objection in WFTU forums to the suppression of left-wing union activity in Spain, Greece, and Tunisia.[27]

From 1945 to early 1948 the CIO followed a divided course with reference to international affairs. Its official statements continued to deplore the growing tensions between the West and the Soviet Union. On the other hand, in its relationships with the U.S. government and its involvement with the specifics of international affairs, its top leaders pursued a de facto anti-Communist path. Thus, even as Murray leaned against the pressure for a confrontation with the CIO's domestic Communists, he consistently chose anti-Communists to represent the industrial union federation in WFTU, governmental, and internal CIO foreign policy activities. He sanctioned close collaboration between CIO functionaries, such as Carey and Ross, and the Department of State aimed at exposing and limiting Soviet influence in the WFTU. He raised no objection when the U.S. military government in occupied Germany dismissed labor advisors from pro-Soviet CIO unions.[28]

The pro-Soviet unions in the CIO acquiesced in these arrangements. So long as the CIO supported Big Three unity and so long as its official statements did not explicitly criticize the USSR, they registered only token objections to these appointments and consultations. The active role played by general counsel Lee Pressman, whose pro-Soviet sympathies remained strong, in wording and rewriting convention resolutions helped to smooth possible conflicts.[29]

By the middle of 1947, however, this approach to foreign policy was becoming untenable. By the spring of that year the Truman administration had made clear its anti-Soviet position. In Germany, Japan, Italy, Greece, France, and elsewhere administration officials enlisted U.S. unionists to cooperate in establishing pro-Western labor movements and to resist Communist unions. President Truman's sweeping call on March 12, 1947, for American military and economic aid to the governments of Greece and Turkey, the "Truman Doctrine," was, in effect, a direct rebuke to the Soviet Union and a pledge of U.S. resistance to the expansion of Communist influence anywhere. Evidence mounted in the conduct of occupation affairs in Germany and Japan that anti-Communism headed the U.S. agenda. Secretary of State George Marshall's proposal on June 5, 1947, that the U.S. extend large-scale aid to the war-ravaged countries of Europe was, in effect, another powerful declaration of the anti-Communist and anti-Soviet foundations of American foreign policy.[30]

Indeed, the debate over the character and purposes of Marshall's proposal eventually forced the issue of Communism into the open in the CIO. With considerable justice the Russian leaders charged that American support for European recovery was part of a broad anti-Soviet initiative. Through the later half of 1947 they subjected the so-called Marshall Plan to harsh abuse, charging that the United States was using Europe's weakness to gain economic domination of the continent and to enlist reluctant Europeans in the American-led anti-Soviet crusade.[31]

Marshall's speech merely indicated the intention of the government to seek public support and eventual congressional funding for aid to Europe. The actual content and character of the program remained uncertain, pending specific proposals and the eventual congressional debate and legislative action. On June 22 President Truman appointed a nineteen-member advisory committee to discuss the program's scope and to rally support. The president appointed two labor representatives, George Meany and James B. Carey, to this committee, which was chaired by Averell Harriman. With Murray's ready support, Carey accepted the appointment, terming the administration's initiative "a most efficacious step to insure the carrying out of our commitment" to building peace and prosperity in Europe. From the start Carey and other CIO officials worked closely with the administration, angrily rejecting charges that the Marshall initiative was anti-Soviet.[32]

Indeed, through much of 1947 the anti-Soviet thrust of the emerging Marshall Plan remained latent. Thus, the CIO did not immediately have to face the internal implications of its growing alignment with the government's foreign policy. Within the Harriman Committee, for example, Carey insisted that American aid be given "without political or economic strings." Murray's lengthy statement of CIO support for the foreign aid program, sent to President Truman on November 14, 1947, was a high-minded appeal for American generosity and sacrifice. Aid, it urged, "should be provided to all nations who need it." "Our outlook," declared Murray, "should be pro-democratic rather than anti this or that."[33]

These sentiments were also reflected in the resolution on foreign policy adopted at the CIO's ninth convention in Boston in mid-October. After a speech by Marshall the delegates unanimously passed a resolution that put aid in the context of peaceful resolution of international tensions, renewal of Big Three unity, and American generosity. It made no mention of any specific plan or program.[34]

Despite the bland character of the resolution, debate over its meaning suggested the disputatious nature of these foreign policy questions. Reuther, for example, pointedly invoked memories of 1940, the last time major foreign policy disputes had racked the CIO. "The very people in the CIO convention who were calling Roosevelt a war monger are now calling Truman a war monger. . . . John Lewis was wrong in 1940 . . . and the Communists were wrong in 1940, when they called Roosevelt a war monger." As for the Marshall Plan, "unless we make [it] . . . succeed[,] . . . there won't be any free trade unions anywhere in Europe, as there aren't any on the other side of the Iron Curtain." To Reuther the Marshall Plan idea was clear and simple: generous U.S. aid to Europe would "explode the propaganda that the choice is between Joe Stalin and Standard Oil."[35]

Pro-Soviet delegates responded sharply. Irving Potash, a Communist and vice-president of the Fur and Leather Workers' Union, pointed to the resolution's stress on disarmament, support for the United Nations, the extension of aid regardless of political affiliation, and Big Three unity. "The resolution," he reminded the delegates, "declares support for a sound program of postwar rehabilitation" and rejects any effort to use aid as a political weapon. It was foolish to rake over the coals of the past and to plant the seeds of divisiveness in CIO ranks.[36]

Murray's closing remarks reflected the bifurcation of the CIO in foreign policy. At one and the same time the CIO head disavowed any CIO involvement in power politics *and* cast Communism beyond the pale of legitimate political choice. The important point to keep in mind, he declared in implicit rebuke to Reuther, was that "the Marshall idea is to give money or food or economic aid to the devastated countries . . . , a means to feed the hungry and clothe the naked and shelter the homeless and give medicine to the sick." What could be less political, less contentious than this generous affirmation of simple human obligation?

Yet, as he concluded, the fundamental anti-Communism that was to him, as to Carey and Reuther, implicit in the government's initiative became obvious. Generous and timely aid, he felt confident, would cause its recipients to reject totalitarianism. "There is," he advised the hundred or so pro-Soviet delegates, "not much you and I can do about it if the people [receiving Marshall Plan aid] make up their minds they don't want Communism when they get plenty of food. . . . That is a fact."[37] Still unwilling to sanction an outright assault on the pro-Soviet left, Murray nonetheless took for granted that Communism was a pathology and, by implication, that Communists, foreign or domestic, were potential enemies rather than firm allies.

THE POLITICAL DIMENSION

In the fall of 1947 the CPUSA, responding to signals from abroad, swung decisively behind the third party option and required its laborites to back independent (later Progressive) candidate Henry Wallace. Meanwhile the embrace by Murray and most other CIO leaders of the Marshall Plan idea tied them to the central foreign policy and, eventually, political objectives of the Truman administration. Neither the CIO leadership nor the pro-Soviet unionists had much influence over the circumstances that dictated these critical decisions. Yet it was in this complex showdown, fought where foreign policy and politics intersected in the troubled world of 1947–48, that the CIO abandoned its decade-long effort to square the circle of left politics and redefined itself as a key component of the emerging liberal anti-Communist consensus.[38]

Throughout the decisive period from September 1947 to November 1948 the CIO's pro-Soviet elements and their critics rarely expressed directly the central issues that divided them. Much of the debate at the October 1947 convention, a January 1948 Executive Board meeting, and other union gatherings invoked such traditional themes as union autonomy, political nonpartisanship, and union discipline. At root, however, was a fundamental conflict. An articulate minority among the CIO's leadership believed that the U.S. political and economic system veered naturally toward imperialism, class domination, and war, and that the Soviet Union was the champion of anticolonialism, economic and social justice, and peaceful international cooperation. A broad majority among the CIO's leadership, however, believed the opposite. Increasingly, Murray came to believe that coalition with pro-Soviet colleagues was impossible. He begged them to drop their third party pipedreams, to "move over just an inch or two – you know what I mean." But he had come to understand that the only "compromise" possible was one that met their nonnegotiable stipulations. Communists and their allies might have kept Murray on the sidelines had they been able to be flexible, declared the CIO president, but such a stance was impossible to those who held that "whatever a particular foreign power has to say with respect to international situations it must forever be right, it is never wrong." During World War II these fundamentally differing conceptions could coexist, but not in the tense climate of the late 1940s.[39]

At the CIO's mid-October annual convention formal unanimity masked deep conflicts. Resolutions endorsing aid to Europe and political nonalignment meant different things to the two sides. To the pro-Soviet minority the foreign policy statement reaffirmed the CIO's adherence to Big Three unity as the key to a peaceful world order. In regard to political action, these men and women believed that the resolution kept possible third party initiatives as a legitimate option.[40]

The non-Communist majority, however, had a different understanding of these resolutions. It was not for nothing that Marshall had been invited to speak and that Secretary-Treasurer Carey was serving on the Harriman Committee. Clearly the resolution aligned the CIO with the Truman administration's European aid initiative. In playing an active role in shaping the emerging European Recovery Program, CIO leaders would no doubt dissent on particulars, but they would do so from within the tent.[41]

With regard to political action, to the mainstream leadership nonpartisanship was a coded reference, not a literal fact. Since its inception the CIO had been part of the Democratic coalition. Nonpartisanship in this context meant continuing to promote the liberal agenda in the only plausible arena, the Democratic Party, whatever its many flaws. Clearly, then, the nonpartisan convention resolution was really a declaration against a *third* party initiative and a reaffirmation of the CIO's efforts to liberalize the Democratic Party.

By the time the Executive Board met three months later, however, the political map had changed. In September 1947 Communist parties representing the Soviet Union, six members of the Soviet bloc, Italy, and France had met in central Poland to reconstitute formally an international Communist organization; the earlier version, the Comintern, had been disbanded by Stalin in 1943. The founding manifesto, which became available to American Communists early in October, bristled with attacks on the West and with calls for proletarian activism. The Marshall Plan, it declared, was "part of a general plan of world expansion being carried out by the U.S.A." that envisaged the "enslavement" of Europe, China, Indonesia, and South America. Social democrats in England, France, Germany, and Italy were "loyal supporters of the imperialists." Communists everywhere, the manifesto went on, "will form the spearhead of the resistance against plans for imperialist expansion."[42]

What did this bitter attack mean in practical terms? "Every concession to the U.S. line," the manifesto warned, "makes the backers of the line more aggressive." By implication, the effort of Communists and their allies in the United States to remain under the Democratic Party's umbrella now appeared misdirected. The manifesto seemed to offer a way out. "The chief danger for the working class at the present moment," it advised, "is that of under-estimating its own forces and over-estimating the forces of the imperialist front." If it meant anything, this manifesto seemed to mean that American Communists should promote a progressive third alternative to the hopeless Republicans and the war-crazed Democrats. If a prominent and popular politician such as Wallace headed such an initiative, clearly Communists, in and out of the labor movement, had to seize the opportunity to implement the indicated strategy.[43]

The Central Committee of the CPUSA actively promoted the creation of a third party. Communists in and out of the labor movement played key roles in convincing Henry Wallace that a mighty progressive groundswell would greet his candidacy, and on December 29, 1947, he announced his intention to run for the presidency. Party leaders told their CIO members to back the third party.[44]

In the past the CIO had been open to advocates of independent or labor party politics. Support for laborite politics had not been confined to Communists and their friends, who, indeed, during World War II had worked to squelch independent political initiatives. But CIO leaders now regarded this third party bid as an invitation to Republican victory. Murray and other top CIO leaders were convinced that the CIO's best hope for advancing its agenda lay within the Democratic Party, although not necessarily with support for Truman's 1948 bid for reelection.[45]

The clash that occurred at the January 1948 Executive Board meeting, however, went well beyond discussion of the wisdom of a third party. At the practical level it defined the basic fault line that, once and for all, separated Communists and their allies from the others. At the institutional level it involved basic questions about the character and purposes of the CIO.

Both sides invoked basic principles of union practice. On the day before the Executive Board meeting, January 21, the nine CIO vice-presidents went beyond reaffirmation of the 1947 convention resolutions. They defined nonpartisanship so as to exclude third party politics and explicitly endorsed the emerging Marshall Plan. On the next day Bridges, speaking for the pro-Soviet minority, criticized the linking of Marshall Plan support with political action, noting correctly that the two items had been separately dealt with in October. He and other Wallace supporters declared that since then the Truman administration had galloped rightward and that the entry of Wallace into the race as a third party candidate had drastically changed the political landscape. Moreover, Bridges and his supporters argued that the linkage of foreign policy and political action would in effect put the CIO in the Truman camp, making a mockery of the putative nonpartisanship of the industrial union organization. Throughout this debate, Bridges and his cohorts stressed the theme of union autonomy, declaring that the vice-presidents' resolution was an attempt to steamroller the affiliates and to impose a degree of centralized control that violated the CIO's traditions of democratic unionism.[46]

Bridges and his allies did not seek a CIO endorsement for Wallace. Rather, they stressed the need for consensus within the CIO's fragile political structure. They urged the Executive Board to reaffirm the autonomy of each union – even of local unions *within* international unions – in political matters. Since the Wallace candidacy was attracting widespread support among CIO members, declared a UE policy statement supporting the Wallace advocates, CIO-PAC could "function effectively" only "in Congressional and Senatorial elections."[47]

The implications of such a course were far reaching. Subjecting CIO-PAC's national endorsements to the de facto veto of a relatively small group of leaders would drastically weaken the industrial union federation's ability to play a serious role in national politics. The CIO's history offered no clear precedents. Almost no one connected with the CIO had dissented from its vigorous efforts in behalf of FDR in 1936 and 1944. In 1940, however, bitter division had prevented any general CIO endorsement. One way of reading this record was to point to the wisdom of making endorsements only when an obvious consensus prevailed. From another viewpoint, however, the whole purpose of having a PAC was to provide a coherent process through which the CIO could play an ongoing role in national politics.

Upholders of the vice-presidents' statement seized upon this institutional dimension. The real issue, declared Reuther, was not autonomy, because no one was suggesting that international unions could not make their own political choices; it was whether the CIO could act in the national political arena in a coherent and disciplined way. Repudiation of the vice-presidents' statement, Reuther declared, would "take the guts out of the CIO." At stake, then, was not Wallace, and not autonomy. It was whether the CIO was a forum for discussion or an authoritative labor center. Reuther, and increasingly Murray himself, challenged the good faith of the pro-Soviet spokesmen. The UAW chief was blunt: Bridges and his ilk were "not fools, they are just prostitutes." Clearly, he charged, they were dancing to tune of the CPUSA, which in turn took its cue from the Cominform.[48]

At the board meeting and at subsequent CIO gatherings Murray, hitherto restrained and at times even jocular in his references to the Communist issue, shifted to a hard-core anti-Communist line. He contrasted the Wallace initiative with the campaign of Senator Robert M. La Follette in 1924, in which Murray had participated. The Wisconsin senator, Murray recalled, had involved labor leaders at every stage in the process. Wallace, in contrast, had never consulted Murray or, apparently, others. Murray denounced "communistic interference with the affairs of the labor movement," which now decrees that "we should fight, we should quarrel, we should split, . . . because this man said something in a radio address."[49]

Later that spring Murray learned some of the details of the process by which the CPUSA Central Committee had forced its labor cadres to embrace Wallace. His chief source of information was TWU president Michael Quill, a hitherto loyal party supporter. Personally sympathetic to Wallace's candidacy, Quill nonetheless believed that the party's insistence that union functionaries risk an open split with the CIO was disastrous. At a decisive meeting in December, he reported, party leaders had brushed aside Quill's objections, disregarding the certain isolation of the pro-Soviet unions in the CIO that support for Wallace would bring. During the spring of 1948 Murray lashed out, charging that "the Communist Party is directly responsible for the organization of a third party in the United Sates" and that the behavior of Bridges and company at the January board meeting was explicable only in light of their thralldom to party bosses.[50]

Now conflict between third party supporters and defenders of the CIO escalated. The linkage of foreign policy issues, notably the Marshall Plan, and the problem of political action was reminiscent of 1940, when Communists and their allies had also opposed an incumbent Democratic president because they deemed his foreign policy inimical to Soviet interests. Anyone who disagreed with them, Murray recollected, was "a Wall Streeter, a warmonger and a traitor. That is what they said to me in 1940," which, he added, was "not so very far back."[51]

According to some of the CIO's most active progressives, however, Murray had it all wrong. UE president Albert Fitzgerald returned from the January board meeting with discouraging reports of "personal attacks . . . [and] red-baiting." Whereas in 1940 John L. Lewis had carefully separated his personal political preferences from his role as CIO head, Murray, Fitzgerald charged, was "usurping power arbitrarily." "The CIO statement," he lamented, "leads to [a] split of [the] CIO as a legislative and organizing center." Some of the most idealistic and effective organizers, PAC operatives, and activists found in the Wallace campaign an opportunity to revitalize a movement that seemingly had degenerated into bureaucratic inertia and had become an appendage of the frightening foreign policy obsessions of the Truman administration. Now was the time to stand against the militaristic tide and to redeem the promise of industrial unionism. "I feel that Murray has surrendered," declared respected PAC operative Palmer Weber. Reactionary priests and the "lousy White House mob" were now calling the shots in the CIO.[52]

Early casualties of the conflict were Bridges and Pressman. In March, Haywood, acting for Murray, removed the ILWU president as California regional director, charging that Bridges's support for Wallace would "divide our forces and jeopardize the accomplishment of our objectives." With greater reluctance Murray dismissed Pressman as CIO and USWA general counsel following Pressman's declaration after the January board meeting that he would support Wallace and run for a Brooklyn congressional seat on the third party slate. The CIO's anti-Communists welcomed the opportunity to eliminate pro-Soviet forces. Declared Bittner, the Wallace issue "was really the first open fight between the trade unionists and the communists and in the end I am sure it will do the CIO a lot of good."[53]

The IUCs and the closely related PAC bodies were critical forums. CIO officials and anti-Communist local unionists now resolved to drive the pro-Soviet influence from among the councils once and for all. For years, charged Jack Altman, a leader in the anti-Communist bloc and vice-president of the United Retail, Wholesale, and Department Store Employees, Communist-dominated councils had repeatedly "disregarded CIO policy and adopted their own foreign policy, thus embarrassing the entire CIO." The Communists and their council allies, veteran Communist-basher Germer snarled, "are for Moscow, not for the U.S.A." For years, Murray had tolerated them, but at last "he refuses to let them run wild."[54]

Communists and their allies had long recognized the political importance of the IUCs. In New York, Los Angeles, San Francisco, Detroit (Wayne County), Minneapolis (Hennepin County), and Milwaukee as well as in state councils in New York, California, Washington, Minnesota, and Wisconsin, Communists and their allies had gained leadership positions through hard work and skillful maneuvering. Council meetings were ideal forums for statements on civil rights, foreign policy, and social justice. A large city council might have several staff positions in which politically sympathetic activists could be placed, and the councils were the keys to labor's involvement in local politics. Thus, for example, the Wayne County Council, controlled by pro-Soviet forces throughout most of the 1940s, provided impetus for the political careers of its Director of Organization Coleman Young and Michigan state senator and CIO organizer Stanley Nowak. In New York Quill used the IUC to good advantage in his election to the city council.[55]

As the CIO became more politically active, however, the mainstream leadership began to pay closer attention to the councils. Kroll's restructuring of PAC operations, especially after the disastrous 1946 elections, tightened council-PAC bonds. In the fall of 1946 the Executive Board unanimously adopted new rules for the councils that explicitly described the councils as creatures of the CIO, declared that their primary function was to implement national CIO policy, and prohibited councils from associating with organizations whose goals and objectives the CIO had not officially endorsed. Clearly, these rules sought to check Communist-oriented councils, which in the past had endorsed pro-Soviet front organizations and adopted highly partisan resolutions in the name of the CIO.[56]

Early in March 1948 Brophy instructed council officers that it was "the obligation of all Councils to take a forthright stand in support of National CIO policies" on the Marshall Plan and the election. "No evasion or compromise is permissible," he warned. Any delay or obstruction of prompt endorsement of national CIO policy "will be regarded as . . . action in conflict with CIO policy."[57]

Third party supporters were outraged. A California local union official, like many associated with the pro-Soviet affiliates, was "indignant" that a supposedly democratic organization such as the CIO would issue "dictatorial orders." Pro-Wallace unionists argued that since they were composed of locals of diverse affiliates, the councils should not be used to implement the CIO's wrongheaded political agenda. The Greater New York Council rejected Brophy's letter outright, as, in effect, did the San Francisco Council, the Wayne County Council, and other Communist-influenced bodies.[58]

Throughout the spring and summer Haywood, Brophy, and perennial troubleshooter Adolph Germer visited councils around the country, seeking to blunt third party and anti–Marshall Plan sentiments. In Detroit, Los Angeles, Portland, and New York, representatives of the central CIO, along with sympathetic local unionists, struggled to wrest control from pro-Soviet leadership. In September, under Germer's direction, pro-Murray forces sought to change the rules on delegate eligibility and to pack the Wayne County IUC meeting with newly enrolled anti–third party delegates, most of them representing Reuther's UAW locals. Thwarted by the incumbent leadership, Germer led a walkout, reconstituting the council on the basis of the new delegates. Haywood promptly issued a charter to this rump group, which immediately endorsed the CIO's Marshall Plan and third party positions.[59]

In San Francisco pro-Soviet forces were too powerful to permit similar machinations. Instead, Bridges's successor as regional director, anti-Communist Steelworker Tim Burke, encouraged unions loyal to the national CIO to disaffiliate and collaborated with dissident groups in pro-Soviet locals seeking to switch international union affiliation. Critics charged that Burke even cooperated with AFL unions in the San Francisco Bay area in some of these raids. In New York and Los Angeles as well, the two sides squared off, with the pro-Soviet forces invoking local autonomy, and the CIO loyalists urging national policy.[60]

Under siege, third party elements assailed the tactics of the national CIO. Phil Connelly, a Communist and secretary of the Los Angeles IUC, alerted California CIO members about the "'crack down' policy instituted by Allan Haywood and John Brophy against Councils which chose to exercise their constitutional right to remain neutral" on the Marshall Plan and the Wallace candidacy. In Detroit, Connelly warned his membership, CIO leaders resorted to "disruption and goon tactics," while in New York they adopted a strategy of "super-legalism" by bringing a laundry list of petty charges against the leadership of the pro-Soviet council. New York Council leaders charged CIO representatives with holding a "kangaroo court," and fights erupted between pro- and anti-national CIO adherents. "I won't stay in this room with you goons," shouted one council member at her national CIO opponents. Indeed, the intervention of Haywood, Brophy, Germer, and their subordinates was often high-handed and manipulative. Brophy

justified virtually any means to foil Communist schemes "to split the progressive vote . . . and make possible the election of an even more reactionary
Congress than ever." [61]

In the event, the actual participation of pro-Soviet CIO unionists in the
Wallace movement was muted and sporadic. Leaders such as Quill, Emspak, Matles, and even Bridges carefully identified their support of Wallace
as being personal, not institutional. UE president Fitzgerald headed the
Wallace campaign's labor division, but he too disavowed any notion that he
represented his 600,000-member union. Only Mine, Mill, FTA, and several
tiny affiliates officially endorsed the former vice-president. [62]

Actually, mainstream CIO leaders shared many of their critics' objections to Truman. He had handled reconversion ineptly, relied on unsavory
machine politicians and conservative businessmen, and during the 1946
coal and rail strikes had expressed stridently antiunion views. Moreover,
the men of the CIO shared the general belief that the Missourian could not
be elected. CIO leaders frantically sought a replacement for the Democratic
nomination. PAC tried unsuccessfully to lure General Dwight Eisenhower
into the contest and then turned to Supreme Court Justice William O.
Douglas. When Douglas too backed off, Kroll and many of the fifty-five
CIO members who attended the July Democratic National Convention as
delegates switched their interest to Florida senator Claude Pepper. TWUA
president Emil Rieve announced early for Truman, but as the convention
opened, Kroll, the CIO's de facto convention spokesman, told a press conference that he "did not take any position for or against Truman" and urged
an open convention. Official CIO endorsement of the president did not
come until the end of August, in a sober and carefully phrased statement. [63]

At the convention CIO delegates were more successful in shaping the
platform. They led the successful fight for a strong civil rights platform
plank, the adoption of which, declared PAC's postmortem, "constituted a
great victory for the liberals." As southern delegates stormed out of the hall
to form a states' rights party, the future of the Democratic Party as the
vehicle of labor-liberalism seemed bright. The "Philadelphia [conven-
tion]," said Kroll, "may have been the beginning of a peaceful revolution
in the political history of our country" and "for transforming the Democratic party." Only the divisiveness of the Communist-dominated Progressive Party, gathering in Philadelphia the week after Truman's nomination,
could ruin this new beginning. [64]

This assessment of progressive possibilities applied to foreign policy as
well. CIO leaders believed that their support for the Marshall Plan and
Carey's participation on the Harriman Committee enabled them to help
to shape the eventual legislation that came before Congress early in 1948.

CIO spokesmen pressed for substantial labor involvement in the development and administration of the European Recovery Program. They opposed business-supported deflationary and underconsumptionist approaches to economic expansion. They stressed the humanitarian nature of the plan, playing down its strategic and military aspects. The basic recovery plan legislation, Senate Bill 2202, Murray declared in March, "is a significant victory for the CIO position on European Recovery," and he urged all CIO members to join immediately in the effort to "roll up a nationwide demand for ACTION NOW."[65]

Their opponents charged that the leadership had become an appendage to the Democratic Party. The CIO leadership, declared Julius Emspak, had "abandoned [the] interests of the membership to become statesmen." Added his colleague James Matles, the "CIO has ceased to be a union . . . [and] has become a labor front." Declared President James Durkin of the Communist-oriented United Office and Professional Workers, the emerging European recovery legislation was "a military plan based on political discrimination and completely at variance with CIO's policies."[66]

It was true that the foreign policy objectives of the Truman administration were not fully compatible with those of the CIO. Murray, Carey, and other pro-administration CIO leaders were not privy to the real nature of their own government's international agenda. At least until a Soviet-engineered coup at the end of February 1948 brought the Communists to power in Czechoslovakia, they continued to harbor hopes that Marshall Plan aid was compatible with U.S.-USSR cooperation, though in fact there remained little sentiment in the administration for such a view. Despite Marshall's uplifting speech at the 1947 CIO convention, the president and his advisors were convinced that the confrontation with the USSR was the central issue of their times and that the CIO was a critical component in rallying support for the administration's policies.[67]

Indeed, the administration's cultivation of labor in behalf of foreign policy objectives was evident in the circumstances surrounding the president's response to the Taft-Hartley Bill. Truman vetoed the measure on June 20, 1947, just two weeks after Marshall's speech floating the concept of European aid and less than a week before a decisive meeting of foreign ministers in Paris. On the eve of his veto measure, reported NLRB member James Reynolds, Truman revealed his innermost thinking about the connection between labor law and foreign policy. Taft-Hartley, he admitted, was essentially a good and needed law, and he was confident that Congress would override his veto. Then he showed Reynolds a globe. He snapped his fingers and said, "You know, Reynolds, . . . the Taft-Hartley [Act] . . . is about that important compared to this," indicating the vast expanse occupied by the USSR. Aid to Europe in the effort to contain Communism "and the preservation of democracy, is the most important thing." If he did not veto Taft-Hartley, he would lose labor support and most likely the election, but "if I veto it, I'm going to hold labor support . . . [and] I'll be re-elected and the Marshall Plan will go forward." [68]

In important respects both the CIO leadership and the pro-Soviet elements were acting in the dark. The desire to align themselves with what they understood to be the correct international analysis of the rapidly developing world crisis, now highlighted by the U.S. Marshall Plan project, impelled CPUSA leaders into the third party venture and forced CIO Communists to confront Murray and the national leadership directly. Thus both the pro-Soviet and pro-administration elements in the CIO were hostage to political forces, namely the international Communist movement and the Truman administration's foreign policy circles.

Yet the two cases were not entirely parallel. The pro-Soviet unionists had no influence over or access to the decision-making process in the Soviet bloc and little influence within CPUSA circles. They could merely accommodate themselves to the party's choices. The position of CIO leaders with reference to the Democratic Party and the Truman administration was different. Carey, after all, was a member of the Harriman Committee, and Murray was fully able to express the CIO's distinctive interpretation of the Marshall Plan initiative. Perhaps Truman did veto the Taft-Hartley Bill in an effort to solidify his labor support. But mixed motives and the accommodation of important constituencies were the essence of politics. The administration's soft-pedaling of the more confrontational aspects of the Marshall Plan initiative in its dealings with CIO leaders was a subcase of its overall effort to sell this far-reaching and unprecedented program to the American people, a correlative of hard-core national security arguments its spokesmen used in persuading conservative Republicans.

Both sides invoked the rank and file to back their position. Endorsement of Truman, pro-Soviet unionists said, would discredit the CIO among ordinary workers. The proceedings of the July convention that created the Progressive Party and officially launched the Wallace campaign, declared a prominent UE leader, constituted "a recording of the voices, sentiments and aspirations of millions speaking through the hundreds of common folk who, as delegates, spoke their piece." In response, national CIO leaders stressed the hopeless nature of the Wallace candidacy. Voters seemed to support this view. A mid-campaign survey showed CIO members who expressed a choice favoring Truman by 55 percent to 38 percent for Dewey, with Wallace registering only 10 percent. Moreover, union members were convinced by a more than two-to-one margin that Wallace's campaign was being run by the Communists, and through the summer and fall they expressed clear hostility toward the Communist Party and the Soviet Union on a variety of issues. In the end, Wallace gained only 2.38 percent of the popular vote and won no electoral votes.[69]

In the complex course of events surrounding the Marshall Plan and the third party controversy, the CIO took a decisive turn. In effect, it was now an integral part of a political coalition. To be players in the game, CIO leaders had to work within the admittedly unsatisfactory Democratic Party. On the whole, they set about to do this willingly enough. PAC operatives saw themselves as vigorous and effective spokesmen for America's working people, trading punches in the central arena in which public policies were debated. CIO operatives believed that in politics, as in collective bargaining, they rarely accomplished their complete agenda. Like organizing and collective bargaining, politics was steady work.

PURGE

"It is . . . Communism and anti-Communism. There is no question about that," said Philip Murray in May 1949. Indeed, the battle that raged in the CIO in the wake of the 1948 election involved conceptions of the left that were fundamentally at odds. Would the CIO continue as a component of a liberal-left coalition in which Communists and their allies were legitimate participants? Put differently, could the American branch of a Leninist movement play a legitimate role in bourgeois labor politics? The "left" invoked union autonomy, the rights of dissent, and the CIO's tradition of political tolerance, while their opponents appealed to majority rule and rejection of outside interference. But in the past the "left" had cheerfully run roughshod over claims of autonomy, the rights of dissent, and appeals to diversity when their goals demanded. For their part, the anti-Communist crusaders resorted to legalistic pettifogging, bullying, and collaborating with illiberal elements in their zeal to destroy their enemies.[70]

After the 1948 elections the CIO leadership stepped up its attacks on pro-Soviet elements and in 1949–50 drove eleven affiliated unions out of the industrial union federation. In this anti-Communist jihad, CIO officials were aided substantially by anti-Communist liberals, ACTU and other Catholic organizations, and, most significantly, agencies of the federal government. In the anti-Communist project, the Executive Board gained broad powers to compel affiliates and councils to conform to CIO policy. At the same time, however, the loss of nearly a million members and the inability of the CIO to recruit new members to replace them underscored the continuing weakness of the CIO as a central labor federation.[71]

The annual CIO convention, held in Portland, Oregon, three weeks after Truman's victory, signaled the start of open warfare against the Communists and their allies. Murray led the attack. "We do not want the Communist party over in New York to be pulling the strings and having them act here like Charlie McCarthys," he insisted. In the debates over resolutions endorsing PAC, the Marshall Plan, and CIO organizing policy, Murray and his chief spokesmen, who now included Carey, Rieve, ACWA head Jacob Potofsky, and Walter Reuther, lashed out repeatedly at the third party advocates, who in defense appealed to the CIO's tradition of political ecumenicalism. These exchanges were often accompanied by loud heckling and even anti-Semitic utterances from the floor when pro-Soviet spokesmen rose to defend themselves.[72]

Some third party advocates seemed to distance themselves from their pro-Soviet colleagues. Thus, to the dismay of his usual allies, UE president Albert Fitzgerald declared that "I think Vishinsky and Molotov are engaging themselves in saber rattling and war mongering." Fitzgerald's administration-supported reelection as one of the CIO's nine vice-presidents suggested that Murray harbored hopes that he might, as Joseph Curran of the NMU had done and as Quill was in the process of doing, split with the pro-Soviet forces in his union and thus bring the energetic UE in line with CIO policy.[73]

Murray and his allies ridiculed the performance of leftist affiliates such as FTA, the Office and Professional Workers, the FE, the United Federal Workers, and Mine, Mill. Organizers from these unions put party activities ahead of legitimate union concerns, charged their critics. "I think," said George Baldanzi, "we are all getting tired of this so-called dialectical minestrone." No one acknowledged the special difficulties associated with organizing food processing, agricultural, and white collar workers, nor were the equally unimpressive performances of politically correct affiliates such as the United Paperworkers, the Marine and Shipbuilding Workers, or the Gas, Coke, and Chemical Workers aired. In his opening remarks, Murray urged "a rebirth of that spirit [of 1936–37] in the CIO." But in fact the conduct of the debate over organizing clearly showed that the leadership was less interested in revitalizing industrial unionism than in bashing the pro-Soviet forces.[74]

Despite the sweeping criticisms of allegedly underachieving leftist affiliates, the CIO did little to promote organizing in such fields as white collar, government, food and agricultural, and service work. For the next several years it largely confined its organizing activities to raiding the dissident affiliates, though it was not only ideological difference that underlay these assaults. Such factors as rivalry with the AFL and the desire of large organizations such as the USWA and the UAW for coherent bargaining arrangements also played a part. There was, for example, no intrinsic reason why iron miners in Alabama should be members of Mine, Mill, while their counterparts in Minnesota were in the USWA, or why some of the CIO's farm equipment workers should be in the UAW and others in the small FE. Die casting, a critical process in much heavy metal work, was organically linked with the building of automobile engine blocks, and yet in 1938 the CIO had chartered a separate die casters' union that Mine, Mill eventually absorbed.

These organizations, granted charters in the CIO's early days of promiscuous organizing, struggled with small memberships. Scattered Mine, Mill locals in metal mining and manufacturing were vulnerable to AFL challenge, employer attack, or the temptation to accept substandard contracts. The same possibilities prevailed with regard to the FE, UAW leaders charged. Nonetheless they clung tenaciously to their charters, despite periodic efforts of the larger affiliates to force them to merge.

The Taft-Hartley Act's non-Communist affidavit intensified the practical and ideological attacks on these unions. The officers of all of the pro-Soviet affiliates refused to sign the non-Communist affidavit, thus depriving them of NLRB rights and laying themselves open to employer-instigated decertification elections and AFL raids. UE director of organization James Matles eloquently advocated a CIO boycott of NLRB proceedings. A vigorous rank-and-file union, he urged, could use its shop-floor power to compel employers to deal with it. His views gained some initial legitimacy by the fact that Lewis, Murray, and the officers of the AFL's International Typographical Union, the nation's oldest continuous labor organization, refused on principle to sign the insulting affidavit.[75]

Most CIO leaders, however, believed Matles's position irresponsible. They believed that the NLRB was a critical component in gaining union recognition. They regarded the willingness of leaders of the "left" to expose their memberships to the disadvantages entailed in noncompliance as further evidence of Communists' disregard for workers' interests. The official CIO stand on the affidavits was to leave the decision on whether or not to sign to the affiliates. Apart from Murray and the heads of a dozen Communist-oriented unions, however, all quickly conformed. From the start, USWA's organizers and regional directors pressured their chief to reconsider, and after the Steelworkers suffered several embarrassing election defeats, Murray reluctantly signed an affidavit on July 29, 1949, leaving the pro-Soviet organizations the only holdouts. Even these unions sought ways around the affidavit. In both FTA and Mine, Mill, for example, party member presidents were replaced by arrangement with non-party sympathizers, who promptly hired them as nonelected adminis-trators.[76]

Walter Reuther quickly began using the affidavit against the nonsigning UE, FE, and Mine Mill locals. Elected UAW president by a narrow margin in 1946, Reuther initially faced a closely divided executive board and a UAW apparatus studded with his enemies. Raiding brought in new locals, invariably with pro-Reuther leadership, thus solidifying his control. Besides, UAW organizers claimed, if the UAW did not step in, the AFL rivals would. Moreover, raiding was a means of bringing major segments of the metalworking sector under UAW control. Reuther believed that with almost three-fourths of workers in basic industry members of unions, the time was ripe for the consolidation of a unified and powerful metal and vehicle workers' union. The anti-Communist affidavit, however repugnant, offered opportunities to achieve this goal.[77]

FE was a prime target. UAW leaders of all ideological persuasions had grumbled about Lewis's sanctioning in 1938 of a separate organizing committee for workers in the agricultural implements field and in 1942 had opposed the granting of a separate charter to FE by the CIO. Yet FE had established a reputation for efficiency and militancy. CIO officials tried sporadically to promote the absorption of FE by the UAW. During the year after Reuther's accession to the UAW presidency, in 1946–47, his opponents negotiated a deal to permit the smaller union to enter the UAW as a virtually autonomous department. Reuther and his allies correctly saw this as a maneuver that would bolster his factional rivals. Reutherites wanted, rather, to bring the FE membership into the UAW on a local-by-local basis, with the process overseen by Reuther-appointed organizers. A UAW membership referendum on the question of en bloc FE affiliation in June and July of 1947 resulted in an overwhelming victory for him.

At the UAW's October 1947 convention Reuther was reelected and drove most of his enemies from the executive board. Securely in power, he went after FE locals. In the spring of 1948 UAW forces ousted the FE in Peoria and Memphis. With FE leaders supporting Wallace, Reuther pressured the CIO to compel FE to merge with the auto union on terms dictated by the UAW. When in March 1949 the FE convention rejected forced merger, the CIO Executive Board endorsed UAW raiding, and at the convention seven months later FE's charter was revoked. Through the early 1950s the two unions fought brutal picket line battles throughout the Midwest. Eventually the UAW absorbed most of the old FE locals but not until after the Autoworkers had suffered a number of humiliating defeats in representation elections.[78]

Mine, Mill faced challenges from several sources. Over the years this affiliate had perplexed the CIO leadership on account of its unlikely mixture of radicalism, factionalism, eccentric and unstable leadership, and racial progressivism. During World War II its membership had peaked at 100,000. It had pockets of strength among the metal mining and smelting workers of Idaho, Montana, Utah, and Ontario and clung to footholds among the impoverished lead miners and smelter workers of Kansas and Oklahoma and among copper miners and refinery workers in Arizona and Texas. In addition, its organizers, many of whom reflected the erratic but pronounced pro-Soviet politics of the top leadership, built large locals among the brass and munitions workers of Connecticut. On Alabama's Red Mountain, which supplied iron ore to the mills and foundries of Bessemer and Birmingham, Mine, Mill had established five locals, representing over 4,000 workers, evenly divided between blacks and whites.[79]

Mine, Mill's president for the decade after it joined the CIO in 1935 was Reid Robinson, an unsteady activist from the fabled Butte, Montana, Miners Union. A faithful spokesman for the pro-Soviet left, Robinson began during World War II to borrow money from employers and in the fall of 1946 resigned the presidency under a cloud. His successor, Maurice Travis, was a Communist Party member, and when Travis stepped down the next year in the wake of controversy over his election, he was replaced by a handpicked successor, John Clark, and assumed the secretary-treasurer post. Meanwhile, dissidents in Connecticut, Alabama, and Utah fought the pro-Soviet leadership, with Connecticut anti-Communists in the large brass workers' locals working closely with Catholic labor action groups and appealing to the CIO to force a change in leadership. In addition, the anti-Communist Marine and Shipbuilding Workers, reeling from the postwar devastation of the shipbuilding industry, sought to pick off locals in Connecticut, Utah, and Nevada. Meanwhile, the UAW moved aggressively against Mine, Mill's Midwestern die casting locals and through the summer of 1948 brought 20,000 former Mine, Mill workers into the auto union.[80]

The most controversial raid on Mine, Mill, however, took place in Alabama. Among the iron miners and foundry workers there, Mine, Mill had built biracial local unions, largely on the basis of solid support among African American workers. Workers in the neighboring locals of the USWA, a substantial majority of whom were white, believed that Mine, Mill's egalitarianism invited conservative attacks on the CIO. Moreover, the existence of vulnerable Mine, Mill locals hindered the USWA in its efforts to improve its contracts covering iron miners and smelter workers in Minnesota.[81]

Many of the white members of Mine, Mill's Red Mountain locals despised their union's Communist orientation and its promotion of racial equality. Mine, Mill leaders, reported one disgruntled white member in 1943, were "trying . . . to change our way of living – the segregation policy that we have been raised up under in the South." Dissidents claimed that they needed CIO help to oust the radical union because "the colored men have the controlling vote and they are being coached how to go."[82]

Unwilling to sanction the breakup of a CIO affiliate, Murray initially held back. In the wake of the events of 1947–48, however, he okayed the issuance of CIO LIU charters on the grounds that these disaffected workers would otherwise be lost to the CIO. USWA representatives actively encouraged the rebellion, acquiescing in the racist agenda of the white rebels. After a savage campaign in which Klansmen and white unionists openly intimidated blacks, the CIO unions defeated the Mine, Mill locals in May 1949 by a vote of 2,996 to 2,233.[83]

This episode was one of the most violent in the CIO's crusade against the pro-Soviet left. Shortly before the Alabama balloting, representatives of the rival forces assembled at a local radio station for an election eve broadcast. According to Murray's personal representatives, after George Elliott, a dissident Mine, Mill member, had spoken in behalf of the CIO, he was accosted by Mine, Mill secretary-treasurer Travis. Travis called Elliott a "popsicle," an epithet denoting lack of manhood and subservience to the company, Tennessee Coal & Iron. Furious, Elliott slugged Travis, and in the ensuing fight Travis was badly injured, eventually losing an eye. Mine, Mill adherents had an entirely different version. In this account, Travis was innocently listening to the broadcast when the Steelworkers' thugs bashed him with a chair and "then proceeded to kick in his face and jump on him. . . . While they were beating Travis the gangsters, led by [Murray's 'personal representative' Nick Zonarich], were calling Travis a 'N —— r lover.' "[84]

Murray quickly accepted Zonarich's version of the incident. The CIO president accused Mine, Mill of "deliberately and methodically and systematically develop[ing] . . . a feeling of racial hatred" and of "calumny," "slander," and "character assassination." He termed Travis's injury "regrettable." But he directed his severest condemnation at Travis's "application of vile language" and at Mine, Mill's press releases and flyers, which featured allegations of USWA complicity with the Ku Klux Klan and "appeals to the prejudices of the colored people."[85]

Another union with a strong record on racial issues, FTA, likewise suffered crippling CIO attacks. Attention was focused on its large biracial Local 22, representing over 12,000 workers at the large R. J. Reynolds Tobacco Company facilities in Winston-Salem, North Carolina. After a strike in the summer of 1947, Local 22 gained significant improvements in wages and working conditions for its members. It developed imaginative educational and community action programs, and its members revitalized the lethargic local chapter of the NAACP. Local 22 activists were instrumental in electing a black minister to the Winston-Salem city council. Communists in FTA and the CPUSA were especially proud of Local 22. Recalled a leading southern party functionary, "Every time someone with a brass-hat brain in New York decided we ought to support this or that international cause, they'd call on . . . Local 22, to . . . pass a resolution of support," thus exposing it to anti-Communist attacks.[86]

Virtually since its inception as the UCAPAWA, FTA had posed problems for the CIO leadership. Murray detested its president, Donald Henderson, a former economics instructor whose lengthy lectures on politics, racial practices, and organizational priorities made him few friends in the CIO. The encouragement of political and union militancy among blacks by FTA in the South clashed with the CIO's more cautious policy of reassuring white workers and community leaders while quietly recruiting blacks.[87]

By 1949 both FTA and its prized Local 22 were in trouble. Raiding by the CIO's Packinghouse Workers and Brewery Workers, as well as by AFL organizations, sapped FTA strength, which declined to under 25,000 members nationally. Cigarette manufacturers mechanized production and thus reduced employment, especially in processes that employed blacks. In Winston-Salem, blacks no longer constituted a majority of the labor force. In 1947 HUAC had conducted hearings in the North Carolina city and highlighted the local's unwavering support for Soviet policies. Employers, civic leaders, and AFL organizers exploited racial prejudice in attacks on Local 22. At the urging of North Carolina CIO officials, Murray and Haywood dispatched Willard Townsend, African American head of the CIO's small UTSE, to provide a legitimate CIO alternative to the controversial FTA.

In the resulting NLRB elections, held in March 1950, Local 22 was defeated, and the CIO presence in Winston-Salem was expunged. In the first balloting, involving Local 22, the UTSE, the AFL Tobacco Workers, and an employer-backed company union, 5,300 workers voted for union representation against 3,400 for "no union" (in effect, a vote for the company union). But the union votes were split, with Local 22 capturing 3,300, the AFL 1,500, and the UTSE a mere 540. In the runoff election two weeks later, with Winston-Salem's mayor urging workers to "drive Stalin's little songbirds from our doorsteps," and with both the AFL and the CIO hoping to pick up the pieces if Local 22 lost to "no union," FTA appeared to have gained a slim majority of the 7,800 votes cast. Several months later, however, the NLRB ruled that 134 disputed ballots be added to the "no union" total. The result was a 60-vote loss for the embattled organization and the effective end of a union presence among the R. J. Reynolds workers. The issues of Communism and foreign policy, seemingly remote from the hot packing sheds, processing rooms, and cigarette machines of North Carolina, thus led directly to the dismantling of this hopeful experiment in biracial unionism.[88]

The CIO's approach to its largest pro-Soviet union, the UE, differed from that exhibited with regard to the smaller affiliates. The UE initially had the leadership and resources necessary to fight off most raiding forays. Moreover, CIO secretary-treasurer James Carey, deposed in 1941 as the union's president, wanted to keep the big union intact while battling within it to supplant the pro-Soviet leadership.

The refusal of the UE's officers to sign Taft-Hartley affidavits nonetheless made the union vulnerable. Indeed, part of Carey's brief against Emspak, Matles, and Fitzgerald was that their refusal to sign exposed the union to AFL raids and to decertification proceedings. In the two years after the passage of Taft-Hartley, UE locals underwent more than 500 raids. Over Carey's objections, the UAW picked off large eastern locals in armaments and office equipment plants. UE officers accused CIO national representatives of participating in "this conspiracy against UE" and charged that "the offenders have connived with dissident and disruptive minorities in these unions." Reuther replied only that "those who willfully and consciously defy the democratic policies of the CIO in order to serve interests contrary to the welfare of their membership must be prepared to reap the wrath of their rank and file."[89]

On the whole, however, the UE managed to retain its membership. In August 1946 Carey and his supporters had formed the UE Members for Democratic Action and ran slates of candidates at each subsequent UE national convention. Not until 1949, however, after the UE had virtually left the CIO, did the dissidents even come close in their efforts.[90]

After the UE had severed its ties with the CIO in the summer of 1949, Murray and Haywood chartered a rival electrical workers' union, the IUE. Throughout the next decade and more, the UE and the IUE battled for the right to represent workers in the nation's electrical, appliance, heavy engine, and related sectors. The UE had an enviable reputation even among its anti-Communist critics for the quality of its contracts and the fiscal honesty and efficiency of its administration. Rooted in the class-conscious labor activism of the 1930s, UE's organizers and operatives drove hard bargains and established vigorous local unions with tough grievance committees.

Carey and the new IUE, on the other hand, were often more responsive to the electrical companies' demands for increased productivity in the face of mounting international competition, although the unpredictable Carey mixed this fundamentally accommodationist stance with militant outbursts. He and his colleagues relied heavily on anti-Communist rhetoric. The contracts they negotiated tended to be less restrictive on matters such as incentive pay plans, time and motion studies, seniority, discipline, and the rights of women workers, who comprised a large proportion of the appliance industry's labor force.[91]

The UE's leaders were experienced and steady union veterans. Carey, in contrast, still a youthful thirty-eight when Murray appointed him to head the fledgling IUE, had been a hands-on union activist only during the 1930s. He had served as CIO secretary since 1938 and was a sharp critic of the Soviet regime and its American apologists, including most notably his former colleagues in the UE. Carey enjoyed close associations with liberal politicians. He chaired the CIO's CARD and was a member of President Truman's Committee on Civil Rights. Now, however, when he sought to move back into the sharply different arenas of organizing and bargaining, he soon proved erratic, histrionic, and gullible.[92]

In the exhausting effort to supplant the UE in dozens of local unions, the rebels gained critical support from Roman Catholic clergy and from the FBI and other federal and state agencies. Carey worked closely with Pittsburgh priest Charles Owen Rice, a long-term supporter of industrial unionism and an increasingly influential anti-Communist figure. Many electrical workers were sons and daughters of early twentieth-century immigrants from central and Eastern Europe, among whom anti-Soviet and anti-Russian feelings were common. Thus, even when they perceived the UE's pro-Soviet leaders as being effective bread-and-butter unionists, many Catholic workers turned against them.[93]

Carey also collaborated extensively with the FBI, other federal agencies, and congressional investigating committees. The IUE president fingered former colleagues as Communists and security risks. He used the notoriously irresponsible proceedings of HUAC and the Senate Committee on Internal Security to discredit his rivals, and he prodded employers and federal agencies involved in military production to bar them from employment on national security grounds. "It is," said Carey in January 1950, "a fight to the finish between democratic American trade unionism and the attempts of the Kremlin to preserve the UE as a mass base for the expression of Soviet foreign policy in this country." Indeed, at least according to one of the country's leading labor journalists, he even told an American Legion convention that "yes, we would join with fascists in order to fight, in a war, Communists."[94]

UE membership fell rapidly while the IUE reached a peak of 325,000 members in 1955. Even so, total membership in the electrical workers' jurisdiction fell by almost 30 percent during this period, and both AFL and other CIO unions continued to recruit members in what once had been unchallenged UE territory. Aggressive corporate labor relations policies, increasing international competition, decentralization of operations into nonunion areas, and, above all, the continuing interunion conflict fragmented a once-cohesive bargaining environment.[95]

Through 1949 and into the next year, the national CIO moved to restrict, isolate, and eventually to expel the pro-Soviet unions. Executive Board resolutions at the May 1949 meeting in effect called for the ouster by rank-and-file workers of officers of affiliates who refused to back CIO convention and Executive Board decisions. This board meeting, according to a CIO press release "one of the most important . . . in [the] organization's recent history," also ended the CIO's membership in the WFTU and endorsed the recently created North Atlantic Treaty Organization. Murray, the CIO spokesman said, was "disgusted with the situation in which some left-wing unions flout policy" and threatened them with more drastic action at the November convention in Cleveland.[96]

Murray was now determined to get rid of the pro-Soviet organizations. He resolved to ask the 1949 convention simply to expel the pro-Soviet unions. But general counsel Arthur Goldberg and others argued that continuing pressure would be more effective. By having the convention establish formal grounds for expulsion and authorize a "legal" trial of each of the offending affiliates, the CIO could reveal to all that men such as Bridges and Ben Gold were party-dominated dupes. Surely these "trials" would trigger membership revolts. And, they pointed out, by keeping the beleaguered unions in the industrial union federation for several additional months, the CIO would continue to collect their monthly per capita dues, which over a year could amount to as much as $200,000. Resolutions adopted at the convention, over the bitter objections of the beleaguered delegates, authorized the Executive Board by a two-thirds majority to refuse to seat anyone "who is a member of the Communist Party . . . or who consistently pursues policies and activities directed toward the achievement of the program or the purposes of the Communist Party." Moreover, the delegates shouted through a companion resolution empowering the board to expel any affiliate it deemed to have been following policies "consistently directed toward the achievement of the program or the purposes of the Communist Party." Armed with these changes in the CIO constitution, Murray and Goldberg could now orchestrate trials of the offending affiliates' officers.[97]

Leaders of some pro-Soviet unions were defiant. Even before the convention, the UE executive board charged that Murray and his allies had become "completely subservient to the dictates of the [Truman] Administration and the Democratic party." They vowed not to "knuckle down" and, after the decisive May board meeting, suspended payment of the UE's monthly dues to the CIO. The convention likewise revoked the FE's charter when it failed to heed the CIO directive that it merge with the UAW.[98] During the debate over the new powers of expulsion, Bridges was defiant: the ILWU, he asserted, "has no plans to leave the CIO. . . . To get rid of us you are going to have to throw us out."[99]

Over the next year, the national CIO leadership proceeded to do precisely that. On the day following the convention, William Steinberg, president of a small affiliate representing several thousand shipboard radio and telegraph operators, filed charges against ten affiliates under the terms of the just-adopted resolutions. Included on Steinberg's list were Mine, Mill, the ILWU, the Office and Professional Workers, FTA, the Fur and Leather Workers, and several small West Coast maritime unions, along with the United Furniture Workers.[100] By this time, of course, both the FE and the UE were no longer in the CIO. Murray appointed four three-man trial committees to assess the charges. Meanwhile, the Research Department gathered evidence of the unions' consistent support for pro-Soviet policies. According to the convention resolutions under which the trials would take place, it was not necessary to demonstrate actual membership in the CPUSA, a virtually impossible task in most cases; the "prosecution" merely needed to show a systematic pattern of pro-Soviet behavior.[101]

In the trials, which took place in the first five months of 1950, Steinberg relied on two kinds of "evidence," documentary material showing the parallels between the positions of the USSR and the CPUSA on one hand and those of the unions on the other, and testimony from union members documenting specific episodes of Communist influence. Steinberg, who was merely the mouthpiece for the CIO's anti-Communist consensus, asserted that from the mid-1930s onward, the accused unions had repeatedly changed their positions to conform to the policies of the USSR and the CPUSA. Steinberg and the researchers who prepared the CIO case focused on specific controversial episodes in which opinion within the industrial union federation was divided and in which shifts in the Soviet line required rapid reversals on the part of Communists. Thus, for example, the U-turn in August 1939 from strident support for U.S. efforts to stop Hitler to equally adamant insistence on American neutrality in a war of "rival imperialisms" indicated that the Communist line, not independent judgment, was dictating their stands. Equally telling was the charge that the sudden embracing of Wallace's candidacy in 1947–48 stemmed directly from the

CPUSA's interpretation of the Cominform's September manifesto and not from personal conviction or consultation with other CIO leaders. In the midst of the case against the Office and Professional Workers, after listening to James Durkin describe disputes about the Marshall Plan, foreign policy, and the Wallace campaign as honest differences of opinion, an irritated Murray interrupted: "The sudden changes, the sudden changes; that's the point." [102]

CIO researchers did little more than compile material from Communist and union newspapers and proceedings. One of the chief investigators, Paul Jacobs, recalled that after Goldberg had directed him to prepare the case against the ILWU, "I spent the next few weeks in the library of the Hoover Institute at Stanford University, reading through old copies of the Communist newspapers." Then he examined Longshoremen's documents at the University of California. Upon arriving in Washington, Jacobs was asked to present the material, which, of course, clearly demonstrated the parallels between the positions of the pro–Soviet unions and those of the Communists. While the cobbling together of parallel statements would hardly have held up in a law court, the reminders of the precise sequencing of the actions of the pro–Soviet unionists and especially of the abrupt and categorical advocacy of positions earlier opposed with equal vehemence were telling. [103]

Testimony from defecting members of the accused unions and lapsed Soviet supporters was more damaging. Ken Eckert and Homer Wilson, former high-ranking officers of Mine, Mill, were particularly effective in documenting specific meetings at which party officials issued instructions to the union's leaders. Testimony from former party supporters Joseph Curran and Michael Quill as to the degree of influence, if not control, exercised by the party in running the NMU and the TWU – both now free of the taint of Communist domination and hence not under trial – was also precise and compelling. Quill, who had been very close to the party for over fifteen years and who enjoyed a reputation for honesty, detailed the party's particular interest in promoting the CIO's public employee unions, often at the expense of his own Transport Workers. He quoted party labor functionary Roy Hudson as directing him in 1941 to stop organizing Detroit street railway men and to help establish a local of a CIO state, county, and municipal workers' union headed by party member Abram Flaxer. "'Detroit is the motor city, a border city. Flaxer has to get a toe-hold,'" Hudson had said. Again, in 1947, Flaxer was given a party dispensation to refrain from attacking the CIO leadership over foreign policy and political questions. Quill reported that party secretary Eugene Dennis told him that "'Flaxer must not upset the applecart, because it is important that he maintain the cloak of [the] CIO in the Canal Zone.'" [104]

The trial proceedings were far from impartial. All twelve members of the trial committees were staunch anti-Communists. The CIO itself functioned as investigator, prosecutor, judge, and executioner. Steinberg's initial charges were vague; at the ILWU trial in May, Bridges, who had survived years of federal prosecution focusing on his political affiliations, exploited the looseness of the charges and the irregular conduct of the proceedings. As the ILWU's two-day session ended, recalled Jacobs, everyone knew "that the decision to expel the union had been made months before." CPUSA officials had advised the accused unionists to cooperate with the trials and to use them to expose the injustice of the proceedings, but at least in this tactical matter the embattled unionists often ignored the party's position. Gold and Bridges hurled defiance at the CIO, while FTA's Henderson presented a sober and detailed defense. Jacob Potofsky, chairing the committee trying FTA, rejected Henderson's request for legal counsel and permitted defendants to call witnesses only after a court order required him to. At the FTA's hearing, Henderson had a hard time making his case, so frequent were the asides and interruptions from trial panel members.[105]

CIO leaders denied accusations of witch hunting. "This is not a purge," insisted Murray. From their perspective, they were simply specifying conditions under which individuals and organizations could participate in the affairs of a private body, the CIO. Were the exclusions of the pro-Soviet unions in principle any different from the exclusions left-wing groups often conducted in efforts to retain a coherent ideological perspective? CIO leaders did not question the right of the accused unions to continue to exist, only their right to claim CIO affiliation. "Damn it," Murray confronted one of the accused leaders, "if you don't like this organization, why do you mess these things up? Why don't you get out?"[106]

Liberal allies of the CIO applauded the expulsion of these affiliates. Ouster of the pro-Soviet unions demonstrated conclusively that the CIO was uncompromised by association with those so deeply entangled in Soviet crimes. Moreover, CIO leaders believed that the expulsion of the pro-Soviet affiliates would permit the CIO and its loyal affiliates to offer the victimized rank-and-file members of these Stalinist labor bodies an alternative, one that they were sure workers would choose if given the chance.

In fact, the CIO did little to provide an alternative to the organizations it was in the process of destroying. Calls for the members of pro-Soviet unions to throw off the yoke of their Stalinist leadership were hollow. The ILWU, the Fur and Leather Workers, the UE, and others had done well by their members. When the CIO and its non-Communist unions did challenge the former affiliates, the pariah unions did surprisingly well. It took the UAW, the most successful of the raiders, almost five years to break the loyalty of FE members in key midwestern locals. The USWA suffered humiliating defeats at the hands of Mine, Mill when it sought to take over the latter's locals in Montana and Connecticut. The IUE enjoyed only spotty success in its battles with the UE. Workers, observed one anti-Communist rank and filer, cared far less about ideology than about competence and performance. "All this flag-waving, breast-beating, and Red-baiting has availed the I.U.E. nothing against the U.E.," asserted this astute Philadelphian. Both the Fur and Leather Workers, which had an avowedly Stalinist leadership, and the ILWU were largely impervious to CIO challenge.[107]

Part of the CIO case against affiliates such as the United Public Workers, FTA, and the Office and Professional Workers was that they had failed to organize their jurisdictions. Intent upon political and ideological matters, the charge went, these unions had languished, with just enough membership to provide sinecures for party functionaries. In expelling these affiliates the CIO pledged to recruit thousands of agricultural and cannery, office and professional, and government workers. At the 1950 convention, Haywood vowed, the CIO would soon go after "that great warrior," Harry Bridges, and he warned the West Coast radical, "Be ready, Harry, we're coming."[108]

In fact the CIO did little organizing. The 1949 convention had increased the per capita tax to ten cents, with the additional two cents to go into organizing. In February 1950 the CIO established a Government and Civic Employees Organizing Committee to challenge the ousted United Public Workers. The CIO made desultory gestures toward reviving its halfhearted program of white collar recruitment. Director of Organization Haywood urged struggling affiliates such as the United Packinghouse Workers, the United Brewery Workers, and the Gas and Chemical Workers to move aggressively into food processing, and the CIO awarded jurisdiction of department store and retail clerks to the ACWA in an effort to counteract a left-wing secession from its almost-moribund Retail, Wholesale, and Department Store Union.[109]

None of these initiatives bore much fruit, however. Despite the ritualistic calls for rekindling the spirit of '37, the CIO, vigorous and effective in its excision of the pro-Soviet organizations, was lethargic and inept in recruiting their jurisdictions or building effective replacements. The CIO left organizing largely to the affiliates, which enjoyed at best spotty success. In the spring of 1950 Michigan IUC leaders begged Haywood for assistance in bringing disaffected locals in the electrical industry and public employment under the CIO banner. "Two or three men [organizers], now, Allan, is all we ask," implored Secretary Barney Hopkins. But Haywood reported that the CIO, far from expanding its organizing activities, was laying off field representatives. "We are very limited in funds," he told Hopkins, and could offer no substantial support.[110]

Some observers believed that the campaign against the pro-Soviet unions would result in the aggrandizement of the CIO's central authority. They pointed to the course that the UMW had followed and to the increasingly centralized character of the USWA and the Reuther-led UAW. In fact, however, as in so many phases of its existence, the CIO remained institutionally frail. In the interests of ideology, politics, and general distaste for the pro-Soviet organizations affiliates could grant the CIO powers to act aggressively. But they had no interest in arming the CIO with far-reaching powers or resources in organizing or collective bargaining.[111]

At the time of the ouster, few on the anti-Communist left shed tears for the expelled unions or their top leaders. True, the rising tide of mindless anti-Communism, as epitomized by Joseph McCarthy, Richard Nixon, and other right-wing zealots, gave reason for caution in expressing anti-Communist sentiments. But to the non-Communist left, the palpable linkage of pro-Soviet unions to the CPUSA and to the USSR made them enemies of genuine progressivism. "Ever since [the 1930s]," asserted one radical commentator, the Communists "have been hanging on to . . . control by a combination of ruthless, bureaucratic rule, clever demagoguery, and a minimum of service to the workers." C. Wright Mills, an independent left-wing scholar, regretted the high-handed nature of the proceedings but bade good riddance to the Communists and their allies, whose manipulation of CIO activities, he believed, had undermined the industrial union federation's ability to establish a legitimate progressive position in American life. Paul Jacobs, a CIO staffer with strong socialist commitments, took a certain pleasure in driving the Communists out of the CIO, "partly out of . . . anger at the way in which the Communists had betrayed our ideals."[112]

The CIO crusade against the Communists and their allies abounded in ironies. For example, in the effort to cleanse the industrial union body of ideological pollution, it was CIO functionaries and supporters who in fact most vigorously brandished the ideological weapon. Thus as Steinberg recounted his litany of charges against the accused unions, he ostentatiously (and selectively) quoted from a dog-eared copy of Lenin's *Left-Wing Unionism: An Infantile Disorder*, while Bridges, Gold, Henderson, and the others portrayed themselves as simple trade unionists who did the bidding of their rank-and-file members. Similarly, during many of the raiding campaigns the CIO unions stressed ideology, appealing to workers to abandon their current affiliations in the service of patriotic Americanism and anti-

Communism. Meanwhile, leaders of the beleaguered unions effectively denounced their rivals for injecting irrelevant abstractions into union affairs.[113]

Another mordant irony involved the resort to the government by CIO leaders in destroying their rivals. Throughout the late 1940s and early 1950s, CIO leaders sought to steer a narrow path between mutually beneficial cooperation with governmental bodies, on one hand, and traditional defense of civil liberties, on the other. CIO leaders made no secret of their intense dislike of Nixon, McCarthy, and other extremists. They opposed repressive legislation and objected to the irresponsible investigations of the HUAC and the Senate Committee on Internal Security.[114]

Even so, CIO functionaries collaborated closely with the government's anti-Communist organs. Carey actively worked with the FBI and with congressional zealots to defeat his enemies in the UE. Both Carey and UAW president Reuther, though publicly deploring the practices of HUAC, used the information and especially the publicity generated by the committee's hearings to undermine their rivals. The policy of Reuther and other CIO leaders who willingly signed the Taft-Hartley affidavit to raid fellow CIO unions, while defensible on tactical grounds, compromised their civil libertarian credentials and legitimated a key feature of this "slave labor law." While Murray himself generally steered clear of direct collaboration with governmental authorities, some of his key aides were not so scrupulous. From the outset of the proceedings against the pro-Soviet unions, USWA staffer Meyer Bernstein and CIO general counsel Arthur Goldberg kept Army Intelligence closely informed. Thus, in November 1949 Bernstein informed General A. H. Bolling, assistant chief of staff of Army Intelligence, that "the job will be a thorough going [*sic*] study of the activities of the Commies, and you people ought to have that." Goldberg consulted regularly with the FBI on CIO affairs.[115]

The anti-Communist crusade was one of the CIO's defining episodes. "They are not trade unionists, they are colonial agents of a foreign government using the trade unions as an operating base," declared Walter Reuther at the CIO's November 1948 convention. Believing that, as the UAW leader did and as Murray came to, there was no choice but to drive the pro-Soviet forces from the CIO. Freed of the pro-Soviet incubus, the CIO could resume the struggle to become a coherent, progressive, and politically powerful labor center. Critics, however, believed that the attack on these unions signaled the effective end of the industrial union project. "It will," said the UE executive board in the spring of 1949, "if permitted to continue, lead to the destruction of the CIO."[116]

Addressing the CIO's annual convention on November 20, 1950, in Chicago, Murray proudly reviewed the successful efforts to thwart the Communist "plot" to take over the CIO. "By removing the obstructionists," he predicted, "we have gained effectiveness and militance." These were dubious assertions. The year before, reporter Blanche Finn had counted the delegates and found that they consisted largely of officers and staff members, with very few rank-and-file representatives and a resultant "lack of spontaneous debate from the floor." The 1950 convention was even more top heavy. Murray was sure that "the history of the CIO gives confidence that our unions will rise to the obligations which the second half of the twentieth century is certain to place upon them," but convention rhetoric alone could not revitalize the industrial union project.[117]

10 The Korean War

Sergeant Harold R. Cross, the last U.S. soldier killed in the Korean War, was a UAW member from Detroit. Indeed, from the outbreak of the conflict in June 1950 the CIO and the workers it represented played critical roles. The unions became more closely integrated into the Democratic Party and the national security state. The government's erratic mobilization and stabilization programs revived the CIO's status as central representative of industrial workers in national forums. At the same time, however, the Truman administration left considerable scope for collective bargaining. For the most part, CIO unions were in theory free to respond to inflationary pressures with broad wage demands and to take their members out on strike. Still, wartime exigencies and their own commitment to the foreign policy goals on which the conduct of the war was based made business as usual impossible.[1]

CIO leaders hoped to translate their support for the war into partnership in the management of the economy upon which the military effort rested. At the same time they were frustrated by legislation that precluded the kinds of arrangements that they believed had served them well during World War II and by a government that rejected partnership even as it cultivated labor support. Moreover, a restive rank and file forced them to sanction large numbers of wartime strikes. CIO leaders raged against the government's reliance on corporate officials in the conduct of its wartime economic programs. Even so, industrial unionists enjoyed considerable success in combining responsiveness to rank-and-file pressures, enlistment of the government in behalf of their collective bargaining goals, and support for the war effort, even if they failed in their efforts to project themselves into basic decision-making forums.

Developments in the steel industry in 1951 and 1952 vividly revealed the CIO's Korean War dilemma. In the spring of 1952, deterioration of wage standards and the Truman administration's confused stabilization programs ultimately compelled Murray to lead a protracted strike against the major steel producers. The resulting settlement owed more to the political alliance between Murray and the CIO on one hand and the Truman-led Democratic Party on the other than to any coherent program of wartime labor relations. Left-wing unionists deplored Murray's repeated postponement of strike deadlines and his willingness to moderate USWA demands. Most observers, however, believed that Murray had shrewdly combined militancy and political leverage to pry concessions from an obdurate employer while escaping the repressive consequences that might have been expected in the waging of a wartime strike of massive proportions. In any event, it was clear to all that the Korean War experience had further solidified the CIO-Democratic alliance and had intensified the CIO's commitment to the government's national security agenda.

INDUSTRIAL RELATIONS MACHINERY

Initially expecting a short-term conflict, the Truman administration only slowly developed regulatory machinery. On September 9, 1950, Congress passed the Defense Production Act, which in theory gave the president vast powers to put the economy on a war footing. The law, however, contained loopholes making true price control impossible. Moreover, it was ambiguous with regard to labor-management disputes. For the first five months of the conflict, the administration counted on patriotism, an early end to hostilities, and stepped-up Conciliation and Mediation Service efforts to keep the factories humming.[2]

On September 9 an executive order did create the Economic Stabilization Administration, under which was subsumed a price stabilization board and a wage stabilization board. It was not until a month later, however, that the president named U.S. commissioner of conciliation Cyrus Ching as director of the wage board. As late as the first week in December, officials in the rudimentary mobilization and stabilization apparatus were reassuring the public that voluntary methods remained the order of the day.[3]

By then, however, Chinese troops had crossed the Yalu River. As United Nations forces retreated, the administration shifted gears. In mid-December, Truman appointed General Electric executive Charles E. Wilson as director of the Office of Defense Mobilization, a superagency that would centralize the economic aspects of the war effort and make the role of the WSB, the only wartime agency on which organized labor had formal representation, uncertain.

Meanwhile, inflationary pressures mounted. Workers demanded wage increases, and strike levels spurted. Observed Art Preis, "The period of the Korean War witnessed more strikes and strikers than any other comparable . . . time in American history." Leaders of the CIO and its affiliated unions, well aware of the dangers that job actions during wartime posed, sought to keep the lid on in the mills and plants while stepping up pressure on the administration to develop authoritative dispute resolution processes.

Labor representation in the administration's mobilization and stabilization programs, along with an effective disputes board, they believed, would help them to keep workers on the job. Ardent supporters of the war and of the foreign policy on which it was based, CIO leaders believed that the administration and the Democratic Party could not afford to be unresponsive to the CIO and working people generally who formed the core of their political strength.[4]

In fact, the workings of the mobilization and stabilization machinery remained problematic. Wilson's appointment angered laborites. IUE leaders had found him intransigent in their relations with General Electric, which had been adopting an unusually tough collective bargaining policy. Moreover, Wilson soon made it clear that he had no room for substantive labor representation in the Office of Defense Mobilization. "Labor," declared Murray before the stabilization agencies were functioning, "must be accorded active participation and leadership in every important facet of our mobilization effort." But Wilson's selection pointed in the opposite direction.[5]

Through the winter and spring of 1950–51 the frustration of CIO leaders mounted. In December the CIO had joined with representatives of the AFL, the railroad brotherhoods, and the temporarily unaffiliated IAM to form the ULPC to coordinate organized labor's relations with wartime agencies. This uncommon gesture toward labor unity, however, failed to convince Wilson to heed demands for stong labor representation in the expanding economic policy bureaucracy.[6]

In January the labor leadership's increasing unhappiness with administration policies came to a head. On the twenty-fifth, the Economic Stabilization Administration, the agency established by Truman under the terms of the Defense Production Act, issued a sweeping wage freeze order. This directive seemed to ignore the ULPC's forcefully expressed views on wage stabilization. Union officials argued that a rigid wage control program would actually encourage job actions and make their own efforts at restraint impossible. Since its inception, the ULPC had stressed that any wage stabilization program had to be part of a broad "equality of sacrifice" program in which real price control was an essential component.[7]

In itself, the Economic Stabilization Administration's action was not overly alarming, since it would be left to the WSB, on which the unions were represented, to give substance to this order. But on February 15, with the industry and public members outvoting the labor contingent, the board handed down General Wage Regulation 6, which spelled out the specific terms of the wage freeze. This ruling limited wage increases that could be granted without board approval to 10 percent and included fringe benefits in the calculation of wage hikes. It seemed to call into jeopardy increases negotiated before January 26 but not scheduled to go into effect until after that date, and it made no clear allowance for improvement of below-average wage rates.[8]

CIO leaders were furious. The Department of Education and Research churned out detailed studies demonstrating the continuing erosion of real wages and booming corporate profits. On February 16, after failing to get the WSB majority to reconsider the January 25 order, the ULPC announced the resignation of labor representatives from the WSB; two weeks later, the ULPC pulled labor representatives from all wartime stabilization agencies.

In its statement explaining the walkout, the ULPC attacked both General Wage Regulation 6 and the Office of Defense Mobilization. "Our decision," the labor leaders insisted, "cannot and must not be interpreted merely as a protest against an unfair and unworkable wage formula." The wage freeze merely capped "a whole series of shocking developments," of which chronic failure to include labor representation in the mobilization apparatus was the most egregious example. The policies of the Office of Defense Mobilization and the Economic Stabilization Administration were "inflexible, inequitable and unworkable." They reflected an "utter lack of concern with the viewpoints and experiences of American labor." Said Murray, "The direction of this defense mobilization program . . . has slipped into the hands of a clique of men who represent only one attitude: the attitude of the top executive offices [of] big business."[9]

These dramatic walkouts, however, did not signal a permanent break with the administration. Labor spokesmen carefully kept their guns trained on the WSB and on Wilson, exempting Truman himself from the heavy artillery. They remained in contact with the president's aides, notably Assistant to the President John R. Steelman, who since 1945 had been Truman's chief advisor on labor policy. In cooperation with administration officials, ULPC members worked to reshuffle and redefine the WSB and to bring about reconsideration of the January 25 wage freeze.[10]

It was critical for CIO leaders to keep collective bargaining within the mobilization and stabilization machinery. Unlike the World War II situation, the labor leadership had not taken a no strike pledge, and now they bowed, though often reluctantly, to the mounting rank-and-file pressure. The great majority of Korean War walkouts were sanctioned strikes, in contrast to the experience of World War II, when wildcats and other unauthorized job actions had predominated.[11]

At the same time, however, institutional and ideological imperatives caused industrial union leaders to attempt to slow the strike wave. The 1950 elections had boosted the power of the conservative coalition, raising fears of further antiunion legislation. In contrast, they believed, effective federal wage and disputes programs offered something of a safe haven from both angry rank and filers and labor-hating legislators.

Beyond these practical considerations, however, lay their commitment to the cause for which U.S. troops were fighting. Murray, Carey, Reuther, and the rest of the CIO leadership considered themselves part of the administration insofar as the Korean war was concerned. The 1950 convention issued an impassioned call for "achieving the inevitable liberation of the Korean nation from Communist oppression." By acting promptly to quell "small fires we prevent the blaze of war from engulfing the world," said a widely circulated CIO statement. With the anticapitalist left largely silenced, CIO officials embraced the Truman administration's version of events in Asia completely and devoted their attention to beating back attacks from the right. They sought to persuade workers that the Democratic conduct of foreign policy since World War II had been wise and resolute, no easy task when large numbers of Americans questioned the patriotism and sagacity of the men linked to the Yalta agreements, the "loss" of China, and the bloody Korean stalemate.[12]

Moreover, CIO leaders shared with administration officials the fear that the "police action" in Korea might well be only the opening round in a decades-long struggle against world Communism. "This mobilization," said Reuther in December, "may last a generation. . . . It is imperative that we keep our productive machine going at full speed." Administration officials believed that it was precisely because of this long-term struggle that they should not employ extraordinary means of dealing with the admittedly difficult economic problems that the Korean conflict brought. Clearly, one Truman aide declared, the government could not forbid strikes or otherwise regiment labor-management affairs "for the *duration* of 'police actions' that may arise in Indo-China, Malaya, Southeast Asia, or Yugoslavia." "It would appear essential," he added ominously, "to save such 'last resort' measures until such time as we face a total war with Russia."[13]

Over the next several months, administration officials and labor leaders repaired the break. In February the Economic Stabilization Administration modified its wage-freeze formula in labor's favor. In March President Truman appointed a sixteen-member panel to make recommendations about the nature of future wage stabilization and dispute resolution machinery. A month later he accepted and implemented its recommendation for the establishment of an expanded WSB, now armed with authority to consider labor-management disputes. On April 21 he reconstituted the WSB, with an expanded tripartite membership and with the power to make recommendations on both wage and noneconomic issues for dispute settlement. Moreover, with reference to disputes, the new board was to report directly to the president, circumventing both the administratively awkward Economic Stabilization Administration and Wilson's Office of Defense Mobilization.[14]

Taken in all, the ULPC walkout, which CIO leaders completely supported, accomplished its purposes. The revisions of General Wage Regulation 6 and the new board's relative autonomy gave laborites room to maneuver. The administration's tacit repudiation of the wage freeze and its revamping of the WSB provided organized labor with an arena in which to fight its wage battles while it reaffirmed its support for the administration's conduct of the war.

Of course, the reconstitution of the WSB did not speak to the broader problem of labor representation in the mobilization apparatus. Initially, CIO influentials saw war mobilization as an opportunity to promote a more rational economic order, with organized labor gaining (in CIO secretary-treasurer James B. Carey's words) "full partnership in the planning." But in fact corporate executives quickly dominated the military production and allocation agencies. "They have locked us out of the war mobilization effort," declared Walter Reuther. "They have a cocktail party in the evening [before a formal committee meeting] and make the decision and meet with the advisory committee the next morning and go through some motions," he fumed. The administration, Emil Rieve said, would give some unionist a janitorial job and claim him as an example of consultation with the labor movement.[15]

Indeed, even administration officials sympathetic to organized labor were skeptical of the demand for such representation. Remarked Steelman's chief assistant, "The entire concept of labor participation is perhaps unfortunate." Whereas corporate business could make available literally thousands of experienced economists, lawyers, managers, and technical experts, organized labor had but a handful of capable administrators. Truman insisted that organized labor's proper role was confined to the representation of union members in collective bargaining and closely related dealings with the government.[16]

As during World War II, when it came to the CIO's ostensible larger agenda, no one was listening. Though Reuther continued to expound a kind of laborite technocracy, the CIO itself, once labor's grievances in the area of wage stabilization were met, backed off from expansive visions. Murray's report to the 1952 convention did include a bland statement in behalf of the general concept of economic "planning," but by that word he meant little more than the use of fiscal measures to smooth the business cycle.[17]

Certainly the CIO gave little evidence of any sustained commitment to its early demands for partnership in the single most important industrial dispute of the Korean War period, the steel strike of 1952. Throughout this complex controversy, neither Murray nor his chief advisor and spokesman, USWA and CIO general counsel Arthur Goldberg, invoked notions of laborite participation in management. From the onset of negotiations between the USWA and U.S. Steel in November 1951 to the end of a fifty-nine-day strike in late July of the next year, the actions of President Truman and other federal officials were decisive. In 1952, as had been the pattern since the mid-1930s, CIO leaders used their influence within a Democratic administration to wrench a favorable settlement from an obdurate employer. That this process further welded the USWA and the CIO to the Truman administration, its national security agenda, and the Democratic Party seemed to Murray and his colleagues to be both unexceptionable and unproblematic.

As they squared off in the fall of 1951 against U.S. Steel, USWA negotiators pressed the case for large wage increases, improvement of the industry's rudimentary fringe benefits, and achievement of the union shop. In more candid moments steel industry leaders acknowledged the legitimacy of the steelworkers' economic demands but insisted that assurances of price relief had to precede serious bargaining. Both sides sought to manipulate the government's elaborate, but thus far largely untested, dispute resolution and economic stabilization machinery.[18]

The controversy was enmeshed in interunion rivalry as well. The USWA still lagged behind both the UMW and the UAW in the scope and quality of the fringe benefits contained in its contracts. Moreover, the UAW had established itself as the CIO's leader in wage negotiations. Its 1948 and May 1950 contracts with GM had provided seemingly generous settlements and had introduced for the first time in mass production industry cost-of-living and annual productivity improvement factor clauses. As president of the CIO, Murray believed that his Steelworkers should lead the way for industrial workers. Skeptical of the kinds of automatic wage adjustments featured in the UAW's recent contracts, Murray and his aides expressed vindication when under the terms of the UAW's 1950 contract, which ran for an unprecedented five years, the cost-of-living and annual productivity improvement factor provisions were inadequate to satisfy inflation-afflicted autoworkers. Bound by the contract's rigid no strike clause, UAW chief Reuther countenanced discipline-eroding wildcat job actions and work-to-rule campaigns in an effort to force the auto giant to reopen the contract.

The UAW dilemma seemed to vindicate Murray's opposition to automatic wage adjustment mechanisms. But if the USWA were now to assert its leadership in collective bargaining, it would need a strong contract settlement from pattern-setting U.S. Steel. Thus as negotiations began at the end of November 1951, the Steelworkers put forth ambitious proposals calling for wage increases of over thirty cents an hour; enhanced pension, insurance, and vacation provisions; and achievement of a full union shop, with dues checkoff features.[19]

U.S. Steel, the industry bellwether, rejected the Steelworkers' demands outright. Company officials declared that they could not contemplate wage increases without prior governmental assurance of compensatory price relief. With 600,000 steelworkers ready to walk out on January 1, 1952, the president remanded the dispute to the WSB and asked Murray to postpone the strike until the board could make recommendations.

Over the next several months the two parties pulled every available lever in the press and within the stabilization bureaucracy. The steel industry won the public relations war. The USWA's legitimate claim that high profits made a generous wage without the need for price increases possible gained little public support. The steel companies' insistence that it had "PROTECTED THE PUBLIC AGAINST A NEW WAGE-PRICE SPIRAL," as one of its widely circulated advertisements asserted, fell on receptive ears. "The propaganda of the companies," admitted one of Truman's aides, "probably has been effective" in obscuring the facts about profits and the illegitimacy of the industry's demand for significant price relief.[20]

The union, however, did better in the governmental arena. Goldberg conferred regularly with Truman's assistants Charles Murphy and James Rowe and with Steelman's assistant, Harold Enarson. At times, aides in the presidential office, who largely agreed with the USWA's analysis of the economics of the case, coordinated strategy with Goldberg as to the timing and character of various maneuvers within the stabilization and congressional arenas. In addition, the USWA found both the WSB and a special panel it created in January to investigate the dispute receptive to its case. Thus in March when the WSB recommended a staggered wage increase of 16.5 cents an hour, improvements in benefits, and a compromise in union security that met the USWA more than halfway, Murray readily accepted them as the basis for a settlement.[21]

The steelmakers also had important allies within the government, however. Congressional conservatives publicized the case for wage restraint and/or price relief. Office of Defense Mobilization chief Wilson actively opposed the WSB's recommendations. With diverse elements of the mobilization and stabilization bureaucracies in conflict, declared Enarson, "the babble of government tongues" discouraged real collective bargaining and made a wartime steel strike a distinct possibility.[22]

Between April and July the administration sought desperately to bring about a settlement. Throughout this period, however, the president refused to wield the government's most potent weapons against the union. He abjured the Taft-Hartley Act's cooling off provisions,[23] and he did not attempt to rally public opinion against the union even after Murray had rejected several compromises. In 1948 Truman had imposed a Taft-Hartley injunction on the UMW. But unlike Lewis, Murray was a loyal Democrat, a vigorous supporter of the government, and an ardent proponent of the administration's foreign policy. The president appeared to sympathize with Murray's goal of achieving contract parity with Lewis's UMW. He seemed to understand that the union security issue had great importance for a USWA constantly measuring itself against the standards of solidarity established by the legendary John L.

Indeed, the administration's most dramatic action, seizure of the steel mills on April 8, was directed primarily at the steelmakers. Unionists cheered the president's late-night takeover order. Eager as most steelworkers were for wage advance, few welcomed the prospect of a long strike. Reported writer Murray Kempton from Homestead, Pennsylvania, steelworkers "were still standing at the [street]corners at midnight talking about Mr. Truman. . . . They had come right under the gun and the President had paid off their patience." Workers harbored plausible hopes that the government would raise wages during its period of operation. There were significant precedents for such a development, most recently in 1946 when the secretary of commerce had negotiated wage increases and pathbreaking pension and retirement provisions with the UMW after Truman had seized the coal mines. Contrasting with the workers' jubilation was the response of steel executives. "I felt physically ill," recalled Inland Steel's Clarence Randall, and he likened Truman to "Caesar . . . and Mussolini and Hitler."[24]

Even after the courts had ruled the steel seizure unconstitutional, thus triggering the actual walkout in June, administration officials still refrained from attacks on the Steelworkers. By late June Steelman had hammered out a generally acceptable wage-benefits package, along with price increase assurances for the steelmakers. Now the main issue was no longer wages but, rather, union security, a matter that members of Congress and the press showed little appreciation for or understanding of. Nonetheless, Truman stuck by the USWA. To those who suggested that the union shop was a frivolous demand, administration spokesmen replied that if this were the case, the steel companies could easily grant it. Early in July, when the steel companies rejected a promising compromise, the president told reporters that "this appears to me to be a conspiracy against the public interest." [25]

Business leaders, editorialists, and political critics unleashed a barrage of antiunion and anti-Truman criticism. Refusal to impose a Taft-Hartley cooling-off order, congressional critics charged, revealed nakedly the president's appeasement of the CIO. Yet Secretary of Defense Robert M. Lovett's July 23 warning of the catastrophic effects of the fifty-one-day strike was free of union bashing. [26]

On July 24 Truman at last announced a settlement. By now both the administration and the union needed an agreement lest their alliance, and the war effort that it supported, suffer. The strike had begun seriously to affect military production. It strained the union's strike support system and ravaged its members' living standards. Despite desultory proposals over the years for the CIO to create a central strike fund, in fact the industrial union federation was able to do little other than offer moral support. Indeed, Murray suffered the indignity of having John L. Lewis offer the USWA a $10 million line of credit. Truman's aides began ostentatiously to draft plans for another government takeover, thus time under the cumbersome but dire stipulations buried in the Selective Service Act, which would have required the mustering of steelworkers and their employers into the armed forces. [27]

The settlement differed little from those that Steelman and his aides been advancing over the previous six weeks. A complex union security provision stopped short of granting the USWA what either the UMW or the UAW had earlier achieved, but it did require new hires to become members after thirty days unless they gave written notice to the company at that time that they did not want to join. Wage and benefits provisions tracked the WSB's March proposals but were not so generous. Some Steelworker dissidents were critical, singling out the contract's initial failure to reaffirm existing shop-floor practices. Silence on this issue, they believed, would give employers a green light to attack hard-won work rules and to reverse the union's relatively successful struggle to rationalize the industry's discriminatory methods of job description and wage payment. [28]

Overall, however, the USWA leadership and most journalistic observers believed that the 1952 steel strike had been a significant victory for organized labor. The "befriending of labor," judged one journalist, "has never been carried so far by any administration as by Harry Truman in his support of Phil Murray's steel strike." In 1951 laborites had forced a favorable reshuffling of the WSB. The USWA had conducted a nine-week steel strike without governmental reprisal. The alliance with the Democratic Party was strengthened, and the USWA and the CIO had, at least to the satisfaction of their leaders, combined undiminished support of the war with an exercise in effective militancy. "This settlement," USWA officials boasted, "will have major and beneficial effects on workers in other industries throughout the years ahead." A *Time* magazine reporter relayed the jubilation of one USWA district official: "Nobody can beat us now, nobody. Nobody is strong enough. We've got the power."[29]

But some unionists voiced doubts. Relying on the government for the achievement of collective bargaining goals was dangerous. Lewis had found this out, for in 1946 his collective bargaining victories during the period of government operation of the mines had been followed by a bitter showdown that had resulted in the courts' imposing staggering fines on both the union and Lewis personally. The injunction against the coal miners in 1948 was one of eighty that Truman had resorted to under the terms of Taft-Hartley in the five years since his veto of the legislation in 1947. The shotgun was always behind the door. Even without the threat of overt repression, reliance on government tended to distance union leadership from rank-and-file workers.[30]

During the Korean conflict the CIO prospered. Membership figures, lagging in the wake of the recession of 1949, moved upward again. Per capita tax payments from the UAW, the USWA, and other war-expanded affiliates grew in 1951 and 1952. In November 1953, despite postwar layoffs, the monthly average membership reported by affiliates to Secretary-Treasurer James Carey was about 4.65 million. Treasury surpluses mounted. After the steel shutdown, though strike totals remained high, most walkouts were short, and none imposed similar strains on military production or on the still-uncertain mobilization and stabilization machinery.[31]

At the same time, however, the course that the CIO followed exacted a heavy price. Pursuit of basic collective bargaining goals primarily through channels of governmental bureaucracy leeched power from labor's grass roots and often made rank-and-file workers spectators in their own drama. Murray's enlistment of the government in behalf of the USWA's goals paid handsome immediate dividends, but it posed troubling problems for the future. As critics pilloried the Truman administration simultaneously for softness on Communism and entanglement in the bloody and protracted Korean conflict, CIO leaders, as ardent defenders of the administration's unpopular limited war strategy, could hardly escape the backlash, even among their own members. Republican victory in November 1952 quickly made reliance on government seem more perilous and problematic than at any time since 1932.

11 The Postwar CIO

During its last half-decade of independent existence, the CIO simultaneously claimed some of its most impressive achievements and exhibited increasing signs of stasis and decay. The economy's central industrial core, practically void of unions before 1935, was now about 70 percent organized. CIO unions gained pension and health care rights for millions of workers. The CIO's role in the Democratic Party and in the congressional and state legislative areas expanded. "This year," boasted the CIO's leaders in 1955, "marks . . . two almost incredible decades, unmatched and unparalleled in the entire history of the American labor movement for economic, social and political progress achieved on behalf of the nation's working men and women."[1]

Nonetheless, the CIO as an institutional entity remained uncertain and adrift. Membership totals and finances fluctuated sharply. The very success of unions such as the USWA and the UAW underlined the marginality of most of the other thirty-odd affiliates. High wage levels and the establishment of pensions, health care, and job security for CIO workers inadvertently contributed to the segmentation of the American labor force. Though political action and lobbying brought the CIO into national and international forums on a wide range of issues, these efforts often ended in frustration and uncertainty.

POLITICS

Throughout the early 1950s CIO leaders looked to the political and legislative arenas for the advancement of workers' interests and perhaps the re-creation of the circumstances necessary for renewed growth and vitality. They worked doggedly for the election of liberal and Democratic candidates on all levels. They lobbied endlessly for a broad range of welfare state and economic growth policies. They hoped that repeal or sharp amendment of Taft-Hartley would trigger union advance. Economic growth would bring a favorable climate for wage gains and organizing initiatives. Civil rights legislation would cement the CIO's alliances with other liberal groups.

Foreign and defense concerns also encouraged the turn toward political action. CIO leaders translated the controversial foreign policy decisions of the government to their own membership and to the voting constituencies with which they were allied. They attacked the militaristic isolationism associated with the Republican right and publicly defended the broad purposes first of the Truman, then of the Eisenhower, administration, often in the face of powerful currents of membership and general public dissent. They embraced a version of the government's Cold War policies that stressed the building of democratic institutions abroad.

At the same time the CIO was deeply enmeshed in the American defense structure. Believing as they did that the USSR and its Chinese ally posed a powerful military and moral threat, CIO leaders embraced the broad foreign and military policies of the government enthusiastically. The UAW, the USWA, and the IUE were firmly implanted in military production. Leaders such as Walter Reuther, Philip Murray, and David J. McDonald (who succeeded Murray in 1952 as USWA president) argued for greater efficiency, less profiteering, and more planning in producing military goods, never for a reduction in the defense effort.

In its political operations during this period, the CIO was more successful in raising funds for Democratic candidates than in mobilizing a consistent and reliable blue collar electoral presence or in influencing party leaders. The prime mechanism for the CIO's political aims remained PAC, directed by Jack Kroll. PAC translated the policy and candidate endorsements of the CIO's Executive Board and convention into practical politicking. It encouraged the affiliated unions to establish PAC bodies and worked closely with state and local IUCs to promote grassroots political action. It was through PAC that the CIO channeled the increasingly large sums necessary for political campaigning to liberal candidates, most of them Democrats. Work with PAC and the political action arms of affiliated unions provided the stepping stones to leadership roles in state and local Democratic Party organizations for some CIO activists.

CIO leaders held a broad vision of political action. They sought to bring working people together in an inclusive political movement. The CIO creed held that the people were inherently progressive and that the CIO was the truest and most effective voice of the people. "We firmly believe," said Kroll in 1950, "that if the majority of the people vote they will vote for liberal, progressive candidates." This assumption, he added, was "fundamental" to industrial unionism's political operations.[2]

CIO-PAC was a body composed of representatives of the CIO's powerful affiliates. The most active among them were USWA secretary-treasurer David J. McDonald, ACWA's Jacob Potofsky, James Carey, TWUA president Emil Rieve, and UAW secretary-treasurer Emil Mazey, a staunch Reuther ally. In addition, both CIO presidents during this period, Murray and Reuther, took an active role in PAC affairs. Director Kroll both oversaw ongoing operations and had a critical role in policymaking. Assistant Director Tilford E. Dudley, a lawyer with extensive Washington experience, and the field representatives were direct employees of PAC and were in almost daily contact with Washington headquarters. Some had been socialists or third party enthusiasts, but now they carried forth the effort to mobilize blue collar voters, establish and sustain regular methods of funding labor's political project, and continue the effort to turn the Democratic Party into a reliable vehicle for anti-Communist labor liberalism.[3]

PAC occupied a suite of rooms in CIO Washington headquarters. During most of this period its permanent staff consisted of about twenty people at headquarters and ten or twelve field representatives. Allocations from the CIO funded its headquarters operations and certain nonpartisan field operations such as voter registration and civic education. PAC work peaked, of course, during election periods. Indeed, it was difficult for PAC to sustain the interest of union leaders, much less rank-and-file members, in political affairs in the long stretches between elections. As a result PAC's operations were characterized by long periods of slow, plodding background activities and hectic spasms of fund raising and electioneering.

The decentralized nature of the American polity insured the CIO's political operations would be complex, expensive, and often frustrating. In the 1950s, voter registration requirements were often confusing and arcane, with lengthy lead times between registration deadlines and elections. In the South, where PAC operatives worked with civil rights organizations, poll tax requirements and racially motivated voter qualification procedures absorbed much manpower and money. Though throughout this period PAC operatives forged alliances with the AFL's Labor's League for Political Education and the political action arms of the railroad brotherhoods, maintaining a common labor front was often impossible in view of the conflicting political agendas of the various labor groups. Indeed, PAC representatives often found that rivalries among CIO unions compromised their efforts. Its conservative critics depicted PAC as a sinister juggernaut, attempting to steamroller a passive working-class electorate, but a more apt metaphor would have been a resourceful mechanic attempting to keep a ponderous and complicated piece of equipment from grinding to a halt.[4]

PAC was closely integrated into the CIO's IUC structure, with officers of one organization often doubling as officers of the other. PAC national field representatives, such as southern director Daniel Powell, worked closely with the PAC and council organizations, and with political action bodies established by the affiliated unions, to collect campaign funds, coordinate CIO efforts with those of other liberal groups and party organizations, and generally stimulate interest in political affairs among the CIO membership. In most industrial states PAC and IUC operatives worked closely with Democratic Party functionaries and with prolabor politicians, with CIO members often gaining formal positions of leadership in the party apparatus. At the 1952 Democratic National Convention, 108 of the 1,600 delegates were CIO members, and in Michigan and other industrial states CIO members served prominently on Democratic governing bodies. Nonetheless, PAC remained officially nonpartisan, whatever the participation of its people in the Democratic Party.[5]

The heart of PAC's activities was its work in behalf of liberal candidates. The money and personnel it used for these purposes came from its "dollar drive," a local-by-local effort to collect a dollar from each union member for campaigning purposes. Half of the money collected was sent to national CIO-PAC, and the other half was retained by the affiliated union and was in most cases itself divided between its national political action arm and that of the local union or council. In 1950, a congressional election year, the affiliated unions sent almost a half-million dollars to national PAC. In theory this meant that a million CIO members had each contributed a dollar. CIO leaders believed that collection of a dollar annually from one in every five rank-and-file members was a reasonable expectation, although in fact the general run of PAC contributions was closer to one in eight. Affiliated unions made up the shortfall, in part by pressuring staff members, field representatives, and local union leaders to set an example by contributing a day's pay or a quarter of the weekly salary. This device provided about 10 percent of the contributions and permitted leaders to say to ordinary members, " 'I have contributed one day's pay to PAC; how about you contributing one buck?' " The relatively low levels of membership contributions troubled CIO leaders, for they called into question the grassroots character of PAC's efforts.[6]

PAC officials ran conferences and seminars on political action, seeking to inform local unionists about labor's political and legislative goals, to recruit rank-and-file workers for precinct work, and to teach techniques of political mobilization. They nagged local unions to join state and local PAC bodies and to participate in the dollar drive. They collaborated with other liberal groups to promote registration and balloting among union members, their families, and other lower-income citizens. PAC bodies on all levels sought to build a political presence through a system of block workers, responsible for telephone solicitation, door-to-door canvassing, and election-day contacts. These men and women, declared a Wisconsin state IUC handbook, were "community stewards," the political counterpart to the unions' in-plant shop stewards. Block workers, according to a 1953 PAC manifesto, were the "central figures" in the CIO's entire political effort.[7]

Both the fund-raising and mobilization efforts suggested a certain gap between the CIO and PAC leadership, on one hand, and rank-and-file members on the other. PAC statements reflected the leadership's essentially class analysis of American politics. At the same time, however, PAC activists increasingly came to question the efficacy of direct class appeals. As one political operative observed after the 1953 elections, "Working class psychology doesn't work. Members are middle class and think middle class." At the same time, issues such as taxation, unemployment, economic development, and social security had powerful class implications about which working people were well aware. The challenge for PAC was to exploit class issues while occupying the broad middle ground of American politics.[8]

Indeed, in the 1950s the political values and behavior of blue collar workers aroused lively public discussion. Political analysts noted the high degree to which lower-income and blue collar Americans expressed feelings of powerlessness and alienation, attitudes that dampened responsiveness to PAC's civic-minded appeals. PAC reports often showed that half of CIO members were not registered to vote and that of those who were, large numbers never showed up at the polls.[9]

Moreover, a large minority of CIO members ignored or disagreed with PAC recommendations. In the 1952 presidential election, a team of political scientists reported, at least 40 percent of Detroit's UAW members either opposed union political activity or "lack[ed] clear convictions and remain[ed] uncommitted." Another 1952 survey reported that seven in ten unionists reported that they felt "little direct contact with their organizations on political matters." Many workers believed that unions had no business involving themselves in political matters.[10]

Even so, the basic PAC analysis that saw blue collar workers as actual or potential Democratic voters was true at the core. Even in 1952, 56 percent of union voters cast their ballots for Stevenson, and in the 1954 congressional elections Democrats garnered 64 percent of union members' votes. Moreover, CIO members regularly proved more committed to the Democratic Party than did their AFL or railroad brotherhood counterparts.[11]

These facts were difficult to interpret. What did the widespread nonvoting mean? The diminishing band of critics on the left argued that emphasis on anti-Communism and willingness to compromise with the Democratic Party's more conservative elements repelled workers.[12] But it was hard to find evidence for such an analysis. On almost every public issue, union officers and political operatives expressed more liberal positions than did rank-and-file workers. Nonvoting among union members seemed to correlate primarily with low levels of education and early socialization in rural surroundings rather than with ideological affinities. True, many workers expressed resentment toward union leaders for stressing political action, but typically these workers rejected the whole notion that a labor organization had any legitimate business concerning itself with politics.[13]

Certainly, the results of some of PAC's most fervent campaigns were deeply frustrating. Thus, for example, efforts in behalf of key senatorial liberals in 1950 failed dismally. Liberal incumbents Frank Graham and Claude Pepper were defeated in the Democratic primaries in North Carolina and Florida, while in Ohio arch-conservative Robert A. Taft crushed his PAC-supported Democratic opponent. In California CIO favorite Helen Gahagan Douglas lost heavily to right-wing Republican congressman Richard M. Nixon. Declared the TWUA's chief PAC operative, despite massive efforts, we got a "punch in the nose" on election day and "we really don't know what happened to us."[14]

In 1952, results seemed at first glance even more devastating, with the GOP regaining control of both houses and Eisenhower piling up a massive victory over Democrat Adlai Stevenson. Here again, however, Kroll remained positive. "CIO members," he reassured his colleagues, "followed the recommendations of the CIO leadership" by over 70 percent. Indeed, one authoritative study of the 1952 results in Detroit showed a solid three-to-one majority in favor of Stevenson. But a detailed postelection survey showed that overall only 57 percent of union voters (including, of course, non-CIO members, who were less solidly Democratic), cast their ballots for Stevenson, while Eisenhower captured 43 percent. This result stood in sharp contrast to that of 1948, when, at least by some accounts, 81 percent of union voters had backed Truman.[15]

Results in 1954 were more heartening, but combined with the erratic patterns of the past, they suggested that while PAC candidates might be successful, direct PAC political influence was as elusive as ever. PAC candidates scored heavily, reflecting a concerted CIO effort to alert industrial workers and their families to the doleful consequences of Eisenhower administration economic policies. Even so, the "labor vote" remained spectral, sometimes potent and visible, often illusory. "There's only one certain place that union leaders can speak for their members," asserted outgoing President Truman in 1953, "and that's economically." Even PAC activists had their doubts. In 1952, lamented southern publicity man Ed Lashman, PAC not only took a terrible beating in the South, but results suggested as well that "the northern CIO victories in the past have been a myth."[16]

Even though PAC could not always deliver the vote, it was a critical source of funds for Democratic candidates. In the 1950 Ohio senatorial race, for example, PAC contributed almost 35 percent of the losing Democratic challenger Joseph Ferguson's total expenditures in the general election. In the 1952 elections PAC and other CIO sources spent somewhere between $500,000 and $1 million in the futile effort to stave off Republican victory. In 1954 PAC pumped $1.5 million into the congressional and state races.[17]

Indeed, by the mid-1950s, labor money, with CIO-PAC disproportionately represented, was by far the single largest component of campaign funds for Democratic congressional candidates.[18] And money talked more loudly than questionable claims of class-conscious labor voting. Candidates could immediately calculate the CIO's financial contribution even when they might doubt that highly visible PAC electioneering was an overall plus.

Indeed, this combination of reliance on labor funds and apprehension over overt identification with labor compromised PAC's activities. True, politicians such as Michigan governor G. Mennen "Soapy" Williams, Minnesota senator Hubert H. Humphrey, and Illinois senator Paul Douglas openly identified themselves with PAC's programs. But too often Republican candidates successfully depicted PAC as a sinister force advancing a cryptosocialist agenda. "Why are we so unsuccessful?" plaintively asked a Michigan PAC leader. "Does the words C.I.O. [sic] instill a fear in the voters?" In the bitter 1950 California senatorial election Nixon scored heavily when he conjured up hordes of PAC campaign workers being imported from the East to work in Helen Douglas's behalf. Of course the southern political establishment had great success in labeling PAC a carpetbagging intrusion. Efforts to register black voters and to support progressive candidates required CIO workers there to remain in the background, quietly supplying funds and campaign resources but keeping the union banner carefully furled.[19]

Kroll and the other PAC professionals tacitly admitted the problematic nature of their appeal in how they referred to the dynamics of political action. In important respects the CIO's political agenda did not spring from the grass roots but, rather, came down from its upper echelons and had to be packaged so as to attract union voters. In 1951 Mazey declared that "our members are still politically inarticulate; they are still politically unconscious as far as the responsibilities of citizenship are concerned." All we ask, Kroll said repeatedly, is that our members have access to our viewpoint, just as they have access to the views of newspapers, radio commentators, and business leaders. He admitted that "the CIO viewpoint" too often encountered "downright hostility" among unionists and their families. Kroll, Mazey, and other CIO political operatives viewed the membership as a passive audience in need of persuasion at the hands of enlightened professionals.[20]

Through the early 1950s, CIO leaders believed that they were making progress. PAC analysts plausibly attributed Eisenhower's victory to factors of personality and circumstance rather than to some basic shift to the right. Rebound in the 1954 elections strengthened the belief of Kroll and his cohorts that PAC was on the right track. "Increased political activity," said Mazey, "offers us the best hope for solving . . . the basic problems that confront us." Added Kroll, "We have developed tens of thousands of CIO members who have become veterans on the political field." The return of a Democratic Congress and the defeat of right-wing candidates "is a good omen for the future."[21]

Yet the actual role of the CIO and of organized labor more generally in American politics remained problematic. Said James Carey, normally an ardent Democratic partisan, in the 1952 election "we compromised with some of the most relentless antagonists of the New Deal and Fair Deal programs," following a path that "brought us nothing but desertions and defeat." As Kroll himself complained, often the CIO had to bargain with party leaders "much as it would with an employer." Domination of the congressional Democratic Party by entrenched southern conservatives continually frustrated the CIO's legislative ambitions.[22]

Despite such disappointments, most CIO leaders believed that there remained no reasonable option but to continue to attempt to shape the Democratic Party into a reliably liberal instrument. Walter Reuther, once a third party advocate, now defined the CIO's political task as that of "making the Democratic party into the kind of political vehicle that will facilitate the forward implantation of our kind of legislative and economic political program." The success of PAC's candidates in 1948 and 1954 and the belief that a united labor movement could build upon the CIO's political initiatives gave plausibility to hopes that labor's power and influence in the Democratic Party could lead the way toward a more liberal future.[23]

THE CIO PROGRAM, 1946–1955

"You simply cannot understand our almost unique American economic system," instructed Walter Reuther in 1954, "unless you realize that our economy must grow and expand every year." In the 1950s, CIO leaders and spokesmen endorsed the American economic system even as they criticized corporate and governmental policies that stifled its expansion and short-changed lower-income people. The most consistent and significant part of the CIO's political program was a commitment to social Keynesianism that posited endless economic growth. To be sure, CIO leaders pressed for an expanded social welfare system, federalization of worker support programs, more progressive tax policies, and other social democratic desiderata. Said the Wisconsin State IUC, "The American dream must be reinterpreted in social welfare terms." But even here, economic growth was the key. "Maximum production and employment," affirmed a basic policy statement, were the keys to "our current struggle for a free world."[24]

By the late 1940s, questions of economic policy dominated the legislative agenda of the CIO. Its spokesmen and lobbyists identified three phases of this subject for particular attention: encouraging economic growth, improving worker support and social welfare programs, and combating excess corporate wealth and influence. CIO spokespersons consistently and explicitly connected these economic policy concerns to the need to buttress American leadership in the anti-Communist world order. "If we permit our economy at home to be weakened," declared a UAW resolution in 1953, "we shall imperil the world-wide battle against Communist dictatorships."[25]

CIO leaders both feared a return to depression conditions and reveled in the great productive capacity of the U.S. economy. They invoked the Employment Act of 1946, which the 1948 convention hailed as one of the "hallmarks in the history of Congressional legislation." The CIO Full Employment Committee met regularly with the president's Council of Economic Advisors, which the 1946 enactment created, to press the case for federal action to achieve and maintain full employment that they believed the law now required.[26]

The industrial union federation's economic policy influentials asserted the key importance of the consumer while downplaying the dangers of inflation. They pressed for a vigorous federal role, through fiscal policies, the expansion and greater federalization of welfare and worker support programs, and accelerated public spending on health care, education, housing, and public works. They assailed corporate leaders and Republican politicians, especially after Eisenhower became president, for their willingness to "accept" high levels of unemployment and for their failure to unleash the full productive capacities of the economy. Indeed, too many fearful business leaders and their Republican allies "do *not* want a consistently expanding economy, do *not* want to provide full employment, . . . and welcome recessions," a UAW statement charged in 1953.[27]

Far from being the grave digger of capitalism, the postwar CIO celebrated America's dynamism and vigor. This was especially true after Walter Reuther succeeded to the presidency in December 1952. Reuther held that the great productive capacity of the American economic machine could be harnessed in behalf of social justice at home and expansion of freedom abroad. "We of the CIO are extremely optimistic about the future and the possibilities of the American economy," he told a congressional committee early in 1954. Reuther stressed improvement of productivity, full employment, and rising levels of consumer spending. "The Republican leadership fails to understand," declared a UAW policy statement early in 1954, "that our dynamic mass production economy cannot stand still. It must expand and go forward or contract and slide backward."[28]

Belief in the power of the U.S. economy did not mean a return to laissez-faire, however. A modern economy, the CIO's chief economic spokesmen held, required extensive governmental action. Without a strong federal presence and a powerful labor movement, wages and buying power would stagnate. Shortsighted corporate decisions involving investment, manpower, and product mix continually threatened to weaken America's competitive posture, spread social misery, and bring discredit upon the free institutions that were embedded in the American economic system. The democratic state, reflecting the demands of workers and consumers, had to play a major role in sustaining economic growth and fair distribution of income. The Reutherite CIO insisted that its economic proscriptions served the broad public interest and furthered the project of free world leadership. "What's Good for America is Good for the CIO," asserted a CIO Legislative Department slogan. Capitalism was too important to be left to the capitalists.[29]

The views on economic policy held by Reuther and by an able group of economists serving in the UAW and CIO research departments remained fixed on the short and medium range. They never spoke of attaining some qualitatively new plateau of human endeavor, nor did they think very seriously about the pollution and resource depletion that unlimited growth threatened. Indeed, they rarely even invoked the traditional goal of shorter hours, at least in its more transformative aspects. There were challenges aplenty in a world suffering from poverty and want. Thus Reuther told a congressional committee in 1954 that "the millions of American families with incomes below $3000 per year constitute the greatest untapped market for goods of all types."[30]

At the same time, Reutherite economic analysis contained a pragmatic visionary component as well. The demands that rising productivity, social justice, and world leadership imposed on American business pushed always in the direction of greater human intervention. Reuther and other CIO leaders harbored no dreams of the eventual creation of some central commissariat of production. But they did press for the guaranteed annual wage, a collective bargaining goal that they believed would reduce workers' insecurity, sustain high levels of purchasing power, and force otherwise wasteful employers to adopt more rational modes of production. They sought a steadily improving minimum wage, unemployment compensation, and old age and retirement provisions that served the same ends. Critical areas of American life such as education, health care, housing, and a broad range of recreational and infrastructural facilities and services required direct state action.

CIO economic spokesmen looked toward the gradual evolution of a new kind of political economy. Increasingly, the private sector would be subjected to demanding tests of the public good while a powerful government, responding primarily to an increasingly articulate and mobilized democratic public, stood ready to intervene where private enterprise proved inadequate. Thus, in response to the serious 1949 recession, the CIO convention passed a resolution urging that if "private enterprise fails or refuses to make investment in new productive capacity that is required for maintaining full production and employment, the government must accept responsibility to see that the necessary productive capacity is provided and used." CIO leaders never articulated a full-blown version of such a vision, but in the 1950s these hopes and expectations infused virtually every major expression emanating from the CIO on questions of political economy.[31]

From the late 1940s onward, CIO leaders lost few opportunities to promote the CIO's version of the emerging political economy. In 1946 Murray appointed the Full Employment Committee, which in 1951 became a standing body and was renamed the Economic Policy Committee. Its members, CIO vice-presidents all, met regularly with governmental officials, notably the members of the Council of Economic Advisors. Executive committee and Executive Board meetings throughout this period devoted much of their attention to Economic Policy Committee reports and to discussion of the economy and economic affairs legislation. Beginning in 1947 the president's report to the annual convention started with lengthy economic analyses, and each convention featured widely publicized resolutions embodying the CIO's perspectives on economic developments. Murray, Reuther, Economic Policy Committee chair Emil Rieve, and CIO and affiliate Research Department staff members regularly made presentations before congressional committees and other public bodies. In addition, the *CIO News* highlighted economic analysis, and since the early 1940s the Research Department had been publishing *Economic Outlook*, a sophisticated monthly analysis of economic trends, legislative developments, and CIO policies. The staffs of the USWA, UAW, and TWUA, moreover, were heavily involved in general economic analysis, and the publications and public statements of the leaderships of these unions reinforced the general CIO perspective. The CIO and its key affiliates employed professional economists, who provided detailed statistical and conceptual substance to the laborite Keynesian analysis.[32]

The recession of 1953–54 provided CIO leaders with opportunities to present the case for deficit spending and improvements in Social Security, minimum wage, and unemployment compensation programs. Research Department and Economic Policy Committee reports documented the lag in production and the growth in joblessness. As early as December 1953 the UAW had begun to mobilize its membership in behalf of assertive federal action. The American economy, declared a UAW action statement, was "a delicate and intricate mechanism." A return to depression conditions would "tip the balance of the cold war in favor of world Communism." The key to recovery lay in "putting more buying power into the hands of the masses of the people," and the UAW issued a seven-point program involving taxes, unemployment compensation, public spending, and improved social benefits that would turn the tide.[33]

In the spring of 1954, as unemployment rose to nearly 6 percent, the CIO, led by Reuther, swung into action. The current downturn, argued Everett Kassalow of the Research Department, was worse than that of 1949, with key indicators showing actual decline in output for the first time since the end of World War II. In February the industrial union federation issued the *CIO's 10 Point Program to Halt Growing Unemployment*, a public statement based on congressional testimony by Reuther. The Eisenhower administration, it charged, failed to heed the clear mandate of the Employment Act by moving quickly to shore up purchasing power. It fought the raising of personal income tax exemptions, a device that would pump billions into the economy. It resisted the CIO's demand for a boost in the minimum wage, another means of expanding lower-income consumption. It rejected the kinds of public works projects that had been so successful in the 1930s.[34]

The CIO pressured Congress. In May 1954 CIO leaders brought over 400 union activists to the Capitol to lobby for extension of unemployment benefits, stepped-up federal spending on public works, lower-income tax relief, expansion of public housing construction, and support for pensioners, farmers, and small businesses. In contrast to some of the angry public demonstrations of the 1930s, this was to be an exercise in responsible civic petition.

The Legislative Department, which coordinated the affair, issued detailed instructions. In visiting congressmen, delegates were to point out specific plant closures or layoffs in the member's district and to ask for support of expanded unemployment benefits and tax relief legislation. Farm state congressmen should be reminded of labor's support for the family farm and of the close links between adequate purchasing power and farm prosperity. In no case should the CIO's men and women appear argumentative, although they should gently remind legislators of the CIO's political and electoral strength.[35]

In the conference's public sessions, CIO leaders blasted the Eisenhower administration. Charged Reuther and other CIO leaders, the administration had adopted a "do-nothing, look-the-other-way" policy, callously consigning millions to joblessness in the name of economic readjustment. Inaction played into the hands of the Communists, who dishonestly but effectively contrasted Soviet "full employment" with the mounting misery in the United States. Participants were also treated to "the battle of the Humphries," as Minnesota senator Hubert H. Humphrey, the CIO favorite, and Eisenhower's Secretary of the Treasury George Humphrey addressed the gathering, with the former frequently interrupted by the unionists' applause.[36]

Unfortunately for the CIO's social and economic agenda, legislative successes were rare during the 1950s. None of the CIO's recession-fighting proposals gained enactment in the Republican Eighty-third Congress. The Eighty-first and Eighty-second Congresses, while nominally Democratic, remained under Dixiecrat-Republican ("Dixiegop," in CIO parlance) control. A 1952 PAC analysis, made before the elections of that year returned a GOP majority, put core CIO-supported strength in the House at about 130 and in the Senate below 20. In 1949, liberals did gain narrow passage of low-cost housing legislation, but neither the Truman nor the Eisenhower administration actually built even a small fraction of the authorized units. Under Eisenhower there were modest advances in minimum wage and social security coverage; on the other hand, unemployment insurance remained firmly under often niggardly and discriminatory state control, coverage remained spotty, and benefit levels slipped below 1938 standards.

On all of these complex issues of taxation and social provision, the CIO Legislative Department worked closely with other liberal groups and maintained constant surveillance of the legislative process. The Legislative Department coordinated the activities of the CIO staff and the Washington representatives of the affiliated unions. A congressional research staff kept track of bill content, voting records, and legislative histories. The Legislative Department also published the biweekly "Report on Congress" and issued periodic "Field Action Requests," asking particular affiliates or IUCs to contact their legislators on matters of pressing importance. But wily southern committee chairmen and their GOP allies manipulated the complex congressional machinery so as to make the disposition of every major domestic policy initiative a cumbersome, nerve-wracking process.[37]

The fate of a spring 1954 tax reform measure demonstrated the frustrations that liberal-labor forces regularly experienced in these years. In an exhausting process of give-and-take, CIO-supported liberals backed off from their demand that the personal tax exemption be raised from $600 to $1,000, settling for a House vote on a modest $100 increase. But then labor-liberal forces lost on the floor of the House 211 to 202. Indeed, throughout this period labor-supported liberals were often hard pressed to prevent further erosion of existing programs.[38]

The postwar CIO legislative and public policy agenda featuring demands for continual economic growth and improved public programs fit squarely into the broad mainstream of American public life. The CIO had little to say to those who were critical of the wastefulness of defense-industry-driven private affluence. CIO leaders often invoked the broad republican traditions of the labor movement, but in both its collective bargaining strategies and the public policies it promoted the CIO helped to fuel the increasingly privatistic, consumer-driven U.S. economic system. Organizers, reported political scientist Samuel Lubell, might complain that "workers have bought so many things on the installment plan that they don't like to go out on strike for fear of falling behind in their payments." But in fact CIO economic policies encouraged the increasing consumerization of the American working class that helped to cut it adrift from its more heroic traditions.[39]

CIO approaches to worker support and public welfare policies also carried problematic implications. In theory industrial unionists articulated the interests not only of their own members but of working- and lower-class Americans generally. Certainly, enhanced Social Security and unemployment benefits helped all covered workers. But as CIO unions became increasingly successful in securing health insurance benefits and as the wage advances gained in collective bargaining put auto, steel, and other central core workers into relatively high income brackets, CIO officials sometimes found it hard to square the interests of their members with the interests of the broader masses of working and lower-income people. Many workers resented efforts to create or expand tax-funded public health care programs, for example, when they themselves already enjoyed contractual insurance benefits. For their part, though they called for public job training programs, labor's lobbyists were chary about sanctioning the use of public funds to train workers, many of whom were members of minority groups, who might well compete with current union members. Even expanded and enhanced minimum wages, a key feature of the CIO economic program, served to protect basic wage rates of currently employed lower-income employees in textile and services at the expense of potential new entrants into the labor market.[40]

The CIO and its allies had little success in their noneconomic legislative goals. The 1948 Democratic platform pledged efforts to repeal Taft-Hartley and to launch civil rights initiatives designed to implement the 1947 recommendations of President Truman's Committee on Civil Rights. With respect to labor law, throughout this period the powerful conservative presence in Congress precluded anything more than token and technical amendment. NLRB proceedings became increasingly protracted and unresponsive, a circumstance that intensified in the Eisenhower administration, whose board appointees had little sympathy for organized labor. Indeed, by the mid-1950s CIO political and legislative functionaries thought themselves fortunate to be able to beat back Republican-sponsored initiatives designed to further weaken union security and, in the words of the TWUA's political representative, to give "almost dictatorial power over unions to the state legislatures."[41]

As for civil rights, the inability of labor-liberals early in the Eighty-first Congress to gain debate-limiting rules changes in the Senate aborted any possibility of federal legislative action. The only successes were within the Democratic Party. The 1948 presidential platform plank, adopted only after resourceful labor-liberal maneuvering, committed the party to a bold civil rights agenda. Moreover, President Truman, albeit with initial reluctance, pledged to introduce legislation to implement the recommendations of the Committee on Civil Rights on which CIO secretary-treasurer James Carey was an outspoken member. Narrower Democratic congressional majorities in 1950 and the return of the GOP to power in 1952, however, ended serious congressional consideration of civil rights, although the labor-liberal resurgence of 1954, following as it did in the wake of the *Brown v. Board of Education* school desegregation decision in May of that year, rekindled hopes that a more northern-centered Democratic congressional leadership might be able to move forward.[42]

In the mid-1950s the CIO record in political and domestic legislative affairs remained mixed. Despite frustrations and setbacks, ten years of PAC activity seemed to have paid off in the 1954 elections. Even if the forward agenda of liberalism was stalled, conservative attacks on Social Security and other federal programs were increasingly futile. The Employment Act of 1946, for all its limitations, provided a useful forum for the expression of CIO full-employment perspectives. Urban liberals continued to gain ground in the Democratic Party. Even as labor-led third party possibilities receded, more modest hopes of continued liberal advance remained strong.

The expansion of the postwar collective bargaining system in the central core of the American economy shifted the focus of union activity. The organizing crusades of the 1930s and high-level engagement with the wartime government had required that the CIO itself take center stage. But after the war the decentralized nature of industrial relations in the United States and the historic traditions of single-union bargaining quickly shifted focus to the affiliated unions, with the national CIO playing a subsidiary role.

Unions such as the UAW and the USWA led in efforts to expand medical, pension, unemployment, and other protections. They pressed for the establishment of the guaranteed annual wage as a means of stabilizing employment and encouraging employers to plan production more coherently. At the same time, unionists, employers, arbitrators, and judges gradually elaborated the rudimentary systems of workplace governance adumbrated in early CIO contracts.

National CIO leaders did make sporadic efforts to create a unified approach to bargaining. During the 1945–46 strike wave, for example, Murray tried to bring the UAW and the UE in line with the general (i.e., Murray's) CIO agenda. In the summer of 1946 he appointed a CIO wage research committee, in anticipation of tough bargaining with employers for 1947 contracts. Immediately after the war, CIO convention resolutions called for united action in behalf of common collective bargaining goals. In 1946 Reuther urged "practical steps in the CIO to get a war chest of about ten or twelve million dollars, which all CIO Unions could have access to . . . [for] making a fight in these basic struggles."[43]

But unified bargaining never got off the ground. Each of the Big Three metal industry unions dealt with its employers within the context of the particular industry's distinctive economic and historical circumstances. Homilies aside, the CIO generated no code of common standards, guidelines, or bargaining strategies.[44]

This was true most importantly in wage bargaining from 1946 through 1955. There was no common front and indeed much interunion rivalry in the patterns achieved in the various "rounds" of negotiation during this period. Thus, for example, in November 1946 Autoworkers struck GM while Murray was still working with President Truman to avert widespread walkouts. Over the next decade the UAW and the USWA scrutinized each other's negotiations closely. UAW wage advances were a constant goad to Murray and his successor David McDonald in steel negotiations. In 1948 and 1950, when the UAW and GM negotiated cost-of-living adjustments and annual improvement factor wage provisions and announced an unprecedented five-year contract, Steelworkers responded with a mixture of envy and disdain. On one hand, they could not help but contrast the still-contentious state of relations in steel with the now-harmonious relationship the UAW had developed with GM. On the other hand, however, Steelworkers, as did John L. Lewis, remained contemptuous about cost-of-living adjustments, believing that they could erode wage standards that should never be held hostage to management's business success.[45]

Affiliates also waged the battle for guaranteed annual wages, long a CIO demand, piecemeal. The national CIO, it was true, promoted the case for the guaranteed annual wage. But the actual achievement of limited employment security owed nothing to any coordinated bargaining strategy. In its protracted struggles with the basic steel industry, the USWA was unable to achieve meaningful discussion of the concept of the guaranteed annual wage, while Reuther's UAW did make a breakthrough in its 1955 negotiations with the automakers. The UAW contracts, however, did not create a true guaranteed annual wage. The plans established were based on supplementing public unemployment assistance for laid off autoworkers through a separate fund established by the company. When layoffs occurred, affected workers would receive up to 95 percent of their weekly wage from unemployment compensation and payments from the negotiated Supplementary Unemployment Benefits fund. Duration of payment and seniority-based eligibility depended on the accumulation of money in the fund.

CIO officials had promoted the concept of a guaranteed annual wage primarily as a means of pressuring employers to establish more carefully planned production schedules. The "main purpose," declared a UAW economist, "was not to get pay for idleness but to compel the industry . . . to schedule steady employment for its workers," but the Supplementary Unemployment Benefits program largely eliminated the incentive a company might have to schedule its activities so as to minimize layoffs. Since the required payments into the Supplementary Unemployment Benefits fund were unavailable to the company in any event and since the company's liability was limited to the amount in the fund, the program could do little to affect the seasonal nature of auto production. Proudly hailed by CIO leaders as a "historic milestone," the Supplementary Unemployment Benefits programs in the 1955 contracts, observed more dispassionate analysts, seemed a frail basis for the guaranteed annual wage concept. In reality they simply divided up the compensation granted by the companies in a different way than would more traditional wage and benefits settlements.[46]

Even though actual bargaining was conducted by the separate affiliates in uncoordinated and even rivalrous fashion, the CIO itself did provide key support. Its spokesmen roused public support for the general wage and negotiating policies shared by all industrial unionists. National CIO organs, especially the Research Department's monthly publication, *Economic Outlook*, put the CIO case before the public with intelligence and vigor. The CIO message was simple: only substantial wage increases could sustain the postwar economy and, in the words of a 1952 document, insure "a more brilliant economic future than was ever envisaged before."[47]

Moreover, the postwar bargaining stress on so-called fringe benefits among industrial unionists was directly related to the political and legislative efforts of the national CIO. When conservative electoral victories made expansion of New Deal programs impossible, CIO leaders turned to collective bargaining but did not give up hope for eventual legislative success. Thus David McDonald told the 1946 convention that "we cannot wait for many years for Congress . . . to pass improved Social Security laws." Added the TWUA's William Pollock, "If we cannot bring this protection to our members by national legislation . . . , we should insist that this become part of our contracts."[48]

From the start, however, industrial unionists saw bargaining for private benefits as complementary to their efforts to advance public provision. Thus, benefit levels in the pioneering pension and employment security programs gained by the Steelworkers and Autoworkers in 1949 and 1955 were pegged to Social Security and unemployment compensation payment levels. Unionists expected that when employers were forced to fund retirement programs, they would become advocates of expanded public benefits so as to reduce their own obligations. Similarly, CIO leaders' despair of immediate passage of public health care provisions impelled them to place employer-provided health care insurance high on their list of collective bargaining demands. Here too, however, they hoped and expected that the resultant expense would cause employers eventually to enlist in the movement for broad health care coverage.[49]

The CIO itself was the least in evidence in negotiations affiliates conducted over work practices, grievance procedures, shop-floor discipline, and the pace and content of work itself. The affiliated unions individually took care of the training of stewards and the processing of grievances. There was an irony in this because it was the sense of victimization and injustice that workers had felt at the point of production that had animated much of the original rank-and-file support for the CIO project. Even through much of World War II, confrontationalism had often characterized shop-floor relations in basic industry.

After the war, however, most major employers in the central industrial core came to accept, however grudgingly, the presence of strong unions.

Some academic observers, such as influential economist Sumner Slichter, believed that the day had dawned when union leaders, backed by well-organized shop-floor power, would be able to achieve a significant voice in the management of the firms whose workers they represented. The wartime surge of union membership, the success of the new unions in the immediate postwar strike wave, and labor's political influence made such judgments seem plausible. Throughout the postwar decade, however, employers fought to limit the potential for the exercise of shop-floor power and to deny the unions any substantive voice in the conduct of business.[50]

For their part, when CIO spokesmen invoked concepts of worker involvement, they usually spoke in generalities. To be sure, the CIO officially promoted the creation of industry councils, labor-management bodies that would consider problems of production, manning, and technology. After the war, Clinton Golden and others in the USWA pressed Murray to put joint industry-union cooperation at the head of the union's agenda. Reuther seldom missed an opportunity to assert the need for worker expertise, as represented by union functionaries, to improve the efficiency of the whole industrial machine.[51]

Still, industrial unionists found that concepts such as "industry councils" and "labor-management partnership" were easier to invoke than to specify or achieve. Thus, for example, in 1946, a widely distributed CIO publication, *Should Labor Have a Direct Share in Management?*, featured Murray's views. The CIO head urged recognition of workers' "citizenship" rights at the job site, but he stopped far short of advocating real union decision-making power. He called only for "a new kind of [industrial] manager," one who would encourage employees to take an active interest in the firm's affairs and who would listen to workers' ideas. "Organized labor," Murray affirmed, "does not question management's right to run business."[52]

Within the unions themselves, issues relating to the day-to-day control of the shop floor and the pacing of work were inherently divisive. Grievances that caused workers in one department to conduct an angry strike might be regarded as trivial among fellow workers elsewhere in the plant. Frequent interruptions of production alienated many workers and might undermine the union's bargaining position in the wage and benefits negotiations that most workers regarded as fundamental. Postwar CIO publications and public statements continually stressed industrial unionism's positive contribution to productivity and industrial citizenship, and the official advice it passed along to its members and activists rarely stressed aggressive assertion of shop-floor rights.[53]

It was also true that employers, government officials, and contract arbitrators placed increasingly sharp boundaries around permissible shop-floor activism. The widespread inclusion of grievance arbitration in CIO contracts, initially a triumph for unionism in that it curbed unilateral managerial authority and subjected it to outside evaluation, undercut direct activism. Decisions by arbitrators and judges reaffirmed the rights of management to direct its business. In addition, these rulings charged union leaders with the responsibility for disciplining members who violated the contract, thus strengthening the hand of union leaders vis-à-vis rank-and-file workers.[54]

Every CIO union faced different job site traditions. Rubber workers, for example, had long used the strategic importance of skilled tire builders to exert informal shop-floor power. "Tire builders are a breed apart," observed one local unionist. "The pitmen are just as independent, they're famous for their walkouts too. . . . They take action on their own." The postwar URW leadership, faced with the rapid geographical dispersal of tire making into nonunion plants, sought to curb this rank-and-file activism in its Akron strongholds. Autoworkers, even with the pioneering long-term contracts negotiated by the Reuther team in 1948 and 1950, retained the right to strike over local conditions. UAW locals and assembly plant managers fought incessantly over work standards, line speed, and related problems of workplace discipline, as high-wage contracts prodded the auto companies toward ever greater mechanization of operations. Local struggles often snarled the international union's agenda. In 1949, for example, even as the UAW sought to negotiate pioneering pension provisions with Ford, thousands of unionists in key Ford plants waged lengthy strikes to protest the assembly line speedups. In addition, the UAW's skilled tradesmen, who had been crucial in the building and leadership of the union, now sought greater autonomy in union affairs so that they could better protect their distinctive work cultures and compensation structures.[55]

Steelworkers faced still different problems. Even with union-induced rationalization of job descriptions and payment methods, steel production remained complex and discontinuous. High proportions of skilled and semiskilled maintenance and repair workers created enclaves of de facto craft unionism in large USWA locals. Workers jealously guarded hard-won work rules, while the steel companies insisted that changing technology and rising international competition required greater workplace flexibility. Throughout the late 1940s and early 1950s the two sides argued endlessly over the inclusion of "managerial rights" provisions in steel contracts and over the description and legitimacy of the complex of shop-floor practices that characterized the production of steel.[56]

These matters were divisive even within particular plants. As a central body, the CIO could only speak to the broadest issues relating to the changing content and structure of work. Thus, for example, the problem of automation occupied the attention of CIO researchers and spokesmen. They aligned themselves with the American economy's vaunted productivity and denied any suggestion that they sought to impede technological progress. Asked if the introduction of labor-saving technology should be curbed, Reuther responded for the CIO that "nothing could be more wicked or foolish." But he insisted that expansion of technology should not pauperize workers. Government, industry, and labor had to promote worker retraining and skill enhancement. Expansionary fiscal and economic policies had to stimulate greater demand. Workers' representatives had to be consulted in the development and implementation of new procedures. In 1954 the CIO president was taken on a tour of an automated Ford engine plant in Cleveland where new machinery had eliminated hundreds of jobs. "You know," said one of Ford's engineers, "not one of those machines pays dues to the United Automobile Workers." Reuther retorted tellingly, "And not one of them buys new Ford cars, either."[57]

CIO leaders, however, had little to say about the internal life of the plants in which their members toiled. As far as most CIO leaders were concerned, the solution to the problem of shop-floor conditions was the grievance procedure. By the 1950s most CIO contracts featured multilevel dispute resolution steps, with the shop steward acting as the worker's initial representative. The contract specified grievable issues. Consultations between the steward and front-line supervision could often hammer out acceptable compromises. For more difficult cases, the procedure involved international union representatives and management officials. Capping most CIO contracts by the mid-1950s was resort to arbitration by a neutral party. Contractual rights, the opportunity to have experienced representation in conflicts with bosses, and the general sense of protection that an effective grievance procedure brought represented a sea change from the old patterns of shop-floor relations.[58]

Accordingly the ideal shop steward in the late CIO was not the fiery tribune of a resentful working class that his 1930s counterpart often appeared. He was a sober, responsible union officer, charged with a particular obligation to know the contract thoroughly and to establish friendly relations with coworkers. It was his[59] job to get the members out to picnics, union meetings, blood drives, and credit union affairs. "As a steward in a CIO union," instructed the CIO, "you are helping to win a free, happy, secure life for everyone."

In reality, however, the front-line steward increasingly found himself bypassed in the industrial relations system of the 1950s. Detailed contracts made it difficult for an ordinary steward to represent his coworkers authoritatively. The discrediting of radical activists removed or discouraged the kinds of men and women who in the 1930s and 1940s had often aggressively pressed workers' claims. With the arbitration system relying so heavily on precedents, top leaders were reluctant to trust even individual grievances, which might have broad implications, to mere rank-and-file representatives. Offering only the opportunity to perform the "nasty jobs . . . such as selling P.A.C. memberships, dance tickets, and raffle chances," noted two academic students of local unionism, stewardships often went begging. "You may as well forget that we have any stewards," declared a local UAW president in the early 1950s. "They're a joke."[60]

By the mid-1950s, academic students of American industrial relations were painting a picture of a harmonious system operating in the core of the manufacturing economy. Just as in the American polity, they held, competing interests had agreed to basic rules that regulated disputes and minimized the dangers of basic conflict. A "workplace rule of law"[61] based on recognition of pluralistic interests prevailed. The system impelled managers to abandon old injustices and to enlist workers positively in the endless project of boosting productivity and economic growth, and it assigned to union leaders the related role of discouraging irrational militancy and assuring order and discipline in the workplace.[62]

Life on the shop floors, however, was often remote from this ideal. Throughout the postwar decade, workers and managers continued their century-long patterns of conflict and accommodation. Workers found ways around the grievance and arbitration procedures, often in collaboration with foremen eager to maintain familiar work routines. Throughout the 1950s, industrial relations studies showed mounting numbers of grievances filed over shop-floor conditions and work norms. Often thousands of individual grievances were grouped together and disposed of in trade-offs between the union and management in the annual contract negotiations, a practice that did give unions some bargaining leverage on wages and benefits but also led to disgruntlement on the part of aggrieved workers and, critics argued, tended to erode the strength and credibility of the shop-floor union presence.[63]

For their part top leaders grew increasingly impatient with localized worker protests. Willingly enough, the great majority of CIO leaders traded off the half-mythical tradition of spontaneous protest for orderly processes. Unauthorized strikes violated contracts, broke faith with employers, and left the union open to public opprobrium, legal action, and bargaining table reprisals. The whole thrust of twentieth-century industrial relations, most decidedly including the great victories won in the 1930s and 1940s, dele-gitimated localistic protest and point-of-production job actions. "Wild-cat strikes," declared new USWA president David J. McDonald in 1953, "must stop in the United Steelworkers Union" because the "word is going around the industry that" the USWA's top leaders were "losing control of the United Steelworkers of America."[64]

Throughout the postwar period, CIO unions, led by the USWA and the UAW, played critical roles in establishing the modern American system of collective bargaining and industrial relations. Wage and benefits bargaining, along with related legislative efforts, advanced the case for demand-driven economic growth. The patterns of wage distribution in the contracts that CIO unions negotiated during this period continued – although with excep-tions as skilled craftsmen grew more assertive – the industrial union mov-ement's stress on narrowing differentials based on skill levels. The success-ful struggles of the UAW and the USWA, along with the breakthroughs achieved by the UMW, introduced a whole range of pension, medical in-surance, and other worker support programs not only to the realm of col-lective bargaining but to the expectations that workers, union members or not, brought to American workplaces. Whatever the constraints and mal-functionings of the emerging grievance and arbitration systems, no worker wanted to go back to the old days.

The achievement of these gains both justified the CIO project and indi-cated its ambiguities and limitations. For the founding generation, good wages, decent working conditions, and a modicum of security had been *basic*, but not *exclusive*, goals. They had seen the industrial union thrust also as a means of creating an active program of collective republican citi-zenship, of bringing blue collar America into effective participation in an economic and political system increasingly dominated by large, cohesive interests. By the mid-1950s their success in winning economic benefits for their members and their embrace of consumer-driven economics threatened to encourage a largely instrumentalist conception of unionism that made its economic payoff the only meaningful measure of performance.

Indeed, in some respects the very success of CIO negotiators threatened to divide their members from the rest of the working class. Even as UAW or USWA contracts gained employer-paid medical and pension benefits, they separated steelworkers and autoworkers from millions of other workers in segmented U.S. labor markets. Would autoworkers and steelworkers continue to support the CIO's expansive political and legislative program when they themselves already enjoyed many of the benefits for which it sought public funding? Would the aging generation of men and women who had built the CIO and who filled its postwar ranks not perhaps become more concerned about the taxes needed to support public programs than the need for equity in access to health care or provision for old age?

CIO leaders thought not. The CIO's growing political strength would result in the expansion of public programs and of the removal of pensions, health care, and related items from the collective bargaining agenda, thus permitting even greater advances in wages and working conditions. The CIO, pledged Reuther to the 1954 convention, would "fight everlastingly for those economic, legislative and political advances which will strengthen labor and therefore strengthen the fabric of democracy in America and, indeed, throughout all the free world." Increasingly, however, outside observers questioned whether the CIO of the mid-1950s could, without drastic restructuring, meet such a challenge.[65]

FOREIGN POLICY

CIO leaders regarded questions of foreign policy as central. They believed that they had both special reasons and special obligations to refute Soviet claims to leadership of the world's working masses. America, Reuther declared in 1951, "must accept the major share [of responsibility] for giving leadership to the building up of the material and productive strength of the free world and mobilizing the spiritual force of free people everywhere." Of all the elements in American society, he asserted, the "CIO is the most articulate, the most potent and I think the most reliable force freedom has."[66]

The CIO provided active support for the broad foreign policy objectives of both the Truman and the Eisenhower administrations. Its operatives lobbied in behalf of a strong military establishment, generous foreign aid provisions, and positive American initiatives in the Third World. The CIO resolutely backed the war in Korea. Its spokesmen bowed to no one in their condemnation of Soviet and Chinese Communism. They embraced the North Atlantic Treaty Organization and fought all efforts to impede the president's ability to conduct foreign policy.[67]

The CIO combined these stands with an active role in the international labor community. Having pulled out of the WFTU early in 1949, CIO leaders helped establish a rival body, the International Confederation of Free Trade Unions, which was founded in December of the same year. Unlike the WFTU, the new body endorsed the U.S.-led anti-Communist version of world order. Through its participation in the affairs of the International Confederation, its relationship to the United Nation's International Labor Organization, and the association its affiliates maintained with the various international trade secretariats, the CIO attempted to promote higher standards for workers, support union movements abroad, and discredit the claims of the USSR as the workers' state. The CIO foreign policy apparatus had regular contact with and some influence in Western European social democratic and trade union circles. Governments and/or opposition parties in Sweden, Norway, West Germany, and the United Kingdom valued a close association with the Reuther-led CIO, and even under Eisenhower, U.S. officials paid attention to the views of CIO functionaries in regard to European developments.[68] A special CIO committee sought to forge close relations with the labor movements in Latin America, while a CIO Free World Labor Fund and other special projects channeled financial and organizational assistance to non-Communist unionists around the world.

Within its broad support of U.S. foreign policy, the CIO nonetheless often found itself at odds with the administration in power. CIO spokesmen believed that the orientation of American policies, especially after the accession of Eisenhower, was too negative and reactive. Congressional conservatives stressed too much the military and repressive aspects of foreign policy. The CIO, in contrast, emphasized such foreign policy initiatives as the Point Four program, inaugurated by the Truman administration, that channeled technical assistance to underdeveloped countries. "Our foreign policy," intoned a 1954 convention resolution, "must be based on the decent aspirations of people everywhere – to live in peace, friendship and harmony with those of other lands, working in brotherhood to raise living standards, to promote freedom and to achieve personal security."[69]

The CIO leaders attempted to inculcate in their members the precepts of a proactive and humane foreign policy. They sponsored international exchanges, entertained labor leaders from abroad, and churned out a steady stream of publications calling on the American people to bear the necessary economic and military burdens. They worked hard to attempt to convince often-skeptical CIO members that Communist success had not resulted, as the extreme right insisted, from the disloyalty of government officials but stemmed, rather, from poverty and despair.[70]

Educating the membership, though, was only part of the CIO's task. In large part, its leaders believed, the nation's failures in foreign policy reflected the shortsightedness of the men who dominated the government's foreign policy machinery, especially after 1953. Since the essential contest in the battle with Communism was for the allegiance of ordinary people, the CIO, with its vast membership among working people, should have a key role in advising policymakers and in implementing foreign assistance programs. Under both Truman and Eisenhower CIO leaders constantly pressed for inclusion in the foreign policy machinery and for participation in the foreign aid and diplomatic missions that proliferated during the late 1940s and early 1950s.[71]

CIO leaders also sought to distinguish themselves from their AFL counterparts. The older federation's chief foreign policy expert, Jay Lovestone, was a particular target because as a former leader of the CPUSA he enjoyed great influence. He and his henchmen, believed the CIO's foreign affairs experts, relentlessly promoted crudely militaristic policies. Thus Victor Reuther, appointed in 1951 to direct the CIO's European office, waged a constant battle against AFL functionaries for influence within the government and the International Confederation of Free Trade Unions. All too often, Victor Reuther believed, a key appointment to an important governmental or international labor post went not to a balanced labor representative but to "a Lovestone stooge," someone for whom bellicose anti-Communism was an end in itself.[72]

Through the International Confederation and the International Labor Organization of the United Nations the CIO championed enhancement of workers' living standards and the rights of workers to organize. CIO leaders did this, however, in a distinctive American idiom. Thus, for example, they implicitly rejected the legitimacy of labor movements that were, as was often the case in the Third World, primarily political vehicles, and they sought always to promote the model of labor relations embedded in the U.S. collective bargaining system. Moreover, they urged a high-productivity, mass-production model of industrial enterprise. Under the auspices of the European Recovery Program established under the Marshall Plan, for example, CIO representatives participated eagerly in productivity committees designed to introduce American methods of production to European business and labor leaders. While less high-handed than their AFL counterparts, CIO representatives abroad nonetheless believed that the fight against Communism required adoption of American-style labor relations regimes.[73]

CIO leaders constantly criticized the government, especially under Eisenhower, for failing to conduct the Cold War more vigorously and imaginatively. Eisenhower and his team, a convention resolution charged, had given "comfort and advantage to the enemies of democracy." The administration missed opportunities to contrast the advances Western workers were making under collective bargaining with growing evidence of working-class disaffection with Communism in Eastern Europe. The 1954 CIO convention charged that "the present Administration . . . [has] achieved an impressive record for vacillating and contradictory policies." Its inaction and confusion were responsible for "the loss of at least half of Indo-China to the Communists."[74]

Statements such as this, however, did not mean support for all of Communism's less savory foes. UAW secretary-treasurer Emil Mazey, a CIO Executive Board member, sought to make this clear. Noting early in 1955 that "there is a lot of talk about a free world versus the slave world," he pointed to the U.S. embrace of such dictators as "Tito of Yugoslavia, Franco of Spain, Peron of Argentina, Batista of Cuba and a whole host of others." CIO leaders condemned talk of using atomic weapons in behalf of the regime of Generalissimo Chiang Kai-shek on the island of Taiwan. Instead of backing dictators or brandishing nuclear warheads, CIO leaders urged, the government should rely on democratic movements and generous economic aid to win the battle against Communism.[75]

In one sense such high-minded views represented an intelligent and principled perspective. The problem was that they often bore little connection to the actual dilemmas facing national policymakers or the peoples of afflicted areas. Apart from Western Europe the CIO had little organic connection with either labor movements or the U.S. government. Its policy statements evidenced little intimate knowledge of the countries involved and regularly avoided tough questions involving trade-offs between democratic ideals and anti-Communist priorities. They failed to contemplate any notion – widespread among progressive forces in the Third World – that justice for emerging colonial peoples might entail bitter sacrifices on the part of Americans.

Unlike their counterparts in the AFL, CIO leaders no longer served as conduits for funds from the Central Intelligence Agency.[76] At the same time, though, they revealed little concern about the methods employed by the U.S. government in the frequent overthrows of nationalist and other revolutionary leaders in the Third World. According to the CIO view of the Third World, it was cynical Communists, on one side, and corrupt corporate lackeys, on the other, who were the primary agents of misery. CIO position papers and resolutions showed little curiosity into the relationship between Third World poverty and Western standards of living.

CIO publications and pronouncements applauded the defeat of allegedly Communist-led or -influenced governments. With regard to Guatemala, for example, the CIO raised no objections to the heavy-handed CIA-inspired overthrow of the leftist government of Jacobo Arbenz in the spring of 1954. Reported a CIO Latin American observer, "The Arbenz government was pretty thoroughly riddled with Communists." True, Mazey and Oil Workers' president Jack Knight raised doubts about the wisdom of unilateral U.S. intervention, however "covert." The effect of our policy, charged Knight, was "to give aid and comfort to the United Fruit company." Mazey went further, declaring, "We have got to stop measuring our foreign policy on what's good for American business." For the most part, however, CIO leaders embraced the government's anti-Communist priorities. They placed their hopes in the responsiveness of the new regime to the plight of the people and urged the Eisenhower administration to press for progressive labor policies and land reform measures. Yet as even CIO observers quickly noted, the prominence of men with close ties to United Fruit both in the new Guatemalan government and in the U.S. foreign policy apparatus offered no hope for optimism on this score.[77]

CIO leaders often writhed uncomfortably in their overall defense of a foreign policy that sanctioned continued Third World dependency and relied heavily on military dictators. They believed that anti-Communism took precedence, that American policies *could* promote progressive ends without jeopardizing U.S. and Western living standards, and that the more underhanded and unsavory methods of U.S. diplomacy were not necessary for pursuing anti-Communist world leadership. Rarely, if ever, did they examine these premises. Insofar as much of the nation's limited foreign policy debate of the 1950s was concerned, the CIO remained a faithful, if occasionally obstreperous, member of the team.

12 The Final Years of the Late, Great CIO

The death of Philip Murray on November 9, 1952, coupled with Republican electoral victory just a few days before, triggered rumors about the impending breakup of the CIO. Speculated *U.S. News and World Report*, "The odds, as of now, . . . seem to favor a collapse of the CIO."[1] In fact, however, obituaries were premature. The industrial union federation's new president, Walter Reuther, was a vigorous spokesman for industrial unionism, and in collective bargaining and political action, and as part of the loyal liberal opposition, the CIO remained effective and enterprising.

Nonetheless, from the time of Murray's death until its merger with the AFL three years later, the CIO as an institutional entity remained uncertain and adrift. Membership totals and finances fluctuated, and industrial unionists failed to expand the boundaries of the organized labor force. Critics charged that the CIO had lost touch with the rank and file, even as the demographic contours of the CIO's membership and general constituency changed.

Yet in the 1950s, even if industrial unionists could not break new ground, collective bargaining had become the norm in the industrial core, and organized labor played an increasingly recognized role in the political arena. The men and women of the CIO stepped up participation in the civic, educational, and religious life of their communities. Clearly, union leaders believed, whatever its problems and disappointments, the CIO was as American as apple pie.

THE REUTHER SUCCESSION

Murray's death unleashed rivalries that brought into the open a growing sense of drift and confusion. For twelve years he had been the central figure in an organization beset with personal, ideological, and institutional conflicts. Steeped in the traditions of adversarial unionism, Murray was nonetheless intensely patriotic, hostile to radicalism, and orthodox in his ambitions for the working class. His modest lifestyle and mild public demeanor provided a sharp contrast with the glowering figure of his predecessor, John L. Lewis, and helped gain for him unusually sympathetic treatment in the press.[2]

Murray's elevation to the CIO presidency in 1940 both coincided with and helped to promote a new role for the industrial union federation. The USWA remained his home base, but it was in his capacity as CIO chief that wartime governmental officials, including most notably the president, dealt with him. Murray shifted resources and personnel between the CIO and the USWA with little regard for accounting niceties. Many of the smaller affiliates were subsidized by the CIO, which, in effect, meant the USWA. The growing importance of the CIO in the Democratic Party strengthened Murray's public role as the leader of industrial workers. Remarked CIO publicity director Henry Fleisher, "The Steelworkers [union] was the bulwark of the CIO . . . and Phil was the fountainhead and the spiritual father of all that."[3]

Within the CIO, Murray had kept the peace. In 1941–42 the CIO had withstood the angry departure of Lewis and the Mine Workers. During a critical period, it was Murray who had kept the split between the CIO's anti-Communist and pro-Soviet factions under control. More recently, Murray had suppressed growing resentment among fellow USWA officers, and among top UAW leaders, that the two huge metalworkers' organizations were getting little in return for their enormous financial outlays to the CIO.[4]

Topping the list of internal divisions that widened with the loss of Murray was the ill feeling between USWA and UAW partisans. The two unions reflected sharply different aspects of the CIO tradition. Linked to the parochial and often authoritarian world of the UMW, the USWA, from its origins in 1936 as an organizing committee, had been a top-down affair. For all his benign demeanor, Murray brooked no opposition and kept close control over the local unions. He suppressed factional and ideological dissent. All dues moneys were sent to Pittsburgh and then redistributed. The national union maintained rigid control over strike authorization. Murray and his aides justified this hierarchical governance on the grounds that the history of unionism in steel had been one of defeat and disaster. Thus a strong, centralized union was necessary in the confrontation with powerful steelmakers.[5]

The UAW tradition was different. The union had grown from the grass roots of militant local activism. The lack of strong central direction in the 1930s had encouraged the emergence of all sorts of dissent on political, personal, and trade union issues. Working in a relatively new sector without steel's long history of union defeat, automobile industry unionists exuded a kind of optimistic militancy, reveling in a degree of disputation and factional conflict unthinkable in the narrower world of the Steelworkers.

Substantive issues divided the two unions as well. They were natural rivals for primacy in collective bargaining. As CIO chief, Murray strove to make Steelworkers' contracts the best in the industrial core. Yet increasingly in the postwar period the UAW extracted settlements from the technologically more advanced automobile industry that surpassed those gained by the USWA. Whether it was basic wage rates, health and pension benefits, employment security, or acquisition of the union shop, by the early 1950s the UAW had become the CIO leader.[6]

Moreover, the accession of Walter Reuther to the UAW presidency underlined the differences between the two organizations. As the USWA's dabbling with ideas of joint labor-management direction of the industry ebbed after the war, Reuther emerged as an articulate champion of stepped-up laborite participation in the direction of the economy. Murray led the Steelworkers in long strikes in 1949 and 1952, while the UAW achieved the union shop virtually without opposition and entered long-term contracts with GM and the other automakers. Moreover, Murray resented Reuther's ambition and his apparent disdain for the great traditions of union struggle associated with the UMW. A widely circulated story captured the Murray-Reuther rivalry. It seems that during the 1946 strikes the two CIO leaders met with President Truman. When Reuther stepped out of the room for a moment, the president, alarmed by the Autoworker's self-confidence, gave friendly counsel to Murray. "Phil," Truman was supposed to have warned, "that young man is after your job." "No, Mr. President," Murray replied, "he really is after *your* job."[7]

In reality Reuther harbored no political ambitions, but Murray's death immediately raised the question of succession in the CIO. Poised to assume Murray's mantle in the USWA was its secretary-treasurer, David J. McDonald. While McDonald showed no interest in leading the CIO, he both hated Reuther and regarded the UAW leader's plans for renewed laborite advance as socialistic nonsense. Vain and self-important, the fifty-year-old McDonald was a skillful political infighter who managed to gain control of the USWA apparatus despite indications that Murray had planned to push him aside. Remarked Lee Pressman, "Both Murray and Lewis treated McDonald as a small boy. . . . David was always the kid who got Phil's tickets and carried his valise." But Murray had put off demoting McDonald, and so the week after Murray's passing the steel union's executive board, cognizant of the power and influence that McDonald wielded as secretary-treasurer, chose him as acting president, with full expectation that he would quickly gain the office in his own right.[8]

Throughout his career in the USWA, McDonald had been active in CIO affairs. He served on the federation's executive committee, was secretary-treasurer of PAC and of SOC, and acted as Murray's lieutenant in dealings with other CIO leaders. Nonetheless, McDonald believed that the CIO's day had passed; Republican victory and organizational stasis dictated retrenchment, not the ambitious agenda associated with Reuther. Moreover, McDonald detested Reuther, whom he regarded as a self-promoting and priggish prima donna. "Don't call him Reuther," McDonald told his aides. "Refer to him as that no good red-headed socialist bastard Reuther." For their part, the Reutherites regarded McDonald as a boozy, self-important fraud. Remarked CIO publicity man Henry Fleisher, "If ever you find a prescription of two people who couldn't last a day on a desert island there they were, heading the two largest unions in the CIO."[9]

Evidence of the Reuther-McDonald conflict permeated Atlantic City when the 1952 CIO convention, postponed by Murray's sudden death, finally assembled in early December. The chief item of business, of course, was the election of a new leader. McDonald urged the delegates to support Allan S. Haywood, the sixty-four-year-old director of organization, for the presidency. As "Mr. CIO," Haywood had spent fifteen years speaking at banquets and midwifing the births of new affiliates. Delegates from the LIUs and IUCs overwhelmingly supported him, as did unionists who shared McDonald's resentment and suspicion of Reuther, despite Haywood's marginal role in top CIO decision making.[10]

As head of the dynamic UAW, Reuther too was an obvious contender for the top position. Reuther saw in the CIO presidency a logical extension of his emerging role as American labor's preeminent public spokesman. Despite labor's recent setbacks, Reuther believed, mass organization remained essential. Perhaps, freed from Murray's parochialism, the CIO could resume its forward march. A vigorous program of organizing and political action might give the industrial union project new life.[11]

On December 4 the delegates chose Reuther as the CIO's third president. But the vote was close, with Reuther outdistancing Haywood by only 52 percent to 48 percent. Joining the Steelworkers were delegates from affiliates that Haywood had helped to establish and had serviced in his capacity as director of organization, notably the Packinghouse Workers, the Paperworkers, the Gas, Coke, and Chemical Workers, the Communications Workers, and the Shipbuilding Workers, as well as most delegates from LIUs and IUCs. In addition to the UAW, those supporting Reuther included the TWUA, the ACWA, the URW, the IUE, and the NMU.[12]

Reuther soon learned that he could not reforge the CIO as a spearhead of laborite advance. At the convention, he had agreed to the creation of a new office, the executive vice-presidency, and to the naming of his erstwhile rival, Haywood, to it. But two months later, CIO leaders were stunned by news of Haywood's death, an event that soon revealed the institutional fragility of the Reuther-led CIO. Haywood's passing virtually invited McDonald now to promote the candidacy of someone from his camp to fill this potentially powerful office.[13]

In theory the executive vice-presidency might have provided Reuther with just the leverage needed to move the CIO project along. With Haywood gone, he might engineer the appointment of one of his more energetic supporters, who could translate Reuther's general vision of a revitalized CIO into specific programs. But McDonald quickly claimed the vacated slot for someone with a UMW-USWA background, settling on John V. Riffe, a forty-nine-year-old veteran organizer and second-level official in the UMW, USWA, and CIO. Reuther had no enthusiasm for the appointment, but McDonald made it clear that unless Riffe or someone very much like him were named, Steelworker disaffection would grow.[14]

Over the next two and a half years McDonald sniped away at Reuther. He maneuvered his personal assistant, Oral Garrison, into the Washington headquarters from whence he received regular reports on all manner of CIO affairs. He kept the pressure on Riffe, nominally the CIO's number two official, to follow the Steelworkers' agenda. For his part, Riffe suffered from ill health and the machinations of Garrison and CIO secretary-treasurer James B. Carey, who was determined to retain his own influence in CIO affairs during this period of transition.[15]

These rivalries often took bizarre forms. At Executive Board meetings, McDonald noisily wisecracked with his colleagues even as Reuther and Carey attempted to carry on business. In May 1954 McDonald rebuked reporters for following the term *United Steelworkers of America* with the letters *CIO* in news stories about his union. "We are an autonomous union," he insisted, while the CIO was merely "a loose association of international unions." For about a year beginning in June 1953 McDonald met ostentatiously with Lewis and the president of the AFL's International Brotherhood of Teamsters, Dave Beck, encouraging press speculation that he was preparing to abandon the CIO and help form a rival labor federation.[16]

McDonald's shenanigans were constant reminders of the CIO's vulnerability. Association of McDonald with Lewis, for example, aligned him in the public eye with one of Reuther's most savage critics. In 1951, at a huge public gathering of autoworkers near Detroit, Lewis had labeled Reuther a "pseudo-intellectual nitwit," while in September 1954 he declared, in a telegram that McDonald cheerfully made public, that the CIO was "a federated group, dominated by intellectual inebriates in frantic pursuit of the butterflies of their own delusions."[17]

Reuther fumed at McDonald's behavior. Constant talk of USWA defection pulled the rug from any positive initiatives Reuther might have contemplated. "I don't want the CIO made over in my [own] image," Reuther assured his fellow unionists in June 1954. Far from pressing an assertive agenda, he said, "I have leaned over backwards to please" the Steelworkers. He pledged to "lay the cards on the table" for McDonald and demand that this sniping at the CIO end. But in fact no showdown ever took place.[18]

Meanwhile, within the CIO apparatus, Riffe began to advance a personal agenda based on his newfound Christian piety. A hard-drinking, poker-playing organizer of the old school, Riffe had recently experienced personal rebirth through the Moral Re-Armament movement. Founded in 1938 by Lutheran clergyman Frank Buchman, MRA was a Protestant initiative that sought to give ideals of honesty, purity, unselfishness, and love practical application. Staunchly anti-Communist, MRA otherwise preached social harmony, holding that racial, international, and industrial conflict would yield to Christly reconciliation under the guidance of MRA-inspired businessmen, diplomats, and labor officials.[19]

For years, MRA's leading spokesman within the CIO was John G. Ramsay, a self-taught Protestant layman and Steelworker activist. Attracted by the charismatic Buchman, Ramsay believed that "God is the forgotten factor" in industrial relations. During World War II he had tried to convince Murray that MRA represented "practical christianity." The staging of the MRA pageant "You Can Defend America" as part of the official proceedings at the founding convention of the USWA in May 1942 reflected its influence. After the war, amid personal and health crises, Riffe became an enthusiastic adherent. Indeed, declared his wife, "John [now] . . . believed with Frank Buchman that it is [either] Moral Re-Armament or Communism."[20]

From the start of his vice-presidency Riffe publicly combined his CIO activities with open endorsement of MRA. "By applying . . . [MRA] principles," he proclaimed in the summer of 1953, "I have been able to accomplish more for my union in the past three months than in the past three years." In September of the next year he addressed the MRA's annual convention at Mackinac Island, Michigan, using his CIO travel budget to finance the trip. "MRA," he declared, "is the only hope I have seen anywhere. It does have the answer." He pledged that he would urge union officials "from Walter Reuther on down" to turn to MRA "for training and to get the answer."[21]

Riffe's effusions made him a laughingstock in labor circles. Reflecting on the vice-president's reputation as a cutthroat poker player, one Packinghouse official mused ruefully that "I wish I had had the opportunity to win back my money from Riffe before he got so pious." Carey, anxious to protect his own turf, lost few opportunities for public ridicule. At last, in December 1954, the Executive Board declared that the CIO was "unsympathetic to Moral Re-Armament" and forced Riffe to tell MRA to stop using his name in its literature. Even so, the specter of the mighty CIO being led by an adherent of a movement preaching personal regeneration and painless social harmony did little to encourage Reuther's hopes for revitalization.[22]

RESHUFFLING THE CIO

From the outset of the Reuther presidency the divisions and weaknesses within the CIO sabotaged hopes for renewed vigor. Reuther's reputation for progressivism and energy encouraged expectations that industrial unionism would gain a new dynamism. But his own lack of commitment to the CIO, along with McDonald's continuing opposition and the structural and organizational weaknesses of key affiliates, insured that there would be no forward march in the 1950s. "We have to recapture the crusading spirit we had in the early days, and we have to take on some of the areas of the unorganized," the new president told the 1952 convention. In fact, however, Reuther moved quickly to restructure the CIO in ways that reduced its organizing presence and, in effect, precluded bold initiatives.[23]

As in the past, so in the 1950s, CIO membership figures were a matter of disputation. One candid delegate to the 1952 convention confirmed suspicions that CIO officials grossly inflated the reported voting strength of small affiliates.[24] According to monthly per capita tax receipts, total membership in 1949, just before the ouster of the pro-Soviet unions, had been 4.2 million. In 1951–52 it stood at a fairly consistent monthly average of 3.5 million, despite extensive CIO raids against the ousted affiliates. The Korean War spurred growth again, and by the spring of 1953 affiliates were paying per capita tax on 4.9 million members, a post–World War II high. The post–Korean War slump, however, took its toll, and in 1954 and 1955 the total fell off by about a million. Veteran labor reporters such as Daniel Bell, Victor Riesel, and Murray Kempton, however, questioned even these figures, mainly because smaller, CIO-subsidized affiliates had a vested interest in claiming inflated memberships.[25]

The UAW and the USWA accounted for almost 60 percent of the CIO's total. The next five largest unions in size (ACWA, TWUA, CWA, URW, and IUE) added an additional 25 percent, which meant that the other twenty-five to twenty-eight affiliates accounted for only 15 percent of CIO membership among them. The CIO was equally concentrated in geographic terms, for as of 1954 over 50 percent of all CIO members worked in four states, Michigan, Ohio, New York, and Pennsylvania. In contrast, the South and Southwest accounted for only 14 percent of the CIO total.[26]

The CIO's preponderance in manufacturing was readily apparent as well. Together, the metal, textile and clothing, meatpacking, rubber, and electrical unions accounted for about 70 percent of the membership. Textiles and apparel apart, these industries were relatively centralized with large numbers of workers per plant, making for cost-effective organizing and servicing. By the mid-1950s, 70 percent of the workers in the nation's 1935 manufacturing establishments employing over 1,000 workers were already unionized. As of 1952, 60 percent of union contracts in manufacturing had union shop or other union security provisions, and unions in the industrial core remained strong and popular: elections required by the Taft-Hartley Act to reconfirm union shop status resoundingly demonstrated blue collar workers' ongoing adherence to industrial unionism.[27]

Throughout his presidency Reuther spoke eloquently of the possibilities of renewing the CIO's mission to organize the unorganized. He believed that the industrial union federation already had the financial resources to forge ahead, for it spent about $3.5 million annually, of total receipts of $5.76 million, for organizing purposes. "Never in the history of a labor movement has a parent body been able to put forth this kind of sustained organizational effort," Reuther declared in March 1954. Such resources "ought to enable us to get moving to organize many hundreds of thousands of workers in these fields." Declared a TWUA official, at one early meeting "brother Ruether [sic] spoke . . . of certain people who had developed what he called 'Modern Organizing Methods.' "[28]

Those who hoped that Reuther's accession would signal a revival of CIO élan, however, were disappointed. Reuther did not in fact attempt to expand the CIO into new fields. Instead he moved quickly to liquidate CIO-directed centralized organizing projects, including the southern campaign. In February 1953 he appointed the Organizing Policy Committee, which developed a program that would eliminate all these special projects. Along with a simultaneously instituted general administrative streamlining, which closed forty-three of the organization's fifty-six regional offices, this move would free up as many as 200 CIO staff representatives. But Reuther's CIO would not employ them in new fields; rather, affiliated unions would come to the Organizing Policy Committee with specific requests for assistance. Meanwhile, the thirteen district directors would play no role in organizing, concentrating instead on political and administrative work. This program, said Reuther in June 1953, was "the most realistic approach to this problem that we have come up with to date." He hinted that the new program would enable the CIO to press ahead in underorganized fields, but in view of the lack of energy and resourcefulness generally displayed by the affiliates with jurisdiction in these areas, in fact the new plan simply insured that the CIO would not seek to occupy new territory.[29]

Although Reuther referred to these changes as technical adjustments, they amounted to a gutting of the institutional CIO as a vehicle for organizing. As early as August, Riffe's assistant Oral Garrison was reporting that "under the new organizational setup . . . , the National Office has more or less lost all contact with the staff." At the same time, Riffe and Reuther pressured LIUs, long a source of financial and convention voting strength to the CIO headquarters, to transfer into affiliated unions. Thus, the whole thrust of the new order, while never acknowledged explicitly by Reuther, was to weaken the CIO as an institutional entity and to shift its resources to the international unions. With the limited Riffe in ostensible command and with centralized organizing campaigns a thing of the past, the CIO as such could play little coherent role in industrial unionism's organizing mission.[30]

Through most of his tenure as executive vice-president, Riffe tinkered with these changes. His optimistic reports, however, were long on elaborate details of administrative restructuring but short on actual organizing initiatives. By October 1954 he was forced to admit "that this plan has not been as successful in operation as it was intended."[31]

The affiliates did not pick up the slack either. The CIO unions with jurisdiction among government, white collar, chemical, service, and goods-handling workers were small, impecunious, ill led, and lacking in energy or imagination. Internal conflict ravaged the Gas, Coke, and Chemical Workers' union. Forever dependent on CIO subsidies, it was unable to develop any coherent challenge to du Pont and other antiunion employers. In a field with almost 2 million unorganized wage workers, the Government and Civic Employees Organizing Committee, which took over the jurisdiction originally granted Communist-tainted public employees' unions, could claim only 15,000 members. "Almost three years of activity," observed an internal CIO report early in the Reuther regime, "have been wasted" since the ouster of the pro-Soviet unions in public employment. With regard to white collar workers, a CIO official admitted to *Fortune* labor editor Daniel Bell that there was "no central effort, no central drive, no power pushing in the field."[32]

In theory there were resources available for launching bold initiatives. True, the CIO itself was a modest operation, with an annual budget a quarter that of the USWA and with only about a third the number of employees of the UAW, which had a payroll of over 1,000. But the USWA and the UAW combined had strike funds and reserves of at least $15 million. In the

1930s the UMW, along with the ACWA and the ILGWU, had launched the CIO on far less.[33]

What was lacking now, however, was the will and the organizational coherence to re-ignite the industrial union project. In view of the CIO's internal rivalries and institutional inertia, there was no one to assume the responsibility for organizing the unorganized. Reuther himself treated the CIO as an afterthought. Confronted with McDonald's hostility and saddled with the limited Riffe as executive vice-president, he made no effort to funnel new resources into the CIO or to spearhead vast new organizing initiatives. Organizing took money and institutional commitment. The big affiliates of the CIO in the 1950s had the former, but no one had the latter.

The unemployment associated with the post–Korean War recession slashed per capita tax payments and plunged the CIO into the red. By February 1954 the industrial union federation was running a monthly deficit of over $80,000. Emergency meetings of the top officers resulted in sharp reductions in subsidies to weak affiliates, the closing of many regional offices, and a general effort, in Reuther's words, to "boil it down." TWU president Michael Quill, who had ridden out many crises during his long association with the CIO, feared that "we'll be drained shortly if we don't do something." Deficits continued through March 1955.[34]

Riffe, ineffective as an innovator, was successful as a budget cutter. Between the onset of the new program in April 1953 and the end of October the next year, he reported, the organizing department had cut seventy-seven people, saving the CIO over $400,000 in salaries and travel expenses. This was probably his most substantial achievement as executive vice-president.[35]

In response to these budgetary embarrassments, rumors continued to circulate about the impending demise of the CIO. "M'Donald Ready to Deliver Death Blow to CIO," headlined Victor Riesel's widely read column in March 1954. In December *U.S. News and World Report* quoted one staff member who said that the annual convention "is being tagged as a wake." The leadership angrily denied these reports. Secretary-Treasurer Carey's deficit-studded reports were invariably accompanied by insistence that the downturn was temporary and that the CIO was alive and well.[36]

It was true that the industrial union federation remained solvent, with cash balances that never dropped below $1.5 million. Its major unions were among the nation's largest and most influential, and the November 1954 elections lent new luster to the CIO's political operations. While reports of disintegration were not literally true, however, by mid-1954 few in the CIO believed that the trajectory of the industrial union federation arced upward. Increasingly, they believed that if industrial unionism was to renew its onward march, it would have to do so as part of a unified American labor movement.

WHAT DO WORKERS WANT?

The changing dynamics of the American workforce proved too hard a challenge for the CIO's postwar leadership. They were unprepared to deal with the growth of service, white collar, and other nonindustrial sectors. They worried endlessly about the declining appeal of unionism for postwar workers. At the same time they ignored low-wage service and white collar sectors, whose large numbers of blacks and women might have offered possibilities for renewal.

Although the CIO was secure in the metalworking heart of the industrial core, it was unable to penetrate most other fields. Insofar as organizing success was concerned, in the words of *Fortune* labor commentator Daniel Bell, "The Cream Is Off." Standard Oil, du Pont, and other major corporations remained nonunion, seemingly with the support of large majorities of their workforces, and in 1952, for the first time, the CIO lost more NLRB representation elections than it won. With manufacturing saturated, the CIO would have to look to the expanding service, retail, government, and white collar areas for continued growth. But these sectors presented significant problems. Shops were smaller, and the cost per worker of organizing was higher. Established AFL unions far outdistanced the CIO among goods-handling, white collar, service, and public workers. Indeed, the lure of an expanding AFL began to pull packinghouse, textile, food processing, and chemical workers away from the once-rebel body. The presence of large numbers of women workers in the service and governmental sectors also posed problems for a union movement rooted so strongly in the metal-bashing industrial core.

At the time of Reuther's accession, the CIO enrolled a mere 26,000 government and civic workers, 4,500 radio technicians and engineers, 20,000 newspaper workers, 7,500 insurance workers, and 8,000 department store clerks. Even in manufacturing, key industries remained outside the fold. In textiles, membership totals were actually declining from wartime peaks as a resurgent AFL United Textile Workers mounted a sustained challenge while southern employers intensified their resistance. Moreover, the CIO had little representation in the vast chemical and petroleum industries, 80 percent of whose 750,000 workers were unorganized.[37]

The CIO's one great postwar organizing success was the affiliation in 1949 of the CWA, representing technicians, repairmen, and telephone operators (most of the latter being women). Faced with the difficult task of wresting collective bargaining contracts from the powerful Bell system, however, the new union's cautious leadership made no effort to energize a general CIO organizing campaign in nonmanufacturing sectors or among women workers.[38]

In the 1950s, workers, whether union members or not, seemed to show little interest in or understanding of unionism. Lamented one Michigan activist, "We are by no means reaching the masses of . . . the workers." Among white collar workers, reported CWA vice-president John J. Moran, "there are still many people who don't belong and don't want to belong to the CWA because it is in the CIO." Union meetings were ill attended, and it was impossible to get members to read the *CIO News* and other union publications.[39]

In December 1953 economist Everett Kassalow, a member of the CIO research department, tried to pinpoint the reasons for the CIO's declining appeal. Noting that "no significant industry or service which was not organized before 1945–46 has been organized since then," Kassalow ran through the usual explanations for the lack of movement: the smaller size of unorganized plants, organizer burnout, and white collar resistance to unions. He quoted a conversation with a veteran organizer, comparing circumstances of the mid-1950s with those prevailing ten or twelve years before. "The era of invincibility is gone," this man had observed. Workers had joined unions in the old days not because organizers' techniques were better but because "the worker assumed up till 1941–42 that labor was on top and management was underneath and you might as well be with the winner."[40]

Then, too, management had smartened up. Nonunion firms often met or exceeded union contract benefits. They had developed sophisticated forms of paternalism. They carefully screened new employees and successfully portrayed unions as violent, radical, and racially suspect. Moreover, the Taft-Hartley Act had strengthened antiunion forces everywhere, with NLRB sanctions increasingly ineffective in cases of worker victimization.[41]

Moreover, in the generally strong economy of the Cold War era, workers often identified positively with their employers in ways that would have been unthinkable twenty years earlier. Textile workers, reported TWUA research director Solomon Barkin, felt indebted to the mill owners for providing whites with relatively well-paid work; in the Piedmont, wages had more than quintupled since the mid-1930s. In August 1955 a Gallup poll found that 80 percent of blue collar workers surveyed believed that their "family income [has n]ever been higher than it is now." A study of a representation election involving Chicago chemical workers indicated how workers could vote against union representation while expressing pro-union sentiments. Detailed interviews found that they believed unions were needed to counter the power of business. Indeed, reported the researchers, "These virtues are almost cliches to these people." In the end, though, a company union that did not rouse management antagonism, required minimal dues, and made no demands on the time or energy of workers was victorious.[42]

Leftist critics of the CIO argued that a return to militant activism was the key to recruitment. They pointed to strike statistics that continued to show high levels of worker discontent through the mid-1950s as evidence that workers would respond to aggressiveness. But all of the polling data and social surveys, to say nothing of the field reports of organizers, suggested the opposite, that it was precisely the CIO's reputation for strikes and confrontation that dissuaded potential members.[43]

One group that did respond positively to the union appeal in the 1950s was African Americans. Yet few in the industrial union federation's leadership actively addressed the economic and workplace issues that most directly affected African American workers, who in the mid-1950s comprised about 10 percent of CIO membership. Reuther and his fellow officers failed to see in the disadvantaged position of African Americans in the U.S. economy any particular opportunity to direct resources toward a group whose grievances might have provided the tinder necessary to revitalize industrial unionism's flagging organizing program.

In the 1930s and 1940s African Africans had played key roles in CIO victories in metalworking, pulp and paper, meatpacking, and other manufacturing areas. In many communities a symbiotic relationship emerged between new biracial industrial unions and a revitalized civil rights movement. But in the 1950s, though the industrial union federation was a significant force in the national civil rights legislative coalition, the CIO relegated African American workers to the margins.

On one level the mature CIO sustained its early focus. Certainly the UAW's 150,000 black members were a vigorous presence in the UAW, which played a prominent role in Michigan and national civil rights activism. In the USWA, in which the blacks were both numerically less significant and politically less visible than in the UAW, they compelled the international union, at least in some instances, to move against discriminatory local unions. The Packinghouse Workers' union stepped up its stress on racial matters in the early 1950s, using the loyalty of its large African American contingent as the key to rebuilding after disastrous strikes in 1948. Certainly, strong industrial union contracts, which generally tended to benefit particularly workers at the lower ends of the wage scales, were instrumental in the dramatic surge in black income. Thus, by the early

1950s, black workers' annual income was 60 percent of that of whites, compared with under 40 percent in 1939.[44]

Moreover, CIO conventions issued strong civil rights statements. The CIO filed an amicus brief in *Brown v. Board of Education*. In 1952 the CIO helped to create the Negro Labor Committee, USA, which brought together unionists from the AFL and the CIO to work "to abolish discrimination within the labor movement and our general community life." The CIO's CARD continued to encourage affiliates and councils to step up their efforts in behalf of racial justice. Murray, Walter Reuther, James Carey, and other CIO leaders frequently and eloquently denounced racism, usually within the context of waging the international battle against Communism. Thus, said Murray in a typical statement during the Korean War, revival of the FEPC "would . . . be worth two or three army divisions," for discrimination was a "national disgrace . . . [and] plays directly into the hands of the Kremlin."[45]

Few in the CIO regarded the concerns of black workers as central, however. Indeed, several factors militated against too strong an interest in racial matters. Since the pro-Soviet unions had highlighted civil rights, ardent racial progressivism might suggest pro-Communist sympathies. PAC operatives believed that forthright CIO support for desegregation could jeopardize the chances of prolabor candidates, and not only in the South. In 1950, for example, the defeat of a strong CIO congressional candidate in Detroit led Michigan State CIO Council director Gus Scholle to the conclusion that "this one issue was primarily responsible."

On the matter of race, CIO unions faced a good deal of internal opposition. In the UAW, for example, Reuther's strong civil rights statements stood in sharp contrast to his unwillingness to challenge the virtually all-white skilled tradesmen. In the USWA, for years the all-white Alabama district leadership ignored blatant racism in grievance handling, local negotiations, and general servicing of the Birmingham area's increasingly restive black iron and steel workers. In northern locals, whites dominated grievance committees, leadership posts, and access to skilled jobs. In neither union were blacks represented among the top leadership. Indeed, the Packinghouse Workers' leaders found themselves suspect because of their emphasis on racial justice, which some in the CIO believed smacked of Communist enthusiasms. In turn, they regarded the CIO's official actions in the civil rights arena as dilatory and often insincere.[46]

When it came to racial matters within the CIO, the response of the white-led federation and its affiliates was modest. CARD, which in 1952 was renamed the Civil Rights Committee, continued in operation under the directorship of George L.-P. Weaver, with CIO secretary-treasurer James

Carey chairing it and serving as the CIO's chief public spokesman in matters relating to civil rights. The committee stressed the CIO's antidiscrimination traditions and devoted most of its energies to the public arena, focusing CIO efforts on executive, legislative, and juridical developments, while steering clear of divisive workplace issues such as hiring and access to skilled jobs.[47]

The CIO also failed to recruit low-wage black workers aggressively. In none of the many discussions of the Reuther regime concerning new approaches to organizing were African Americans mentioned. The CIO did have a potential means of appealing to black workers, the black-led UTSE. But this struggling organization received little of the support that the CIO granted favored affiliates. Between October 1952 and March 1953 the CIO paid out $460,000 to affiliates in direct subsidies, organizers' salaries and expenses, and loans, and another $480,000 to the southern organizing campaign. The UTSE share in this largess amounted to less than $10,000, and even this money came as a result of the CIO's "borrowing" its organizers. Indeed, UTSE leaders experienced the indignity of watching the Brewery Workers, a new affiliate that received substantial subsidies despite its record of racial discrimination, gain CIO blessings in its attempt to carve out locals among black North Carolina tobacco workers. CIO officials gave little support to, and often actively opposed, efforts by the racially progressive Packinghouse Workers to organize sugar and other food processing workers.[48]

Reuther and other UAW officers were vocal supporters of civil rights legislation. The auto union's internal record, however, was less than spectacular. Its leaders were proud of its efforts to integrate bowling alleys. They ordered desegregation of facilities in the union halls of southern locals. The union created the Fair Practices Committee to consider complaints of mistreatment of black workers within the UAW. But Reuther and most of his leadership team believed that insofar as the workplace was concerned, blacks would rise with their white coworkers as unions achieved higher wages and better conditions for all. Thus they opposed earmarking a seat on the international executive board for an African American on grounds that to single out blacks would amount to reverse discrimination. Reuther did not challenge the lily-white skilled tradesmen, whose crafts remained more heavily segregated than even the notorious AFL building trades. In his appointments of blacks to staff positions, Reuther invariably chose men known for caution and bureaucratic correctness. Reuther showed no sign of committing the resources of the UAW or the CIO to an organizing campaign that would target the low-wage industries in which so many blacks toiled.[49]

African American unionists grew frustrated. Black CIO dissidents were active in the National Negro Labor Council, established in 1951 to "pursue . . . a militant struggle to improve our conditions" and to compel the diffident white leadership of the unions to respond to the needs of black workers. CIO leaders quickly denounced the council, whose origins and membership did draw heavily from the former CIO pro-Soviet affiliates, as subversive and inauthentic. But sharp criticism of the CIO's lack of focus and commitment in racial matters came from within the industrial union federation as well. Thus, that same year, a Philadelphia activist lashed out at the CIO for indifference and hypocrisy. In a letter to top CIO officers, URW member James Hill pointed out accurately that none of the federation's leadership was African American. The handful of black organizers and staff members seemed more like tokens than integral parts of the CIO apparatus. CARD was really just a "smokescreen . . . , a fatuous, self-righteous organization." Its officers said the right things in public, but the CIO held out little real hope for black workers.[50]

UTSE president Willard Townsend, a dutiful CIO loyalist, also grew impatient with the federation's lack of focus and energy. A faithful follower of the standard CIO line, Townsend agreed that racial injustice was at root an economic problem and shared the animus toward Communists and their allies. Even so, he asserted in a heretical 1955 outburst, "there is one thing that is certain – they did keep the civil rights question alive," which was more than the current leadership could claim.[51]

Critics black and white charged that the CIO was increasingly functioning as a protective association for white workers. True, African Americans fortunate enough to be employed in large central core CIO-organized firms enjoyed high wages and good benefits. But the unwillingness and inability of the CIO to carry industrial unionism into the economy's tertiary sectors in effect rendered it at best a marginal participant in the postwar struggles of African Americans for economic justice.[52]

Even in the core industries the CIO role became ever more problematic. For example, automobile corporations were decentralizing production and introducing greater mechanization in the labor-intensive operations that traditionally employed most blacks. The dispersal of production from inner cities hit black workers with particular force. Victimized by discrimination in housing and hiring practices, urban blacks watched the high-wage, union jobs they had struggled to gain slip away. Largely denied entry into the skilled trades, trapped in the declining northern cities, blacks suffered disproportionately when the Korean War boom ended and the second major postwar recession began in the fall of 1953.

Standard union practices also often had an adverse impact on the CIO's

African American members. World War II-era contracts had typically established seniority provisions that were based on departmentwide job rights. That is, when faced with layoffs, veteran employees had the right to "bump" less experienced workers only within a given component of a large plant. In some cases such provisions could protect black workers from displacement by less veteran but more highly skilled whites. But widespread mechanization resulted in heavy job loss for those, such as blacks, who performed the affected tasks. Seniority was no help because it was limited to the department in which the job loss was taking place.

Similar developments affected most major basic industries. Meatpackers mechanized the kill floors and front-end butchering operations, strong outposts of black employment, even as they pulled operations out of cities such as Chicago, Fort Worth, and Omaha and began moving them to remote feedlots. In steel, departmentwide seniority also affected black workers. Postwar innovation brought the closing of antiquated plants and the redesign of front-end operations, with the result that black employment began to decline. Mechanization of log handling, debarking, and chipping operations in the pulp mills dried up traditional African American jobs. Expanding employment in manufacturing and assembly operations might have upgraded rather than displaced blacks, but requirements for these jobs often entailed educational credentials that blacks were less likely to have. Thus blacks found the promise inherent in the great CIO breakthrough at best only spottily fulfilled in the changing postwar economy.[53]

If the CIO leadership was desultory in its acknowledgment of racial matters, it hardly recognized a gender component to the American labor force. As of the mid-1950s about 600,000 of the CIO's approximately 4 million members were women. The ACWA, the TWUA, and the CWA had the highest proportions of female membership, with the ACWA leading at about 40 percent. Other unions with substantial female membership included the IUE, the UAW, and the Packinghouse Workers. Few women served in leadership positions in any of these organizations.[54]

CIO leaders largely ignored gender in attempting to respond to the problems of postwar organizing. On the whole the ousted pro-Soviet unions, notably the UE and FTA, had done the best job among CIO affiliates in accommodating the special bargaining concerns of women workers and developing female leadership. After the departure of the UE, the IUE, about a third of whose members were women, proved much less responsive to the bargaining priorities of its female members. The UAW did a better job but only because active women's caucuses hammered away in behalf of equal pay, ending gender segregation in job lines, and asserting female members' recall and seniority rights. The new CWA harbored energetic female activists and staff members but like the ACWA and the TWUA, the CWA had few women in leadership posts. While the CWA's male officials were sensitive to the interests of the female membership, they did not provide the CIO with an energetic or imaginative voice in behalf of systematic recruitment of women workers.[55]

At CIO conventions fewer than 5 percent of the delegates were women, and between 1946 and 1954 the participation of female unionists actually declined. The CIO Washington staff of forty or so economists, lawyers, researchers, publicists, and legislative experts had only one woman, Katherine Ellickson, who was the number two person in the research department. At any given time, only a handful of women were employed as organizers. Discussion of special problems or opportunities involving women workers played no role in the lengthy annual state of the CIO addresses by Murray and Reuther. Each year a convention resolution opposing the Equal Rights Amendment but upholding the rights of women workers was passed with little interest or debate, sometimes as part of a convention-ending omnibus motion.[56]

Of course, the new organizing program insured that little would change. In allocating staff to affiliated unions, few of which had ever shown much interest in white collar or clerical workers, the CIO reinforced existing male-dominated patterns of membership and recruitment. Even though female membership had surged during World War II, few in the CIO regarded this development as permanent or hopeful. True, the 1946 convention adopted a resolution attacking employers who "attempted to dislodge and downgrade women" and pledging to "fight to insure the protection and achievement of equal rights of women both on and off the job." But in fact most CIO leaders watched with equanimity as female factory workers lost their jobs after the war.

Always ready to acknowledge the importance of the working man's wife in her capacity as an auxiliary to the union and as a voter, CIO leaders were committed to traditional family wage concepts and displayed little awareness of the growing presence of women in the labor force. In their mind they had built their unions with little help from women, whom they tended to regard as a weak link in the workingman's commitment to the union cause. The 1952 election returns reinforced traditional gender assumptions, for they revealed that wives of unionists supported General Eisenhower at much higher rates than did their husbands. As a result, CIO political operatives intensified their home-and-family appeals to women. Thus even at a time when saturation of the industrial core might have encouraged CIO leaders to think more creatively about sectors of the economy employing large numbers of women, they remained wedded to their traditional views about gender.[57]

STAFFERS AND CITIZENS

In the 1950s the CIO presented itself as a mainstream American institution. Throughout the brief Reuther era the CIO leadership sought to convince a skeptical press and public that the CIO had put aside its confrontational heritage and had earned a right to full participation in the American consensus. CIO leaders joined in charitable drives, served on community boards, and endorsed all manner of good causes. Booths at fairs and expositions, attendance of field representatives and council officers at devotional breakfasts, and participation of industrial unionists in charity drives worked, in Riffe's words, to "acquaint the general public with the wholesome work of our organization." "CIO activities and interests," declared a 1953 pamphlet, "are woven into the entire fabric of American life [and are aimed at] . . . lifting the educational and cultural standards of the people." The men and women who represented the CIO in the field closely reflected these mainstream values, both in their formal political and social beliefs and in the styles of life they followed.[58]

Apart from pushing the revamping of the CIO's organizing program, Reuther's major innovation as CIO chief was the development of an expensive radio and public relations campaign. In 1948 the UAW bought FM station WDET in Detroit and attempted in its broadcasts to combine new approaches to media-conscious union members with cultural and public service programming designed to enhance the auto union's image as a good citizen. Soon after gaining the presidency, Reuther pressed for an ambitious CIO radio and public relations initiative along similar lines. In 1953 the CIO officers came to an agreement with radio commentator John W. Vandercook, a progressive veteran of the airwaves, to sponsor a weekly program. By March 1954 a weekly CIO radio program was heard on 155 stations in forty-one states and the District of Columbia. The cost of this and related public relations efforts, however, was staggering, amounting to over $1 million a year, a sum equal to 20 percent of the CIO's annual receipts. The response did not seem to justify such outlays. Reuther's CIO assistant, Robert Oliver, told his chief that "confidentially, I have not found anyone [other than those in the CIO Publicity Department] . . . who thinks the program is worth a damn." Indeed, audience surveys in New York and Detroit showed the CIO's program attracting little attention.[59]

CIO efforts to integrate industrial unionism into American life were not confined to the airwaves. Pamphlets, filmstrips, and the regular participation of its operatives in religious, educational, and civic organizations reinforced its role as a legitimate member of the community. "Labor organizations can make more friends at County Fairs than any other single way," asserted a Michigan IUC functionary. In 1952 the Michigan CIO set up a tent at nine such events. Unionists showed films, gave away balloons, and held raffles. A wire recorder was a big attraction, with visitors being given a disc that they could take home to play for their friends, and "while so doing, – CIO would reach that many more people." At an Indiana county fair, unionists raffled off a tractor umbrella. Reported Michigan unionists, students and teachers seemed receptive to the CIO message, though it was true that "many farmers that visited our tent were not overwhelmed with the CIO."[60]

On the national level, the National CIO Community Services Committee, established in 1941 as the War Relief Committee, worked with IUCs and international unions to collect and distribute funds for charitable efforts at home and abroad. It provided support for unemployed and striking CIO members and trained thousands of unionists to help afflicted coworkers to gain access to public benefits. Increasingly, however, it focused on promoting good citizenship. Marking the tenth anniversary of the Community Services Committee in 1951, National Director Leo Perlis boasted that over the past decade CIO members had contributed more than $300 million to charitable, war relief, and community improvement projects. By the mid-1950s thousands of CIO members were serving on the national or local boards of such organizations as the American Red Cross, the United Services Organization, Travellers Aid, and the Boy Scouts. The main task of the Community Services Committee, Perlis remarked in 1955, was "to discover areas of agreement in our communities so that all sections of our population could learn to work in harmony for the common good." Perhaps more important than the money collected, the blood donated, and the influence exerted, Perlis believed, were the intangibles: "The good word and the warm heart and the firm grip."[61]

Religion played a major role in the CIO's community presence. Cultivation of enlightened religious leaders was critical to combat business's influence in the churches. The flood of corporate money into the coffers of religious bodies, warned one of the CIO's most active religionists, threatened to create "religious fascism" in the United States. The adherence of top CIO officials such as Philip Murray and James B. Carey to Catholic social gospel as articulated in papal encyclicals was widely known. As a poor youngster working in the coal mines of Scotland, Murray recalled, "in the evening by the light of a kerosene lamp I would read the family Bible," along with his father's union papers. "Churches and labor unions should work hand in hand because of their common concern for the family life," he urged. Few CIO gatherings were complete without invocations and blessings from the clergy. Appeals to workers' religious feeling was a key element in CIO efforts to take over the memberships of purged unions suffering under the control of irreligious Communists. Declared CWA head Joseph Beirne, a devout Roman Catholic, in December 1953, "We sort of look at our community service work as – well – practicing Christianity, if you will." [62]

John G. Ramsay devoted much of his career in the CIO to linking Christian principles with labor activism. Working with SOC in the late 1940s and early 1950s, Ramsay had as his special assignment the cultivation of southern clergymen. He urged repeatedly that the CIO establish a religion and labor committee, solicited and publicized statements of religious belief from Murray and other CIO leaders, and attended meetings, served on panels, and maintained contact with religious leaders of all faiths around the country. "Clergymen who stand out for social justice need our support," he insisted. [63]

The vast majority of its institutional operatives and IUC leaders expressed active religious commitment. In the spring of 1954 Ramsay conducted a survey of CIO officials, field representatives, regional directors, and IUC leaders with the object of establishing a profile of the CIO's role in the communities in which it operated. Circulating a voluntary questionnaire to 450 participants in seven regional meetings, Ramsay sought "to find out how the leadership of CIO councils in their normal every day life took responsibility for their respective local communities." Of the 294 unionists who returned a questionnaire, 251 claimed to be "members of Religions." Eighty-three were Catholics, while mainstream Protestant denominations claimed another 120. Four Jews, 6 Mormons, 2 Christian Scientists, and a Unitarian were among the others. Few unionists belonged to fraternal or veterans' organizations, but about 40 percent listed membership in the PTA. Pointing out that the 85 percent of CIO leaders who "were members of Religions" far exceeded national norms, Ramsay was delighted, for this fact established that the "CIO is not separate, but [is] an important and integrated part of the whole community." Presidential assistant Victor Reuther was happy to learn about the high levels of religious participation revealed in Ramsay's survey. "Such material," he declared, "answers the general prejudices aroused against unions and their leaders, . . . to create the picture of the trade unionist as the 'bomb-carrying rabble-rouser.'" [64]

Indeed, the 200 or so CIO field representatives were a quite different breed from the fabled proletarian organizers of the New Deal era. Gone were the Communists and those who identified with them. By the mid-1950s, few CIO organizers admitted to any politics left of the liberal wing of the Democratic Party. Though everyone said that organizing was the main priority, field representatives spent much of their time working on contract administration, education, internal CIO matters, political action, and community service. Much organizing work had less to do with making fiery speeches and mobilizing pickets than with quiet, practical appeals based on immediate dollars-and-cents concerns.

In attempting to organize a new plant, a team of field representatives would take up residence in a low-rent motel and attempt to form in-plant committees, get workers to sign cards, neutralize the antiunion utterances of community influentials, and prepare for an NLRB election. At best organizing was slow and frustrating work, especially since the Taft-Hartley Act had enhanced employers' ability to resist unionization. Training sessions for organizers now stressed the increasingly arcane procedures into which Taft-Hartley and a growing body of court decisions directed union recruitment.[65]

Idealistic and progressive in outlook, CIO representatives functioned as intermediaries in a world bounded on one side by the harsh realities of daily work in the mill or plant and on the other by the increasing affluence of American life. As white collar representatives of a large, bureaucratic institution, they had to work hard to retain a sense of solidarity with the men and women who toiled in the plants, shops, and offices. It was easy to become disdainful of the lack of sophistication and the lethargy that workers appeared to exhibit. Organizers' reports as often featured complaints about workers' indifference and lassitude as about employers' machinations or workplace outrages. There was little turnover among the CIO organizing staff, and, reported close observer Daniel Bell in 1953, "morale and efficiency have been declining" among the "aging" field staff.[66]

Organizers and other field representatives typically earned anywhere from $85 to $130 a week at a time when the average weekly straight-time wage of an autoworker was about $100. Regional directors earned $7,000 a year. Under Reuther, the CIO developed a pension plan for its staff members. Even so, organizers had only tenuous job security, as the widespread layoffs brought about by the 1954 recession and CIO budget cuts attested. Few field representatives welcomed a return to regular jobs in the auto plants or steel mills, but for most there was little possibility of rising within the CIO or its affiliates, for jobs on the unions' research, legal, publicity, and technical staffs increasingly fell to people with advanced education.

The reports that field representatives and regional directors sent back to their superiors revealed the changing nature of the organizing lifestyle. Like middle class Americans everywhere in the 1950s, organizers struggled to make house, car, and furniture payments, often using advances of their salaries as an informal banking system. Again like most Americans in the 1950s, CIO representatives often had to pay out of pocket for medical emergencies. Field representatives juggled several distinct identities. They were the front-line cadres of organized labor and retained a sense of being fighters for social justice. In income, work situations, and lifestyles, however, they were middle class Americans. They were, as sociologist C. Wright Mills observed, "managers of discontent," mediating between rank-and-file discontents and bureaucratic institutions that privileged order, regularity, and stability. Sensitive to injustice and conscientious in seeking a better life for their clients, they nonetheless responded as much to the institutional needs of their employer as to the circumstances of working people.[67]

"We are engaged in C.I.O.'s No. 1 job," a group of organizers displeased with the financial aspects of the new setup reminded Reuther in the fall of 1953.[68] But in fact by the mid-1950s the CIO's main jobs had to do with politics and public relations. With the Communists driven out, with the central industrial core largely organized, and with no dynamic outside force impelling it to expand its boundaries, the CIO settled into its role as a functioning part of a complex corporate and international order.

To some activists these developments were sources of bitter disappointment. Unionists from the ousted left-wing unions were not alone in criticizing the CIO. In March 1953 former CIO education director Kermit Eby decried the loss of energy, the bureaucratization of the industrial unions, and the growing tendency to defer to the upper leadership. "God is in his heaven and Walter Reuther is in Detroit," Eby declared, seemed to be the new slogan of the once-turbulent industrial workers.[69]

The CIO's top leadership, however, focused instead on the industrial union federation's accomplishments. Collective bargaining gains, vigorous political action programs, and a positive and growing CIO presence in the community attested to the success of the great project. Proclaimed President Reuther at the December 1954 convention in Los Angeles, the "CIO is strong." Community action, anti-Communism, adherence to the doctrine that "what is good for America is good for the CIO," and continued advances in political action and collective bargaining were forcing even skeptics "to recognize the CIO as a major force for good in the nation." The CIO, proclaimed James Carey in 1955, "came as a mighty, surging answer to despair and desperation." Whatever its current travails, the CIO could claim "two almost incredible decades, unmatched and unparalleled in the entire history of the American labor movement."[70]

Despite these ebullient words, however, by the fall of 1954 CIO leaders were turning their main focus on prospects of merger with the once-despised AFL. In this difficult task, how much of the CIO's historic, but of late subdued, commitment to expansion, broad-ranging political action, and racial justice would remain? Indeed, would a CIO presence survive at all, as stronger AFL affiliates destroyed or absorbed marginal CIO unions? Thus, beginning as early as mid-1953 and with sharpening focus thereafter, Reuther and his associates turned their attention to these questions as they engaged the AFL's new leadership in increasingly portentous negotiations about the institutional fate of the modern American labor movement.

13 Merger and Beyond

The merger of the AFL and the CIO, which was consummated at a convention held in New York City during the first week in December 1955, marked an end not only to the conflict between the two wings of organized labor but to the period of experimentation and expansion that the birth of the CIO had inaugurated two decades earlier. As final unity arrangements were being made, Reuther told his executive board that "we want a new labor movement that breaks with the past." Reuther and others in the CIO initially hoped that unification would revive the spirit of the 1930s, that the new labor movement would "accept the challenge that millions of unorganized workers represent in America." By the time of the merger, however, they had made compromises insuring that no such development would occur.[1]

Indeed, on the CIO side, David McDonald played a more central role in the merger process than did Reuther himself. McDonald's disruptive role within the CIO conditioned the merger process and undercut CIO efforts to gain strong provisions governing civil rights, jurisdictional disputes, and industrial unionism. Collaborating with him was general counsel Arthur J. Goldberg, who used his detailed knowledge of the ongoing negotiations to shape an emerging consensus in behalf of unification.

UNITY DISCUSSIONS, 1937–1952

Earlier unity discussions had ended badly. In the late 1930s they were hostage to Lewis's often mystifying agenda and his penchant for insulting AFL officers. For their part, AFL president William Green and his cohorts insisted that the CIO disband and that its members be incorporated piecemeal into existing AFL unions. During World War II Lewis's bizarre "accouplement" scheme, along with continuing rivalry between the AFL and the CIO on a broad range of issues, further soured relations. Moreover, according to a veteran CIO staff member, Murray regarded AFL secretary-treasurer George Meany, the main federation representative on joint wartime bodies, "as some kind of loud-mouth bum from New York. . . . 'That damn Meany,'" he fulminated, "'I can't stand him . . . [I] don't want to have anything to do with him.'"[2]

Indeed, Murray was never enthusiastic about unity. Through at least the late 1940s he believed that the industrial union federation was on an upward arc. While political and public relations demands forced Murray to enter into at least a semblance of negotiations with the AFL, most close observers believed that he had little personal commitment to the project. "I think," observed CIO staffer Henry Fleisher, "if Phil Murray had lived forever the merger would have been postponed a long time."[3]

When they did consider the possibility of accommodation with the AFL, Murray and his CIO cohorts talked of "functional unity." Thus Murray held that the two federations should collaborate in political, legislative, and perhaps international affairs, deferring contentious issues of philosophy and structure, perhaps indefinitely. Functional unity would confirm the CIO's coequal status while exhibiting its genuine interest in labor unity.[4]

In contrast AFL leaders spoke of "organic unity." While dropping their insistence that the CIO unions formally acknowledge the primacy of the AFL, they resented any notion of parity between the two federations. Organic unity would inevitably highlight the AFL's longer existence, its greater numbers, and, implicitly, the CIO's character as an ephemeral, "dual" union.[5]

Between 1946 and 1952 the two labor centers spasmodically negotiated, with Murray and Green each appointing members of a joint unity committee. Stultifying debates on functional versus organic unity alternated with charges of bad faith. To a limited extent, however, the two federations did cooperate. In 1949 they both helped to form the International Confederation of Free Trade Unions and in July of the next year the AFL and the CIO issued a joint statement pledging cooperation in legislative, political, and international affairs. During the first year of the Korean War the CIO and the AFL joined in the ULPC to assert a united voice in the government's economic mobilization and stabilization forums. Even after the AFL pulled out of the committee in August 1951, mutual consultation continued, although the joint unity committee itself became inactive.[6]

Eisenhower's election and the deaths of Murray and Green, all of which occurred during a three-week span in November 1952, renewed talk of labor unification. The passing of the leaders of the CIO and the AFL removed some of the personal animosity characterizing earlier unification initiatives. Thus it came as no surprise when early in December the two new leaders, Reuther and the AFL's George Meany, announced that they would meet early in the new year.[7]

Talk of renewed unity discussions highlighted the fact that many of the formal issues that had animated the initial break no longer seemed important. "Industrial unionism" faded as a rallying cry. AFL organizations such as the Electrical Workers, Carpenters, and Machinists had enrolled hundreds of thousands of semiskilled workers. The Teamsters were pioneering the organization of service, goods-handling, and even production workers. At the same time, skilled workers in the UAW, USWA, and other CIO affiliates clamored for recognition of the distinctive problems of the tool-and-die makers, millwrights, and other skilled tradesmen who comprised up to 20 percent of the major industrial unions.[8]

Moreover, CIO criticisms that the AFL ignored the unorganized seemed increasingly hollow. Indeed, the CIO found itself steadily outstripped by its once-lethargic rival. By 1950 the AFL legitimately claimed twice the membership of the CIO, and its organizations of clerks, public employees, and service workers, although hardly models of dynamism, easily outdistanced the CIO's feeble efforts in these fields.[9]

CIO criticisms of the AFL's racial policies and its tolerance of corrupt activities among its affiliates were still pertinent. With regard to the former, however, there was some narrowing of the differences. True, several AFL unions retained openly discriminatory practices of recruitment, apprenticing, and union governance. Building trades unions practiced blatant de facto discrimination. Even official AFL support for fair employment practices legislation was conditioned on excluding unions from its provisions. Nonetheless, by 1950 the AFL had more black members than did the CIO, and Meany, both as secretary-treasurer and as president, had established a positive reputation among civil rights groups and black unionists, including the AFL's influential A. Philip Randolph, head of the Brotherhood of Sleeping Car Porters. With the CIO emphasizing legislative aspects of civil rights, the two labor centers seemed to be drawing closer even in this area.[10]

The problem of union corruption also seemed more susceptible to compromise. Industrial unions were less vulnerable to penetration by criminal elements than were the AFL's trucking, longshoring, building, and entertainment trades unions. "For decades," charged a CIO statement, "William Green disgracefully condoned . . . flagrant racketeering and gangsterism" in the East Coast longshoremen's union, while "the AFL ignored or winked at corruption in the . . . Teamsters, the Carpenters and others." But Meany's ascendancy had brought change. He launched a vigorous campaign to clean up the New York-based ILA and persuaded the AFL Executive Council to empower the federation to act against wrongdoing in its affiliates. The problem of corruption in the Teamsters, led by the shrewd and unscrupulous Dave Beck, was particularly acute, for the union was as dynamic as it was crime ridden. As Meany became increasingly critical of the sprawling union – now among the largest in the entire labor movement – some in the CIO believed that unification would help to contain its pernicious influence. The wholesome reputation of the CIO, believed Carey, would strengthen the well-intentioned Meany in his confrontations "with the Becks and others more or less of his kind." [11]

Thus the time seemed ripe for accommodation. Organized labor faced its greatest political challenge in a generation. The passing of Green and Murray and the ascendancy of new leaders eliminated some of the purely personal and historical animosities that had impeded earlier unity discussions. The narrowing of ideological and policy differences made unification increasingly seem to be a question of detail rather than of basic principle.

THE MERGER PROCESS

From the first meeting of Meany and Reuther in January 1953 to the effectuation of merger in December 1955, negotiations proceeded in irregular spasms. Within the CIO, outbursts of hostility toward the AFL increasingly gave way to a sense of inevitability. By 1955 only TWU president Michael Quill spoke against the merger. [12]

At first the reconstituted joint unity committee concentrated on producing a no-raiding pact, which was accomplished in the late fall of 1953. Then the AFL and CIO leadership spent six months getting affiliated unions to agree to participate in the apparatus that the agreement established. Although initially harmonious work on this project encouraged hopes that unification would soon follow, through the summer and early fall of 1954 there was little movement. By October, however, Steelworkers' president David McDonald was hinting that continued USWA membership in the CIO depended on rapid progress toward merger. With Goldberg serving as chief draftsman, the joint unity committee adopted a statement endorsing a merger of the AFL and the CIO and appointing a subcommittee to draft specific proposals. Early in February 1955 Reuther and Meany approved the document, and before the month was over, the executive bodies of the two federations had approved a basic merger agreement. Under Goldberg's guidance the joint unity committee prepared a constitution for the merged body, which the two federations' executive bodies endorsed in May. The two organizations rescheduled their fall conventions for the week of December 1, agreeing that a joint convention of the now-unified labor movement would begin on December 5. The joint committee had difficulty devising a name for the merged body, eventually settling on American Federation of Labor–Congress of Industrial Organizations (AFL–CIO). [13]

Even as a subcommittee charged with developing a no-raiding agreement worked through the spring of 1953, forces in both federations looked toward eventual merger. After Murray's death AFL insiders believed that the

CIO was on the verge of disintegration and urged Meany to bide his time. "'Get them one by one,'" advised Jay Lovestone, the federation's behind-the-scenes ideology and foreign policy expert. But Meany believed that the destruction of the rival federation would weaken organized labor. The sixty-year-old Meany had come from the New York City building trades of the 1920s. His appearance and demeanor seemed to reflect the hard-bitten business unionism and racial insensitivity of this ultraconservative wing of organized labor. But in fact Meany recognized that the growing political role of organized labor required that it come to public arenas with clean hands. No crusader, he recognized nonetheless that African Americans were important allies of the labor movement and that the evidences of overt racism in the unions were damaging. Both he and Reuther were free of the complex legacies of loyalty and betrayal that entangled Green, Lewis, and Murray, the UMW triumvirate that since 1924 had dominated the nation's labor leadership.[14]

Within the CIO the pressure for unification was even more direct. At its heart stood McDonald, who lost few opportunities to express his disdain for Reuther and his alienation from the CIO. His broad hints that the USWA would pull out of the industrial union body convinced CIO insiders that he meant business. When not hobnobbing with Lewis and Dave Beck, McDonald was musing that while the steel union might not withdraw from the CIO, suspension of its monthly per capita tax payments of around $100,000 might be an appropriate way to begin recovery of USWA resources that Murray had diverted to the CIO.[15]

Faced with McDonald's obduracy, Reuther had little choice but to pursue merger. His executive assistant in the CIO, Robert Oliver, grew frustrated at Reuther's accommodation of McDonald. "'Walter,'" he insisted, "'we've got two million dollars in the treasury. . . . We ought to . . . invest all of our money and all of our energies and all of our drive into building this CIO of ours without any worrying about what David J. McDonald . . . is going to do.'" But in fact Reuther was unwilling to call McDonald's bluff, to commit UAW resources or top-level personnel to the CIO, or to devote sustained attention to CIO affairs.[16]

Initially most CIO leaders insisted that any unity agreement incorporate certain basic principles: explicit institutional commitment to industrial unionism, authoritative mechanisms to eliminate jurisdictional conflicts, firm guarantees against racial discrimination, and specific mechanisms with which to combat corruption. Implicit in these stipulations was the underlying notion that a united labor movement must embark on a vigorous campaign of organizing the unorganized. Reuther was at his eloquent best in enunciating these principles, but it was McDonald who determined the pattern of discussion that led eventually to the merger agreement and the constitution, in which these basic CIO principles were only partially addressed.[17]

McDonald influenced events both through his gestures of hostility toward the CIO and through repeated insistence on rapid progress toward organic unity. At the USWA convention in September 1954 he called for prompt and authoritative merger negotiations through the joint unity committee. The Steelworkers, he said, were committed to "complete, immediate, organic unity. Talk about waiting around for a year or two . . . is pure, unadulterated bunk." The CIO should scrap its insistence on specific guarantees, and the two federations should get on with the project. "Unity," McDonald insisted, "could be worked out in a matter of weeks, not years."[18]

As a direct result of McDonald's urgings the joint committee resumed detailed discussions in October 1954. In the end, the USWA chief was right: the basic agreement to bring the AFL and CIO together was drafted over a three-month period. This document, which was approved by the joint united committee and signed by Meany and Reuther on February 9, 1955, represented a mixed bag insofar as the "basic" CIO principles were concerned. It did contain a strong statement on corruption and did provide specific mechanisms by which the merged organization's executive body could investigate, charge, and suspend offending affiliates. On the questions of raiding and racial discrimination, however, it was more equivocal.[19]

CIO unionists were particularly concerned with the former for quite practical reasons. Powerful AFL unions such as the Teamsters, the Carpenters, and the Electrical Workers had been expanding aggressively in jurisdictions claimed by a number of struggling CIO affiliates such as the Woodworkers, the Utility Workers, and the Brewery Workers. Quite apart from matters of principle, the officers and staff members of these organizations worried about their jobs. The merger documents did uphold the principle of individual union integrity and autonomy; merger at the top entailed no requirement that affiliates amalgamate or disband. Moreover, the merger agreement did contain a broad declaration endorsing the CIO's strong anti-raiding position. Still, it left to the new body's executive officers the job of establishing machinery for settling interunion disputes. Meany's agenda in the AFL had included the ending of the ferocious jurisdictional conflicts that had been the federation's long-term bane, but many in the CIO remained skeptical of the ability of the new mechanism to curb the appetite of Beck's Teamsters, merger or no merger.[20]

The merger documents' provisions regarding discrimination were even more problematic. It was true that both the merger agreement and the constitution for the first time in the history of the major labor federations explicitly declared, in the words of the constitution, that "all workers whatever their race, color, creed or national origin are entitled to share in the full benefits of trade union organization." But such a declaration, perhaps revolutionary in 1920 or 1930, was commonplace by the mid-1950s. More importantly, the unity documents provided for no specific enforcement mechanism, nor were the remaining AFL affiliates that continued to bar or segregate African Americans required to abandon their racist practices. AFL spokesmen defended the provisions relating to race by arguing that traditions of union autonomy prevented the establishment of any disciplinary mechanism. Critics, however, tellingly pointed to the provisions in the merger document and the constitution that were created specifically for the investigation and punishment of affiliates accused of corruption or Communist influence. Was racial justice, they asked, less important than these other concerns?

Despite the CIO's historic commitment to racial equality, however, rarely did its leaders foreground the question of racial discrimination in their deliberations regarding merger. On more than one occasion it was left to the Executive Board's one black member, Willard Townsend, to remind his colleagues of the need to insist on strong antidiscrimination provisions. Secretary-Treasurer Carey, long the CIO's point man in public civil rights matters, pressed for a more vigorous stand, but in the end McDonald's insistence on bypassing contentious issues in the name of rapid organic unity prevailed on this, as on other, questions. Indeed, Reuther himself seemed to echo the traditional AFL invocation of union autonomy in matters of race. "He agreed," stated a summary of the May 1955 executive committee meeting, that "the primary responsibility [to fight discrimination] was in each individual International Union." Reuther erroneously insisted that the merger agreement did provide specific mechanisms for the disciplining of discriminatory affiliates when in fact it merely charged the executive council with the responsibility to exercise broad oversight in upholding the general philosophy of the new labor federation.[21]

Whatever the problems on these issues, Reuther professed confidence that the merger itself would generate forward motion for organized labor. The unification of organized labor, he believed, could unleash enormous new energy. Combined, the two federations commanded vast resources and "we have got to find a way to zip open those money bags [and] . . . to get these resources dedicated to an organizational crusade."[22]

The problem was how to accomplish this feat. From the outset of merger talks CIO leaders had insisted that the new central labor body include a distinct industrial union component, perhaps a "Council of Industrial Organizations," a vehicle for keeping alive the CIO heritage and spearheading forward movement. Of course, Reuther told his fellow officers in July 1955, the character of this organ "will be determined in large measure by the per capita decision." From the beginning of the unity discussions it was clear that each affiliate would pay a monthly per capita tax of four cents, the amount currently paid by AFL unions to the central body, instead of the ten cents per member per month currently paid by CIO unions. Reuther and other optimists hoped that the difference of six cents could be paid into this industrial union arm to support organizing activities. If AFL organizations with substantial industrial memberships participated, this new body could have an annual income of over $5 million, ample funds, in the words of the ACWA's Frank Rosenblum, to launch "an organizational campaign with imagination and ingenuity."[23]

Again, however, McDonald balked. He would be no happier about a lavishly financed Reuther-dominated industrial union vehicle than he would have been with an aggressive CIO. Supported by smaller affiliates eager to cut their dues by 60 percent, McDonald argued that the industrial union component should be akin to the existing AFL departments for the building trades, metal trades, railway employees, and consumer products unions. These were financed by a monthly tax of a penny or two. Declared McDonald in March, "We do not want a super-duper organization within the new parent body." Indeed, given McDonald's refusal to contemplate a more ambitious industrial union presence within the merged federation, Reuther's subsequent hints of a more ambitious enterprise were actually misleading.[24]

If the Industrial Union Department, which was the body established under the new constitution, could not serve as the spearhead for laborite advance, perhaps the very fact of labor unity would be the catalyst. Perhaps the merged federation's organizing department, enriched by special contributions representing the savings in per capita tax, would lead the way. With relatively little sacrifice, Reuther asserted, the new federation could amass $15 million "to launch a comprehensive, effective organizational crusade to carry the message of unionism in the dark places of the South, into the vicious company towns, in the textile industry, in the chemical industry." The UAW, he announced, had pledged $1.5 million as a contribution to such a campaign. The momentum generated by the merger process, he believed, would permit "[us to] organize from two to four million new workers in America" by the time of the merged federations' second convention, scheduled for December 1957.[25]

As the merger negotiations proceeded, Reuther made it clear that he would not be a candidate for either of the two leadership posts of the joint organization. He did insist, however, that he be named chair of the Industrial Union Department and that the CIO be responsible for the appointment of its director and for that of the director of the new federation's organizing department. CIO control of organizing, he urged, would enable industrial unionists to "keep the flame of those ideals . . . that make the CIO the force that it is burning brightly." If the merger led to such a result, Reuther would not be presiding over the dissolution of the CIO. He would be engineering its transformation into a dynamic new phase.[26]

If Reuther truly held such a vision, however, his actions in the final stages of the merger process sabotaged it. In regard to the Industrial Union Department, he not only acquiesced in McDonald's limited vision of its functions but agreed to letting the Steelworkers' chief name its first director. McDonald's choice, a little-distinguished district director in a secondary area of USWA activity, quickly limited Industrial Union Department activities to research, publicity, and legal and legislative advising. Indeed, McDonald informed his fellow Steelworkers, "Its functions . . . are not going to be many. . . . It will be sort of a symbol."[27]

As for the new AFL–CIO's organizing department, Reuther did indeed select its director. At an executive committee meeting six weeks before the merger was to take place, McDonald initially put Riffe forward for the job, but the CIO's ailing executive vice-president declined. Reuther then named his choice, John W. Livingston, then serving as a UAW vice-president and director of the crucial GM Department. On paper Livingston looked well qualified. Forty-seven years old, he had begun as a rank-and-file activist in St. Louis and by the mid-1950s had logged broad experience in the automotive, aircraft, farm equipment, and auto parts sectors. In addition he was experienced in relations with governmental bodies and had played significant roles in the UAW's innovative programs of outreach to European and other international labor bodies.[28]

The CIO executives quickly ratified Reuther's selection. Potofsky believed that Livingston was the "best man we have available in [the] CIO." Livingston was just the leader to "capture [workers'] imagination" and "challenge [the] Du Ponts [sic] [and the] textile barons." He was, according to McDonald (who claimed credit for bringing Livingston's name up in the first place), a "hell of a man."[29]

The character and performance of the director of organization, Reuther asserted, "either make labor unity worthwhile or make it just an academic matter." If the CIO president truly believed that, however, Livingston was a perplexing choice for such an ostensibly significant job. A competent functionary, he was more of a caretaker in the GM Department than a dynamic innovator. Far from being a key man in Reuther's emerging UAW empire, Livingston was something of an outsider who owed his position to the internal politics of the auto union, not to close ties with its dynamic chief. In the decade and a half before his selection, Livingston had been little involved in organizing and had shown no evidence of imagination or even particular interest in the organizing functions of the UAW. Reuther, critics rumored, was happy to shove Livingston aside to make room in the UAW for his own supporters. McDonald and Meany embraced Livingston precisely because his choice permitted them to support a UAW man for a putatively top AFL–CIO post while at the same time not being saddled with an ardent Reutherite. Shut off from the new federation's inner councils, Livingston quickly became an isolated figure, and of course no vast war chest or dynamic organizing campaign materialized.[30]

Why did Reuther fail to follow through on his verbally ambitious hopes of a renewal of CIO-type organizing? His critics believed that the pattern of grandiloquent rhetoric followed by lack of practical follow-through was one of his characteristic faults. He had spent little time on CIO affairs, and the main drift of the organizational reforms that he and Oliver had undertaken had been to weaken the central direction of CIO organizing activities. He had paid much attention to budget balancing and little to practical revitalization of the CIO. Finding the resonating rhetoric with which to outline labor's mission was the easy part; establishing real guarantees of a progressive and dynamic postmerger labor movement, however, called for sacrifices and commitments that Reuther was not prepared to make.

His bitterest critic within the CIO, TWU president Michael Quill, personalized his attack on Reuther, whom he accused of selling out the basic CIO principles in his haste to bring about merger. "He rode roughshod over the corpse of Allen [sic] Haywood to get in," Quill unfairly proclaimed, but now the UAW head was attempting to "lead us into a blind-alley merger with the AFL." Referring to the Miami-area locale in which the basic merger agreement was signed in February 1955, Quill called the agreement "the surrender of Indian Creek."[31]

In the final analysis, however, Reuther had little choice. McDonald's constant threats to pull out or withhold per capita tax, and general unwillingness to cooperate with the Reuther-led CIO, severely narrowed Reuther's options. McDonald defended his activities on the grounds that he was trying to play a positive role in ending the split in the House of Labor. Thus, he pursued his highly publicized association with Beck and Lewis because "I wanted it to cause some consternation. . . . All I was doing was playing some cards in order to bring about a merger." In effect, by the fall of 1954 Reuther had virtually no support for a struggle to assert a vital continuing CIO presence. Observed one CIO staff member, "Reuther found himself in a no-win situation."[32]

Given these constraints, why did Reuther posit such a bright future for the new AFL–CIO? In part, it was his style. He believed that his role was to project an ambitious agenda for organized labor. Clearly it was the CIO that had brought vigor, imagination, and energy to the labor movement. Veteran CIO functionary Jacob Clayman reported that the common feeling among CIO people was that the new organization would soon take on a CIO coloration. "I heard this discussion many, many times in many, many areas, at many, many levels," Clayman recalled. The sixty-one-year-old Meany would surely give way before too long. Whatever the details of the merger, the CIO was the wave of the future.[33]

To the extent that Reuther shared such a view, he was wildly out of touch with the central tendencies of the labor movement of the mid-1950s. The most expansionary American union was the International Brotherhood of Teamsters, whose membership total had reached that of the UAW and whose trajectory pointed upward. Few in the CIO wanted to see *its* influence expand, nor could they realistically hope that the corruption-plagued organization would generously open its bulging coffers to finance general organizing in the name of the new AFL–CIO.

Moreover, Teamster organizing went against the grain of the CIO traditions. The Teamsters, as CIO leaders recognized, did not organize workers; as Reuther himself observed, "they organize the boss," using open-ended grievance procedures, selective work stoppages, boycotts, and strong-arm tactics to impose union shop agreements on reluctant truckers and warehousers. All good CIO men abhorred these practices, yet the Teamsters had pioneered new forms of cross-craft organization and were enrolling thousands of service, clerical, and other nonmanufacturing workers.[34]

Along with Reuther, his CIO colleagues pinned their hopes on renewed organizing on tapping into the funds accumulating in large AFL affiliates. "The only practical way to organize . . . [the chemical industry]," declared Jack Knight of the Oil, Chemical and Atomic Workers, "is by the same techniques that the Steelworkers and the Automobile Workers were organized." Knight hoped that he and his colleagues could "persuade the AFL to raise the per capita tax to 10 cents as soon as possible." Added L. S. Buckmaster of the URW, "We will have to educate the . . . AFL that they will have to spend more money." Reuther often invoked the prospect of collecting a dollar from each member of the new AFL–CIO, thus creating an organizing fund of $15 million. In fact, however, these were fantasies. The whole tradition of the AFL spoke against centralized organizing campaigns, and any possibility of CIO-type efforts – which in any event, as Operation Dixie had indicated, were highly problematic – were precluded by the decisions Reuther and his fellow CIO officers had felt themselves obliged to make concerning the character and personnel of the Industrial Union Department and the AFL–CIO's Department of Organization.[35]

Even on Reuther's own terms the targets of the putative campaigns that he identified belonged to the receding industrial order. Thus, for example, his calls for revitalization invariably invoked textiles and petrochemicals; he never highlighted clerical, white collar, service, and government employment. Beyond a call for accumulating vast amounts of money and inventing new ways of establishing priorities, targeting key groups of workers, and developing a coherent basic strategy, Reuther never got beyond generalities based on unrealistic financial projections.[36]

The truth was that the merger was not about organizing but about consolidating and focusing organized labor's political, legislative, and general public presence. After all, for most of the two previous decades, rivalry in the organizing field had been a positive development. It was the threat of the CIO that had pushed AFL unions forward. In recent years, however, competition had largely degenerated into expensive and exhausting cross-federation raiding of existing unions. An authoritative study of recent experience revealed that it cost a union an average of $500 for each worker recruited through raiding. Unions were spending over a million and a half dollars a year to effect a change in total membership amounting to under 2 percent of the number of workers involved. The first significant step toward eventual merger had been the negotiation of a no-raiding pact in 1953 and 1954. But there was no sense during these negotiations or at a lavish dinner held in June 1954 celebrating the achievement that the resources saved would be earmarked for a new organizing crusade.[37]

Certainly Meany seldom bothered to pay lip service to labor's organizing mission. He believed that lavish organizing budgets were bad investments and that the day of mass recruitment was past. Not everyone in the CIO disagreed with such a perspective. Thus, remarked the NMU's Joseph Curran during the CIO's internal discussions of merger, his colleagues were indulging in "wishful thinking on organizing drives. . . . Conditions are not such that we can go out on organizational drives as in the old days." Economist and staff member Jack Barbash concurred: the hope that the merger would lead to a new organizing surge, he believed, was "naive [and] ahistorical," especially since the basic per capita tax was being slashed by 60 percent. "The CIO spirit was the product of an historical moment . . . which will never be recaptured," Barbash insisted.[38]

The final merger arrangements included no mandate for an expansion of organizing. As the CIO entered its last weeks of separate existence and as the merger process locked into place, Reuther acknowledged limitations of the merger. "The AFL," he admitted to his executive board early in November, "has not moved in the right direction as far as we would like." In view of the absence of a vigorous industrial union body or of a firm commitment to marshal the new AFL–CIO's financial resources, he was reduced to pleading that "somewhere down the road . . . we've got to change the basic character of the whole labor movement."[39]

MIRACLE ON 34TH STREET

In the fall of 1955 the merger of the AFL and the CIO was the source of extensive public commentary. Columnists speculated on the effects of the merger; editorialists affirmed that workers were now part of the country's broad middle class. During the combined convention, which began on December 5, a live message from President Eisenhower, beamed to the 1,400 delegates, 4,500 guests, and 250 media representatives who gathered at the 71st Regiment Armory at Park Avenue and 34th Street in Manhattan, warned laborites not to abuse their new power. One journalist calculated that the combined weight of the AFL–CIO's twenty-seven-member Executive Council was three tons, no doubt an exaggeration.[40]

The CIO had already held its final convention on December 1 and 2. On the first day Reuther ticked off accomplishments of the past year in collective bargaining, organizing, community relations, and political action. The afternoon session was given over to honorific speeches and to a lengthy pageant, written by Hyman Bookbinder, a USWA staff member, and narrated by actor Melvyn Douglas and with songs, some of them specially written for the occasion, by folklorist Joe Glazer, backed up by a chorus from the Workmen's Circle. Reminiscences and tributes from old CIO hands such as Adolph Germer and John Brophy followed. Walter Reuther's father, Valentine Reuther, addressed the convention.

The gathering's main business, however, took place the next morning. The time had come to liquidate the CIO and to unite it with its old nemesis. Appropriately the chairman of the convention's resolutions committee was David J. McDonald, who, Reuther observed in his introductory remarks, "has done a good deal to facilitate the work of our [joint unity] committee." Said McDonald, "This is the moment of destiny," and he called upon the Resolutions Committee secretary Joseph Curran to read the text of the resolution.

Only Michael Quill spoke against adoption. He dropped his personal animosity toward Reuther. Rather, he said, his attitude was one of "pity

[for] all of us who are in this plight . . . , including the President of the CIO." He cast the unification process not as a merger but as CIO capitulation to the AFL under the terms of a constitution that "had to be tailored to meet the approval of the top command of the American Federation of Labor." It failed to meet CIO specifications on organizing, jurisdictional conflict, racial discrimination, and corruption. Indeed, according to Quill, "This document is not a constitution. This is a license for inter-union warfare; a license for racketeering and a license for discrimination against minority groups." The merger document, he declared, was unworthy of the struggle that had created and sustained the CIO. "I feel sorry," he concluded, "that after 20 years of struggle . . . we are marching down the road back to the AFL."[41]

Reuther rejected these charges. The CIO leader affirmed that in the final analysis, "this is a matter of believing. . . . This is no time for doubt." To be sure, CIO negotiators had had to compromise; had anyone in the hall ever signed an agreement that was not a compromise? The merger was the key to moving forward. CIO unions had pledged over $4 million "to launch an organizational crusade" that would begin as soon as the convention was over. The merger was no sellout to the AFL; it was "the beginning of the building of a stronger, finer, more dedicated labor movement."[42]

Shortly after, the vote was taken. Union after union weighed in for the merger until Quill moved that the roll call be suspended in favor of a show of hands. James Carey's final tally, reflecting the inflated membership figures characteristic of the CIO, showed 5,712,077 in favor and 120,002, representing the TWU's book membership along with the votes of two "one lungers" representing IUCs in Springfield, Illinois, and Wilkes-Barre, Pennsylvania, opposing.[43]

Walter Reuther had the final word. He recapitulated the CIO's proud heritage, invoking the memories of Murray and Hillman, omitting any reference to John L. Lewis, who, save for a passing reference or two the day before,[44] was a nonperson insofar as the historical ledger was concerned. Affirming that "this is not the end," Reuther urged his listeners to "go forward and remain true to the things that we believe in." "This," he affirmed, "is one of those glorious hours." After John Ramsay offered a brief closing prayer, Reuther, as his final act in the CIO, urged the delegates to join in the singing of "Solidarity Forever" and to exit the hall "marching and singing together."[45]

Alas, all did not go smoothly in these final rites. McDonald, convinced that Reuther's men had systematically slighted Lewis and Murray, and hence the Steelworkers, in the pageant and closing ceremonies, walked out and brought most of the USWA delegation with him. Moreover, Quill's angry diatribe left few delegates in the mood for singing heroic songs. Reported the *New York Times*, "only a small group gathered near the platform for the finale." When the huge joint merger convention opened on Monday morning at the armory, CIO delegates, accustomed in their gatherings to preassigned seating arrangements, found that the AFL first-come, first-served system now prevailed, with the result that most were relegated to the back of the cavernous hall.[46]

Despite these hitches and despite Quill's mordant predictions, most CIO leaders expressed hopes for a brighter future. But was their optimism perhaps the product of necessity? What expectations could they realistically entertain that the merger would carry forth the CIO heritage? Back in November, at one of the last meetings of the CIO executive committee, Reuther had asked his colleagues, "Is the CIO's imagination going to be lost? Is the CIO going to be absorbed?" Though he meant these questions to be rhetorical, he and his fellow officers had cause to worry that they might be prophetic.[47]

Conclusion

The CIO[1] was a positive force in American life. In the twenty years of its separate existence, it made six major contributions. In the 1930s it brought an angry, but often inchoate, working class activism into coherent and politically effective focus, creating permanent labor unions for the first time in mass production industry. During World War II it helped significantly to win the war against fascism. It created and sustained organized labor's first and most enduring modern political action vehicle, which itself was a significant component of postwar progressive politics. It embraced the aspirations of African Americans as had no previous sustained American labor organization and played a positive role in the struggle for civil rights. It opposed Stalinism at home and abroad at a time when many of the left were beguiled by the Soviet mystique. Its collective bargaining achievements, especially those of the post–World War II period, established new standards of material well-being, personal dignity, and workplace decency for its members and for workers everywhere.

In view of the great difficulty organized labor has almost always faced in establishing and sustaining unions in America, these were great achievements. Permanent unions in the automotive, steel, electrical, rubber, and other mass production industries brought an industrial working class into national economic and political arenas on a potent and long-term basis. The participation of these workers and unions in the necessary fight against fascism, even as they frequently protested specific mobilization and stabilization policies, demonstrated positively how a labor movement could combine citizenship and self-interest in a time of national peril. The creation of an energetic political action arm, along with vehicles for promoting the CIO's legislative agenda, made the CIO a key part of postwar liberalism.

The CIO allied itself with the NAACP and other mainstream civil rights groups to a degree unparalleled by a major labor body in American history. It kept its faith with the democratic left by rejecting continued affiliation with those who apologized for Stalinism and who ignored or denied its profoundly reactionary character. The CIO paid off for its members, attaining wage levels, pensions, access to health care, and patterns of workplace governance that have, in effect, created legitimate entitlements for working people everywhere.

It is important to keep these achievements in mind especially in the mid-1990s. The dizzying decline of private-sector unionism and the two-decade-long erosion of workers' standards may make the CIO achievement of material gains and social and political power seem ephemeral or insubstantial. Moreover, the fact that each of these achievements carried with it high costs and, in many cases, closed off other, more far-reaching possibilities also leads in some quarters to emphasis on the CIO's failures rather than its successes.

Indeed, the tendency to discount the CIO's contributions is natural for both friends and opponents of organized labor. If the industrial union surge of the 1930s and 1940s had real possibilities of being a more powerful and far-reaching phenomenon than were actually realized, CIO achievements in collective bargaining, public influence, and political presence must seem disappointing. Thus it is plausible to see the decline of the labor movement over the past two decades as being rooted in – indeed, made inevitable by – the flawed performance of the CIO in this pregnant period. From such a perspective, then, what is remarkable about the CIO project is not its success but its shortcomings, compromises, and disastrous choices.

It is true that CIO success was limited and CIO victories were partial. Each of its major achievements came at a heavy price, and in each area of success there were plausible, if not necessarily realistic, alternatives. Thus even the very existence of the CIO as an authoritative and structured organizational entity did preclude the possibility of a more decentralized, syndicalist-like, perhaps regionally diverse response to the circumstances of the 1930s. If it is true that in the militancy of workers in the 1930s lay the seeds of far-reaching shop-floor unionism, constituting a basic challenge to the structures of capitalist power, then the CIO, by insisting on orderly, even bureaucratic procedures and by confining such potentially radical initiatives as the sit-down strike to purely tactical uses, did indeed channel it toward more "responsible" and less system-challenging paths.

Similarly, the degree of union recognition and institutional stability gained in the 1930s and especially during World War II under the aegis of the federal government also exacted a price. To the extent that CIO leaders relied on the NLRB, the NWLB, and other personal and institutional forces in government, they accepted limits to the exercise of worker power. Likewise, the CIO's repeated eschewal of sustained third party activity in favor of participation in a deeply flawed Democratic coalition inevitably softened labor's voice and entailed compromise with a wide range of awkward allies.

The racial arena is a particularly poignant one in which to observe the limitations of the CIO. It was Communists and their allies, after all, who created and sustained the most principled biracial unions of the CIO era, unions that in some cases pioneered in promoting egalitarian workplace practices and in energizing somnolent civil rights organizations. However, most CIO unionists downplayed the race card and subsumed concern for black workers under class appeals that ignored or evaded confrontation with racist forces in the community and on the shop floor.

Even the important collective bargaining achievements of the CIO had a downside. Failure to gain broad public health, pension, and unemployment provisions forced CIO negotiators to become parties to the creation of what one historian has termed a private feudal system[2] of employer-provided benefits. Success in this kind of benefit provision increasingly isolated organized workers from ill-paid and benefit-poor workers in less favored sectors. Arbitration provisions in CIO contracts eroded shop-floor power, encouraging a clientlike relationship between the union and its members. Far from serving as the militant tribunes of worker discontent, CIO leaders increasingly functioned as administrative bureaucrats.

Even the CIO's harshest critics do not deny that in each of these areas achievements were made, although in all cases they object to the price paid and to the alternatives spurned. With regard to the "achievement" of repudiating the Communists and their allies, however, there is no such consensus. Of all the phases of the CIO's history, the role of the pro-Soviet left in the industrial union federation remains the most contentious. There is no doubt that the internal warfare that led in 1949–50 to the purging of ten affiliates and the loss of over 1 million members was a damaging and even enervating affair. Moreover, even some of the pro-Soviet left's fiercest critics have conceded that Communist-influenced unions were among the most egalitarian, the most honest and well-administered, the most racially progressive, and the most class conscious. The argument that in casting out the Communists and their allies, the CIO deprived itself of some of its most dynamic elements while at the same time enlisting in the frightening Cold War governmental apparatus has achieved widespread endorsement.

While the stress on the limitations of the CIO project is often intriguing, it is, in my view, not persuasive. I do not believe that there was a leftward-tending working-class militancy in the 1930s that CIO bureaucracy defanged or diverted. Rather, I believe, with Lewis and Hillman, that the AFL's failures made the greatest threat the abatement of class-based activism and the resurgence of corporate ideological hegemony. Furthermore, I find little evidence that industrial workers had much stomach for the kinds of root-and-branch confrontation with the American state that a more radical program would have required. Relatedly, I believe that the pro-union activities of the federal government in the 1930s and during World War II

(Handwritten annotation at top:) state action crucial, yes — but state action that favored UWC was produced from below, not above. When CIO clearly,

(Handwritten annotation right margin:) state action / yes / US / in nature / (however → / TH)

were absolutely crucial for the achievement of permanent industrial unions and that union behaviors that accommodated themselves to this circumstance were in general appropriate and necessary. Moreover, working within the Democratic Party was an obvious necessity to all but a handful of doctrinaire activists. The CIO rightly acted in this period as if the state and the political system were open to the influence of industrial workers, that they had a right to contest for influence within its structures, and that to attempt to operate in sustained fashion outside these structures was to invite futility and marginalization.

The strongest argument for missed opportunities was in the area of civil rights. Black workers responded eagerly to the CIO appeal and might have formed the vanguard of continued postwar organizing success. By the 1950s, CIO leaders were seemingly unaware of both the changing macroeconomic dynamics and the ongoing workplace conditions that threatened African Americans. Sharing the affliction of undue "moderation" on racial issues common among postwar liberals, CIO leaders failed to provide the leadership that might have made the industrial unions a more potent force in the great movement for civil rights of the 1950s and 1960s.

Still, even on these issues the CIO record, and the postmerger heritage of industrial unionists, was positive. Recruitment of black workers on an equal basis in the 1930s was something new in the mainstream labor movement. Forthright opposition to the hate strikes of World War II and vigorous efforts in behalf of the FEPC were important contributions. The CIO never wavered in its formal support for court decisions and national legislation attacking segregation and discrimination even when these stands cost it heavily among white workers, and not only in the South. In Washington, D.C., and in state capitals CIO (and later AFL–CIO) legislative representatives played significant roles in the enactment of civil rights laws whose provisions are now commonplace but that were in the 1950s and 1960s great victories for human rights. In retrospect it seems clear that the few episodes of aggressive biracial unionism were the products of situations in which black workers constituted the majority and would have been impossible to replicate in the ordinary workplaces and communities in which the racial attitudes of most white workers sharply reduced the social space needed for bold advance.

One of the most frequently cited reasons for lamenting the purging of the pro-Soviet unions in the late 1940s is the strong record many of these affiliates compiled in the racial arena. Indeed the Steelworkers' destruction of Alabama's biracial Mine, Mill locals as well as the CIO assault on racially progressive FTA locals in North Carolina cigarette factories constitute some of the most unsavory episodes in CIO history. The admirable, and on the whole sincerely compiled, record of Communist-oriented affiliates along with the often courageous and principled actions of many pro-Soviet individuals on racial matters make the strongest case for repudiating the anti-Communist purge.

Race, however, was not the only issue facing the labor left in the New Deal–World War II era. Even if its primacy is asserted, how long could a CIO tainted with the practical and moral incubus of Communist association have remained an effective force? Being a Communist in the 1930s and the 1940s was not just being a liberal in a hurry. The importance of Communism lay precisely in its connection to the Soviet empire and to the stature achieved by the Stalinist apparatus. To be a Communist, or even to be a consistent ally and defender of Communists, was to link yourself to Stalinism. It meant that you either denied Soviet crimes that killed and imprisoned millions or you justified them.

In the CIO the battle over Communism was fought in the idiom of other issues, notably political endorsements and response to key foreign policy initiatives such as the Marshall Plan. Beneath these disagreements over policies, however, lay fundamental disagreements over the bases of progressive politics. The members of this generation of labor leftists had to choose where they stood in the great divide marked by Stalinism. In the final analysis it was a matter not susceptible to nuanced preferences. Of course, in the not-so-long run, the continuance of a strong pro-Soviet bloc in the CIO would have surely crippled its political operations and would have invited increasing repression. Repression can be an honorable price to pay for principled commitments, but by 1949 there was little honor in association with Communists and their consistent allies.

The failure of the CIO on the Communist issue lay not in purging the pro-Soviet unions from its ranks. Rather, it lay in not following this necessary action with renewed commitment to organize the unorganized. The CIO and its affiliates expended millions of dollars in attempting to raid the memberships of such pro-Soviet organizations as the UE, Mine, Mill, and the FE. These actions did nothing to advance the cause of the industrial working class and invited employers' counterattacks. But failure to follow the ouster of the Communist-leaning affiliates with bold and principled mass organization, lamentable as it is, does not invalidate the initial repudiation of the Stalinoid impulse.

To mount a modest defense of the CIO record, however, is not to withhold criticism. In key areas the industrial union project fell short of legitimate expectations. Race, of course, was one of them, and another lay in the realm of gender. Innovative and imaginative in many areas of tactics and structure, CIO men failed to grasp the importance of women's growing role in the labor force and the possibilities for even more effective activism and organization that responsiveness to women's economic and political concerns might have afforded.

Failure to organize white collar, service, and government workers, of course, was related to the failure of imagination in gender matters. Under Lewis, Murray, and Reuther the CIO remained wedded to traditionally masculine notions of labor activism. Its few gestures toward nonindustrial workers failed to address the distinctive concerns of female workers. In effect the CIO left a vast segment of the labor force outside its boundaries, not by conscious decision but by virtue of its inability to transcend its origins.

Other limitations are clear in retrospect. The ambitions of some leaders for a codeterminative role for organized labor made little impact. Strong contracts backed by arbitration leeched power from front-line union representatives and channeled it upward into the union hierarchy. A union such as the UAW found in the 1980s that decades of erosion of power at the point of production required a campaign of "organizing the organized," that is, attempting to rebuild grassroots strength in the face of aggressive corporate efforts to transform workplaces. The ardent embrace of economic growth, combined with the de-emphasis on redistributionist goals, helped pave the way for the contemporary assault on organized labor and the decline of union sentiment among workers. Defensible as the isolation of the Communists and their allies was, the participation of some in the CIO in red-baiting and radical-bashing helped to marginalize even the non-Communist left and to make even the ardent advocacy of racial justice a ground for suspicion.

In the final analysis, however, all institutions are flawed. The CIO was the product of a period of incessant and harrowing crisis. For the most part its leaders were men of humble origins who had to struggle against daunting odds in their efforts to build and sustain mass unions. I believe that they were on the right side of most of the important issues, even though they too often spoke in an idiom and acted in a fashion that I find uncongenial. My own experience in political and labor organizing causes me to be impressed with their achievements rather than angry at their failures. Bottom line, and to paraphrase that man of the loading dock, Archie Bunker, "Mister, we could use a man like Walter Reuther again."

Notes

Abbreviations

In addition to the abbreviations found in the text, the following abbreviations are used in the notes.

DEPOSITORY DESIGNATIONS

ALUAWSU	Archives of Labor and Urban Affairs, Wayne State University, Detroit, Mich.
CUA	Catholic University of America, Washington, D.C.
GMMA	George Meany Memorial Archives, Silver Spring, Md.
LMDC	Labor-Management Documentation Center, Martin P. Catherwood Library, New York State School of Industrial and Labor Relations, Cornell University, Ithaca, N.Y.
PSULA	Pennsylvania State University Labor Archives, University Park, Pa.
SHSW	State Historical Society of Wisconsin, Madison, Wisc.

COLLECTION DESIGNATIONS

ACWA-LMDC	Amalgamated Clothing Workers of America Papers, Labor-Management Documentation Center, Martin P. Catherwood Library, New York State School of Industrial and Labor Relations, Cornell University, Ithaca, N.Y.
AG	Adolph Germer Papers, State Historical Society of Wisconsin, Madison, Wisc.
CIOEB-WSU	CIO Executive Board Minutes, Archives of Labor and Urban Affairs, Wayne State University, Detroit, Mich.
CIOEB-IUE	CIO Executive Board Minutes, IUE headquarters, Washington, D.C.
CIOFJLL	CIO Files of John L. Lewis, microfilm
CIOPROC	Proceedings of CIO annual conventions
CIOST	CIO Secretary-Treasurer Papers, Archives of Labor and Urban Affairs, Wayne State University, Detroit, Mich.
CIOWO	CIO Washington Office Papers, Archives of Labor and Urban Affairs, Wayne State University, Detroit, Mich.
COHC	Columbia Oral History Collection, Columbia University, New York, N.Y.
DBC-NYU	Daniel Bell Collection, Robert F. Wagner Labor Archives, New York University, New York, N.Y.
DMD-PSULA	David McDonald Papers, Pennsylvania State University Labor Archives, University Park, Pa.
DPP-SHC	Daniel Powell Papers, Southern Historical Collections, University of North Carolina, Chapel Hill, N.C.
HSTPL	Harry S. Truman Presidential Library, Independence, Mo.
ILGWU-LMDC	International Ladies' Garment Workers' Union Papers, Labor-Management Documentation Center, Martin P. Catherwood Library, New

	York State School of Industrial and Labor Relations, Cornell University, Ithaca, N.Y.
ILWUPSF	International Longshoremen's and Warehousemen's Union Papers, ILWU headquarters, San Francisco, Calif.
IUMSWPMD	International Union of Marine and Shipbuilding Workers Papers, University of Maryland, College Park, Md.
JBC	James B. Carey Papers, Archives of Labor and Urban Affairs, Wayne State University, Detroit, Mich.
JKPLC	Jack Kroll Papers, Library of Congress, Washington, D.C.
KPE	Katherine Pollak Ellickson Papers, Archives of Labor and Urban Affairs, Wayne State University, Detroit, Mich.
MSAFL–CIO	Michigan State AFL–CIO Papers, Archives of Labor and Urban Affairs, Wayne State University, Detroit, Mich.
NIU-CUA	CIO National and International Unions Papers, Catholic University of America, Washington, D.C.
NWLB-NA	National War Labor Board Records, Record Group 202, National Archives, Washington, D.C.
PAM-L	*Pamphlets in American History – Labor* (microfiche)
PRC	Paul R. Christopher Papers (AFL–CIO Region VIII Papers), Southern Labor Archives, Georgia State University, Atlanta, Ga.
SLA-GSU	Southern Labor Archives, Georgia State University, Atlanta, Ga.
SOC-DU	Southern Organization Committee (Operation Dixie) Papers, Duke University, Durham, N.C.
TWUA	Textile Workers Union of America Papers, State Historical Society of Wisconsin, Madison, Wisc.
UEUP	United Electrical, Radio and Machine Workers Papers, University of Pittsburgh, Pittsburgh, Pa.
UMWA-A	United Mine Workers of America Papers, Alexandria, Va.
UPWA	United Packinghouse Workers Papers, State Historical Society of Wisconsin, Madison, Wisc.
USWA-IEB	United Steelworkers of America, International Executive Board Minutes, Pennsylvania State University Labor Archives, University Park, Pa.

JOURNALS

JAH	*Journal of American History*
LH	*Labor History*

Bibliographical Note

The two articles cited in note 4 of the introduction provide a survey of CIO bibliography and a guide to archival collections. The list below cites major books appearing since the second of these articles, as well as some publications omitted from them. The first citation to any work in each chapter is complete.

Babson, Steve. *Building the Union: Skilled Workers and Anglo-Gaelic Immigrants in the Rise of the UAW*. New Brunswick: Rutgers University Press, 1991.
Carew, Anthony. *Walter Reuther*. Manchester, U.K.: Manchester University Press, 1993.
Cohen, Lizabeth. *Making a New Deal: Industrial Workers in Chicago, 1919–1939*. Cambridge: Cambridge University Press, 1990.

Dubofsky, Melvyn. *The State and Labor in Modern America*. Chapel Hill: University of North Carolina Press, 1994.

Faue, Elizabeth. *Community of Suffering and Struggle: Women, Men, and the Labor Movement in Minneapolis, 1915–1945*. Chapel Hill: University of North Carolina Press, 1991.

Fraser, Steven. *Labor Will Rule: Sidney Hillman and the Rise of American Labor*. New York: Free Press, 1991.

Gabin, Nancy F. *Feminism in the Labor Movement: Women and the United Auto Workers, 1935–1975*. Ithaca: Cornell University Press, 1990.

Honey, Michael K. *Southern Labor and Black Civil Rights: Organizing Memphis Workers*. Urbana: University of Illinois Press, 1993.

Kelley, Robin D. G. *Hammer and Hoe: Alabama Communists during the Great Depression*. Chapel Hill: University of North Carolina Press, 1990.

Klehr, Harvey, and John Earl Haynes. *The American Communist Movement: Storming Heaven Itself*. New York: Twayne, 1992.

MacShane, Denis. *International Labour and the Origins of the Cold War*. Oxford: Clarendon Press, 1992.

Meyer, Stephen. *"Stalin over Wisconsin": The Making and Unmaking of Militant Unionism, 1900–1950*. New Brunswick: Rutgers University Press, 1992.

Ottanelli, Fraser M. *The Communist Party of the United States: From the Depression to World War II*. New Brunswick: Rutgers University Press, 1991.

Reed, Merl E. *Seedtime for the Modern Civil Rights Movement: The President's Committee on Fair Employment Practice, 1941–1946*. Baton Rouge: Louisiana State University Press, 1991.

Renshaw, Patrick. *American Labor and Consensus Capitalism, 1935–1990*. Jackson: University Press of Mississippi, 1991.

Romero, Federico. *The United States and the European Trade Union Movement, 1944–1951*. Translated by Harvey Fergusson II. Chapel Hill: University of North Carolina Press, 1992.

Rosswurm, Steven, ed. *The CIO's Left-Led Unions*. New Brunswick: Rutgers University Press, 1992.

Scales, Junius Irving, and Richard Nickson. *Cause at Heart: A Former Communist Remembers*. Athens: University of Georgia Press, 1987.

Zieger, Robert H., ed. *Organized Labor in the Twentieth-Century South*. Knoxville: University of Tennessee Press, 1991.

Introduction

1. Thomas Geoghegan, *Which Side Are You On?: Trying to Be for Labor When It's Flat on Its Back* (New York: Penguin, 1991), 3, 7.

2. Remarks of Everett Kassalow, quoting an unnamed organizer, ca. Dec. 1, 1953, CIOWO, box 59: 11.

3. Ruth McKenney, *Industrial Valley* (New York: Harcourt, Brace, 1939), 373; Edward Levinson, *Labor on the March* (New York: Harper, 1938), 141; John P. Burke, quoted in Robert H. Zieger, *American Workers, American Unions, 1920–1985* (Baltimore: Johns Hopkins University Press, 1986), 69.

4. See Robert H. Zieger, "Toward the History of the CIO: A Bibliographical Report," *LH* 26, no. 4 (Fall 1985): 487–516, and Robert H. Zieger, "The CIO: A Bibliographical Update and Archival Guide," *LH* 31, no. 4 (Fall 1990): 413–40.

5. Remarks of Michael Quill, CIOPROC, 1955, 301–4; [James Carey], "The Historic Meaning of the CIO," [Fall 1955], JBC, addition 3, box 26; remarks of Walter Reuther, CIOPROC, 1955, 304–8.

6. Robert H. Zieger, *American Workers, American Unions*, 2d ed. (Baltimore: Johns Hopkins University Press, 1994), chap. 7.

Chapter One

1. Remarks of Max Zaritsky, Nov. 7, 1936, Katherine Pollak Ellickson meeting notes, KPE, box 14: 26. At his union's 1930 convention, UMW leader John L. Lewis had told the delegates that, despite the UMW's temporary setbacks, he would continue to speak out for the workers and "not in the quavering tones of a feeble mendicant asking alms, but in the thundering voice of the captain of a mighty host." Quoted in Robert H. Zieger, *John L. Lewis: Labor Leader* (Boston: Twayne, 1988), 49.

2. Irving Bernstein, *The Lean Years: A History of the American Worker, 1920–1933* (Boston: Houghton Mifflin, 1960), 52–54; Rhonda Levine, *Class Struggle and the New Deal: Industrial Labor, Industrial Capital, and the State* (Lawrence: University Press of Kansas, 1988), 20–46; Stanley Lebergott, *The Americans: An Economic Record* (New York: Norton, 1984), 431–43; Zieger, *Lewis*, 76; John L. Lewis speech, Dec. 7, 1934, reprinted in *United Mine Workers Journal*, Dec. 1934.

3. Robert S. Lynd and Helen Merrell Lynd, *Middletown: A Study in Modern American Culture* (New York: Harcourt, Brace, 1929), 75. See also Richard Jensen, "The Lynds Revisited," *Indiana Magazine of History* 75 (Dec. 1979): 303–19, and Dwight W. Hoover, *Middletown Revisited* (Muncie, Ind.: Ball State University, 1990; Ball State Monograph No. 34), 3–10.

4. The theme of "de-skilling" is a lively and contested one among labor historians. See, e.g., Gavin Wright, "Labor History and Labor Economics," in *The Future of Economic History*, ed. Alexander J. Field (Boston: Kluwer-Nijhoff, 1987), 332–34; Andrew Dawson, "The Paradox of Dynamic Technological Change and the Labor Aristocracy in the United States, 1880–1914," *LH* 20, no. 3 (Summer 1979): 325–51; Margo Conk, *The United States Census and Labor Force Change: A History of Occupation Statistics, 1870–1940* (Ann Arbor: UMI Research Press, 1980), esp. 41–46; David Gartman, *Auto Slavery: The Labor Process in the American Automobile Industry, 1897–1950* (New Brunswick: Rutgers University Press, 1986); and Steve Babson, *Building the Union: Skilled Workers and Anglo-Gaelic Immigrants in the Rise of the UAW* (New Brunswick: Rutgers University Press, 1991), 1–62.

5. Richard J. Jensen, "The Causes and Cures of Unemployment in the Great Depression," *Journal of Interdisciplinary History* 19, no. 4 (Spring 1989): 561; Wright, "Labor History and Labor Economics," 332–37; Lizabeth Cohen, *Making a New Deal: Industrial Workers in Chicago, 1919–1939* (Cambridge: Cambridge University Press, 1990), 159–211.

6. Thomas Göbel, "Becoming an American: Ethnic Workers and the Rise of the CIO," *LH* 29, no. 2 (Spring 1988): 173–98; Ewa Morawska, "East European Labourers in an American Mill Town, 1890–1940: The Deferential-Proletarian-Privatized Workers?," *Sociology* 19, no. 3 (Aug. 1985): 364–83; John Bodnar, "Immigration, Kinship, and the Rise of Working-Class Realism in Industrial America," *Journal of Social History* 14 (Fall 1980): 45–65; John Bukowczyk, "The Transformation of Working-Class Ethnicity: Corporate Control, Americanization, and the Polish Immigrant Middle Class in Bayonne, New Jersey, 1915–1925," *LH* 25, no. 1 (Winter 1984): 53–82; Cohen, *Making a New Deal*, 53–98.

7. August Meier and Elliott Rudwick, *Black Detroit and the Rise of the UAW* (New York: Oxford University Press, 1979), 3–33; Peter Gottlieb, *Making Their Own Way: Southern Blacks' Migration to Pittsburgh, 1916–30* (Urbana: University of Illinois Press, 1987), 1–116; James Grossman, *Land of Hope: Chicago, Black Southerners, and the Great Migration* (Chicago: University of Chicago Press, 1989), 13–119; Dennis C. Dickerson, *Out of the Crucible: Black Steelworkers in Western Pennsylvania, 1875–1980* (Albany, N.Y.: SUNY Press, 1986), 85–118; Dennis Nordin Valdes,

"Betabeleros: The Formation of an Agricultural Proletariat in the Midwest, 1897–1930," *LH* 30, no. 4 (Fall 1989): 536–62.

8. David Montgomery, *Workers' Control in America: Studies in the History of Work, Technology, and Labor Struggles* (Cambridge: Cambridge University Press, 1979), 91–112; David Montgomery, *The Fall of the House of Labor: The Workplace, the State, and American Labor Activism, 1865–1925* (Cambridge: Cambridge University Press, 1987), 310–457.

9. U.S. Department of Commerce, Bureau of the Census, *Historical Statistics of the United States, 1789–1945* (Washington, D.C.: Government Printing Office, 1949), 73.

10. Wright, "Labor History and Labor Economics," 335–37; Lebergott, *The Americans*, 380–81, 431–38. But see Frank Stricker, "Affluence for Whom? Another Look at Prosperity and the Working Classes in the 1920s," *LH* 24, no. 1 (Winter 1983): 5–33.

11. Bernstein, *Lean Years*, 47–74; Stricker, "Affluence for Whom?"; Robert H. Zieger, *Republicans and Labor, 1919–1929* (Lexington: University of Kentucky Press, 1969), 216–47, 249–59.

12. Zieger, *Republicans and Labor*, 249–59; David Montgomery, "Thinking about American Workers in the 1920s," *International Labor and Working Class History* 32 (Fall 1987): 4–24; Bernstein, *Lean Years*, 1–43; James O. Morris, *Conflict within the AFL: A Study of Craft Versus Industrial Unionism, 1901–1938* (Ithaca: Cornell University Press, 1958), 86–116; Roger Keeran, *The Communist Party and the Auto Workers Unions* (Bloomington: Indiana University Press, 1980), 28–59.

13. Hoover quoted in Robert H. Zieger, "Solving the Labor Problem: Herbert Hoover and the American Worker in the 1920's," in *Herbert Hoover Reassessed: Essays Commemorating the Fiftieth Anniversary of the Inauguration of Our Thirty-First President* (Washington, D.C.: Government Printing Office, 1981), 177; Robert H. Zieger, "Herbert Hoover, the Wage-Earner, and the 'New Economic System,' 1919–1929," in *Herbert Hoover as Secretary of Commerce: Studies in New Era Thought and Practice*, ed. Ellis W. Hawley (Iowa City: University of Iowa Press, 1981), 80–114.

14. Lynd and Lynd, *Middletown*, 78; John T. Walker, "Socialism in Dayton, Ohio, 1912 to 1925: Its Membership, Organization, and Demise," *LH* 26, no. 3 (Summer 1985): 384–405; Errol Wayne Stevens, "Labor and Socialism in an Indiana Mill Town, 1905–1921," *LH* 26, no. 3 (Summer 1985): 353–83; Michael Nash, *Conflict and Accommodation: Coal Miners, Steel Workers, and Socialism, 1890–1920* (Westport, Conn.: Greenwood Press, 1982); Richard W. Judd, *Socialist Cities: Municipal Politics and the Grass Roots of American Socialism* (Albany, N.Y.: SUNY Press, 1989); John T. Cumbler, *A Social History of Economic Decline: Business, Politics, and Work in Trenton* (New Brunswick: Rutgers University Press, 1989), 93–111.

15. Ronald Edsforth, *Class Conflict and Cultural Consensus: The Making of a Mass Consumer Society in Flint, Michigan* (New Brunswick: Rutgers University Press, 1987), 87–96. Joyce Shaw Peterson, *American Automobile Workers, 1900–1933* (Albany, N.Y.: SUNY Press, 1987), posits a similar trade-off but sees the autoworkers' bargain less enthusiastically made. See also Gilman Ostrander, *American Civilization in the First Machine Age, 1890–1940* (New York: Harper and Row, 1970), 199–219, and Cohen, *Making a New Deal*, 99–158. For an intriguing episode of the role of consumer culture in the generation and shaping of worker protest, see Jacquelyn Dowd Hall, "Disorderly Women: Gender and Labor Militancy in the Appalachian South," *JAH* 73, no. 2 (Sept. 1986): 377–80.

16. Daniel Nelson, *American Rubber Workers and Organized Labor, 1900–1941* (Princeton: Princeton University Press, 1988), 77–110.

17. Ronald W. Schatz, *The Electrical Workers: A History of Labor at General Electric and Westinghouse, 1923–1960* (Urbana: University of Illinois Press, 1983), 38–48.

18. I. A. Newby, *Plain Folk in the New South: Social Change and Cultural Persistence, 1880–1915* (Baton Rouge: Louisiana State University Press, 1989), 568–69; Jennings J. Rhyne, *Some Southern Cotton Mill Workers and Their Villages* (Chapel Hill: University of North Carolina Press, 1930), 7–19, 205–6, 212; Harriet L. Herring, *Welfare Work in Mill Villages: The Story of Extra-*

Mill Activities in North Carolina (Chapel Hill: University of North Carolina Press, 1929; Montclair, N.J.: Patterson Smith, 1968); Gavin Wright, "Cheap Labor and Southern Textiles, 1880–1930," *Quarterly Journal of Economics* 96 (Nov. 1981): 605–29.

19. On packinghouse workers in the 1920s, see Rick Halpern, "The Iron Fist and the Velvet Glove: Welfare Capitalism in Chicago's Packinghouses, 1921–1954," *Journal of American Studies* 26, no. 2 (Aug. 1992): 159–84. For the experiences of pulp and paper workers, see Robert H. Zieger, *Rebuilding the Pulp and Paper Workers' Union, 1933–1941* (Knoxville: University of Tennessee Press, 1984), 41.

20. H. M. Gitelman, "Welfare Capitalism Reconsidered," *LH* 33, no. 1 (Winter 1992): 5–31; David Brody, "The Rise and Decline of Welfare Capitalism," in *Workers in Industrial America: Essays on the Twentieth-Century Struggle*, by David Brody (New York: Oxford University Press, 1980), 48–81; Daniel Nelson, "The Company Union Movement, 1900–1937: A Reexamination," *Business History Review* 56, no. 3 (Autumn 1982): 335–57.

21. Schatz, *Electrical Workers*, table, 61; Nelson, *American Rubber Workers*, 113; Peterson, *American Automobile Workers*, 131–32.

22. On this theme, see Cohen, *Making a New Deal*, 214–89.

23. On the AFL, see Philip A. Taft, *The A.F. of L. in the Time of Gompers* (New York: Harper and Bros., 1957); Philip A. Taft, *The A. F. of L. from the Death of Gompers to the Merger* (New York: Harper and Bros., 1959), 1–85; Lewis L. Lorwin, *The American Federation of Labor: History, Policies, and Prospects* (Washington, D.C.: Brookings Institution, 1933); Craig Phelan, *William Green: Biography of a Labor Leader* (Albany, N.Y.: SUNY Press, 1989); and William E. Forbath, *Law and the Shaping of the American Labor Movement* (Cambridge, Mass.: Harvard University Press, 1991).

24. The standard history of the IWW is Melvyn Dubofsky, *We Shall Be All: A History of the Industrial Workers of the World* (Chicago: Quadrangle, 1969). On the Knights of Labor, see Leon Fink, *Workingmen's Democracy: The Knights of Labor and American Politics* (Urbana: University of Illinois Press, 1983).

25. Morris, *Conflict within the AFL*; Christopher Tomlins, "AFL Unions in the 1930s: Their Performance in Historical Perspective," *JAH* 65, no. 4 (Mar. 1979): 1021–42. On steel, see David Brody, *Labor in Crisis: The Steel Strike of 1919* (Philadelphia: Lippincott, 1965); on packinghouse workers, see James R. Barrett, *Work and Community in the Jungle: Chicago's Packinghouse Workers, 1894–1922* (Urbana: University of Illinois Press, 1987), 188–202. Mass production unionism in the World War I period is charted in Montgomery, *Fall of the House of Labor*, 370–89, and Bruno Ramirez, *When Workers Fight: The Politics of Industrial Relations in the Progressive Era, 1896–1916* (Westport, Conn.: Greenwood Press, 1978), 104–22, 194–205.

26. Harvey Klehr, *The Heyday of American Communism: The Depression Decade* (New York: Basic Books, 1984), 28–48; David Brody, "The Emergence of Mass-Production Unionism," in *Workers in Industrial America: Essays on the Twentieth Century Struggle*, by David Brody (New York: Oxford University Press, 1980), 82–119; David Brody, "The Expansion of the American Labor Movement: Institutional Sources of Stimulus and Restraint," in *Institutions in Modern America*, ed. Stephen E. Ambrose (Baltimore: Johns Hopkins University Press, 1967), 11–36.

27. Morris, *Conflict within the AFL*, 63–67; Phelan, *Green*, 57–62.

28. Green's remarks are quoted in Phelan, *Green*, 53.

29. Ibid., 52–53.

30. Hillman quoted in Steve Fraser, "From the 'New Unionism' to the New Deal," *LH* 25, no. 3 (Summer 1984): 408–9. See also Steve Fraser, "The 'New Unionism' and the 'New Economic Policy,'" in *Work, Community, and Power: The Experience of Labor in Europe and America, 1900–1925*, ed. James E. Cronin and Carmen Sirianni (Philadelphia: Temple University Press, 1983), 173–96; Steve Fraser, "Dress Rehearsal for the New Deal: Shop-Floor Insurgents, Politi-

cal Elites, and Industrial Democracy in the Amalgamated Clothing Workers," in *Working-Class America: Essays on Labor, Community, and American Society*, ed. Michael H. Frisch and Daniel J. Walkowitz (Urbana: University of Illinois Press, 1983), 212–55; Steve Fraser, "Sidney Hillman: Labor's Machievelli," in *Labor Leaders in America*, ed. Melvyn Dubofsky and Warren Van Tine (Urbana: University of Illinois Press, 1987), 207–33; and Steven Fraser, *Labor Will Rule: Sidney Hillman and the Rise of American Labor* (New York: Free Press, 1991), 191–282.

31. Fraser, "From the 'New Unionism' to the New Deal," 413.

32. Ibid., 414.

33. Allan J. Lichtman, "Critical Election Theory and the Reality of American Presidential Politics, 1916–1940," *American Historical Review* 81, no. 2 (Apr. 1976): 317–51; Richard Oestreicher, "Urban Working-Class Political Behavior and Theories of American Electoral Politics, 1870–1940," *JAH* 74, no. 4 (Mar. 1988): 1257–86; David Burner, *The Politics of Provincialism: The Democratic Party in Transition, 1918–1932* (New York: Knopf, 1968), 178–243; Kristi Andersen, *The Creation of a Democratic Majority, 1928–1936* (Chicago: University of Chicago Press, 1979); and Gerald H. Gamm, *The Making of New Deal Democrats: Voting Behavior and Realignment in Boston, 1920–1940* (Chicago: University of Chicago Press, 1989), 3–40.

34. Melvyn Dubofsky and Warren Van Tine, *John L. Lewis: A Biography* (New York: Quadrangle, 1977), 148–49, 175–77; Zieger, *Republicans and Labor*, 256–58; Zieger, *Lewis*, 33–36.

35. See Phelan, *Green*, 64–67; Dubofsky and Van Tine, *Lewis*, 182–86; Irving Bernstein, *Turbulent Years: A History of the American Worker, 1933–1941* (Boston: Houghton Mifflin, 1969), 27–36; Bernard Bellush, *The Failure of the NRA* (New York: Norton, 1975), 14–27; John Kennedy Ohl, *Hugh S. Johnson and the New Deal* (DeKalb: Northern Illinois University Press, 1985), 96–108.

36. Bernstein, *Turbulent Years*, 37–171; U.S. Department of Commerce, *Historical Statistics*, 72–73; Zieger, *Rebuilding the Pulp and Paper Workers' Union*, 66–94.

37. Bernstein, *Turbulent Years*, 172–317.

38. U.S. Department of Commerce, *Historical Statistics*, 73; Peterson, *American Automobile Workers*, 129–39; Dubofsky and Van Tine, *Lewis*, 170–72; Bernstein, *Lean Years*, 1–43.

39. Bernstein, *Turbulent Years*, 292.

40. Bernard Sternsher, "Victims of the Great Depression: Self-Blame/Non-Self-Blame, Radicalism, and Pre-1929 Experiences," *Social Science History* 1 (Winter 1977): 137–77; Bodnar, "Immigration, Kinship, and the Rise of Working-Class Realism"; Gary Gerstle, *Working-Class Americanism: The Politics of Labor in a Textile City, 1914–1960* (Cambridge: Cambridge University Press, 1989), 96–150; Cohen, *Making a New Deal*, 267–93.

41. Eugene T. Sweeney, "The A.F.L.'s Good Citizen, 1920–1940," *LH* 13, no. 2 (Spring 1972): 200–216; Warren Van Tine, *The Making of the Labor Bureaucrat: Union Leadership in the United States, 1870–1920* (Amherst: University of Massachusetts Press, 1973); Walter Licht and Hal Seth Barron, "Labor's Men: A Collective Biography of Union Officialdom during the New Deal Years," *LH* 19, no. 4 (Fall 1978): 532–45; Gary Fink, "The American Labor Leader in the Twentieth Century: Quantitative and Qualitative Portraits," in *Biographical Dictionary of American Labor*, ed. Gary Fink, 2d ed. (Westport, Conn.: Greenwood Press, 1984), 3–67; David Brody, "Career Leadership and American Trade Unions," in *The Age of Industrialism in America: Essays in Social Structure and Cultural Values*, ed. Frederic Cople Jaher (New York: Free Press, 1968), 288–305. See also the biographical studies in Dubofsky and Van Tine, *Labor Leaders in America*.

42. Zieger, *Rebuilding the Pulp and Paper Workers' Union*, quoting President John P. Burke of the International Brotherhood of Pulp, Sulphite, and Paper Mill Workers, 76; Bernstein, *Turbulent Years*, 352–90; Phelan, *Green*, 75–95; Walter Galenson, *The CIO Challenge to the AFL: A History of the American Labor Movement, 1935–1941* (Cambridge, Mass.: Harvard University Press, 1960). For a more positive view of AFL policies and performance, see Tomlins, "AFL Unions in the 1930s."

43. Zieger, *Rebuilding the Pulp and Paper Workers' Union*, 76; Phelan, *Green*, 101–5.

44. In 1933, the ACWA was admitted to the AFL.

45. Dubofsky and Van Tine, *Lewis*, 203–17; Fraser, "Sidney Hillman," 216–20; Licht and Barron, "Labor's Men," 538–42; Fink, "American Labor Leader," 46–51.

46. Quoted in Robert H. Zieger, *American Workers, American Unions, 1920–1985* (Baltimore: Johns Hopkins University Press, 1986), 38.

47. Gerald Zahavi, *Workers, Managers, and Welfare Capitalism: The Shoemakers and Tanners of Endicott Johnson, 1890–1950* (Urbana: University of Illinois Press, 1988), 99–176; Elizabeth Fones-Wolf, "Industrial Recreation, the Second World War, and the Revival of Welfare Capitalism, 1934–1960," *Business History Review* 60, no. 2 (Summer 1986): 232–57; Stuart Chase, *A Generation of Industrial Peace: 30 Years of Labor Relations at Standard Oil Company (NJ)* (New York: Standard Oil of New Jersey, 1947); John N. Schacht, *The Making of Telephone Unionism, 1920–1947* (New Brunswick: Rutgers University Press, 1985), 40–46; and Sanford M. Jacoby and Anil Verma, "Enterprise Unions in the United States," *Industrial Relations* 31, no. 1 (Winter 1992): 138–43.

48. Dubofsky and Van Tine, *Lewis*, 203–21; Zieger, *Lewis*, 76–83; notes on CIO meeting, Nov. 7–8, 1936, KPE, box 14: 25.

Chapter Two

1. The standard accounts of the struggle over industrial unionism in the AFL are Melvyn Dubofsky and Warren Van Tine, *John L. Lewis: A Biography* (New York: Quadrangle, 1977), 197–221; Irving Bernstein, *Turbulent Years: A History of the American Worker, 1933–1941* (Boston: Houghton Mifflin, 1969), 352–98; and James O. Morris, *Conflict within the AFL: A Study of Craft Versus Industrial Unionism, 1901–1938* (Ithaca: Cornell University Press, 1958), 136–211. Lewis's speech is printed in American Federation of Labor, *Report of the Proceedings of the 1935 Convention* (1935), 534–40.

2. The best account of the Lewis-Hutcheson affray is in Dubofsky and Van Tine, *Lewis*, 220–21. See also Louis Stark, "Fist Fight Puts A.F. of L. in Uproar," *New York Times*, Oct. 20, 1935.

3. There is a vivid account of Lewis's motives, allegedly in his own words, in Saul Alinsky, *John L. Lewis: An Unauthorized Biography* (New York: G. P. Putnam's Sons, 1949), 77–80, but Alinsky's book is of questionable reliability. See Dubofsky and Van Tine, *Lewis*, 217–21, for a more authoritative account. De Caux's comments occur in Len De Caux, *Labor Radical: From the Wobblies to CIO, a Personal History* (Boston: Beacon Press, 1970), 216.

4. Lewis at the 1935 AFL convention, as quoted in Robert H. Zieger, *John L. Lewis: Labor Leader* (Boston: Twayne, 1988), 82.

5. Zieger, *Lewis*, 77; W. Jett Lauck, "Memorandum as to Statement," Oct. 9, 1935, W. Jett Lauck Papers, Alderman Library, University of Virginia, Charlottesville, Va., box 40: Suggested Program for 1934–1935.

6. Lauck, "Memorandum."

7. Ibid.

8. Edward Wieck to Oscar Ameringer, Feb. 8, 1936, Edward Wieck Papers, ALUAWSU, box 15: Lewis.

9. Dubofsky and Van Tine, *Lewis*, 181–232.

10. For a profile of Dubinsky, see Bernstein, *Turbulent Years*, 77–82.

11. Howard typescript statements, Dec. 1935–Feb. 1936, ACWA-LMDC, box 74: 36; "Charles Perry Howard," in *Biographical Dictionary of American Labor*, ed. Gary Fink, 2d ed. (Westport, Conn.: Greenwood Press, 1984), 304.

12. Matthew Josephson, *Sidney Hillman: Statesman of American Labor* (Garden City: Doubleday, 1952), 311–26; Steven Fraser, *Labor Will Rule: Sidney Hillman and the Rise of American Labor* (New York: Free Press, 1991), 198–237.

13. Fraser, *Labor Will Rule*, 289–348.

14. On Brophy, see Sr. M. Camilla Mullay, "John Brophy, Militant Labor Leader and Reformer: The CIO Years" (Ph.D. dissertation, Catholic University of America, 1966), and John Brophy, *A Miner's Life: An Autobiography*, edited and supplemented by John O. P. Hall (Madison: University of Wisconsin Press, 1964). The quotes are from, respectively, McAlister Coleman, *Men and Coal* (New York: Farrar and Rinehart, 1943), 162, and John Brophy interview, May 2, 1955, COHC, 621.

15. On Germer, see Lorin Lee Cary, "Institutionalized Conservatism in the Early C.I.O.: Adolph Germer, a Case Study," *LH* 13, no. 4 (Fall 1972): 475–504.

16. Coleman, *Men and Coal*, 109–12, 161–63; Stephen H. Norwood, "Powers Hapgood," in Fink, *Biographical Dictionary*, 279–80.

17. Robert H. Zieger, "Katherine Pollak Ellickson," in Fink, *Biographical Dictionary*, 206–7; Robert H. Zieger, "Leonard Howard De Caux," in Fink, *Biographical Dictionary*, 179; De Caux, *Labor Radical*.

18. Green to Roy O. Howard, Mar. 13, 1933, International Brotherhood of Teamsters Papers, SHSW, series IIIA, box 8.

19. Bernstein, *Turbulent Years*, 423; Craig Phelan, *William Green: Biography of a Labor Leader* (Albany, N.Y.: SUNY Press, 1989), 130–31. The AFL's unshakable sense of its own exclusive legitimacy as the repository of the hopes of the American working class is skillfully analyzed in David Brody, "The Expansion of the American Labor Movement: Institutional Sources of Stimulus and Restraint," in *Institutions in Modern America*, ed. Stephen E. Ambrose (Baltimore: Johns Hopkins University Press, 1967), 11–36.

20. Minutes, CIO meeting, Dec. 9, 1935, JBC, box 89.

21. "Summary of Conference on Auto Situation," Nov. 26, 1935, attached to Brophy to Germer, Nov. 27, 1935, and David Land to Germer, Dec. 10, 1935, AG, box 2. There are dozens of other communications from auto and rubber workers' activists along these lines in the Germer papers. See also unsigned report [from Germer?], Jan. 9, 1936, NIU-CUA, box 23, and memoranda by John Brophy on the auto industry, Nov. 15 and Nov. 27, 1935, ACWA-LMDC, box 68: 40. The complex story of union activism in the auto industry, 1933–36, is best conveyed in Bernstein, *Turbulent Years*, 94–99, 181–82, 499–509, and Sidney Fine, *The Automobile under the Blue Eagle: Labor, Management, and the Automobile Manufacturing Code* (Ann Arbor: University of Michigan Press, 1963).

22. Germer to Brophy, Dec. 8, 1935, AG, box 2. On the Mechanics Educational Society, see Steve Babson, *Building the Union: Skilled Workers and Anglo-Gaelic Immigrants in the Rise of the UAW* (New Brunswick: Rutgers University Press, 1991), 116–17, 148–50.

23. Dubofsky and Van Tine, *Lewis*, 223–26, covers the opening stages of the Green-Lewis confrontation; Lewis's letter of Dec. 7, quoted above, is quoted extensively at 225. See also Lewis's remarks, Minutes, CIO meeting, Dec. 9, 1935, JBC, box 89.

24. Minutes, CIO meeting, Dec. 9, 1935, JBC, box 89.

25. Ibid.; report by director for meeting of Dec. 9, 1935; report of director, Jan. 9, 1936; report by director for meeting of Feb. 21, 1936, all in JBC, box 89.

26. The authoritative account of the origins of the URW and of the 1936 Goodyear strike is Daniel Nelson, *American Rubber Workers and Organized Labor, 1900–1941* (Princeton: Princeton University Press, 1988), 143–203.

27. The sources cited in n. 25 above present a running account of Germer's reports.

28. Rose Pesotta, *Bread upon the Waters* (New York: Dodd, Mead, 1944; Ithaca: ILR Press, 1987), 205.

29. Lewis speech quoted in Nelson, *American Rubber Workers*, 181; Lewis speech, Jan. 19, 1936, copy in UMWA-A (CIO, 1936). See also Dubofsky and Van Tine, *Lewis*, 228–29.

30. Report of director, Jan. 9, 1936; report by director . . . , Feb. 21, 1936; report by director . . . , Apr. 14, all in JBC, box 89; CIO expenditures, Nov. 15, 1935–Mar. 31, 1936, KPE, box 14: 12. See also Bernstein, *Turbulent Years*, 589–96, and Pesotta, *Bread upon the Waters*, 195–226.

31. Nelson, *American Rubber Workers*, 190–93; Pesotta, *Bread upon the Waters*, 212–13.

32. Pesotta, *Bread upon the Waters*, 224; Nelson, *American Rubber Workers*, 194–203; Germer to Brophy, Mar. 25, 1936, AG, box 2. See also Cary, "Institutionalized Conservatism," 491–92.

33. On the history of labor relations in steel, see David Brody, *Steelworkers in America: The Nonunion Era* (Cambridge, Mass.: Harvard University Press, 1960); David Brody, *Labor in Crisis: The Steel Strike of 1919* (Philadelphia: Lippincott, 1965); and David Brody, "The Origins of Modern Steel Unionism: The SWOC Era," in *Forging a Union of Steel: Philip Murray, SWOC, and the United Steelworkers*, ed. Paul F. Clark, Peter Gottlieb, and Donald Kennedy (Ithaca: ILR Press, 1987), 13–29. Robert R. R. Brooks, *As Steel Goes, . . . : Unionism in a Basic Industry* (New Haven: Yale University Press, 1940), 21–45, and Clinton S. Golden and Harold J. Ruttenberg, *The Dynamics of Industrial Democracy* (New York: Harper and Bros., 1942), 109–13, contain vivid firsthand steelworkers' remembrances.

34. Golden and Ruttenberg, *Dynamics of Industrial Democracy*, 112; Brody, "Origins of Modern Steel Unionism," 17. See also Richard Oestreicher, "Working-Class Formation, Development, and Consciousness in Pittsburgh, 1790–1960," in *City at the Point: Essays in the Social History of Pittsburgh*, ed. Samuel P. Hays (Pittsburgh: University of Pittsburgh Press, 1989), 138.

35. Bernstein, *Turbulent Years*, 92–94, 197–99, 369–72; Clinton S. Golden to William P. Mangold, Mar. 12, 1936, in Thomas R. Brooks, *Clint: A Biography of a Labor Intellectual, Clinton S. Golden* (New York: Atheneum, 1978), 141–42; Brophy to William Green, Jan. 10, 1936, American Federation of Labor Papers, SHSW, series 11C, box 1.

36. Bernstein, *Turbulent Years*, 432–37.

37. Report by director for meeting of Apr. 14, 1936, and supplementary report on the steel situation, Apr. 13, 1936, JBC, box 89; Brophy quoted in Brody, "Origins of Modern Steel Unionism," 17.

38. Dubofsky and Van Tine, *Lewis*, 234–41. As late as June, Dubinsky insisted that no campaign to organize steel could succeed outside the AFL (Dubinsky to Brophy, June 1, 1936, ILGWU-LMDC, box 15: 3A). I examined these papers when they were housed at the ILGWU headquarters in New York City.

39. Dubofsky and Van Tine, *Lewis*, 236–38; Clinton Golden to Heber Blankenhorn, May 20, 1936, Clinton Golden Papers, PSULA, box 6.

40. Minutes of the Organizational Meeting of the Steel Workers Organizing Committee . . . , June 17, 1936, NIU-CUA, box 33: USWA 1; Brody, "Origins of Modern Steel Unionism," 20; Bernstein, *Turbulent Years*, 440–41.

41. The Green-Lewis correspondence is cited at length in Dubofsky and Van Tine, *Lewis*, 238–39.

42. Phelan, *Green*, 134–36, presents the SWOC controversy from Green's perspective.

43. Minutes . . . , June 17, 1936, NIU-CUA.

44. Staughton Lynd, "Personal Histories of the Early CIO," *Radical America* 5, no. 3 (May–June 1971): 53–58, 72–75; Staughton Lynd, "Guerrilla History in Gary," *Liberation* 14, no. 7 (Oct. 1969): 17–21; Staughton Lynd, "The Possibility of Radicalism in the Early 1930's: The Case of Steel," *Radical America* 6, no. 6 (Nov.–Dec. 1972): 37–64. On SWOC's governing structure, see Lloyd Ulman, *The Government of the Steel Workers' Union* (New York: John Wiley and Sons, 1962), 3–39, and Golden and Ruttenberg, *Dynamics of Industrial Democracy*, 48–118.

45. Thomas R. Brooks, *Clint*, 158–60; Bernstein, *Turbulent Years*, 448–55; Max Gordon, "The

Communists and the Drive to Organize Steel, 1936," *LH* 23, no. 2 (Spring 1982): 254–65; minutes of CIO meeting, Washington, July 2, 1936, JBC, box 89.

46. Benjamin Stolberg, *The Story of the CIO* (New York: Viking, 1938), 88–89, and David J. McDonald, *Union Man* (New York: Dutton, 1969), 93–101, discuss the reactions of UMW organizers and the difficulties of early SWOC organizing. Walter Galenson, *The CIO Challenge to the AFL: A History of the American Labor Movement, 1935–1941* (Cambridge, Mass.: Harvard University Press, 1960), 91, quotes organizer Meyer Bernstein. Murray's remarks are quoted in Brody, "Origins of Modern Steel Unionism," 20–21. Membership estimates are given in Brody, "Origins of Modern Steel Unionism," 21, and Stolberg, *Story of the CIO*, 72. A candid assessment of SWOC's early difficulties appears in Philip Murray statement, Nov. 8, 1936, NIU-CUA, box 33: USWA 1.

47. The best treatment of LNPL is in Dubofsky and Van Tine, *Lewis*, 248–53, which includes accounts of the speeches cited.

48. Ibid., 251–53; Irving Bernstein, *The Lean Years: A History of the American Worker, 1920–1933* (Boston: Houghton Mifflin, 1960), 454. Although virtually all commentators agree that "labor" was crucial to Roosevelt's massive victory, no one has sought to identify the distinctive impact of *organized* labor's financial and organizational efforts. For standard accounts, see William E. Leuchtenberg, *FDR and the New Deal, 1932–1940* (New York: Harper Torchbooks, 1963), 188–89; Arthur M. Schlesinger, Jr., *The Age of Roosevelt: The Politics of Upheaval* (Boston: Houghton Mifflin, 1960), 424; James MacGregor Burns, *Roosevelt: The Lion and the Fox* (New York: Harcourt, Brace and World, 1956), 276, 286–87; Murray Edelman, "New Deal Sensitivity to Labor Interests," in *Labor and the New Deal*, ed. Milton Derber and Edwin Young (Madison: University of Wisconsin Press, 1957), 181–82. David Plotke, "The Wagner Act, Again: Politics and Labor, 1935–1937," in *Studies in American Political Development*, ed. Stephen Skowronek and Karen Orren (New Haven: Yale University Press, 1989), 3: 140–41, contains a succinct recent statement.

49. Minutes of CIO meeting, Nov. 7–8, 1936, KPE, box 14: 25. The words attributed to Lewis were transcribed by Ellickson.

50. Report of director for CIO meeting, Nov. 7 and 8, 1936, part 1, "Review of the Past Year," ACWA-LMDC, box 209: 4; Murray statement, Nov. 8, 1936, NIU-CUA, box 33: USWA 1.

51. Notes on CIO meeting, Nov. 7, 1936, KPE, box 14: 25. Ellickson quoted Hillman's remarks when she typed up her notes in 1968.

Chapter Three

1. Robert Stuart McElvaine, "Thunder without Lightning: Working-Class Discontent in the United States, 1929–1937" (Ph.D. dissertation, SUNY-Binghamton, 1974), esp. 73–124.

2. Helen Heaton Vorse, *Labor's New Millions* (New York: Modern Age Books, 1938), 58; Edward Levinson, *Labor on the March* (New York: Harper, 1938), 141, 165; Len De Caux, *Labor Radical: From the Wobblies to CIO, a Personal History* (Boston: Beacon Press, 1970), 242. Graphic evidence of Pentecostlike worker activism is abundant. See, e.g., Steve Babson, *Working Detroit: The Making of a Union Town* (New York: Adama Books, 1984), 80–81; Carlos Schwantes, "'We've Got 'em on the Run, Brothers': The 1937 Non-Automotive Sit Down Strikes in Detroit," *Michigan History* 58 (Fall 1972): 179–99; Irving Bernstein, *Turbulent Years: A History of the American Worker, 1933–1941* (Boston: Houghton Mifflin, 1969), 447; Ruth McKenney, *Industrial Valley* (New York: Harcourt, Brace, 1939), 373–79; Bruce Nelson, "'Pentecost' on the Pacific: Maritime Workers and Working-Class Consciousness in the 1930s," in *Political Power and Social Theory: A Research Annual*, ed. Maurice Zeitlin and Howard Kimeldorf (Greenwich, Conn.: JAI Press, 1984), 4: 141–82.

3. Richard J. Jensen, "The Causes and Cures of Unemployment in the Great Depression," *Journal of Interdisciplinary History* 19, no. 4 (Spring 1989): 553–83; Bernard Sternsher, "Victims of the Great Depression: Self-Blame/Non-Self-Blame, Radicalism, and Pre-1929 Experiences," *Social Science History* 1 (Winter 1977): 137–77; William R. Phillips and Bernard Sternsher, "Victims of the Great Depression: The Question of Blame and First-Person History," in *Hitting Home: The Great Depression in Town and Country*, ed. Bernard Sternsher, rev. ed. (Chicago: I. R. Dee, 1989), 267–84; John Bodnar, *Workers' World: Kinship, Community, and Protest in an Industrial Society, 1900–1940* (Baltimore: Johns Hopkins University Press, 1982), 165–91; George H. Gallup, *The Gallup Poll: Public Opinion, 1935–1971*, vol. 1, *1935–1948* (New York: Random House, 1972), 62–63. McElvaine, "Thunder without Lightning," samples and excerpts many workers' letters to FDR and Eleanor Roosevelt. He interprets them as displaying radical-tending sentiments, but many excerpts suggest a combination of appeals to paternal authority and parochial resentment.

4. Clinton S. Golden and Harold J. Ruttenberg, *The Dynamics of Industrial Democracy* (New York: Harper and Bros., 1942), 111–17; David J. McDonald, *Union Man* (New York: Dutton, 1969), 93–96; steelworker Orville Rice, quoted in Bodnar, *Workers' World*, 150–51.

5. Daniel Nelson, "The CIO at Bay: Labor Militancy and Politics in Akron, 1936–1939," *JAH* 71, no. 3 (Dec. 1984): 571, 582–84; Daniel Nelson, *American Rubber Workers and Organized Labor, 1900–1941* (Princeton: Princeton University Press, 1988), 204–33.

6. Sidney Fine, *Sit-Down: The General Motors Strike of 1936–1937* (Ann Arbor: University of Michigan Press, 1969), 144–46, 168–69, 228–29.

7. Claude E. Hoffman, *Sit-Down in Anderson: UAW Local 663, Anderson, Indiana* (Detroit: Wayne State University Press, 1968), 36–79; John G. Krutchko, *The Birth of a Union Local: The History of UAW Local 674, Norwood, Ohio, 1933–1940* (Ithaca: New York State School of Industrial and Labor Relations, 1972); Peter Friedlander, *The Emergence of a UAW Local, 1936–1939: A Study in Class and Culture* (Pittsburgh: University of Pittsburgh Press, 1975), 33–70, quote, 34; Clayton Fountain, *Union Guy* (New York: Viking Press, 1949), 58–61, 227; Fountain, letter to *Detroit News*, Jan. 17, 1937, quoted in George Douglas Blackwood, "The United Automobile Workers of America, 1935–1941" (Ph.D. dissertation, University of Chicago, 1952), 79; Henry Kraus, *The Many and the Few: A Chronicle of the Dynamic Auto Workers* (Los Angeles: Plantin Press, 1947).

8. Ronald W. Schatz, *The Electrical Workers: A History of Labor at General Electric and Westinghouse, 1923–1960* (Urbana: University of Illinois Press, 1983), 66–76; James A. Hodges, *New Deal Labor Policy and the Southern Cotton Textile Industry, 1933–1941* (Knoxville: University of Tennessee Press, 1986), 147–68.

9. Friedlander, *Emergence of a UAW Local*, 66–70; Ray Boryczka, "Militancy and Factionalism in the United Auto Workers Union, 1937–1941," *Maryland Historian* 8 (Fall 1977): 13–25; Orville Rice, oral history, in Bodnar, *Workers' World*, 143–52; Nelson, *American Rubber Workers*, 263–88; John Bodnar, "Power and Memory in Oral History: Workers and Managers at Studebaker," *JAH* 75, no. 4 (Mar. 1989): 1204–14. See Victor Reuther, *The Brothers Reuther and the Story of the UAW: A Memoir* (Boston: Houghton Mifflin, 1976), 150–82, for an account that both acknowledges the hesitancy of rank-and-file workers and stresses their pro-UAW sentiments.

10. The best accounts of the auto industry's development as related to work processes and labor relations through the first third of the century are Sidney Fine, *The Automobile under the Blue Eagle: Labor, Management, and the Automobile Manufacturing Code* (Ann Arbor: University of Michigan Press, 1963), and Steve Babson, *Building the Union: Skilled Workers and Anglo-Gaelic Immigrants in the Rise of the UAW* (New Brunswick: Rutgers University Press, 1991). See also David Gartman, *Auto Slavery: The Labor Process in the American Automobile Industry, 1897–1950* (New Brunswick: Rutgers University Press, 1986).

11. Fine, *Blue Eagle*; Ronald Edsforth, *Class Conflict and Cultural Consensus: The Making of a*

Mass Consumer Society in Flint, Michigan (New Brunswick: Rutgers University Press, 1987), 79–126; Joyce Shaw Peterson, *American Automobile Workers, 1900–1933* (Albany, N.Y.: SUNY Press, 1987); William E. Chalmers, "Labor in the Automobile Industry" (Ph.D. dissertation, University of Wisconsin, 1932).

12. Edsforth, *Class Conflict and Cultural Consensus*, 79–102; Peterson, *American Automobile Workers*, 46–107.

13. The deterioration of working conditions, the collapse of workers' security, and the growing harshness of industrial life for autoworkers are amply documented in Fine, *Blue Eagle*, 1–43; Peterson, *American Automobile Workers*, 130–48; Reuther, *Brothers Reuther*, 124–42; and Babson, *Working Detroit*, 52–60.

14. There is a splendid account of the large-scale Briggs strike in Peterson, *American Automobile Workers*, 139–49, while Alex Baskin, "The Ford Hunger March – 1932," *LH* 13, no. 3 (Summer 1972): 331–60, highlights a dramatic Detroit-area mass protest. For the surge of union sentiment, see Fine, *Blue Eagle*, 429; Bernstein, *Turbulent Years*, 95; David Land to Adolph Germer, Dec. 10, 1935, AG, box 2.

15. Tracy Doll, quoted in Fine, *Blue Eagle*, 291; Wyndham Mortimer, open letter to Flint autoworkers, Nov. 10, 1936, AG, box 3.

16. There are no reliable membership totals for autoworker federal labor unions in Flint or elsewhere. Some local activists asserted that as many as 20,000 Flint autoworkers had joined such post-NRA unions in the Michigan city (David Land to Adolf Germer, Dec. 10, 1935, AG, box 2).

17. Ibid.

18. Green quoted (July 1935) in Melvyn Dubofsky and Warren Van Tine, *John L. Lewis: A Biography* (New York: Quadrangle, 1977), 215

19. The varieties of auto industry unionism in 1933 are well charted in Bernstein, *Turbulent Years*, 94–98, 502–9; Fine, *Blue Eagle*, 23–25, 155–75, 299–300; Kraus, *Many and Few*, 13–14; and Babson, *Building the Union*, 109–12, 141–42, 167–70. The apprehensions of CIO representatives are a running theme in Adolph Germer's reports from Detroit, Flint, Toledo, and other auto centers. See, e.g., Germer to John Brophy, Dec. 8, 1935, and Matt Smith to Germer, Jan. 13, 1936, AG, box 2.

20. Brophy to Germer, Feb. 13, 1936, AG, box 2. Stanley Vittoz, "The Economic Foundations of Industrial Politics in the United States and the Emerging Structural Theory of the State in Capitalist Society: The Case of New Deal Labor Policy," *Amerikastudien/American Studies* 27 (1982): 365–412, stresses the favorable economic climate. See also Stanley Vittoz, *New Deal Labor Policy and the American Industrial Economy* (Chapel Hill: University of North Carolina Press, 1987), 153–64.

21. Kraus, *Many and Few*, 39–41 (on FDR election), 47–55 (on the new spirit in the plants [quote, 55]); Fine, *Sit-Down*, 115–18.

22. Kraus, *Many and Few*, 42.

23. The classic treatment of the Flint sit-down strike is Fine, *Sit-Down*, while Kraus, *Many and Few*, is a vivid firsthand account that also makes use of documentary material. See also Bernstein, *Turbulent Years*, 519–51.

24. Quote from Dubofsky and Van Tine, *Lewis*, 258.

25. Dubofsky and Van Tine, *Lewis*, 255–71.

26. Telephone conversation between John L. Lewis and Governor Murphy of Michigan, Jan. 9, 1937, 10:45 A.M., UMWA-A (Central Labor Unions, UAW, 1937).

27. Fine, *Sit-Down*; Bernstein, *Turbulent Years*, 549–51; Dubofsky and Van Tine, *Lewis*, 268–70.

28. Bernstein, *Turbulent Years*, 551–54.

29. For accounts of the UAW's post-Flint activism, see Boryczka, "Militancy and Factionalism," and Babson, *Working Detroit*, 80–92.

30. Nelson Lichtenstein, "The Promise of Industrial Democracy and Its Demise" (unpublished paper in Zieger's possession), stresses GM's uncompromising bargaining strategy, while Boryczka, "Militancy and Factionalism," chronicles ill-advised post-Flint initiatives. Germer's observations are contained in letters to Brophy, Oct. 25 and 28, 1937, AG, box 3.

31. Lewis's remarks, report of SWOC-CIO conference, Pittsburgh, Nov. 11, 1936, CIOST, box 59: SWOC, 1937. The observations in this paragraph on the sense of legitimacy that characterized CIO leaders and on the CIO's firm location within the House of Labor rest in part on three splendid essays by David Brody. See "The Emergence of Mass-Production Unionism," in *Workers in Industrial America: Essays on the Twentieth Century Struggle*, by David Brody (New York: Oxford University Press, 1980), 82–119; "The Expansion of the American Labor Movement: Institutional Sources of Stimulus and Restraint," in *Institutions in Modern America*, ed. Stephen E. Ambrose (Baltimore: Johns Hopkins University Press, 1967), 11–36; and "The Origins of Modern Steel Unionism: The SWOC Era," in *Forging a Union of Steel: Philip Murray, SWOC, and the United Steelworkers*, ed. Paul F. Clark, Peter Gottlieb, and Donald Kennedy (Ithaca: ILR Press, 1987), 13–29.

32. A SWOC press release of Nov. 8, 1936, drove home the vast dimensions of FDR's victory and the role of steelworkers in achieving it. In Weirton, W.Va., Roosevelt outpolled Landon by 3 to 1; in Aliquippa, Pa., 2 to 1; in Homestead, over 4 to 1; in Lackawanna, N.Y., 4 to 1; and in Pittsburgh's heavily industrial 17th ward, home of a large Jones and Laughlin plant, almost 7 to 1 (CIOFJLL, part 1, reel 12).

33. The course of SWOC and CIO activities in steel, 1936–37, is treated in Bernstein, *Turbulent Years*, 432–98; Dubofsky and Van Tine, *Lewis*, 272–77; Brody, "Origins of Modern Steel Unionism"; Walter Galenson, *The CIO Challenge to the AFL: A History of the American Labor Movement, 1935–1941* (Cambridge, Mass.: Harvard University Press, 1960), 75–105; and Robert R. R. Brooks, *As Steel Goes, . . . : Unionism in a Basic Industry* (New Haven: Yale University Press, 1940).

34. Minutes, CIO meetings, Washington, D.C., July 2 and Aug. 10, 1936, JBC, box 86; minutes, SWOC meeting, Pittsburgh, Sept. 29, 1936, NIU-CUA, box 33: USWA 1; auditor's report, Oct. 14, 1936, UMWA-A (CIO, 1936).

35. Golden and Ruttenberg, *Dynamics of Industrial Democracy*, 48–51, 110–12; Murray statement, Sept. 29, 1936, CIOFJLL, part 1, reel 12.

36. Dubofsky and Van Tine, *Lewis*, 276–77; Golden and Ruttenberg, *Dynamics of Industrial Democracy*, 112–18; Brody, "Origins of Modern Steel Unionism," 20–21; Judith Stein, "Southern Workers in National Unions: Birmingham Steelworkers, 1936–1951," in *Organized Labor in the Twentieth-Century South*, ed. Robert H. Zieger (Knoxville: University of Tennessee Press, 1991), 188–90. For an inside account of the comradeship and mutuality that characterized much of the labor process in basic steel through the 1920s and 1930s, see Charles Rumford Walker, *Steel: The Diary of a Furnace Worker* (Boston: Atlantic Monthly Press, 1922).

37. Golden and Ruttenberg, *Dynamics of Industrial Democracy*, 110–17; Murray, report to SWOC, Nov. 8, 1936, NIU-CUA, box 33: USWA, 1.

38. Murray, report to SWOC, Nov. 8, 1936, NIU-CUA, box 33: USWA, 1; Benjamin Stolberg, *The Story of the CIO* (New York: Viking, 1938), 88–89.

39. The best accounts of the company union movement in steel are in Bernstein, *Turbulent Years*, 455–68, and Brooks, *As Steel Goes*, 75–109. See also David Brody, "The Rise and Decline of Welfare Capitalism," in Brody, *Workers in Industrial America*, 48–81.

40. Brooks, *As Steel Goes*, 75–109, and the oral histories cited in n. 41 below describe these developments.

41. For Murray's injunctions to organizers with reference to company unions, see Murray memo to SWOC subregional directors, Sept. 11, 1936, Harold Ruttenberg Papers, PSULA, box 3. On the activities within the ERPs, the following oral histories, on file at PSULA, are illumi-

nating: Albert Atallah (Sept. 20, 1967); Elmer Maloy (Nov. 7, 1967); Gene Di Cola (Aug. 1966); John Mullen (Feb. 1966); and George Patterson (Oct. 31, 1967, and Feb. 1–2, 1969). The interviews collected in and relied upon by Staughton and Alice Lynd help to document the ferment in the ERPs but stress a higher degree of spontaneous activism than most participants and observers reported. See Alice Lynd and Staughton Lynd, eds., *Rank and File: Personal Histories by Working-Class Organizers* (Boston: Beacon Press, 1973), esp. 130–48, 165–75; Staughton Lynd, "Guerrilla History in Gary," *Liberation* 14, no. 7 (Oct. 1969), 17–21; and Staughton Lynd, "Personal Histories of the Early CIO," *Radical America* 5, no. 3 (May–June 1971): 49–76. See also David Brody, "Radical Labor History and Rank-and-File Militancy," *LH* 16, no. 1 (Winter 1975): 117–26.

42. Dubofsky and Van Tine, *Lewis*, 280–99; Robert H. Zieger, *John L. Lewis: Labor Leader* (Boston: Twayne, 1988), 46–49, 52–60.

43. The story of the Lewis-Taylor negotiations is told in Bernstein, *Turbulent Years*, 46–48, 470–73, and Dubofsky and Van Tine, *Lewis*, 272–77.

44. The precise role of Murray in the agreement remains unclear. In a recollection soon after the episode, Taylor, who otherwise tended to magnify the one-on-one character of the negotiations, did recall Murray being in on the final stages of the deal in Taylor's New York residence. Lee Pressman, however, in a 1957 oral history account, contrastingly remembered the agreement as being announced rather peremptorily to himself and Murray by Lewis after Lewis's final meeting with Taylor. Even Harold Ruttenberg, SWOC's economist and a staunch Murray loyalist, recalled in a 1989 interview that Murray's only knowledge of the negotiations came from UMW secretary-treasurer Thomas Kennedy, who processed Lewis's expense vouchers and shared what he learned through this indirect means with his long-term friend, Murray. Neither the existing papers of Philip Murray nor those of John L. Lewis nor any of the copious *contemporary* records of various CIO bodies and individuals associated with them shed light on this matter. The general Lewis-Murray relationship is examined in Melvyn Dubofsky, "Labor's Odd Couple: Philip Murray and John L. Lewis," in Clark et al., *Forging a Union of Steel*, 30–44. Pressman's recollections are in Lee Pressman interview, COHC, 80–82, while Ruttenberg's are in an interview with historian Gilbert J. Gall, July 16, 1989 (copy of transcript in Zieger's possession). Taylor's account is contained in Myron Taylor, *Ten Years of Steel: Extension of Remarks to Annual Meeting to Stockholders of the United States Steel Corporation* (Hoboken, N.J.: n.p., 1938).

45. Brody, "Origins of Modern Steel Unionism," 23–24; but see Brooks, *As Steel Goes*, 193–96, for a less sanguine view of U.S. Steel's post-agreement behavior.

46. Golden to Katherine Pollak, June 3, 1937, CIOST, box 59: SWOC, 1937.

47. Bernstein, *Turbulent Years*, 473–77 (Murray is quoted on 473); "Barry Malone" to Clinton Golden, Apr. 18 and May 11, 1937, Golden Papers, PSULA, box 6.

48. The standard account of the Little Steel strikes is Donald G. Sofchalk, "The Little Steel Strike of 1937" (Ph.d. dissertation, Ohio State University, 1961). See also James L. Baughman, "Classes and Company Towns: Legends of the 1937 Little Steel Strike," *Ohio History* 87, no. 2 (Spring 1978): 175–92.

49. Brooks, *As Steel Goes*, 138–39. See also Dubofsky and Van Tine, *Lewis*, 312–14, for an assessment of the distinct roles of Lewis and Murray in the onset of the strike.

50. Baughman, "Classes and Company Towns," 188–91; Sofchalk, "Little Steel Strike," 70–84, 158–61, 208–262; Galenson, *CIO Challenge*, 103–5.

51. The figure of 550 is a low estimate based on the material in Philip Taft and Philip Ross, "American Labor Violence: Its Causes, Character, and Outcome," in *Violence in America: Historical and Comparative Perspectives – A Report Submitted to the National Commission on the Causes and Prevention of Violence*, ed. Hugh Davis Graham and Ted Robert Gurr (New York: Bantam Books, 1970), 281–396. Taft and Ross count over 700 people killed in labor violence from the mid-1870s through the 1960s. About 90 of these were killed after the summer of 1937. Of the

remaining 600+, at least 90 percent died at the hands of employers, their agents, or public authorities protecting employers' property.

52. The story of the newsreel is told in Jerold S. Auerbach, *Labor and Liberty: The La Follette Committee and the New Deal* (Indianapolis: Bobbs-Merrill, 1966), 121–28. The reporter, who published his story in the *St. Louis Post-Dispatch*, July 17, 1937, anonymously, was Paul Y. Anderson. This report is reprinted in Richard Hofstadter and Michael Wallace, eds., *American Violence: A Documentary History* (New York: Alfred A. Knopf, 1970), 179–84. See also Daniel J. Leab, "The Memorial Day Massacre," *Midcontinent American Studies Journal* 8 (Fall 1967): 3–17, and Donald G. Sofchalk, "The Chicago Memorial Day Incident: An Episode of Mass Action," *LH* 6, no. 1 (Winter 1965): 3–43. Lewis's response is in a press release of June 1, 1937, CIOFJLL, part 1, reel 13.

53. On Massillon, see Brooks, *As Steel Goes*, 130–34, 138–44.

54. Bernstein, *Turbulent Years*, 478–96; Brooks, *As Steel Goes*, 130–52; Sofchalk, "Little Steel Strike."

55. Bernstein, *Turbulent Years*, 497–98; Brooks, *As Steel Goes*, 158–62; Brody, "Origins of Modern Steel Unionism," 23–26; summary of SWOC income and expenses as of Nov. 30, 1937, NIU-CUA, box 33: USWA, 1.

56. Brooks, *As Steel Goes*, 145–52, 253–55, has a good account of the importance of the NLRB to the CIO in steel in the aftermath of the Little Steel strike. See also Richard Cortner, *The Wagner Act Cases* (Knoxville: University of Tennessee Press, 1964).

57. These criticisms are outlined in Gilbert J. Gall, "CIO Leaders and the Democratic Alliance: The Case of the Smith Committee and the NLRB," *Labor Studies Journal* 14, no. 2 (Summer 1989): 3–27; Cletus E. Daniel, *The ACLU and the Wagner Act: An Inquiry into the Depression-Era Crisis of American Liberalism*, Cornell Studies in Industrial and Labor Relations, no. 20 (Ithaca: ILR Press, 1980); Brooks, *As Steel Goes*, 143–52; and Christopher L. Tomlins, *The State and the Unions: Labor Relations, Law, and the Organized Labor Movement in America, 1880–1960* (Cambridge: Cambridge University Press, 1985), 132–47. Tomlins and other students of the system of industrial relations that emerged from the New Deal–World War II era have argued that the Wagner Act and related developments in labor law and court decisions have, on the whole, ill served the American working class. See Ronald Schatz, "Into the Twilight Zone: The Law and the American Industrial Relations System since the New Deal," *International Labor and Working Class History* 35 (Fall 1989): 51–60, for synopses and citations.

58. Brooks, *As Steel Goes*; Richard Cortner, *The Jones and Laughlin Case* (New York: Knopf, 1970); Cortner, *Wagner Act Cases*.

Chapter Four

1. Murray speech, CIO conference, Atlantic City, Oct. 12, 1937, KPE, box 17: 15. The precise bases for Murray's claims are not entirely clear; they are cited here to exemplify the ebullience of the CIO's leadership in 1937. For a more restrained assessment of CIO membership, see n. 8 below.

2. Brophy report to CIO executives, Mar. 9, 1937, KPE, box 14: 30; Brophy report to CIO, Oct. 11, 1937, KPE, box 17: 14; Clinton Golden to Katherine Pollak [Ellickson], June 3, 1937, CIOST, box 59: SWOC, 1937; Ellickson notes of Lewis remarks, CIO meeting, Mar. 9, 1937, KPE, box 14: 29; Murray speech, CIO conference, Oct. 11, 1937, KPE, box 17: 15.

3. Ellickson notes on CIO meeting of Mar. 9, 1937, KPE, box 14: 29; Germer to Lewis, Apr. 14, 1937, UMWA-A (CIO, Mar. 1937); Ellickson memo, May 1, 1937, KPE, box 17: 7; Golden to Ellickson, June 3, 1937, CIOST, box 59: SWOC, 1937; Brophy report to CIO executives, Mar. 9, 1937, KPE, box 14: 30.

4. Dubinsky's unease with the drift toward separate status for the CIO is indicated in Jay Lovestone to John Brophy, Mar. 23, 1937, NIU-CUA, box 1937–38: CIO, Brophy. On alternative visions of organizing strategy, see, for example, Mark Naison, "The Southern Tenants Farmers' Union and the C.I.O.," 1968, pamphlet in Zieger's possession (originally published in *Radical America*, Sept.–Oct. 1968). On the problem of expulsion of CIO unions from central labor bodies and the effort to create separate CIO organizations, see "Industrial Councils," 1937–39, ILGWU-LMDC, box 2: 16A; Warren Van Tine, "The CIO Split from the AFL in Columbus [Ohio]" (unpublished paper, ca. 1992, in Zieger's possession); Gary M. Fink, "The Unwanted Conflict: Missouri Labor and the CIO," *Missouri Historical Review* 64 (July 1970): 432–47. Brophy's commitment to standard procedures is indicated in Brophy report, Mar. 9, 1937, KPE, box 14: 30.

5. Katherine Ellickson notes, CIO meeting, Mar. 9, 1937, KPE, box 14: 29; Ellickson, "Notes on Conference with Mr. Howard," Mar. 24, 1937, KPE, box 17: 17; Brophy to Industrial Union Councils, June 14, 1937, KPE, box 17: 1; Katharine Pollak [Ellickson] to Walter Smethurst, June 15, 1937, and Walter Smethurst to A. F. Whitney, Oct. 5, 1937, CIOST, box 58: Railroad Brotherhoods, 1937; C.I.O. Organizers *Bulletin*, May 19, 1937, KPE, box 17: 12.

6. Brophy report to CIO, Oct. 11, 1937, KPE, box 17: 14.

7. Gary Gerstle, *Working-Class Americanism: The Politics of Labor in a Textile City, 1914–1960* (Cambridge: Cambridge University Press, 1989), 103–229; Rick Halpern and Roger Horowitz, "The Austin Orbit: Regional Union Organizing in Meatpacking, 1933–1943" (unpublished paper, ca. 1986–89, in Zieger's possession).

8. CIO membership figures for the 1930s – indeed, throughout its history – were unreliable. The figure of 225,000 LIU members is Brophy's, appearing in his report to the CIO of Oct. 11, 1937, KPE, box 17: 14. The membership total of 3 million for the CIO is my estimate and is based on a variety of claims, reports, per capita tax statements, and similar material appearing in the documents cited in the preceding notes. The "official" estimate of CIO membership claimed in Brophy's statement, cited above, was 3.8 million, but extrapolations from scattered membership figures used by various CIO unions in computing their per capita monthly tax indicate that this figure is high by at least 30 percent. My estimates are that as of October 1937 the CIO had about 1 million members in its "old," original unions (the UMW, the ACWA, and the ILGWU) and an equal number in its "new" unions (the UAW, SWOC, TWOC, and others). Even these figures may be on the high side since SWOC, TWOC, and other new unions often did not collect dues during the early stages of their operations, but they did often count membership cards signed as an indication of membership. See packet of material prepared by J. C. Bell and/or Thomas Kennedy on CIO finances, ca. Oct. 1, 1937, UMWA-A, UMW secretary/treasurer records (CIO, 1937).

9. The expansion of the LIUs is summarized in Brophy report, Oct. 11, 1937, KPE, box 17: 14. Dues levels are indicated in Lewis to Murray, June 7, 1937, NIU-CUA, box 33: USWA, 1. Background material on directly affiliated unions is available from James O. Morris, *Conflict within the AFL: A Study of Craft Versus Industrial Unionism, 1901–1938* (Ithaca: Cornell University Press, 1958), esp. 150–209, and Robert H. Zieger, *Madison's Battery Workers: A History of Federal Labor Union 19587* (Ithaca: New York School of Industrial and Labor Relations, 1977), esp. 33–35, 83–87.

10. Ellickson memo re federal labor union finances, Feb. 5, 1936, KPE, box 15: 15; "A.F.L. Is Hostile to Industrial Unions," Dec. 3, 1936, KPE, box 15: 1; "Rights of Federal Locals," Mar. 22, 1937, KPE, box 18: 8.

11. Ellickson memo to Brophy, "Basic Matters of Policy to Be Decided," Apr. 16, 1937, KPE, box 17: 17.

12. CIO Organizers *Bulletin*, May 19, 1937, KPE, box 17: 12; Brophy report, Oct. 11, 1937, KPE, box 17: 14. Six weeks later the number of IUCs had grown to 116 ("List of Industrial Union

Councils," Nov. 22, 1937, KPE, box 17: 5). For accounts of the early formation of IUCs, see Van Tine, "CIO Split," and Darryl Holter, "Sources of CIO Success: The New Deal Years in Milwaukee," *LH* 29, no. 2 (Spring 1988): 199–224.

13. Clinton Golden to John Brophy, July 17, 1937, NIU-CUA, box 33: USWA, 1; Richard Francis, Washington State CIO director, to John L. Lewis, ca. Jan. 1, 1938, UMWA-A; Murray speech, CIO conference, Oct. 12, 1937, KPE, box 17: 15.

14. The CIO Washington staff's reliance on AFL precedents in arranging the new body's affairs is revealed throughout the papers of Katherine Pollak Ellickson, who prepared the action drafts of most of the documents describing the CIO's structural, procedural, and jurisdictional concerns. See, for example, the following items in KPE: Ellickson memo, "Suggestions by Hugh Thompson on Local Union Set-Ups," Aug. 6, 1937 (box 18: 11); Ellickson to Brophy, Oct. 9, 1937 (box 17: 1); Ellickson, handwritten notes re state federations and state IUCs, ca. Spring 1937 (box 17: 2). Also, see McDonald's elaborate proposal, May 17, 1937, UMWA-A (CIO Organizing Structure), and Brophy "Notes for CIO Speakers," in Brophy to Lewis, Aug. 26, 1937, UMWA-A (CIO, 1937, General Office). For an astute assessment of the importance of regular procedures and adherence to past precedents in the early CIO, see Lorin Lee Cary, "Institutionalized Conservatism in the Early C.I.O.: Adolph Germer, a Case Study," *LH* 13, no. 4 (Fall 1972): 475–504.

15. See, for example, Len De Caux, *Labor Radical: From the Wobblies to CIO, a Personal History* (Boston: Beacon Press, 1970), 236–44, who sharply distinguishes the spontaneous and democratic militancy of industrial workers and their rank-and-file spokesmen from the "swivel-chair tribe" that administered the CIO and, in his view, soon shaped it into a variant of business unionism.

16. Report of Richard Francis, Washington State CIO director, ca. Jan. 1, 1938; Harry Bridges to John L. Lewis, Dec. 29, 1937; Walter Smethurst to John L. Lewis, weekly memorandum, Sept. 22, 1937 (CIO, 1937, General Office), all in UMWA-A.

17. Basic sources for the development of West Coast waterfront and marine unionism in the 1930s and its relationship to the CIO include Charles P. Larrowe, *Harry Bridges: The Rise and Fall of Radical Labor in the United States*, rev. ed. (New York: Lawrence Hill, 1977); Howard Kimeldorf, *Reds or Rackets?: The Making of Radical and Conservative Unions on the Waterfront* (Berkeley: University of California Press, 1988), 80–126; and Bruce Nelson, *Workers on the Waterfront: Seamen, Longshoremen, and Unionism in the 1930s* (Urbana: University of Illinois Press, 1988), 127–273. Also see Irving Bernstein, *Turbulent Years: A History of the American Worker, 1933–1941* (Boston: Houghton Mifflin, 1969), 252–98, 572–89.

18. The intricacies of craft demarcations and ideological stances that characterized union development on the West Coast are best followed in Bernstein, *Turbulent Years*, 572–89. Moreover, as Bernstein relates, developments on the Atlantic and Gulf Coast waterfronts both paralleled and interacted with those in the West, making the whole marine and waterfront scene one that even knowledgeable observers often despaired of untangling (*New Yorker* columnist Howard Brubaker, quoted in Bernstein, *Turbulent Years*, 588–89).

19. Louis Goldblatt and Roger Lapham, respectively, quoted in Nelson, *Workers on the Waterfront*, 221, 220. See also Harvey Schwartz, *The March Inland: Origins of the ILWU Warehouse Division, 1934–1938* (Los Angeles: UCLA Institute of Industrial and Labor Relations, 1978).

20. Recent evidence indicates that Bridges was in fact a member of the Communist Party, although efforts on the part of the U.S. government in the 1930s and 1940s to document his membership failed in a series of protracted court proceedings. See Harvey Klehr and John Haynes, "The Comintern's Open Secrets," *American Spectator*, Dec. 1992, 34–35.

21. See Bernard Matthew Mergen, "A History of the Industrial Union of Marine and Shipbuilding Workers of America, 1933–1951" (Ph.D. dissertation, University of Pennsylvania, 1968), 226–34. Bridges's disdain for the Shipbuilding Workers' Union is expressed, for example, in Bridges to Lewis, Sept. 4, 1936, ILWUPSF (ILWU History: . . . UMW), and Bridges to John

Brophy, Mar. 30, 1937, ILWUPSF (ILWU History: CIO). For the Marine and Shipbuilding Workers' furious dissent, see Philip Van Gelder to John Brophy, Mar. 25, 1937, and Van Gelder and John Green to Lewis, May 7, 1937, both in NIU-CUA: IUMSWA; Van Gelder to Lewis, May 7, 1937, and Van Gelder to Benjamin Carwardine, July 12, 1937, IUMSWPMD, series I, subseries 2, box 1: CIO National Office, May–June and July, 1937. Nelson, *Workers on the Waterfront*, 228–37, discusses Lundeberg's role.

22. See, e.g., I. Lutsky, manager, Los Angeles Joint Board, ILGWU, to David Dubinsky, July 19, 1937, ILGWU-LMDC, box 14: 5C.

23. For the CIO officials' tilt toward Bridges and Bridges's affiliation with the CIO in the summer of 1937, see Lewis to Bridges, Sept. 14, 1936, CIOFJLL, part 1, reel 19 (ILA, 1936); Bridges statement, May 29, 1937, CIOFJLL, part 1, reel 19 (ILWU); Mervyn Rathbone to Harry Bridges, Dec. 3, 1937, with draft of Rathbone letter to ILWU locals, Nov. 29, 1937, ILWUPSF (ILWU History: Trade Union Relations, CIO Maritime Committee); Bridges to Lewis, Dec. 29, 1937, UMWA-A; and Nelson, *Workers on the Waterfront*, 228–39. In August 1937, Bridges's union received a CIO charter as the ILWU, thus formalizing the West Coast locals' rupture with the ILA.

24. On Communists in the early CIO, see John Brophy interviews, May 15, 19, 23, 1955, COHC, 671–72, 773–77, 798–806; Harvey A. Levenstein, *Communism, Anticommunism, and the CIO* (Westport, Conn.: Greenwood Press, 1981), 37–38; and Bert Cochran, *Labor and Communism: The Conflict That Shaped American Unions* (Princeton: Princeton University Press, 1977), 82–102. Part of the deal that brought Bridges and the ILA/ILWU into the CIO included CIO support for an ILWU effort to supplant the ILA in the Atlantic and Gulf ports. The savage conflict between Bridges's men and the brutal regime of ILA president Joseph Ryan, who enjoyed the full support of the AFL, is outlined in Kimeldorf, *Reds or Rackets?*, 123–25; Al Lannon, "General Longshore Report," week of Sept. 13, 1937, and Al Lannon, "Some Points on Policy," ca. Oct. 1, 1937, CIOFJLL, part 1, reel 19 (ILA-ILWU); and Felix Siren to John L. Lewis, June 28, 1938, UMWA-A.

25. On the distinctive political role of the South, both in Congress and more generally, in the shaping of the modern American welfare state that emerged in the 1930s, see, e.g., Lee J. Alston and Joseph P. Ferrie, "Resisting the Welfare State: Southern Opposition to the Farm Security Administration," in *Emergence of the Modern Political Economy*, ed. Robert Higgs (*Research in Economic History: A Research Annual*, supp. 4; Greenwich, Conn.: JAI Press, 1985): 83–120; Roger Biles, "The Urban South in the Great Depression," *Journal of Southern History* 56, no. 1 (Feb. 1990): 71–100; and the essays in *The Politics of Social Policy in the United States*, ed. Margaret Weir, Ann Shola Orloff, and Theda Skocpol (Princeton: Princeton University Press, 1988), especially those by Jill Quadagno ("From Old-Age Assistance to Supplemental Security Income: The Political Economy of Relief in the South, 1935–1972," 235–63) and Kenneth Finegold ("Agriculture and the Politics of U.S. Social Provision: Social Insurance and Food Stamps," 199–234).

26. F. Ray Marshall, *Labor in the South* (Cambridge, Mass.: Harvard University Press, 1967), 20–133; Michael K. Honey, *Southern Labor and Black Civil Rights: Organizing Memphis Workers* (Urbana: University of Illinois Press, 1993), 13–64. The best treatment of the 1934 textile strike is James A. Hodges, *New Deal Labor Policy and the Southern Cotton Textile Industry, 1933–1941* (Knoxville: University of Tennessee Press, 1986), 43–140. The classic account of the Piedmont rebellion of 1929–31 is Tom Tippett, *When Southern Labor Stirs* (New York: Jonathan Cape and Harrison Smith, 1931). See also Irving Bernstein, *The Lean Years: A History of the American Worker, 1920–1933* (Boston: Houghton Mifflin, 1960), 1–43, and Jacquelyn Dowd Hall, James Leloudis, Robert Korstad, Mary Murphy, Lu Ann Jones, and Christopher B. Daly, *Like a Family: The Making of a Southern Cotton Mill World* (Chapel Hill: University of North Carolina Press, 1987), 328–55.

27. Hodges, *New Deal Labor Policy*, 148–53; Paul David Richards, "The History of the Textile Workers Union of America, CIO, in the South, 1937 to 1945" (Ph.D. dissertation, University of Wisconsin, 1978), 37–75.

28. On racial patterns in the southern mills, see David L. Carlton, *Mill and Town in South Carolina, 1880–1920* (Baton Rouge: Louisiana State University Press, 1982); Mary Frederickson, "Four Decades of Change: Black Workers in Southern Textiles, 1941–1981," in *Workers' Struggles, Past and Present: A "Radical America" Reader*, ed. James Green (Philadelphia: Temple University Press, 1983), 62–82; and I. A. Newby, *Plain Folk in the New South: Social Change and Cultural Persistence, 1880–1915* (Baton Rouge: Louisiana State University Press, 1989), 462–89.

29. The literature on mill village life is surveyed in Robert H. Zieger, "From Primordial Folk to Redundant Workers: Southern Textile Workers and Social Observers," in *Cultural Perspectives on the American South*, ed. Charles Reagan Wilson (forthcoming). Recent scholarship has stressed positive aspects of mill village life. See, e.g., Hall et al., *Like a Family*, and Newby, *Plain Folk*, with the latter providing the more clearheaded account. On labor protest, see Newby, *Plain Folk*, 519–67, and Hodges, *New Deal Labor Policy*, 104–18.

30. The AFL's and the United Textile Workers' role among textile workers is capably discussed in George Sinclair Mitchell, *Textile Unionism and the South* (Chapel Hill: University of North Carolina Press, 1931), and Marshall, *Labor in the South*, 101–33. See also Robert Sidney Smith, *Mill on the Dan: A History of Dan River Mills, 1882–1950* (Durham: Duke University Press, 1960), 51–53, 294–324. The quote is from Bernstein, *Turbulent Years*, 617.

31. Bernstein, *Turbulent Years*, 616–19.

32. Ibid., 616–17.

33. Steven Fraser, *Labor Will Rule: Sidney Hillman and the Rise of American Labor* (New York: Free Press, 1991), 373–99.

34. Richards, "History of the Textile Workers Union," 42–64; Hodges, *New Deal Labor Policy*, 148–51.

35. Hodges, *New Deal Labor Policy*, 150–51; Bernstein, *Turbulent Years*, 617; Richards, "History of the Textile Workers Union," 42–46; John A. Salmond, *Miss Lucy of the CIO: The Life and Times of Lucy Randolph Mason, 1882–1959* (Athens: University of Georgia Press, 1988), 75–100.

36. Lucy Randolph Mason to Jacob Potofsky, Sept. 17, 1937, ACWA-LMDC, box 220: 9; Hodges, *New Deal Labor Policy*, 154–66, quote at 154.

37. Paul Christopher to G. W. Smith, Apr. 9, 1937, and TWOC Weekly Letter, May 1, 1937, PRC, box 7: 1935–37; TWOC Weekly Letters, Apr. 1–Sept. 11, 1937, ILGWU-LMDC, box 169: 2; Paul Christopher to Francis Gorman, Dec. 18, 1937, PRC, box 44: Gorman; Solomon Barkin to Ralph Hetzel, Dec. 31, 1937, TWUA, installment 3, box 43: John L. Lewis-1; Hodges, *New Deal Labor Policy*, 163.

38. Quoted in Hodges, *New Deal Labor Policy*, 154.

39. Mason to Kathryn Lewis, June 25, 1938, CIOFJLL, part 1, reel 15 (TWOC); Hillman quoted in Hodges, *New Deal Labor Policy*, 162.

40. For this perspective on southern organizing, see William Edward Regensburger, "'Ground into Our Blood': The Origins of Working Class Consciousness and Organization in Durably Unionized Southern Industries, 1930–1946" (Ph.D. dissertation, UCLA, 1987), 17, 57–62, 71–76, 95–86, 94, 96, 113–14, 196.

41. "The CIO in the South," *CIO News*, July 9, 1938.

42. Luigi Antonini, "Mr. Lewis Drops In," *Justice*, Jan. 15, 1937, clipping in UMWA-A (CIO-ILG, 1937).

43. Ronald W. Schatz, *The Electrical Workers: A History of Labor at General Electric and Westinghouse, 1923–1960* (Urbana: University of Illinois Press, 1983), 53–79, quote at 66; Bernstein, *Turbulent Years*, 603–15; James B. Carey to John L. Lewis, June 22, 1936, and J. Behman to

Lewis, July 23, 1936, CIOFJLL, part 1, reel 4 (UE-1936); Julius Emspak interview, July 22, 1959, COHC, 159–223; James B. Carey interview, July 26, 1956, COHC, 132–47; James J. Matles and James Higgins, *Them and Us: Struggles of a Rank-and-File Union* (Boston: Beacon Press, 1975), 30–53. The death toll in the South is indicated in George Brown Tindall, *The Emergence of the New South, 1913–1945* (Baton Rouge: Louisiana State University Press, 1967), 529–30.

44. James R. Barrett, *Work and Community in the Jungle: Chicago's Packinghouse Workers, 1894–1922* (Urbana: University of Illinois Press, 1987); David Brody, *The Butcher Workmen: A Study of Unionization* (Cambridge, Mass.: Harvard University Press, 1964), 34–105; Lizabeth Cohen, *Making a New Deal: Industrial Workers in Chicago, 1919–1939* (Cambridge: Cambridge University Press, 1990), 43–46; Rick Halpern, *Down on the Killing Floor: Black and White Workers in Chicago's Packinghouses, 1904 to 1954* (University of Illinois Press, forthcoming).

45. Cohen, *Making a New Deal*, 296–97; Paul Street, "Breaking up Old Hatreds and Breaking through the Fear: The Emergence of the Packinghouse Workers Organizing Committee in Chicago, 1933–1940," *Studies in History and Politics* 5 (1986): 63–82; St. Clair Drake and Horace R. Cayton, *Black Metropolis: A Study of Negro Life in a Northern City* (New York: Harcourt, Brace, 1945), 302–9.

46. Street, "Breaking up Old Hatreds," 65–66; Van A. Bittner to John L. Lewis, Oct. 18, 1937, and Lewis response, Oct. 21, 1937, CIOFJLL, part 1, reel 13 (PWOC). Initial CIO hesitation to become involved in meatpacking is indicated in Katherine Pollak Ellickson, "Notes on Conference with Mr. [Charles] Howard," Mar. 24, 1937, KPE, box 17: 17, and Ellickson file memos of May 3 and 18, 1937, KPE, box 18: 14.

47. Joshua Freeman, *In Transit: The Transport Workers Union in New York City, 1933–1966* (New York: Oxford University Press, 1989); Jerry Lembcke and William M. Tattam, *One Union in Wood: A Political History of the International Woodworkers of America* (New York: International Publishers, 1984); Vicki L. Ruiz, *Cannery Women, Cannery Lives: Mexican Women, Unionization, and the California Food Processing Industry, 1930–1950* (Albuquerque: University of New Mexico Press, 1987); Cletus E. Daniel, *Bitter Harvest: A History of California Farmworkers, 1870–1941* (Ithaca: Cornell University Press, 1981), 276–81; Vernon H. Jensen, *Nonferrous Metals Industry Unionism, 1932–1954: A Story of Leadership Controversy*, Cornell Studies in Industrial and Labor Relations, vol. 5 (Ithaca: Cornell University Press, 1954), 41–42; Horace Huntley, "Iron Ore Miners and Mine, Mill in Alabama, 1932–1952" (Ph.D. dissertation, University of Pittsburgh, 1976), 48–96; Sharon Hartman Strom, "Challenging 'Woman's Place': Feminism, the Left, and Industrial Unionism in the 1930s," *Feminist Studies* 9, no. 2 (Summer 1983): 359–86; Sharon Hartman Strom, "'We're No Kitty Foyles': Organizing Office Workers for the Congress of Industrial Organizations, 1937–1950," in *Women, Work, and Protest: A Century of U.S. Women's Labor History*, ed. Ruth Milkman (Boston: Routledge and Kegan Paul, 1985), 206–34; Cohen, *Making a New Deal*, 298–301; James Nelson, *The Mine Workers' District 50: The Story of the Gas, Coke, and Chemical Workers of Massachusetts and Their Growth into a National Union* (New York: Exposition Press, 1955); Robert Ozanne, *A Century of Labor-Management Relations at McCormick and International Harvester* (Madison: University of Wisconsin Press, 1967), 195–99.

48. Carey interview, July 27, 1956, COHC, 135–36; Emspak interview, Aug. 15, 1959, COHC, 159–62; Freeman, *In Transit*, 102–3, quote at 103.

49. On meatpacking, see Street, "Breaking up Old Hatreds"; Rick Halpern, "Interracial Unionism in the Southwest: Fort Worth's Packinghouse Workers, 1937–1954," in *Organized Labor in the Twentieth-Century South*, ed. Robert H. Zieger (Knoxville: University of Tennessee Press, 1991), 158–64; and Roger Horowitz, "'It Is Harder to Struggle Than to Surrender': The Rank and File Unionism of the United Packinghouse Workers of America, 1933–1948," *Studies in History and Politics* 5 (1986): 85–86. On the establishment of white collar, agricultural, woodworking, and government employees' unions, see CIO Organizers *Bulletin*, June 24 and July 22, 1937, ILGWU-LMDC, box 16: 5, and Jerrell H. Shofner, "Communists, Klansmen, and the CIO

in the Florida Citrus Industry," *Florida Historical Quarterly* 71, no. 3 (Jan. 1993): 300–309. As of October 1, 1937, the CIO had advanced the new federal workers' affiliate $23,000, its state and local government employees' counterpart $10,000, and the Agricultural, Cannery, and Packing Workers $9,000 (packet on CIO finances as of Oct. 1, 1937, UMWA-A, secretary-treasurers' office [CIO, 1937]). See also list of financial dealings with each affiliate, Sept. 30, 1940, CIOST, box 71: Comptroller's Department, 1941.

50. Walter Smethurst to Van Bittner, Nov. 5, 1937, NIU-CUA, box 30; Brophy remarks, "Digest of Proceedings . . . ," Apr. 12–13, 1938, UMWA-A (CIO conference, Washington, Apr. 1938).

51. There is an able summary of the partial nature of the CIO's 1937 breakthroughs in Nelson N. Lichtenstein, *Labor's War at Home: The CIO in World War II* (Cambridge: Cambridge University Press, 1982), 9–25. See Gerald A. Rose, "The Westwood Lumber Strike," *LH* 13, no. 2 (Spring 1972): 171–99, and Robert H. Zieger, *Rebuilding the Pulp and Paper Workers' Union, 1933–1941* (Knoxville: University of Tennessee Press, 1984), 180–90, for examples of successful AFL counterattack.

52. I. Lutsky to Dubinsky, Aug. 8, 1938, ILGWU-LMDC, box 14: 5C; Walter Smethurst to Lewis, Brophy, Pressman, and others, Nov. 17, 1937, UMWA-A (CIO, 1937, General Office). On the TWU, see Freeman, *In Transit*, 44–53, 128–34. On the UE, see Levenstein, *Communism, Anticommunism, and the CIO*, 60–63. On the general topic, see Harvey Klehr, *The Heyday of American Communism: The Depression Decade* (New York: Basic Books, 1984), 223–51.

53. There are many letters from Lovestone to Lewis's speechwriter, confidant, and advisor W. Jett Lauck, 1937 and 1938, in the W. Jett Lauck Papers, Alderman Library, University of Virginia, Charlottesville, Va., box 40: Lovestone. See also Jay Lovestone to John Brophy, Mar. 23 and Apr. 28, 1937, John Brophy Papers, CUA, box 1937–38: CIO-Brophy. Stolberg's articles appeared, for example, in the *Washington Daily News* and the *New York World Telegram*, ca. Jan. 10–22, 1938, and were widely discussed in labor circles. His criticism of Brophy appears in the January 10 article, and his characterization of Communist machinations is in the January 12 piece. A full file of the Stolberg articles appears in the Lauck papers, box 209: Stolberg Articles. They were quickly gathered together into a book, Benjamin Stolberg, *The Story of the CIO* (New York: Viking, 1938). On Stolberg's life, see his obituary in the *New York Herald Tribune*, Jan. 23, 1951, a copy of which, with intriguing reflections on Stolberg's interviewing techniques, appears in the Brophy papers, CUA, box 1951: P-W.

54. Lewis's attitudes toward and relationships with Communists are ably summarized in Melvyn Dubofsky and Warren Van Tine, *John L. Lewis: A Biography* (New York: Quadrangle, 1977), 288–89, and Bernstein, *Turbulent Years*, 782–83. Lewis's bird dog quip is based on widely reported hearsay and, even if not authoritatively documentable, is reflective of his attitude. For the vigor and effectiveness of Communists in CIO unions, see Judith Stepan-Norris and Maurice Zeitlin, "'Who Gets the Bird?' or, How the Communists Won Power and Trust in America's Unions: The Relative Autonomy of Intraclass Political Struggles," *American Sociological Review* 54, no. 4 (Aug. 1989): 503–23.

55. Sumner M. Rosen, "The CIO Era, 1935–1955," in *The Negro and the American Labor Movement*, ed. Julius Jacobson (Garden City: Anchor Books, 1968), 188–96; F. Ray Marshall, *The Negro and Organized Labor* (New York: John Wiley and Sons, 1965), 34–41; Herbert G. Gutman, "The Negro and the United Mine Workers of America," in Jacobson, *The Negro and the American Labor Movement*, 49–127; Herbert Hill, "Myth-Making as Labor History: Herbert Gutman and the United Mine Workers of America," *International Journal of Politics, Culture, and Society* 2, no. 2 (Winter 1988): 132–200; Sterling D. Spero and Abram L. Harris, *The Black Worker: The Negro and the Labor Movement* (New York: Columbia University Press, 1931), 352–82; Ronald L. Lewis, *Black Coal Miners in America: Race, Class, and Community Conflict, 1780–1980* (Lexing-

ton: University Press of Kentucky, 1987), 173–76; Walter Licht and Hal Seth Barron, "Labor's Men: A Collective Biography of Union Officialdom during the New Deal Years," *LH* 19, no. 4 (Fall 1978): 532–45.

56. There is no authoritative survey of the industrial employment of blacks in the 1930s. The figures cited here are from Spero and Harris, *Black Worker*; Marshall, *The Negro and Organized Labor*, 35; and Judith Stein, "Blacks and the Steelworkers Organizing Committee" (paper presented at the North American Labor History Conference, Detroit, Oct. 1985, in Zieger's possession); August Meier and Elliott Rudwick, *Black Detroit and the Rise of the UAW* (New York: Oxford University Press, 1979), 5–9; and Street, "Breaking up Old Hatreds," 69–74.

57. Lewis, *Black Coal Miners*, 173–76; Drake and Cayton, *Black Metropolis*, 313–15; Meier and Rudwick, *Black Detroit*, 25–28; Van A. Bittner, *Industrial Unionization of Steel and the Negro Worker*, pamphlet, ca. June 1936, CIOFJLL, part 1, reel 12 (SWOC).

58. Huntley, "Iron Ore Miners," 48–83; Lewis, *Black Coal Miners*, 192; Street, "Breaking up Old Hatreds," 67.

59. Horace R. Cayton and George S. Mitchell, *Black Workers and the New Unions* (Chapel Hill: University of North Carolina Press, 1939), 104–78, quote at 169.

60. Cayton and Mitchell, *Black Workers and the New Unions*, 199–216, quote at 212; mimeo statement by Philip Murray for CIO conference, Nov. 8, 1936, KPE, box 14: 26.

61. Meier and Rudwick, *Black Detroit*, 8–16.

62. Lloyd N. Bailer, "Negro Labor in the Automobile Industry" (Ph.D. dissertation, University of Michigan, 1943), 191–203; Meier and Rudwick, *Black Detroit*, 34–61. The quote by Homer Martin is in *Black Detroit* at 38, and that from the Pittsburgh *Courier* (Mar. 27, 1937) is on the same page.

63. Meier and Rudwick, *Black Detroit*, 34–107.

64. Ibid., 78–82; Stein, "Blacks and the Steelworkers Organizing Committee"; Nancy Weiss, *Farewell to the Party of Lincoln: Black Politics in the Age of FDR* (Princeton: Princeton University Press, 1983), 180–235, esp. 203; John B. Kirby, *Black Americans in the Roosevelt Era: Liberalism and Race* (Knoxville: University of Tennessee Press, 1980), 152–84, esp. 167. For the greater emphasis on the part of some radical laborites on the distinctive role of the black working class, see Regensburger, "'Ground into Our Blood,'" 18–25, 48, 101, 107, 113–16, 125–26, 196.

65. U.S. Department of Commerce, Bureau of the Census, *Historical Statistics of the United States, 1789–1945* (Washington, D.C.: Government Printing Office, 1949), 63; Alice Kessler-Harris, *Out to Work: A History of Wage-Earning Women in the United States* (New York: Oxford University Press, 1982), 266–69; Ruth Milkman, *Gender at Work: The Dynamics of Job Segregation by Sex during World War II* (Urbana: University of Illinois Press, 1987), table, 13; Schatz, *Electrical Workers*, 30–33; Strom, "'We're No Kitty Foyles,'" 206–34; Ruiz, *Cannery Women*.

66. Henry Kraus, *The Many and the Few: A Chronicle of the Dynamic Auto Workers* (Los Angeles: Plantin Press, 1947), 18–23; Sidney Fine, *Sit-Down: The General Motors Strike of 1936–1937* (Ann Arbor: University of Michigan Press, 1969), 201; John Bodnar, *Workers' World: Kinship, Community, and Protest in an Industrial Society, 1900–1940* (Baltimore: Johns Hopkins University Press, 1982), 165–91; Van Bittner, *The Drive to Organize Steel and Its Significance to Our Women*, pamphlet, ca. Aug. 1936, CIOFJLL, part 1, reel 12; organizers' reports, Jan. 11, 1937, United Steelworkers of America District 31 Papers, Chicago Historical Society, series I, box 124: SWOC Field Workers Staff Meetings.

67. Martha May, "Bread before Roses: American Workingmen, Labor Unions, and the Family Wage," in Milkman, *Women, Work, and Protest*; Milkman, *Gender at Work*, 40; UAW Local 2 vice-president Mike Mannini, quoted in Kessler-Harris, *Out to Work*, 269.

68. Mary Voltz quoted in Milkman, *Gender at Work*, 35; Patricia Cooper, "The Faces of Gender: Sex Segregation and Work Relations at Philco, 1928–1938," in *Work Engendered: Toward a*

New History of American Labor, ed. Ava Baron (Ithaca: Cornell University Press, 1991), 320–50; Rose Pesotta to David Dubinsky, Feb. 20, 1941, quoted in Ann Schofield, introduction to Rose Pesotta, *Bread upon the Waters* (Ithaca: ILR Press, 1987), ix.

69. David J. McDonald, *Union Man* (New York: Dutton, 1969), 30–45; Katherine Pollak Ellickson interview, Dec. 15, 1974 (with Philip Mason), ALUAWSU, 15, 47–48, 51, 60–61; Katherine Pollak Ellickson interview, Jan. 10, 1976 (with Dennis East), ALUAWSU, 8–10. There were some intriguing exceptions to the UMW rules about women. For example, Lewis respected and consulted frequently with Josephine Roche, who had inherited Colorado coal properties and whose recommendation was apparently influential in his decision to engage Lee Pressman as the CIO's legal counsel. In addition, Lewis's daughter Kathryn, who was twenty-four years old when the CIO was founded, was increasingly important to him as a kind of informal administrative assistant, personnel manager, and gatekeeper. On Roche, see Dubofsky and Van Tine, *Lewis*, 329, 362, and W. Jett Lauck, diary entries for Jan. 8, 14, and 16, 1936, Lauck papers, box 449. On Kathryn Lewis's role, see Dubofsky and Van Tine, *Lewis*, 293–95, 308–9; "Kathryn Lewis," in *Biographical Dictionary of American Labor*, ed. Gary Fink, 2d ed. (Westport, Conn.: Greenwood Press, 1984), 355; and Ellickson interview, Dec. 15, 1974, ALUAWSU, 51–61.

70. The post-Flint sit-down wave in Detroit is described in Carlos A. Schwantes, "'We've Got 'em on the Run, Brothers': The 1937 Non-Automotive Sit Down Strikes in Detroit," *Michigan History* 58 (Fall 1972): 179–99. For the experiences of clerical workers, see Strom, "'We're No Kitty Foyles,'" 218–20, while the role of women in early electrical industry organizing and in the UAW is discussed in Milkman, *Gender at Work*, 34–40, and Ruth Meyerowitz, "Organizing the United Automobile Workers: Women Workers at the Ternstedt-General Motors Parts Plant," in Milkman, *Women, Work and Protest*, 235–58. For agricultural and cannery workers, see Ruiz, *Cannery Women*, 69–85. The quote is from Milkman, *Gender at Work*, 40.

71. Strom, "Challenging 'Woman's Place,'" stresses the lack of a feminist agenda even in left-wing CIO unions, while Lizabeth Cohen, "Reflections on the Making of *Making a New Deal*," *LH* 32, no. 4 (Fall 1991): 592–94, notes that in her study of working-class *mentalité* in Chicago, "gender never became as central a category of analysis . . . [as] class, race and ethnicity" because she could find little evidence that working people there, male or female, dissented from the labor movement's notions of gender. For a discussion of the possibilities of a more gender-conscious approach in one important CIO area, see Elizabeth Faue, *Community of Suffering and Struggle: Women, Men, and the Labor Movement in Minneapolis, 1915–1945* (Chapel Hill: University of North Carolina Press, 1991), 100–146.

72. Record of CIO Washington conference, Apr. 12–13, 1938, UMWA-A (CIO: CIO conference, Washington); Lee Pressman, draft, and Call for Constitutional Convention, both Oct. 5, 1938, UMWA-A (CIO, 1st Constitutional Convention, 1938).

Chapter Five

1. *New York Times*, Nov. 13, 14, 1938; Richard D. Ketchum, *The Borrowed Years, 1938–1941: America on the Way to War* (New York: Random House, 1989), 144–47; Melvyn Dubofsky and Warren Van Tine, *John L. Lewis: A Biography* (New York: Quadrangle, 1977), 307–9; CIOPROC, 1938.

2. James B. Carey interview, Aug. 2, 1957, COHC, 192–93. The constitution appears in CIOPROC, 1938, 126–54.

3. On the institutional character of the AFL, see Lewis L. Lorwin, *The American Federation of Labor: History, Policies, and Prospects* (Washington, D.C.: Brookings Institution, 1933); Philip A. Taft, *The A.F. of L. in the Time of Gompers* (New York: Harper and Bros., 1957); and Philip A. Taft, *The A. F. of L. from the Death of Gompers to the Merger* (New York: Harper and Bros., 1959).

For patterns of institutional continuity between the AFL and the CIO, see David Brody, "The Expansion of the American Labor Movement: Institutional Sources of Stimulus and Restraint," in *Institutions in Modern America*, ed. Stephen E. Ambrose (Baltimore: Johns Hopkins University Press, 1967), 11–36.

4. John Brophy interviews, May 16, 1955, COHC, 662–63, and May 23, 1955, COHC, 814–15; Katherine Pollak Ellickson interview, Dec. 15, 1974, ALUAWSU, 18–19, 51, 61–62. There is much evidence of the quotidian expansion of the roles of Bell, Smethurst, Dennie Lewis, and Kathryn Lewis in UMWA-A, CIOFJLL, and CIOST. On Pressman's role, see Ellickson interview, 52–53, 61–62; Brophy interviews, May 16, 1955, 665–78, and May 18, 1955, 773–74, 806. Pressman's interview, Mar. 19, 1957, COHC, 198–99, claims that when Lewis suffered a heart attack in 1941, he and Murray were the only nonfamily members permitted to see him. "I . . . will always be convinced that you are the leader not merely of labor but of the common people of this nation," Pressman told Lewis in October 1940 (Pressman to Lewis, Oct. 26, 1940, UMWA-A (1940–42, General Office).

5. John L. Lewis to Eli Oliver, executive vice-president, Labor's Non-Partisan League, July 23, 1938, ACWA-LMDC, box 77: 2; Gardner Jackson interview, Nov. 6, 1954, COHC, 720–22, 727–28, 749; "Labor's Non-Partisan League: Its Origins and Growth," [1939], UMWA-A (CIO miscellaneous, 1935–39: LNPL, 1939). Lewis's unfocused political ambitions and his lack of consultation with his fellow CIO officers are indicated in Lee Pressman interview, COCH, 104–7.

6. Woll report on 1939 CIO convention in Woll to Green, Nov. 1, 1939, AFL Papers, SHSW, series 11C, box 24: Correspondence, 1939–41; Benjamin Stolberg, "Lewis Fights Labor Peace," *American Mercury*, Mar. 1940, 347.

7. Lewis remarks, Apr. 13, 1938, CIO conference, Washington, D.C., Apr. 12–13, UMWA-A (CIO conference, 1938).

8. In 1941 Carey was defeated for the UE presidency but retained his CIO position, the salary for which the CIO now paid.

9. Carey interview, May 16, 1957, COHC, 192, 198–99; Brophy interviews, May 16, 1955, COHC, 662–63, and May 18, 1955, COHC, 765–68.

10. CIOEB-WSU, June 15, 1939, 306.

11. Frey to William Green, Nov. 29, 1938, AFL Papers, SHSW, series 11C, box 24: Correspondence, 1939–41. In the CIO's first three years of operations, the ILGWU had advanced it over $100,000, and in the period after June 1937 had been its third highest contributor of per capita tax (J. R. Bell to Lewis, May 11, 1938, UMWA-A [CIO/ILG-3]; Lee Pressman to Philip Murray, Mar. 20, 1942, CIOST, box 71: Comptroller, 1942).

12. Patterns of membership and per capita tax collection can be traced in CIOFJLL, part 2, Audits and Accounting section for each year (e.g., 1938, reel 3; 1939, reel 4; 1940, reel 6; 1941, reel 7). See also unorganized materials in UMWA-A (CIO, 1940–42/Audits and Accounts, dated May 7, 1940, and Oct. 1941) and in CIOST, box 71: Comptroller files for 1941 and 1942.

13. In 1937, for example, reports by journalists friendly to the CIO credited the struggling TWOC with having as many as 270,000 workers under contract and with having enrolled as many as a half-million members. See Edward Levinson in the *Philadelphia Record*, Oct. 13, 1937, and Jefferson G. Bell in the *New York Times*, Oct. 13, 1937, clippings in W. Jett Lauck Papers, Alderman Library, University of Virginia, Charlottesville, Va., box 209. SWOC's status in 1938 is indicated in audit and accounting material, Oct.–Dec. 1938, CIOFJLL, part 2, reel 3, and in David J. McDonald to Lewis, Oct. 18, 1938, CIOFJLL, part 1, reel 13. Benjamin Stolberg, "Lewis Fights Labor Peace," 347, put the CIO dues-paying membership figure at a reasonably accurate 1.5 million.

14. Robert R. R. Brooks, *As Steel Goes, . . . : Unionism in a Basic Industry* (New Haven: Yale University Press, 1940), 161–62. Brooks makes careful distinctions among the various categories of membership: workers under contract, number of signed cards, and dues-paying members. As

of early 1940 SWOC claimed about a half-million workers in the first two, partially overlapping, categories and 225,000 in the third, although SWOC dues-paying membership, as reported to the CIO through its monthly per capita tax, remained at under 100,000 through that year.

15. Len De Caux to Lewis, Oct. 21, 1938, CIOFJLL, part 2, reel 3 (on *CIO News*); miscellaneous information on CIO finances [prepared by J. R. Bell and/or Thomas Kennedy], Fall 1937, UMWA-A, UMW Secretary-Treasurer (CIO, 1937); report of the special [CIO] committee on finance, ca. Oct. 1, 1937, UMWA-A; financial reports in Bell to Lewis, May 11, 1938, UMWA-A (CIO-ILGWU); financial and auditing material, 1940, CIOFJLL, part 2, reel 6.

16. UMW loans to the CIO are listed in J. R. Bell to Esther Cossel, Aug. 14, 1941, UMWA-A (UMW-CIO Finances, 1935–55). Per capita dues collections can be followed in the annual CIO audit files, CIOFJLL, part 2. See especially the material in this file for 1941, which summarizes payments made by affiliates from May 1937 through September 1941.

17. CIO subsidies are indicated in the financial and auditing material, CIOFJLL, part 2, reel 6 (CIO, Audits and Accounting, 1940), and in a report on assistance to affiliates, Oct. 1941, UMWA-A (CIO, 1940–42 [loose material]). The early financing of the textile drive is indicated by reporter Jefferson Bell, *New York Times*, Oct. 13, 1941, clipping in Lauck papers, box 209; and by J. R. Bell to Lewis, Mar. 13, 1939; Lewis to Bell, Mar. 13, 1939; and Emil Rieve to Bell, July 20, 1939, CIOFJLL, part 1, reel 15.

18. The CIO affiliate that combined the greatest amount of cash absorbed with the fewest members in the shortest time was indeed UCWOC, which, since its formal launching in September 1939 had claimed over $168,000 in CIO funds while paying per capita tax on an average of about 2,600 members a month. By Oct. 1941 the expenses for UCWOC had mounted to $313,000, the largest amount funneled to any new union other than SWOC (report on assistance to affiliates, Oct. 1941, UMWA-A [CIO, 1940–42 (loose material)]). See also financial and accounting material, CIOFJLL, part 2, reel 6 (CIO Audits and Accounting, 1940).

19. Harry Bridges to Walter Smethurst, Jan. 21, 1939, ILWUPSF (History . . . CIO); Louis Goldblatt to Bridges, Mar. 29, 1940, ILWUPSF (History – Goldblatt, 1938–40); Bjorne Halling to J. R. Robertson, Aug. 28, 1940, ILWUPSF (History . . . CIO Maritime Committee, 1937–43); CIO Committee on Appeals, memo dated Dec. 30, 1940, CIOST, box 58: Retail, Wholesale.

20. UCWOC, "Rules and Regulations," ca. Aug. 1, 1939; UCWOC press release, Aug. 2, 1939, CIOFJLL, part 1, reel 13; *Program of the United Construction Workers Organizing Committee* [pamphlet], Mar. 1, 1940, Lauck papers, box 216: Building Trades.

21. Brophy interview, May 19, 1955, COHC, 818. Dubofsky and Van Tine, *Lewis*, esp. 157, 165, 194, assess Dennie Lewis's capabilities and functions. For Lewis's vigorous advocacy of the UCWOC cause, see Minutes of the Meeting of the Executive Board . . . , Oct. 14, 1939, JBC, box 89.

22. Brophy interview, May 23, 1955, COHC, 810–28.

23. Minutes of special meeting of the Executive Board, Oct. 8, 1939, JBC, box 89.

24. Accounts of the complex conflict within the UAW include Christopher Johnson, *Maurice Sugar: Law, Labor, and the Left in Detroit, 1912–1950* (Detroit: Wayne State University Press, 1988), 227–38; Roger Keeran, *The Communist Party and the Auto Workers Unions* (Bloomington: Indiana University Press, 1980), 186–205; Bert Cochran, *Labor and Communism: The Conflict That Shaped American Unions* (Princeton: Princeton University Press, 1977), 127–43; Harvey A. Levenstein, *Communism, Anticommunism, and the CIO* (Westport, Conn.: Greenwood Press, 1981), 81–84; and Martin Halpern, *UAW Politics in the Cold War Era* (Albany, N.Y.: SUNY Press, 1988), 22–29.

25. The demographic nature of Martin's rank-and-file support, and indeed of the support for either faction, remains murky. However, Steve Fraser, "'The Labor Question,'" in *The Rise and Fall of the New Deal Order, 1930–1980*, ed. Steve Fraser and Gary Gerstle (Princeton: Princeton University Press, 1989), 72, suggests the nature of his appeal. There is a vivid sketch of Martin

in Irving Bernstein, *Turbulent Years: A History of the American Worker, 1933–1941* (Boston: Houghton Mifflin, 1969), 506–9 and 559–69.

26. There are many communications from Lovestone to Lauck, 1937–38, Lauck papers, box 40: Lovestone.

27. Robert Alexander, "Jay Lovestone," in *Biographical Dictionary of the American Left*, ed. Bernard K. Johnpoll and Harvey Klehr (New York: Greenwood Press, 1986), 253–54; Robert Alexander, *The Right Opposition: The Lovestoneites and the International Communist Opposition in the 1930s* (Westport, Conn.: Greenwood Press, 1981), 56–59.

28. Ray Boryczka, "Militancy and Factionalism in the United Auto Workers Union, 1937–1941," *Maryland Historian* 8 (Fall 1977): 13–25. Thus, although UAW officials of all persuasions continued to claim membership totals of nearly 400,000, by January 1939 the union was officially reporting and paying dues on only 13 percent of that total. George Addes to CIO, Mar. 20, 1939, CIOFJLL, part 1, reel 3 (UAW).

29. Addes to Brophy, July 28, 1938, John Brophy Papers, CUA, box 1937–38; Dick [last name undecipherable] to Adolph Germer, June 17, 1938, AG, box 3. The correspondent was Germer's Detroit office assistant.

30. CIOFJLL, part 1, reels 2 and 3 (UAW), contain dozens of reports and other communications from Germer, Hillman, and Murray as well as all manner of material from both pro- and anti-Martin UAW officials and local unionists. Lovestone's efforts to play a role in the conflict and his promotion of his adherents in the Martinite UAW are revealed in his many verbose communications with Jett Lauck and John Brophy in Lauck papers, box 40: Lovestone.

31. Wyndham Mortimer, *Organize!: My Life as a Union Man*, ed. Leo Fenster (Boston: Beacon Press, 1971), 162 65; Levenstein, *Communism, Anticommunism, and the CIO*, 82–85.

32. Lewis's role in the UAW conflict is discussed in Dubofsky and Van Tine, *Lewis*, 317–19. For a detailed account of the convention, see Martin Halpern, "The 1939 UAW Convention: Turning Point for Communist Power in the Auto Union?," *LH* 33, no. 2 (Spring 1992): 190–216.

33. In addition to the sources cited in n. 24 above, see Bernstein, *Turbulent Years*, 554–69. For the tool-and-die strike, see John Barnard, "Rebirth of the United Automobile Workers: The General Motors Tool and Diemakers' Strike of 1939," *LH* 27, no. 2 (Spring 1986): 165–87, and Kevin Boyle, "Rite of Passage: The 1939 General Motors Tool and Die Strike," *LH* 27, no. 2 (Spring 1986): 188–203.

34. At least, at its maximum pre–World War II strength, the ILGWU paid the CIO per capita tax on 250,000 members ($12,500 monthly). The Roosevelt recession hit Dubinsky's organization hard, however, and between November 1937 and April 1938 it averaged only 134,000 dues-paying members and $6,695 per month. J. R. Bell to John L. Lewis, May 11, and Aug. 22, 1938, CIOFJLL, part 1, reel 5 (ILGWU).

35. Dubinsky's remarks are from his speech of January 11, 1938, reprinted in an ILGWU-published pamphlet, *The Position of the International Ladies' Garment Workers' Union in Relation to CIO and AFL, 1934–1938* (1938), copy in the CIOFJLL, part 1, reel 5 (ILGWU). There is a spirited account of the ILGWU's course in and out of the CIO in Benjamin Stolberg, *Tailor's Progress: The Story of a Famous Union and the Men Who Made It* (Garden City: Doubleday, Doran, 1944), 261–76.

36. Dubofsky and Van Tine, *Lewis*, 302–6; Bernstein, *Turbulent Years*, 708–10. Dubinsky's role in the 1937 unity talks is indicated in the copious materials, including his handwritten notes and summaries, Oct. 26 and after, 1937, ILGWU-LMDC, box 16: 2C. His belief in Lewis's culpability for sabotaging the talks with the AFL is indicated in a typescript letter from Max Danish, editor of the ILGWU newspaper *Justice*, Jan. 26, 1938, ILGWU-LMDC, box 16: 2B, and Dubinsky's January 11, 1938, speech reprinted in *Position of the International Ladies' Garment Workers' Union*. This publication constituted a documentary record of the ILGWU's role in unity talks and the union's widening dissent from Lewis and the drive to create a separate CIO.

37. David Dubinsky to John Owens, CIO Ohio regional director, Jan. 10, 1938, ILGWU-LMDC, box 16: 2B; typescript of Dubinsky speech and related correspondence, ILGWU-LMDC, box 16: 1B, 1C; John L. Lewis to Dubinsky, Aug. 16, 1938, and newspaper clippings (e.g., Drew Pearson in the *New York Mirror*, Aug. 26, 1938), ILGWU-LMDC, box 14: 3B; typescript "Resolution unanimously adopted by General Executive Board . . . ," Nov. 11, 1938, ILGWU-LMDC, box 14: 3A; "Not a Withdrawal," from radio address by David Dubinsky on WEVD, Nov. 13, 1938, UMWA-A (CIO-ILG, 1937 [*sic*]). This address was subsequently published in the ILGWU pamphlet *Position of the International Ladies' Garment Workers' Union.* The ILGWU reaffiliated with the AFL in 1940.

38. *New York Times*, Mar. 16, 1937; typescripts of Lewis speeches, Apr. 26 and June 18, 1941, John L. Lewis Papers (microfilm), reel 1 (Speeches); United Mine Workers of America, *Proceedings* . . . (1940), 295. Lewis's aides regularly fed his conspiratorial inclinations. See., for example, Pressman to Lewis, May 22, 1940, and Jan. 1, 1941, UMWA-A (CIO, 1940–42, Legislative/Legal); Ralph Hetzel to Lewis, Oct. 28, 1938, CIOFJLL, part 2, reel 2.

39. On Hillman, see Steven Fraser, *Labor Will Rule: Sidney Hillman and the Rise of American Labor* (New York: Free Press, 1991).

40. Ibid., 441–58.

41. Ibid., 432–51; Dubofsky and Van Tine, *Lewis*, 339–57; Pressman interview, June 20, 1957, COHC, 235–386.

42. Pressman interview; Dubofsky and Van Tine, *Lewis*, 307–11, 319–23; Matthew Josephson, *Sidney Hillman: Statesman of American Labor* (Garden City: Doubleday, 1952), 483; Saul Alinsky, *John L. Lewis: An Unauthorized Biography* (New York: G. P. Putnam's Sons, 1949), 192–84, quotes Lewis at length on these matters, but historians have learned to be cautious of Alinsky's documentation.

43. UMW, *Proceedings*, 312, 314; Nelson N. Lichtenstein, *Labor's War at Home: The CIO in World War II* (Cambridge: Cambridge University Press, 1982), 31.

44. The Lewis-Roosevelt correspondence is summarized and reprinted in U.S. House, Special Committee to Investigate the National Labor Relations Board, *Hearings*, 76th Cong., 3d sess., 1941, vol. 28, appendix, 7412–24.

45. "Chronology of Record of Activities on Labor Policies," ca. Oct. 15, 1940, ACWA-LMDC, box 78: 12. Josephson, *Hillman*, 512–21, reprints the document quoted at 520.

46. Hillman's Oct. 1, 1940, remarks are quoted in Josephson, *Hillman*, 521; Lewis's objections are contained in his letter to Hillman, Oct. 7, 1940, ACWA-LMDC, box 78: 2.

47. Josephson, *Hillman*, 521–22; Steve Fraser, "Sidney Hillman: Labor's Machiavelli," in *Labor Leaders in America*, ed. Melvyn Dubofsky and Warren Van Tine (Urbana: University of Illinois Press, 1987), 221–24; "Chronology of Record of Activities on Labor Policies," ACWA-LMDC, box 78: 2; Philip Murray, petition to the [Labor] Advisory Commission to the Council of National Defense [*sic*], ca. Nov. 1, 1940, ACWA-LMDC, box 102: 9. Hillman denied that he had caved in to the Smith Committee, telling Lewis that "contrary to your contention [in a report Lewis was preparing for the upcoming CIO convention], my testimony at the Smith hearing did not contradict the principles contained in the statement on labor policy" that the president had signed and the NDAC had issued earlier (Hillman to Lewis, Nov. 19, 1940, ACWA-LMDC, box 78: 2 [the letter is marked "Never sent out"]). Hillman's testimony appears in U.S. House, *Hearings*, 7271–86.

48. Josephson, *Hillman*, 474–86.

49. Typescripts of Lewis speeches, Apr. 1 and June 18, 1940, Lewis papers, reel 1 (Speeches).

50. *New York Times*, Oct. 26, 1940.

51. Dubofsky and Van Tine, *Lewis*, 357–60; *New York Times*, Oct. 26, 27, 1940; Allan S. Haywood to Lewis, and Lee Pressman to Lewis, Oct. 26, 1940, CIOFJLL, part 2, reel 5. See also Pressman interview, Dec. 12, 1957, COHC, 385–89. For two astute, but conflicting, views of

Lewis's motivations and expectations, see Pressman interview, esp. 356–95, and John Brophy interview, May 23, 1955, COHC, esp. 840–927.

52. Irving Bernstein, "John L. Lewis and the Voting Behavior of the CIO," *Public Opinion Quarterly* 5 (June 1941): 233–49, and Bernstein, *Turbulent Years*, 720, note patterns of labor support.

53. This account is taken from Josephson, *Hillman*, 492–93.

54. CIOPROC, 1940, 162.

55. Ibid., 183–92; Josephson, *Hillman*, 496–502; Fraser, *Labor Will Rule*, 450–51.

56. Bernstein, *Turbulent Years*, 724–26; Fraser, *Labor Will Rule*, 449–51. Dubofsky and Van Tine, *Lewis*, 364–69, believe that Lewis neither sought to encourage a draft nor would have accepted another term as CIO president.

57. CIOPROC, 1940, 271–74.

Chapter Six

1. U.S. Department of Commerce, Bureau of the Census, *Historical Statistics of the United States, 1789–1945* (Washington, D.C.: Government Printing Office, 1949), 64, lists 11.94 million in manufacturing, 3.510 million in construction, 4.15 million in transportation, and 1.11 million in mining.

2. Richard W. Steele, "'No Racials': Discrimination against Ethnics in American Defense Industry, 1940–42," *LH* 32, no. 1 (Winter 1991): 66–90.

3. Ewa Morawska, "East European Labourers in an American Mill Town, 1890–1940: The Deferential-Proletarian-Privatized Workers?," *Sociology* 19, no. 3 (Aug. 1985): 364–83; John Bodnar, "Immigration, Kinship, and the Rise of Working-Class Realism in Industrial America," *Journal of Social History* 14 (Fall 1980): 45–65; Thomas Göbel, "Becoming an American: Ethnic Workers and the Rise of the CIO," *LH* 29, no. 2 (Spring 1988): 173–98; Kristi Andersen, *The Creation of a Democratic Majority, 1928–1936* (Chicago: University of Chicago Press, 1979); John W. Jeffries, *Testing the Roosevelt Coalition: Connecticut Society and Politics in the Era of World War II* (Knoxville: University of Tennessee Press, 1979); Peter Friedlander, *The Emergence of a UAW Local, 1936–1939: A Study in Class and Culture* (Pittsburgh: University of Pittsburgh Press, 1975), esp. 26–28, 42–43, 72–74. On the aging of the industrial labor force, see Ronald W. Schatz, *The Electrical Workers: A History of Labor at General Electric and Westinghouse, 1923–1960* (Urbana: University of Illinois Press, 1983), 109.

4. Victor B. Nelson-Cisneros, "UCAPAWA and Chicanos in California: The Farm Worker Period, 1937–1940," *Aztlan* 7, no. 3 (Fall 1976): 453–77; Vicki L. Ruiz, *Cannery Women, Cannery Lives: Mexican Women, Unionization, and the California Food Processing Industry, 1930–1950* (Albuquerque: University of New Mexico Press, 1987); Clete Daniel, *Chicano Workers and the Politics of Fairness: The FEPC in the Southwest, 1941–1945* (Austin: University of Texas Press, 1991), 1–37; Mario T. Garcia, "Border Proletarians: Mexican-Americans and the International Union of Mine, Mill, and Smelter Workers, 1939–1946," in *Labor Divided: Race and Ethnicity in United States Labor Struggles, 1835–1960*, ed. Robert Asher and Charles Stephenson (Albany, N.Y.: SUNY Press, 1990), 83–104, 315–21; Sarah Deutsch, *No Separate Refuge: Culture, Class, and Gender on an Anglo-Hispanic Frontier in the American Southwest, 1880–1940* (New York: Oxford University Press, 1987), 170–73; Luis Leobardo Arroyo, "Chicano Participation in Organized Labor: The CIO in Los Angeles, 1938–1950. An Extended Research Note," *Aztlan* 6, no. 2 (1975): 277–303; Lizabeth Cohen, *Making a New Deal: Industrial Workers in Chicago, 1919–1939* (Cambridge: Cambridge University Press, 1990), 324–25, 338–39.

5. Michael K. Honey, *Southern Labor and Black Civil Rights: Organizing Memphis Workers* (Urbana: University of Illinois Press, 1993), 16–18, 150–54; Robert Korstad and Nelson Lichten-

stein, "Opportunities Found and Lost: Labor, Radicals, and the Early Civil Rights Movement," *JAH* 75, no. 3 (Dec. 1988): 788–91; Horace Huntley, "The Red Scare and Black Workers in Alabama: The International Union of Mine, Mill, and Smelter Workers, 1945–53," in Asher and Stephenson, *Labor Divided*, 129–45, 327–31; William Edward Regensburger, "'Ground into Our Blood': The Origins of Working Class Consciousness and Organization in Durably Unionized Southern Industries, 1930–1946" (Ph.D. dissertation, UCLA, 1987).

6. Peter Gottlieb, *Making Their Own Way: Southern Blacks' Migration to Pittsburgh, 1916–30* (Urbana: University of Illinois Press, 1987), 217–23; Horace R. Cayton and George S. Mitchell, *Black Workers and the New Unions* (Chapel Hill: University of North Carolina Press, 1939); St. Clair Drake and Horace R. Cayton, *Black Metropolis: A Study of Negro Life in a Northern City* (New York: Harcourt, Brace, 1945), 214–62; Cohen, *Making a New Deal*, 331–33, 335–36; Rita Helmbold, "Downward Occupational Mobility during the Great Depression: Urban Black and White Working Women," *LH* 29, no. 2 (Spring 1988): 135–72.

7. Herbert R. Northrup, "Blacks in the United Automobile Workers Union," in *Black Workers and Organized Labor*, ed. John H. Bracey, Jr., August Meier, and Elliott Rudwick (Belmont, Calif.: Wadsworth Publishing, 1971), 155–70; Paul Street, "Breaking up Old Hatreds and Breaking through the Fear: The Emergence of the Packinghouse Workers Organizing Committee in Chicago, 1933–1940," *Studies in History and Politics* 5 (1986): 63–82; Bernard Matthew Mergen, "A History of the Industrial Union of Marine and Shipbuilding Workers of America, 1933–1951" (Ph.D. dissertation, University of Pennsylvania, 1968), 138–44; William H. Harris, "Federal Intervention in Union Discrimination: FEPC and West Coast Shipyards during World War II," *LH* 22, no. 3 (Summer 1981): 325–47; Robert Ozanne, *A Century of Labor-Management Relations at McCormick and International Harvester* (Madison: University of Wisconsin Press, 1967), 184–90.

8. Alice Kessler-Harris, *Out to Work: A History of Wage-Earning Women in the United States* (New York: Oxford University Press, 1982), 217–75 (quote at 275); Nancy F. Gabin, *Feminism in the Labor Movement: Women and the United Auto Workers, 1935–1975* (Ithaca: Cornell University Press, 1990), 8–46.

9. U.S. Department of Commerce, *Historical Statistics*, 67–69.

10. Richard J. Jensen, "The Causes and Cures of Unemployment in the Great Depression," *Journal of Interdisciplinary History* 19, no. 4 (Spring 1989): 556–97; U.S. Department of Commerce, Bureau of the Census, *Statistical Abstract of the United States, 1942* (Washington, D.C.: Government Printing Office, 1943), 387; Robert A. Margo, "The Microeconomics of Depression Unemployment," NBER Working Paper Series on Historical Factors in Long Run Growth, No. 18 (Washington, D.C.: NBER, Dec. 1990).

11. Harold J. Ruttenberg and Stanley Ruttenberg, "War and the Steel Ghost Towns," *Harper's*, Jan. 1940, 147–55; Clinton S. Golden and Harold J. Ruttenberg, *The Dynamics of Industrial Democracy* (New York: Harper and Bros., 1942), 151–54, 164–69; Mark Reutter, *Sparrows Point: Making Steel – The Rise and Ruin of American Industrial Might* (New York: Summit Books, 1988), 265–79; U.S. Department of Commerce, *Statistical Abstract*, 385.

12. U.S. Department of Commerce, *Historical Statistics*, 67; Ruttenberg and Ruttenberg, "War and the Steel Ghost Towns," 147–48.

13. Richard Polenberg, *One Nation Divisible: Class, Race, and Ethnicity in the United States since 1938* (New York: Viking, 1980), 18–19.

14. U.S. Department of Labor, Bureau of Labor Statistics, *Wages in Cotton-Goods Manufacturing*, Bulletin No. 663 (Washington, D.C.: Government Printing Office, Nov. 1938): 63–64.

15. Mark McColloch, "Consolidating Industrial Citizenship: The USWA at War and Peace, 1939–1946," in *Forging a Union of Steel: Philip Murray, SWOC, and the United Steelworkers*, ed. Paul F. Clark, Peter Gottlieb, and Donald Kennedy (Ithaca: ILR Press, 1987), 63.

16. U.S. Department of Agriculture, Bureau of Human Nutrition and Home Economics, *Con-*

sumer Purchases Study, Urban, Rural, and Farm: Family Expenditures for Automobile and Other Transportation, Five Regions, misc. pub. 415 (Washington, D.C.: Government Printing Office, 1941), 40–41; U.S. Department of Agriculture, Bureau of Human Nutrition and Home Economics, *Consumer Purchases Study, Family Housing and Facilities, Urban, Village, Farm: Five Regions*, misc. pub. 399 (Washington, D.C.: Government Printing Office, 1940), 81–194.

17. See Daniel Levine, *Poverty and Society: The Growth of the American Welfare State in International Comparison* (New Brunswick: Rutgers University Press, 1988), 229–58; Edwin Amenta and Theda Skocpol, "Redefining the New Deal: World War II and the Development of Social Provision in the United States," in *The Politics of Social Policy in the United States*, ed. Margaret Weir, Ann Shola Orloff, and Theda Skocpol (Princeton: Princeton University Press, 1988), 81–122; David Brody, "The New Deal and World War II," in *The New Deal*, vol. 1, *The National Level*, ed. John Braeman, Robert H. Bremner, and David Brody (Columbus: Ohio State University Press, 1975), 267–309; Harry A. Millis and Royal E. Montgomery, *The Economics of Labor*, vol. 2, *Labor's Risks and Social Insurance* (New York: McGraw-Hill, 1938).

18. Users of summary Gallup poll survey data must be cautious. For some well-advised admonitions, see Daniel Bell, "Industrial Conflict and Public Opinion," in *Industrial Conflict*, ed. Arthur Kornhauser, Robert Dubin, and Arthur M. Ross (New York: McGraw-Hill, 1954), 240–56, and Tom Nissiter, "Surveys and Opinion Polls," in *Contemporary History: Practice and Method*, ed. Anthony Seldon (Oxford: Basil Blackwell, 1988), 55–69.

19. "Social and Economic Class," Apr. 2, 1938, in *The Gallup Poll: Public Opinion, 1935–1971*, vol. 1, *1935–1948*, by George H. Gallup (New York: Random House, 1972), 148.

20. On support for FDR and the Democrats: "President Roosevelt's Voter Appeal," Feb. 19, 1939, 140, and "Presidential Trial Heat," Sept. 13, 1939, 241; on the Wagner Act: "Wagner Labor Act," Mar. 10, 1939, 144; on the role of the federal government: "Government Spending," Dec. 26, 1937, 80–81; "Government Spending," June 17, 1938, 107; "Federal Budget," Feb. 19, 1940, 210–11; "Government Spending," Mar. 6, 1940, 212; and "Wage and Price Controls," Apr. 9, 1941, 273; on corporate wealth: "Corporate Salaries," Mar. 30, 1938, 95; on presidential power: "Presidential Power," Apr. 8, 1938, 96; on food and health: "Food," Dec. 5, 1941, 310, all in ibid.

21. On fairness of wages: "Wages and Hours Law," Jan. 2, 1939, 133, and "Wage and Price Control," Nov. 10, 1941, 305; on a better life with the Republicans: "Business Prosperity," June 7, 1939, 158; on military expenditures: "Federal Budget," 210; on participation in European war: "European War," July 7, 1940, 231; on defeating Germany: "European War," Nov. 2, 1941, 304, all in ibid. Robert Stuart McElvaine, "Thunder without Lightning: Working-Class Discontent in the United States, 1929–1937" (Ph.D. dissertation, SUNY-Binghamton, 1974), 251–59, stresses the radical content of these polls and related evidences of working-class opinion.

22. On favoring unions: "Labor Unions and Strikes," Nov. 17, 1941, 306; on WPA strikes: "Works Progress Administration," July 26, 1939, 169; on defense strikes: "Defense Industries," Jan. 5, 1941, 257–58, "Labor Strikes," Nov. 3, 1941, 304, and "Labor Unions and Strikes," Nov. 17, 1941, 306; on HUAC: "The Dies Committee," Dec. 11, 1938, 128; on Communists: "Communist Party," June 18, 1941, 285; on Green over Lewis: "William Green and John L. Lewis," Oct. 7, 1938, 120–21; on the captive mine strike: "John L. Lewis," Nov. 21, 1941, 307, all in Gallup, *Gallup Poll*, vol. 1.

23. There have been few detailed studies of the theme of workers' control or of workers' attitudes toward employers and supervisors as related to the 1930s and the World War II period. For a discussion of the theme of control as related to the CIO era, see Robert H. Zieger, "Toward the History of the CIO: A Bibliographical Report," *LH* 26, no. 4 (Fall 1985): 504–10. Two recent works illuminating the responses of depression-era workers and employers to the problems of the workplace regime are Jensen, "Causes and Cures," 559–64, and Sanford Jacoby, *Employing Bureaucracy: Managers, Unions, and the Transformation of Work in American Industry, 1900–1945*

(New York: Columbia University Press, 1985). A classic rumination on alienation in the modern workplace is Daniel Bell, "Work and Its Discontents: The Cult of Efficiency in America," in *The End of Ideology: On the Exhaustion of Political Ideas in the Fifties*, by Daniel Bell (New York: Collier, 1962), 227–72, while Daniel T. Rodgers, "Tradition, Modernity, and the American Industrial Worker: Reflections and Critique," *Journal of Interdisciplinary History* 7, no. 4 (Spring 1977): 655–81, is an insightful reflection.

24. Detailed accounts of employer efforts to meet the problem of shop-floor governance in mass production industries are found in Daniel Nelson, *American Rubber Workers and Organized Labor, 1900–1941* (Princeton: Princeton University Press, 1988), 57–59, 103–10, and Ozanne, *A Century of Labor-Management Relations*, 245–48. See also Daniel Nelson, "The Company Union Movement, 1900–1937: A Reexamination," *Business History Review* 56, no. 3 (Autumn 1982): 335–57; John N. Schacht, *The Making of Telephone Unionism, 1920–1947* (New Brunswick: Rutgers University Press, 1985), 40–46; Stuart Brandes, *American Welfare Capitalism, 1880–1940* (Chicago: University of Chicago Press, 1976); and David Brody, "The Rise and Decline of Welfare Capitalism," in *Workers in Industrial America: Essays on the Twentieth Century Struggle*, by David Brody (New York Oxford University Press, 1980), 48–81.

25. John R. Commons, *Industrial Goodwill* (New York: McGraw-Hill, 1919), 26; Richard C. Wilcock, "Industrial Management's Policies toward Unionism," in *Labor and the New Deal*, ed. Milton Derber and Edwin Young (Madison: University of Wisconsin Press, 1957), 307. The consistent two-thirds or better support for labor unions in the Gallup polls, cited above, suggests that skepticism of employers' benevolence was widespread.

26. On electrical appliances: Schatz, *Electrical Workers*, 11–24; on automobiles: Nelson Lichtenstein, "Great Expectations: The Promise of Industrial Jurisprudence and Its Demise, 1930–1960," in *Industrial Democracy in America: The Ambiguous Promise*, ed. Nelson Lichtenstein and Howell John Harris (Washington, D.C., and Cambridge: Woodrow Wilson Center Press and Cambridge University Press, 1993), 122–28; Nelson Lichtenstein, "'The Man in the Middle': A Social History of Automobile Industry Foremen," in *On the Line: Essays in the History of Auto Work*, ed. Nelson Lichtenstein and Stephen Meyer (Urbana: University of Illinois Press, 1989), 153–89; Steve Jefferys, "'Matters of Mutual Interest': The Unionization Process at Dodge Main, 1933–1939," in Lichtenstein and Meyer, *On the Line*, 102–12; Carl Gersuny and Gladis Kaufman, "Seniority and the Moral Economy of U.S. Automobile Workers, 1934–1946," *Journal of Social History* 18 (Spring 1985): 463–75; Stephen Meyer III, *The Five Dollar Day: Labor, Management, and Social Control in the Ford Motor Company, 1908–1921* (Albany, N.Y.: SUNY Press, 1981); Friedlander, *Emergence of a UAW Local*, 3–53; and David Gartman, *Auto Slavery: The Labor Process in the American Automobile Industry, 1897–1950* (New Brunswick: Rutgers University Press, 1986). The Studebaker Corporation followed still another approach, one of small-town, family-based loyalty combined with a desire to avoid labor unrest at virtually any cost. See John Bodnar, "Power and Memory in Oral History: Workers and Managers at Studebaker," *JAH* 75, no. 4 (Mar. 1989): 1204–8; Alan R. Raucher, *Paul G. Hoffman: Architect of Foreign Aid* (Lexington: University Press of Kentucky, 1985), 25–27; and Howell John Harris, *The Right to Manage: Industrial Relations Policies of American Business in the 1940s* (Madison: University of Wisconsin Press, 1982), 15–40.

27. Richard A. Lauderbaugh, *American Steel Makers and the Coming of the Second World War* (Ann Arbor: UMI Research Press, 1980), 121–69; Golden and Ruttenberg, *Dynamics of Industrial Democracy*, esp. 162–74; Reutter, *Sparrows Point*, 275–79, quote at 277; Robert R. R. Brooks, *As Steel Goes, . . . : Unionism in a Basic Industry* (New Haven: Yale University Press, 1940), 190–240.

28. Bruce Nelson, *Workers on the Waterfront: Seamen, Longshoremen, and Unionism in the 1930s* (Urbana: University of Illinois Press, 1988), 183–85; Bruce Nelson, "'Pentecost' on the Pacific: Maritime Workers and Working-Class Consciousness in the 1930s," in *Political Power and Social*

Theory: A Research Annual, ed. Maurice Zeitlin and Howard Kimeldorf (Greenwich, Conn.: JAI Press, 1984), 4:141–82; Howard Kimeldorf, *Reds or Rackets?: The Making of Radical and Conservative Unions on the Waterfront* (Berkeley: University of California Press, 1988), 110–20; Steve Babson, *Working Detroit: The Making of a Union Town* (New York: Adama Books, 1984), 88–101; Lichtenstein, "Great Expectations"; Ray Boryczka, "Militancy and Factionalism in the United Auto Workers Union, 1937–1941," *Maryland Historian* 8 (Fall 1977): 13–25; Jefferys, "'Matters of Mutual Interest'"; Street, "Breaking up Old Hatreds," 69–75; Daniel Nelson, "The CIO at Bay: Labor Militancy and Politics in Akron, 1936–1938," *JAH* 71, no. 3 (Dec. 1984): 565–86.

29. Golden and Ruttenberg, *Dynamics of Industrial Democracy,* 82–118,

30. James A. Hodges, *New Deal Labor Policy and the Southern Cotton Textile Industry, 1933–1941* (Knoxville: University of Tennessee Press, 1986), 177–79; Joshua Freeman, *In Transit: The Transport Workers Union in New York City, 1933–1966* (New York: Oxford University Press, 1989), 113–20. There is a good discussion of the goals of auto union activists in Jefferys, "'Matters of Mutual Interest,'" 105–12. See also William Serrin, "Working for the Union: An Interview with Douglas Fraser," *American Heritage* 36 (Feb.–Mar. 1985): 58. Thus, observes Thomas Göbel ("Becoming an American," 196–97), the CIO was "not just . . . a union movement trying to increase the wages of workers but [w]as something of a civil crusade, a movement that promised a sense of dignity and power to a great number of people previously excluded from full participation in American life"; he adds that "the CIO produced a kind of 'worker's control'" through its achievement of seniority, written contracts, and grievance procedures.

31. Gersuny and Kaufman, "Seniority," 467–69.

32. Steve Babson, "British and Irish Militants in the Detroit UAW in the 1930s," in Asher and Stephenson, *Labor Divided,* 227–45, 349–51.

33. See, e.g., Friedlander, *Emergence of a UAW Local,* 26–29, and Charles Sabel, *Work and Politics: The Division of Labor in Industry* (Cambridge: Cambridge University Press, 1982), 138–41.

34. See, e.g., Boryczka, "Militancy and Factionalism"; Ray Boryczka, "Seasons of Discontent: Auto Union Factionalism and the Motor Products Strike of 1935–1936," *Michigan History* 61 (Spring 1977): 3–32; Steve Babson, *Building the Union: Skilled Workers and Anglo-Gaelic Immigrants in the Rise of the UAW* (New Brunswick: Rutgers University Press, 1991), 126–33.

35. Cyrus Ching, *Review and Reflection: A Half-Century of Labor Relations* (New York: B. C. Forbes, 1953), 40–48.

36. For the General Electric contract, see Schatz, *Electrical Workers,* 74. On the elaboration of personnel policies in some firms, see Richard Edwards, *Contested Terrain: The Transformation of the Workplace in the Twentieth Century* (New York: Basic Books, 1979), 130–62. Forms of company unionism, often with de facto contractual provisions that mimicked those found in union contracts, were strong and successful in the meatpacking (Swift), telephone, shoe, oil, and photographic industries. See D. Nelson, "Company Union Movement"; Stuart Chase, *A Generation of Industrial Peace: 30 Years of Labor Relations at Standard Oil Company (NJ)* (New York: Standard Oil of New Jersey, 1947); Schacht, *Making of Telephone Unionism,* 34–40; and Gerald Zahavi, *Workers, Managers, and Welfare Capitalism: The Shoeworkers and Tanners of Endicott Johnson, 1890–1950* (Urbana: University of Illinois Press, 1988), 126–210. For the survival of welfare capitalism through the 1930s, see Elizabeth Fones-Wolf, "Industrial Recreation, the Second World War, and the Revival of Welfare Capitalism, 1934–1960," *Business History Review* 60, no. 2 (Summer 1986): 232–57; Sanford Jacoby and Anil Verma, "Enterprise Unions in the United States," *Industrial Relations* 31, no. 1 (Winter 1992): 139–42; and Jacoby, *Employing Bureaucracy,* 226–28.

37. Roger Keeran, *The Communist Party and the Auto Workers Unions* (Bloomington: Indiana University Press, 1980), 205–25; Philip Bonofsky, *Brother Bill McKie: Building the Union at Ford*

(New York: International Publishers, 1953); Babson, *Building the Union*, 211; Christopher Johnson, *Maurice Sugar: Law, Labor, and the Left in Detroit, 1912–1950* (Detroit: Wayne State University Press, 1988), 245–49.

38. Johnson, *Sugar*, 245–49; Irving Bernstein, *Turbulent Years: A History of the American Worker, 1933–1941* (Boston: Houghton Mifflin, 1969), 741–43.

39. August Meier and Elliott Rudwick, *Black Detroit and the Rise of the UAW* (New York: Oxford University Press, 1979), 34–107.

40. Bernstein, *Turbulent Years*, 734–51; Ross Gregory, *America 1941: A Nation at the Crossroads* (New York: Free Press, 1989), 59–60. Gregory quotes UAW members cited in the *Detroit Free Press*, Apr. 3, 6, 1941.

41. Bernstein, *Turbulent Years*, 727–34; McColloch, "Consolidating Industrial Citizenship," 46–49; Art Preis, *Labor's Giant Step: Twenty Years of the CIO*, rev. ed. (New York: Pathfinder Press, 1972), 111; *CIO News*, Apr. 4, May 12, 19, June 23, 1941.

42. McColloch, "Consolidating Industrial Citizenship," 49–50; Bernstein, *Turbulent Years*, 727–31.

43. Bernstein, *Turbulent Years*, 750–51; Walter Galenson, *The CIO Challenge to the AFL: A History of the American Labor Movement, 1935–1941* (Cambridge, Mass.: Harvard University Press, 1960), 183–84.

44. Bernstein's account (*Turbulent Years*, 748–51) relies on the recollections of Ford's production chief, Charles Sorenson, who credits Ford's wife, Clara, with changing her husband's mind. The controversy over the reasons for Henry Ford's acceptance of the contract illustrates the combination of Victorian sentimentality and modernistic innovation that characterized much of Ford's life and career. Sorenson's tale – told to him by Henry Ford – of Clara Ford's last-minute intervention brings the perils of Pauline to the usually humdrum world of collective bargaining. At the same time, the Ford contract *was*, in effect, the prototype for post–World War II contracts, and such features as union security, dues checkoff, and cooperative grievance handling later became the focal points of criticism of the neosyndicalist labor historians of the 1970s who attacked the CIO-era dispensation in industrial relations. See, e.g., Nelson Lichtenstein, "UAW Bargaining Strategy and Shop-Floor Conflict, 1946–1970," *Industrial Relations* 24, no. 3 (Fall 1985): 360–81; Nelson Lichtenstein, "Life at the Rouge: A Cycle of Workers' Control," in *Life and Labor: Dimensions of American Working-Class History*, ed. Charles Stephenson and Robert Asher (Albany, N.Y.: SUNY Press, 1986), 237–59; and Christopher L. Tomlins, *The State and the Unions: Labor Relations, Law, and the Organized Labor Movement in America, 1880–1960* (Cambridge: Cambridge University Press, 1985), 247–326.

45. Nelson N. Lichtenstein, *Labor's War at Home: The CIO in World War II* (Cambridge: Cambridge University Press, 1982), 46–47; Galenson, *CIO Challenge*, 219–25, 366–67, 403–4, 423–26, 446–48; Joel Seidman, *American Labor from Defense to Reconversion* (Chicago: University of Chicago Press, 1953), 53–61. The *CIO News* through the spring of 1941 carries details of CIO success.

46. Murray's and Bittner's remarks, Nov. 23, 1940, CIOEB-WSU, 201, 222, respectively; Lewis's remarks, CIO legislative conference, July 7, 1941, JBC, box 89.

47. "Defense Industries," Jan. 5, 1941, 257–58; "Labor Strikes," Nov. 3, 1941, 304; "Labor Unions and Strikes," Nov. 17, 1941, 306, all in Gallup, *Gallup Poll*, vol. 1. Between July 1939 and December 1941 at least four dozen antiunion bills were introduced. One of the more punitive proposals, introduced by Representative Howard Smith, appeared on the verge of passage at the time of Pearl Harbor and served as the basis for the antiunion Smith-Connally Act of 1943. See Steven Fraser, *Labor Will Rule: Sidney Hillman and the Rise of American Labor* (New York: Free Press, 1991), 459–63; James C. Foster, *The Union Politic: The CIO Political Action Committee* (Columbia: University of Missouri Press, 1975), 10; and Lee Pressman's remarks, Dec. 13, 1941, morning session, CIO Executive Board minutes, JBC, box 93.

48. Stephen Meyer, *"Stalin over Wisconsin": The Making and Unmaking of Militant Unionism, 1900–1950* (New Brunswick: Rutgers University Press, 1992), 78–120; Matthew Josephson, *Sidney Hillman: Statesman of American Labor* (Garden City: Doubleday, 1952), 538–66; Lichtenstein, *Labor's War at Home*, 49–50; Fraser, *Labor Will Rule*, 464–65.

49. Mark Perlman, *The Machinists: A New Study in American Trade Unionism* (Cambridge, Mass.: Harvard University Press, 1961), 3–97; Jacob Vander Meulen, *The Politics of Aircraft: Building an American Military Industry* (Lawrence: University Press of Kansas, 1991), 147–81.

50. Galenson, *CIO Challenge*, 506–9; Arthur P. Allen, Arthur Schneider, and Betty V. H. Schneider, *Industrial Relations in the California Aircraft Industry* (Berkeley: Institute of Industrial Relations, 1956), 8–18; Jacob Vander Meulen, "West Coast Aircraft Workers and the Early Warfare State, 1935–1941" (unpublished paper, 1992, in Zieger's possession).

51. B. Nelson, *Workers on the Waterfront*, 223–73; Ruiz, *Cannery Women*, 69–85; Harvey Schwartz, *The March Inland: Origins of the ILWU Warehouse Division, 1934–1938* (Los Angeles: UCLA Institute of Industrial and Labor Relations, 1978), 125–37; Bert Cochran, *Labor and Communism: The Conflict That Shaped American Unions* (Princeton: Princeton University Press, 1977), 176–84; Jerry Lembcke and William M. Tattam, *One Union in Wood: A Political History of the International Woodworkers of America* (New York: International Publishers, 1984), 47–102.

52. David Dubinsky to J. W. Buzzell, Mar. 15, 1938, ILGWU-LMDC, box 14: 4A; I. Lutsky to Dubinsky, Aug. 31, 1938, ILGWU-LMDC, box 16: 2A; Adolph Germer to Allan S. Haywood, Sept. 24, 1940, AG, box 4; Harry Bridges to John L. Lewis, Oct. 9, 1940, ILWUPSF (History, TUR-UMW). See also Mergen, "History of the International Union," 226–37.

53. Wyndham Mortimer, *Organize!: My Life as a Union Man*, ed. Leo Fenster (Boston: Beacon Press, 1971), 166–73; Victor Reuther, *The Brothers Reuther and the Story of the UAW: A Memoir* (Boston: Houghton Mifflin, 1976), 223–24; Keeran, *Communist Party and the Auto Workers Unions*, 214–18; Maurice Isserman, *Which Side Were You On?: The American Communist Party during the Second World War* (Middletown, Conn.: Wesleyan University Press, 1982), 92.

54. Allen et al., *Industrial Relations*, 14–18, outlines the favorable wage provisions and collaborationist tenor of key IAM contracts. See also Vander Meulen, *Politics of Aircraft*, 212–16.

55. This account is taken from Isserman, *Which Side Were You On?*, 96–98; Frankensteen is quoted at 98. See also Fraser, *Labor Will Rule*, 465–67.

56. The Communist Party quote is from Isserman, *Which Side Were You On?*, 99; Lewis quoted from CIO Legislative Conference, July 7, 1941, JBC, box 89. On Hillman's role, see Josephson, *Hillman*, 544–46, and Fraser, *Labor Will Rule*, 465–67. See also Lichtenstein, *Labor's War at Home*, 58–63.

57. The emerging literature on the CIO, often so brilliant and provocative in its critique of labor's enmeshment in the national security state, is curiously obtuse in its lack of sympathy for those public men and women, in the labor movement and out, for whom the scope and implications of Axis military success controlled their approach to labor relations and other contemporary issues. This observation holds for such works as Lichtenstein, *Labor's War at Home*; Fraser, *Labor Will Rule*; and Melvyn Dubofsky and Warren Van Tine, *John L. Lewis: A Biography* (New York: Quadrangle, 1977), for each, while duly noting the international context, does so within a rhetorical frame that elevates highly specific labor issues, such as the demand for union security or jurisdictional disputes, to a level of importance comparable to the threat that an ascendant Hitler posed. Liberal and social democratic CIO leaders such as Hillman, Murray, and Walter Reuther – and, after June 22, Communists and their allies such as Joseph Curran, Michael Quill, and Julius Emspak – did not make this mistake. See CIOPROC, Nov. 18, 1941, 142.

58. See McColloch, "Consolidating Industrial Citizenship," 46–51, for shrewd observations on the limits of existing scholarship in explaining and analyzing this outburst of laborite activism on the part of workers who had often in the period after 1937 evidenced only episodic and often grudging support for SWOC.

59. Preis, *Labor's Giant Step*, 112.

60. The steelworker is quoted in an article in the *Nation* of Apr. 24, 1937, as cited in Richard C. Cortner, *The Wagner Act Cases* (Knoxville: University of Tennessee Press, 1964), 180. The other quote is from Murray's report to the 1941 CIO convention (CIOPROC, 1941, 88).

61. In the existing literature there is a tendency for historians to ignore or bypass discussion of this vulnerability. Widespread shop-floor militancy is taken to be a source of unambiguous strength; the ignorance of defense mobilization bureaucrats and congressional critics of labor affairs is taken as somehow rendering them trivial or ineffectual; the powerful nonunion habits of the vast majority of the American working class are ignored; the widespread condemnation of defense strikes and skepticism of labor leaders and unions among blue collar people are unacknowledged. See, for example, Lichtenstein, *Labor's War at Home*, and Preis, *Labor's Giant Step*. More balanced treatments are found in Gilbert J. Gall, "CIO Leaders and the Democratic Alliance: The Case of the Smith Committee and the NLRB," *Labor Studies Journal* 14, no. 2 (Summer 1989): 3–27, and Foster, *Union Politic*, 10.

62. A considerable literature has sprung up reexamining the once-commonplace view that the National Labor Relations Act and the NLRB were crucial and positive components in the building of effective industrial unions in the 1930s and 1940s. See Zieger, "Toward the History of the CIO," 507, n. 42, and Robert H. Zieger, "The CIO: A Bibliographical Update and Archival Guide," *LH* 31, no. 4 (Fall 1990): 414–16, nn. 4–7, for key citations. David Plotke, "The Wagner Act, Again: Politics and Labor, 1935–1937," in *Studies in American Political Development*, ed. Stephen Skowronek and Karen Orren (New Haven: Yale University Press, 1989), 3:105–56, however, is a useful reminder of the reinforcing role Wagner Act litigation played.

The actual course by which the NLRB and the courts addressed the cases forming the backdrop to the 1941 surge is outlined in Bernstein, *Turbulent Years*, 727–28, 741–43; Gall, "CIO Leaders and the Democratic Alliance"; James A. Gross, *The Reshaping of the National Labor Relations Board: National Labor Policy in Transition, 1937–1947* (Albany, N.Y.: SUNY Press, 1981), 13–14, 16–20, 30–39; Cortner, *Wagner Act Cases*, 180–81. Melvyn Dubofsky, *The State and Labor in Modern America* (Chapel Hill: University of North Carolina Press, 1994), 137–68, is an authoritative and balanced treatment, but see also Tomlins, *The State and the Unions*, 103–281, for a contrasting view.

63. Gall, "CIO Leaders and the Democratic Alliance"; Gross, *Reshaping the NLRB*, 151–225.

64. Hatton W. Summers quoted in Seidman, *American Labor*, 44; Josephson, *Hillman*, 541; Fraser, *Labor Will Rule*, 462. Pressman's comments are in CIO Executive Board Minutes, Dec. 13, 1941, JBC, box 93.

65. Recent biographers of Lewis, Murray, and Hillman stress the acuteness of Lewis's critique of the CIO's relations with the national security state and the high price paid by the CIO for governmental support. See Dubofsky and Van Tine, *Lewis*, 339–70; Ronald W. Schatz, "Philip Murray and the Subordination of the Industrial Unions to the United States Government," in *Labor Leaders in America*, ed. Melvyn Dubofsky and Warren Van Tine (Urbana: University of Illinois Press, 1987), 234–57; and Fraser, *Labor Will Rule*, 441–68. See also Lichtenstein, *Labor's War at Home*, 26–43. Murray's presidential report to the 1941 CIO convention stresses the positive benefits of governmental action for the CIO during the defense mobilization process and the success of CIO leaders, including Hillman, in fending off antilabor actions (CIOPROC, Nov. 17, 1941, 39–120).

66. For Hillman's general approach to organization and union behavior, see Fraser, *Labor Will Rule*; Steve Fraser, "Dress Rehearsal for the New Deal: Shop-Floor Insurgents, Political Elites, and Industrial Democracy in the Amalgamated Clothing Workers," in *Working-Class America: Essays on Labor, Community, and American Society*, ed. Michael H. Frisch and Daniel J. Walkowitz (Urbana: University of Illinois Press, 1983), 212–55; and Steve Fraser, "Sidney Hillman: Labor's Machievelli," in Dubofsky and Van Tine, *Labor Leaders in America*, 207–33. For Hillman's role

in the North American Aviation and construction workers' controversies, see Fraser, *Labor Will Rule*, 465–67, 487–88, and Josephson, *Hillman*, 544–46, 548–50. Indicative of Lewis's savage attack on Hillman for his role in the North American Aviation strike are his remarks, July 7, 1941, draft minutes, CIO Legislative Conference, JBC, box 89.

Fraser views Hillman's activities in this period more darkly than I do and stresses the degree to which he, and the industrial union movement more generally, were encoiled in governmental priorities. Since he acknowledges labor's vulnerability and steers clear of most of the traps outlined in n. 61 above, Fraser implicitly takes a profoundly pessimistic view of the CIO's resolution of its opportunities and dilemmas as it entered World War II.

67. CIOEB-WSU, Nov. 23, 1940, 203, 205.

68. Lewis's words are in CIOEB-WSU, Nov. 15, 1940, 14. See also *Time* correspondent (Ed Townsend?), "John L. Lewis and the CIO," notes of informal interview, July 11, 1941, ACWA-LMDC, box 209: 11. See also Lewis's remarks, legislative conference, July 7, 1941, JBC, box 89. For some of the reverberations of the Lewis-Hillman conflict in the IUCs, see, e.g., Leonard H. Goldsmith to Lewis, Nov. 26, 1940; Goldsmith to Lewis, July 22, 1941, with attached clipping from *Newark Sunday Call*, July 20, 1941; and William Ross to Lewis, Oct. 25, 1940, with attached resolution by the Greater Newark Industrial Union Council, all in UMWA-A.

69. Lewis's remarks, CIO Legislative Conference, July 7, 1941, JBC, box 89; Fraser, *Labor Will Rule*, 463 (quote), 466–67.

70. CIOEB-WSU, June 5, 1940, 50–51; *CIO News*, July 28, Aug. 8, Sept. 22, Oct. 13, 20, 27, Nov. 24, 1941. As of October 1941 UCWOC had absorbed at least $313,000 in CIO subsidies, the largest total given to any affiliate other than the Steelworkers, and had paid a total of $6,700 into the CIO in per capita tax (receipts, disbursements as of Sept. 30, 1941, CIOST, box 71 [Comptroller], and loose material relating to finances, Oct. 1941, UMWA-A [CIO, 1940–42]).

71. Hillman to Frances Perkins, July 22, 1941, and Office of Production Management press release, July 24, 1941, ACWA-LMDC, box 101: 12; notes of afternoon session CIO Executive Board meeting, Detroit, Nov. 16, 1941 (quoting Dennie Lewis), JBC, box 93; *CIO News*, Oct. 27, 1941. Fraser, *Labor Will Rule*, 487–88, seems to accept UCWOC as a credible organization.

72. The exchange on finances is in CIOEB-WSU, Nov. 15, 1940, 8–50.

73. Debate over the creation of an IUC in New York State revolved around the fear of Hillman and other needle trades unionists that it would, as had similar councils in Michigan, California, Washington, Wisconsin, and elsewhere, provide Communists with a new and effective organ in the CIO. See, e.g., CIOEB-WSU, Nov. 17, 1940, 103–59. See "CIO Union Split on New Council," *New York Journal American*, July 25, 1940, and related clippings, ILGWU-LMDC, box 16: 4a, and "State Convention of C.I.O. Is Put Off," *New York Times*, Sept. 16, 1941.

74. CIOEB-WSU, Nov. 15, 1940, 32. While Lewis was right in pointing to the textile campaign, it was also true that TWOC and its successor, the TWUA, did pay substantial per capita tax to the CIO and represented a far lower cost-return loss than did Lewis's pet, the United Construction Workers. See receipts, disbursements, as of Sept. 30, 1941, CIOST, box 71: Comptroller Dept., 1941.

75. For Murray's role in the captive mines dispute, see Dubofsky and Van Tine, *Lewis*, 402. A *Time* reporter (Ed Townsend?) cited Lewis's characterization of Murray in his interview notes, July 11, 1941, ACWA-LMDC, box 209: 11. Throughout 1941 the *CIO News* foregrounded UMW, District 50, and UCWOC activities.

76. The quotes from Lewis are in *Time* correspondent interview (Ed Townsend?) with Lewis, July 11, 1941, ACWA-LMDC, box 209: 11. On Murray, see Richard Rovere, "Philip Murray Takes Over," *New Republic*, Nov. 29, 1941, 531–33.

77. Rose Stein, "Lewis and the Communists," *Nation*, Aug. 16, 1941, 140–42. On August 5 Lewis signed an anti-aid statement issued under Republican auspices.

78. The best accounts of the captive mines strike are in Dubofsky and Van Tine, *Lewis*,

397–404; Bernstein, *Turbulent Years*, 752–67; Golden and Ruttenberg, *Dynamics of Industrial Democracy*, 190–230; Fraser, *Labor Will Rule*, 430. Lewis's bitter critique of the government is indicated in *Time* correspondent (Townsend?) interview notes, July 11, 1941, ACWA-LMDC, box 209: 11.

79. CIOPROC, Nov. 17–22, 1941, 9–10, 189, 205–6; *CIO News*, Nov. 24, 1941; Rovere, "Philip Murray Takes Over," 532; Dubofsky and Van Tine, *Lewis*, 403–4.

80. CIOPROC, 1941, 205–6, 146, 168; *CIO News*, Dec. 15, 1941.

81. Lewis to Brophy, June 18, 1941; Brophy to Lewis, June 19, 1941; Lewis to Brophy, July 3, 1941; Brophy to Lewis, July 7, 1941; Lewis to Brophy, July 12, 1941, all in UMWA-A. The complex and disputed Lewis-Murray confrontation of 1941–42 is most authoritatively treated in Dubofsky and Van Tine, *Lewis*, 405–12, but see also Sanford D. Horwitt, *Let Them Call Me Rebel: Saul Alinsky, His Life and Legacy* (New York: Knopf, 1989), 217–21, and Melvyn Dubofsky, "Labor's Odd Couple: Philip Murray and John L. Lewis," in Clark et al., *Forging a Union of Steel*, 30–44.

82. Brophy interview, May 23, 1955, COHC, 867–73; Dubofsky and Van Tine, *Lewis*, 410; Robert H. Zieger, *John L. Lewis: Labor Leader* (Boston: Twayne, 1988), 118–20; Lewis to Michael Widman, Oct. 30, 1941, UMWA-A (steel cabinet, CIO miscellaneous); James B. Carey to Ora Gassaway, president, District 50, Apr. 28, 1942, CIOST, box 61: Transport, 1937–43.

83. Zieger, *Lewis*, 121–23.

84. CIOEB-WSU, Jan. 24, 1942, 95–96. The correspondence between Lewis and Murray on this matter (Lewis to Murray, Jan. 17; Murray to Lewis, Jan. 19; Lewis to Murray, Jan. 23) is reprinted in ibid., 15–19. See also Dubofsky and Van Tine, *Lewis*, 405–7. The correspondence relating to these financial matters is contained in draft minutes of CIO Executive Board meeting, Apr. 21, 1942, JBC, box 93. Murray's letter to Thomas Kennedy, UMW secretary-treasurer, is Mar. 16, 1942, while the resolution quoted was adopted on Apr. 21, 1942. Lewis's words, quoted in this resolution, were from his Nov. 15, 1940, remarks to the Executive Board. The most authoritative listing of UMW financial advances to the CIO is "Loans Made to Congress of Industrial Organizations by the United Mine Workers of America," Aug. 11, 1941, attached to J. R. Bell to Esther Cossel, Aug. 14, 1941, UMWA-A (steel cabinet, UMW-CIO Finances, 1935–1955). The $1.665 million total is confirmed in CIO auditing committee (John O'Leary, John Ghizzori, and David McDonald) to CIO, Nov. 7, 1941, UMWA-A (loose CIO material, box for 1940–41). There is a lengthy discussion of the history of UMW-CIO financial affairs in CIOEB-WSU, June 5, 1942, 326–88.

85. The "lost soul" quote is in CIOEB-WSU, Mar. 24, 1942, 241–69; the "perfectly wicked" quote is in CIOEB-WSU, June 5, 1942, 326–88.

86. Dubofsky and Van Tine, *Lewis*, 410–11.

87. Ibid., 410–12; Bernstein, *Turbulent Years*, 785–86.

88. Murray remarks, Bellaire, Ohio, June 21, 1942, teletype news report, June 22, 1942, CIOFJLL, part 2, reel 7; United Mine Workers of America, *Proceedings . . .* (1942), 190–91.

89. Robert H. Zieger, "Showdown at the Rouge," *History Today* 40 (Jan. 1990): 49–50; Bruce Nelson, "'Give Us Roosevelt': Workers and the New Deal Coalition," *History Today* 40 (Jan. 1990), picture at 47; James Wechsler, *Labor Baron: A Portrait of John L. Lewis* (New York: William Morrow, 1944), 72; Heywood Broun, "Mr. Lewis and Mr. Green," *Nation*, Nov. 28, 1936, 634.

90. CIOEB-WSU, Nov. 23, 1940, Mar. 24, 1942, 241, 244; CIO Comptroller's Department, cash analysis, ca. Jan. 1, 1941, CIOST Papers, box 71: Comptroller; report of the Comptroller, Jan. 26, 1942, CIOEB-WSU, 305–8.

91. On this last point, see Dubofsky and Van Tine, *Lewis*, 411; Dale Kramer, "John L. Lewis: Last Bid?," *Harper's*, Aug. 1942, 283.

92. Reid Robinson, June 5, 1942, in CIOEB-WSU, 365.

Chapter Seven

1. Nelson Lichtenstein, "The Making of the Postwar Working Class: Cultural Pluralism and Social Structure in World War II," *Historian* 51, no. 4 (Nov. 1988): 42–63; Gary Gerstle, *Working-Class Americanism: The Politics of Labor in a Textile City, 1914–1960* (Cambridge: Cambridge University Press, 1989), 289–301.

2. CIOPROC, 1942, 39.

3. For a succinct statement of the central role that patriotic support for the war played in the shaping of CIO responses, see Joshua Freeman, "Delivering the Goods: Industrial Unionism during World War II," *LH* 19, no. 4 (Fall 1978): 590–91. Freeman's 1978 observation that much of the revisionist literature emerging since the 1960s fails to factor in this bedrock reality remains as true now as it did in 1978.

4. See Chapter 6 for a discussion of antilabor congressional and popular sentiments.

5. Typescript minutes of CIO Executive Board meeting, Dec. 13, 1941, JBC, box 93.

6. Murray to Sidney Hillman, JBC, box 93; Victor Reuther, *The Brothers Reuther and the Story of the UAW: A Memoir* (Boston: Houghton Mifflin, 1976), 244, as quoted in Freeman, "Delivering the Goods," 590. See also Ronald W. Schatz, "Philip Murray and the Subordination of the Industrial Unions to the United States Government," in *Labor Leaders in America*, ed. Melvyn Dubofsky and Warren Van Tine (Urbana: University of Illinois Press, 1987), 246–47.

7. Bittner remarks, Mar. 24, 1942, CIOEB-WSU, 26; Bridges and Emspak remarks, minutes of legislative conference, Mar. 23, 1942, held as part of the Executive Board meeting, CIOEB-WSU, 44, 64, respectively. References to CIO criticism of political and corporate foot-dragging are found, for example, in Reuther's remarks, CIOEB-WSU, 46–51. Philip Murray's addresses and reports at the wartime CIO conventions elaborate on these themes. See CIOPROC, 1942, 13–18, 39–45; CIOPROC, 1943, 8–12, 33–37; and CIOPROC, 1944, 10–16, 36–40.

8. Schatz, "Philip Murray," 248; Neil Betten, *Catholic Activism and the Industrial Worker* (Gainesville: University Presses of Florida, 1976), 112–14.

9. "500 Planes a Day: A Program for the Utilization of the Automobile Industry for Mass Production of Defense Planes," in *Walter P. Reuther: Selected Papers*, ed. Henry M. Christman (New York: Macmillan, 1961), 1–12; Nelson N. Lichtenstein, *Labor's War at Home: The CIO in World War II* (Cambridge: Cambridge University Press, 1982), 85–86; Nelson Lichtenstein, "Walter Reuther and the Rise of Labor-Liberalism," in Dubofsky and Van Tine, *Labor Leaders in America*, 286–88; David Brody, "The New Deal and World War II," in *The New Deal*, vol. 1, *The National Level*, ed. John Braeman, Robert H. Bremner, and David Brody (Columbus: Ohio State University Press, 1975), 282–87.

10. Address by President Philip Murray on Industry Council Plan, July 7, 1941, CIO legislative conference, JBC, box 89; Reuther's remarks, CIO legislative conference, Mar. 23, 1942, CIOEB-WSU, 46–51; Howell John Harris, *The Right to Manage: Industrial Relations Policies of American Business in the 1940s* (Madison: University of Wisconsin Press, 1982), 71–72. See also Paul A. C. Koistinen, "Mobilizing the World War II Economy: Labor and the Industrial-Military Alliance," *Pacific Historical Review* 42, no. 4 (Nov. 1973): 450–51.

11. Lichtenstein, *Labor's War at Home*, 80, citing Leo Troy, *Trade Union Membership, 1897–1962* (New York: National Bureau of Economic Research, Occasional Paper 92, 1965). Troy's (and hence Lichtenstein's) estimates for 1939 would appear high in light of the material presented in Chapter 5 above. In February 1943 Murray declared that when he assumed the CIO presidency in December 1940, the CIO had only 1.3 million members (Feb. 5, 1943, CIOEB-WSU, 181). Murray's reading of membership growth appears Oct. 28, 1943, CIOEB-WSU, 10–11, while James Carey's cash flow figures are in CIOEB-WSU, Jan. 28, 1944, 351–52.

12. Clinton S. Golden and Harold J. Ruttenberg, *The Dynamics of Industrial Democracy* (New

York: Harper and Bros., 1942), 190–91. The union shop should not be confused with the closed shop in which the employer agreed to *hire* only union members.

13. Ibid., 212; Murray's remarks, verbatim transcript, Bethlehem Steel Corporation et al. and SWOC, May 14, 1942, Headquarters Records, Dispute Case Files, Transcripts of Hearings in Dispute Cases, 1942–1945 (PI entry 12), NWLB-NA.

14. Golden and Ruttenberg, *Dynamics of Industrial Democracy*, 226; Joel Seidman, *American Labor from Defense to Reconversion* (Chicago: University of Chicago Press, 1953), 91–108; Lichtenstein, *Labor's War at Home*, 20–25.

15. Murray's remarks, Dec. 28, 1941, minutes of Executive Board meeting, JBC, box 93; Seidman, *American Labor*, 80–81.

16. Seidman, *American Labor*, 91–108, cites the key cases and arguments. Lichtenstein, *Labor's War at Home*, 20–25, takes a more critical view. CIO objections to certain NWLB limitations on maintenance of membership are indicated in Lee Pressman to Roland J. Thomas, Mar. 30, 1942, with attached statement on union security, Records of Benjamin C. Sigal, series 406, box 2778, NWLB-NA. While NWLB maintenance of membership provisions applied to both AFL and CIO unions, they were more central to the latter organizations. Many AFL construction unions operated under closed shop arrangements or used the pension and benefits features common among craft unions to secure members' allegiance. In the shipyards, the AFL Metal Trades Department negotiated contracts that obligated thousands of as yet unhired workers to pay dues to its affiliates, notably the Boilermakers, as naval vessel production came on line and new hiring expanded geometrically. Throughout the war, the CIO railed against this practice as an abuse of legitimate union security and because it crippled the Marine and Shipbuilding Workers' efforts to compete with the racially discriminatory and often collusive Boilermakers and other AFL metalworking organizations. Since these agreements were freely signed by Henry J. Kaiser's shipyards and hence involved no labor-management dispute, they did not fall under the purview of the NWLB, although the NLRB did, until its ability to do so was curtailed by congressional action, invalidate some notoriously collusive AFL arrangements. See Seidman, *American Labor*, 179–82, and William H. Harris, "Federal Intervention in Union Discrimination: FEPC and West Coast Shipyards during World War II," *LH* 22, no. 3 (Summer 1981): 325–47; and CIOEB-WSU, Oct. 29, 1943, 231–34.

17. CIOEB-WSU, Oct. 29, 1943, 284.

18. CIOEB-WSU, Jan. 24, 1942.

19. Ronald Edsforth, *Class Conflict and Cultural Consensus: The Making of a Mass Consumer Society in Flint, Michigan* (New Brunswick: Rutgers University Press, 1987), 157–89; Steve Babson, *Working Detroit: The Making of a Union Town* (New York: Adama Books, 1984), 76–133; Robert H. Zieger, "The Union Comes to Covington: Virginia Paperworkers Organize, 1933–1952," *Proceedings of the American Philosophical Society* 126, no. 1 (1982): 72–80; Robert Korstad and Nelson Lichtenstein, "Opportunities Found and Lost: Labor, Radicals, and the Early Civil Rights Movement," *JAH* 75, no. 3 (Dec. 1988): 788–93; Rick Halpern, "Interracial Unionism in the Southwest: Fort Worth's Packinghouse Workers, 1937–1954," in *Organized Labor in the Twentieth-Century South*, ed. Robert H. Zieger (Knoxville: University of Tennessee Press, 1991), 164–69; Michael K. Honey, *Southern Labor and Black Civil Rights: Organizing Memphis Workers* (Urbana: University of Illinois Press, 1993), 177–213; Wilson J. Warren, "The Heyday of the CIO in Iowa: Ottumwa's Meatpacking Workers, 1937–1954," *Annals of Iowa* 51 (1992): 363–89.

20. CIOPROC, 1944, 60; Harry A. Millis and Royal E. Montgomery, *Organized Labor* (New York: McGraw-Hill, 1945), 301–5, 313–15; Murray Emanuel Polakoff, "The Development of the Texas State C.I.O. Council" (Ph.D. dissertation, Columbia University, 1955), 1–19.

21. The files of the Wayne County and Michigan State IUCs are at ALUAWSU, while those of the ILWU at the union's San Francisco headquarters contain much material on the Bay Area and other West Coast councils. Some of the left-right controversies that characterized the Los

Angeles IUC are revealed, for example, in I. Lutsky to David Dubinsky, Aug. 31, 1938, ILGWU-LMDC, box 16: 2A, while the controversy over the Greater New York council is indicated in clippings from New York newspapers, July 25, 26, Aug. 8, 27, 1940, ILGWU-LMDC, box 16: 4A. Among the few studies of IUCs are Polakoff, "Development of the Texas State C.I.O. Council," which details the chronic tensions between the council and the CIO's state and regional directors. The CIO Industrial Union Council files, housed at Catholic University of America, contain sketchy material reflective of these themes, though largely for the post–World War II period.

22. Walter Yonn, "The San Francisco CIO and the 1948–50 Purge" (paper presented at the Seventeenth Annual Southwest Labor Studies Conference, Stockton, Calif., Mar. 23, 1991, in Zieger's possession) is an illuminating discussion of the ways in which the San Francisco IUC functioned in the 1940s. See also Philip Murray, "Report of President . . . ," CIOPROC, 1946, 25–28. Pleas for local unions to affiliate and for international unions to pressure their locals to affiliate with IUCs became almost ritualistic at CIO gatherings. See, for example, CIOPROC, 1942, 57.

23. Office of Facts and Figures, Bureau of Intelligence, report, May 6, 1942, in Osgood Nichols to Thomas Kennedy, May 22, 1942, Records of the National Wage Stabilization Board 1946–47, Records of Benjamin C. Sigal (series 406), NWLB-NA, box 2778; Pete Daniel, "Going among Strangers: Southern Reactions to World War II," *JAH* 77, no. 3 (Dec. 1990): 886–911; Alan Clive, *State of War: Michigan in World War II* (Ann Arbor: University of Michigan Press, 1979), 36–42, 101–16, 193–98; James N. Gregory, *American Exodus: The Dust Bowl Migration and Okie Culture in California* (New York: Oxford University Press, 1989), 173–82; Gerald D. Nash, *The American West Transformed: The Impact of the Second World War* (Bloomington: Indiana University Press, 1985), 37–55, 69–73; Lichtenstein, *Labor's War at Home*, 138–39; Mark McColloch, "Consolidating Industrial Citizenship: The USWA at War and Peace, 1939–1946," in *Forging a Union of Steel: Philip Murray, SWOC, and the United Steelworkers*, ed. Paul F. Clark, Peter Gottlieb, and Donald Kennedy (Ithaca: ILR Press, 1987), 55–62; Merl E. Reed, "The FEPC, the Black Worker, and the Southern Shipyards," *South Atlantic Quarterly* 74, no. 4 (Autumn 1975): 446–47, 464–65; Joshua B. Freeman and Steven Rosswurm, "The Education of an Anti-Communist: Father John F. Cronin and the Baltimore Labor Movement," *LH* 33, no. 2 (Spring 1992): 220–25. The quoted words concluding this paragraph are from Lowell J. Carr and James E. Stermer, *Willow Run: A Study of Industrialization and Cultural Inadequacy* (New York: Harper and Bros., 1952), 77, in Clive, *State of War*, 127. See also Evelyn Miller, "Report . . . Community Organization Project, Delaware County, Penna. . . . ," Oct. 1943, Records of Benjamin C. Sigal, Records of the Labor Members, Records of the Officers of the Board (Industrial Unions), NWLB-NA.

24. Nelson Lichtenstein, "Auto Worker Militancy and the Structure of Factory Life, 1937–1955," *JAH* 67, no. 2 (Sept. 1980): 335–49, quote at 342; Nelson Lichtenstein, "'The Man in the Middle': A Social History of Automobile Industry Foremen," in *On the Line: Essays in the History of Auto Work*, ed. Nelson Lichtenstein and Stephen Meyer (Urbana: University of Illinois Press, 1989), 169–72. See also Lichtenstein, *Labor's War at Home*, 110–35. For similar conditions in another CIO center, Baltimore, see Freeman and Rosswurm, "Education of an Anti-Communist," 223–25.

25. U.S. Department of Commerce, Bureau of the Census, *Historical Statistics of the United States, 1789–1945* (Washington, D.C.: Government Printing Office, 1949), 73; Robert H. Zieger, *John L. Lewis: Labor Leader* (Boston: Twayne, 1988), 140–41. The best account of the 1943 coal strikes is Melvyn Dubofsky and Warren Van Tine, *John L. Lewis: A Biography* (New York: Quadrangle, 1977), 415–40.

26. Clive, *State of War*, 74–77; Lichtenstein, *Labor's War at Home*, 121–27; Murray, Jan. 28, 1944, CIOEB-WSU, 216. Freeman, "Delivering the Goods," 581–88, offers a shrewd assess-

ment of these issues. But see Martin Glaberman, *Wartime Strikes: The Struggle against the No-Strike Pledge in the UAW during World War II* (Detroit: Bewick, 1980), 98–134, for a different view.

27. Standard accounts of wartime strikes are Lichtenstein, *Labor's War at Home*, 110–35, and Seidman, *American Labor*, 131–51. A vivid and politically engaged account that contains important documentary and statistical information is Glaberman, *Wartime Strikes*.

28. See tables 2–4 in Lichtenstein, *Labor's War at Home*, 133–35, and surrounding discussion, as well as 194–97; Freeman, "Delivering the Goods," 583. Soldier quoted in Clive, *State of War*, 79; see also 75–82.

29. Lichtenstein, *Labor's War at Home*, table 3, 134, 181–82, 197–201; CIOEB-WSU, June 18, 1944, 225–27, and Mar. 11, 1945, 125–30.

30. Ronald W. Schatz, *The Electrical Workers: A History of Labor at General Electric and Westinghouse, 1923–1960* (Urbana: University of Illinois Press, 1983), 140–44; Howard Kimeldorf, *Reds or Rackets?: The Making of Radical and Conservative Unions on the Waterfront* (Berkeley: University of California Press, 1988), esp. 134; Joshua Freeman, *In Transit: The Transport Workers Union in New York City, 1933–1966* (New York: Oxford University Press, 1989), 228–48; Freeman, "Delivering the Goods," 591–92. Quill's words are in CIOEB-WSU, July 7, 1943, 31.

31. McColloch, "Consolidating Industrial Citizenship," 53; Lichtenstein, *Labor's War at Home*, 122, 131–33, 171; Murray's comments, Jan. 28, 1944, CIOEB-WSU.

32. George H. Gallup, *The Gallup Poll: Public Opinion, 1935–1971*, vol. 1, *1935–1948* (New York: Random House, 1972), entries for Mar. 13, 1942 (325); Jan. 20, 1943 (365); May 5, 1943 (383); May 28, 1943 (386); June 18, 1943 (389); June 2, 1944 (447–48); remarks of Reid Robinson, June 18, 1944, CIOEB-WSU, 151–52, and of Murray, CIOEB-WSU, 215.

33. Sumner M. Rosen, "The CIO Era, 1935–1955," in *The Negro and the American Labor Movement*, ed. Julius Jacobson (Garden City: Anchor Books, 1968), 200–201; Philip Foner, *Organized Labor and the Black Worker, 1619–1973* (New York: International Publishers, 1974), 243; Robert C. Weaver, *Negro Labor: A National Problem* (New York: Harcourt Brace, 1946), 80–81, table 1.

34. There are no definitive figures for African American membership in the CIO. CIO claims tended, understandably, to be exaggerated. See CIO, *The CIO and the Negro Worker: Together for Victory*, PAM-L, 480. On the UAW, see August Meier and Elliott Rudwick, *Black Detroit and the Rise of the UAW* (New York: Oxford University Press, 1979), 212; on the USWA, see May 5, 1944, USWA-IEB, 96. Estimates for black membership in other CIO unions are based on the figures in Lichtenstein, *Labor's War at Home*, 80, table 1. Elsewhere Lichtenstein speaks of "the half million black workers who joined unions affiliated with the Congress of Industrial Organizations" (Nelson Lichtenstein, "Uneasy Partners: Walter Reuther, the United Automobile Workers and the Civil Rights Movement" [paper presented at the annual meeting of the American Historical Association, Cincinnati, Dec. 1988, in Zieger's possession, 3]), but here he may be referring to all those who passed through the CIO during its first fifteen years and not to actual membership at any given time. Some CIO unions made sweeping claims. Thus, for example, Richard Carter, a black member of the Marine and Shipbuilding Workers' executive board, implied that that union had 80,000 African American members (CIOPROC, 1944, 291), although in fact the Marine and Shipbuilding Workers' peak wartime total membership was 209,000, and all evidence indicates that no more than 10 percent of the total was comprised of African Americans.

35. Meier and Rudwick, *Black Detroit*, 108–206; Korstad and Lichtenstein, "Opportunities Found and Lost," 788–99; Donald T. Critchlow, "Communist Unions and Racism: A Comparative Study of the Responses of the United Electrical, Radio and Machine Workers and the National Maritime Union to the Black Question during World War II," *LH* 17, no. 2 (Spring 1976): 230–44; August Meier and Elliott Rudwick, "Communist Unions and the Black Community: The Case of the Transport Workers Union, 1934–1944," *LH* 23, no. 2 (Spring 1982): 165–97;

Bruce Nelson, "Organized Labor and the Struggle for Black Equality in Mobile during World War II," *JAH* 80, no. 3 (Dec. 1993): 952–88; Honey, *Southern Labor and Black Civil Rights*, 198–202; William Edward Regensburger, "'Ground into Our Blood': The Origins of Working Class Consciousness and Organization in Durably Unionized Southern Industries, 1930–1946" (Ph.D. dissertation, UCLA, 1987), 101–40.

36. Quoted in Korstad and Lichtenstein, "Opportunities Found and Lost," 789.

37. Korstad and Lichtenstein, "Opportunities Found and Lost," 793–99; Meier and Rudwick, *Black Detroit*, 108–206.

38. Halpern, "Interracial Unionism in the Southwest," 164–69; Paul Street, "Breaking up Old Hatreds and Breaking through the Fear: The Emergence of the Packinghouse Workers Organizing Committee in Chicago, 1933–1940," *Studies in History and Politics* 5 (1986): 63–82; Honey, *Southern Labor and Black Civil Rights*, 177–213; Horace Huntley, "The Red Scare and Black Workers in Alabama: The International Union of Mine, Mill, and Smelter Workers, 1945–53," in *Labor Divided: Race and Ethnicity in United States Labor Struggles, 1835–1960*, ed. Robert Asher and Charles Stephenson (Albany, N.Y.: SUNY Press, 1990), 129–45; Judith Stein, "Southern Workers in National Unions: Birmingham Steelworkers, 1936–1951," in Zieger, *Organized Labor*, 192–98; Bruce Nelson, "'Pentecost' on the Pacific: Maritime Workers and Working-Class Consciousness in the 1930s," in *Political Power and Social Theory: A Research Annual*, ed. Maurice Zeitlin and Howard Kimeldorf (Greenwich, Conn.: JAI Press, 1984), 4: 141–82; Kimeldorf, *Reds or Rackets?*, 146; Michael Torigian, "National Unity on the Waterfront: Communist Politics and the ILWU during the Second World War," *LH* 30, no. 3 (Summer 1989): 411–25.

39. Halpern, "Interracial Unionism in the Southwest," 164–69; Floyd Brouillard to Samuel Sponseller, Mar. 20, 1943, United Packinghouse Workers of America Papers, SHSW, box 2: 3; Nelson, "Organized Labor and the Struggle for Black Equality"; Herbert R. Northrup, *Organized Labor and the Negro* (New York: Harper and Bros., 1944), 210–18; Merl E. Reed, "Black Workers, Defense Industries, and Federal Agencies in Pennsylvania, 1941–1945," *LH* 27, no. 3 (Summer 1986): 370–72; Reed, "The FEPC, the Black Worker, and the Southern Shipyards"; Lucien Koch to John Green, Feb. 21, 1946, IUMSWPMD, series II, subseries 7, box 1: Washington Office, Jan.–June 1946.

40. CIO Committee to Abolish Racial Discrimination, *Working and Fighting Together Regardless of Race, Creed, or National Origin* (1943) *PAM-L*, 3120.

41. Merl E. Reed, *Seedtime for the Modern Civil Rights Movement: The President's Committee on Fair Employment Practice, 1941–1946* (Baton Rouge: Louisiana State University Press, 1991), 10–76; Meier and Rudwick, *Black Detroit*, 120–21 (Dodge), 155–56 (Rouge); Marshall Stevenson, "Challenging the Roadblocks to Equality: Race Relations and Civil Rights in the CIO, 1935–1955" (Ohio State University Center for Labor Research, Working Paper 006 [1993]); Marshall Stevenson, "Challenging the Roadblocks to Equality: Race Relations and Civil Rights in the CIO, 1935–1955" (unpublished paper in Zieger's possession, 37–38 [on rubber, steel]).

42. Lichtenstein, *Labor's War at Home*, 125–26; Clive, *State of War*, 141–42; Meier and Rudwick, *Black Detroit*, 121–36; Dominick J. Capeci, Jr., *Race Relations in Wartime Detroit: The Sojourner Truth Housing Controversy of 1942* (Philadelphia: Temple University Press, 1984), 70–74.

43. Reed, "The FEPC, the Black Worker, and the Southern Shipyards," 454–55; Foner, *Organized Labor and the Black Worker*, 264–65; Freeman and Rosswurm, "Education of an Anti-Communist," 223; Meier and Rudwick, "Communist Unions and the Black Community," 182–95; Freeman, *In Transit*, 256–58. Other episodes are alluded to in Philip Murray's remarks, Nov. 6, 1943, CIOEB-WSU, 375–77.

44. CIO convention resolution quoted in Foner, *Organized Labor and the Black Worker*, 257; CIO, *The CIO and the Negro Worker*, 480.

45. This account of the founding of CARD follows closely Stevenson, "Challenging the Road-

blocks" (unpublished version), 22–33. On Townsend and Wilson, see "Willard Saxby Townsend," in *Biographical Dictionary of American Labor*, ed. Gary Fink, 2d ed. (Westport, Conn.: Greenwood Press, 1984), 554–55, and Dennis C. Dickerson, "Boyd L. Wilson," in Fink, *Biographical Dictionary*, 586–87. Murray's account of his meeting with the black steelworkers, May 5, 1944, USWA-IEB, 94–98.

46. CIOPROC, 1942, 177–84 (Reuther's remarks, 183–84).

47. CARD, *Working and Fighting Together*; CARD, *Report of the National CIO Committee to Abolish Discrimination*, Sept. 1945, *PAM-L*, 2599.

48. CARD, *Report*; Stevenson, "Challenging the Roadblocks" (unpublished version), 31–34; Foner, *Organized Labor and the Black Worker*, 256.

49. Stevenson, "Challenging the Roadblocks" (unpublished version), 33; CARD, *Report*.

50. Stevenson, "Challenging the Roadblocks" (unpublished version), 39–41.

51. Clete Daniel, *Chicano Workers and the Politics of Fairness: The FEPC in the Southwest, 1941–1945* (Austin: University of Texas Press, 1991), 12–15, 115–18, 186–88; Reed, *Seedtime*.

52. Meier and Rudwick, *Black Detroit*, 156–74; Daniel, *Chicano Workers and the Politics of Fairness*, 35–37; Reed, *Seedtime*, 33, 114, 150, 353. On the AFL unions and the railroad brotherhoods, see Foner, *Organized Labor and the Black Worker*, 243–52; Stevenson, "Challenging the Roadblocks" (unpublished version), 38; and Reed, *Seedtime*, 34–36, 37–38, 164–65, 267–317.

53. Stevenson, "Challenging the Roadblocks" (unpublished version); CARD, *Report*; CARD, *Working and Fighting Together*; Foner, *Organized Labor and the Black Worker*, 258–59.

54. On the class-essentialist assumptions of the CIO leadership, see Lichtenstein, "Uneasy Partners"; CARD, *Working and Fighting Together*.

55. Stevenson, "Challenging the Roadblocks" (unpublished version), 25–31; May 5, 1944, USWA-IEB, 94–96; Critchlow, "Communist Unions and Racism," 230–44; Meier and Rudwick, *Black Detroit*, 209–12; Roger Keeran, *The Communist Party and the Auto Workers Unions* (Bloomington: Indiana University Press, 1980), 231–35.

56. Michael Honey, "Industrial Unionism and Racial Justice in Memphis," in Zieger, *Organized Labor*, 142–46, contrasts the handling of racial issues in several CIO affiliates. See also Korstad and Lichtenstein, "Opportunities Found and Lost," 786–89; Huntley, "Red Scare and Black Workers," 129–45, 327–31; Stevenson, "Challenging the Roadblocks" (unpublished version), 26–27; John Cort, "Two Conventions: The Auto Workers and the AFL," *Commonweal*, Nov. 12, 1943, 88. Cort's contemporary assessment is echoed by historian Nelson Lichtenstein, who judges that in their policies and attitudes toward African Americans, Communists held a complicated position that was "one part political opportunism, but probably two parts strategic vision and commitment" (Lichtenstein, "Uneasy Partners").

57. See the suggestive discussion of this theme in Gerstle, *Working-Class Americanism*, 289–301, 330–31.

58. Lichtenstein, "Uneasy Partners," 17–19; Stevenson, "Challenging the Roadblocks" (unpublished version); CIOPROC, 1944, 287–93; Henry Lee Moon, *Balance of Power: The Negro Vote* (Garden City: Doubleday, 1948), 132–35.

59. Lichtenstein, *Labor's War at Home*, 178–202.

60. Murray's remarks Nov. 17, 1944, CIOEB-WSU, 239, and June 13–15, 1944, USWA-IEB, 45–50, 62.

61. "Presidential Trial Heat," Oct. 18, 1944, 466, reporting CIO members in support of FDR by a 72 percent to 28 percent margin; "Third Party Vote," Oct. 24, 1944, 466, reporting only .7 percent of those polled planning to vote for a third party; "War Bonds," July 4, 1943, 391, reporting on purchases made over the previous six months, all in Gallup, *Gallup Poll*, vol. 1. See remarks of Sidney Hillman, July 7, 1943, CIOEB-WSU, 54–58.

62. At least this was true *attitudinally*, as evidenced in polling data and general rhetoric. See, e.g., Gerstle, *Working-Class Americanism*, 278–309. Lichtenstein, "Making of the Postwar Work-

ing Class," 57–59, stresses ongoing and even continued resistance by white workers to the industrial and residential inroads of blacks during the war. However, as Lichtenstein points out elsewhere (*Labor's War at Home*, 125–26), hate strikes became rare after 1943 and "many white workers did accept blacks as part of the factory work environment," even though residential integration remained an explosive issue. The meager polling data points toward rising levels of acceptance. See Mildred A. Schwartz, *Trends in White Attitudes toward Blacks*, National Opinion Research Center Report no. 119 (Chicago: University of Chicago Press, 1967), 20–21, 54–55, 71–87, 131, 133.

63. The figures cited do not include the results of the 150,000 ballots sent to UAW members serving in the armed forces. Of the 11,300 of these returned, 93 percent supported the pledge. See Glaberman, *Wartime Strikes*, 104–20.

64. "Problems of Organized Labor," Feb. 6, 1942, 320, in Gallup, *Gallup Poll*, vol. 1.

65. "Labor Union Dues," Feb. 7, 1942, 321; "Featherbedding," July 9, 1943, 392; "Closed Shop," Aug. 10, 1945, 519, all in ibid. The term *closed shop* may well have been interpreted by those questioned as signifying any sort of vigorously enforced union security. See also "Union Finances," Dec. 23, 1942, 360 (response is for "manual workers," who favored the proposition by a 77 percent to 8 percent margin, with 15 percent undecided), and "Labor Unions," June 2, 1943, 387 (response of union members is 80 percent to 12 percent, with 8 percent undecided, in favor of regulation and financial oversight), in ibid.

66. "Strikes in War Industries," Mar. 13, 1942, 325; "Strikes," May 5, 1943, 383; "Strikes," May 28, 1943, 386, all in ibid.

67. "Labor Unions," May 31, 1943, 386–87, in ibid.

68. Zieger, *Lewis*, 45, 49.

69. CIOPROC, 1944, 146. Wartime Gallup polls showed union members in war production plants supporting legislation barring strikes in war industries by better than two-to-one majorities. See "Strikes," May 5, 1943, 383, and "Labor Strikes," June 2, 1944, 447–48, in Gallup, *Gallup Poll*, vol. 1.

70. James C. Foster, *The Union Politic: The CIO Political Action Committee* (Columbia: University of Missouri Press, 1975), 10–12; Lichtenstein, *Labor's War at Home*, 167–68; "Strikes in War Industries," Mar. 13, 1942, 325; "Labor Union Finances," Apr. 3, 1942, 328; "Union Finances," Dec. 23, 1942, 360; "Labor Unions," May 14, 1943, 384; "Labor Unions," June 2, 1943, 387; "Featherbedding," July 9, 1943, 392; "C.I.O. Political Endorsement," July 11, 1944, 453; "Labor Unions," Aug. 12, 1945, 519, all in Gallup, *Gallup Poll*, vol. 1. See also Murray's remarks, Mar. 24, 1942, CIOEB-WSU, 114.

71. Throughout the war, laborites were disappointed at the limited role awarded to organized labor in the government's general mobilization, stabilization, and planning apparatus. See Brody, "New Deal and World War II," 267–309, and Koistinen, "Mobilizing the World War II Economy," 443–78. For the official documentary record of the NWLB, see U.S. Department of Labor, *Termination Report of the National War Labor Board: Industrial Disputes and Wage Stabilization in Wartime, January 12, 1941–December 31, 1945*, 3 vols. (Washington, D.C.: [1947–48]).

72. Created in April 1941 as the Office of Price Administration and Civilian Supply; renamed in January 1942 as the Office of Price Administration.

73. Timothy Alan Willard, "Labor and the National War Labor Board, 1942–1945: An Experiment in Corporatist Wage Stabilization" (Ph.D. dissertation, University of Toledo, 1984), 200–206; James MacGregor Burns, *Roosevelt: The Soldier of Freedom* (New York: Harcourt Brace Jovanovich, 1970), 255–62; Mark H. Leff, "The Politics of Sacrifice on the American Home Front in World War II," *JAH* 77, no. 4 (Mar. 1991): 1296–1306.

74. Willard, "Labor and the National War Labor Board," 230–36; Lichtenstein, *Labor's War at Home*, 116.

75. [CIO], *Procedure and Preparation of Cases before the National War Labor Board* (pamphlet, Dec. 1942), Records of the Vice-chairman (PI 39), CIO files, NWLB-NA.

76. Willard, "Labor and the National War Labor Board," 329–426.

77. R. J. Thomas, "What Labor Did," in *While You Were Gone: A Report on Wartime Life in the United States*, ed. Jack Goodman (New York: Simon and Schuster, 1946), 198–99.

78. Tom De Lorenzo, quoted in Robert H. Zieger, *American Workers, American Unions, 1920–1985* (Baltimore: Johns Hopkins University Press, 1986), 91; Murray quoted in ibid., 85–86. Polling data regularly indicated strong support on the part of lower-income citizens generally and often union members specifically for antistrike legislation, labor conscription, and compulsory arbitration of industrial disputes. See, for example, "Strikes," Aug. 24, 1945, 521, in Gallup, *Gallup Poll*, vol. 1.

79. On premium pay, see Lichtenstein, *Labor's War at Home*, 96–103; quote is at 103.

80. Ibid., 103–6; Willard, "Labor and the National War Labor Board," 203–4; United States Conciliation Service Commissioner Jennings to John Steelman, Sept. 8, 1942, General Correspondence, Apr. 10, 1942–May 18, 1943 (PI 31), NWLB-NA.

81. Seidman, *American Labor*, 121–22; Lichtenstein, *Labor's War at Home*, 145–51; Schatz, *Electrical Workers*, 141–44; McColloch, "Consolidating Industrial Citizenship," 69–70.

82. Thomas, "What Labor Did," 200.

83. Seidman, *American Labor*, 113–30; Willard, "Labor and the National War Labor Board," 145–56; Lichtenstein, *Labor's War at Home*, 70–72.

84. They were William Davis, a New York lawyer and former head of the now-defunct NDMB; Frank Graham, the liberal president of the University of North Carolina; Wayne Morse, an Oregon labor arbitrator of strong pro-union sympathies; and George Taylor, a University of Pennsylvania economist who had worked closely with CIO unionists in establishing arbitration machinery in the clothing and automobile industries.

85. Quote is Lewis's from testimony before the U.S. Senate Committee to Investigate the National Defense Program, Mar. 26, 1943, reprinted in United Mine Workers of America, *Proceedings . . .*, 1944 convention, 131. See also Dubofsky and Van Tine, *Lewis*, 415–25; Willard, "Labor and the National War Labor Board," 260–66; and Zieger, *Lewis*, 142–44.

86. CIOEB-WSU, Nov. 17, 1944, 239.

87. Willard, "Labor and the National War Labor Board," 282–92, quoting Neil Brant at 292; Murray remarks, June 18, 1944, 159–70; Nov. 17, 1944, 238–39; Nov. 19, 1944, 254–68, all in CIOEB-WSU; Murray remarks, CIOPROC, 1944, 45–47.

88. Draft resolution, July 7, 1943, 16; Baldanzi's remarks, 18–20, 31–32; Rieve's remarks, 27–29, all in CIOEB-WSU; Lichtenstein, *Labor's War at Home*, 152–55.

89. Rieve, Mar. 11, 1945, in CIOEB-WSU, 125–30; Lichtenstein, *Labor's War at Home*, 152–55; Glaberman, *Wartime Strikes*, 100–115.

90. Murray's remarks, June 18, 1944, 168 (obnoxious directives), 169–70 (end); Murray's remarks, Nov. 19, 1944, 271 (nothing happens), all in CIOEB-WSU.

91. Lichtenstein, *Labor's War at Home*, 182–85; Murray's remarks, Jan. 27, 1944, CIOEB-WSU, 81–91, 99–104, 167–75, 181–93 (quote at 104).

92. Murray's remarks, Oct. 29, 1943, CIOEB-WSU, 231–32, 242–43. Here the pro-Soviet elements, including Reid Robinson, whose Mine, Mill was directly affected, hastened to dampen Murray's verbal militancy. "We did not contemplate any strike action," declared Robinson of a situation at a Basic Magnesium plant in Nevada. Bridges added that "you have to choose some other form of weapon. . . . [The CIO cannot] deviate from the no-strike pledge" (CIOEB-WSU, 237–38; 268–74).

93. Hillman's remarks, July 7, 1943, 54–58 (quote at 58); Reuther's remarks, May 14, 1943, 81, in CIOEB-WSU.

94. Murray's remarks, Mar. 11, 1945, 92–125 (quotes at 123, 119–20, respectively); Bittner's remarks, Mar. 11, 1945, 145–46, in ibid.

95. Robinson's remarks, 35–38; Bridges's remarks, Jan. 27, 1944, 144–61, 194–95; ILWU statement in support of FDR plan reprinted, 196–99, all in ibid. There has been considerable debate over the character and meaning of wartime policies and actions of pro-Soviet unions. The most balanced treatments are found in Maurice Isserman, *Which Side Were You On?: The American Communist Party during the Second World War* (Middletown, Conn.: Wesleyan University Press, 1982), 136–41, and Harvey A. Levenstein, *Communism, Anticommunism, and the CIO* (Westport, Conn.: Greenwood Press, 1981), 156–83. Bert Cochran, *Labor and Communism: The Conflict That Shaped American Unions* (Princeton: Princeton University Press, 1977), 196–247, offers a scathing critique of pro-Soviet behavior, while Keeran, *Communist Party and the Auto Workers Unions*, 226–49, is more sympathetic. On Bridges, see also Torigian, "National Unity," 418–21.

96. I highlight the Trotskyist critique in part because it establishes one extreme boundary in the wartime debate over labor's role in the war effort. In addition, however, the Trotskyist perspective has been influential in the emerging historiography of the CIO's World War II experience. See, e.g., Art Preis, *Labor's Giant Step: Twenty Years of the CIO*, rev. ed. (New York: Pathfinder Press, 1972), 147–253 (quote at 131–32); Glaberman, *Wartime Strikes*; and Lichtenstein, *Labor's War at Home*, a book derived from the author's 1974 doctoral dissertation, "Industrial Unionism under the No-strike Pledge: A Study of the C.I.O. during the Second World War" (Ph.D. dissertation, University of California-Berkeley, 1972), a work that more explicitly employs a Trotskyist perspective. See also Mike Stevens, "Behind the Murray-Lewis Dispute," *Labor Action*, Aug. 31, 1942, 3; and reports on the UE convention (ca. Aug.–Sept. 1943), *Labor Action*, Sept. 20, 1943, 1, and Sept. 27, 1943, 1.

97. Irving Howe, "Split Crisis Grows Sharper in the CIO," *Labor Action*, June 15, 1942, 1, 2; Mike Stevens, "District 50 . . . : A Vital Factor in the American Labor Movement," *Labor Action*, Oct. 5, 1942, 3.

98. For examples of widespread District 50 agitation, see, e.g., Rick Halpern, *Down on the Killing Floor: Black and White Workers in Chicago's Packinghouses, 1904 to 1954* (University of Illinois Press, forthcoming); Zieger, "Union Comes to Covington," 72–75; Grant Oakes and Gerald Fielde to James B. Carey, July 6, 1943, CIOST, box 52: FE; Allan Haywood to Grant Oakes, Aug. 6, 1943, CIOST, box 50: FE-UAW; Anthony Esposito to Haywood, Mar. 20, 1944, CIOST, box 58: Playthings. Bittner's remarks, Nov. 6, 1943, 432; Thomas's remarks, Mar. 11, 1945, 220–21; Murray remarks, May 14, 1943, 153, all in CIOEB-WSU.

99. Lichtenstein, *Labor's War at Home*, 102–3; Joseph Goulden, *Meany* (New York: Atheneum, 1972), 97–107; John N. Schacht, *The Making of Telephone Unionism, 1920–1947* (New Brunswick: Rutgers University Press, 1985), 100–129.

100. Murray's remarks, Mar. 11, 1945, CIOEB-WSU, 104–5. There is a convenient summary of membership gains in Lichtenstein, *Labor's War at Home*, 80–81, although Lichtenstein's figures show CIO membership at 2.659 million in 1941 and at 3.847 million in 1945. Murray's estimate of 1.5 million in December 1940 seems reasonable in light of the problems of recruitment and dues collection described in Chapter 5 above. Recall too that Lichtenstein's 1941 figures included about 600,000 UMW members who were, of course, no longer in the CIO in 1945.

101. See below, 181ff.

102. CIO program and Executive Board resolution, July 13, 1945, 88a; Hillman's remarks, 73, in CIOEB-WSU.

103. Lichtenstein, *Labor's War at Home*, 80–81; CIOPROC, 1944, 56; June 5, 1942, 316; Mar. 12, 1945, 297; July 13, 1945, 7–8, CIOEB-WSU; Paul David Richards, "The History of the Textile Workers Union of America, CIO, in the South, 1937 to 1945" (Ph.D. dissertation, Uni-

versity of Wisconsin, 1978), 150–82; Van Bittner's remarks, Mar. 11, 1945, CIOEB-WSU, 150. On the expansion of arbitration, see Katherine Van Wezel Stone, "The Post-War Paradigm in American Labor Law," *Yale Law Journal* 90, no. 7 (June 1981): 1523, and Matthew W. Finkin, "Revisionism in Labor Law," *Maryland Law Review* 43 (1984): 71–74.

104. Murray's remarks, June 18, 1944, CIOEB-WSU, 165–66.

105. McColloch, "Consolidating Industrial Citizenship," 62–76; Willard, "Labor and the National War Labor Board," 126–29; Schatz, *Electrical Workers*, 142–43 (quote at 143); Freeman, *In Transit*, 242–48; Patrick Renshaw, "Organised Labour and the United States War Economy, 1939–1945," *Journal of Contemporary History* 21 (Jan. 1986): 15; William Davis to Osgood Nichols, Aug. 6, 1943, Records of William H. Davis, NWLB-NA.

106. McColloch, "Consolidating Industrial Citizenship," 64–69; Willard, "Labor and the National War Labor Board," 126–29. Remarks Willard, "In the end, the period of wage stabilization during the war, which labor complained about so bitterly, resulted in greater economic gains for most workers than the massive strike wave of the postwar years" (129).

107. Reuther's remarks on arbitration are in verbatim transcript, NDMB Transcripts of Hearings, case 2025, NWLB Records (RG 202), Suitland, Md., 470–71. His remarks on policing are in complete transcript of Joint Press Conference Held by C. E. Wilson . . . and Walter P. Reuther . . . in the Auditorium of the General Motors Building, Detroit, Mar. 31, 1942, NWLB Records, Records of the Vice-Chairman (PI 39) (General Motors [general]), NWLB-NA. For an incisive discussion of the tensions between shop-floor activism and the national leadership in the UAW during World War II, see Nelson Lichtenstein, "Conflict over Workers' Control: The Automobile Industry in World War II," in *Working-Class America: Essays on Labor, Community, and American Society*, ed. Michael H. Frisch and Daniel J. Walkowitz (Urbana: University of Illinois Press, 1983), 284–311, and Lichtenstein, "Auto Worker Militancy," 335–53.

108. The wide-ranging discussion, July 10–14, 1945, CIOEB-WSU, focuses on these themes.

109. Haywood's remarks, July 13, 1945, 84; Murray's remarks, July 13, 17–51 (quote at 42), in CIOEB-WSU.

110. This was regarding the 1944 strike by the United Retail, Wholesale, and Department Store Employees, a 60,000-member affiliate, against the Montgomery Ward Company, whose chairman, Sewell L. Avery, repudiated a 1942 contract with the union and defied both NWLB and presidential directives and conducted a campaign of harassment, firings, and refusal to bargain with the union. The ILWU, which had a long history of jurisdictional conflict with the United Retail, Wholesale, and Department Store Employees, ignored the CIO's strike endorsement and ordered ILWU-organized Ward workers in Minnesota to put in overtime to handle work shunted there from strike-torn Chicago. See Lichtenstein, *Labor's War at Home*, 208–9, 213.

111. Ibid., 211–12. Murray's militant remarks of Oct. 28, 1943, CIOEB-WSU, 231–34.

112. June 13–15, 1944, USWA-IEB, 45–72.

113. Jan. 28, 1944, 229, and June 18, 1944, 167–68, CIOEB-WSU.

114. CIOPROC, 1944, 82–86, 94–96; Lichtenstein, *Labor's War at Home*, 89–90; H. J. Harris, *Right to Manage*, 72; Seidman, *American Labor*, 175–79.

115. Millis and Montgomery, *Organized Labor*, 470; Freeman, "Delivering the Goods," 591; Bridges remarks, Mar. 24, 1942, CIOEB-WSU, 142–43, 149.

116. Foster, *Union Politic*, 6; Dubofsky and Van Tine, *Lewis*, 249, 251–52, 327–28, 333, 348, 360; Millis and Montgomery, *Organized Labor*, 233–38; Steven Fraser, *Labor Will Rule: Sidney Hillman and the Rise of American Labor* (New York: Free Press, 1991), esp. 361–64, 374–78.

117. Lichtenstein, *Labor's War at Home*, 152–56, 175, 287 n. 60; Irving Martin Abella, *Nationalism, Communism, and Canadian Labour: The CIO, the Communist Party, and the Canadian Congress of Labor, 1935–1956* (Toronto: University of Toronto Press, 1973), 73–78.

118. Isserman, *Which Side Were You On?*, 203–5, 208–13.

119. Remarks of Joseph D. Cannon, CIOPROC, 1942, 211.

120. Foster, *Union Politic*, 10–12; Seidman, *American Labor*, 188–89; special meeting, July 7, 1943, CIOEB-WSU, 60–84. See also Murray's remarks, Mar. 23, 1942, CIOEB-WSU, 76.

121. Fraser, *Labor Will Rule*, 503–6; Foster, *Union Politic*, 5–7; Joseph Gaer, *The First Round: The Story of the CIO Political Action Committee* (New York: Duell, Sloan and Pearce, 1944), xi–xv. The Gallup poll reported that only 42 percent of war plant workers voted in the 1942 elections. Of the 58 percent nonvoters, three-quarters indicated that they favored the Democrats in 1944 ("Voter Interest," May 12, 1943, 384, in Gallup, *Gallup Poll*, vol. 1). More recently, however, historians have tended to discount the putatively Democratic character of the nonvoting members of the electorate in 1942. See, e.g., John W. Jeffries, *Testing the Roosevelt Coalition: Connecticut Society and Politics in the Era of World War II* (Knoxville: University of Tennessee Press, 1979), 136–39. Lichtenstein, *Labor's War at Home*, 172–73, stresses the role of anti–third party machinations in pushing Murray and Hillman to create a formal political action arm, but I believe that he overestimates both the grassroots strength of third party sentiment in the CIO and the seriousness with which CIO leaders regarded it. In view of the results of the 1942 elections, the passage of Smith-Connally, the generally bitterly antilabor tenor of political discourse, and the critical nature of the impending 1944 presidential election, the building of an effective CIO political action machine was an obvious necessity, regardless of the isolated, if sometimes vociferous, third party sentiment that cropped up here and there.

122. Foster, *Union Politic*, 5–9.

123. Ibid., 12–13; July 7, 1943, CIOEB-WSU, 145–49. Technically the committee appointed on July 7 had the job of investigating the feasibility of creating a permanent PAC, holding regional conferences at which to gather information, and making recommendations to the November 1943 CIO convention. In reality, however, the unanimous approval of the PAC resolution established the committee on a de facto basis. The subsequent convention unanimously ratified the board's action.

124. Hillman's remarks, CIOPROC, 1943, 243, 247.

125. "Will workers be better off if Democrats or Republicans win presidential election in 1944?," July 3, 1943, 391; "Presidential Trial Heat," Sept. 20, 1944, 462; "Presidential Trial Heat," Oct. 18, 1944, 466, all in Gallup, *Gallup Poll*, vol. 1.

126. Minutes, meeting of CIO-PAC, Philadelphia, July 17, 1943, DMD-PSULA, box 39: CIO-PAC.

127. Foster, *Union Politic*, 23–28; "Political Action," ca. Fall 1943; Thomas Burns to McDonald, Jan. 31, 1944; Fred J. Hart to George Roberts, Feb. 22, 1944; Hart to Roberts, Apr. 19, 1944; William Moran to McDonald, May 17, 1944, all in DMD-PSULA, box 39: CIO-PAC.

128. Foster, *Union Politic*, 23–28; Robert H. Zieger interview with Tilford E. Dudley, Washington, D.C., July 17, 1984 (in Zieger's possession). PAC's claim of responsibility for the departure of Dies from Congress, however, was seriously exaggerated. See Dennis K. McDaniel, "The C.I.O. Political Action Committee and Congressman Martin Dies' Departure from Congress: Labor's Inflated Claims," *East Texas Historical Journal* 32, no. 2 (1993): 48–56.

129. Hillman's remarks, CIOPROC, 1943, 248; CIO Political Action Committee financial statement, Dec. 31, 1943, DMD-PSULA, box 39: CIO-PAC; Gaer, *First Round*, 176–82. Fraser, *Labor Will Rule*, 537, says that PAC and the allied National Citizens Political Action Committee spent $1.5 million on the election.

130. Gaer, *First Round*, 57–60; J. Raymond Walsh, "Forward," in Gaer, *First Round*, viii; Thomas, "What Labor Did," 210–11.

131. *This Is Your America*, reprinted in Gaer, *First Round*, 17–48. For commentary, see Fraser, *Labor Will Rule*, 512–13.

132. *This Is Your America.*

133. CIO Department of Research and Education, *Political Action for All Americans, PAM-L*, 491.

134. *Every Worker a Voter* appears in Gaer, *First Round*, 112–34.

135. *A Woman's Guide to Political Action*, reprinted in Gaer, *First Round*, 403–48.

136. For a different view of CIO wartime graphics on the issue of gender, see Elizabeth Faue, *Community of Suffering and Struggle: Women, Men, and the Labor Movement in Minneapolis, 1915–1945* (Chapel Hill: University of North Carolina Press, 1991), 168–88.

137. *The Negro in 1944*, reprinted in Gaer, *First Round*, 449–78.

138. See Gerstle, *Working Class Americanism*, 289–301, for an illuminating discussion of the changing nature of laborite rhetoric during World War II. A partial exception to the deemphasis on heroic depictions of industrial workers can be found in the remarkable wartime political posters done by Ben Shahn. These often show industrial workers in vigorous workplace settings and reflect the traditional view of the worker as a strong, manly figure. Even here, however, Shahn did not endow his figures with superhuman attributes. His brilliant mixture of realism and stylization depicted the worker as an ordinary person, and hence as hard working and idealistic, and yet as a man confronted by a difficult task, whether on the job or in wider arenas. Of course, Shahn's posters were aimed at promoting political action and were not produced in the service of strike support or picket line heroics. See Kenneth Wade Preston, *The Complete Graphic Works of Ben Shahn* (New York: Quadrangle, 1973), and Lichtenstein, *Labor's War at Home*, 175.

139. Fraser, *Labor Will Rule*, 537; Lichtenstein, *Labor's War at Home*, 175–76; Dudley interview.

140. Fraser, *Labor Will Rule*, 520–34; "C.I.O. Political Endorsement," July 11, 1944, 453, in Gallup, *Gallup Poll*, vol. 1.

141. Remarks of Murray and Hillman, CIOPROC, 1944, 12–13, 206–9.

142. Murray's remarks, CIOPROC, 1944, 12–13; Foster, *Union Politic*, 42–44, 208–13. Jeffries, *Testing the Roosevelt Coalition*, 198–99, gives PAC much credit for Roosevelt's narrow victory in Connecticut.

143. Foster, *Union Politic*, 41–44 (quote at 42); Fraser, *Labor Will Rule*, 536–37.

144. Hillman's remarks, CIOPROC, 1944, 209.

145. On McDonald, see Donald G. Sofchalk, "David John McDonald," in Fink, *Biographical Dictionary*, 375–76; John Herling, *Right to Challenge: People and Power in the Steelworkers Union* (New York: Harper and Row, 1972); and David J. McDonald, *Union Man* (New York: Dutton, 1969).

146. CIOPROC, 1944, 278–86; McDonald, *Union Man*, 165–68.

147. McDonald, *Union Man*, 168.

Chapter Eight

1. CIOPROC, 1946, 5.

2. Joel Seidman, *American Labor from Defense to Reconversion* (Chicago: University of Chicago Press, 1953), 221; U.S. Department of Commerce, Bureau of the Census, *Historical Statistics of the United States, 1789–1945* (Washington, D.C.: Government Printing Office, 1949), 73.

3. Nelson N. Lichtenstein, *Labor's War at Home: The CIO in World War II* (Cambridge: Cambridge University Press, 1982), 221–30; Seidman, *American Labor*, 213–53; George Lipsitz, *Class and Culture in Cold War America: "A Rainbow at Midnight"* (New York: Praeger/Bergin, 1981), 14–86.

4. For Reuther's sweeping vision of a reordered postwar structure of economic decision making and social policy, see Victor Reuther, *The Brothers Reuther and the Story of the UAW: A Memoir*

(Boston: Houghton Mifflin, 1976), 246–48; John Barnard, *Walter Reuther and the Rise of the Auto Workers* (Boston: Little, Brown, 1983), 101–9; and Nelson Lichtenstein, "Walter Reuther and the Rise of Labor-Liberalism," in *Labor Leaders in America*, ed. Melvyn Dubofsky and Warren Van Tine (Urbana: University of Illinois Press, 1987), 286–90. For Murray, see, for example, his remarks, May 24, 1945, USWA-IEB, 20–32. See also Morris L. Cooke and Philip Murray, *Organized Labor and Production: Next Steps in Industrial Democracy* (New York: Harper, 1940); and Ronald W. Schatz, "Philip Murray and the Subordination of the Industrial Unions to the United States Government," in Dubofsky and Van Tine, *Labor Leaders in America*, 248. But see the "Comments" of Harold J. Ruttenberg in *Forging a Union of Steel: Philip Murray, SWOC, and the United Steelworkers*, ed. Paul F. Clark, Peter Gottlieb, and Donald Kennedy (Ithaca: ILR Press, 1987), 126–30, which emphasize Murray's distrust of corporate leaders and his unwillingness to "cross what he perceived as the 'Great Divide'" that separated workers from employers.

5. The postwar strike wave awaits its detailed chronicler. Standard extant accounts include Seidman, *American Labor*, 213–53; Lichtenstein, *Labor's War at Home*, 203–32; Lipsitz, *Class and Culture*, 14–86; and several articles by Barton J. Bernstein, notably "The Removal of War Production Controls on Business," *Business History Review* 39, no. 2 (Summer 1965): 243–60; "The Truman Administration and Its Reconversion Wage Policy," *LH* 6, no. 3 (Fall 1965): 214–31; "The Truman Administration and the Steel Strike of 1946," *JAH* 52, no. 4 (Mar. 1966): 791–803; and "Walter Reuther and the General Motors Strike of 1945–1946," *Michigan History* 49, no. 3 (Sept. 1965): 260–77.

6. Lipsitz, *Class and Culture*, 37–86; Art Preis, *Labor's Giant Step: Twenty Years of the CIO*, rev. ed. (New York: Pathfinder Press, 1972), 257–83.

7. Thus, polls conducted by *Fortune* magazine over the year between November 1945 and November 1946 revealed increasing percentages of respondents voicing sympathy with labor in the strikes that dominated news headlines that year, with poor and lower-income groups strongly prolabor. Cited in Lipsitz, *Class and Culture*, 52–55. Other polls, however, revealed much public hostility toward and suspicion of unions. See George H. Gallup, *The Gallup Poll: Public Opinion, 1935–1971*, vol. 1, *1935–1948* (New York: Random House, 1972), 539, 547, 553–54, 563–64, 567–68, 570, 573, 580–81, 583, 608. As the passage late in May 1946 of the harshly antiunion Case Bill indicated, there was little sense in Congress that union bashing was bad politics.

8. Seidman, *American Labor*, 213–17, quote from *Economic Outlook*, 215; Lipsitz, *Class and Culture*, 37–38; Lichtenstein, *Labor's War at Home*, 203–6; Arthur F. McClure, *The Truman Administration and the Problems of Postwar Labor, 1945–1948* (Rutherford, N.J.: Fairleigh Dickinson University Press, 1969), 68–69; Bernstein, "Truman Administration and Reconversion Wage Policy," 225. Robert H. Zieger's interviews with Everett Kassalow (Mar. 16, 1983) and Stanley Ruttenberg (Aug. 27, 1983) (in Zieger's possession), influential CIO economic policy advisors in 1946, indicate the drift from planning approaches toward de facto Keynesianism in 1945 and after.

9. CIOEB-WSU, Nov. 1, 1945, 74–84 (Murray's quoted remarks at 84).

10. Recent discussions of the struggle within the Democratic coalition between groups, such as the CIO, that stressed a planning-regulatory approach and those pressing a more consumer-market driven approach include Alan Brinkley, "The New Deal and the Idea of the State," in *The Rise and Fall of the New Deal Order, 1930–1980*, ed. Steve Fraser and Gary Gerstle (Princeton: Princeton University Press, 1989), 85–121, and Ira Katznelson and Bruce Pietrykowski, "Rebuilding the American State: Evidence from the 1940s," *Studies in American Political Development* 5, no. 2 (Fall 1991): 301–39.

11. On full-employment and the guaranteed annual wage, see CIOEB-WSU, July 13, 1945, 17–89 (Baldanzi's remarks quoted at 44). The basic CIO line in regard to wage demands, economic policy, and governmental action is seen, for example, in Nathan Cowan to House and Senate members, Aug. 10, 1945, in CIO Press Release, Aug. 13, 1945, and CIO Release, "National

Wage Policy," Nov. 1, 1945, MSAFL–CIO, series 1, box 1: 8 (CIO National, 1945); testimony of
Philip Murray, Aug. 22, 1945, in U.S. Senate, Committee on Banking and Currency, *Hearings
on . . . S. 380* (Full Employment Act of 1945), 79th Cong., 1st sess. (Washington, D.C.: Government Printing Office, 1945), 223–37; testimony of James B. Carey, Aug. 30, 1945, in U. S. House,
Committee on Ways and Means, *Hearings on HR 3736* (Unemployment Compensation Act of
1945), 79th Cong., 1st sess. (Washington, D.C.: Government Printing Office, 1945), 94–104. See
also Everett Kassalow, "The Great Depression and the Transformation of the American Labor
Movement," testimony delivered before the U.S. Congress Joint Economic Committee, Nov. 28,
1980, *Industrial Relations Research Institute*, Reprint No. 234 (Madison, Wisc.: IRRI, n.d.),
332–36.

12. Bittner's remarks, Nov. 1, 1945, CIOEB-WSU, 111; *CIO News*, Apr. 1, 1945, quoted in
Lichtenstein, *Labor's War at Home*, 217.

13. Howell John Harris, *The Right to Manage: Industrial Relations Policies of American Business
in the 1940s* (Madison: University of Wisconsin Press, 1982) 110–111; Lichtenstein, *Labor's War
at Home*, 216–18; CIOEB-WSU, July 13, 1945, 17–89, Nov. 1, 1945, 81–84; Murray's remarks
on Labor-Management agreement, May 24, 1945, USWA-IEB, 23–32.

14. Lichtenstein, *Labor's War at Home*, 222–24.

15. Bernstein, "Truman Administration and Reconversion Wage Policy," 220.

16. Truman's opening address, Nov. 5, 1945, in U.S. Department of Labor, Bureau of Labor
Statistics, *The President's National Labor-Management Conference, November 5–30, 1945*, Bulletin
No. 77 (Washington, D.C.: Government Printing Office, 1946), 37–40. Schatz, "Philip Murray,"
234–57, uses the term *corporatism* to characterize Murray's perspective. Murray himself, however, never accepted such a characterization, properly regarding the term in its 1945 context as
having fascist overtones (USWA-IEB, Dec. 10, 1945, 17–18). In my view Schatz's designation,
while intended in a generic and presumably nonpejorative sense, is problematic. If corporatism
means that spokesmen for large organizations acknowledge and seek to exploit a natural governmental interest in their affairs and that they attempt to gain standing and recognition on high-
level deliberations on basic economic and social matters, Murray was a corporatist, but then so
was virtually everyone. Murray readily proved, by virtue of his angry reaction to Truman's handling of the 1945–46 strikes and his vigorous leadership of the USWA's massive walkout, that his
reasonable hope to avoid a massive and risky test of strength at a time of enormous press and
political hostility toward organized labor did not compromise his willingness to act as a traditional
labor activist. Murray was not a consistent social thinker, but he was a pretty good seat-of-the-
pants historian of labor-management-government relations in the twentieth century.

17. Truman's opening address.

18. Harris, *Right to Manage*, 112–18.

19. Bernstein, "Truman Administration and Reconversion Wage Policy," 229–30; Murray remarks, Dec. 10, 1945, USWA-IEB, 15–18.

20. Bernstein, "Truman Administration and Reconversion Wage Policy," 229–30; Murray's
remarks, Dec. 10, 1945, USWA-IEB, 17–23; Lewis quoted in Melvyn Dubofsky and Warren Van
Tine, *John L. Lewis: A Biography* (New York: Quadrangle, 1977), 456–57; Ross Shearer to David
Stowe, Nov. 10, 1945, Papers of David H. Stowe, HSTPL, box 6: President's National Labor-
Management Conference.

21. *New York Times*, Nov. 16, 20, 21, 1945 (Ruch's words, Nov. 16; Romney's remarks,
Nov. 21).

22. Lichtenstein, *Labor's War at Home*, 222–23.

23. Ibid., 222–24.

24. Reuther, *Brothers Reuther*, 248–56; Victor Reuther quoted in Lichtenstein, *Labor's War at
Home*, 224.

25. For Reuther's agenda, see Lichtenstein, "Walter Reuther and the Rise of Labor-Liberal-

ism," esp. 289–91; Barnard, *Walter Reuther*, 101–17; Frank Cormier and William J. Eaton, *Reuther* (Englewood Cliffs, N.J.: Prentice Hall, 1970), 218–30; and Kevin Gerard Boyle, "Politics and Principle: The United Automobile Workers and American Labor-Liberalism, 1948–1968" (Ph.D. dissertation, University of Michigan, 1990), 25–41.

26. Reuther, *Brothers Reuther*, 248–56; Lichtenstein, "Walter Reuther and the Rise of Labor-Liberalism," 289–90; Barnard, *Walter Reuther*, 105–8; Cormier and Eaton, *Reuther*, 219–23.

27. Barnard, *Walter Reuther*, 88–90; Lichtenstein, "Walter Reuther and the Rise of Labor-Liberalism," 280–302; Lichtenstein, *Labor's War at Home*, 221–28; Reuther, *Brothers Reuther*, 248–56.

28. Criticisms of Reuther's role in the 1945–46 strike are outlined in Martin Halpern, *UAW Politics in the Cold War Era* (Albany, N.Y.: SUNY Press, 1988), 51–93; Lichtenstein, *Labor's War at Home*, 225–30; and Lipsitz, *Class and Culture*, 46–52. See also Harris, *Right to Manage*, 73–74, 139–40.

29. Murray's remarks, Mar. 3, 1946, CIOEB-IUE, 305–6; Preis, *Labor's Giant Step*, 268–70.

30. Murray's remarks, Dec. 10, 1945, USWA-IEB, 27–28.

31. Seidman, *American Labor*, 225–26 (Truman quoted at 225).

32. Murray's remarks, Dec. 10, 1945, USWA-IEB, 26; Gallup, *Gallup Poll*, 1:553–54.

33. Seidman, *American Labor*, 226–27; Preis, *Labor's Giant Step*, 271.

34. Seidman, *American Labor*, 228–29; U.S. Department of Commerce, Bureau of the Census, *Historical Statistics of the United States: Colonial Times to 1970* (Washington, D.C.: Government Printing Office, 1975), part 1, 179.

35. "Strike Arrangements" [Jan. 1946], United Steelworkers of America District 31 Papers, Chicago Historical Society, series I, box 127. 6 (1946 strike, Feb. 1946).

36. Preis's reports are reprinted in *Labor's Giant Step*, 277–78.

37. Lichtenstein, *Labor's War at Home*, 229–30; Preis, *Labor's Giant Step*, 268–70; Reuther, *Brothers Reuther*, 254–55; UE to All Local Unions, Feb. 13, 1946, District 8, Philip Murray/64, and UE to All International Representatives, Field Organizers . . . , Feb. 25, 1946, UEUP, file PM/65. The sincerity and plausibility of Reuther's 1945–46 goals remain a question of considerable debate. The case for Reuther is well stated in Reuther, *Brothers Reuther*, 250–56. See also Cormier and Eaton, *Reuther*, 218–30, and Barnard, *Walter Reuther*, 101–9. More critical assessments are offered in Halpern, *UAW Politics*, 51–70, and Preis, *Labor's Giant Step*, 265. See also Harris, *Right to Manage*, 139–40.

38. USWA-IEB, Dec. 10, 1945, 29–34, 41; McDonald to district directors, Sept. 29, 1945, USWA District 31 Papers, Chicago Historical Society, series I, box 127: 4 (Strike of 1946, 1945 data).

39. Murray remarks, Dec. 10, 1945, USWA-IEB, 28; Murray's remarks, Mar. 15, 1946, CIOEB-IUE, 309.

40. Murray in *CIO News*, Jan. 21, 1946, as quoted in Seidman, *American Labor*, 228; Murray's remarks, Jan. 23, 1946, USWA-IEB, 1946, 43.

41. Transcript of UAW-GM bargaining session, Feb. 12, 194[6], Papers of John W. Gibson, HSTPL, box 19: General Motors. This carbon copy is misdated Feb. 12, 1945.

42. Preis, *Labor's Giant Step*, 278.

43. Everett Kassalow to Katherine Ellickson, Mar. 21, 1946, CIOST, box 53: Glass, 1945–46.

44. Harris, *Right to Manage*, esp. 151–52.

45. Seidman, *American Labor*, 229–30 (quote at 229); Nelson Lichtenstein, "Great Expectations: The Promise of Industrial Jurisprudence and Its Demise, 1930–1960," in *Industrial Democracy in America: The Ambiguous Promise*, ed. Nelson Lichtenstein and Howell John Harris (Washington, D.C., and Cambridge: Woodrow Wilson Center Press and Cambridge University Press, 1993), 128–39; Nelson Lichtenstein, "UAW Bargaining Strategy and Shop-Floor Conflict, 1946–1970," *Industrial Relations* 24, no. 3 (Fall 1985): 360–81; Nelson Lichtenstein, "Life at the

Rouge: A Cycle of Workers' Control," in *Life and Labor: Dimensions of American Working-Class History*, ed. Charles Stephenson and Robert Asher (Albany, N.Y.: SUNY Press, 1986), 237–59; Nelson Lichtenstein, "Auto Worker Militancy and the Structure of Factory Life, 1937–1955," *JAH* 67, no. 2 (Sept. 1980): 335–53; Nelson Lichtenstein, "'The Man in the Middle': A Social History of Automobile Industry Foremen," in *On the Line: Essays in the History of Auto Work*, ed. Nelson Lichtenstein and Stephen Meyer (Urbana: University of Illinois Press, 1989), 165–81; Harris, *Right to Manage*, 132–48.

46. See Lichtenstein, "UAW Bargaining Strategy," and Carl Gersuny and Gladis Kaufman, "Seniority and the Moral Economy of U.S. Automobile Workers, 1934–1946," *Journal of Social History* 18 (Spring 1985): 463–75.

47. The southern drive still awaits its definitive historian. Barbara S. Griffith, *The Crisis of American Labor: Operation Dixie and the Defeat of the CIO* (Philadelphia: Temple University Press, 1988), contains generous selections from the author's interviews with SOC organizers. F. Ray Marshall, *Labor in the South* (Cambridge, Mass.: Harvard University Press, 1967), 254–69, contains important material. Michael Goldfield, "The Failure of Operation Dixie: A Critical Turning Point in American Political Development?," in *Race, Class, and Community in Southern Labor History*, ed. Gary M. Fink and Merl E. Reed (Tuscaloosa: University of Alabama Press, 1994), 166–89, is scathingly critical of the CIO's efforts. See also Michael Honey, "Operation Dixie: Labor and Civil Rights in the Postwar South," *Mississippi Quarterly* 45, no. 4 (Fall 1992): 443–50. But see Solomon Barkin, remarks, "'Operation Dixie': Two Points of View," *LH* 31, no. 3 (Summer 1990): 378–85, and Bruce Raynor, comment, session on "Textiles and Politics in the Modern South," Southern Labor Studies Conference, Atlanta, Oct. 12, 1991 (Zieger notes).

48. U.S. Department of Commerce, Bureau of the Census, *Sixteenth Census: Population*, vol. 3, *Labor Force*, part 1, *U.S. Survey* (Washington, D.C.: Government Printing Office, 1943), 192; George Brown Tindall, *The Emergence of the New South, 1913–1945* (Baton Rouge: Louisiana State University Press, 1967), 433–72, esp. 457–58, 463–67, and 471; "Labor Drives South," *Fortune*, Nov. 1946, 134–40, 246.

49. Tindall, *Emergence of the New South*, 440–41; Glen Lawhon Parker, *The Coal Industry: A Study in Social Control* (Washington, D.C.: American Council on Public Affairs, 1940), 105–10, 125, 131–33, 143–49; Philip Taft, *Organizing Dixie: Alabama Workers in the Industrial Era*, rev. and ed. by Gary M. Fink (Westport, Conn.: Greenwood Press, 1981), 82–95.

50. Judith Stein, "Southern Workers in National Unions: Birmingham Steelworkers, 1936–1951," in *Organized Labor in the Twentieth-Century South*, ed. Robert H. Zieger (Knoxville: University of Tennessee Press, 1991), 187–92; Robin D. G. Kelley, *Hammer and Hoe: Alabama Communists during the Great Depression* (Chapel Hill: University of North Carolina Press, 1990), 142–44, 148; Taft, *Organizing Dixie*, 101–10.

51. James A. Hodges, *New Deal Labor Policy and the Southern Cotton Textile Industry, 1933–1941* (Knoxville: University of Tennessee Press, 1986), 141–79; Marshall, *Labor in the South*, 169–71; Emil Rieve to John L. Lewis, May 25, 1939, and to J. R. Bell, July 20, 1939, TWUA, installment 3, box 43: John L. Lewis.

52. "The CIO in the South," *CIO News*, July 9, 1938; Michael K. Honey, *Southern Labor and Black Civil Rights: Organizing Memphis Workers* (Urbana: University of Illinois Press, 1993), 67–144; Horace Huntley, "The Red Scare and Black Workers in Alabama: The International Union of Mine, Mill, and Smelter Workers, 1945–53," in *Labor Divided: Race and Ethnicity in United States Labor Struggles, 1835–1960*, ed. Robert Asher and Charles Stephenson (Albany, N.Y.: SUNY Press, 1990), 135–36; Horace Huntley, "Iron Ore Miners and Mine, Mill in Alabama, 1932–1952" (Ph.D. dissertation, University of Pittsburgh, 1976), 84–96; Robert Korstad, "Daybreak of Freedom: Tobacco Workers and the CIO in Winston-Salem, North Carolina, 1943–1950" (Ph.D. dissertation, University of North Carolina, 1987); Taft, *Organizing Dixie*, 114–16; Vernon H. Jensen, *Nonferrous Metals Industry Unionism, 1932–1954: A Story of Lead-*

ership Controversy, Cornell Studies in Industrial and Labor Relations, vol. 5 (Ithaca: Cornell University Press, 1954), 41–42; and William Edward Regensburger, "'Ground into Our Blood': The Origins of Working Class Consciousness and Organization in Durably Unionized Southern Industries, 1930–1946" (Ph.D. dissertation, UCLA, 1987), 31–38, 57–99.

53. Honey, *Southern Labor and Black Civil Rights*, 87–91; Robert H. Zieger, *Rebuilding the Pulp and Paper Workers' Union, 1933–1941* (Knoxville: University of Tennessee Press, 1984), 98, 113, 183; Bruce Nelson, "Class and Race in the Crescent City: The ILWU, from San Francisco to New Orleans," in *The CIO's Left-Led Unions*, ed. Steven Rosswurm (New Brunswick: Rutgers University Press, 1992), 19–46; Daniel Nelson, "The Rubber Workers' Southern Strategy: Labor Organizing in the New Deal South, 1933–1943," *Historian* 46, no. 3 (May 1984): 319–38; Charles H. Martin, "Southern Labor Relations in Transition: Gadsden, Alabama, 1930–1943," *Journal of Southern History* 47, no. 4 (Nov. 1981): 545–68; Taft, *Organizing Dixie*, 116–19; Hodges, *New Deal Labor Policy*, 157–79; Tindall, *Emergence of the New South*, 513–22; "The CIO in the South," *CIO News*, July 9, 1938, 4. The figures here are estimates based on the sources cited in this note and in the previous notes in this chapter and on Frank T. De Vyver, "The Present Status of Labor Unions in the South," *Southern Economic Journal* 5, no. 4 (Apr. 1939): 485–98.

54. The figure 225,000 is my estimate. Marshall states that "the CIO probably had some 400,000 members in the south at the end of the war" (Marshall, *Labor in the South*, 227); but the basis on which he arrives at that figure is unclear, and the surrounding text (226–41) makes a more modest figure seem likely. See also Tindall, *Emergence of the New South*, 515–16, 520–21; Stein, "Southern Workers in National Unions," 192–98; Paul David Richards, "The History of the Textile Workers Union of America, CIO, in the South, 1937 to 1945" (Ph.D. dissertation, University of Wisconsin, 1978), 167–75; Robert Korstad and Nelson Lichtenstein, "Opportunities Found and Lost: Labor, Radicals, and the Early Civil Rights Movement," *JAH* 75, no. 3 (Dec. 1988): 790–93; Bernard Matthew Mergen, "A History of the Industrial Union of Marine and Shipbuilding Workers of America, 1933–1951" (Ph.D. dissertation, University of Pennsylvania, 1968), 139–42; Bruce Nelson, "Organized Labor and the Struggle for Black Equality in Mobile during World War II," *JAH* 80, no. 3 (Dec. 1993): 952–88; Jensen, *Nonferrous Metals Industry Unionism*, 234; Huntley, "Iron Ore Miners," 111; Robert H. Zieger, "The Union Comes to Covington: Virginia Paperworkers Organize, 1933–1952," *Proceedings of the American Philosophical Society* 126, no. 1 (1982): 72–77; Daniel B. Cornfield, *Becoming a Mighty Voice: Conflict and Change in the United Furniture Workers of America* (New York: Russell Sage Foundation, 1989), 98; Honey, *Southern Labor and Black Civil Rights*, 211, 216; D. Nelson, "Rubber Workers' Southern Strategy," 336–38; Frank T. De Vyver, "The Present Status of Labor Unions in the South – 1948," *Southern Economic Journal* 16, no. 1 (July 1949): 1–9; and H. M. Douty, "Development of Trade Unionism in the South," *Monthly Labor Review* 63, no. 4 (Oct. 1946): 576–80.

55. Michael Widman, Allan S. Haywood, and Walter Smethurst to Emil Rieve, Dec. 19, 1939, TWUA, installment 3, box 43: Haywood; John L. Lewis, "Labor Looks South," *Virginia Quarterly Review* 15, no. 4 (Oct. 1939): 526–34; CIOPROC, 1941, 306–8; CIOPROC, 1943, 50.

56. See, for example, the remarks of Walter Smethurst, June 13, 1939, CIOEB-WSU, 36B–C, and those of Thomas Burns, vice-president of the United Rubber Workers, Oct. 12, 1939, CIOPROC, 1939, 194–95, and D. Nelson, "Rubber Workers' Southern Strategy," 335–38. The quote is in Michael Widman, Allan Haywood, and Walter Smethurst to Rieve, Dec. 19, 1939, TWUA, installment 3, box 43: Haywood.

57. Lee J. Alston and Joseph P. Ferrie, "Resisting the Welfare State: Southern Opposition to the Farm Security Administration," in *Emergence of the Modern Political Economy*, ed. Robert Higgs (*Research in Economic History: A Research Annual*, supp. 4; Greenwich, Conn.: JAI Press, 1985): 83–120; James C. Cobb, "'Somebody Done Nailed Us on the Cross': Federal Farm and Welfare Policy and the Civil Rights Movement in the Mississippi Delta," *JAH* 77, no. 3 (Dec. 1990): 912–15; Kenneth Finegold, "Agriculture and the Politics of U.S. Social Provision: Social

Insurance and Food Stamps," in *The Politics of Social Policy in the United States*, ed. Margaret Weir, Ann Shola Orloff, and Theda Skocpol (Princeton: Princeton University Press, 1988), 199–234; Ann Shola Orloff, "The Political Origins of America's Belated Welfare State," in Weir et al., *Politics of Social Policy*, 60–80; Jill Quadagno, "From Old-Age Assistance to Supplemental Security Income: The Political Economy of Relief in the South, 1935–1972," in Weir et al., *Politics of Social Policy*, 235–63; Margaret Weir, "The Federal Government and Unemployment: The Frustration of Policy Innovation from the New Deal to the Great Society," in Weir et al., *Politics of Social Policy*, 149–90; Bruce J. Schulman, *From Cotton Belt to Sunbelt: Federal Policy, Economic Development, and the Transformation of the South, 1938–1980* (New York: Oxford University Press, 1991), 31–35, 56–66.

58. Robert A. Garson, *The Democratic Party and the Politics of Sectionalism, 1941–1948* (Baton Rouge: Louisiana State University Press, 1974), 75–78 (Bailey quoted at 78). See also Joseph Gaer, *The First Round: The Story of the CIO Political Action Committee* (New York: Duell, Sloan and Pearce, 1944), 154–55, 231–32, 266–67; Political Action Committee syllabus, 1951, DPP-SHC, University of North Carolina, series 1: Political Action School.

59. Garson, *Democratic Party and the Politics of Sectionalism*, 143–47; A. Cash Koeniger, "The New Deal and the States: Roosevelt versus the Byrd Organization in Virginia," *JAH* 68, no. 4 (Mar. 1982): 876–96; James T. Patterson, *Congressional Conservatism and the New Deal: The Growth of the Conservative Coalition in Congress, 1933–1939* (Lexington: University Press of Kentucky, 1967), 250–337; Katznelson and Pietrykowski, "Rebuilding the American State," 325–36; Haywood to Paul R. Christopher, July 25, 1945, PRC, box 33: Haywood.

60. McDonald's remarks, Mar. 13, 1946, CIOEB-IUE, 172–74; George Baldanzi to Emil Rieve, Mar. 18, 1946, TWUA, supplement 3, box 40: CIO Organizing Committee, Georgia.

61. McDonald's remarks, Mar. 13, 1946, CIOEB-IUE, 172–74.

62. "Southern Organizing Campaign," ca. Mar. 10, 1946, and David J. McDonald assessment letter, Mar. 12, 1946, DMD-PSULA, box 22: South; Paul J. Christopher memorandum to all CIO Regional Directors in the Southeastern States, Feb. 13, 1946, PRC, box 52A: 1946.

63. Griffith, *Crisis of American Labor*, 24, 27; "Minutes, Southern CIO Organizing Committee," Washington, D.C., Apr. 11, 1946, DMD-PSULA, box 22: Southern Campaign. Problems associated with recruiting organizers were chronic. See, for example, Baldanzi to Bittner, May 8, 1946, TWUA, supplement 3, box 40: CIO Organizing Committee-Georgia, and David J. McDonald to James Feeney, June 2, 1946, DMD-PSULA, box 22: South. As late as mid-July Bittner pleaded with fellow CIO executives not to send him "organizers that are not good enough for your own Union" (CIOEB-IUE, July 17, 1946, 57). For patterns of applications and lists and brief biographies of applicants for organizing positions, see, for example, "List of Persons Interested in Working in CIO Southern Organizing Drive," ca. Spring 1946, and much related material in TWUA, supplement 3, box 40: CIO Organizing Committee-Georgia. In July, Bittner reported that 85 percent of SOC's organizers were from the South and that military veterans made up 75 percent of the force (Bittner remarks, July 18, 1946, CIOEB-IUE, 40).

64. Paul Christopher to All CIO Regional Directors in the Southeastern States, Feb. 13, 1946, PRC, box 52a: 1946; *Wall Street Journal*, Apr. 24, 1946, copy in DMD-PSULA, box 22: South; minutes of the Virginia State Organizing Committee, Richmond, May 5, 1946, SOC-DU, Virginia, box 256: Virginia Organizing Committee; Van A. Bittner, to the Directors and Field Workers, CIO Organizing Committee, June 3, 1946, SOC-DU, South Carolina, box 102: Bittner, June–Dec. 1946. See also Allan S. Haywood, "We Propose to Unionize Labor in the South," *Labor and Nation*, Apr.–May 1946, 35–37.

65. There is a sober and astute assessment of the problems of southern organizing in "Labor Drives South," 135–40, 237. For a good recent statement of these problematics, see Honey, "Operation Dixie," 439–52.

66. David McDonald letter to SOC principals, Mar. 12, 1946, DMD-PSULA, box 22: Campaign in South; McDonald remarks, Mar. 13, 1946, CIOEB-IUE, 179–91; *CIO News* quoted in Griffith, *Crisis of American Labor*, 41.

67. CIOEB-IUE, Mar. 13, 1946, 198.

68. On the NLRB's post–World War II drift to the right, see James A. Gross, *The Reshaping of the National Labor Relations Board: National Labor Policy in Transition, 1937–1947* (Albany, N.Y.: SUNY Press, 1981), 246–48.

69. See, for example, Bittner's remarks, Nov. 20, 1946, CIOPROC, 1946, 190–91; Steven Rosswurm, "The Catholic Church and the Left-Led Unions: Labor Priests, Labor Schools, and the ACTU," in Rosswurm, *CIO's Left-Led Unions*, 130–31; Harvey A. Levenstein, *Communism, Anticommunism, and the CIO* (Westport, Conn.: Greenwood Press, 1981), 208–15.

70. "Minutes, Southern CIO Organizing Committee," Washington, D.C., Apr. 11, 1946, DMD-PSULA, box 22: Southern Campaign.

71. Korstad and Lichtenstein, "Opportunities Found and Lost," 790–93; Huntley, "Red Scare and Black Workers," 129–45; Michael Honey, "Industrial Unionism and Racial Justice in Memphis," in Zieger, *Organized Labor*, 142–47; Donald T. Critchlow, "Communist Unions and Racism: A Comparative Study of the Responses of United Electrical, Radio and Machine Workers and the National Maritime Union to the Black Question during World War II," *LH* 17, no. 2 (Spring 1976): 242–44; Bittner to Franz Daniel, July 3, 1946, SOC-DU, South Carolina, box 102: Bittner, June–Dec. 1946; Reid Robinson to Philip Murray, May 17, 1946, DMD-PSULA, box 22: South; exchange among FTA president Donald Henderson, NMU president Joseph Curran, and CIO secretary-treasurer James B. Carey, Feb. 5, 1943, CIOEB-WSU, 169–75; W. A. Copeland to Paul R. Christopher, Mar. 26, 1945, PRC, box 44: Letters, 1945; Copeland to Christopher, Mar. 31, 1945, PRC, box 58: Loose leaf-CIO, 1945–46.

72. Bittner's remarks, July 18, 1946, CIOEB-IUE, 41–42; Bittner to Donald Henderson, Oct. 18, 1946, Philip Murray papers, CUA, box A4: 31, Bittner. The pragmatic character of most CIO unions' relations with black workers during this period is suggested in Stein, "Southern Workers in National Unions," 192–98; Rick Halpern, "Interracial Unionism in the Southwest: Fort Worth's Packinghouse Workers, 1937–1954," in Zieger, *Organized Labor*, 164–69; and Honey, "Industrial Unionism and Racial Justice," 140, 144–47.

73. Richard L. Rowan, "The Negro in the Textile Industry," in *Negro Employment in Southern Industry: A Study of Racial Policies in Five Industries*, by Herbert R. Northrup and Richard L. Rowan (Philadelphia: Industrial Research Unit, Wharton School of Finance and Commerce, University of Pennsylvania, 1970), 53–65; Mary Frederickson, "Four Decades of Change: Black Workers in Southern Textiles, 1941–1981," in *Workers' Struggles, Past and Present: A "Radical America" Reader*, ed. James Green (Philadelphia: Temple University Press, 1983), 62–71; Baldanzi to Lewis Conn, May 6, 1946, and William Smith to Van Bittner, May 26, 1946, in TWUA, supplement 3, box 40: CIO Organizing Committee-Georgia. On southern blacks' support for the CIO, see, for example, Regensburger, "'Ground into Our Blood,'" 18–22, 48, 101, 105–7, 113–27, 141–42; Stein, "Southern Workers in National Unions," 191–202; and B. Nelson, "Organized Labor and the Struggle for Black Equality." See also Michael Goldfield, "Race and the CIO: The Possibilities for Racial Egalitarianism during the 1930s and 1940s," *International Labor and Working Class History* 44 (Fall 1993): 1–32.

74. David McDonald to James Feeney, June 3, 1946, DMD-PSULA, box 22: South. Patterns of recruitment of organizers are evident in TWUA, supplement 3, box 40: CIO Organizing Committee-Georgia. Haywood's remarks are in his article "We Propose to Unionize Labor in the South," 37.

75. Haywood remarks, Mar. 13, 1946, CIOEB-IUE, 197; William Smith to North Carolina Field Representatives, June 18, 1946, TWUA, supplement 3, box 40: CIO Organizing Commit-

tee-Georgia. Contrast this casual approach to training with, for example, the intense precampaign training undergone by Freedom Summer volunteers in 1964. Observes Nelson Lichtenstein, "To have organized the South in the late 1940s would have required a massive, socially disruptive interracial campaign reminiscent of the CIO at its most militant in the late 1930s, indeed a campaign not dissimilar from that which the modern civil rights movement would wage in the 1960s" (Lichtenstein, "Labor in the Truman Era: Origins of the 'Private Welfare State,'" in *The Truman Presidency*, ed. Michael J. Lacey [Washington, D.C., and Cambridge: Woodrow Wilson International Center for Scholars and Cambridge University Press, 1989], 144).

76. CIOPROC, 1946, 211–14; Bittner's remarks, July 18, 1946, CIOEB-IUE, 45–46; Rieve's remarks, Mar. 13, 1946, CIOEB-IUE, 205; Baldanzi to Bittner, Aug. 9, 1946, TWUA, installment 3, box 40: CIO Organizing Committee-Georgia. On Lucy Randolph Mason, see Mary Frederickson, "Heroines and Girl Strikers: Gender Issues and Organized Labor in the Twentieth-Century American South," in Zieger, *Organized Labor*, 87–88, 90, 91–93, and John A. Salmond, *Miss Lucy of the CIO: The Life and Times of Lucy Randolph Mason, 1882–1959* (Athens: University of Georgia Press, 1988), 75–145. The CIO circulated widely a pamphlet titled *The Church and the CIO Must Cooperate: A Vital Message to Southern Ministers*, ca. Aug. 1946. It stated that "the CIO feels that the Church should help unions develop the right type of leadership." Copy in Murray papers, CUA, box A4: 31, Bittner.

77. *One Out of Every Six*, a pamphlet on "The Story of Gadsden, Alabama, and the CIO," ca. July 1946, SOC-DU, South Carolina, box 102: Bittner, 1948–49; Tindall, *Emergence of the New South*, 523–25; Lucy Randolph Mason, *To Win These Rights: A Personal Story of the CIO in the South* (Westport, Conn.: Greenwood Press, 1970), 183; James C. Cobb, *The Selling of the South: The Southern Crusade for Industrial Development, 1936–1980* (Baton Rouge: Louisiana State University Press, 1982), 106–7; Marshall, *Labor in the South*, 251–52, 261; Griffith, *Crisis of American Labor*, 88–105; Southern States Industrial Council circular, *The Kiss of Death*, quoted in Garson, *Democratic Party and the Politics of Sectionalism*, 188–89.

78. McDonald remarks, Mar. 13, 1946, CIOEB-IUE, 175–79.

79. Griffith, *Crisis of American Labor*, 29–32.

80. Quoted in Griffith, *Crisis of American Labor*, 31–32, 37. Griffith's interviews with organizers provide invaluable material on the conduct of the campaign.

81. Dalrymple to William Pollock, June 21, 1946, TWUA, installment 3, box 41: CIO-Atlanta; Smith to Baldanzi, July 3, 1946, TWUA, box 40: CIO Organizing Committee-Georgia; press release, July 30, 1946, DMD-PSULA, box 22: South; Bittner remarks, July 17, 1946, CIOEB-IUE, 51; Smith to Bittner, Aug. 8, 1946, SOC-DU, North Carolina, box 53: Bittner.

82. Griffith, *Crisis of American Labor*, 28–33; Bittner to State Directors and Field Representatives, June 18, 1946, and to Franz Daniel, Nov. 4, 1946, SOC-DU, South Carolina, box 102: Bittner, June–Dec. 1946.

83. See David Plotke, "The Wagner Act, Again: Politics and Labor, 1935–1937," in *Studies in American Political Development*, ed. Stephen Skowronek and Karen Orren (New Haven: Yale University Press, 1989), 3: 144–51.

84. See Hodges, *New Deal Labor Policy*, 157–79; Bittner to Franz Daniel, Aug. 21, 1946, SOC-DU, South Carolina, box 102: Bittner, Dec. 1946. The uncertain nature of NLRB election campaigns is revealed in copious material, including Tennessee director Paul R. Christopher's illuminating written commentary on southern drive labor board proceedings in Tennessee, 1946–49 (SOC-DU, Tennessee, box 128: Bittner, election results). These situation reports and other communications reveal the success employers had in protracting board proceedings even before the passage of the Taft-Hartley Act in June 1947 and indicate that a high proportion of NLRB cases involved raids on established AFL locals or defenses of CIO locals from AFL raids.

85. Griffith, *Crisis of American Labor*, 33–36. Baldanzi did not regard these defeats as reflections on SOC, arguing that all three campaigns had begun before the southern drive was in gear.

Baldanzi to Bittner, Aug. 9, 1946, TWUA, installment 3, box 40: CIO Organizing Committee-Georgia.

86. Organizers' reports quoted in Griffith, *Crisis of American Labor*, 53–56; Smith to Bittner, Oct. 10, 1946, SOC-DU, North Carolina, box 53: Bittner.

87. Griffith, *Crisis of American Labor*, 42, 57; SOC press release, Aug. 20, 1946, TWUA, installment 3, box 41: CIO-Atlanta; Franz Daniel to Bittner, Aug. 10, 1946, SOC-DU, South Carolina, box 102: Bittner, June–Dec. 1946; Alan L. Swim to State Directors, Sept. 16, 1946, SOC-DU, Tennessee, box 128: Bittner memos; Bittner to Baldanzi, Aug. 23, 1946, TWUA, installment 3, box 41: CIO-Atlanta; Smith to Bittner, October 10, 1946, SOC-DU, North Carolina, box 53: Bittner.

88. Ray Marshall, "Some Factors Influencing the Growth of Unions in the South," in Industrial Relations Research Association, *Proceedings of the Thirteenth Annual Meeting*, St. Louis, Dec. 28–29, 1960 (Madison: IRRA, [1961]), 166–82. Griffith, *Crisis of American Labor*, 42, 56, 193, gives somewhat contradictory figures. An indication of SOC's financial trajectory is found in Bittner's remarks, Jan. 23, 1948, CIOEB-WSU, 354–73. Organizers were typically paid $63 per week, out of which they were to pay their own lodging expenses. They received three cents a mile for use of their own automobiles and a daily food allowance of $3 to $5. Baldanzi to Edmund F. Ryan, Jr., May 13, 1946, TWUA, installment 3, box 30: CIO Organizing Committee-Georgia.

89. Bittner remarks, Nov. 13, 1946, CIOEB-IUE, 25, 38–39; Marshall, *Labor in the South*, 256–58; Griffith, *Crisis of American Labor*, 36, 41–42.

90. Griffith, *Crisis of American Labor*, 42–43; Bittner's remarks, Nov. 13, 1946, CIOEB-IUE, 25–40; Murray's remarks, Nov. 20, 1946, CIOPROC, 1946, 221.

91. CIOPROC, 1947, 13–17, 76; Bittner's remarks, Oct. 17, 1947, CIOEB-WSU, 234–41 (quote at 241); Griffith, *Crisis of American Labor*, 42; Marshall, *Labor in the South*, 264–65; De Vyver, "Present Status of Labor Unions – 1948," 1–22. Bittner's claim of 280,000 new southern members is suspect. De Vyver's tabulation of NLRB elections between March 1946 and August 1947, based on his examination of board files, shows that the CIO won 534 elections in eleven southern states (not including Texas) with a total vote of just under 72,000. Since it is unlikely that many of these victories quickly brought union shop contracts, the new membership gained through these elections was certainly less than this figure. How many southern recruits came into the CIO as a result of the southern organizing campaign and how many through ongoing recruitment and affiliation is impossible to judge.

92. De Vyver, "Present Status of Labor Unions – 1948," 12; Charles Hathaway to Ralph Helstein, Dec. 31, 1946, UPWA, box 38: 6.

93. Murray's remarks, CIOPROC, 1946, 224.

94. Bittner to Paul Christopher, Mar. 7, 1947, SOC-DU, Knoxville, box 128: Bittner, May 1946–Apr. 1947.

95. Griffith, *Crisis of American Labor*, 27, 139–60; Goldfield, "Failure of Operation Dixie"; Honey, "Industrial Unionism and Racial Justice," 145–51; "'Operation Dixie': Two Views," *LH* 31, no. 3 (Summer 1990): 373–78 (comments by Michael Honey); Vicki L. Ruiz, *Cannery Women, Cannery Lives: Mexican Women, Unionization, and the California Food Processing Industry, 1930–1950* (Albuquerque: University of New Mexico Press, 1987), 41–57, 112–19; Regensburger, "'Ground into Our Blood,'" 57–62, 128–37, 255–72; Karl Korstad, "Black and White Together: Organizing in the South with the Food, Tobacco, Agricultural, and Allied Workers Union (FTA-CIO), 1946–1952," in Rosswurm, *CIO's Left-Led Unions*, 75–86. There is no convenient, explicit *contemporary* statement of these views. Pro-Soviet unionists, at least in their public statements, generally voiced support for the southern campaign, though often complaining about red-baiting, jurisdictional matters, lack of élan, and their own marginalization. See, e.g., statements by James Matles (207–9), Joseph Stack (214–15), and Donald Henderson (217–18), CIOPROC, 1946, and Henderson remarks, Nov. 17, 1948, CIOEB-WSU, 41–42. The strong support of the CPUSA-

oriented unionists for biracial unionism and their belief that recruitment of black workers held the key to CIO success in the South is indicated, for example, in the remarks of Henderson and NMU president Joseph Curran, Feb. 5, 1943, CIOEB-WSU, 169–71, 174–75.

96. Schulman, *From Cotton Belt to Sun Belt*. See also "'Operation Dixie': Two Views," 378–85 (remarks by Barkin).

97. Sidney Hillman, "What Will PAC Do Now?," ca. Feb. 1, 1945, in Joseph Gaer to Daniel Schwartz, Feb. 3, 1945, ACWA-LMDC, box 70: 25; Hillman remarks, July 14, 1945, CIOEB-WSU, 342. The standard account of the CIO's political activities is James C. Foster, *The Union Politic: The CIO Political Action Committee* (Columbia: University of Missouri Press, 1975).

98. Hillman, willing to cooperate with Communists and their allies, steadfastly opposed third party initiatives. In the period from the 1944 election to his death in July 1946 he struggled to retain influence within the Democratic Party, to sidetrack third party enthusiasts, and to shield PAC from those in the CIO who wanted to truncate or even eliminate it as a permanent organ. See Steven Fraser, *Labor Will Rule: Sidney Hillman and the Rise of American Labor* (New York: Free Press, 1991), 568–71, and Matthew Josephson, *Sidney Hillman: Statesman of American Labor* (Garden City: Doubleday, 1952), 660–62. Hillman's close cooperation with Democratic leaders and his determination "to stop a Third Party movement and to persuade [*sic*] our people to cooperate with the regular democratic [*sic*] organization" are revealed in aide Palmer Weber's memo, ca. Oct. 1945, to Hillman, ACWA-LMDC, box 212: 5.

99. The Brophy report is cited and discussed in Foster, *Union Politic*, 58. The CIO leadership's linkage of third party discussion to the goals of the Communist Party and of those Communists and their allies operating in the CIO did not become explicit until the later part of 1947.

100. Foster, *Union Politic*, 61–62; Fraser, *Labor Will Rule*, 567–71.

101. Quote is in Steve Babson, *Working Detroit: The Making of a Union Town* (New York: Adama Books, 1984), 128. See also Palmer Weber to Sidney Hillman, ca. Oct. 1945, ACWA-LMDC, box 212: 5; Foster, *Union Politic*, 58–60; Steve Babson, "Detroit's Municipal Elections and the CIO, 1937–1950," Dec. 7, 1981 (unpublished paper in Zieger's possession); Wilber H. Baldinger, "A Labor Variation on an Horatio Alger Theme: A Letter from Detroit," *Labor and Nation*, Oct. 1945, 53–54. For a shrewd discussion of the political hopes that CIO activists harbored and the sharp constraints under which they operated, see Daniel Nelson, "The CIO at Bay: Labor Militancy and Politics in Akron, 1936–1938," *JAH* 71, no. 3 (Dec. 1984): 565–86. See also Hugh Lovin, "CIO Innovators, Labor Party Idealogues, and Organized Labor's Muddles in the 1937 Detroit Elections," *Old Northwest* 8 (Fall 1982): 223–43.

102. CIO press release on CIO-PAC postwar agenda, July 12, 1945, and Murray testimony, Aug. 22, 1945, on S. 380, typescript, MSAFL–CIO, series 1, box 1: 8, CIO National-1945. These files contain extensive verbatim testimony by Murray, Carey, Legislative Director Nathan Cowan, and other CIO leaders on a wide range of immediate postwar economic, civil rights, housing, and regional development legislation.

103. CIO Executive Board statement, Nov. 2, 1945, mimeo, on atomic energy, MSAFL–CIO, series 2, box 61: Brophy-7. Remarks journalist-historian Robert J. Donovan, "No one who lived through the political storms of the Roosevelt and Truman administrations . . . is likely to forget the intensity with which questions like FEPC, welfare, public works, and government controls were fought over" (Donovan, *Conflict and Crisis: The Presidency of Harry S. Truman, 1945–1948* [New York: Norton, 1977], 114).

104. Roland Young, *Congressional Politics in the Second World War* (New York: Columbia University Press, 1956), 197–217; Merl E. Reed, *Seedtime for the Modern Civil Rights Movement: The President's Committee on Fair Employment Practice, 1941–1946* (Baton Rouge: Louisiana State University Press, 1991), 337–43; Katznelson and Pietrykowski, "Rebuilding the American State," 301–39; Bert Cochran, *Harry Truman and the Crisis Presidency* (New York: Funk and Wagnalls, 1973), 199–200; Alonzo Hamby, *Beyond the New Deal: Harry S. Truman and American*

Liberalism (New York: Columbia University Press, 1973), 59–85; Lichtenstein, "Labor in the Truman Era"; mimeographed copy of Carey testimony, Aug. 30, 1945, House Committee on Ways and Means, MSAFL–CIO, series 1, box 1: National CIO, 1945.

105. On the shift in liberal-labor thinking on political economy, see Brinkley, "New Deal and the Idea of the State," 85–121. On the CIO's role in the battle over the Employment Act of 1946, see Stephen Kemp Bailey, *Congress Makes a Law: The Story Behind the Employment Act of 1946* (New York: Columbia University Press, 1950), 92–96. Murray's testimony was reprinted and widely distributed. See testimony of Philip Murray, Aug. 22, 1945, MSAFL–CIO, series 1, box 1: 8, CIO National-1945.

106. Bailey, *Congress Makes a Law*, 80, 92–96; "Employment Act of 1946," in *The Truman Administration: A Documentary History*, ed. Barton J. Bernstein and Allen J. Matusow (New York: Harper, 1966), 47–48; Hamby, *Beyond the New Deal*, 79–80; Bernstein, "Removal of War Production Controls," 243–60; Kassalow, "Great Depression and Transformation," 332–35; CIO, "Background of Inflation," Aug. 15, 1946, and "Wage and Price Program," Aug. 15, 1946, MSAFL–CIO, series 2, box 104: 6, PAC-1946.

107. Kroll statement "PAC Today," ca. Jan. 1946, JKPLC, box 4: 1946.

108. Foster, *Union Politic*, 61–63; minutes of regional CIO staff conference, Houston, Tex., Sept. 14, 1946, Walter P. Reuther Papers, ALUAWSU, box 57: 14, CIO-1946; "Political Participation," June 30, 1946, 586, and "Voter Interest," Oct. 4, 1946, 602, in Gallup, *Gallup Poll*, vol. 1; Julius Emspak to General Executive Board, Aug. 27, 1946, UEUP, District 8, box PM: 78.

109. The subject of postwar Communism and anti-Communism will be treated at greater length in Chapter 9 below. Foster, *Union Politic*, 65–66, 68–69, stresses the importance of the Communist issue in the 1946 elections. See also Rosswurm, "Catholic Church and Left-Led Unions," 128–37.

110. Foster, *Union Politic*, 65–69; Murray to Industrial Union Councils, Aug. 1, 1946, MSAFL–CIO, series 2, box 99: 1, National CIO-1945–46; Kroll speech, Sept. 26, 1946, and "Outline of Remarks," Oct. 7, 1946, JKPLC, box 4: 1946; CIO-PAC, *The People's Program for 1946* and *Elections: 1946*, PAM-L, 562, 569.

111. Foster, *Union Politic*, 67–70; Kroll statement, Nov. 6, 1946, JKPLC, box 5: 1946.

112. "Most Important Problem," Oct. 22, 1945, 534–35; "Most Important Problem," Jan. 16, 1946, 553–54; "Most Important Problem," Aug. 3, 1946, 555; "Labor Disputes," Jan. 6, 1946, 567–68; "Strikes," Apr. 5, 1946, 590; "Wagner Act," Jan. 10, 1947, 618, all in Gallup, *Gallup Poll*, vol. 1; R. Alton Lee, *Truman and Taft-Hartley: A Question of Mandate* (Lexington: University Press of Kentucky, 1966), 30–44; Foster, *Union Politic*, 49–70; Gross, *Reshaping the NLRB*, 251–54; CIO, CIOPROC, 1946, 284. See also Melvyn Dubofsky, *The State and Labor in Modern America* (Chapel Hill: University of North Carolina Press, 1994), 199–208.

113. On union security, the standard work is Gilbert J. Gall, *The Politics of Right to Work: The Labor Federations as Special Interests, 1943–1979* (New York: Greenwood Press, 1988), 13–54. For a sympathetic assessment of the enactment, see James T. Patterson, *Mr. Republican: A Biography of Robert A. Taft* (Boston: Houghton Mifflin, 1972), 352–66.

114. There is a convenient rundown of key provisions of Taft-Hartley in Lee, *Truman and Taft-Hartley*, 75–77, while Charles O. Gregory, *Labor and the Law*, 2d rev. ed. (New York: Norton, 1958), discusses Taft-Hartley at length and reprints in comparative format key sections of the Wagner and Taft-Hartley Acts.

115. Murray testimony, Feb. 19, 1947, in U.S. Senate, Committee on Labor and Public Welfare, *Hearings . . . on S. 55 and S. J. Res. 22*, 80th Cong., 1st sess. (Washington, D.C.: Government Printing Office, 1947), part 2, 1089–1145. The quotes here are from Murray's written statement, 1121–22. The testimony of other CIO leaders, notably George Baldanzi, Walter Reuther, Donald Henderson, Oil Workers president O. A. Knight, James Matles, and Jacob Potofsky, is contained in ibid., part 3.

116. Lee Pressman, memorandum on Ball-Taft-Smith Bill (S. 55), in ibid., part 2 (Feb. 11–12, 14–15, 18–19, 1947), 1154–55; Pressman's remarks, May 17 and June 27, 1947, CIOEB-WSU, 270–91, and 1–129, respectively.

117. Pressman's remarks, CIOEB-WSU, June 27, 1947, 82–83; Murray's remarks, CIOEB-WSU, May 17, 1947, 292–306; Bittner's remarks, CIOEB-WSU, 311–12; copy of minutes, Oil Workers International Union, District 5 Council meeting, Apr. 27, 1947, CIOST, box 56: Oil Workers, 1947–49.

118. Executive Board resolution, Mar. 13, 1947, and CIO release, Mar. 13, 1947, MSAFL–CIO, series 2, box 99: National CIO, 2-1947; Kroll to Daniel Powell, Mar. 26, 1947, DPP-SHC, series 2: National PAC Correspondence, 1945–1955; Kroll to IUC and PAC bodies, May 22, 1947, MSAFL–CIO, series 2, box 104: 16, PAC-1947; Preis, *Labor's Giant Step*, 314.

119. Preis, *Labor's Giant Step*, 312–14; Lipsitz, *Class and Culture*, 112–36; Halpern, *UAW Politics*, 201–4.

120. Tilford E. Dudley to Daniel Powell, Apr. 17, 1947, DPP-SHC, series 2, National PAC Correspondence, 1945–1955; Irwin L. De Shetler to Allan S. Haywood, May 19, 1947, DMD-PSULA, box 63: Haywood, 1947–51; remarks of Allan S. Haywood, May 17, 1947, CIOEB-WSU, 323–27; remarks of Murray, CIOEB-WSU, 342–48; June 27, 1947, 141 (first quote), and Oct. 13, 1947, CIOPROC, 1947, 78 (second quote).

121. The quote is in Preis, *Labor's Giant Step*, 314.

122. Murray's remarks, May 17, 1947, CIOEB-WSU, 341–48.

123. Ibid.; "Labor," May 23, 1947, in Gallup, *Gallup Poll*, 1:648–49.

124. CIOPROC, 1947, 78–79, 108–10. Jack Kroll to Louis Goldblatt, June 10, 1947, IL-WUPSF, ILWU History (Political Action: U.S., 1945–48), outlines the kinds of step-by-step programs of voter education, fund raising, and multilevel coordination among CIO organs that the leadership sought to implement in the wake of Taft-Hartley.

125. Julius Emspak to UE officers and representatives, June 23, 1947, UEUP, Region 8, file PM/107; McDonald's remarks, July 2, 1947, USWA-IEB, 11–12; Murray's remarks, CIOPROC, 1947, 203.

126. Matles's remarks, Oct. 14, 1947, CIOPROC, 1947, 197–99; James Matles and James Higgins, *Them and Us: Struggles of a Rank-and-File Union* (Boston: Beacon Press, 1975), 166–70.

127. Kroll speech, Feb. 1, 1948, JKPLC, box 4: Jan.–July 1948; Kroll release, Seattle, Nov. 17, 1947, JKPLC, box 4: 1947.

Chapter Nine

1. The most cogent account of the international left in the World War II era is Julius Braunthal, *History of the International*, vol. 3, *1943–1968* (Boulder, Colo.: Westview Press, 1980), 1–212. See also Denis MacShane, *International Labour and the Origins of the Cold War* (Oxford: Clarendon Press, 1992), esp. 97–143.

2. The problem of terminology when referring collectively to those who were members of the CPUSA, or who were loyal to its programs and policies even when not formal members, or who regularly and consistently cooperated with Communists and characteristically awarded the Soviet Union the benefit of the doubt, remains troubling. The best discussion of those who consistently allied themselves with Communists and affiliated themselves with Communist positions is David Caute, *The Fellow-Travellers: Intellectual Friends of Communism*, rev. ed. (New Haven: Yale University Press, 1988), esp. 1–16, but this book deals primarily with intellectuals in the United Kingdom. Steven Rosswurm, "Introduction: An Overview and Preliminary Assessment of the CIO's Expelled Unions," in *The CIO's Left-Led Unions*, ed. Steven Rosswurm (New Brunswick:

Rutgers University Press, 1992), 7, terms "trade unionists, who quite freely and consciously worked with CP members, . . . 'independent leftists,' " but since many anticapitalist leftists abhorred the Communist Party and fought its influence in the CIO, this terminology hardly seems helpful.

3. On the initial reluctance of the Communist Party to join in the CIO project, see Bert Cochran, *Labor and Communism: The Conflict That Shaped American Unions* (Princeton: Princeton University Press, 1977), 345–47. There is a vast literature on the role of Communists in the CIO. In addition to the works cited in the notes below, see Harvey Klehr, *The Heyday of American Communism: The Depression Decade* (New York: Basic Books, 1984), esp. 223–51; Melvyn Dubofsky and Warren Van Tine, *John L. Lewis: A Biography* (New York: Quadrangle, 1977), 288–89, 318–19, 363–69; Steven Fraser, *Labor Will Rule: Sidney Hillman and the Rise of American Labor* (New York: Free Press, 1991), 417–20, 434–35, 444–46, 517–23; Bruce Nelson, *Workers on the Waterfront: Seamen, Longshoremen, and Unionism in the 1930s* (Urbana: University of Illinois Press, 1988), 251–64; Fraser M. Ottanelli, *The Communist Party of the United States: From the Depression to World War II* (New Brunswick: Rutgers University Press, 1991), 140–53; Joshua Freeman, *In Transit: The Transport Workers Union in New York City, 1933–1966* (New York: Oxford University Press, 1989). Two collections of essays, *Political Power and Social Theory: A Research Annual*, vol. 4, ed. Maurice Zeitlin and Howard Kimeldorf (Greenwich, Conn.: JAI Press, 1984), and Rosswurm, *CIO's Left-Led Unions*, provide a sampling of recent scholarship. The Zeitlin and Kimeldorf volume also contains some critical commentary, including Robert H. Zieger, "The Popular Front Rides Again," 297–302. Robert H. Zieger, "Toward the History of the CIO. A Bibliographical Report," *LH* 26, no. 4 (Fall 1985): 491–500, provides commentary on scholarly and autobiographical literature, as does Michael Goldfield, "Recent Historiography of the Communist Party U.S.A.," in *The Year Left: An American Socialist Yearbook*, ed. M. Davis, F. Pfeil, and M. Sprinker (London: Verso/New Left Books, 1985), 315–58. A contemporary example of anti-Communist criticism is U.S. Chamber of Commerce, Confidential Report No. 2, "Communism in the Labor Movement: A Handbook . . . ," Report of the Committee on Socialism and Communism, 1947, in Association of Catholic Trade Unionists-Detroit Papers, ALUAWSU, box 14: Communist Control in Labor, 1947.

4. The best account of Communist activities during World War II is Maurice Isserman, *Which Side Were You On?: The American Communist Party during the Second World War* (Middletown, Conn.: Wesleyan University Press, 1982).

5. Joseph Starobin, *American Communism in Crisis, 1943–1957* (Berkeley: University of California Press, 1975), 107–94, conveys something of the texture of party developments and their role in the labor movement during this period. The most recent general account of the CPUSA is Harvey Klehr and John Earl Haynes, *The American Communist Movement: Storming Heaven Itself* (New York: Twayne, 1992), esp. 96–147. For Communist activity in the CIO, see Rosswurm, "Introduction," 2–5; Judith Stepan-Norris, "Left Out: The Consequences of the Rise and Fall of Communist Union Leaders in the CIO" (Ph.D. dissertation, UCLA, 1988); and Daniel Bell notes on interview with Lewis Merrill, 1955, DBC-NYU, 1982 addition, box 2: 55. Merrill said that at one point half of the United Office and Professional Workers' organizers were party members. The ACTU's hostile but well-informed estimates of Communist influence appear in the association's newspaper, *Wage Earner*, Oct. 4, 1946. For Loftus's assessment, see "Issue of Communism Is Left Open by CIO," *New York Times*, Nov. 24, 1946.

6. Early critiques of Communist behavior in the labor movement are Max Kampelman, *The Communist Party vs. the C.I.O.* (New York: Praeger, 1957), and David Saposs, *Communism in American Unions* (New York: McGraw-Hill, 1959). See also Cochran, *Labor and Communism*, and Irving Howe and Lewis Coser, *The American Communist Party: A Critical History*, rev. ed. (New York: Praeger, 1962), 368–401. Harvey A. Levenstein, *Communism, Anticommunism, and the CIO*

(Westport, Conn.: Greenwood Press, 1981) is a balanced account, while a recent update in this vein is Leo Ribuffo, "The Complexity of American Communism," in *Right Center Left: Essays in American History*, by Leo Ribuffo (New Brunswick: Rutgers University Press, 1992), 129–60.

7. The words quoted are those of Monsignor Charles Owen Rice, "Confessions of an Anti-Communist," *LH* 30, no. 3 (Summer 1989): 452, 455. The second quote is from Junius Irving Scales and Richard Nickson, *Cause at Heart: A Former Communist Remembers* (Athens: University of Georgia Press, 1987), 208. These generalizations are based on recent literature reexamining the day-to-day role of Communists and their allies in and around the labor movement. See, for example, Judith Stepan-Norris and Maurice Zeitlin, "'Who Gets the Bird?' or, How the Communists Won Power and Trust in America's Unions: The Relative Autonomy of Intraclass Political Struggles," *American Sociological Review* 54, no. 4 (Aug. 1989): 503–24; Judith Stepan-Norris and Maurice Zeitlin, "'Red Unions' and 'Bourgeois' Contracts?," *American Journal of Sociology* 96, no. 5 (Mar. 1991): 1151–1200; Vicki L. Ruiz, *Cannery Women, Cannery Lives: Mexican Women, Unionization, and the California Food Processing Industry, 1930–1950* (Albuquerque: University of New Mexico Press, 1987); Jerry Lembcke and William M. Tattam, *One Union in Wood: A Political History of the International Woodworkers of America* (New York: International Publishers, 1984), esp. 18, 46; Jerry Lembcke, "Uneven Development, Class Formation and Industrial Unionism in the Wood Products Industry," in Zeitlin and Kimeldorf, *Political Power and Social Theory*, 183–216; James R. Prickett, "New Perspectives on American Communism and the Labor Movement," in Zeitlin and Kimeldorf, *Political Power and Social Theory*, 2–36; Ronald W. Schatz, *The Electrical Workers: A History of Labor at General Electric and Westinghouse, 1923–1960* (Urbana: University of Illinois Press, 1983); Roger Keeran, *The Communist Party and the Auto Workers Unions* (Bloomington: Indiana University Press, 1980); Robin D. G. Kelley, *Hammer and Hoe: Alabama Communists during the Great Depression* (Chapel Hill: University of North Carolina Press, 1990), 228–31; Horace Huntley, "The Red Scare and Black Workers in Alabama: The International Union of Mine, Mill, and Smelter Workers, 1945–53," in *Labor Divided: Race and Ethnicity in United States Labor Struggles, 1835–1960*, ed. Robert Asher and Charles Stephenson (Albany, N.Y.: SUNY Press, 1990), 129–45; Martin Halpern, *UAW Politics in the Cold War Era* (Albany, N.Y.: SUNY Press, 1988), esp. 266–67; Michael K. Honey, *Southern Labor and Black Civil Rights: Organizing Memphis Workers* (Urbana: University of Illinois Press, 1993); Karl Korstad, "Black and White Together: Organizing in the South with the Food, Tobacco, and Agricultural and Allied Workers Union (FTA-CIO), 1946–1952," in Rosswurm, *CIO's Left-Led Unions*, 69–94; Robert Korstad and Nelson Lichtenstein, "Opportunities Found and Lost: Labor, Radicals, and the Early Civil Rights Movement," *JAH* 75, no. 3 (Dec. 1988): 786–811; Paul Lyons, *Philadelphia Communists, 1936–1956* (Philadelphia: Temple University Press, 1982); Mark Naison, *Communists in Harlem during the Depression* (Urbana: University of Illinois Press, 1983), esp. 171; Charles H. Martin, "The International Labor Defense and Black America," *LH* 26, no. 2 (Spring 1985): 165–94; William Edward Regensberger, "'Ground into Our Blood': The Origins of Working Class Consciousness and Organization in Durably Unionized Southern Industries, 1930–1946" (Ph.D. dissertation, UCLA, 1987), esp. 221–74. For a skeptical contrasting recent perspective on Communist sensibility, see Aileen Kraditor, *"Jimmy Higgins": The Mental World of the American Rank-and-File Communist, 1930–1958* (New York: Greenwood Press, 1988).

8. See the sources cited in n. 6 above. On the Packinghouse Workers, see Rick Halpern, "The Iron Fist and the Velvet Glove: Welfare Capitalism in Chicago's Packinghouses, 1921–1954," *Journal of American Studies* 26, no. 2 (Aug. 1992): 159–84; Roger Horowitz, "The Path Not Taken: A Social History of Industrial Unionism in Meatpacking, 1930–1960" (Ph.D. dissertation, University of Wisconsin, 1990); Roger Horowitz, "'It Is Harder to Struggle than to Surrender': The Rank and File Unionism of the United Packinghouse Workers of America, 1933–1948," *Studies in History and Politics* 5 (1986): 83–96; and Paul Street, "Breaking up Old Hatreds and Breaking through the Fear: The Emergence of the Packinghouse Workers Organizing Committee

in Chicago, 1933–1940," *Studies in History and Politics* 5 (1986): 63–82. On Communists' sensitivity to gender, race, and new frontiers of organizing, see Rosswurm, "Introduction"; Mark McColloch, "White Collar Unionism, 1940–1950," *Science and Society* 46, no. 4 (Winter 1982–83): 405–19; and Donald T. Critchlow, "Communist Unions and Racism: A Comparative Study of the Responses of the United Electrical, Radio and Machine Workers and the National Maritime Union to the Black Question during World War II," *LH* 17, no. 2 (Spring 1976): 230–44.

9. In 1945 the CIO did establish a special White Collar Committee, chaired by Carey, and in 1946 reconstituted it as a permanent body, but it was among the least active of CIO committees. George L.-P. Weaver to Carey, Nov. 23, 1948, JBC, box 90: EB Minutes, Nov. 15, 1946; minutes, CIO Vice-Presidents' Meeting, Dec. 14, 1948, JBC, box 93; [Daniel Bell], "Organizing: The Cream Is Off," *Fortune*, Apr. 1950, 54.

10. Starobin, *American Communism in Crisis*, 71–152; Klehr and Haynes, *American Communist Movement*, 96–109; Howe and Coser, *American Communist Party*, 437–55. The standard works on the early history of the party are Theodore Draper, *The Roots of American Communism* (New York: Viking, 1957), and Theodore Draper, *American Communism and Soviet Russia: The Formative Period* (New York: Viking, 1960). Among the more thoughtful recent overviews of the history of U.S. Communism are Goldfield, "Recent Historiography," and Ribuffo, "Complexity of American Communism."

11. On the Communist issue in the UAW, see MacShane, *International Labour*, 105–11, 114–15, summarizing recent scholarship. On Catholics and the CIO, see Neil Betten, *Catholic Activism and the Industrial Worker* (Gainesville: University Presses of Florida, 1976); Douglas P. Seaton, *Catholics and Radicals: The Association of Catholic Trade Unionists and the Labor Movement, from Depression to Cold War* (Lewisburg, Pa.: Bucknell University Press, 1981); Steven Rosswurm, "The Catholic Church and the Left-Led Unions: Labor Priests, Labor Schools, and the ACTU," in Rosswurm, *CIO's Left-Led Unions*, 119–38; and Joshua B. Freeman and Steven Rosswurm, "The Education of an Anti-Communist: Father John F. Cronin and the Baltimore Labor Movement," *LH* 33, no. 2 (Spring 1992): 217–47. The files of ACTU's Detroit branch, AL-UAWSU, chart the diverse stands of postwar Catholic anti-Communism. See especially the reports and correspondence of Fr. Charles Owen Rice, 1948–49, in box 33. On the Committee for Renovative Trade Unionism, see Levenstein, *Communism, Anticommunism, and the CIO*, 212–13.

12. Draper, *American Communism and Soviet Russia*; Klehr and Haynes, *American Communist Movement*, 43–44, 60–62; Fraser, *Labor Will Rule*, 178–83.

13. Murray's distaste for ideological bloodletting is indicated, e.g., in his remarks of Nov. 15, 1946, CIOEB-IUE, 112–33.

14. The postwar conflicts involving liberals and Communists are charted from different perspectives in Alonzo Hamby, *Beyond the New Deal: Harry S. Truman and American Liberalism* (New York: Columbia University Press, 1973), 87–119, and Norman Markowitz, *The Rise and Fall of the People's Century: Henry A. Wallace and American Liberalism, 1941–1948* (New York: Free Press, 1973), 200–265.

15. See, for example, Louis Stark, "Murray Undecided on Keeping CIO Post," *New York Times*, Sept. 19, 1946; Joseph Loftus, "CIO Committee to Attempt Purge of Communist Ties," *New York Times*, Nov. 16, 1946; Joseph Loftus, "Issue of Communism Is Left Open by CIO," *New York Times*, Nov. 24, 1946; Louis Stark, "CIO in Tough Fight with Its Communists," *New York Times*, Sept. 23, 1947; James Higgins, "How Long Can He Compromise?," *New Republic*, Oct. 10, 1947, 12–15.

16. See Win Booth to Don Bermingham, May 27, 1949, DBC-NYU, original series, box 7: Bridges, for reports on continued CIO support for Bridges in his fight against deportation. Murray's remarks on Communists in unions are in Apr. 2, 1946, USWA-IEB, 151–64, and Nov. 15, 1946, CIOEB-IUE, 112–33. MacShane, *International Labour*, 121, quotes Murray on not criti-

cizing the USSR. See also Philip Murray, "If We Pull Together," *American Magazine*, June 1948, 21, 134.

17. CIOPROC, 1946, 113–14; "brief from remarks[,] Mr. Murray's talk to Ex. Bd. . . . ," Nov. 15, 1946, JBC, box 90; William Goldsmith notes of interview with John Brophy, Nov. 11, 1955, DBC-NYU, "closed" files, box 7: Brophy; Germer to Clinton Golden, Nov. 26, 1947, Jan. 8, [1948], Clinton Golden Papers, PSULA, box 3: CIO, 1947–48. The vociferous anti-Communism of Murray's second-line leadership is revealed vividly in USWA-IEB, Apr. 2, 1946, 103–49, while Murray's responsiveness to Catholic anti-Communism is outlined in Rosswurm, "Catholic Church and Left-Led Unions," 129–32.

18. Robert Alexander, "Jay Lovestone," in *Biographical Dictionary of the American Left*, ed. Bernard K. Johnpoll and Harvey Klehr (New York: Greenwood Press, 1986), 253–55; Frank Cormier and William J. Eaton, *Reuther* (Englewood Cliffs, N.J.: Prentice Hall, 1970), 236; Robert H. Zieger, "George Meany: Labor's Organization Man," in *Labor Leaders in America*, ed. Melvyn Dubofsky and Warren Van Tine (Urbana: University of Illinois Press, 1987), 331–32; Federico Romero, *The United States and the European Trade Union Movement, 1944–1951*, trans. Harvey Fergusson II (Chapel Hill: University of North Carolina Press, 1992), esp. 12–16, 23–24, 88–90, 92–96.

19. Cormier and Eaton, *Reuther*; John Barnard, *Walter Reuther and the Rise of the Auto Workers* (Boston: Little, Brown, 1983); Nelson Lichtenstein, "Walter Reuther and the Rise of Labor-Liberalism," in Dubofsky and Van Tine, *Labor Leaders in America*, 280–302; Victor Reuther, *The Brothers Reuther and the Story of the UAW: A Memoir* (Boston: Houghton Mifflin, 1976).

20. On Reuther's complex relationship to radical currents in the 1930s, see Kevin Boyle, "Building the Vanguard: Walter Reuther and Radical Politics in 1936," *LH* 30, no. 3 (Summer 1989): 433–48.

21. CIOPROC, 1940, 230–31; Isserman, *Which Side Were You On?*, 159–61. The most succinct public statement of Reuther's anti-Communism is Walter P. Reuther, "How to Beat the Communists," *Colliers*, Feb. 28, 1948, 11, 44–45, 48–49. Historian John Lewis Gaddis comments astutely on the legitimate ideological and political hostility to Stalinism that motivated U.S. policymakers, and implicitly people such as Reuther, in "The Tragedy of Cold War History," *Diplomatic History* 17, no. 1 (Winter 1993): 1–16.

22. MacShane, *International Labour*, 105–11, is good on these themes. See also Victor Reuther, *Brothers Reuther*, 188–91, 214–19, 261–63, 267–68; Irving Howe and B. J. Widick, *The UAW and Walter Reuther* (New York: Random House, 1949), 149–71, 187–204; Boyle, "Building the Vanguard," 433–48. Far more critical of Reuther are Halpern, *UAW Politics*, 122–23, 127–28, and Keeran, *Communist Party and the Auto Workers Unions*, 206–7, 261–65. For a scathing contemporary judgment emanating from the pro-Soviet left, see Lincoln Fairley, "A Few Facts about Walter Reuther," Mar. 30, 1949, ILWUPSF, ILWU History (TUR UAW).

23. Murray to Clinton Golden, Nov. 24, 1947, Golden papers, PSULA, box 3: CIO, 1947–48. Recent accounts of the CIO's role in postwar foreign policy developments are MacShane, *International Labour*, 97–143, and Romero, *United States and the European Trade Union Movement*, esp. 7–14, 25–28, 37–41, 83–90, 94–96, 114–15, 118–24, 126–31.

24. CIO, *Report of the CIO Delegation to the Soviet Union*, by James B. Carey, PAM-L, 520; CIO, *Everybody's Business: World Plan for Peace and Security*, PAM-L, 517; CIO-PAC, *The People's Program for 1946*, by Joseph Gaer, PAM-L, 562; CIOPROC, 1946, 277–81; Romero, *United States and the European Trade Union Movement*, 9–12. MacShane points out, however, that pro-Soviet and anti-Communist participants in the visit to the USSR differed sharply over the tone and content of the report and that, as was often the case, Pressman was successful in enhancing its pro-Soviet cast (MacShane, *International Labour*, 122–23). See also Carey interview, May 9, 1958, COHC, 340–51.

25. CIO, *Report on World Unity*, report of the CIO delegation to the WFTU Conference, Paris,

presented at the CIO Executive Board meeting, Nov., 1945, *PAM-L*, 518; James Carey interviews, Oct. 16, 1957, May 9, 1958, COHC, 299–309, 340–51. See also Romero, *United States and the European Trade Union Movement*, 17–21, MacShane, *International Labour*, 119–22, and Fraser, *Labor Will Rule*, 546–50.

26. Carey interviews, Oct. 16, 1957, May 9, 1958, COHC; Carey speech, Dec. 18, 1945, American Society for Russian Relief, New York, in Harry Read to Paul Webber, Dec. 14, 1945, ACTU-Detroit Papers, ALUAWSU, box 11: Carey, 1943–47; Sigmund Diamond, "Labor History vs. Labor Historiography: The FBI, James B. Carey, and the Association of Catholic Trade Unionists," in *Religion, Ideology, and Nationalism in Europe and America: Essays Presented in Honor of Yehoshua Arieli* (Jerusalem: Historical Society of Israel and the Zalman Shazar Center for Jewish History, 1986), 299–315.

27. Anthony Carew, "The Schism within the World Federation of Trade Unions: Government and Trade-Union Diplomacy," *International Review of Social History* 29, part 3 (1984): 297–335, is the most balanced account of these developments. See also MacShane, *International Labour*, 125–28; Peter Weiler, "The United States, International Labor, and the Cold War: The Breakup of the World Federation of Trade Unions," *Diplomatic History* 5, no. 1 (Winter 1981): 1–22, and Julius Braunthal, *History of the International*, 3:11–14. The growing unhappiness with the drift of the WFTU on the part of key CIO foreign affairs functionaries is revealed in, for example, Elmer F. Cope to Clinton Golden, Dec. 8, 1947; Michael Ross to Golden, Dec. 19, 1947; and Golden to Ross, Jan. 24, 1948, all in Golden Papers, PSULA, box 3: CIO, 1947–45.

28. See Carolyn Eisenberg, "Working-Class Politics and the Cold War: American Intervention in the German Labor Movement, 1945–49," *Diplomatic History* 7, no. 1 (Winter 1983): 284–89; Howard B. Schonberger, *Aftermath of War: Americans and the Remaking of Japan, 1945–1952* (Kent, Ohio: Kent State University Press, 1989), 114–23; Thomas R. Brooks, *Clint: A Biography of a Labor Intellectual, Clinton S. Golden* (New York: Atheneum, 1978), 249–314; and Thomas A. Dietz, "James B. Carey, the C.I.O., and the Marshall Plan" (unpublished paper, Dec. 7, 1981, in Zieger's possession).

29. Gilbert J. Gall, "A Note on Lee Pressman and the FBI," *LH* 32, no. 4 (Fall 1991): 551–61; Gilbert J. Gall, "Communication," *LH* 33: 2 (Spring 1992): 319–20; Murray Kempton, *Part of Our Time: Some Monuments and Ruins of the Thirties* (New York: Dell, 1955), 70–71; Daniel Bell, notes of interview with James B. Carey, Oct. 27, 1955, DBC-NYU, original series, box 4; Meyer Bernstein to Clinton Golden, Sept. 2, 1947, Golden papers, PSULA, box 3: CIO, 1947–48; Daniel Bell interview with Clinton Golden, Oct. 26, 1955, DBC-NYU, original series, box 4.

30. Melvyn P. Leffler, *A Preponderance of Power: National Security, the Truman Administration, and the Cold War* (Stanford: Stanford University Press, 1992), 182–219; Schonberger, *Aftermath of War*, 111–33; Eisenberg, "Working-Class Politics and the Cold War," 283–306; Weiler, "United States, International Labor, and the Cold War," 1–22; Anthony Carew, *Labour under the Marshall Plan: The Politics of Productivity and the Marketing of Management Science* (Detroit: Wayne State University Press, 1987), 19–39; Ronald Filippelli, "Luigi Antonini, the Italian-American Labor Council, and Cold-War Politics in Italy, 1943–1949," *LH* 33, no. 1 (Winter 1992): 102–25; Romero, *United States and the European Trade Union Movement*, 81–87, 118–24; MacShane, *International Labour*, 119–43.

31. Michael Hogan, *The Marshall Plan: America, Britain, and the Reconstruction of Western Europe, 1947–1952* (Cambridge: Cambridge University Press, 1987), 51–53; Leffler, *Preponderance of Power*, 182–219.

32. Carey to Truman, July 7, 1947, quoted in Dietz, "James B. Carey, the C.I.O., and the Marshall Plan," 5; Alan R. Raucher, *Paul G. Hoffman: Architect of Foreign Aid* (Lexington: University Press of Kentucky, 1985), 60–61; Rudy Abramson, *Spanning the Century: The Life of W. Averell Harriman, 1891–1986* (New York: William Morrow, 1992), 416–19; Carew, *Labour under the Marshall Plan*, 70–79.

33. Dietz, "James B. Carey, the C.I.O., and the Marshall Plan"; Philip Murray memorandum on Basic Principles Which Must Govern a Foreign Aid Program . . . Submitted to the President . . . , Nov. 14, 1947, MSAFL–CIO, series 1, box 21: 4, National CIO, 1947.

34. CIOPROC, 1947, 260–63, 274–76, 290–93. Murray said that the resolution was hammered out in a lengthy preconvention session that included a wide variety of opinion. It is likely that Pressman actually drafted the text of the resolution. See Kempton, *Part of Our Time*, 71, 75–76.

35. Reuther's remarks, CIOPROC, 1947, 284–87.

36. Remarks of Irving Potash and Joseph Kehoe, ibid., 287–90 and 281–84, respectively.

37. Murray's remarks, ibid., 290–92.

38. There continues a bitter and finally unresolvable controversy over the issue of Communism in the CIO and the circumstances surrounding the split that led to the ouster of eleven affiliates during 1947–50. Even the term by which the minority of unionists who opposed the emerging mainstream of CIO policy are to be addressed is problematic. *Communist* is not accurate, for many of them were not party members. *Left* is not accurate for two reasons: (1) their positions on many issues before and during the decisive 1947–50 period were often in fact to the right of those of other laborites; (2) significant groups of socialists, Trotskyists, and independent leftists assuredly comprised part of the left and fought bitterly with them. Where in fact a group of dissidents in the CIO *were* party members, I do use the term *Communists*. More often, I employ the term *Communists and their allies*, which in my usage denotes party members and those labor activists who regularly and habitually cooperated with party members and held uncritical views of the Soviet Union. I also use the term *pro-Soviet*, which, I recognize, is problematic. It was a characteristic, however, of Communists and their allies that the policies of the Soviet Union and the behavior of its leading figures, notably Joseph Stalin, were *never* referred to critically. I believe that the charge of anti-Communist liberals and laborites that these men and women refused to acknowledge problematic aspects of Soviet society and Soviet policies is both accurate and of critical importance in how we should think about the complex and highly charged issues of the day. I share the perspective on both the importance of terminology and the problems with most recent usage expressed by Rice, "Confessions of an Anti-Communist," 449–62.

39. I believe that Anthony Carew's characterization of the reasons for the breakup of the WFTU is applicable to the Communist/non-Communist split in the CIO. "Between the Leninist model of trade unionism as adapted to Stalinist totalitarianism and the model of unionism practiced under capitalism there was little common ground. [In the absence of a powerful fascist enemy] they had little in common. It is hard to see how a headlong clash between these two rival conceptions of trade unionism could have been avoided for any length of time. . . . The breakup . . . is best seen not as something for which one or another side was responsible, but rather as an inevitable outcome" (Carew, "Schism within the World Federation," 334–35. The recent literature on Communism and the CIO generally does not agree with Carew's (and my) premise. See, for example, Mary Sperling McAuliffe, *Crisis on the Left: Cold War Politics and American Liberals, 1947–1954* (Amherst: University of Massachusetts Press, 1978), and Rosswurm, "Introduction," 1–18. An earlier generation of scholars, in my view with more perspicacity, however, insisted on this point. The best statements are Howe and Coser, *American Communist Party*; Theodore Draper, "American Communism Revisited," *New York Review of Books*, May 9, 1985, 32–37, and Theodore Draper, "The Popular Front Revisited," *New York Review of Books*, May 30, 1985, 44–50. A lively exchange between Draper and critics of his article appears in *New York Review of Books*, Aug. 15, 1985, 40–44. See also Sean Wilentz, "Red Herrings Revisited: Theodore Draper Blows His Cool," *Voice Literary Supplement* 36 (June 1985), 5–7. Cochran, *Labor and Communism*, and Levenstein, *Communism, Anticommunism, and the CIO*, would likely reject Carew's formulation as applied to the CIO and the Communists but are critical

of both camps on other grounds. Murray's remarks of Aug. 31, 1948, are in CIOEB-WSU, 133–57, 212–28.

40. The resolutions and debates on foreign policy and political action appear in CIOPROC, 1947, 274–93, and 303–27, respectively.

41. There is an astute analysis of the powerful anti-Communist subtext of the resolution and the circumstances surrounding it in John Herling, "Two Conventions: AFL and CIO," *Labor and Nation*, Nov.–Dec. 1947, 14–16.

42. The manifesto, dated Sept. 21–27, 1947, is reprinted in Braunthal, *History of the International*, 3 : 549–51.

43. Braunthal analyzes the creation of the Cominform in ibid., 144–81. See also Klehr and Haynes, *American Communist Movement*, 114–15, and Starobin, *American Communism in Crisis*, 170–71.

44. Klehr and Haynes, *American Communist Movement*, 114–15; Starobin, *American Communism in Crisis*, 170–77; Levenstein, *Communism, Anticommunism, and the CIO*, 221–24; Freeman, *In Transit*, 292–92; and David Shannon, *The Decline of American Communism: A History of the Communist Party of the United States since 1945* (New York: Harcourt, Brace, 1959), 134–40. Like many key episodes in the history of the CPUSA, the third party decision and the precise circumstances surrounding it are still disputed subjects. The testimony of TWU president Michael J. Quill as to the sequence of events and the nature of the relationship between party headquarters and unionists such as himself, while challenged on specific points of timing and locale, is generally credible and has been accepted by most reputable commentators. Curtis D. MacDougall, *The Components of the Decision*, vol. 1 of *Gideon's Army* (New York: Marzani and Munsell, 1965), 259–63, is skeptical about, but does not refute, Quill's version.

45. See, for example, Philip Murray, *No Third Party in '48*, pamphlet (text of a radio address), Jan. 30, 1948, MSAFL–CIO, series 3, box 106: 4, PAC 1948, and MacDougall, *Components of Decision*, 174–76. A recent treatment that assesses progressive electoral prospects more optimistically than did Murray and his associates is Stephen Paul Cameron, "The Liberal-Labor-Democratic Alliance, 1945–1952: Anti-Communism as a Flawed Unifying Theme" (Ph.D. dissertation, University of Pennsylvania, 1988).

46. CIOEB-WSU, Jan. 22, 1947, 76–84, 91–132, 138–48.

47. Statement on Autonomy of CIO International Unions in Julius Emspak to UE functionaries and local officers, Jan. 22, 1948, UEUP, file PM/126.

48. Reuther's statements, Jan. 22, 23, 1948, CIOEB-WSU, 54–76, 274–76.

49. Murray's remarks, Jan. 22, 1948, CIOEB-WSU, 221–40. According to MacDougall, Wallace had in fact talked with Murray on the phone and had sought additional audiences (MacDougall, *Components of Decision*, 175).

50. Murray quoted in Starobin, *American Communism in Crisis*, 174–75. On Quill's role, see the sources cited in n. 44 above and interview by "Levering" with Michael Quill, Oct. 31, 1948, DBC-NYU, original section, box 7: Quill.

51. CIOEB-WSU, Aug. 31, 1948, 219–20.

52. Palmer Weber to Jack Kroll, Apr., 1948, JKPLC, box 1: 1948; Polly Hayden to Daniel Powell, DPP-SHC, series 2, correspondence: PAC, 1945–51; Curtis D. MacDougall, *The Campaign and the Vote*, vol. 3 of *Gideon's Army* (New York: Marzani and Munsell, 1965), 611–28.

53. CIO release, including Haywood to Bridges, Mar. 5, 1948, Americans for Democratic Action Papers, SHSW, series 2, box 30: CIO, 1946–49; Cochran, *Labor and Communism*, 303; Kempton, *Part of Our Time* 75–77; Murray's remarks, Feb. 16, 1948, USWA-IEB, 25–29; FBI summary of Pressman interview, Aug. 30–31, 1950, reprinted in Gall, "Note on Lee Pressman and the FBI," 559–60; Ernest De Maio penciled notes, UE General Executive Board Minutes, Feb. 1, 1948, Ernest De Maio Papers, Chicago Historical Society, box 1: GEB Minutes, 1947–49;

Bittner to Clinton Golden, Feb. 4, 1948, Golden papers, PSULA, box 3: CIO, 1947–48. A widely read magazine article by Reuther, "How to Beat the Communists," gave expression to the sense of relief that anti-Communists felt now that disagreements over the Marshall Plan and the Wallace candidacy permitted direct confrontation.

54. Germer to Clinton Golden, Nov. 26, 1947, Jan. 8, 1948, Golden papers, PSULA, box 3: CIO, 1947–48; Jack Altman, "CIO and Political Discipline," *Labor and Nation*, May–June, 1948, 28–29; resolution on Greater New York IUC in Jack Altman to Philip Murray, Mar. 13, 1947, CIOST, box 58: Retail, Wholesale, 1946–47. There is a vivid account of the inner workings of the pro-Soviet Los Angeles IUC and of the machinations on both sides to retain or seize control of it in Paul Jacobs, *Is Curly Jewish?: A Political Self-Portrait Illuminating Three Turbulent Decades of Social Revolt, 1935–1965* (New York: Atheneum, 1965), 184–86. The grievances against the pro-Soviet forces and the range of tactics employed by the national CIO and disaffected local unionists are candidly revealed in the informal minutes of a meeting held on Dec. 2, 1948, in Los Angeles, attended by Brophy, Germer, and CIO regional director Irwin L. De Shetler, a leading West Coast anti-Communist (CIO Industrial Union Council Papers, CUA, box 6: Los Angeles).

55. W. A. Copeland to Paul R. Christopher, Oct. 16, 1946, in Van Bittner to Donald Henderson, Oct. 18, 1946, Philip Murray Papers, CUA, box A4: 3, Bittner; Steve Babson, "Coleman Alexander Young," in *Biographical Dictionary of American Labor*, ed. Gary Fink, 2d ed. (Westport, Conn.: Greenwood Press, 1984), 598–99; Walter Yonn, "The San Francisco CIO and the 1948–1950 Purge" (paper presented at the Seventeenth Annual Southwest Labor Studies Conference, Stockton, Calif., Mar. 23, 1991, in Zieger's possession); Halpern, *UAW Politics*, 207, 216–20, 245–46; Levenstein, *Communism, Anticommunism, and the CIO*, esp. 169, 209–11; Freeman, *In Transit*, 195–97; John Earl Haynes, *Dubious Alliance: The Making of Minnesota's DFL Party* (Minneapolis: University of Minnesota Press, 1984), 111–72.

56. CIOPROC, 1946, 58–61. On associations with outside organizations, see George L.-P. Weaver to Louis Goldblatt, Mar. 13, 1947, ILWUPSF, ILWU History, CIO; James C. Foster, *The Union Politic: The CIO Political Action Committee* (Columbia: University of Missouri Press, 1975), 62; Fred Pieper to John Brophy and Jack Kroll, Mar. 18, 1948, DPP-SHC, series 1: Louisiana, 1946–53; Jack Kroll, "Outline of Remarks," Oct. 7, 1946, JKPLC, box 4: 1946; Altman, "CIO and Political Discipline," 28–29; Loftus, "CIO Committee to Attempt Purge."

57. Brophy to industrial union councils, Mar. 8, 1948, Walter P. Reuther Papers, ALUAWSU, box 58: 3.

58. H. A. McKittrick to Brophy, Mar. 19, 1948, and Brophy to McKittrick, Apr. 9, 1948, in Brophy papers, CUA, box 1948: California, M.; Julius Emspak to Philip Murray, Mar. 16, 1948, UEUP, District 8, file PM/133; Albert J. Fitzgerald and Julius Emspak to All UE Local Unions, Apr. 12, 1948, UEUP, District 8, file PM/136; Harry Bridges to Philip Murray, Mar. 18, 1948, ILWUPSF, ILWU History, Political Action, 1945–48; Yonn, "San Francisco CIO"; Halpern, *UAW Politics*, 245; Freeman, *In Transit*, 296–97; Levenstein, *Communism, Anticommunism, and the CIO*, 225–26.

59. Halpern, *UAW Politics*, 245–46; Proceedings . . . Annual Convention, Greater Detroit and Wayne County Industrial Union Council, Sept. 5, 1948, MSAFL–CIO, series 1, box 17: 9, Wayne County IUC, 1948.

60. Yonn, "San Francisco CIO"; Freeman, *In Transit*, 296–97; unidentified memo, Mar. 15, 1948, CIO Industrial Union Council Papers, CUA, box 14: Greater New York IUC; Phil Connelly, "A Report on the Detroit and New York CIO Councils," Oct. 8, 1948, AG, box 19: CIO Western Region (California), 1948–1952; Halpern, *UAW Politics*, 245–46; Levenstein, *Communism, Anticommunism, and the CIO*, 209–11, 215–16, 225–26, 263.

61. Connelly, "A Report on the Detroit and New York CIO Councils"; clipping, *Washington Star*, Oct. 15, 1948, MSAFL–CIO, series 1, box 21: 11, Scholle personal; notes of meeting (of Los Angeles council oppositionists), Dec. 2, 1948, CIO Industrial Union Council Papers, CUA,

box 6: Los Angeles; Brophy to McKittrick, Apr. 9, 1948, Brophy papers, CUA, box 1948: California, M.; minutes of the Portland, Oregon, Industrial Union Council, Apr. 27, 1948, AG, box 19: Western Region, 1940–53.

62. See MacDougall, *Campaign and the Vote*, 611–28.

63. "A Day to Day Account of the Activities of CIO-PAC at the Democratic National Convention," [1948], JKPLC, box 7: CIO-PAC, 1945–49; "Recommendations of the Executive Officers to the Meeting of the CIO Executive Board," Aug. 30–31, 1948, David McDonald Papers, PSULA, box 33: CIO, Dec. 1947–Dec. 1948.

64. "Day to Day Account"; Kroll speech, Milwaukee, July 22, 1948, JKPLC, box 4: Jan.–July, 1948; Robert H. Zieger interview with Tilford E. Dudley, Washington, D.C., July 17, 1984 (in Zieger's possession).

65. On the efforts of CIO officers in behalf of the European Recovery Program, see CIOPROC, 1948, 53–54. On CIO efforts within the Harriman Committee, see Meyer Bernstein to Clinton Golden, Oct. 30, 1947, Golden papers, PSULA, box 3: CIO, 1947–48. On CIO efforts within the WFTU, see Michael Ross to Clinton Golden, Dec. 19, 1947, and Elmer Cope to Golden, Dec. 8, 1947, Golden papers, PSULA, box 3: CIO, 1947–48; and "Text of Conversations between James B. Carey . . . and Giuseppe de Vittorio . . . and Fernando Santi . . . ," London, Mar. 12, 1948, Clark Clifford Papers, HSTPL, box 9: Labor-General. Murray quoted, Murray to CIO Members (mimeographed), Mar. 10, 1948, MSAFL-CIO, Series 2, box 99:4—National CIO, 1948. The best overall accounts of the CIO's role in the development of the Marshall Plan and its relation to the WFTU are in Carew, "Schism within the World Federation"; Carew, *Labour under the Marshall Plan*, 70–91; and MacShane, *International Labour*, 119–43. For a contrasting view, see Weiler, "United States, International Labor, and the Cold War."

66. Ernest De Maio penciled notations, UE General Executive Board meeting, June 21–22, 1948, De Maio papers, Chicago Historical Society, box 1: GEB Minutes, 1947–49; James H. Durkin to Philip Murray, Mar. 24, 1948, CIO Industrial Union Council Papers, CUA, box 14: Greater New York Council.

67. Leffler, *Preponderance of Power*, 182–219; Hogan, *Marshall Plan*, 26–53. Marshall's speech appears in CIOPROC, 1947, 260–63. The close cooperation between CIO officials such as Carey, Michael Ross, Clinton Golden, and Murray and administration officials during the formative stages of the Marshall Plan program is discussed in Dietz, "James B. Carey, the C.I.O., and the Marshall Plan," and Carew, *Labour under the Marshall Plan*, 70–79. See also the works cited in nn. 5 and 6 above.

68. Reynolds quoted in James A. Gross, *The Reshaping of the National Labor Relations Board: National Labor Policy in Transition, 1937–1947* (Albany, N.Y.: SUNY Press, 1981), 258–59. R. Alton Lee, *Truman and Taft-Hartley: A Question of Mandate* (Lexington: University Press of Kentucky, 1966), 89–105, stresses the sincerity and vigor of Truman's veto, while Susan M. Hartmann, *Truman and the 80th Congress* (Columbia: University of Missouri Press, 1971), 87–90, highlights the inadequacy of Truman's efforts to shape the original legislation and to prevent the override. Truman's own brief discussion of the episode occurs in Harry S. Truman, *Memoirs*, vol. 2, *Years of Trial and Hope* (Garden City: Doubleday, 1956), 29–30. Gross to Zieger, July 15, 1992, says, "I would have confidence in the Reynolds' interview. He was a respected member of the Board in the 1940's who was no ideologue. . . . His [overall] interview is not self-serving or apologetic. Reynolds' recollection of Truman's remarks . . . are consistent with other evidence concerning Truman's attitudes toward union leaders and the need for some check on certain actions of some unions."

69. Remarks of Bridges and Fitzgerald, Jan. 22, 1948, CIOEB-WSU, 76–84, 107–32; William Sentner to Russ Nixon, July 26, 1948, UEUP, District 8, file 100. Polling data is found in "President Truman's Popularity," Apr. 23, 1948, 727–28; "Presidential Trial Heat," May 10, 1948, 732; "Russia," July 5, 1948, 742–43; "Leadership of Political Parties," July 21, 1948 ("Do you think

that the Henry Wallace third party is run by communists?"), 745–46; "Berlin," July 30, 1948, 748–49; "Presidential Trial Heat," Aug. 11, 1948, 750–51; "Presidential Trial Heat," Oct. 9, 1948 (gives CIO breakdown), 763, all in *The Gallup Poll: Public Opinion, 1935–1971*, vol. 1, *1935–1948*, by George Gallup (New York: Random House, 1972). MacDougall, *Campaign and the Vote*, 611–28, assesses patterns of labor support. Vincent Silverman, in "Stillbirth of a World Order: Union Internationalism from War to Cold War in the United States and Britain, 1939–1949" (Ph.D. dissertation, University of California-Berkeley, 1990), argues that working-class opinion in the United States in these years was inchoate and fragmented, but examination of Gallup poll material indicates strongly that there was a broad anti-Communist, anti-Soviet current, which translated into suspicion and hostility toward the Wallace initiative.

70. Murray's remarks, May 19, 1949, CIOEB-IUE, 1949, 798. I believe that recent historians have neglected the ideological component of the left/right conflict. While it is true that most ordinary union leaders, much less rank-and-file workers, rarely spoke in ideological terms, the emergence of Stalinism, with its peculiar combination of antifascist cachet and unspeakable brutality, dominated the life of the left in the era of World War II and its aftermath. The left, as Communists constantly insisted, was an international movement, and no amount of tactical maneuvering could long prevent the character and behavior of the Soviet regime from becoming the crucial determinant in the politics of the CIO. From his first utterances at CIO conventions in 1940, Reuther insisted on the centrality of this perspective, and after 1947 Murray increasingly came to embrace it, though always in less ideological and more practical bureaucratic terms than Reuther.

71. The campaign against the "left" remains, like the other subjects in this chapter, almost as controversial today as it was when it took place. "The implications of the expulsions," declares a recent scholar, "were devastating," and he goes on to lay at the door of the expulsions the full range of ills that have beset the American working class and the labor movement over the past two decades (Rosswurm, "Introduction," 13–16). See Frank Emspak, "The Breakup of the CIO," in Zeitlin and Kimeldorf, *Political Power and Social Theory*, 101–40, for a fuller statement of this view. See Diana Trilling, "How McCarthyism Gave Anti-Communism a Bad Name," *Newsweek*, Jan. 11, 1993, 32–33, for a suggestive defense of liberal anti-Communism.

72. Murray's remarks, CIOPROC, 1948, 166. Alfred Fitzgerald's distress at heckling and anti-Semitic remarks are in ibid., 280. He referred in part to anti-Semitic remarks overheard during comments by Abe Feinglass, ibid., 242–44.

73. For Fitzgerald's remarks, see ibid., 281; also *Labor Action*, Dec. 6, 1948, 4. On Fitzgerald's reelection, see Robert Bendiner, "Murray's Limited Purge," *Nation*, Dec. 18, 1948, 68.

74. Murray's remarks, CIOPROC, 1948, 18, 176, 164; Baldanzi's remarks, ibid., 217.

75. CIOPROC, 1947, 196–200; James Matles memo to UE organizers, "Securing Recognition without NLRB," Aug. 29, 1947, UEUP, District 8, file PM/112. See also James J. Matles and James Higgins, *Them and Us: Struggles of a Rank-and-File Union* (Boston: Beacon Press, 1975), 166–70.

76. Murray's remarks, Oct. 14, 1947, CIOEB-WSU, 203–4. See also Ellen W. Schrecker, "McCarthyism and the Labor Movement: The Role of the State," in Rosswurm, *CIO's Left-Led Unions*, 146–52.

77. Barnard, *Walter Reuther*, 126–28, 133.

78. Levenstein, *Communism, Anticommunism, and the CIO*, 199, 202–3, 205, 270–72; Donald G. Sofchalk, "Grant Wilson Oakes," in Fink, *Biographical Dictionary*, 441–42; Steven Rosswurm and Toni Gilpin, "The FBI and the Farm Equipment Workers: FBI Surveillance Records as a Source for CIO Union History," *LH* 27, no. 4 (Fall 1986): 485–505; Cochran, *Labor and Communism*, 275–77, 309; Robert Ozanne, *A Century of Labor-Management Relations at McCormick and International Harvester* (Madison: University of Wisconsin Press, 1967), 216–21. The course of the FE-UAW controversy can be traced in CIOST, box 50: UAW-FE, 1948–49, and in Report

of Committee Dealing with UAW-FE Dispute, Apr. 4, 1949, DMD-PSULA, box 33: Dec. 1948–May 1949.

79. Vernon H. Jensen, *Nonferrous Metals Industry Unionism, 1932–1954: A Story of Leadership Controversy*, Cornell Studies in Industrial and Labor Relations, vol. 5 (Ithaca: Cornell University Press, 1954), 41–44; Huntley, "Red Scare and Black Workers," 129–45; Mario T. Garcia, "Border Proletarians: Mexican-Americans and the International Union of Mine, Mill, and Smelter Workers, 1939–1946," in Asher and Stephenson, *Labor Divided*, 83–104; Laurel Sefton MacDowell, *"Remember Kirkland Lake": The History and Effects of the Kirkland Lake Gold Miners' Strike, 1941–42* (Toronto: University of Toronto Press, 1983), 56–64, 215–18; Donald G. Sofchalk, "Edward Theodore Cheyfitz," in Fink, *Biographical Dictionary*, 152–53; Jeremy Brecher, Jerry Lombardi, and Jan Stackhouse, eds. and comps., *Brass Valley: The Story of Working People's Lives and Struggles in an American Industrial Region* (Philadelphia: Temple University Press, 1982), 172–90; George G. Suggs, Jr., *Union Busting in the Tri-State: The Oklahoma, Kansas, and Missouri Metal Workers' Strike of 1935* (Norman: University of Oklahoma Press, 1986), 218–29; Gerald Markowitz and David Rosner, "'The Street of Walking Death': Silicosis, Health, and Labor in the Tri-State Region, 1900–1950," *JAH* 77, no. 2 (Sept. 1990): 525–52; Stanley S. Phipps, *From Bull Pen to Bargaining Table: The Tumultuous Struggle of the Coeur D'Alenes Miners for the Right to Organize, 1887–1942* (New York: Garland, 1988), 209–79; Clete Daniel, *Chicano Workers and the Politics of Fairness: The FEPC in the Southwest, 1941–1945* (Austin: University of Texas Press, 1991).

80. Donald G. Sofchalk, "Maurice Eugene Travis," in Fink, *Biographical Dictionary*, 556–57; Donald G. Sofchalk, "Reid Robinson," in Fink, *Biographical Dictionary*, 488–89; notes of Theodore Draper interview with Reid Robinson, Mar. 28, 1955, Theodore Draper Collection, Woodruff Library, Emory University, Atlanta, box 15: 33; Donald G. Sofchalk, "International Union of Mine, Mill, and Smelter Workers," in *Labor Unions*, ed. Gary Fink (Westport, Conn.: Greenwood Press, 1977), 223–25. The best account of these complex developments remains Jensen, *Nonferrous Metals Industry Unionism*. See also Brecher et al., *Brass Valley*, 175–76, and Levenstein, *Communism, Anticommunism, and the CIO*, 272–75.

81. Levenstein, *Communism, Anticommunism, and the CIO*, 274–75; Jensen, *Nonferrous Metals Industry Unionism*.

82. Notes on a meeting held Saturday . . . , July 10, 1943, in the office of Noel R. Beddow, Birmingham, Alabama, Murray papers, CUA, box A4: 2, Beddow. See also Beddow to Mercedes Daughtery (Murray's secretary), July 27, 1943, and Beddow to Murray, Dec. 1, 1943, ibid.

83. Levenstein, *Communism, Anticommunism, and the CIO*, 288–89. Arthur W. Hepner, "Union War in Bessemer," *Reporter*, July 5, 1949, while critical of Mine, Mill's pro-Soviet and third party stands, finds USWA claims of innocence unpersuasive. The Steelworkers could not be on the ballot because of Murray's refusal to sign the Taft-Hartley affidavit; hence the resort to LIUs to challenge Mine, Mill.

84. Levenstein, *Communism, Anticommunism, and the CIO*, 289–90. Murray's remarks, May 17, 1949, CIOEB-IUE, 13–48. See also USWA-IEB, May 5, 1948, 83–114, for substantially the same account by USWA counsel Arthur Goldberg and Secretary-Treasurer David J. McDonald. Mine, Mill widely circulated a flyer, featuring a picture of the bloody and battered Travis, titled "Why Did You Join CIO?," a copy of which is in the ACWA-LMDC, box 212: 3.

85. Murray's remarks, May 17, 1949, CIOEB-IUE, 13–48; remarks of Goldberg and McDonald, May 3, 1949, USWA-IEB, 83–114. The extent to which USWA officials were aware of or encouraged overt racial appeals is unclear. By 1949 the USWA had a sizable contingent of black members in Alabama. In the various collective bargaining and institutional issues in which race played a part in District 31 (Alabama), the international union and its representatives proved more responsive to the concerns of African American steelworkers, and local white unionists and regional functionaries tolerated discrimination and frequently exhibited overtly racist patterns of

speech and behavior. See Judith Stein, "Southern Workers in National Unions: Birmingham Steelworkers, 1936–1951," in *Organized Labor in the Twentieth-Century South*, ed. Robert H. Zieger (Knoxville: University of Tennessee Press, 1991), 192–206, and Robert J. Norrell, "Caste in Steel: Jim Crow Careers in Birmingham, Alabama," *JAH* 73, no. 3 (Dec. 1986): 680–88. The most balanced account of the Red Mountain episode is Jensen, *Nonferrous Metals Industry Unionism*, 233–50.

86. Philip Foner, *Organized Labor and the Black Worker, 1619–1973* (New York: International Publishers, 1974), 260–61, 280–81; Julius Scales quoted in Levenstein, *Communism, Anticommunism, and the CIO*, 285–86; Korstad and Lichtenstein, "Opportunities Found and Lost," 790–93, 801–5; Scales and Nickson, *Cause at Heart*, 204–5 (second quote).

87. Merl E. Reed, "Donald James Henderson," in Fink, *Biographical Dictionary*, 290–91; Ruiz, *Cannery Women*, 41–57, 112–18; Michael Honey, "Industrial Unionism and Racial Justice in Memphis," in Zieger, *Organized Labor*, 142–43, 145–50. Low-keyed CIO-PAC efforts to register African American voters are evident, for example, in Jack Kroll to Fred C. Pieper, Sept. 19, 1947, DPP-SHC, series 1: Louisiana, 1946–53, and much additional material in this collection.

88. Foner, *Organized Labor and the Black Worker*, 282; Levenstein, *Communism, Anticommunism, and the CIO*, 286; Korstad, "Black and White Together," 88–93; Scales and Nickson, *Cause at Heart*, 206–8 (songbird quote, 208); Robert Korstad, "Daybreak of Freedom: Tobacco Workers and the CIO in Winston-Salem, North Carolina, 1943–1950" (Ph.D. dissertation, University of North Carolina, 1987), 326–408.

89. Levenstein, *Communism, Anticommunism, and the CIO*, 180–81; Emspak to Murray, Mar. 16, 1948, UEUP, file PM/133; Reuther response to Murray, Mar. 30, 1948, UEUP, file PM/138.

90. Schatz, *Electrical Workers*, 180–85.

91. Mark McColloch, "The Shop-Floor Dimension of Union Rivalry: The Case of Westinghouse in the 1950s," in Rosswurm, *CIO's Left-Led Unions*, 183–99; Lisa Kannenberg, "The Impact of the Cold War on Women's Trade Union Activism: The UE Experience," *LH* 34, no. 2–3 (Spring–Summer 1993): 309–23.

92. Schatz, *Electrical Workers*, 167–243; notes of Daniel Bell interview with James B. Carey, Oct. 27, 1955, DBC-NYU, original section, box 4; Win Booth to Don Bermingham, Nov. 4, 1949, DBC-NYU, box 4: CIO National; Carey interviews, July 24, 1956–May 9, 1958, COHC; Julius Emspak interview, July 30–Dec. 23, 1959, COHC; "James Barron Carey," in Fink, *Biographical Dictionary*, 144–45; Rice, "Confessions of an Anti-Communist," 455–57; Herbert L. Northrup, "The Case for Boulwarism," *Harvard Business Review* 41 (Sept.–Oct. 1963): 86–97, reprinted in *Labor: Readings on Major Issues*, ed. Richard A. Lester (New York: Random House, 1965), 397–419, esp. 404–9.

93. Schatz, *Electrical Workers*, 188–221; Rice, "Confessions of an Anti-Communist"; interview with Charles Owen Rice, Oct. 17, 1967, PSULA; [Daniel Bell], "The Labor Priests," *Fortune*, Jan. 1949, 150–52. There is a file of Father Rice's reports and letters on the subject of Communism in the UE in ACTU-Detroit Papers, ALUAWSU, box 33: Rice. Recent examinations of the role of the Catholic clergy in the postwar affairs of the CIO include Rosswurm, "Catholic Church and Left-Led Unions"; Freeman and Rosswurm, "Education of an Anti-Communist"; Betten, *Catholic Activism and the Industrial Worker*, 108–45; and Seaton, *Catholics and Radicals*, 187–247.

94. Carey to Congressman Franklin D. Roosevelt, Jr., Jan. 14, 1950, CIOST, box 51: IUE, 1950. A version of this letter, which also called for a congressional investigation of alleged collusion between the UE and major corporations, dated Jan. 16, 1950, was publicly released. The American Legion quote, which was widely circulated by his union foes, is repeated in [Daniel Bell], "The I.U.E.'s Live Wires," *Fortune*, June 1950, 48. For the IUE's FBI and Roman Catholic connections, see Schatz, *Electrical Workers*, 182–201; Diamond, "Labor History vs. Labor Historiography," 299–328; Schrecker, "McCarthyism and the Labor Movement," 145, 146, 154, 155;

David Caute, *The Great Fear: The Anti-Communist Purge under Truman and Eisenhower* (New York: Simon and Schuster, 1978), 376–91; Gardner Jackson to Edwin Darby, Oct. 30, 1951, Gardner Jackson Papers, Franklin D. Roosevelt Presidential Library, Hyde Park, N.Y., box 37: IUE.

95. Schatz, *Electrical Workers*, 225–43; McColloch, "Shop-Floor Dimension of Union Rivalry," 183–99; Northrup, "Case for Boulwarism"; Caute, *Great Fear*, 376–83.

96. CIOEB-IUE, May 17–20; "Inside America" (CIO press release), May 20, 1949, DMD-PSULA, box 33: CIO, Dec. 1948–May 1949.

97. Robert H. Zieger interview with Arthur Goldberg, Aug. 24, 1983 (in Zieger's possession); Win Booth to Don Bermingham, Nov. 5, 1949, DBC-NYU, original section, box 4: CIO National; Arthur J. Goldberg, *AFL–CIO: Labor United* (New York: McGraw-Hill, 1956), 178–87. In 1948 delegates to the annual convention had voted for a temporary increase from five cents to eight cents in the monthly per capita tax paid by affiliates, and at the 1949 meeting it was raised another two cents. Thus the 150,000 to 200,000 members of the pro-Soviet affiliates would be paying monthly per capita tax to the CIO of about $15,000, or $180,000 over the course of the year. At the time it discontinued paying its per capita tax in mid-1949, the UE was paying $40,000 monthly, a sum that the 1949 increase would have raised by $10,000.

98. Soon after, it merged with the UE.

99. James Matles to UE organizers and officers, May 20, 1949, UEUP, District 8, file PM/173; Ernest De Maio penciled minutes, Mar. 17–19, Apr. 21, Aug. 10, 1949, UE IEB Minutes, De Maio papers, Chicago Historical Society, box 1: GEB Minutes, 1947–48; Bridges's remarks, CIO-PROC, 1948, 252–57.

100. Early in 1950 the United Furniture Workers ousted its pro-Soviet leadership and thus escaped charter revocation. See F. S. O'Brien, "The 'Communist-Dominated' Unions in the United States since 1950," *LH* 9, no. 2 (Spring 1968): 184–209.

101. Paul Jacobs, "The Due Processing of Harry Bridges," *Reporter*, Mar. 8, 1956, 36–39.

102. Murray's remarks, Feb. 15, 1950, CIOEB-WSU, 326.

103. Jacobs, *Is Curly Jewish?*, 188–89.

104. Levenstein, *Communism, Anticommunism, and the CIO*, 305 (Ken Eckert misnamed as William); Emil Mazey summarizes Eckert's testimony, Feb. 15, 1950, CIOEB-WSU, 256–59; Quill on Public Workers, CIOEB-WSU, 539–46; Quill on Wallace campaign, Aug. 29, 1950, CIOEB-WSU, 68–69; Hedley Stone on Bridges, in Jacobs, *Is Curly Jewish?*, 190–93; "Why C.I.O. Expelled Mine Mill," n.d., enclosed in Ken Eckert to "Sir and Brother," Apr. 28, 1950, CIOST, box 50: UAW, 1950–51.

105. Levenstein, *Communism, Anticommunism, and the CIO*, 302–6; Jacobs, *Is Curly Jewish?*, 188–92; Robert H. Zieger interview with Everett Kassalow, Mar. 16, 1983 (in Zieger's possession). The transcripts of the trials and related documents are in the CIOST, and discussions and votes are recorded, Feb. 15–16, 1950, and Aug. 28–29, 1950, CIOEB-WSU. A printed version of the transcripts and reports appears in U.S. Senate, *Communist Domination of Certain Unions*, 82 Cong., 1st sess., doc. 89 (Washington, D.C.: Government Printing Office, 1951). In September 1954 the CIO reissued it as a pamphlet: *Official Reports on the Expulsion of Communist Dominated Organizations from the CIO, PAM-L*, 509.

106. Murray's remarks, Feb. 16, 15, 1950, CIOEB-WSU, 566–75 (quote at 574), and 335, respectively.

107. [Daniel Bell], "Civil War in C.I.O.," *Fortune*, Nov. 1949, 204–6; [Daniel Bell], "Why a Copper Strike?," *Fortune*, Oct. 1951, 59–60; O'Brien, "'Communist-Dominated' Unions"; Schatz, *Electrical Workers*, 188–226; McColloch, "Shop-Floor Dimension of Union Rivalry"; Ronald Johnson, "Organized Labor's Postwar Red Scare: The UE in St. Louis," *North Dakota Quarterly* 48 (Winter 1980): 28–39; Gerald Zahavi, "Fighting Left-Wing Unionism: Voices from the Opposition to the IFLWU in Fulton County, New York," in Rosswurm, *CIO's Left-Led*

Unions, 183–200; Gerald Zahavi, "'Communism Is No Bug-a-Boo': Communism and Left-Wing Unionism in Fulton Country, New York, 1933–1950," *LH* 33, no. 2 (Spring 1992): 179–89; Levenstein, *Communism, Anticommunism, and the CIO*, 269–79; Ozanne, *A Century of Labor-Management Relations*, 217–19; Jensen, *Nonferrous Metals Industry Unionism*, 273–78; "Berkman" to *Time*, Inc., Oct. 14, 1950, and unidentified report on Mine, Mill-Steelworkers election in Montana, Fall 1950, DBC-NYU, original section, box 6: Communist Unions, Mine, Mill; Ken Hillyer, "UAW Drive on FE Flops: Relied on Red-Baiting Line," *Labor Action*, May 30, 1949. Philadelphia URW member James H. Hill expressed his views to Murray and Carey in a letter of Oct. 21, 1951, CIOST, box 59: URW, 1942–55.

108. Haywood's remarks, CIOPROC, 1950, 272–73.

109. See the entries for the Retail, Wholesale, and Department Store Union, and the Food, Tobacco, and Allied Workers, in Fink, *Labor Unions*, 330–32, 106–9; Allan S. Haywood to Gus Scholle, Feb. 28, 1950, MSAFL–CIO, series 1, box 30: 8, National CIO-1949–50; George L.-P. Weaver to James B. Carey, Nov. 23, 1948, JBC, box 90: Executive Board minutes, Nov. 15, 1946 (on background of white collar organizing); [Bell], "Civil War in C.I.O.," 204, 206. In the Fall of 1950, FTA merged with the Office and Professional Workers and a pro-Soviet segment of the Retail, Wholesale, and Department Store Union centered in New York City. The resulting organization was called the Distributive, Processing, and Office Workers and had about 55,000 members ([Daniel Bell], "Build-Up," *Fortune*, Nov. 1950, 50–52).

110. Gus Scholle to Allan Haywood, Mar. 2, 1950, and Haywood to Scholle, Mar. 7, 1950, MSAFL–CIO, box 30: CIO, National-1949–50; Barney Hopkins to Haywood, Apr. 4, 1950, and Haywood to Scholle, Apr. 21, 1950, MSAFL–CIO, box 99: CIO, National-1950. There is a shrewd assessment of the CIO's organizing failures in [Bell], "Civil War in C.I.O."

111. See [Daniel Bell], "The Centralization of Power," *Fortune*, Mar. 1950, 158–60, in a rare misreading of the way things were in the CIO, and Cochran, *Labor and Communism*, 311–12, for astute, if brief, observations.

112. Gordon Haskell, "Murray's Assault on the CP Marks End of CIO Era," *Labor Action*, Dec. 13, 1948; "It's CIO vs CP . . . ," *Labor Action*, Nov. 14, 1949. See also Art Preis, *Labor's Giant Step: Twenty Years of the CIO*, rev. ed. (New York: Pathfinder Press, 1972), 397–413; C. Wright Mills, *The New Men of Power: America's Labor Leaders* (New York: Harcourt, Brace, 1948), 194–99; and Jacobs, *Is Curly Jewish?*, 185–86, 188, for leftist hostility toward the CIO's pro-Soviet elements.

113. Levenstein, *Communism, Anticommunism, and the CIO*, 305. Journalists and academic observers frequently commented on the ideological character of much of the local-level effort to unseat pro-Soviet leaders or replace Communist and allied leadership. See, e.g., unidentified report re the Steelworkers' campaign against Mine, Mill in Montana, Fall 1950, and "Berkman" to *Time*, Inc., Oct. 14, 1950, DBC-NYU, original section, box 6: Communist Unions, Mine, Mill; Hillyer, "UAW Drive on FE Flops"; Jensen, *Nonferrous Metals Industry Unionism*, 270–94.

114. See, for example, the resolution and debate on civil liberties and internal security, CIO-PROC, 1950, 265–69.

115. Diamond, "Labor History vs. Labor Historiography," 309–19, quoting Bernstein at 317; Caute, *Great Fear*, 358–59, 376–91; Keeran, *Communist Party and the Auto Workers Unions*, 272–77; Halpern, *UAW Politics*, 262–63; William D. Andrew, "Factionalism and Anti-Communism: Ford Local 600," *LH* 20, no. 2 (Spring 1979): 227–55; Robert H. Zieger, "Showdown at the Rouge," *History Today* 40 (Jan. 1990): 55; Paul Sifton to Walter Reuther, Nov. 23, 1954, CIOWO, box 81: 20; IUE telegram to Sen. Leverett Saltonstall, Oct. 26, 1953, and typescript memo, ca. 1951–52, both in Jackson papers, Franklin D. Roosevelt Presidential Library, box 37: IUE; reports of Fred Collins to Barron Beshoar, Mar. 14, 15, 17, 19, 1952, DBC-NYU, original section, box 7: Reuther, 1952. See also Schrecker, "McCarthyism and the Labor Movement."

116. Reuther's remarks, CIOPROC, 1948, 170; mimeographed minutes, UE GEB meeting, Apr. 21, 1949, De Maio papers, Chicago Historical Society, box 1: GEB minutes, 1947–49.

117. Murray's remarks, CIOPROC, 1950, 68–70; Blanche Finn to Don Bermingham, Nov. 4, 1949, DBC-NYU, original section, box 4: CIO National.

Chapter Ten

1. On Sergeant Cross, see CIO radio spot, ca. Apr. 14, 1954, in Al Zack to Gus Scholle, MSAFL–CIO, series 1, box 55: Scholle, 1954.

2. There is a good discussion of the Defense Production Act's labor relations provisions in Maeva Marcus, *Truman and the Steel Seizure Case: The Limits of Presidential Power* (New York: Columbia University Press, 1977), 6–9. For the CIO critique, see, e.g., Nathan Goldfinger memo "Loopholes in the Defense Production Act," ca. 1951, Research Department Files, and Goldfinger to Stanley Ruttenberg, Nov. 24, 1951, Nathan Goldfinger Papers, GMMA, box 2: 13.

3. Jack Stieber, "Labor's Walkout from the Korean War Wage Stabilization Board," *LH* 21, no. 2 (Spring 1980): 243–44; Marcus, *Truman and the Steel Seizure*, 9–11.

4. CIO Executive Board statement on foreign policy, Aug. 29, 1950, MSAFL–CIO, series 2, box 99: 11, National CIO-1950; CIO-PAC, *Questions about the Battle in Korea*, ca. 1950–51, *PAM-L*, 561; CIOPROC, 1950, 357–65; CIOPROC, 1951, 483; CIOPROC, 1952, 475–76; Art Preis, *Labor's Giant Step: Twenty Years of the CIO*, rev. ed. (New York: Pathfinder Press, 1972), 419–21

5. Philip Murray, "A Program for Economic Mobilization," Oct 2, 1950, National Securities Resource Board Records (RG 304), National Archives, Office of the Chairman (Kassalow Correspondence with Unions: Murray).

6. Murray's remarks, Nov. 16, 1950, CIOEB-WSU, 55–77; Rieve's remarks, CIOEB-WSU, 53–54.

7. Stieber, "Labor's Walkout," 247–53.

8. Ibid., 250–53.

9. CIO release, "Statement by United Labor Policy Committee," Feb. 16, 1951, and Murray speech, Mar. 21, 1951, MSAFL–CIO, series 1, box 32: ULPC; ULPC statement quoted at length in Stieber, "Labor's Walkout," at 253–54.

10. Stieber, "Labor's Walkout," 258–60; Marcus, *Truman and the Steel Seizure*, 21–24.

11. Preis, *Labor's Giant Step*, 421.

12. CIOPROC, 1950, 289; CIOPROC, 1951, 483; CIOPROC, 1952, 375–76; CIO-PAC, *Questions about the Battle in Korea*, Fall 1950, *PAM-L*, 561; rev. ed., May 1951, copy in MSAFL–CIO, series 1, box 14: National CIO-PAC, 1951.

13. Harold Enarson to John Steelman, Feb. 15, 1951, Harold Enarson Papers, HSTPL, box 4: Memoranda, 1950–51.

14. Marcus, *Truman and the Steel Seizure*, 22–25; Stieber, "Labor's Walkout," 258–60; Arthur Goldberg remarks, Mar. 15, 1951, CIOEB-WSU, 45–79.

15. James B. Carey to Stuart Symington, July 10, 1950, NSRB Records, Central Files, 1949–53 (Industrial Relations, General); CIO Executive Board Economic Policy Statement, Aug. 29, 1950, MSAFL–CIO, series 2, box 99: 1, National CIO-1950; speech by Walter Reuther, Mar. 21, 1950 (stenographic transcript of extemporaneous remarks), MSAFL–CIO, series 1, box 32: 26, ULPC; CIO Department of Education and Research, *Economic Outlook*, Apr. 1951, copy in MSAFL–CIO, series 2, box 100: 2, National CIO-1951; "CIO Official Hits Delays, Confusion," press release, Dec. 5, 1951, Walter P. Reuther Papers, ALUAWSU, box 58: 15. There is a thoughtful analysis of organized labor's second-class status in the government arenas in Textile Workers Union of America Research Department, "Outline re American Trade Unions Face Another

Emergency," May 25, 1951, [by Solomon Barkin?], NSRB Records, Office of Chairman (Kassalow, Labor-TWUA).

16. Harold Enarson memorandum, Oct. 30, 1950, Enarson papers, HSTPL, box 4: Memoranda, 1950–51; John Herling, "Labor Independence at Polls Hailed by Truman in Interview," *Evening Star* (Washington), Jan. 14, 1953.

17. CIOPROC, 1952, 61–62. Reuther's continued advocacy of labor involvement in economic decision making is revealed, for example, in his testimony in U.S. Senate, Committee on Banking and Currency, *Defense Production Act Amendments of 1951*, part 3, 82d Cong., 1st sess. (Washington, D.C.: Government Printing Office, 1951), 2131–86; Walter P. Reuther, "Article for *New York Times*," Oct. 20, 1953, typescript, Walter Reuther Papers, ALUAWSU, box 566: 5; and Reuther testimony, U.S. Senate, Committee on Foreign Relations, *Mutual Security Act of 1956*, 84th Cong., 2d sess. (Washington, D.C.: Government Printing Office, 1956), 680–82.

18. Marcus, *Truman and the Steel Seizure*, 58–82, has a succinct account of the events leading up to the strike. She quotes U.S. Steel executive Benjamin Fairless on the legitimacy of the Steelworkers' claims for wage relief (58–59). See also Frederick H. Harbison and Robert C. Spencer, "The Politics of Collective Bargaining: The Postwar Record in Steel," *American Political Science Review* 48, no. 3 (Sept. 1954): 705–20.

19. See, for example, [Daniel Bell], "The Main Event," *Fortune*, Nov., 1951, 49–50; John Barnard, *Walter Reuther and the Rise of the Auto Workers* (Boston: Little, Brown, 1983), 135–44; and "The Treaty of Detroit," *Fortune*, July 1950, 53–55. For steel, see Harold L. Enarson to file, Feb. 19, 1952, Enarson papers, HSTPL, box 4: Letters, 1951–52; Edward Robert Livernash, *Collective Bargaining in the Basic Steel Industry: A Study of the Public Interest and the Role of Government* (Westport, Conn.: Greenwood Press, 1976), 274–76. Livernash's appendices (pp. 231–307) provide a splendid account of the history and development of collective bargaining in steel, 1937–59.

20. Advertisement quoted in Marcus, *Truman and the Steel Seizure*, 64; Enarson to Steelman, Jan. 9, 1952, Enarson papers, HSTPL, box 4: Letters, 1951–52.

21. Marcus, *Truman and the Steel Seizure*, 54–57, 64–67; Enarson file memo, Mar. 5, 1952, Enarson papers, HSTPL, box 5: Steel Negotiations, 1951–52.

22. Enarson to Steelman, Jan. 9, 1952, Enarson papers, HSTPL, box 4: Letters, 1951–52; Marcus, *Truman and the Steel Seizure*, 69–71.

23. The USWA leadership agreed to postpone the strike on several occasions, amounting to about 100 days. Truman and his advisors believed that invocation of Taft-Hartley provisions would unfairly penalize the union for its cooperation and would remove all incentives for the steel companies to bargain in good faith.

24. Kempton quoted in Marcus, *Truman and the Steel Seizure*, 87–88; Randall quoted in ibid., 88.

25. Truman quoted in Livernash, *Collective Bargaining*, 282.

26. Ibid., 278–83. On the administration's problems with union security, see Enarson to "Vic," ca. May 26, 1952, Enarson papers, HSTPL, box 3: Letters, 1951–52.

27. Lewis telegram to Murray, June 17, 1952, and related communications, June–July 1952, UMWA-A, steel file cabinets (folder for USWA, 1949–52). In fact, while acknowledging the UMW's public expression of support for the steelworkers, Murray did not request any financial aid from Lewis. On the settlement, see Livernash, *Collective Bargaining*, 283–84, and Marcus, *Truman and the Steel Seizure*, 252–53.

28. Preis, *Labor's Giant Step*, 449–51; Marcus, *Truman and the Steel Seizure*, 252–53; Livernash, *Collective Bargaining*, 283–84; Bill Jacobs to Marshall Berger (*Time* magazine background report), July 26, 1952, DBC-NYU, original series, box 19: Steelworkers; USWA-IEB, Aug. 20, 1952, 224–32.

29. Murray's report, CIOPROC, 1952, 83; Bookman to Berger, July 25, 26, 1952, DBC-NYU, original series, box 19: Steelworkers-Murray.

30. Bookman to Berger, July 26, 1952, DBC-NYU, original series, box 19: Steelworkers-Murray; Preis, *Labor's Giant Step*, 450–51; Ronald W. Schatz, "Philip Murray and the Subordination of the Industrial Unions to the United States Government," in *Labor Leaders in America*, ed. Melvyn Dubofsky and Warren Van Tine (Urbana: University of Illinois Press, 1987), 254–55. Murray gives an unintendedly revealing glimpse of the condescending attitudes that could so easily develop in dealing with mere rank and filers in USWA-IEB, Aug. 20, 1952, 224–32.

31. Carey report, Nov. 12, 1953, CIOEB-WSU, 32–33. For a discussion of CIO membership levels in the 1950s, see Robert H. Zieger, "Leadership and Bureaucracy in the Late CIO," *LH* 31, no. 3 (Summer 1990): 269; [Daniel Bell], "Why Reuther?," *Fortune*, Jan. 1953, 68. See also Leo Troy, *Trade Union Membership, 1897–1962* (New York: National Bureau of Economic Research, Occasional Paper 92, 1965), 8–9.

Chapter Eleven

1. Carey notes, "The Historic Meaning of CIO," 1955, JBC, addition 3, box 26: Merger, 1955.

2. Kroll's remarks, Feb. 1950, JKPLC, box 4: 1950.

3. The standard account of CIO-PAC is James C. Foster, *The Union Politic: The CIO Political Action Committee* (Columbia: University of Missouri Press, 1975). See also Fay Calkins, *The CIO and the Democratic Party* (Chicago: University of Chicago Press, 1952). This paragraph also rests on the author's interview with Tilford E. Dudley, Washington, D.C., July 17, 1984 (in Zieger's possession) and on the routine materials in the Jack Kroll Papers and the Daniel Powell Papers. Powell was PAC's southern director during this period. For an example of lingering third party sentiment, see the remarks of Michael Quill, CIOPROC, 1954, 479–81.

4. These impressions are drawn from copious materials in the Powell and Kroll papers, from UPWA, box 54: first folder, which contains a wealth of PAC materials for 1949–50, and from material in CIOWO, box 26 and box 27, covering PAC operations in 1954.

5. Statements by Kroll, Aug. 14, 1952, CIOEB-WSU, 102 (on CIO delegates), and Reuther, CIOPROC, 1954, 483–88 (on de facto Democratic partisanship). For the heavy involvement of PAC in Michigan Democratic politics, see Dudley W. Buffa, *Union Power and American Democracy: The UAW and the Democratic Party, 1935–1972* (Ann Arbor: University of Michigan Press, 1984), 3–51, and Calkins, *CIO and the Democratic Party*, 112–46.

6. Lewis J. Clark to Ralph Helstein, Aug. 30, 1950, UPWA, box 61: 1; David McDonald's remarks, Apr. 19–20, 1951, USWA-IEB, 178–82. [Daniel Bell], "The Unions and the Election," *Fortune*, Oct. 1952, 89, cites the one-in-eight figure.

7. Wisconsin State Industrial Union Council, *Citizenship In Operation*, ca. 1953, PAM-L, 589; PAC organizational program for 1952, ca. Nov. 1951, JKPLC, box 7: CIO-PAC, 1950–53. The materials in the Powell papers provide a running record of Powell's activities as southern director for these years, as well as syllabi of political action workshops, minutes of local PAC meetings, correspondence detailing voter registration and voter mobilization efforts, and financial matters.

8. PAC, "Report on 1953 Elections," Jan. 1, 1954 (penciled notes from PAC conference, Atlantic City, Jan. 6–7, 1954), CIOWO, box 27: 3; Foster, *Union Politic*, 181–95; Angus Campbell, Gerald Gurin, and Warren E. Miller, *The Voter Decides* (Evanston, Ill.: Row, Peterson, 1954), 153–54.

9. PAC program outline for 1952, Nov. 1951, JKPLC, box 7: CIO-PAC, 1950–53; Arthur Kornhauser, Albert J. Mayer, and Harold L. Sheppard, *When Labor Votes: A Study of Auto Workers* (Evanston, Ill.: University Books, 1956), 267.

10. Kornhauser et al., *When Labor Votes*, 262; Elmo Roper, "Roper Survey: Does Labor Vote What Leaders Say?," *New York Herald Tribune*, June 2, 1952.

11. Angus Campbell and Homer C. Cooper, *Group Differences in Attitudes and Votes* (Ann Arbor: Survey Research Center, University of Michigan, 1956), esp. 28–37; Angus Campbell, Philip E. Converse, Warren E. Miller, and Donald E. Stokes, *The American Voter* (New York: John Wiley and Sons, 1960), 312.

12. Art Preis, *Labor's Giant Step: Twenty Years of the CIO*, rev. ed. (New York: Pathfinder Press, 1972), esp. 461–511; Mike Davis, "The Barren Marriage of American Labour and the Democratic Party," *New Left Review* 124 (Nov.–Dec. 1980): 434–84; David Milton, *The Politics of U.S. Labor: From the Great Depression to the New Deal* (New York: Monthly Review Press, 1982), 139–67; David Montgomery, "American Workers and the New Deal Formula," in *Workers' Control in America: Studies in the History of Work, Technology, and Labor Struggles*, by David Montgomery (Cambridge: Cambridge University Press, 1979), 153–80.

13. Samuel Lubell, *The Future of American Politics*, 3d rev. ed. (New York: Harper Colophon, 1965), 174–89; Kornhauser et al., *When Labor Votes*, 264–65.

14. Lubell, *Future of American Politics*, 183–87, and Calkins, *CIO and the Democratic Party*, 12–36 (on Ohio); Foster, *Union Politic*, 143–45 (on California); Julian M. Pleasants and Augustus M. Burns III, *Frank Porter Graham and the 1950 Senate Race in North Carolina* (Chapel Hill: University of North Carolina Press, 1990), 49–50, 160–61, 214, and Graham election materials, DPP-SHC, series 1 (on North Carolina and Florida); John Edelman to Al Barkan, Nov. 10, 1950, John Edelman Papers, ALUAWSU, box 4: Barkan.

15. Campbell et al., *Voter Decides*, 73–75; Kornhauser et al., *When Labor Votes*, 29–75; Foster, *Union Politic*, 171–75. Kroll's analysis of the 1952 results and the statistical data supporting it are in CIOPROC, 1952, 422–31. The quote is in "Election Results," ca. Nov.–Dec. 1952, JKPLC, box 7: CIO-PAC, 1950–53.

16. John Herling, "Labor Independence at Polls Hailed by Truman in Interview," *Evening Star* (Washington), Jan. 14, 1953; Ed Lashman to Dan Powell, Nov. 6, 1952, DPP-SHC, series 1, North Carolina, 1947–55.

17. [Daniel Bell], "Picking up the Pieces," *Fortune*, Dec. 1952, 84; Foster, *Union Politic*, 194; Calkins, *CIO and the Democratic Party*, 19; PAC report, Aug. 14, 1952, CIOEB-WSU, 106–21.

18. PAC report, Mar. 23, 1954, CIOEB-WSU, 157–58; G. R. Hathaway, report on the CIO Executive Board meeting . . . , June 29, 1954, UPWA, box 102: 5.

19. Tilford E. Dudley to Daniel Powell, July 3, 1950, DPP-SHC, series 2, National PAC Correspondence, 1945–55; remarks [by Barney Hopkins?], ca. late 1951, MSAFL–CIO, series 2, box 107: 4, PAC-1951.

20. Dudley interview; Kroll general letter, Feb. 3, 1954, CIOWO, box 27: 4; Emil Mazey's remarks, CIOPROC, 1951, 509–12.

21. Foster, *Union Politic*, 189–95; Mazey's remarks and Kroll's remarks, CIOPROC, 1954, 483, 477–78, respectively.

22. Carey speech, Aug. 19, 1953, MSAFL–CIO, series 1, box 46: National CIO-PAC; Kroll memo, ca. Nov. 4, 1955, cited in Foster, *Union Politic*, 199–201.

23. Reuther's remarks, June 29, 1954, CIOEB-WSU, 37–38; Robert Bendiner, "The Labor Vote – Monopoly or Myth?," *Reporter*, Nov. 3, 1955, 21.

24. Reuther's statement before Joint Congressional Committee on the Economic Report and Proposals of the President, Feb. 17, 1954, pamphlet reprint, *PAM-L*, 1506; Wisconsin State IUC, CIO Program, Dec. 1949, pamphlet, *PAM-L*, 584; CIO, *Keep Our Nation Prosperous*, Dec. 1952, *PAM-L*, 655. See Robert Oliver to Paul Derrick, Aug. 3, 1953, Nathan Goldfinger Papers, GMMA, box 1: 21, for a succinct statement of the CIO's basic approach to the American economy. The implicit international context in which laborite Keynesianism flourished is outlined in Charles S. Maier, "The Politics of Productivity: Foundations of American International Eco-

nomic Policy after World War II," in *In Search of Stability: Explorations in Historical Political Economy*, by Charles S. Maier (Cambridge: Cambridge University Press, 1987), 121–52.

25. Everett Kassalow, "The Great Depression and the Transformation of the American Union Movement," testimony delivered before the U.S. Congress Joint Economic Committee, Nov. 28, 1980, *Industrial Relations Research Institute*, Reprint No. 234 (Madison, Wisc.: IRRI, n.d.), 333–37; Robert H. Zieger interview with Everett Kassalow, Mar. 16, 1983 (in Zieger's possession); Robert H. Zieger interview with Stanley Ruttenberg, Aug. 27, 1983 (in Zieger's possession); Resolution: UAW National Conference to Fight for Full Employment, "To Keep America Strong and Prosperous – Keep America at Work," Dec. 6–7, 1953, MSAFL–CIO, series 1, box 55:9, UAW.

26. Kassalow, "Great Depression and Transformation," 335–36; CIOPROC, 1948, 374–75.

27. UAW-CIO Washington office, "Seven Legislative and Administrative Ways to Promote Full Employment," ca. Dec. 1953, MSAFL–CIO, series 1, box 55: 9-UAW.

28. Reuther statement before the Joint Committee on the Economic Report and Proposals of the President, "CIO's Program to Halt Unemployment," Feb. 17, 1954, MSAFL–CIO, series 2, box 101: 7, National CIO-1954; UAW Administrative Letter, Feb. 17, 1954, MSAFL–CIO, series 1, box 55: 10-UAW. The best treatment of Reuther's postwar views on political economy is Kevin Gerard Boyle, "Politics and Principle: The United Automobile Workers and American Labor-Liberalism, 1948–1968" (Ph.D. dissertation, University of Michigan, 1990), esp. 2–18, 53–54. See also Seth Marks Wigderson, "The UAW in the 1950s" (Ph.D. dissertation, Wayne State University, 1989).

29. CIO Legislative Department, "The CIO Legislative Action Program," Jan. 28, 1954, MSAFL–CIO, series 2, box 101: 7, National CIO-1954; Boyle, "Politics and Principle," 174–82.

30. Ruttenberg interview; Kassalow interview; Walter Reuther statement, "CIO's Program to Halt Unemployment," Feb. 2, 1954, MSAFL–CIO, series 2, box 101: 7, National CIO, 1954.

31. Henry C. Fleisher to Stanley Ruttenberg, Oct. 21, 1954, Research Department, Stanley Ruttenberg Papers, GMMA, box 1: 47, listing CIO releases during 1949 recession; quote in CIOPROC, 1949, 412, as cited in Kassalow, "Great Depression and Transformation," 335. See also Nelson Lichtenstein, "Walter Reuther and the Rise of Labor-Liberalism," in *Labor Leaders in America*, ed. Melvyn Dubofsky and Warren Van Tine (Urbana: University of Illinois Press, 1987), 280–81, 287, and Boyle, "Politics and Principle," 174–82.

32. Kassalow interview; Ruttenberg interview; Katherine Pollak Ellickson interview (with Dennis East), Jan. 10, 1976, ALUAWSU; Kassalow, "Great Depression and Transformation," 336. Economist Everett Kassalow served as executive secretary of the Economic Policy Committee and as editor of *Economic Outlook*. Materials in CIOWO, box 24: 1 and 2 contain a good sampling of the detailed, Keynes-inspired materials that Kassalow and other members of the CIO Department of Research supplied regularly to CIO leaders. See also Kassalow to Robert Oliver, Oct. 26, 1953, CIOWO, box 24: 1, and Kassalow memo and report, Apr. 2, 1954, Irwin De Shetler Papers, ALUAWSU, box 21: CIO CEP. Stanley Ruttenberg to Walter Reuther, Dec. 12, 1952, Ruttenberg papers, GMMA, box 2: 5, outlines the ongoing economic policy work of the Department of Research.

33. "To Keep America Strong and Prosperous – Keep America at Work"; Boyle, "Politics and Principle," 174–76.

34. Everett Kassalow, memo and report, Apr. 2, 1954, De Shetler papers, ALUAWSU, box 21: CIO CEP; *CIO's 10 Point Program to Halt Growing Unemployment*, pamphlet, 1954, CIOWO, box 24: 7; Reuther's remarks, Feb. 17, 1954, and CIO Legislative Department, "Report on Congress," Mar. 22, 1954, MSAFL–CIO, series 2, box 101: 7, National CIO-1954.

35. *CIO's 10 Point Program*; CIO Legislative Department, "Visits to Congressmen," ca. 1954, De Shetler papers, ALUAWSU, box 22. Box 22 of the De Shetler papers contains a detailed record of both the subject matter and the patterns of operation relating to CIO congressional legislative activities, 1954–55. De Shetler was California regional director in these years.

36. Call to Full-Employment Conference, Apr. 14, 1954; Program for Full-Employment Conference, May 11–12, 1954; "Program for Prosperity in Peacetime," May 11–12 (proceedings of conference), all in De Shetler papers, ALUAWSU, box 21: Full Employment Conference; "Unemployment Conference," CIO Executive Committee Minutes, Apr. 14, 1954, JBC, box 94; G. R. Hathaway, "Report on the CIO Unemployment Conference, May 11, 1954," UPWA, box 102: 5.

37. CIO Legislative Department, "The CIO Legislative Program," Jan. 28, 1954, and CIO Legislative Department, "Report on Congress," Aug. 2, 1954, Ruttenberg papers, GMMA, box 1: 43. From its inception in 1943 until early 1953 the department was headed by USWA staffer Nathan Cowan. After Reuther's accession to the presidency, Cowan was replaced with Reuther's chief CIO aide, Robert Oliver, who acted as coordinator of CIO legislative activities. "Reorganization of the Legislative Department," ca. early 1953, CIOWO, box 25: 24; CIO Legislative Department, "The CIO Legislative Action Program," Jan. 28, 1954, MSAFL–CIO, series 2, box 101: 7, National CIO-1954. The analyses of core strength in Congress are contained in a series of PAC reports, MSAFL–CIO, series 1, box 38: 14, National CIO-PAC-1952. Included in this folder are legislative histories, analyses of key votes, issue breakdowns, assessments of support, and detailed commentary on a wide range of issues.

38. Robert Oliver to CIO officials, Jan. 15, 1954, Ruttenberg papers, GMMA, box 1: 42; Boyle, "Politics and Principle," 82–90; CIO-PAC, "Senate Votes – 82d Cong., 1st Sess. (Votes 23–37)," Mar. 1952, MSAFL–CIO, series 1, box 38: 14, National CIO-PAC-1952; CIO Legislative Department, "Report on Congress," Mar. 22, 1954, MSAFL–CIO, series 2, box 101: 7, National CIO; CIO Legislative Department, *Report on Congress: The CIO Looks at the 83d Congress*, Sept. 1954, *PAM-L*, 503; CIO, *Report on Congress: The CIO Looks at the 84th Congress*, 1955, *PAM-L*, 513.

39. Robert H. Zieger, *American Workers, American Unions, 1920–1985* (Baltimore: Johns Hopkins University Press, 1986), 138–40; Lubell, *Future of American Politics*, 182. See also Daniel Bell, *The End of Ideology: On the Exhaustion of Political Ideas in the Fifties*, rev. ed. (New York: Collier, 1962), 211–26.

40. These problems were often commented upon in the early 1950s by *Fortune*'s labor editor, Daniel Bell. On the tensions between benefits gained through collective bargaining and organized labor's quest for public provision, see Hugh Mosley, "Corporate Social Benefits and the Underdevelopment of the American Welfare State," *Contemporary Crises* 5 (1981): 139–54, and Beth Stevens, "Labor Unions, Employee Benefits, and the Privatization of the American Welfare State," *Journal of Policy History* 2, no. 3 (1990): 233–60. On the problematic nature of organized labor's legislative agenda, see Karen Orren, "Union Politics and Postwar Liberalism in the United States, 1946–1979," in *Studies in American Political Development: An Annual*, ed. Karen Orren and Stephen Skowronek (New Haven: Yale University Press, 1986), 1: 228–45, and Jill S. Quadagno, *The Transformation of Old Age Security: Class and Politics in the American Welfare State* (Chicago: University of Chicago Press, 1988), 125–77.

41. Gerald Pomper, "Labor and Congress: The Repeal of Taft-Hartley," *LH* 2, no. 3 (Fall 1961): 323–43; Gerald Pomper, "Labor Legislation: The Revision of Taft-Hartley in 1953–1954," *LH* 6, no. 2 (Spring 1965): 143–58; Benjamin Aaron, "Amending the Taft-Hartley Act: A Decade of Frustration," *Industrial and Labor Relations Review* 11, no. 3 (Apr. 1958): 327–38; Gilbert J. Gall, *The Politics of Right to Work: The Labor Federations as Special Interests, 1943–1979* (Westport, Conn.: Greenwood Press, 1988), 47–69 (John Edelman quoted at 68); Alan Draper, *A Rope of Sand: The AFL–CIO Committee on Political Education, 1955–1967* (New York: Praeger, 1988), 30–32; CIO, *Worse than Taft-Hartley* (testimony of Arthur Goldberg and Walter Reuther re S. 2650), 1954, *PAM-L*, 505; Harold Enarson and Milton Kayle to David Stowe, Jan. 14, 1952, Harold L. Enarson Papers, HSTPL, box 4: Letters, 1951–52; Robert H. Zieger interview with Arthur J. Goldberg, Aug. 24, 1983 (in Zieger's possession).

42. Foster, *Union Politic*, 116; William C. Berman, *The Politics of Civil Rights in the Truman Administration* (Columbus: Ohio State University Press, 1970), 55–240; Dudley interview; CIO-PROC, 1954, 382–89; Steven F. Lawson, *Running for Freedom: Civil Rights and Black Politics in America since 1941* (Philadelphia: Temple University Press, 1991), 32–41; Charles V. Hamilton, *Adam Clayton Powell, Jr.: The Political Biography of an American Dilemma* (New York: Atheneum, 1991), 168–73, 188–235.

43. Murray's remarks, Dec. 10, 1945, USWA-IEB, 27–31; Everett Kassalow, "New Patterns of Collective Bargaining," in *Insight into Labor Issues*, ed. Richard A. Lester and Joseph Shister (New York: Macmillan, 1948), 120–26; CIOPROC, 1946, 185–88, 234–53, Reuther quote, 245; CIOPROC, 1947, 236–37; David Brody, "The Uses of Power I: The Industrial Battleground," in *Workers in Industrial America: Essays on the Twentieth Century Struggle*, by David Brody (New York: Oxford, 1981), 176–78.

44. Philip A. Taft, *Organized Labor in American History* (New York: Harper, 1964), 634–35; CIO Department of Education and Research, *CIO's Two-Way Drive for Social Security*, PAM-L, 502.

45. On the general development of wage bargaining during this period, see John E. Maher, "The Wage Pattern in the United States, 1946–1957," *Industrial and Labor Relations Review* 15, no. 1 (Oct. 1961): 3–20; Robert M. Macdonald, "Collective Bargaining in the Postwar Period," *Industrial and Labor Relations Review* 20, no. 4 (July 1967): 553–77; Edward Robert Livernash, *Collective Bargaining in the Basic Steel Industry: A Study of the Public Interest and the Role of Government* (Westport, Conn.: Greenwood Press, 1976), esp. 246–94; Robert M. Macdonald, *Collective Bargaining in the Automobile Industry: A Study of Wage Structure and Competitive Relations* (New Haven: Yale University Press, 1963); Brody, "Uses of Power," 191–92. Another source of USWA jealousy of UAW success was the contrast between the UAW's relatively easy achievement of the union shop and the bitter struggles in the steel industry to gain the same recognition.

46. CIO, *Guaranteed Wages the Year Round*, 1945, PAM-L, 519; CIO Department of Education and Research, *Progress toward Guaranteed Wages and Employment*, 1955, PAM-L, 543; Reuther report to convention, CIOPROC, 1955, 218–21; Macdonald, *Collective Bargaining*, 36–39, 55–58, 79–82; Wayne A. Leeman, "The Guaranteed Annual Wage, Employment and Economic Progress," *Industrial and Labor Relations Review* 8, no. 4 (July 1955): 565–71; Frank Cormier and William J. Eaton, *Reuther* (Englewood Cliffs, N.J.: Prentice Hall, 1970), 327–36. Quoted is Nat Weinberg at 328.

47. Kassalow interview; Ruttenberg interview; Kassalow, "New Patterns of Collective Bargaining," 119–27; Robert R. Nathan and Oscar Gass, *A National Wage Policy for 1947: Analysis Prepared for the Congress of Industrial Organizations* (N.p: Dec. 1946); CIO Committee on Economic Policy, *Maintaining Prosperity* (booklet, 1953); CIO Department of Education and Research, *Wage Policy in Our Expanding Economy* (booklet, 1952), quote at 9.

48. On pensions, see remarks of David McDonald, CIOPROC, 1946, 186; on health care, see William Pollock's remarks, CIOPROC, 1946, 187. See also Mosley, "Corporate Social Benefits"; Stevens, "Labor Unions, Employee Benefits"; and Nelson Lichtenstein, "Labor in the Truman Era: Origins of the 'Private Welfare State,'" in *The Truman Presidency*, ed. Michael J. Lacey (Washington, D.C., and Cambridge: Woodrow Wilson International Center for Scholars and Cambridge University Press, 1989), 148–54.

49. *CIO's Two-Way Drive for Social Security*; CIO, *Meeting the Attack on Old Age Security*, ca. 1952, PAM-L, 654; CIO, *Progress toward Guaranteed Wages and Employment*; Marjorie Thines Stanley, "The Amalgamation of Collective Bargaining and Political Activity by the UAW," *Industrial and Labor Relations Review* 10, no. 1 (Oct. 1956): 40–47; Sanford M. Jacoby, "Employers and the Welfare State: The Role of Marion B. Folsom," *JAH* 80, no. 2 (Sept. 1993): 527; Alan Derickson, "Health Security for All?: Social Unionism and Universal Health Insurance, 1935–1958," *JAH* 80, no. 4 (Mar. 1994): 1333–56.

50. Brody, "Uses of Power," 177–88; Howell John Harris, *The Right to Manage: Industrial Relations Policies of American Business in the 1940s* (Madison: University of Wisconsin Press, 1982); Nelson Lichtenstein, "UAW Bargaining Strategy and Shop-Floor Conflict: 1946–1970," *Industrial Relations* 24, no. 3 (Fall 1985): 360–69.

51. Gilbert Gall interview with Harold Ruttenberg, July 16, 1989 (copy in Zieger's possession); Thomas R. Brooks, *Clint: A Biography of a Labor Intellectual, Clinton S. Golden* (New York: Atheneum, 1978), 224–48; William Serrin, *Homestead: The Glory and Tragedy of an American Steel Town* (New York: Vintage, 1993), 241–57; [Daniel Bell], "Labor's Coming of Middle Age," *Fortune*, Oct. 1951, 114–15, 137–38; Walter Reuther, "Our Social Setup Lags behind our Technological Progress," *Labor and Nation*, Jan.–Feb. 1947, 9–10, copy in Walter P. Reuther Papers, ALUAWSU, box 565: 10; Walter P. Reuther, "Survival or Democratic Survival?," in CIO, Department of Education and Research, *Homes for People; Jobs for Prosperity; Planes for Peace* (pamphlet, 1949), copy in Reuther papers, ALUAWSU, box 565: 15.

52. CIO, Department of Education and Research, *Should Labor Have a Direct Share in Management?*, Fall 1946, *PAM-L*, 3155.

53. For a good statement of these problems, see Jeffrey Haydu, *Between Craft and Class: Skilled Workers and Factory Politics in the United States and Britain, 1890–1922* (Berkeley: University of California Press, 1992), 4–5, 13–15, 19.

54. Brody, "Uses of Power," 194–209; Katherine Van Wezel Stone, "The Post-War Paradigm in American Labor Law," *Yale Law Journal* 90 (1981): 1509–80; Lichtenstein, "UAW Bargaining Strategy," 369–75.

55. [Daniel Bell], "Labor Notes," *Fortune*, July 1952, 60; [Daniel Bell], "Labor Notes," *Fortune*, Oct. 1952, 94, both on rubber, along with Brody, "Uses of Power," 205 (tire builder quote). On auto, see Lichtenstein, "UAW Bargaining Strategy," 366–68; Nelson Lichtenstein, "Auto Worker Militancy and the Structure of Factory Life, 1937–1955," *JAH* 67, no. 2 (Sept. 1980): 349–53; William Gould, *Black Workers in White Unions: Job Discrimination in the United States* (Ithaca: Cornell University Press, 1977), 80–88, 371–88; Bill Goode, "The Skilled Trades: Reflections," in *Auto Work and Its Discontents*, ed. B. J. Widick (Baltimore: Johns Hopkins University Press, 1976), 34–44; Steve Babson, *Building the Union: Skilled Workers and Anglo-Gaelic Immigrants in the Rise of the UAW* (New Brunswick: Rutgers University Press, 1991), 243–44.

56. Brody, "Uses of Power," 195–200, 201–2; Victor Forberger, "Craftsmen and Contractual Relations at the Duquesne Steel Works, 1950s and 1960s" (Master's paper, University of Florida, 1992); Livernash, *Collective Bargaining*, 113–17, 300–307.

57. John Barnard, *Walter Reuther and the Rise of the Auto Workers* (Boston: Little, Brown, 1983), 154, quotes Reuther's retort to the engineer, while Cormier and Eaton, *Reuther*, 309–10, cites his views on technology. See also Walter Reuther, "The Impact of Automation," Oct. 17, 1955, in *Walter P. Reuther: Selected Papers*, ed. Henry M. Christman (New York: Macmillan, 1961), 67–100; CIO Economic Policy Committee, *Automation*, 1955, *PAM-L*, 541; and CIOPROC, 1954, 80–81, where Reuther shares his visit to the Cleveland engine plant. See also Nathan Goldfinger to Carroll Coburn, Oct. 26, 1955, Goldfinger papers, GMMA, box 1: 16; Goldfinger to H. L. Luedicks, Apr. 25, 1955, Goldfinger papers, GMMA, box 1: 52; and David F. Noble, *Forces of Production: A Social History of Industrial Automation* (New York: Knopf, 1984), 74–76 and 252–53.

58. For contemporary accounts of grievance machinery, see John T. Dunlop, *Collective Bargaining: Principles and Cases* (Chicago: Richard D. Irwin, 1949), 78–86, and Leonard R. Sayles and George Strauss, *The Local Union: Its Place in the Industrial Plant* (New York: Harper and Bros., 1953), 27–33. The virtues and liabilities of the grievance arbitration system that emerged in the 1940s and 1950s are discussed in Brody, "Uses of Power," 194–211; Stone, "Post-War Paradigm"; Matthew W. Finkin, "Revisionism in Labor Law," *Maryland Law Review* 43 (1984): 23–92; and Steven Tolliday and Jonathan Zeitlin, "Shop Floor Bargaining, Contract Unionism,

and Job Control: An Anglo-American Comparison," in *On the Line: Essays in the History of Auto Work*, ed. Nelson Lichtenstein and Stephen Meyer (Urbana: University of Illinois Press, 1989), 219–44. See also Nelson Lichtenstein, "Great Expectations: The Promise of Industrial Jurisprudence and Its Demise, 1930–1960," in *Industrial Democracy in America: The Ambiguous Promise*, ed. Nelson Lichtenstein and Howell John Harris (Washington, D.C., and Cambridge: Woodrow Wilson Center Press and Cambridge University Press, 1993), 128–41.

59. All CIO-produced literature directed at stewards that I have seen assumed that the reader would be a male. Indeed, it often pointedly, if unconsciously, trivialized the concerns of women workers. "If Jane and Mary can't agree whether the window should be open or shut – that's not a grievance," a 1954 steward's guide instructed.

60. The steward's role is outlined in CIO, *The Shop Steward: Key to a Strong Union*, ca. 1954, *PAM-L*, 542; Sidney Peck, *The Rank-and-File Leader* (New Haven: College and University Press, 1963), esp. 29–34; Eli Chinoy, *Automobile Workers and the American Dream* (Boston: Beacon Press, 1965), 96–109; and Sayles and Strauss, *Local Union*, 34–42. Quotes are from the latter, at 42 and 34, respectively.

61. The phrase is David Brody's in "Uses of Power."

62. See, for example, Richard Lester, *As Unions Mature: An Analysis of the Evolution of American Unionism* (Princeton: Princeton University Press, 1958), and, though more skeptical, Sayles and Strauss, *Local Union*, 21–24. For more current critical commentary on the "post-war paradigm," see esp. Karl E. Klare, "Traditional Labor Law Scholarship and the Crisis of Collective Bargaining Law: A Reply to Professor Finkin," *Maryland Law Review* 44 (1985): 731–840; Matthew W. Finkin, "Does Karl Klare Protest Too Much?," *Maryland Law Review* 44 (1985): 1100–1110; Katherine Van Wezel Stone, "Re-envisioning Labor Law: A Response to Professor Finkin," *Maryland Law Review* 45 (1986): 978–1013; James B. Atleson, "Reflections on Labor, Power, and Society," *Maryland Law Review* 45: 841–72; and Lichtenstein, "Great Expectations." James B. Atleson, *Values and Assumptions in American Labor Law* (Amherst: University of Massachusetts Press, 1983), and Christopher L. Tomlins, *The State and the Unions: Labor Relations, Law, and the Organized Labor Movement in America, 1880–1960* (Cambridge: Cambridge University Press, 1985), offer sharp critiques of the role of law in the limitation of workers' rights in the post–World War II era.

63. For the theme of continuing shop-floor conflict, see Brody, "Uses of Power," 201–11; Lichtenstein, "UAW Bargaining Strategy," 371–81; Nelson Lichtenstein, introduction to Harvey Swados, *On the Line*, ed. Nelson Lichtenstein (Urbana: University of Illinois Press), vii–xxviii; Charles R. Walker and Robert H. Guest, *The Man on the Assembly Line* (Cambridge, Mass.: Harvard University Press, 1952); and Forberger, "Craftsmen and Contractual Relations."

64. David McDonald's remarks, Oct. 23, 1953, USWA-IEB, 132. For a ringing attack on these by-now commonplace attitudes, see Preis, *Labor's Giant Step*, 438–51. Lichtenstein, "UAW Bargaining Strategy," stresses the persistence of shop-floor conflict and the unresponsiveness of the UAW's international officers to these endemic problems, while Atleson, *Values and Assumptions*, indicates the prioritization of productionist values by courts and arbitrators.

65. Reuther report, CIOPROC, 1954, 46; Daniel Bell, "The Next American Labor Movement," *Fortune*, Apr. 1953, 120–23, 101–2, 204, 206; [Daniel Bell], "Labor's New Men of Power," *Fortune*, June 1953, 148–51; [Daniel Bell], "The AFL Inflates," *Fortune*, Oct. 1953, 118–20; Kermit Eby, "The 'Drip' Theory in Labor Unions," *Antioch Review* 13, no. 1 (Mar. 1953): 95–102.

66. Reuther testimony, U.S. Senate, Committee on Banking and Currency, *Defense Production Act Amendments of 1951*, part 2, 82d Cong., 1st sess. (Washington, D.C.: Government Printing Office, 1951), 2131; Reuther's remarks, Aug. 20, 1953, CIOEB-WSU, 57.

67. CIO-PAC, *Questions about the Battle in Korea*, Sept. 1950, *PAM-L*, 561; CIOPROC, 1951, 481–88; CIOPROC, 1953, 481–92; CIOPROC, 1954, 628–42.

68. Victor G. Reuther, Edgar de Lasalle, and Frank Bellanca, "Summary Report and Recommendations of Special CIO Committee to Europe," Spring 1951, copy in UPWA, box 71: 9; "CIO Activity in Europe," Spring 1951, UPWA, box 71: 9; Victor Reuther, *The Brothers Reuther and the Story of the UAW: A Memoir* (Boston: Houghton Mifflin, 1976), 329–59; Anthony Carew, *Labour under the Marshall Plan: The Politics of Productivity and the Marketing of Management Science* (Detroit: Wayne State University Press, 1987); Milton Zatinsky to Victor Reuther, Apr. 5, 1955, CIOWO, box 44: 5. The files in CIOWO, box 55, broadly reflect the themes in this and the next paragraph.

69. CIOPROC, 1954, 628–29.

70. CIO, *The CIO Says: The Odds Are Up to You – for Peace and Security in the World*, ca. 1953, *PAM-L*, 538.

71. Testimony of James B. Carey with reference to the Defense Production Act, May 21, 1951, U.S. Senate Committee on Banking and Currency, copy in National Security Resources Board Records (RG 304), National Archives, Office of Chair: Kassalow Labor (CIO Testimony).

72. Victor Reuther to Walter Reuther, Aug. 26, 1955, CIOWO, box 59: 10. This whole file is filled with material reflecting Victor Reuther's energetic role in CIO and UAW foreign affairs activities.

73. Carew, *Labour under the Marshall Plan*, 57–59, 120–23; Anthony Carew, "The Anglo-American Council on Productivity, 1948–1952: The Ideological Roots of the Post-War Debate on Productivity in Britain," *Journal of Contemporary History* 26 (1991): 49–69.

74. CIOPROC, 1954, 629; Victor Reuther to Walter Reuther, Oct. 6, 1953, CIOWO, box 59: 3.

75. Debate on "Formosa," Feb. 2, 1955, CIOEB, copy in JBC, box 92: CIOEB.

76. Versions of the exposé of the Reuther brothers' serving as conduits for CIA money on one occasion in the early 1950s include Barnard, *Walter Reuther*, 128; Cormier and Eaton, *Reuther*, 358–60; and Reuther, *Brothers Reuther*, 424–26. For the AFL's record of long-term involvement with the CIA, see Ronald Radosh, *American Labor and U.S. Foreign Policy* (New York: Knopf, 1969), 438–49; Henry Berger, "Organized Labor and American Foreign Policy," in *The American Working Class: Prospects for the 1980s*, ed. Irving Louis Horowitz, John C. Leggett, and Martin Oppenheimer (New Brunswick: Transaction Books, 1979), 204–5; and Denis MacShane, *International Labour and the Origins of the Cold War* (Oxford: Clarendon Press, 1992), esp. 69–74. See also Thomas W. Braden, "I'm Glad the CIA Is 'Immoral,'" *Saturday Evening Post*, May 20, 1967, 10–12.

77. Daniel Benedict, Associate Director, CIO Department for International Affairs, report to CIO Committee on International Affairs and Latin American Sub-Committee on trip to Central America, July 8–23, 1954, copy in DMD-PSULA, box 35: CIO, Oct. 1953–Sept. 1954; CIO-PROC, 1954, 638–41; Blanche Wiesen Cook, *The Declassified Eisenhower: A Divided Legacy* (Garden City: Doubleday, 1981), 217–92; Richard H. Immerman, *The CIA in Guatemala: The Foreign Policy of Intervention* (Austin: University of Texas Press, 1982). Knight and Mazey are quoted in Radosh, *American Labor and U.S. Foreign Policy*, 388–89.

Chapter Twelve

1. "Is CIO Cracking Up?," *U.S. News and World Report*, Feb. 20, 1953, 81; Stanley Levy, "Steel, Mine Unions Hold Secret Talks," *New York Times*, June 26, 1953.

2. For biographical sketches of Murray, see Irving Bernstein, *Turbulent Years: A History of the American Worker, 1933–1941* (Boston: Houghton Mifflin, 1969), 441–47; Ronald W. Schatz, "Philip Murray and the Subordination of the Industrial Unions to the United States Government," in *Labor Leaders in America*, ed. Melvyn Dubofsky and Warren Van Tine (Urbana: University of Illinois Press, 1987), 234–57; and Melvyn Dubofsky, "Labor's Odd Couple: Philip

Murray and John L. Lewis," in *Forging a Union of Steel: Philip Murray, SWOC, and the United Steelworkers*, ed. Paul F. Clark, Peter Gottlieb, and Donald Kennedy (Ithaca: ILR Press, 1987), 30–44. John Chamberlain, "Philip Murray," *Life*, Feb. 11, 1946, 78–90, reflects journalistic treatment. Murray's core values are outlined in Philip Murray, "If We Pull Together," *American Magazine*, June 1948, 21, 133–36.

3. Murray's hundreds of speeches before union bodies, notably those delivered between 1940 and 1952 (the last read into the record after his death) at the CIO annual conventions, copiously document these attributes. John G. Ramsay to Stanley H. Ruttenberg, Aug. 3, 1950, with enclosed statement, John G. Ramsay Papers, SLA-GSU, box 1556: 1, outlines Murray's religious views. On Murray's handling of USWA-CIO affairs, see Robert Oliver interview with Frank Fernbach, Sept. 17, 1979, 28–29, and Henry Fleisher interview with Don Kennedy, May 4, 1979, 16, both at GMMA.

4. James B. Carey to David McDonald, Dec. 10, 1951, DMD-PSULA, box 34: 1951–53; audit report, Mar. 31, 1955, CIOWO, box 21: 16.

5. Lloyd Ulman, *The Government of the Steel Workers' Union* (New York: John Wiley and Sons, 1962), 49–54.

6. Nelson Lichtenstein, "UAW Bargaining Strategy and Shop-Floor Conflict: 1946–1970," *Industrial Relations* 24, no. 3 (Fall 1985): 369–75. See the shrewd comments of Clinton S. Golden and Harold J. Ruttenberg, *The Dynamics of Industrial Democracy* (New York: Harper and Bros., 1942), 110–18, on the contrasts between Pittsburgh and Detroit. [Daniel Bell], "The CIO's New Line-Up," *Fortune*, Jan. 1951, 50, notes a "Catholic"-"socialist" ideological split in the CIO, with Murray and the USWA hospitable to Catholic corporatist ideas and the UAW reflecting a thoroughly secular, technocratic brand of unionism.

7. [Daniel Bell], "Labor's Coming of Middle Age," *Fortune*, Oct. 1951, 137; Nelson Lichtenstein, "Walter Reuther and the Rise of Labor-Liberalism," in Dubofsky and Van Tine, *Labor Leaders in America*, 286–95; Walter Reuther, "Our Social Setup Lags behind Our Technological Progress," *Labor and Nation*, Jan.–Feb. 1947, copy in Walter P. Reuther Papers, ALUAWSU, box 565: 10. The apocryphal Truman story is told in Robert H. Zieger, *American Workers, American Unions, 1920–1985* (Baltimore: Johns Hopkins University Press, 1986), 107.

8. Robert H. Zieger, "Leadership and Bureaucracy in the Late CIO," *LH* 31, no. 3 (Summer 1990): 258–59, quoting Pressman. On McDonald, see Donald G. Sofchalk, "David John McDonald," in *Biographical Dictionary of American Labor*, ed. Gary Fink, 2d ed. (Westport, Conn.: Greenwood Press, 1984), 375–76, and David J. McDonald, *Union Man* (New York: Dutton, 1969). On McDonald's relationship with Murray, see William Serrin, *Homestead: The Glory and the Tragedy of an American Steel Town* (New York: Vintage, 1993), 257–70. On wages in the two industries, see Nathan Goldfinger, "Average Straight-Time Hourly Earnings," ca. early 1952, Philip Murray Papers, CUA, box A4: 136, USWA.

9. Robert H. Zieger interview with Ralph Helstein, Chicago, Mar. 19, 1983 (in Zieger's possession); [Daniel Bell], "Labor's New Men of Power," *Fortune*, June 1953, 148–51, 160–62; David J. McDonald interview with Anthony Luchek, Feb. 7, 1979, GMMA, esp. 3–4; Fleisher interview, 16.

10. Zieger, "Leadership and Bureaucracy," 255–56; Marion Heimlich to Dan Seligman, Oct. 9, 1951, DBC-NYU, original series, box 19: CIO Leaders.

11. The anti-McDonald motivation behind Reuther's nomination is indicated in Jack Conway interview with Alice Hoffman, May 23, 1979, GMMA, 2–3. To what extent Reuther seriously thought that he could advance his broad hopes for organized labor primarily through the CIO is unclear. None of his biographers devotes much attention to his CIO presidency or to his motives for seeking it. See John Barnard, *Walter Reuther and the Rise of the Autoworkers* (Boston: Little, Brown, 1983), 132–33; Lichtenstein, "Walter Reuther and the Rise of Labor-Liberalism," 295–96; Anthony Carew, *Walter Reuther* (Manchester, U.K.: Manchester University Press,

1993); Frank Cormier and William J. Eaton, *Reuther* (Englewood Cliffs, N.J.: Prentice Hall, 1970), 315–24; and Kevin Gerard Boyle, "Politics and Principle: The United Automobile Workers and American Labor-Liberalism, 1948–1968" (Ph.D. dissertation, University of Michigan, 1990).

12. The Helstein interview provided details about the atmosphere of the convention, the character of the Haywood vote, and doubts about Reuther. For the vote, see CIOPROC, 1952, 491–511, and tally sheet, [Dec. 4, 1952], UPWA, box 79: CIO convention. F. W. Dowling, a Packinghouse Workers' district director, reported considerable support for Reuther even in unions that voted for Haywood. Moreover, he pointed out that the mystifying CIO vote-weighing formula, which was designed to suggest greater membership totals than were in fact the case, inflated the vote totals for the smaller affiliates, most of which backed Haywood. F. W. Dowling to All Staff Representatives, Dec. 9, 1952, UPWA, box 79: 10. The McDonald interview, 8–9, outlines his activities at the convention and his objections to Reuther.

13. Zieger, "Leadership and Bureaucracy," 255–70; Oliver interview, 7–8.

14. Zieger, "Leadership and Bureaucracy," 261–62; Oliver interview, 8; Robert H. Zieger, "John Vernon Riffe," in Fink, *Biographical Dictionary*, 486–87; William Grogan, *John Riffe of the Steelworkers: American Labor Statesman* (New York: Coward-McCann, 1959).

15. Oral Garrison to David J. McDonald, Apr. 13, 1953, box 58: Ga–Gk, Apr. 1953–May 1955; Garrison to McDonald, Mar. 27, 1953, box 58: Sept. 1951–Apr. 1953; Garrison to McDonald, Nov. 19, 195[3], box 35: CIO, Nov. 1953–Feb. 1954, all in DMD-PSULA; Riffe to Reuther, May 11, 1954, CIOWO, box 24: 16; Robert Oliver to Reuther, May 21, 1954, with copy of Garrison to McDonald, May 21, 1954, CIOWO, box 28: 2. See also Zieger, "Leadership and Bureaucracy," 261–62.

16. Zieger, "Leadership and Bureaucracy," 255–58; Vin Sweeney to USWA district directors, Mar. 1, 1954, DMD-PSULA, box 35: CIO, Mar. 1953–Jan. 1955; Oral Garrison to David McDonald, May 21, 1954, in Robert Oliver to Walter Reuther, May 21, 1954, CIOWO, box 28: 2. On McDonald's behavior at board meetings, see C. R. Hathaway, report, Mar. 22, 1954, UPWA, box 102: 4. R. J. Thomas, appointed CIO assistant director of organization after his defeat in 1946 by Reuther in the UAW, comments sharply on the role of McDonald and Garrison in promoting conflict within the CIO and in the general disarray in the industrial union federation after Murray's death (R. J. Thomas interview, Fall 1956, COHC, 248–68).

17. Robert H. Zieger, "Showdown at the Rouge," *History Today* 40 (Jan. 1990): 49–54; Zieger, "Leadership and Bureaucracy," 259.

18. Penciled notes, CIO Executive Committee meeting, June 9, 1954, JBC, box 94.

19. On MRA, see Walter Huston Clark, *The Oxford Group: Its History and Significance* (New York: Bookman Associates, 1951). See also Zieger, "Leadership and Bureaucracy," 262–65.

20. Ramsay resume notes, ca. 1941; James Wechsler, "John Ramsay Is a Buchmanite Preaching to Bethlehem . . . ," *PM*, Feb. 21, 1941, clipping; Ramsay speech in untitled MRA pamphlet, ca. 1938, all in Ramsay papers, SLA-GSU, box 1590: 367. On the pageant at the Steelworkers' founding convention, see "Uncle Frank" (Buchman) to Ramsay, June 26, 1942, ibid. On Riffe's conversion, see Rae Riffe to "Zona," Oct. 3, 1959, Ramsay papers, SLA-GSU, box 1590: 371.

21. Riffe's activities and remarks are documented in Zieger, "Leadership and Bureaucracy," 264–65, nn. 24 and 25.

22. Ibid., 264–65; G. R. Hathaway, report on the National CIO Executive Board Meeting, Mar. 22, 1954, UPWA, box 102: 4.

23. CIOPROC, 1952, 484.

24. [Daniel Bell], "Labor Notes," *Fortune*, Feb. 1952, 66; [Daniel Bell], "Unionism on a Plateau," *Fortune*, Nov. 1952, 80; Victor Riesel, "CIO Girding to Push War against AFL," *Philadelphia Inquirer*, Dec. 2, 1952, clipping in Reuther papers, ALUAWSU, box 286: 1; *Detroit Labor*

Trends, Dec. 6, 1952, copy in DBC-NYU, original series, box 19: AFL–CIO; F. W. Dowling to All Staff Representatives, Dec. 9, 1952, UPWA, box 79: 10.

25. The figures in these two paragraphs are derived from examination of audits and reports by the secretary-treasurer as they appeared in CIOEB minutes and in the CIOWO papers. Particularly revealing are Report of CIO Membership by State and Congressional District, Jan. 8, 1954, CIOWO, box 84: 1; audit report, Oct. 1, 1954–Mar. 31, 1955, CIOWO, box 21: 16; James B. Carey report, July 20, 1955, CIOEB-WSU, 10; and Nov. 2, 1955, CIOEB-WSU, 5–6. For skeptical journalists' views, see [Bell], "Labor Notes," 66; [Bell], "Unionism on a Plateau," 80; Riesel, "CIO Girding to Push War"; *Detroit Labor Trends,* Dec. 6, 1952. See also Leo Troy, *Trade Union Membership, 1897–1962* (New York: National Bureau of Economic Research, Occasional Paper 92, 1965), 16–17. The Report of CIO Membership by State gives the total as of Jan. 1954, as about 3,733,000, though some of the information on which it is based goes back to 1949.

26. On the distribution of membership among affiliates, see, for example, CIOEB-WSU, Dec. 1, 1954, 13–15. On geographical distribution, see Report of CIO Membership by State and Congressional District, Jan. 8, 1954, CIOWO, box 84: 1. For a shrewd contemporary assessment, see [Bell], "Unionism on a Plateau."

27. [Daniel Bell], "Organizing: The Cream Is Off," *Fortune,* Apr. 1950, 54; [Daniel Bell], "Big Business Is Organized – by Labor," *Fortune,* June 1952; "12-month average paid membership," Nov. 12, 1953, CIOEB-WSU, 32–33. Union success in Taft-Hartley-mandated elections is cited in Clyde W. Sumers, "A Survey Evaluation of the Taft-Hartley Act," *Industrial and Labor Relations Review* 11, no. 3 (Apr. 1958): 408. See also Melvyn Dubofsky, *The State and Labor in Modern America* (Chapel Hill: University of North Carolina Press, 1994), 209.

28. Reuther's remarks, Mar. 23, 1954, CIOEB-WSU, 266; CIOPROC, 1952, 184; Zieger, "Leadership and Bureaucracy," 266; Reuther to Elwood Swisher, Mar. 18, 1953, CIOWO, box 39: 1; Reuther's remarks, Apr. 6, 1953, CIOEB-WSU, 11; "Statement Showing Expenditures for National Unions, LIU's, and IUC's from Sept. 30, 1952 through Mar. 31, 1953," ca. May 1953, CIOWO, box 25: 1; Boyd E. Payton to William Pollock, Apr. 24, 1953, CIOWO, box 37: 1.

29. "On CIO Organizational Matters," ca. Apr. 1953, CIOWO, box 26: 11; Organizing Policy Committee memorandum, Apr. 21, 1953, Irwin De Shetler Papers, ALUAWSU, box 30: Henry Santiestevan, 1953–54; "Memo on Organizational Matters as Adopted by Organizing Policy Committee," Apr. 21, 1953, CIOWO, box 23: 5; Riffe's remarks, June 4, 1953, CIOEB-WSU, 46–60, and Reuther's remarks, CIOEB-WSU, 60–61; Reuther's remarks, Feb. 5, 1953, CIOEB-WSU, 19–24. Riffe's memo, ca. mid-June 1953, to regional directors and industrial union councils, CIOWO, box 23: 5, explains the new setup. In his 1979 oral history Robert Oliver, Reuther's executive assistant at the CIO, stated that he had devised the actual program of administrative and organizational restructuring (Oliver interview, 35–36).

30. Garrison to Reuther, Aug. 18, 1953, CIOWO, box 25: 2; report of Joseph Childs, Mar. 23, 1954, CIOEB-WSU, 230–45, on the LIUs and the implications surrounding their fate. Members of LIUs paid their monthly per capita tax of $1 directly to the CIO, which provided negotiating, research, publicity, and strike support services. Since as of mid-1953 the LIU membership of about 30,000 paid over $350,000 annually into the CIO coffers, collectively the members of these organizations regularly paid more dues into the industrial union federation than all affiliates save the UAW and the USWA. LIU support for Haywood in his contest with Reuther in 1952 reflected the strong sense of identity as members of the CIO held by members of these organizations. See Allan Haywood's remarks, Oct. 31, 1951, CIOEB-WSU, 165–66. On liquidation, see Harold Jack to James B. Carey, July 20, 1954, CIOST, box 61: LIU.

31. Riffe's June 28, 1954, report to the CIO Operating Committee, CIOWO, box 26: 8, is typical of many such reports. The quote is from Riffe to Reuther, Oct. 26, 1954, Reuther papers, ALUAWSU, box 290: 7. See also Riffe to Reuther, Jan. 7, 1955, CIOWO, box 24: 17.

32. Reuther to Elwood Swisher, Mar. 18, 1953, CIOWO, box 39: 1; "Program for Organizing Government Workers," ca. Jan. 1953, CIOWO, box 26: 10; [Daniel Bell], "Insurance Men Strike, Too," *Fortune*, Mar. 1952, 50; [Daniel Bell], "The Last Frontier," *Fortune*, Jan. 1950, 44, 48; Benjamin C. Sigal to James B. Carey, Aug. 13, 1952, CIOST, box 52: Gas, Coke, 1949–54; discussion of Gas, Coke, Chemical situation, penciled notes, Oct. 27, 1953, CIO Executive Committee meeting, JBC, box 94.

33. James B. Carey, "Data on the Staff of CIO International Unions," June 1953, CIOWO, box 22: 9; Ely Chinoy, *Automobile Workers and the American Dream* (Boston: Beacon Press, 1965), 99; Ulman, *Government of the Steel Workers' Union*, 44–47; summary of UAW International Executive Board meeting, Sept. 8–11, 1953, CIOWO, box 37: 20, listing the net worth of UAW as of July 31 as $18,167,500, which included $5,338,000 in the general fund, $8,790,000 in the strike fund, and $450,000 in miscellaneous accounts.

34. Reuther to Riffe, Jan. 11, 1954, and "Decisions of Officers['] Meeting of Feb. 3, 1954," CIOWO, box 23: 6; penciled notes, Feb. 16, 1954, JBC, box 94: Executive Council-CIO; audit report by Main and Company, May 4, 1955, CIOWO, box 21: 16.

35. Riffe memo regarding payroll changes since Apr. 1, 1953, Mar. 22, 1954, CIOWO, box 25: 4; Riffe, "Memorandum . . . with Respect to Personnel Changes, Financial Saving and General Operation of the Organization Department . . . , Apr. 1, 1953 to Date," Oct. 26, 1954, Reuther papers, ALUAWSU, box 290: 17.

36. Clipping, newspaper unidentified, February 26, 1954, in Les Finnegan to Carey, Mar. 9, 1954, CIOWO, box 35: 8; "Are the CIO's Days Numbered?," *U.S. News and World Report*, Dec. 3, 1954, 86; Carey, financial report, Mar. 22, 1954, JBC, box 94: Executive Committee; Carey report, Mar. 23, 1954, CIOEB-WSU, 248–53.

37. On NLRB losses, see R. J. Thomas to Regional Directors, Jan. 16, 1953, Reuther papers, ALUAWSU, box 290: 12. On patterns of organizing and membership, see [Bell], "Cream Is Off"; CIOEB-WSU, Nov. 29, 1952, 8–10; "12-Month Average Paid Membership," Nov. 12, 1953, CIOEB-WSU, 32–33; "Membership Voting," Dec. 1, 1954, CIOEB-WSU, 13–14; [Daniel Bell], "Textile's Tribulations," *Fortune*, Apr. 1952, 56, 58–59; [Bell], "Unionism on a Plateau," 80; Bell(?) handwritten notes of conversation with Emil Rieve, May 24, 1954, DBC-NYU, original series, box 19: Union Democracy. See Everett Kassalow's extended remarks on organizing, ca. Dec. 1, 1953, CIOWO, box 59: 11, for an astute commentary on the changed environment of the 1950s, and Robert H. Zieger interview with Everett Kassalow, Mar. 16, 1983 (in Zieger's possession).

38. Thomas R. Brooks, *Communications Workers of America: The Story of a Union* (New York: Mason/Charter, 1977), 110–90; John N. Schacht, *The Making of Telephone Unionism, 1920–1947* (New Brunswick: Rutgers University Press, 1985), 174–80.

39. John J. Moran's remarks, Feb 5, 1953, CIOEB-WSU, 69; discussion, Feb. 6, CIOEB-WSU, 193; Barney Hopkins to Gus Scholle, Aug. 26, 1953, MSAFL–CIO, series 1, box 44: 15, MIUC correspondence-1953.

40. Kassalow remarks, ca. Dec. 1, 1953, CIOWO, box 59: 11; Kassalow interview.

41. Solomon Barkin to Stanley Ruttenberg, May 11, 1953, and Barkin to Reuther, May 15, 1953, CIOWO, box 26: 15. See also Elizabeth Fones-Wolf, "Industrial Recreation, the Second World War, and the Revival of Welfare Capitalism, 1934–1960," *Business History Review* 60, no. 2 (Summer 1986): 232–57.

42. "Family Income," Aug. 14, 1955, in *The Gallup Poll: Public Opinion, 1935–1971*, vol. 2, *1949–1958*, by George H. Gallup (New York: Random House, 1972), 1353–54; Union Research and Education Projects, University of Chicago, "Why Some Workers Don't Join Unions," Dec. 1956, Gardner Jackson Papers, Franklin D. Roosevelt Presidential Library, Hyde Park, N.Y., box 73: Union Affairs. Though this study examined a campaign conducted several months after the merger of the AFL and CIO in December 1955, it reported that workers showed little awareness

of the identity of the international union involved, the Oil, Atomic, and Chemical Workers, and referred only to the "CIO."

43. Art Preis, *Labor's Giant Step: Twenty Years of the CIO*, rev. ed. (New York: Pathfinder Press, 1972), 495–96.

44. Gains in wages are cited in Sumner M. Rosen, "The CIO Era, 1935–1955," in *The Negro and the American Labor Movement*, ed. Julius Jacobson (Garden City: Anchor Books, 1968), 200–201, while Gilbert Wesley Moore, "Poverty, Class Consciousness, and Racial Conflict: The Social Bases of Trade Union Politics in the UAW-CIO, 1937–1955" (Ph.D. dissertation, Princeton University, 1978), 166, indicates the number of black autoworkers. On the UAW's civil rights focus, see Nelson Lichtenstein, "Uneasy Partners: Walter Reuther, the United Automobile Workers and the Civil Rights Movement" (paper delivered at the annual meeting of the American Historical Association, Cincinnati, Dec. 1988, copy in Zieger's possession), and Boyle, "Politics and Principle," 185–90. On the Steelworkers, see Judith Stein, "Southern Workers in National Unions: Birmingham Steelworkers, 1936–1951," in *Organized Labor in the Twentieth-Century South*, ed. Robert H. Zieger (Knoxville: University of Tennessee Press, 1991), 198–208. On the Packinghouse Workers' vigorous program of biracial activism, see Roger Horowitz, "The Path Not Taken: A Social History of Industrial Unionism in Meatpacking, 1930–1960" (Ph.D. dissertation, University of Wisconsin, 1990), 663–78, and Rick Halpern, "Interracial Unionism in the Southwest: Fort Worth's Packinghouse Workers, 1937–1954," in Zieger, *Organized Labor*, 164–76.

45. James B. Carey to CIO representatives and councils, Sept. 3, 1952, with attached brochure (reporting on NLCUSA), MSAFL–CIO, series 2, box 100: 11, National CIO-1953; Murray press release, June 21, 1951, Delmond Garst Papers, ALUAWSU, box 5: 25, Murray- 1951; press releases, Dec. 2, 1953, and Mar. 2, 1954, CIOWO, box 23: 12; letter to regional directors, Feb. 18, 1954, CIOWO, box 23: 12. This file has many similar statements and communications on civil rights, desegregation, and related matters.

46. Gus Scholle to Jack Kroll, Apr. 17, 1950, MSAFL–CIO, series 1, box 30: 13, National CIO-PAC-1950; Ralph Helstein to Joseph Beirne, Jan. 20, 1954, copy enclosed in Beirne to Walter Reuther, Feb. 5, 1954, CIOWO, box 39: 17; Russell R. Lasley to A. T. Stephens and Ralph Helstein, June 29, 1953, UPWA, box 96: 8; Ralph Helstein to Walter Reuther, Jan. 25, 1954, UPWA, box 102: 3; G. R. Hathaway to George L.-P. Weaver, June 10, 1954, UPWA, box 102: 3; UPWA Research Department, "Organizing the South – The Problem of Discrimination," Sept. 1955, UPWA, box 116: 7. On the Steelworkers, see Robert J. Norrell, "Caste in Steel: Jim Crow Careers in Birmingham, Alabama," *JAH* 73, no. 3 (Dec. 1986): 675–79, 685–88. Stein, "Southern Workers in National Unions," however, stresses the international union's efforts to end overt discrimination in the Alabama mills. On the subtleties of maintaining segregated job lines in a large northern mill, see Victor Forberger, "Craftsmen and Contractual Relations at the Duquesne Steel Works, 1950s and 1960s" (Master's paper, University of Florida, 1992).

47. The activities of CARD and the Civil Rights Committee are outlined in the annual convention proceedings. The files of George L.-P. Weaver, a subset of the CIO Secretary-Treasurer's Papers, ALUAWSU, bulge with public statements, transcripts of testimony in support of civil rights legislation, records of regional and national civil rights meetings, and correspondence with organizations such as the NAACP, with which the CIO maintained close and friendly relations. For UPWA disdain for official CIO civil rights efforts, see, for example, G. R. Hathaway to George L.-P. Weaver, June 10, 1954, UPWA, box 102: 3, and Ralph Helstein to Riffe, May 18, 1954, UPWA, box 96: 11. See also Marshall Stevenson, "Challenging the Roadblocks to Equality: Race Relations and Civil Rights in the CIO, 1935–1955" (Ohio State University Center for Labor Research, Working Paper Series [1992–93]), 39–48.

48. Allan Haywood to Karl F. Feller, Lewis J. Clark, and Martin Kyne, Mar. 23, 1950, UPWA, box 72: 23; Willard Townsend to Allan Haywood, Jan. 8, 1951, SOC-DU, box 57: Haywood;

Russell R. Lasley to A. T. Stephens and Ralph Helstein, June 29, 1953, UPWA, box 96: 8; Ralph Helstein to John Riffe, May 18, 1954, UPWA, box 96: 11; Ralph Helstein to Joseph Beirne, Jan. 20, 1954, CIOWO, box 39: 17. Important CIO leaders, notably Carey and Riffe, believed the Packinghouse Workers' union to be Communist dominated and, hence, an undesirable candidate for CIO support (John Riffe to Ralph Helstein, May 6, 1953, DMD-PSULA, box 34: CIO, Mar.–June 1953; David Burgess, executive secretary, Georgia State Industrial Union Council, to Robert Oliver, Aug. 14, 1953, CIOWO, box 39: 12; "Report [of] Committee on Packinghouse," CIO Executive Committee Minutes, Oct. 27, 1953, JBC, box 94). On subsidies, see Harold Jack to Carey, CIO financial statement, Mar. 3, 1953, JBC, box 94: Executive Committee; "Statement Showing Expenditures for National Unions . . . ," ca. May 1953, CIOWO, box 25: 1; and "Staff Assigned to Internationals," June 17, 1953, CIOWO, box 25: 2. Memorandum of Activities of CIO Organizational Staff . . . [June 15, 1954], JBC, addition 3, box 22: CIO Organizing and Operating, shows none of the 138 organizers whose activities are detailed assigned to UTSE or other black-oriented projects. CIO records for February 1954, however, do reveal that UTSE was one of only two CIO affiliates then getting a monthly subsidy; in both cases the amount was $1,000 monthly (Carey report, Apr. 1, 1954, Reuther papers, ALUAWSU, box 289: 23).

49. Lichtenstein, "Uneasy Partners"; Boyle, "Politics and Principle," 185–90. Seth Marks Wigderson, "The UAW in the 1950s" (Ph.D. dissertation, Wayne State University, 1989), 311–20.

50. On the National Negro Labor Council, see Philip Foner, *Organized Labor and the Black Worker, 1619–1973* (New York: International Publishers, 1974), 293–311, quote at 299; James H. Hill to Murray and to Carey, Oct. 21, 1951, CIOST, box 59: URW, 1942–55. Packinghouse officials echoed Hill's analysis. See also Research Department, UPWA, "Main Points Shown by Statistics on the South," ca. 1955, UPWA, box 116: 7.

51. Townsend to Robert Oliver, Feb. 12, 1955, CIOWO, box 41: 13.

52. Foner, *Organized Labor and the Black Worker*, 269–74, 287–92.

53. Eva Mueller and William Ladd, "Negro–White Differences in Geographic Mobility," in *Negroes and Jobs: A Book of Readings*, ed. Louis A. Ferman, Joyce L. Kornbluh, and J. A. Miller (Ann Arbor: University of Michigan Press, 1968), 382–400; Alan B. Batchelder, "Decline in the Relative Income of Negro Men," in Ferman et al., *Negroes and Jobs*, 65–91; Rosen, "CIO Era," 200–208; Sidney M. Peck, "The Economic Situation of Negro Labor," in Jacobson, *The Negro and the American Labor Movement*, 209–31; Harold M. Baron and Bennett Hymer, "The Negro Worker in the Chicago Labor Market," in Jacobson, *The Negro and the American Labor Movement*, 232–85; Herbert Hill, "Race, Ethnicity, and Organized Labor: The Opposition to Affirmative Action," *New Politics*, n.s., 1, no. 2 (Winter 1987): 68–74; William B. Gould, *Black Workers in White Unions: Job Discrimination in the United States* (Ithaca: Cornell University Press, 1977), 21, 371–405.

54. These are my estimates based on historic patterns of membership in the various unions. See CIOPROC, 1952, 281; Charles Fischer to Stanley Ruttenberg, May 1, 1951, UPWA, box 72: 1; Ruth Milkman, *Gender at Work: The Dynamics of Job Segregation by Sex during World War II* (Urbana: University of Illinois Press, 1987), 155–56; Nancy Gabin, *Feminism in the Labor Movement: Women and the United Auto Workers, 1935–1975* (Ithaca: Cornell University Press, 1990), 145–55.

55. Gabin, *Feminism in the Labor Movement*, 111–57; Lisa Kannenberg, "The Impact of the Cold War on Women's Trade Union Activism: The UE Experience," *LH* 34, no. 2–3 (Spring–Summer 1993): 309–23; Mark McColloch, "The Shop-Floor Dimension of Union Rivalry: The Case of Westinghouse in the 1950s," in *The CIO's Left-Led Unions*, ed. Steven Rosswurm (New Brunswick: Rutgers University Press, 1992), 194–99; Rosswurm, preface to *CIO's Left-Led Unions*, xv–xvi; "Dorothy Jacobs Bellanca," in Fink, *Biographical Dictionary*, 108; Nina Lynn Asher, "Dorothy Jacobs Bellanca: Feminist Trade Unionist" (Ph.D. dissertation, SUNY-

Binghamton, 1982), 269–71; Horowitz, "Path Not Taken," 678–93; Brooks, *Communications Workers of America*, 135–36, 162–63, 179, 200.

56. "International Headquarters Staff," Dec. 8, 1952, CIOWO, box 25: 1; "Staff Assigned to Internationals," June 17, 1953, CIOWO, box 25: 2. At the 1946 convention a woman delegate counted 25 females among the 516 delegates, while in 1954 there were 9 among 471. In that year, the UAW, the ACWA, the IUE, the Packinghouse Workers, the TWUA, and the CWA, the unions with the largest female membership contingents, had a total of 1 woman delegate among them. Delegates are listed by name in the annual proceedings of CIO conventions.

57. CIOPROC, 1946, 76; Gabin, *Feminism in the Labor Movement*, 111–42; Alan Clive, "Women Workers in World War II: Michigan as a Test Case," *LH* 20, no. 1 (Winter 1979): 69. The UE, with 200,000 female members, compiled a better record in defending women's postwar job rights than did any other CIO affiliate. See Milkman, *Gender at Work*, 104–12, and Ronald W. Schatz, *The Electrical Workers: A History of Labor at General Electric and Westinghouse, 1923–1960* (Urbana: University of Illinois Press, 1983), 119–27. The generalizations in this paragraph are based on the *absence* of engaged concern with gender issues throughout a wide range of documented CIO activities.

58. Riffe to Murray, Aug. 27, 1952, copy in SOC-DU, North Carolina, box 78: Riffe, 1952; CIO, *The CIO: What It Is and What It Does*, 1953–54, *PAM-L*, 503.

59. Remarks by Walter Reuther, Feb 5, 1953, and by Joseph Beirne, Feb. 6, CIOEB-WSU, 69–74, 178–96; Reuther's remarks, June 4, 1953, CIOEB-WSU, 221–22; John Riffe to Delmond Garst, June 22, 1953, Garst papers, ALUAWSU, box 1: 37, Correspondence-1953; Robert Oliver to Walter Reuther, Feb. 2, 1954, CIOWO, box 26: 4; report by Henry C. Fleisher, Mar. 23, 1954, CIOEB-WSU, 331–35; Barney Hopkins to Gus Scholle, Aug. 26, 1953, MSAFL–CIO, series 1, box 44: 15, MIUC correspondence-1953; Mildred Jeffrey and J. A. Rightley to international representatives and local union presidents, Jan. 28, 1950, MSAFL–CIO, series 1, box 32: 11, UAW-1950.

60. R. E. Dingwell and Marvin Metzer, "The Michigan CIO Council at County Fairs," ca. Jan. 1953, MSAFL–CIO, series 1, box 44: 14, MCIOIUC Officers-1953.

61. The activities of the Community Services Committee are briefly outlined each year between 1946 and 1955 in the proceedings of the CIO's annual convention. See especially CIO-PROC, 1946, 87–89, and CIOPROC, 1951, 203–6. "CIO-CSC Today . . . A Report," mimeo, in Leo Perlis to Joseph Beirne, Apr. 21, 1955, Reuther papers, ALUAWSU, box 291: 10, CWA; Walter Reuther speech to CIO Community Services Institute, Apr. 15, 1954, CIOWO, box 23: 17.

62. Minutes of Community Relations meeting, Jan. 15, 1954, CIOWO, box 57: 4; Schatz, *Electrical Workers*, 97–99, 194–221; Schatz, "Philip Murray," 248. Murray's boyhood recollections are in John G. Ramsay to Stanley H. Ruttenberg, Aug. 3, 1950, with attached statement, Ramsay papers, SLA-GSU, box 1556: 1. Beirne's statement in transcript of radio interview with Joseph Beirne, Dec. 20, 1953, Reuther papers, ALUAWSU, box 29: 10, CWA.

63. John Ramsay, "Activities for the month of July," in Ramsay to John Riffe, Aug. 20, 1950, Murray papers, CUA, box A4: 79, CIO Committee-Organizing; Elwood Swisher to Ramsay, July 9, 1954, Ramsay papers, SLA-GSU, box 1557: 24. The words quoted are in John Ramsay to John Riffe, May 26, 1953, Ramsay papers, SLA-GSU, box 1556: 1. The activities of Ramsay and his associates Charles Webber and Jules Weinberg are outlined in Ramsay to Riffe, Nov. 15, 1954, Ramsay papers, SLA-GSU, box 1556: 3.

64. Ramsay's remarks appear in John Ramsay to regional directors, Apr. 29, 1954, Ramsay papers, SLA-GSU, box 1560: 66. Victor Reuther's statement is in his memo of Apr. 12, 1954, CIOWO, box 57: 6. The surveys themselves are collected in the Ramsay papers, SLA-GSU, box 1560: 66, and CIOWO, box 57: 6.

65. "Staff Assigned to Internationals," June 17, 1953, CIOWO, box 25: 2; Riffe report,

Aug. 28, 1953, CIOEB-WSU, 19–23; Don Stevens to Gus Scholle, ca. Nov. 1, 1953, and Oct. 1953, MSAFL–CIO, series 1, box 44: 15, MIUCOS-1953. See MSAFL–CIO, series 1, box 44, folders 18–20, for weekly, monthly, and special reports by Michigan IUC officers and field representatives. Report of John V. Riffe on Meetings of General Organizing Committee and Operating Committee, June 1–2, 15, 1954, JBC, addition 3, box 22: CIO Organizing and Operating, is an eight-page rundown of the uses to which 138 organizers were being put by twenty-two affiliates about a year after the new plan went into effect. There is much material in CIOWO, box 37, reporting on methods of organizing, experiences of organizers, and difficulty in making progress in the southern textile industry, which both during and after the liquidation of SOC employed a large contingent of CIO organizers. See, for example, Boyd E. Payton's reports to Emil Rieve and to Robert Oliver, Oct. 29, 1953–Oct. 5, 1954. See also the reports on southern organizing in CIOWO, box 26, esp. Riffe to R. J. Thomas, Mar. 20, 1953, and Lorne H. Nelles to Riffe, Apr. 8, 15, 1953; "Hank" [Rabun] to Robert Oliver, Feb. 4, 1953, CIOWO, box 41: 1; "Memorandum for Special Committee on Organizing Program," Oct. 1954, and Henry Paley, Research and Education Director of the United Paperworkers, to Oliver, July 13, 1954, CIOWO, box 26: 7; John V. Riffe, "A Staff Training Program for CIO," ca. May 1, 1953, CIOWO, box 22: 4; Riffe to members of CIO Organizing Committee, June 28, 1954, JBC, addition 3, box 22: CIO Organizing.

66. [Daniel Bell], "The Next American Labor Movement," *Fortune*, Apr. 1953, 202; Chinoy, *Automobile Workers and the American Dream*, 96–109.

67. Carey report, CIOEB, ALUAWSU, June 4, 1953, 37–41 (on salaries, per diem); Carey, "Data on Staffs of CIO International Unions," June 1953, CIOWO, box 29: 9; Carey to Reuther, Feb. 23, 1955, CIOWO, box 22: 10. This box contains copious materials giving salaries, assignments, and other quotidian details relating to field representatives and regional directors. The papers of Daniel A. Powell, PAC's southern director, and those of Paul R. Christopher, a southern regional director, provide a rich record of the personal and financial lives of conscientious CIO representatives struggling to balance family life with assignments that entailed much time away from home. Chinoy, *Automobile Workers and the American Dream*, 96–109, documents the lack of upward career mobility. On rationalization of per diem expenses and fringe benefits, see CIOEB, ALUAWSU, June 4, 1953, 37–43; H. W. Denton to Riffe, Sept. 28, 1953, CIOWO, box 25: 3 (complaint about new financial arrangements; activities and difficulties of field reps). C. Wright Mills, *The New Men of Power: American's Labor Leaders* (New York: Harcourt, Brace, 1948), 9, uses the term "managers of discontent."

68. Hugh M. Brown, Jr., William Mayo, John J. Maurillo, and A. R. Kinstley to Walter Reuther, Sept. 30, 1953, CIOWO, box 25: 2.

69. Kermit Eby, "The 'Drip' Theory in Labor Unions," *Antioch Review*, 13, no. 1 (Mar. 1953): 95–102.

70. Reuther report in CIOPROC, 1954, 45–46; Carey notes, 1955, "Historic Meaning of CIO," Carey Papers, addition 3, box 26: Merger, 1955.

Chapter Thirteen

1. Reuther's remarks, July 20, 1955, CIOEB-WSU, 20–21, 34.

2. Philip A. Taft, *Organized Labor in American History* (New York: Harper, 1964), 646–52; Henry Fleisher interview with Don Kennedy, May 4, 1979, GMMA, 16.

3. Fleisher interview, 16; Tom Harris interview with Frank Fernbach, Aug. 10, 1979, GMMA, 6.

4. Arthur J. Goldberg, *AFL–CIO: Labor United* (New York: McGraw-Hill, 1956), 62–71.

5. Taft, *Organized Labor*, 650–52; *New York Times*, Dec. 8, 1952, clipping in ILGWU-

LMDC, box 207: 5, quoting Meany as saying that the CIO had resulted from "a bid for power by John L. Lewis and Sidney Hillman"; George Meany to Walter Reuther, Jan. 21, 1953, CIOWO, box 15.

6. Taft, *Organized Labor*, 650–52; Stanley Ruttenberg interview with Don Kennedy, July 20, 1979, GMMA, 16. On the ULPC, see Jack Stieber, "Labor's Walkout from the Korean War Wage Stabilization Board," *LH* 21, no. 2 (Spring 1980): 239–60, and [Daniel Bell], "End of 'Functional Unity,'" *Fortune*, Oct. 1951, 64.

7. "Meany Would Quit to Aid Labor Unity," *New York Times*, Dec. 8, 1952; George Meany to Walter Reuther, Jan. 21, 1953, CIOWO, box 21: 15; Reuther's remarks, Feb. 5, 1953, CIOEB-WSU, 54–61.

8. A. H. Raskin interview with Jon Bloom, Apr. 18, 1979, GMMA, 5; "Harris" to "Beshoar," June 6, 1953, DBC-NYU, original series, box 19: Merger; Arthur Goldberg's remarks, Mar. 22, 1954, CIOEB-WSU, 74–75.

9. AFL membership list, ca. Jan. 1, 1953, CIOWO, box 21: 15; [Daniel Bell], "Organizing: The Cream Is Off," *Fortune*, Apr. 1950, 51–54; [Daniel Bell], "Unionism on a Plateau," *Fortune*, Nov. 1952, 80; Leo Troy, *Trade Union Membership, 1897–1962* (New York: National Bureau of Economic Research, Occasional Paper 92, 1965), 5–9.

10. Philip Foner, *Organized Labor and the Black Worker, 1619–1973* (New York: International Publishers, 1974), 281; Marc Karson and Ronald Radosh, "The AFL and the Negro Worker, 1894–1949," in *The Negro and the American Labor Movement*, ed. Julius Jacobson (Garden City: Anchor Books, 1968), 155–87; Joseph Goulden, *Meany* (New York: Atheneum, 1972), 305–9. See also Robert H. Zieger, "George Meany: Labor's Organization Man," in *Labor Leaders in America*, ed. Melvyn Dubofsky and Warren Van Tine (Urbana: University of Illinois Press, 1987), 342–44.

11. James Carey notes, "The Historic Meaning of CIO," JBC, addition 3, box 26: Merger, 1955; John Hutchinson, *The Imperfect Union: A History of Corruption in American Trade Unions* (New York: Dutton, 1970), 294–98, 312–13; Goulden, *Meany*, 186–94; Vernon H. Jensen, *Strife on the Waterfront: The Port of New York since 1945* (Ithaca: Cornell University Press, 1974), 105–35; Carey's remarks, May 7, 1955, CIOEB-WSU, 67–68.

12. On the details of the merger, see Goldberg, *AFL–CIO*, and Taft, *Organized Labor*, 655–63. Goulden, *Meany*, 181–206, contains vivid material drawn from the author's extensive interviews with the AFL president.

13. Goldberg, *AFL–CIO*, provides a chronological account of the merger process (72–102) and reprints the AFL–CIO constitution and other key documents relating to the merger (235–97). See also Taft, *Organized Labor*, 645–62. On Goldberg's role, see Raskin interview, 7; Jack Barbash interview with Jim Cavanaugh, Feb. 2, 9, 1979, GMMA, 5–6; Jack Conway interview with Alice Hoffman, May 23, 1979, GMMA, 10–11; Robert H. Zieger interview with Arthur J. Goldberg, Aug. 24, 1983 (in Zieger's possession); and Arthur J. Goldberg interview with Alice Hoffman, Oct. 9, 1979, GMMA. On the debate over nomenclature, see, for example, Minutes, CIO Executive Committee meeting, May 2, 1955, JBC, box 94.

14. Lovestone quoted in Goulden, *Meany*, 186; A. H. Raskin, "Meany Infuses New Spirit into A.F.L. in All Fields," *New York Times*, June 15, 1953, clipping in ILGWU-LMDC, box 205: 5.

15. Robert H. Zieger, "Leadership and Bureaucracy in the Late CIO," *LH* 31, no. 3 (Summer 1990): 255, 256–61; George L.-P. Weaver interview with Paul Addis, May 18, 1979, GMMA, 10; Les Finnegan to Robert Oliver, Mar. 9, 1954, with clipping of Victor Riesel, "M'Donald Ready to Deliver Death Blow to CIO," *New York Mirror*, Feb. 26, 1954, CIOWO, box 35: 8. McDonald's abrupt withdrawal of USWA staff members assigned by Murray to CIO work set the tone. It was, said Robert Oliver, Reuther's chief CIO aide, "the first act of aggression . . . and unfortunately expressed in large measure his attitude toward the CIO" (Robert Oliver interview with Frank Fernbach, Sept. 17, 1979, GMMA, 29). Arthur Goldberg insisted that McDonald never seriously

contemplated pulling the USWA out of the CIO (Goldberg interview with Hoffman, 5). Of course, McDonald's threat to suspend dues payments paralleled John L. Lewis's 1942 claim for reimbursement by the CIO to the UMW, presented just as the UMW was pulling out of the industrial union federation.

16. Oliver interview, 30–31.

17. On the four basic principles, see Walter Reuther's remarks before UAW convention, Mar. 22, 1953, typescript, CIOWO, box 21: 17, and the discussion in Minutes of CIO Executive Committee, Feb. 1, 1955, JBC, box 94. McDonald's understanding of his role in speeding up the pace of unity talks is found in USWA-IEB, Mar. 2, 1955, 38–42.

18. McDonald quoted in Goldberg, *AFL–CIO*, 84–85; McDonald's remarks, Mar. 2, 1955, USWA-IEB, 38–45.

19. Goldberg, *AFL–CIO*, 83–95. This book reprints the February 1955 merger agreement and the implementation agreement, dated Nov. 30, 1955 (235–70).

20. On the apprehensions of smaller CIO affiliates, see, for example, CIOEB-WSU, May 10, 1954, 9–65.

21. Reuther's remarks (as summarized by George L.-P. Weaver), May 2, 1955, JBC, box 94. On Carey's and McDonald's roles, see Weaver interview, 18–19. Townsend's reminders appear, for example, in CIOEB-WSU, Feb. 5, 1953, 62–64, and Aug. 20, 1953, 91–93. See also Goldberg interview with Hoffman, 18, in which he affirms that the constitution of the merged federation was only advisory on the racial practices of affiliates, although in his 1956 account of the merger Goldberg suggested otherwise (Goldberg, *AFL–CIO*, 148–49). See Foner, *Organized Labor and the Black Worker*, 311–15, for a stinging critique of the merger's antidiscrimination features.

22. Reuther's remarks, May 7, 1955, CIOEB-WSU, 38–47.

23. Walter Reuther to Executive Board members, July 8, 1955, CIOWO, box 21: 1; Jacob Potofsky's and Frank Rosenblum's remarks, Executive Committee notes, July 19, 1955, JBC, box 94.

24. McDonald's remarks, Mar. 2, 1955, USWA-IEB, 43–44.

25. Reuther's remarks, May 7, 1955, CIOEB-WSU, 38–47.

26. Reuther's remarks, CIOEB-WSU, Nov. 2, 1955, 93–106.

27. McDonald's remarks, Dec. 7, 1955, USWA-IEB, 14; Al Whitehouse address, opening session, first Executive Board meeting of the Industrial Union Department, AFL–CIO, Mar. 15, 1956, ILGWU-LMDC, box 206: 3B.

28. "John William Livingston," in *Biographical Dictionary of American Labor*, ed. Gary Fink, 2d ed. (Westport, Conn.: Greenwood Press, 1984), 359–60; John W. Livingston interview with Paul Addis, Sept. 28, 1979, GMMA.

29. Penciled notes on Executive Committee meeting by James Gildea, Oct. 26, 1955., JBC, box 94: CIO-EC.

30. Reuther's remarks, Nov. 2, 1955, CIOEB-WSU, 26; Raskin interview, 26–27; Conway interview, 11–13; Livingston interview, 25–27.

31. Quill press statement, Feb. 16, 1955, CIOST, box 61: Transport, 1954 [*sic*]; Quill mimeographed letter, Aug. 29, 1955, with reprint of Quill's column in *TWU Express*, Aug. 1955, CIOWO, box 37: 15; CIOPROC, 1955, 301–4.

32. Virtually all of the oral histories on the merger, recorded in 1979 and collected at the George Meany Memorial Archives, stress the importance of McDonald's role. According to Carey's aide George Weaver, "If the merger hadn't come about the Steelworkers would have pulled out; there's no question in my mind about it." Said CIO staffer Jacob Clayman, "I suspect the most important figure was Dave McDonald" (Jacob Clayman interview with Don Kennedy, Aug. 30, 1979, 2, 3). See also the oral histories of Henry Fleisher, Tom Harris, Stanley Ruttenberg, and John Edelman (Apr. 18, 1957, COHC). McDonald's remarks are in David McDonald interview with Anthony

Luchek, Feb. 7, 1979, GMMA, 3–4. See also David J. McDonald, *Union Man* (New York: Dutton, 1969), 241–42, 247–48.

33. Clayman interview, 3.

34. See Estelle James, "Jimmy Hoffa: Labor Hero or Labor's Own Foe?," in Dubofsky and Van Tine, *Labor Leaders in America*, 310–17; Reuther's remarks, Dec. 10, 1954, CIOEB-WSU, 38.

35. Knight's remarks, CIO Executive Committee meeting minutes, July 19, 1955, JBC, box 94; Buckmaster's remarks, penciled notes, CIO Executive Committee meeting minutes, July 19, 1955, JBC, box 94: CIOEC-July 19, 1955.

36. Reuther's remarks, July 20, 1955, CIOEB-WSU, 32–37.

37. The NLRB study is cited in Goldberg, *AFL–CIO*, 76–77. A copy of the report based on the study, ca. early 1953, is found in UPWA, box 72: 3.

38. Zieger, "George Meany," 341–42; Curran's and Knight's remarks, penciled notes, CIO Executive Committee meeting, July 19, 1955, JBC, box 94; Barbash interview, 17.

39. Reuther's remarks, Nov. 2, 1955, CIOEB-WSU, 97–106.

40. *New York Times*, Dec. 1, 1955, 1, 26–27; Dec. 2, 1955, 1, 20–21; Dec. 3, 1955, 1, 11; Dec. 4, 1955, 1 and sect. 4, 2, 9; Dec. 5, 1955, 1; Dec. 6, 1955, 1, 22–24, 26, 36.

41. CIOPROC, 1955, 301–4.

42. Ibid., 304–8.

43. Ibid., 326.

44. The most pointed and generous reference, interestingly, came from the lips of Valentine Reuther, praising the Mine Worker for launching the CIO (ibid., 256).

45. Ibid., 334–36.

46. McDonald, *Union Man*, 248; *New York Times*, Dec. 3, 1955, 11, and Dec. 6, 1955, 24

47. Reuther's remarks, Nov. 2, 1955, CIOEB-WSU, 97–106.

Conclusion

1. What do I mean by the term *CIO* in this context? How to refer to the diverse activities and components of a large institutional entity has been a continuing problem in my many years of thinking about the "CIO." Throughout this book I have attempted to specify exactly who or what I was referring to. In most cases, I referred to CIO leaders or CIO spokesmen or convention delegates or Executive Board majorities. We are all too familiar with modern bureaucratic institutions to make the mistake of personifying them. I know too much about tensions among ordinary members, elected leaders, and hired staff to ever speak confidently about "the CIO" as a self-explanatory entity.

Here, however, in assessing the significance of the CIO in American history, I fuse the various subcategories. There was an entity called the CIO that was something other than its constituent elements, be they rank-and-file members, headquarter staffers, elected leaders, or affiliated unions and *their* component parts. True, elected leaders often faced rank-and-file opposition, notably during World War II when workplace and racial tensions sparked rebellious outbursts. Leaders and ordinary members frequently exhibited differing views in public opinion polls. But I believe that in their broad direction of CIO affairs the leadership legitimately spoke in behalf of the membership. After World War II, CIO members overwhelmingly reselected their unions as bargaining agents in ballots required by the Taft-Hartley Act for reaffirmation of union shop status. Though CIO conventions became increasingly reflective of union bureaucracies rather than workers as such, they were open, participatory gatherings, with policies freely debated and voted on. While members of the headquarters staff, most notably Lee Pressman and Arthur Goldberg, were extremely influential and in some cases decisively shaped the wording, and thus at times the content, of resolutions and statements, there was never any Praetorian guard or self-perpetuating inner circle unresponsive to elected leaders. Thus, in my view at least, in regard to the broad direction of CIO affairs and the most important subjects to which the CIO addressed itself, it is legitimate to speak of the CIO as a cohesive entity. Thus, in this conclusion, and here only, I use the term *the CIO* without reference to organizational divisions or levels of participation.

2. Nelson Lichtenstein, "Labor in the Truman Era: Origins of the 'Private Welfare State,'" in *The Truman Presidency*, ed. Michael J. Lacey (Washington, D.C., and Cambridge: Woodrow Wilson International Center for Scholars and Cambridge University Press, 1989), 148–54.

Index

South Carolina, 234, 235

Southeast Asia, 130

Southern States Industrial Council, 235

Soviet Union, 20, 102, 103, 136, 179, 244, 252, 253, 254, 255, 256, 258, 259, 261, 262–63, 264–65, 275, 276, 277, 288–89, 291, 306, 328, 329

Spain, 263, 331

Sparrows Point, Md., 118, 155

Stalin, Joseph, 253, 259, 261, 266, 268

Stalingrad, 187

Stalinism, 372, 376

Stamford, Conn., 214

Standard Oil Company, 120, 266, 343

Stanford University, 288

State, U.S. Department of, 263, 264

Steel industry, 2, 29, 30, 34–39, 40, 41, 42, 54–65, 74, 78, 83, 84, 103, 106, 111, 112, 123–24, 126, 131, 139, 154, 163, 166, 320–21; processes and conditions, 6, 41, 113, 114, 118, 115, 152, 175, 228, 327; strikes, 9, 10, 35, 42, 44, 56, 60–63, 84, 124, 152, 168, 213, 214, 221, 222, 223, 224, 294–96, 300–304, 327, 335. *See also* Steel Workers Organizing Committee; United Steelworkers of America

Steelman, John R., 136, 297, 299, 301, 302, 303

Steel mills: seizure of, 302

Steel Workers Organizing Committee (SWOC), 29, 34–39, 42, 44, 54–65, 66, 67, 68, 70, 71, 73, 75, 78, 79, 80, 81, 85, 86, 92, 93, 94, 95, 106, 110, 118, 121, 122, 124–25, 128, 135, 138, 143, 152, 188, 228–29, 233, 259. *See also* Steel industry; United Steelworkers of America

Steinberg, William, 287–88, 289, 291

Stevenson, Adlai: workers support for, 309, 310

Stewards: role in late CIO, 325–26

Stimson, Henry L., 107, 134

Stolberg, Benjamin, 82, 92, 96

Strikes, 9, 10, 17, 18, 87, 97, 163, 177–78, 214; during World War II, 150–52, 161–62, 171, 172, 173, 176, 297; 1945–46, 212–28, 232, 251, 320; during Korean War, 294–96, 300–304

Supplementary Unemployment Benefits, 321

Supreme Court, 41, 63

Sweden, 329

Swift and Company, 80, 121

Swope, Gerard, 13

Taft, Senator Robert A., 310

Taft-Hartley Act, 241, 246–48, 251, 275, 276, 279, 284, 292, 302, 303, 305, 319, 340, 344, 354

Taiwan, 331

Tampa, Fla., 149

Taylor, Myron, 54, 58–59, 60, 228

Teamsters, International Brotherhood of, 94, 337, 359, 362, 367

Tennessee, 1, 228–29

Tennessee Coal and Iron, 282

Tennessee Valley Authority, 241

Texas, 229, 230, 231, 238, 281

Textiles industry, 151, 228, 368; workers, 12, 42, 44, 68, 74–76, 77, 111–12, 139, 229, 235, 343, 344; CIO in, 66, 75–78, 81, 82, 94, 122, 145, 174, 216, 228–29, 230, 231, 232, 234–35, 237, 238, 239, 240. *See also* Textile Workers Organizing Committee (TWOC); Textile Workers Union of America (TWUA)

Textile Workers Organizing Committee (TWOC), 75, 76, 77, 78, 81, 94, 216, 228

Textile Workers Union of America (TWUA), 128, 216, 242, 257, 310, 315, 319, 336, 339, 340, 344, 349, 350; in World War II, 145, 170, 172, 174, 177, 240; in South, 174, 229, 230, 231, 232, 237, 238, 243, 344

Third party: CIO and, 241–42, 266–77, 278, 288–89, 312, 319

Third World, 328, 330, 331, 332

This Is Your America (PAC pamphlet), 183–84

Thomas, Roland J., 100, 128, 160, 166, 168, 173, 181, 219, 220, 231, 260

Tighe, Michael, 36

Time, 304

Timken Roller Bearing, 155

Tito (Josef Broz), 331

Tobacco workers, 74, 78, 80, 83, 114, 228, 229, 234, 238, 240, 282–83, 347

Tobacco Workers International Union (AFL), 240, 283

Toledo, Ohio, 70, 100

Townsend, Willard, 156, 158, 283, 348, 363

United Services Organization, 352

United States Chamber of Commerce, 216

United States Conciliation and Mediation Service, 136, 246, 295

United States Steel Corporation, 24, 42, 43, 54, 56–57, 58–59, 61, 66, 78, 80, 103, 121, 124, 125, 225, 227, 228, 300–304

United Steelworkers of America (USWA), 3, 182–83, 216, 229, 232, 251, 257, 259, 271, 273, 279, 281, 282, 290, 315, 323, 327, 334–36, 359, 367, 375; institutional character, 139, 188, 291, 324, 334, 339, 341–42, 359; during World War II, 144–78 passim; role in CIO, 149, 334, 335, 336–38, 360–62, 364–66, 369–70; African American workers in, 153, 154, 156, 157, 159, 346; collective bargaining activities, 214, 221, 223–24, 295, 300–304, 305, 320–21, 322, 327, 335. *See also* McDonald, David J.; Murray, Philip; Steel industry; Steel Workers Organizing Committee (SWOC)

United Transport Service Employees of America (UTSE), 153, 156, 283, 347, 348

Unity Caucus: in UAW, 98

U.S. News and World Report, 333, 342

Utah, 281

Utility Workers Union of America, 362

Vandercook, John W., 351

Vanzetti, Bartelemeo, 10

Virginia, 230, 231

Voltz, Mary, 87

Vorse, Mary Heaton, 43

Wages of industrial workers, 8, 9, 113–15, 125, 128, 215–16, 228, 237, 305, 314, 315, 316, 318–19, 320, 321, 322, 347, 348; during World War II, 164–76; and postwar strikes, 224–26; during Korean War, 297–300

Wagner Act. *See* National Labor Relations Act

Wallace, Henry A., 258, 266, 268, 269, 270, 271, 273, 274, 276–77, 288, 289

Wall Street Journal 232

Walsh, Raymond, 181, 183

Walsh-Healey Act, 106

War, U.S. Department of, 107

War Manpower Commission, 157, 164, 175

War Production Board, 164, 178

Warren, Ohio, 63

Washington, D.C., 52

Washington State, 71, 272

Washtenaw County, Mich., 149

Wayne County, Mich., 148, 272, 273

Wayne University, 260

WDET (radio station), 351

Weaver, George L.-P., 156, 157, 158, 159, 346–47

Weber, Palmer, 271

Webster, Milton, 158

Welfare capitalism, 9–10, 13, 120

Westinghouse Corporation, 12, 79, 121, 122

Wheeler, Burton K., 108

Wheeling, W.Va., 260

White collar workers, 82, 86, 343, 344, 368; and CIO, 80, 81, 96, 256, 350. *See also* United Office and Professional Workers; United Public Workers; Government and Civic Employees Organizing Committee

Widman, Michael, 123

Williams, G. Mennan, 311

Willkie, Wendell, 108, 179

Willow Run (aircraft plant), 149, 215

Wilson, Boyd L., 156, 159

Wilson, Charles E. (General Motors executive), 224

Wilson, Charles E. (General Electric executive; head of ODM), 295, 297, 299, 301

Wilson, Homer, 288

Wilson Company, 80

Winston-Salem, N.C., 147, 153, 229, 255, 282–84

Wisconsin, 272, 313

Woman's Guide to Political Action (PAC pamphlet), 184, 185

Women's Emergency Brigade, 51

Women workers, 8–9, 114, 152, 154, 343; and CIO, 85–88, 113, 184–85, 255–56, 349–51

Wood products industry, 78, 82, 125, 163, 228, 238, 240

Working and Fighting Together Regardless of Race, Creed, or National Origin (pamphlet), 156–57

Workmen's Circle, 369

Workplace rule of law, 326, 327

Works Progress Administration, 116, 230

World Federation of Trade Unions (WFTU), 262–63, 264, 286, 328

World War I, 106, 174

World War II, 102, 103, 110–90, 212, 229–30, 294, 350, 372, 373. *See also* National War Labor Board (NWLB); No Strike Pledge

Yalta agreements, 298
Young, Coleman, 272
Young, Ruth, 87

Youngstown, Ohio, 61, 62, 63
Youngstown Sheet and Tube Company, 61, 124, 168
Yugoslavia, 298, 331

Zaritsky, Max, 6, 24
Zonarich, Nicholas, 282